The Past in Perspective

The Past in Perspective

An Introduction to Human Prehistory

KENNETH L. FEDER

Central Connecticut State University

SIXTH EDITION

New York Oxford

OXFORD UNIVERSITY PRESS

Oxford University Press is a department of the University of Oxford.
It furthers the University's objective of excellence in research,
scholarship, and education by publishing worldwide.

Oxford   New York
Auckland   Cape Town   Dar es Salaam   Hong Kong   Karachi
Kuala Lumpur   Madrid   Melbourne   Mexico City   Nairobi
New Delhi   Shanghai   Taipei   Toronto

With offices in
Argentina   Austria   Brazil   Chile   Czech Republic   France   Greece
Guatemala   Hungary   Italy   Japan   Poland   Portugal   Singapore
South Korea   Switzerland   Thailand   Turkey   Ukraine   Vietnam

For titles covered by Section 112 of the US Higher Education
Opportunity Act, please visit www.oup.com/us/he for the latest
information about pricing and alternate formats.

Published by Oxford University Press
198 Madison Avenue, New York, New York 10016
http://www.oup.com

Library of Congress Cataloging-in-Publication Data
Feder, Kenneth L.
   The past in perspective : an introduction to human prehistory / Kenneth L. Feder.—
Sixth edition.
       pages cm
   Summary: "Textbook for introduction to archaeology and world prehistory
courses"—Provided by publisher.
   ISBN 978-0-19-995073-7
   1. Prehistoric peoples. 2. Human evolution. 3. Fossil hominids. 4. Human remains
(Archaeology) I. Title.
   GN766.F43 2013
   569.9—dc23
                                                                2013014192

Printing number: 9 8 7 6 5 4 3 2 1

Printed in the United States of America
on acid-free paper

For Josh and Jacob

Contents

4

The Human Lineage 96

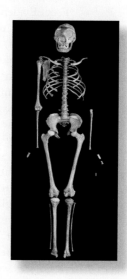

5

The First Humans 128
The Evolution of _Homo sapiens_

6

Expanding Intellectual Horizons 168
Arts and Ideas in the Upper Paleolithic and Late Stone Age

7

Expanding Geographic Horizons 198
New Worlds

8

After the Ice 238
The Food-Producing Revolution

9

Roots of Complexity 300
The Origins of Civilization

10

An Explosion of Complexity 340
Mesopotamia, Africa, and Europe

11

An Explosion of Complexity 384
The Indus Valley and China
CHAPTER OVERVIEW 384

12

An Explosion of Complexity 402
Mesoamerica

Evolutionary Epilogue 491

Preface

"The past is a bucket of ashes," wrote the poet Carl Sandburg in his poem *Prairie*. Surely he was wrong. The past is not cold, dead, and spent. It is alive in everything we are and will be. We live in a universe filled with its traces. The stars in the night sky shine with a light that began its journey millions of years ago. The fossilized remnants of remarkable creatures that once walked the earth lie entombed in the soil beneath our feet. Cooking hearths and food scraps, pyramids and pottery, stone tools and bone awls, cave paintings and ivory sculptures—all date to the ancient human past yet continue to exist in the present. The past is not a bucket of ashes, but rather, as writer L. P. Hartley put it in his 1953 novel *The Go-Between*, "the past is a foreign country." In this book, we will visit that country.

The Past in Perspective: An Introduction to Human Prehistory focuses on the dim echoes of the human past, presenting an accessible chronicle of human physical and cultural evolution. The readers of this text are undergraduates with no previous coursework in archaeology; for many it will be their only academic exposure to our prehistoric past. Rather than overwhelm beginning students with an all-inclusive, detailed, or encyclopedic survey of human antiquity, this text focuses on the major themes of the human evolutionary story. It begins with the evolution of our earliest hominid ancestors, traces the evolution of the modern human species, and follows the various pathways our ancestors took in the development of food-producing societies and complex civilizations. My goal throughout is to instill in readers an appreciation for the long chronicle of humanity and the ongoing processes we use to construct and assess that story.

How the Text Is Organized

Chapters 1 and 2 provide context and background for the discussion of human prehistory. Chapter 1 places the study of the human past in the context of science, specifically the science of anthropology. Chapter 1 also explains how a scientific approach to the study of prehistory developed. Chapter 2 is a brief overview of key methodologies employed by archaeologists and paleoanthropologists in their study of the human past. It represents a brief introduction to archaeology.

Following these introductory chapters, Chapters 3 through 14 go on to present a chronological survey of the human past. Each chapter follows a consistent format with these headings: Prelude, Chronicle, Issues and Debates, Case Study Close-up, Summary, and To Learn More. A consistent format provides a pedagogical advantage, and the trajectory of human physical and cultural evolution becomes far more apparent and connected. What we know, what we don't know, and what are still topics of vigorous debate will be clear to the reader.

 The **PRELUDE** represents a conscious attempt on my part to provide a pedagogical "hook" for each chapter. Personal anecdotes or fascinating historical incidents, for example, immediately engage students in the key issue or issues of the chapter, whether it is upright locomotion, the origins of artistic expression, or the power of ancient civilizations.

 The **CHRONICLE** presents in narrative form a consensus view of that part of the human past that is the chapter's focus. It represents the heart of each chapter, providing our current understanding of the time period covered, the hominids discussed, and the cultural evolutionary developments reflected in the time period.

 ISSUES AND DEBATES discusses the answers we have been able to provide for key questions about human physical and cultural evolution as well as the unresolved issues that remain and the ongoing debates. These sections provide differing—and sometimes competing—perspectives. Students are thus exposed to the sometimes messy, always exciting, and inevitably human process of science fraught with disagreements, reassessments, shifting paradigms, and only hard-won consensus.

 The **CASE STUDY CLOSE-UP** is a detailed examination of one or more sites considered diagnostic or emblematic of the time period or primary issue of the chapter.

Each chapter's **Summary** provides a brief recapitulation of the key issues in the chapter.

To Learn More provides suggestions for further reading in professional journals, academic texts, and trade books.

Additional Features

In addition to a consistent chapter format, I've included a number of other features that make this text a more useful learning tool.

A timeline opens every chapter and helps place the key events and sites mentioned in the body of the chapter within a global historical context.

To help students better orient themselves on the world stage, I've included abundant maps throughout the book. Each chapter (3–14) presents a map or, in some cases, multiple maps in which each of the sites mentioned in the chapter is located. Chapters 3 through 14 also include a list of sites—broken out by continent, region, or country—that are mentioned in the chapter, along with the page number where they can be found.

A list of Key Terms at the end of each chapter provides an alphabetical listing of important terms that appear in boldfaced type within the chapters and includes page numbers for where they can be found. Definitions can be found in the end-of-book Glossary.

The text's visual appeal enhances its readability. Full-color photographs are cross-referenced to pertinent text discussions. Detailed, colorful charts and drawings, as well as abundant color photographs, underscore significant points in the text. Captions add information rather than simply label the art.

The Glossary, References, and a comprehensive Index make information readily accessible.

What's Different about the Sixth Edition?

A new edition of a textbook is a collaborative effort between the author and the faculty who use the book or who might consider using the book in their classes. Along with the usual and obligatory updates, the majority of the changes made in the sixth edition of *The Past in Perspective* have been the result of the many substantive and thoughtful suggestions made by colleagues who used the fifth edition and who contacted me with comments, as well as the very thoughtful and detailed revisions proposed by reviewers who were approached by the publisher. This book has been revised and greatly improved through this process and I owe those who generously—and gently—suggested improvements. Specifically:

- **Chapter 2:** I have greatly expanded the discussion of noninvasive techniques in the discovery, analysis, and interpretation of archaeological sites (a big thanks to Jarrod Burks for this!). Also, as a result of reviewer suggestions, I've added a section on archaeological ethics. It was the ethical thing to do.
- **Chapter 3:** I've expanded much of the discussion of carbon isotope analysis, bipedality, australopithecine diet and possible tool use, and the use of strontium isotope analysis to gauge hominid movement and territoriality.
- **Chapter 4:** I've included the latest information about the oldest handaxes (1.76 million years ago) and the geographic distribution of handaxe technology.
- **Chapter 5:** I added a bunch of new stuff on the spread of hominids into the Arabian Peninsula and Europe as well as an extensive discussion of the genomic analysis of human beings and our ancestors.
- **Chapter 6:** I have thoroughly reworked and reorganized my comparison between Middle Paleolithic and Middle Stone Age culture on the one hand and Upper Paleolithic and Late Stone Age culture on the other. Students should be able to understand the differences far more readily now.
- **Chapter 7:** This is one of the most thoroughly revised chapters in the book. I have updated and clarified the earliest human settlement of the Pacific and revised, reworked, reorganized, rethought, and thoroughly rewritten the sections about the earliest settlement of the New World (Michael Waters's work has been crucial in my reevaluation of the pre-Clovis settlement of the Americas and in the revision of my presentation of the data and controversies). I've also replaced the Case Study Close-up with a discussion of the Gault site (another thanks to Michael Waters).
- **Chapter 8:** I've added material on the genetic analysis of the first European farmers. I've also put together a new table that will be very useful

to students; it's a listing of the modern world's most economically important domesticated plants including a column with the estimated dating of the earliest evidence for their domestication. As part of a basic reorganization of the discussion, my coverage of Göbekli Tepe and the earliest mound builders in North America has been shifted to the next chapter.

- **Chapter 9:** As just noted, I have shifted my discussion of Göbekli Tepe to this chapter on the origins of complexity and I have greatly enhanced and expanded my treatment of (and added photographs of) this amazing site. Also, reflecting this same change in organization, I've moved the discussion of the earliest signs of complexity in North America to this chapter; this is where it should always have been.
- **Chapter 10:** In Issues and Debates, I've included a new discussion provocatively titled "Was the Development of Civilization a Good Thing?" Also, based on very sensible suggestions by reviewers, I've shifted my discussion of Minoan Crete from Chapter 11 to this chapter. I've also moved Great Zimbabwe to here from Chapter 14.
- **Chapter 11:** I've expanded and updated my treatment of both the Indus Valley and, especially, the development of the state in ancient China.
- **Chapter 12:** I've added a section on Monte Alban and significantly expanded my treatment of the Aztec empire.
- **Chapter 13:** One of the most significant expansions to this book is my presentation of the Inca. Here, I have added significantly to my discussion of the Inca political and economic systems, including inheritance and the maintenance of their colonial empire (thanks especially to Brian Siegel for his extremely helpful comments and his strong opinions on this point). I've included a new Case Study Close-up: Inca child sacrifice.
- **Chapter 14:** Now focused exclusively on North America, I have thoroughly reorganized the chapter. The new organization makes more sense and students should find it a better match for the organization of the rest of the book's chapters. Mound 72 at Cahokia is now the Case Study Close-up.

Supplementary Material for Students and Instructors

A companion website for *The Past in Perspective* is available at www.oup.com/us/feder. On the website, students will find multiple-choice quizzes, chapter summaries, interactive timelines, and vocabulary flashcards. For instructors, the website contains PowerPoint presentations for each chapter, as well as links to professional resources.

A personal goal of mine in writing this book has been to inspire among its readers a life-long interest in the past. As a result, I have included a resource in the accompanying website called "Visiting the Past." In it, I provide information about actually visiting some of the sites featured in the text. I have always found it terrifically gratifying when I hear from past students a year, five years, or even longer after taking one of my courses that as a result of interest kindled there, they have visited archaeological sites open to the public—often sites I highlighted in class and of which I showed photos from my own visits. I realize that the vast majority of this book's readers will not go on to careers in archaeology, but I hope that many will be similarly inspired by the material presented here to personally experience some of the significant sites discussed in its pages. Of course, I have an ulterior motive; I hope that students who visit sites like the ones discussed in this book recognize their significance on multiple levels and become citizens committed to their protection and preservation.

An Instructor's Manual and Computerized Test Bank on CD-ROM is available with the text and includes multiple-choice and short-answer/essay questions, as well as chapter overviews, lists of key words, and suggested sources for videos, CD-ROMs, and Internet sites. To receive the manual and test bank, please contact your OUP representative.

Acknowledgments

Jan Beatty is, in many ways, responsible for the existence of this book. I can't thank Jan enough for her vision and support in this and many other projects.

A million thanks to Sherith Pankratz, Keith Faivre, and Katy Albis at Oxford University Press. This book was truly a collaborative effort and they deserve recognition for all of the work they put into making the book look great and, I think, read so well. Thanks, guys!

I am extremely grateful to many colleagues and students, as well as to my late father, all of whom have shared their thoughts, suggestions, and, yes, pointed criticisms about *The Past in Perspective*. I am also indebted to my many colleagues who provided some of the spectacular photographs that grace the pages of this book. In particular, for this sixth edition, I would like to thank Jarrod Burks, Jenn Davis, Jon Erlandson, M. H. Feder, Sonja Gray, Chris Lepre, Brian Siegel, Pierre-Jean Texier, Liz Throop, Paola Villa, and Michael Waters.

I would also like to thank the reviewers of the sixth edition: Britt Bousman, Texas State University; Jonathan Mark Kenoyer, University of Wisconsin, Madison; Kelly Knudson, Arizona State University; Marc Levine, University of Colorado at Boulder; Ian Lindsay, Purdue University; Mark A. Rees, University of Louisiana at Lafayette; Jim G. Shaffer, Case Western Reserve University; LuAnn Wandsnider, University of Nebraska–Lincoln; and Dean H. Wheeler, Glendale Community College. I took their counsel seriously and am in their debt for the many useful suggestions they made.

In the area of personal thanks, I am grateful for having a colleague like Michael Alan Park. My sense of excitement about the world around me was kindled by my parents, and I thank them both. Special thanks goes to my globetrotting father for his wonderful photographs. Of course, no acknowledgments are complete without crediting one's immediate family. Thanks to my kids, Josh and Jacob, whose mere existence reminds me of my own very small place in evolution's drama. And expansive thanks to my wife, Melissa, the sweetest person on the planet. I can't lift heavy objects or fix cars, but I can write books. I think she's impressed. Finally, I must acknowledge my multiple partners in crime, kitties Randolph, Harpo, Groucho, and Buster, who are gone now, but who, in sharing their lives with me, disabused me of any foolish notion I may have had about the superiority of the human species. And thanks to our current generation of Aslan and little Xander ("little" is a euphemism; he's a massive, 20-pound Maine Coon cat, but his brain is little) who are quick to remind me that a scratch behind the ear and a clean litter box are far more pressing than whatever it is I am staring at on the computer screen.

The Past in Perspective

1

Encountering the Past

CHAPTER OVERVIEW

This book focuses on the work of archaeologists. Archaeology is a subdiscipline within the broader field of anthropology—the study of humanity. Whereas other anthropologists study living people, archaeologists concentrate on the cultural evolution of past human beings. Archaeologists accomplish this through the study of our ancestor's biological remains and, especially, the analysis of the physical objects that they made, used, and left behind.

Recognizing that the world and humanity were ancient, and understanding that elements of this ancient past were preserved and could be studied in the present, was difficult for past thinkers whose concepts of time were constrained by their traditional beliefs. Some viewed the world as the static product of a relatively recent, divine creation. Others came to understand that the earth is the result of slow-acting, natural causes that continue to operate in the present. In this now-accepted view, the world and all of its inhabitants, including human beings, have a lengthy history and are ever changing. Only by recognizing that the world is vastly ancient and characterized by change can the lengthy archaeological record of an ancient humanity be accommodated.

	1640	1650	1660	1670	1680	1690	1700
GEOLOGY		Bishop Ussher determines that creation took place in 4004 B.C., 1650				*The Wisdom of God* by John Ray is published, 1691 William Whiston proposes that a collision between earth and a comet caused Noah's flood, 1696	
BIOLOGY							
ARCHAEOLOGY							

1710	1720	1730	1740	1750	1760	1770	1780	1790	1800	1810	1820	1830	1840	1850	1860	1870	1880

Theory of the Earth by James Hutton published, 1788

Principles of Geology by Charles Lyell published, 1830

William Smith's stratigraphic tables first circulated, 1799

William Smith's stratigraphic tables published, 1815

Linnaeus publishes his taxonomy for all living things, 1758

Philosophie Zoologique by Jean-Baptiste Lamarck published, 1809

Darwin begins his voyage on the *Beagle*, 1831

Darwin writes a synopsis of his theory of evolution, 1844

The Origin of Species by Charles Darwin published, 1859

The Descent of Man by Charles Darwin published, 1872

John Frere finds flint tools in soil layer deep in quarry in Hoxne, England, 1797

Flint tools and bones of extinct animals found in Kent's Cavern, England, 1824

C. J. Thomsen publishes museum guide and introduces three-age system, 1836

Primitive skull found in Neander Valley, Germany, 1856

Ancient Society by Lewis Henry Morgan published, 1877

Human bones found with bones of extinct animals in French cave, 1828

Geological Evidences of the Antiquity of Man by Charles Lyell published, 1863

Boucher de Perthes finds ancient flint axes, 1837

Researches in the Early History of Mankind by Edward Tyler published, 1865

PRELUDE

THE PAST IS DEAD AND GONE. At least that's what we usually think and say. Surely there is nothing much left of it beyond our dim memories. Perhaps the past is like the faces of people in an old printed photograph, people we once knew—people we once were. The image is crisp soon after the photo is taken but gradually fades as time hurries on, blurring into indistinct splotches of color on photo paper. Ultimately, the past, like these images, grows faint, becoming little more than an indecipherable haze. Indeed dead. Indeed gone. But is this common impression entirely accurate?

In fact, it isn't. In a very real way, the past sometimes and unexpectedly endures into the present. When we are lucky, its image can be brought into sharp focus again.

For example, take a walk out toward the margins of just about any modern town. Follow a trail into the desert or deep into the piney woods and recognize that, in a sense, the trail conveys the hiker back through time.

Consider my own town of Simsbury, Connecticut. In the rural, northwest corner of town, out beyond the beautiful homes with their splendid views of the valley below, a trail meanders through the McLean Game Refuge, a 4,000-acre sanctuary for animals, fish, birds, and trees. The trail into the refuge surges downhill, propelling the hiker past stands of hemlock, white and red pine, maple, and oak. As you gaze around the curiously broad trail and scan the higher ground on either side, you notice that this uninhabited woodland bears witness to something far different in its past. Low-lying stone walls demarcate the edges of the wide path, and that in itself is a puzzle (Figure 1.1). No one in living memory built these walls, yet there they stand, mysteriously lining the edges of a hiking trail far wider than it needs to be, in the middle of a game refuge. And there is more. Look beyond the walls that border the trail and you will notice a web of more stone walls, often rather elaborate and well made, in some cases stretching for more than 100 feet before intersecting with yet other fieldstone walls. These walls serve to enclose segments of land, each several acres in size, as if demarcating the property holdings of invisible homesteads. But whose property? Whose homesteads?

▲ **Figure 1.1**
Now deep in the forest, stone walls like this one once lined the roadways and gridded the fields used by the inhabitants of Pilfershire and hundreds of other communities scattered throughout New England. (K. L. Feder)

Again, mysterious. Why would anyone feel compelled to do all the work necessary to segregate sections of land by piling up thousands of heavy fieldstones in the middle of what now is a thickly treed, uninhabited game refuge?

As you continue farther along the trail into the woods, the stone walls seem to loom larger around you. They are taller, more elaborately made, and increasingly out of place in the apparent long-standing wilderness that surrounds you. Then, in the distance, along the trail, an opening in the trees becomes apparent. Arriving at the clearing, you spy a complex, well-made, fieldstone foundation of a large structure with a substantial square block of stones presenting fireplaces on each of its four faces (Figure 1.2, top). It is obviously the remnant of the center chimney of a house whose superstructure, likely wood-framed and sheathed in clapboard siding, is gone now, but whose stone-piled foundation clearly indicates its size and configuration. Walking around the foundation, it is easy to locate the well. Sprinkled about you on the ground, mixed in with oak and maple leaves, pine cones and needles, are bits and pieces of ceramic vessels; large chunks of thick-walled, utilitarian stoneware crocks; more delicate shards of plain, white-glazed dishes; spalls of oddly thick, green glass; and deeply rusted iron nails, not round like our modern ones but squared off, looking more like little wedges of metal than nails (Figure 1.2, bottom; the Swiss Army knife is for scale).

◀ **Figure 1.2**
This stone foundation (top) is all that remains of one of the structures that made up the long-since-deserted Pilfershire community located in north-central Connecticut. Stone walls, foundations, and wells, along with the objects used and then lost, abandoned, or discarded by the inhabitants of the community, represent that part of the past which endures into the present (bottom). This book presents what we know about the grand sweep of human history through the analysis of the enduring physical remains of the past. (K. L. Feder)

Curious enough that this foundation sits in the middle of the woods, a healthy walk from the nearest inhabited home, but even more curious when you continue past the large foundation and realize it is but one of several embedded deeply in the woods, some distance from the modern neighborhood of elegant homes.

What was this place? When was it inhabited? Who lived here? What happened to their seemingly once thriving small community? Why was it abandoned? Where did the inhabitants go? These are vexing questions, but one thing is certain: The past is not dead and gone here. Though now little more than a collection of stone walls and cellar holes in the middle of the woods, 200 years ago, in fact, this was the nucleus of a thriving community called Pilfershire, with homes, cleared fields, farms, barns, a cider mill, a school, various small industries, and shops. The children of Pilfershire once ran along village paths that are now hiking trails in a wildlife sanctuary. The path taken to get to this place, curiously broad for a simple hiking trail and mysteriously bounded by stone walls, is what remains of the old coach road that conveyed people and goods to and from the village. People

▲ **Figure 1.3**
Hidden in a niche in a cliff in northern Arizona, Montezuma's Castle was not really a fortress of the Aztec king Montezuma. It was, instead, a small community of Native Americans of the Sinagua culture (see Chapter 14) who inhabited the area more than 600 years ago (left). This Easter Island Moai (right) was never completed and still rests in the quarry where it was being sculpted nearly a thousand years ago. Ancient communities and places of work, like quarries, mines, hunting grounds, and so forth, can all become part of the archaeological record. (Left, K. L. Feder; right, Sonja Gray)

worked, prayed, laughed, loved, lived out their lives, and ultimately died at this place. Now they are ghosts, and their community is little more than a point of interest in a nature trail guide. Oh, and one more thing: What was once their community is now an **archaeological site**, an enchanted place where the past has not evaporated, is not dead and gone, but continues to reside in the present.

A Foreign Country

In the wonderful title of David Lowenthal's (1988) book whose wording he took from the English novelist L. P. Hartley, it is phrased in this way: *The Past Is a Foreign Country*. With that literary image in mind, we might say that the site where the remnants of the Pilfershire community can be found today represents a place where we in the present can visit that exotic land that is the past.

In a sense, Pilfershire represents an abandoned, forgotten part of human history, but it is not unique. All over Connecticut, throughout New England, scattered around the United States, and, in fact, dispersed across the globe, there are innumerable "lost villages," places where the detritus of past people lies abandoned in the woods, nestled under meters of sand, ensconced in ancient layers of soil, hidden deep in the recesses of dark caverns, and even embedded in rock (Figure 1.3). The pasts reflected in these lost villages—and lost quarries, encampments, fishing stations, sacred places (see Figure 1.4), trading posts, mines, hunting camps, and burial grounds (Figure 1.5)—reside in our present in the form of material remains left behind by human beings who lived their lives centuries, millennia, and even millions of years ago. The remnants of their homes and possessions—even the remains of their own bodies—continue their slow descent into oblivion, but

▲ **Figure 1.4**
Quartzite picks used to quarry soapstone at 3,000-year-old site located in northwest Connecticut (left; and see Figure 2.1, middle, for examples of the quarrying process from the same site). A spectacular petroglyph—art etched into the surface of a rock face—from McKee Springs, located in Dinosaur National Monument in Utah (right). (Both photographs by K. L. Feder)

▶ **Figure 1.5**
People in the distant past left memorials to those they loved and respected and for whom they grieved; here, a burial mound in Illinois marks the location of a buried leader of his community (top). A cemetery used in the eighteenth and nineteenth centuries in New Hartford, Connecticut (bottom). The cemetery is a site; the gravestones are artifacts. (K. L. Feder)

at least for some of them, we have arrived before they have become dust, before they are, in fact, dead and gone. In these providential instances, we have arrived in time to tell their stories.

This book strives to accomplish that task of storytelling through the application of the sciences of **paleoanthropology** and **archaeology**. This book is not about a single time or place but of all the times and all the places of humanity. It is a travelogue, of sorts, in which together we will visit the "foreign country" that is our species' enduring past.

An Anthropological Perspective

Paleoanthropology and archaeology are subfields within the broader discipline of **anthropology** (Figure 1.6). Contemporary anthropology is the study of people. Of course, the other social sciences—economics, political science, psychology, sociology—also study people but from very particular perspectives, focusing on specific aspects of human behavior. Anthropology, on the other hand, attempts to be **holistic** and **integrative** in its approach. If other social scientists specialize in the workings of specific systems within human society, anthropologists tend to be generalists who want to know how human society, with all its interrelated parts, works as a whole and how it came into existence.

Some anthropologists—called **ethnographers**—study humans by residing in particular societies and observing the behaviors of the people living in them. For example, projects conducted by ethnographers in my anthropology department have included the investigation of the religion of the Maya people of Mexico, the lives of coal miners in Romania, political activists in India, and African American hairdressers in Connecticut. Researchers who go beyond examining a particular group of people to compare the behaviors of different cultures are conducting **ethnology**. An ethnologist might take the work of several ethnographers who have conducted detailed studies of specific human groups and investigate, for example, how those various peoples deal with death, discipline their children, choose a mate, or build their houses. A highly specialized subfield of anthropology is **anthropological linguistics**. Here, the focus is language—how it evolved and the historical relationships among the known languages.

Primatologists also live with the groups they study. Instead of living among and studying people, these anthropologists focus their attention on the group of animals called the nonhuman **primates**. Prosimians, monkeys, apes, and humans are all primates (see Chapter 3). Primatologists aim to better understand our nearest living relatives. Believing that all primates share a common evolutionary heritage, primatologists hope to gain insights into our ancestral line. Jane Goodall (Figure 1.7), who has devoted much of her life to living among and learning about chimpanzees in the wild, is perhaps the best-known primatologist. Dian Fossey

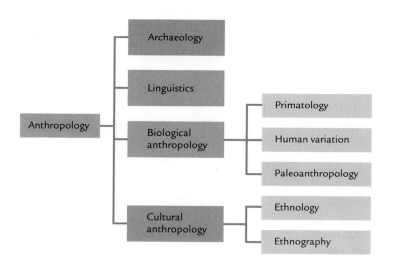

◄ **Figure 1.6**
The major subdivisions of the field of anthropology, including the two that are the focus of this book: paleoanthropology and archaeology. While these subdivisions represent distinct approaches, there is a great amount of connectivity among them. Each of these subdivisions can, in turn, be further subdivided into various anthropological specialities.

▶ **Figure 1.7**
Jane Goodall is among the field's best-known primatologists. Goodall's work among the chimpanzees has directly provided enormous insight into the lives of the chimps, and, indirectly, into the lives of our ancient ancestors. (Karl Ammann: Corbis)

▲ **Figure 1.8**
Don Johanson's work in east Africa has revealed the remains of some of our most ancient hominid ancestors. He is shown here at Hadar, a fossil locality that has provided the remains of Lucy and other members of the species *Australopithecus afarensis* (see Chapter 5). (© Institute of Human Origins, Arizona State University)

lived and worked with gorillas in the African nation of Rwanda. Her life and work as a primatologist was the subject of a biography by Farley Mowat, *Woman in the Mists* (1987), and the Hollywood movie *Gorillas in the Mist* (Phelan 1988).

If you watch the popular TV show *Bones*, you see the work of another kind of biological anthropologist: a **forensic anthropologist**. "Forensic" literally means the application of scientific procedures in the solution of a crime. *Bones* is based on the work of a real forensic anthropologist, Kathy Reichs. Using their knowledge of the human skeleton, especially skeletal trauma and pathology, forensic anthropologists work with law enforcement in investigating crimes. For example, a Connecticut colleague of mine, Al Harper (1999), was able to contribute to the solution of a murder in which a woman's body was run through a wood chipper by her husband. Though the vast majority of the murdered woman's skeleton had been pulverized, using standard techniques applied by archaeologists and paleotanthropologists (see Chapter 2), Al and his team recovered a tooth and a fingertip (with a manicured nail) that they were able to trace to the missing flight attendant. Her husband, who had claimed that his wife wasn't dead, just missing, was arrested, tried, and convicted of the murder.

Paleoanthropologists and archaeologists investigate the evolutionary history of humanity, both the biological evolution of our species and its **cultural evolution**. Paleoanthropologists have as their database the biological history of our species, often as reflected in the skeletal remains of our ancient human ancestors (Figure 1.8). Paleoanthropologists search for and analyze the fossils of our ancestors, and they rely increasingly on the analysis of modern human DNA in an attempt to solve the puzzle of our genetic roots. In a few lucky instances, they have even been able to extract DNA from ancient bones, reading the genetic instructions for some of our ancestors (see Chapter 5).

Archaeologists rely on the material remains left behind by past peoples, including those same varieties of human beings whose bones the paleoanthropologists unearth (Figure 1.9). Material remains may include the things people made and used, from simple stonecutting tools to complex monuments. Although archaeology is often perceived as being a romantic enterprise, it is perhaps better described as the study of "other people's garbage," as a PBS TV documentary called it (PBS 1980).

We humans are not only biological organisms whose adaptation is rooted in our genes but also cultural organisms whose uniquely great intelligence allows us to invent much of our strategy for survival. As researchers first recognized in the eighteenth century, these invented

adaptations—our **cultures**—have evolved just as surely as have our bodies and brains. Not only did our human ancestors leave behind their physical remains, which reflected their biological adaptation, but also they left behind the material objects they made and used as part of their cultural adaptation. The study of these two sources of information—their bones and **artifacts**—allows us to paint a picture of the lives of our ancient human ancestors.

▲ **Figure 1.9**
Archaeologist Melinda Zeder of the Smithsonian Institution has worked extensively in the Middle East, exploring some of the world's most ancient Neolithic sites (see Chapter 8, especially that chapter's Case Study Close-Up). (Courtesy of Melinda Zeder)

An Ancient World

An understanding of the context of time is crucial in our journey to the "foreign country" of the past. How deep is the human story? How far back in time can we trace our species? Any discussion of ancient societies requires the recognition that time itself is ancient, and this recognition is relatively recent in Western thought.

The Age of the Earth

It was commonly believed by Europeans in the sixteenth and seventeenth centuries that the world was only a few thousand years old. In 1642 John Lightfoot calculated creation's date at 3928 B.C., making the world 5,570 years old at that time (Brice 1982:19). There were other, similar estimates.

Most people in the Western world came to accept the very precise determination of Irish archbishop James Ussher who, in 1650, calculated that the earth had been created in 4004 B.C. and that God had begun the work "upon the entrance of the night preceding the twenty-third day of October" (from Archbishop Ussher's *Annales*, in Brice 1982:18). Beginning in 1701, this date was printed as a marginal note in English bibles. Though Ussher's precise figure is often maligned by modern scientists and writers, he arrived at it in 1650 through detailed historical research, analysis of astronomical cycles, and reference to biblical genealogies (Gould 1991).

Along with a young earth, many Western thinkers believed the world to have been created by God, just as we now see it, during the creation week discussed in the Old Testament of the Bible. Most believed that the world was "fixed" or set at creation and that, apart from minor, cyclical changes, like the alternation of the seasons, everything that was a part of that world—plant and animal species, as well as human beings—had changed little, if at all, since creation less than 6,000 years previously. John Ray, a reverend, naturalist, and scientist, was perhaps the most eloquent spokesman for this **creationist** perspective. In his view (1691, Preface), the world around him reflected "the works created by God at first and by him conserved to this day in the same state and condition in which they were first made."

A Wreck of a World

Some Western thinkers disagreed with Ray's perspective, believing, instead, that the earth had changed radically from the original creation and that this change had been decidedly for the worse. They agreed that the world God created had been perfect and that some of that perfection could still be seen and used as an argument for God's existence, but they also viewed the modern world as a pale reflection of the perfect place God had created. Many naturalists in the late seventeenth through eighteenth centuries were **catastrophists**. They believed the world had changed dramatically since creation through a series of catastrophic, natural processes set in motion by God upon his original creation of the world. Perhaps most important from our perspective here, catastrophists generally believed that these natural processes could be understood through careful study.

Noah's Flood

One example catastrophists pointed to as evidence of the process of catastrophic deterioration of the earth was Noah's flood. The Bible states that God decided to destroy the world and all its living things through a great universal deluge, saving only the family of Noah and representatives of each kind of animal. Though the flood was viewed by catastrophists as a supernatural event caused by God, some believed that God had used a natural process to initiate it. Astronomer Edmund Halley (after whom Halley's comet is named) proposed in 1694 that a comet crashing into the earth (sent, of course, by God) might have initiated the great flood.

Some catastrophists believed that great floods, like Noah's but of a smaller magnitude, had been the primary natural agency by which God caused his creation to wind down. Imagine devastating tsunamis, like the one that struck the Pacific coast of Japan in March 2011; the tragic impact of Hurricane Katrina in 2005; or the powerful earthquake that killed more than 230,000 people on the island nation of Haiti in 2010, afflicting the planet on a frequent basis.

Catastrophists faced a problem of scale and timing. Flooding is a natural phenomenon that often causes great destruction, and volcanoes and earthquakes are capable of incredible devastation; but these processes seemed to be too infrequent and far too limited in power to produce, in the accepted time frame provided by Bishop Ussher, the kinds of planetary deterioration catastrophists believed characterized the earth. Though enormous on a human scale, great floods, powerful volcanic eruptions, and devastating earthquakes seemed trifling on a planetary scale. Certainly, the Great East Japan earthquake and the subsequent tsunami were devastating natural events. Nearly 20,000 people were killed, another 30,000 injured, and 130,000 buildings were destroyed. But even this incredible catastrophe was largely local in its impact. The 2011 tsunami and the 2010 Haitian earthquake still were not catastrophes on a planetary scale. Most of the earth and most of its people did not suffer direct effects from these disasters. Catastrophists had to posit that calamities—the likes of which human history had never witnessed or recorded—had occurred in the past on a fairly regular basis in order to produce the degree of degeneration they perceived in the physical world.

Equable and Steady Change

Scottish scientist James Hutton became one of the first proponents of a hypothesis that stood in opposition to catastrophism (Figure 1.10). In his view, first espoused in his seminal and revolutionary work *Theory of the Earth*, "The operations of nature are equable and steady," not unpredictable and catastrophic (1795:19). This viewpoint, held by others as well, gave rise to the new perspective of **uniformitarianism**.

Hutton viewed the world as a marvelously constructed, perfectly synchronized machine—not merely switched on at creation and destined to run down, but brilliantly conceived to readjust and re-create itself continually. Hutton proposed a world designed by a creator so clever that slow and steady processes of decay were eternally offset by the slow and steady cycle of rejuvenation. In a conceivably indirect criticism of Bishop Ussher's calculation of a young earth, Hutton maintained that "time, which means everything in our ideas and is often deficient in our schemes, is to nature, endless" (1795:15). Processes like **erosion** and **weathering**—seen every day in rivers cutting their channels, in tides sculpting the shore, or in wind carving canyons—could have produced the present appearance of the earth if afforded sufficient time (Figure 1.11). Hutton argued that once it was accepted that these ordinary processes were responsible for earth's alteration since creation, our planet's actual age could be deduced. Through the careful scientific study of the rates and patterns

▲ **Figure 1.10**
Eighteenth-century Scottish geologist James Hutton, one of the first and most persuasive proponents of the perspective of uniformitarianism. (James Hutton, *Theory of the Earth*, 1795)

▶ **Figure 1.11**
I may be biased, but I think there's no better place on earth to see the incredible combination of time and erosion than the American Southwest. The only appropriate word to apply to Delicate Arch in Arches National Park in Utah is phantasmagoric (top); it looks like something you'd expect to see on Mars. The remarkable beauty of the delicate spires of Bryce Canyon, also in Utah, is another remarkable example of nature's ability to sculpt the planet (bottom). I've traveled a bunch but I don't think I've ever seen a more beautiful vista. (K. L. Feder)

of ordinary processes of erosion and weathering, "we find . . . means for conclud-ing a certain portion of time to have necessarily elapsed, in the production of those events of which we see the effects" (1795:19).

For the earth to have attained its appearance, modern observable phenom-ena must have been operating long enough to have produced mountain chains, meandering rivers, great canyons, and eroded valleys. Because the rates of ero-sion and weathering could be measured, one needed only to ask how long such processes must have been operating in order for modern features to have formed.

Fairy Stones?

If the earth was far more ancient than Bishop Ussher's calculation suggested, where did human beings fit in? Throughout the sixteenth and seventeenth cen-turies, beautifully chipped, symmetrical stone "axes" were found across Europe, often buried deeply in the soil. Perhaps these were the product of human man-ufacture from an ancient period before the use of metal. Many seventeenth-century observers rejected this—after all, the Bible didn't mention a "stone age," a period of time when people made only stone tools—and proposed, instead, that these objects had been fashioned not by ancient people but by elves and fairies! In the mid-1600s, in a more naturalistic explanation, Ulisse Aldrovandi suggested that such objects were produced by nature when lightning strikes the ground; this was only a slightly more reasonable hypothesis than one suggesting that fair-ies were responsible.

Other scientists in the seventeenth century were not quite so enamored of explanations that relied on fairies and elves or thunder and lightning. They sug-gested that these flint objects had been made by people in the past. But this explanation still was hampered by the restriction that a previous race of stone-tool-using humans could be no more than about 6,000 years old because that was the age of the earth and the universe that God had created.

John Frere's Discovery

In 1797, only two years after the publi-cation of Hutton's expanded version of *Theory of the Earth*, John Frere, a young Englishman, found some of these curi-ous stone axes in a brick-earth quarry in the small English village of Hoxne (Figure 1.12). His letter describing the artifacts to the London Society of Anti-quaries was read before the group in the same year and printed in its journal in 1800 (Frere 1800).

What made Frere's discovery so sig-nificant was that for perhaps the first time, primitive stone tools had been excavated at great depth (in this case, 12 feet below the surface) and that the bones of extinct animals were found

▼ **Figure 1.12**
Two views of one of the flint implements found and reported on in 1797 by John Frere. Frere suggested that the great depth of the implements as well as their position in a soil layer beneath one in which the bones of extinct animals were found suggested great antiquity for the makers of such tools. (© Society of Antiquaries, London)

above the tools, in more recently deposited soil layers. Frere recognized that from a uniformitarian perspective, this placement implied a great age for the tools and, in turn, a significant age for the humans who had made them.

Frere's argument for the antiquity of the artifacts he found was based on their **stratigraphic** position in the quarry. Frere and members of the London Society of Antiquaries may have been aware of the work of British surveyor William Smith, who a few years earlier had recognized that the soil beneath the earth's surface occurred in layers and that the layers produced ordered and regular groups of fossils. Smith showed that the layers could be identified and distinguished by their population of fossil species, with sequentially lower layers representing increasingly ancient time periods. In 1799 Smith circulated a handwritten table showing the order of strata he had encountered, but he did not publish a detailed report until 1815, laying the groundwork for the analysis of **stratigraphy** (see Chapter 2; Grayson 1983).

More Stone Tools . . . and Bones

Jacques Boucher de Perthes was a French customs official with a passion for artifact collecting, finding hundreds of flint implements in his excavations in the high gravel terraces overlooking the River Somme in northern France. In the title of the book he wrote presenting his work, published in 1847, he labeled these chipped stone tools *antediluvian*, meaning, literally, "from before the flood." Certainly the tools appeared to be primitive and ancient, but, just as important, like Frere, Boucher de Perthes found the artifacts in deep excavations, in the same layers where he also recovered the bones of extinct animals, including those of bison, woolly mammoth, woolly rhinoceros, and cave bears (Boucher de Perthes 1864). The stratigraphic context and association of the tools with fossil bones provided strong evidence for their great antiquity, dating, in fact, from a time when people relied on stone, not metal, for their weapons and tools and when animals long since extinct roamed the European countryside.

Frere's and Boucher de Perthes's discoveries implied a greater antiquity for the human species than was allowed for in Bishop Ussher's biblically based chronology. Their unearthing of tools and bones seemed to place our species deep in time in Hutton's uniformly changing, ancient earth.

The Slow Agency of Existing Causes

Hutton had fired the first salvos in a revolution in thinking about the processes responsible for the physical features of the earth and the age of the planet. The brilliant British geologist Charles Lyell (Figure 1.13) continued this revolution in thinking about the past. To come to a rational understanding of the earth, Lyell felt it necessary to dispense entirely with "imaginary pictures of catastrophes and confusion such as haunted the imagination of the early cosmogonists" (1990:72). His fundamental assertion was that "all past changes on the globe had been brought about by the slow agency of existing causes" (1830:63). That really was the heart of Lyell's argument: explaining the appearance of the earth by reference to existing processes that acted slowly over vast spans of time.

Perhaps the most revolutionary and problematic deduction from such a hypothesis concerned the time necessary to produce the kinds of geological

▲ **Figure 1.13**
Nineteenth-century
English geologist
Charles Lyell. Lyell was
the most eloquent
and thorough of the
uniformitarianists. In
his view, the appearance
of the modern world
was due not to ancient
catastrophes but to
"the slow agency of
existing causes." This led
him to the conclusion
that the earth was far
more ancient than
was generally believed.
(Charles Lyell, *Principles of
Geology*, 1830)

features seen on the earth if only the "slow agency of existing causes" was considered. Lyell himself admitted, "The imagination was first fatigued and overpowered by endeavoring to conceive the immensity of time required for the annihilation of whole continents by so insensible a process" (1990:63). But he went on to apply his fundamental axiom of uniformitarianism to estimate the ages of significant geological features. In a work published in 1863, for example, Lyell calibrated the modern rate at which the Mississippi Delta was growing and concluded that at its current rate of growth it must have taken 100,000 years to have attained its size.

Uniformitarianists who followed Lyell applied a similar approach: measure current erosion or deposition rates and calculate how long those processes of erosion or deposition must have been ongoing to produce the size of the particular geological feature. For example, in the late nineteenth century, British geologist Archibald Geikie examined the erosion rate of the Colorado River in the Grand Canyon. Based on that rate, he estimated that it took about 1,200 years for the river to cut one vertical foot into the underlying rock, making the mile-deep canyon, by this calculation, a little more than 6 million years old (5,280 feet × 1,200 years = 6,336,000 years; Atkinson and Leeder 2008). (More recent research indicates that the age of the Grand Canyon is closer to 20 million years old; Polyak, Hill, and Asmerom 2008.)

Needless to say, these estimated ages for the Mississippi Delta and Grand Canyon were shocking to those who accepted Bishop Ussher's determination for the age of the entire earth; 100,000 years is nearly eighteen times longer and 6 million years is about 1,000 times longer than the entire duration of earth's history if you accepted Ussher's calculation. Lyell was viciously attacked in print and charged with heresy, but such allegations rang hollow. Though the Bible measures the period of creation as six days, it does not place that creation week in time; nowhere does the Bible actually record the age of the universe, earth, or life. Hutton and Lyell's view and that of uniformitarianism may have contradicted the interpretation of an archbishop, but they did not disclaim the word of God.

Lyell was a great scientist and a persuasive proponent of the uniformitarian perspective. His work resonated in the minds of many geologists, biologists, and archaeologists and freed them from the perspective of a recent earth into whose chronology all of their observations and deductions had to be crammed. Charles Darwin later was to state, without too much exaggeration, "The science of geology is enormously indebted to Lyell—more so, as I believe, than to any other man who ever lived" (F. Darwin 1961:51).

Ancient Humans Revisited

With Lyell, uniformitarianism was to become the orthodox perspective in geology. The earth was old, and its story could be read in its ancient layers. With the discovery of clusters of such stone tools ensconced in deep stratigraphic layers and with no evidence of the use of metals found alongside, it became increasingly clear to many that human beings had been around for far longer than 5,700 years and that their cultures had changed dramatically since the makers of those stone tools had lived.

Cultures Ancient and Changing

Just six years after the initial publication of Lyell's *Principles of Geology*, a guidebook was published describing the artifacts that could be seen in the Danish National Museum in Copenhagen. Written by Danish museum curator Christian Jurgensen Thomsen, the guidebook organized the museum's collection chronologically into three prehistoric ages—stone, bronze, and iron—based on the most-favored raw materials used to make tools during each of the three epochs. Inherent in Thomsen's **three-age system** was the notion that culture had changed through time, in a predictable sequence. The three ages were developmental as well as chronological. There was an implied succession of increasing technological sophistication, an evolution toward tools that were better (more effective, more durable) but also more difficult to manufacture.

That culture had been undergoing great change during human tenure on the planet was no more evident in the nineteenth century than was the notion of an ancient earth. Thomsen deserves credit for recognizing and making explicit in his guidebook that the archaeological record clearly shows great changes in human technological abilities.

Thomsen's three-age system became the first in a series of approaches to the changes in culture that can be labeled **unilineal evolution**, based on the assumption that there was a single pathway of technological progress along which all cultures passed. Perhaps the best-known unilineal cultural evolutionary sequence was suggested in the nineteenth century by Lewis Henry Morgan (1877), who posited that all cultures progress through a series of fixed stages of development that he called savagery, barbarism, and civilization. According to Morgan, cultures at the savagery stage subsisted on fruits, nuts, and fish; used fire for cooking, heating, and light; and developed the bow and arrow. At the barbarism stage, societies developed agriculture and the ability to make ceramics and forge iron. Finally, upon reaching the civilization stage in Morgan's sequence, people developed a system of writing. In Morgan's view, due to the lack of some key technological invention, some cultures became stuck at either the savagery or barbarism stages, thus accounting for the presence of "primitive" people in the modern world. As we will see throughout this book, the unilineal approach is not supported by the archaeological record, which reflects, instead, the many and diverse pathways in which different people adapted to their surroundings and adjusted to change. The modern view, in contrast to the unilineal model, is multilinear. If unilineal evolution can be seen as a single ladder of progress up which all people climb, **multilineal evolution** can be represented as a dense bush of many branches growing in myriad directions.

Charles Darwin and the Antiquity of Life

In 1828 a bright, young Englishman entered Cambridge University in pursuit of a degree in theology. His name was Charles Darwin (Figure 1.14). Darwin took a natural science course at Cambridge with John Stephens Henslow, a remarkable teacher who became a mentor to many of his students. Henslow genuinely liked Darwin and felt that he had a knack for observing nature. He recommended his young student to a position aboard a British government survey

▲ **Figure 1.14**
Charles Darwin, the
father of modern
biological evolutionary
theory. (Neg. #108781,
courtesy of Department of
Library Services, American
Museum of Natural History)

ship, the *Beagle*, which was to produce detailed sailing charts of the coast of South America and then circumnavigate the world. The voyage would begin in 1831, when Darwin was just 22 years old. Despite some initial misgivings on the part of his father, who was still supporting him financially, Darwin accepted the position and began a mission that was supposed to last 2 years but actually lasted closer to 5. Though officially hired to be a companion to the ship's young captain, Darwin's training was as a naturalist, and he spent much of his time on the voyage around the world observing nature and collecting plant and animal specimens in places far removed from England. Thus, events had conspired to push the young theology student to collect the data that would, 28 years later, lead to one of the most important books ever published in the name of science.

An Evolutionary Philosophy

Evolution is the focus of Darwin's work and the organizing theme of this book. The term itself evokes so much emotion and misunderstanding that it is important first to put it in context, especially here, in a book whose underlying outline is based on the physical and cultural evolution of our species (Park 2012).

Biological evolution simply implies a process of systematic change through time. The natural world is vast and diverse, and many living things are born into it. Some of those living things possess characteristics that improve the chance of their survival and of their having descendants who share those advantageous characteristics. By chance, an individual may be faster, stronger, more dexterous, or able to move more efficiently through its habitat. It may be better camouflaged, have better visual acuity, be better at attracting a mate, or possess greater intelligence. These advantages may make it more likely to survive and more likely, therefore, to pass those characteristics on to subsequent generations.

Over vast spans of time, an entire species can be moved toward these advantageous characteristics, because those who lack them tend to die more quickly—often before becoming old enough to mate and produce descendants who also lack them. Through the slow and steady accumulation of advantageous characteristics or as the result of the rapid appearance of a dramatically different and advantageous feature, a species can become so different that it no longer is even the same kind of animal. It has become a new and different species: It has evolved.

The varied and changing natural world provides the context in which an organism must live and to which it must adjust. Biological evolution is not directed; species do not actively develop strategies for survival—called **adaptations**. And biological evolution has no direction; species do not inevitably become bigger, stronger, or faster. In fact, the fossil record shows that most species become extinct. Those that survive do so because at least some individual members are lucky enough to possess physical or behavioral adaptations that allow them to.

For some species, the means of adjustment go beyond the solely biological. Such species are able, as a result of their great intelligence, to develop new adaptations virtually instantly. They can invent new ways of surviving and teach these new ways to other members of their species and to their offspring. These survival methods are not genetically determined in the manner of a thick coat of fur, powerful jaws, or grasping hands and feet; they are cultural. Though made possible by the biological feature of a large and complex brain, culture represents a strategy for survival beyond that which is provided by an animal's physical characteristics. Modern human beings rely, as did our ancient human ancestors, on cultural adaptations for survival. A discussion of these adaptations and how they, too, have systematically changed through time makes up a large portion of this book.

The Mutability of Species

Although he didn't think it was important at the time, Darwin recognized that animals he encountered on islands off the coast of South America resembled, but were not identical to, animals found on the mainland, where they must have originated. The island descendants of mainland species seemed to have altered from their original state after migrating. The descendants must have become better adjusted, or **adapted**, to the different environmental conditions in their new habitats. Even on different islands within island chains, individual kinds of animals resembled each other, though differing in significant attributes from island to island.

For example, on the Galápagos Islands, 500 miles west of the northwestern coast of South America, Darwin found that tortoises living on each of the dozen large islands could be differentiated, and so could finches—small birds whose source was certainly the mainland. The finches did not look precisely like any other South American finch, and they differed in form and behavior among islands. How had each type of finch become uniquely adjusted to the particular features of its island if the finch species was immutable and fixed at creation? This mystery simply could not be explained within the accepted paradigm of the fixity of species.

In 1836, after a long and successful voyage, Darwin and the *Beagle* returned triumphantly to England. Many of Darwin's reports and specimens had preceded him, and he returned to find his work roundly praised by the scientific community. Darwin met and was befriended by geologist Charles Lyell, who was extremely grateful that Darwin's geological observations matched precisely his uniformitarian view of the evolution of the earth.

The Origin of Species

Darwin's masterpiece, *The Origin of Species by Means of Natural Selection*, was published in 1859. In the introduction to the book, Darwin succinctly articulates the essence of his theory:

> As many more individuals of each species are born than can survive; and as, consequently, there is a frequently recurring struggle for existence, it follows that any being, if it vary, however slightly in any manner profitable to itself, under the complex and sometimes varying conditions of life, will have a better chance of surviving, and thus be *naturally selected*. From the strong principle of inheritance, any selected variety will tend to propagate its new and modified form. (Darwin 1859:7)

As Darwin saw it, variation within a species—of tortoises, finches, and so on—provided some individuals with characteristics that allowed them a better chance for survival under the conditions established by nature. He called this process "**natural selection**" because, in essence, those individuals were passively "selected" by nature to survive and pass along their advantageous characteristics to their offspring. In this way, for example, finches of a single species might lose their way in a storm and get blown to an island where conditions were quite different from those at their mainland home. Many of the finches would die, unable to survive in their new circumstances; but a few might, by chance, possess characteristics that would enable them to endure. They would pass those features on to their offspring; and over many generations, birds with those qualities would continue to be selected for—that is, to survive. After a time, the island finches would no longer resemble the mainland finches. Given sufficient time, they might become so different that they would be a different species entirely.

Human Evolution

Darwin understood the controversy that would erupt if this evolutionary perspective were to be applied to human beings. In 1857 he wrote to his colleague Alfred Russell Wallace: "You ask whether I shall discuss 'man.' I think I shall avoid the whole subject, as so surrounded with prejudices; though I fully admit that it is the highest and most interesting problem for the naturalist" (Bowlby 1990:325). He hinted at the applicability of natural selection to humanity in *Origin* when he concluded that, by the application of the theory, "Much light will be thrown on the origins of man and his history" (Darwin 1859:243). As we will see throughout this book, Darwin was right.

In fact, in 1856, the year before Darwin indicated to Wallace his desire to steer clear of any mention of humanity in his discussion of evolution, a partial fossil skull was found in the Neander Valley in Germany (see Figure 5.7). At least two similar skulls had been found previously in Europe (in Belgium and on Gibraltar). The Neander Valley skull, like those found previously, was as large as a modern human skull, though it looked quite different. Some saw it as representative of an ancient and primitive race of humans.

With the notion of a uniformly changing, very ancient earth in place, the skeletal evidence began to convince many people of the great antiquity of the human species. There still was substantial debate over what "great antiquity" meant on any kind of a fixed time scale. No date could be assigned to the early humans who had made the stone tools, nor could any age be assigned to the German skull. But scientists were clearly shifting their opinion and beginning to view the earth and the human species as ancient—far older than Ussher's 5,700 years.

Cultures Evolving

Led first by Hutton and then Lyell, the uniformitarianists had shown that the earth was old; the pages of its ancient history were the strata that lay beneath our feet. Archaeologists had discovered human-made objects on those ancient pages, proving the great antiquity of humanity within the stratigraphic history of the planet. Darwin had gone on to show that within the lengthy history of the earth, plants and animals had changed dramatically; they had, in fact, evolved. And now, the ancient human-made objects found by the early archaeologists—the stone tools—provided clear evidence that human culture had evolved over an enormous period of time as well. As Charles Lyell himself pointed out (1863:379), if culture had remained constant throughout human history, then archaeologists should have been finding "buried railways or electrical telegraphs" along with other scientifically advanced artifacts in ancient stratigraphic layers. Instead, archaeologists were finding stone tools, admittedly finely made but technologically simple, associated with the bones of extinct animals in ancient soil layers. Clearly this was evidence of great change from the culture of the earliest humans to that of the modern (nineteenth-century) world. As surely as geologists had shown that the earth had sustained enormous change over a vast expanse of time and as surely as biologists now were showing that life itself had experienced great change, so archaeologists were showing that human behavior had also changed greatly during our species' history on earth.

Our Modern View

We began our historical discussion with a belief in an unchanging universe that was created less than 6,000 years ago by an omnipotent God and that was populated by plants, animals, and people whose forms and qualities were forever fixed at creation. That universe was simple, predictable, and reassuring.

We now hold the modern scientific view of the universe and life, initially espoused by Lyell and Darwin, as ancient and dynamic, unpredictable and serendipitous, awesome and awful.

What we have lost in terms of a pleasant and comforting view of the world and the human species' place in it is more than made up for in the infinitely fascinating story we can now tell of the evolution of our species. And, as seventeenth-century scientist and clergyman John Ray stated, "Those who scorn and decry knowledge should remember that it is knowledge that makes us men, superior to the animals and lower than the angels, that makes us capable of virtue and happiness such as animals and the irrational cannot attain" (Raven 1950:251).

Summary

Though many people assume that the past is merely dead and gone, in fact it can endure into the present in the form of the material remains of the things ancient people made and used. The sciences of archaeology and paleoanthropology endeavor to find and analyze those remains in an attempt to tell the story of human antiquity. That story is the focus of this book. Time is the backdrop against which the story of humanity is played out, and until fairly recently the depth of time was unknown. Most Western thinkers in the seventeenth century believed that the world and all life within it had been established during a creation week that had occurred not even 6,000 years previously. They further believed that their world was just as God had made it and reflected the perfection of creation.

Some natural scientists, on the other hand, saw the world as a "wreck," which had decayed since the time of creation. Viewing the world as quite young, perhaps no more than 6,000 years old, these thinkers suggested that the history of the earth had been marked by a string of catastrophes.

James Hutton and Charles Lyell were spokesmen for a different perspective. Rejecting claims of hypothetical catastrophes, they explained the appearance of the earth on the basis of observable, slow, steady, and uniform natural processes. They asserted that such observable natural phenomena could produce the current state of the earth if afforded sufficient time. They measured the age of the earth not in thousands of years but in hundreds of thousands and even millions of years. Especially during the nineteenth century, researchers began uncovering tantalizing bits of evidence—in the form of flint implements together with the bones of extinct animals and even those of human beings—that suggested this ancient earth had been populated by early forms of humanity.

Charles Darwin viewed the biological world as the result of natural processes of change. His theory of natural selection provided an overarching explanation for the diversity of life on the planet. With the amount of time provided by Hutton and Lyell's perspective of earth history, the process of natural selection could have produced the great diversity of life seen on the planet, the differences and similarities among different kinds of organisms, even the evolution of humanity.

TO LEARN MORE

Two excellent sources on the history of archaeological and paleoanthropological thoughts are Glyn Daniel and Colin Renfrew's *The Idea of Prehistory* (1988) and William Stiebing Jr.'s *Uncovering the Past: A History of Archaeology* (1993). For more detailed coverage of the early history of the discipline, see Donald Grayson's *The Establishment of Human Antiquity* (1983) and A. Bowdoin Van Riper's *Men Among the Mammoths: Victorian Science and the Discovery of Human Prehistory* (1993). If you are interested in a detailed discussion of the life of Charles Darwin, John Bowlby's 1990 monograph, *Charles Darwin: A New Life*, is simply terrific. For a wonderful summary of the evolutionary perspective (with lots of amazing photographs), take a look at *Exploring Evolution* by my friend and colleague, Michael Park (2012).

Web links for this chapter can be found at www.oup.com/us/feder

KEY TERMS

adaptation, 18
adapted, 19
anthropological
   linguistics, 9
anthropology, 9
archaeological site, 7
archaeology, 8
artifact, 11
catastrophist, 12
creationist, 12

cultural evolution, 10
culture, 11
erosion, 13
ethnographer, 9
ethnology, 9
evolution, 18
forensic anthropologist, 10
holistic, 9
integrative, 9
multilineal evolution, 17

natural selection, 20
paleoanthropology, 8
primate, 9
primatologist, 9
stratigraphic, 15
stratigraphy, 15
three-age system, 17
uniformitarianism, 13
unilineal evolution, 17
weathering, 13

2

Probing the Past

CHAPTER OVERVIEW

Paleoanthropologists and archaeologists study the actual physical remains of human beings and those of our evolutionary ancestors. They also examine the material remains of the behavior of these ancient ancestors: the things that past humans made and used and then lost or discarded. By the investigation of the bones of humans and human ancestors as well as analysis of the objects they left behind—tools, weapons, items of adornment, works of art, structures, and so on—paleoanthropologists and archaeologists hope to better understand the ways in which our ancestors evolved and adapted. This chapter summarizes many of the most important and widely used techniques relied on by these scientists to paint a picture of the human past.

Applicable range of major dating techniques

2 million   1 million

Radiocarbon Radioactive decay	
Archaeomagnetism Alignment of particles in cultural deposits with the earth's magnetic field	
Dendrochronology Counting of annual growth rings of trees	
Uranium series* Radioactive decay	▪ ▪ ▪ ▪ ▪ ▪
Obsidian hydration Chemical process: accumulation of weathering rind on artifact	
Fission track Radioactive decay leaves microscopic tracks in crystals at known rate	▬▬▬▬
Luminescence Radiation damage: accumulation of energy in crystals	
Electron spin resonance Radiation damage: accumulation of unpaired electrons in crystals	◀━━━
Potassium argon (K/Ar) Radioactive decay	◀━━━
Paleomagnetism Alignment of particles in natural deposits with the earth's magnetic field	◀━━━

*Uranium series results older than 300,000 years are statistically questionable.

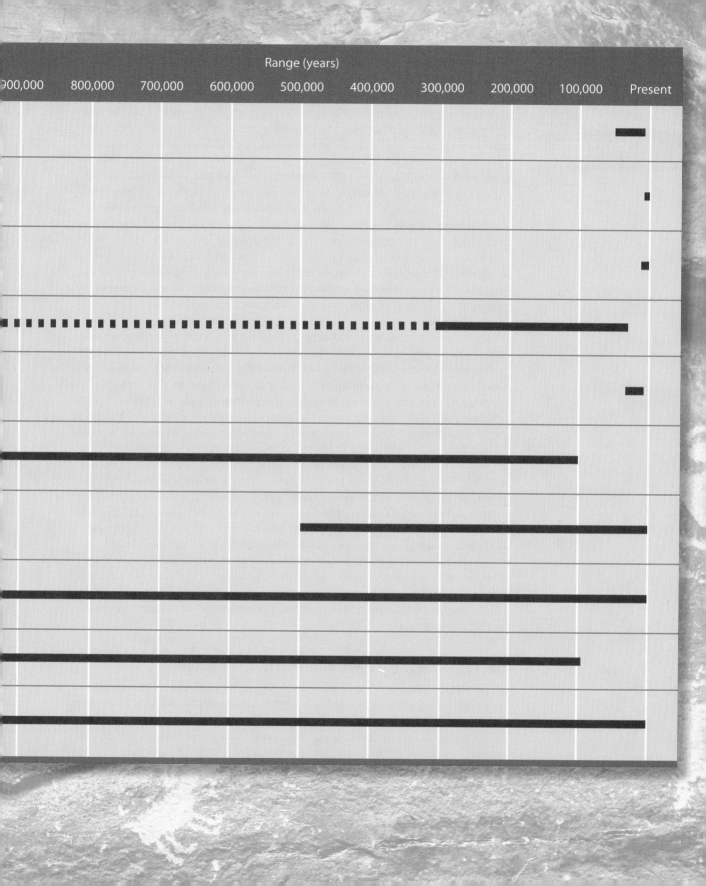

900,000	800,000	700,000	600,000	500,000	400,000	300,000	200,000	100,000	Present

ONE OF MY FAVORITE TELEVISION SHOWS when I was a kid was the cartoon series *Rocky and Bullwinkle*. Don't tell anybody, but actually it remains one of my favorite shows to this day. Smart, funny, and subversive, the cartoons were laced with adult humor, puns, and politically astute commentary, all from a smart-ass talking squirrel and a goofy moose. My favorite segment of the show was Peabody's Improbable History. Mr. Peabody was a bipedal, talking dog who happened to be a genius (you could tell by his glasses) and who, with his boy Sherman (whom he adopted from the local pound), would time travel in one of Mr. Peabody's inventions, the Way Back Machine. After setting a date and place on the machine's control panel, Peabody and Sherman would travel back, for example, to the sixteenth century to help Galileo figure out gravity, or they'd visit Columbus in the fifteenth century and point the way to the New World.

I bring this up because, as a prehistorian, I have to admit I'd love to have a Way Back Machine. It would render my profession so much easier. Instead of the slow and laborious process of looking for paleoanthropological and archaeological sites, excavating them, analyzing the artifacts we recover, and trying to come up with a comprehensible story of the biological evolution and cultural development of our species, we could simply travel back in time with Sherman and Peabody and be eyewitnesses to antiquity.

But we don't have a Way Back Machine. Instead, we must rely on some extremely cool real-world techniques to find archaeological sites and then extract information from the stones, bones, soils, and plant materials left behind. It can be a daunting process, but we rely on an approach that authors Michael Shermer and Alex Grobman (2000) characterize as "a convergence of evidence." In each historical discipline, including archaeology, paleoanthropology, historical geology, and history, we search for knowledge and meaning along different, independent pathways. We are confident in our conclusions when different and independent streams of data point to the same conclusion, when they converge at the same point. It is, for example, difficult to figure out when the first people entered the New World and where they came from (see Chapter 7), but when geological data, archaeological investigations in the Old and New Worlds, and genetic information from both ancient bones and modern people separately and independently point to the same scenario, when they converge on the same story, we can be pretty confident that our reconstruction matches the way things really were. This chapter is a very brief summary of how we obtain the information necessary for that convergence.

Epistemology: How We Know What We Know

Every field of scientific study presents its own set of challenges. Researchers in each branch of science must develop a specific set of methods for data collection as well as techniques of analysis and interpretation. Archaeology and paleoanthropology are no different. Our data are the objects that ancient humans and human ancestors made, used, lost, abandoned, or discarded; environmental data that informs us about the natural conditions our ancient forebears experienced and to which they adapted; and their actual biological remains. Archaeologists and paleoanthropologists have developed procedures for finding this ancient evidence along with techniques for extracting from it information about the lives of our ancient ancestors. This chapter summarizes some of the more significant methods used in archaeology and paleoanthropology for data collection and analysis.

The "Science" in the Study of the Past

Science often begins with objective observation of the world or universe. For example, biologists examine living things; astronomers focus on other planets, stars, and galaxies; and geologists observe the earth itself. Anthropologists, on the other hand, concentrate on humanity, with paleoanthropologists and archaeologists focusing more specifically on humanity's past.

All scientists observe the world and look for patterns or correlations, cause-and-effect relationships, trends, and trajectories in an attempt to puzzle out the rules that govern how the world works—how the earth was formed, how rivers flow, how life originated, how humanity evolved, or how people adapt through their cultures. To be sure, scientists are not blank slates or passive receptors of the data they encounter in research. Dominant perspectives called **paradigms**—think of a paradigm as a scientific worldview or conceptual framework—play a significant role in how we structure our research, in the kinds of research that receive funding, in what kinds of evidence we look for, and in how we interpret and interpolate what we do find. The hallmark of science, however, rests in its open-mindedness to new data and ideas, in its constant testing, probing, reassessment, and revision. New approaches and new interpretations, in archaeology, paleoanthropology, and all other sciences, are constantly being proposed and then tested. One of the great strengths of science rests in its ability to accept data—and explanations of these data—that are surprising and unexpected.

From the things they observe and the patterns they perceive, scientists come up with general explanations, or **hypotheses**, for what they have observed. Scientists are not content, however, just to generalize about the world. They also need to test these hypotheses by predicting what additional data will be found if a hypothesis is valid, if it accurately explains how things work. Paleoanthropologists and archaeologists accomplish these tasks by applying the procedures outlined in this chapter and by a rigorous adherence to the scientific method.

The fact that in archaeology and paleoanthropology we are examining our own human past and time periods enormously distant from our own poses a unique challenge. It is one thing for a chemist to examine a chemical reaction and suggest a rule that governs how those reactions progress; it is one thing for a microbiologist to focus on a colony of bacteria and suggest a hypothesis for how those bacteria react to heat or an overabundance of food. These chemical reactions and bacteria are of the here and now, and they are apart from us. It is quite another thing for paleoanthropologists and archaeologists to gaze back across the centuries, millennia, and eons of human history where the data are ancient, elusive, and rare and where our interpretations impinge on how we view ourselves. Did we humans begin our journey as a "killer ape," and what does it mean to us if we did? Were the world's first civilizations dependent on slavery and warfare, and if so what does this knowledge tell us about our twenty-first-century civilization?

As scientists, we must always be aware of and try to transcend our own preconceptions of what we think the past *should* tell us—or what we would like it to tell us—about ourselves. Our constructs of the past should be objective and free of our own temporal and cultural biases. This ideal is not easy to achieve, and we archaeologists and paleoanthropologists have sometimes fallen short of these goals. Further, we must recognize that our interpretations of the human past are approximations subject to continual refinement, major overhaul, or even complete abandonment as new data and new ways of looking at the same data come to the fore.

Paleoanthropological and Archaeological Sites

I use the term "site" quite frequently in this book. Paleoanthropological and archaeological **sites** are places where physical evidence of a past human presence can be recovered. Such evidence consists of (1) the skeletal remains of human beings or human ancestors, (2) **artifacts**—objects made and used by past peoples (Figure 2.1), and (3) **ecofacts**—environmental elements that exhibit traces of human use or activity, such as the bones of butchered animals.

Wherever people lived or worked, they used material from the surrounding environment: stone, clay, metal, wood, bone, plant fiber, seeds, antler, animal hides, and so on. These materials ultimately are lost, used up and discarded, abandoned, or hidden away for future use. Where conditions in the soil allow for their preservation, these items can be found and recovered for analysis by scientists who study the human past. Together, these physical remnants make up the archaeological site. A site was once a home, a community, a place of work. It now is a place where data can be collected that will enable us to tell the story of that home, that community, and that workplace.

Sites are defined not only by the recovered objects themselves but also by the physical arrangement of the remains. The preserved spatial context of archaeological remains—where things were used and left by an ancient people—allows us to reconstruct the activities that took place at a site. Most reconstructions of past times are based on analysis of human remains, artifacts, and ecofacts, as well as their spatial arrangement at sites where people lived or performed special tasks. Sites can be small and short-term, like hunting camps, or large and permanent, like the sites of the world's first cities in Mesopotamia (see Chapter 10). Pilfershire, discussed in Chapter 1, is an example of an archaeological site.

How Sites Are Formed

Sites come into existence through a series of site formation processes (Schiffer 1976). Tools can be discarded or lost; food remains can be thrown in a trash pit or pile; dead bodies may be casually abandoned or intentionally and ceremonially buried; valuable objects may be "cached," or hidden away, for a future retrieval that never takes place; human ancestors may be killed by animals and their remains dragged into a lair; and so forth. The study of how paleontological remains ended up in a particular place is called **taphonomy**; we can also apply this term to the study of how paleoanthropological or archaeological remains came to rest in their place of discovery. Recognition of how items became part of the paleoanthropological or archaeological record provides insights into the behavior of the human beings who left those artifacts behind.

Archaeological artifacts and ecofacts used or produced together to accomplish a task—to make stone tools, to prepare food, to carry out a ceremony—often are deposited together on the ground in a pattern that reflects the spatial

◀ **Figure 2.1**
Artifacts are objects that human beings manufactured. The eight long stone blades shown here are part of a cluster of thirty such artifacts, found in an ancient site in southern New England (top). A feature is an archaeological deposit that reflects a human activity or series of activities that occurred at a specific place. Here (middle) are shown two "unharvested" soapstone bowl blanks from a 3,000-year-old site in Barkhamsted, Connecticut (see Figure 1.4, left, for the tools used to quarry the soapstone at this site). These two impressive stone towers (bottom) are among a series of such towers constructed by Native Americans in southeast Utah, at the Hovenweep site.
(K. L. Feder)

arrangement of the activity. These clusters of archaeological material are called **features** and can be analyzed in our attempt to reconstruct a particular activity or set of behaviors. When **activity areas** are intact—in other words, where the items used together and deposited together are left exactly where they fell by ancient people—we use the term **primary refuse**. The next time you see inconsiderate folks leave the remnants of their picnic lunch behind on the ground, don't think of it as a gross mess; think of it as primary refuse. The remnants of that lunch, the waste flakes resulting from the production of stone tools left where they fell, and the skeletal elements of an animal left where it was butchered are examples of primary refuse.

The trash dump in my town, now called the Simsbury landfill, was used as the collective garbage disposal point for residents of my town for more than 90 years. The landfill began as a deep, broad depression where, beginning in 1920, residents would simply haul their trash for disposal. Slowly, the depression became filled with trash, but town residents kept coming; and by 1988, what was once a trash pit had become a substantial trash mountain more than 60 feet high. The Simsbury landfill and countless others throughout the world represent **secondary refuse** accumulations, places where members of a community collectively disposed of their trash. Just like us in the modern world, ancient people also often cleaned up the places where they carried out tasks, removing the objects used and produced from their primary contexts to a designated refuse area or areas. Just as we use refuse dumps and recycling facilities in our towns and cities, people in the past often took their trash to a pile or pit, removing from the immediate vicinity of their living quarters material that might be dangerous, that might attract wild animals or noxious insects, or that might simply otherwise be a nuisance (perhaps because of its smell).

Understand that archaeological sites are, essentially, repositories of the material remnants of people living out their lives. "Material remnants" is the key part of the site definition. As such, it must be admitted that the archaeological record is an imperfect and incomplete record of a way of life; behaviors or activities that don't involve any material objects may not leave behind any direct evidence. An elder sitting under a tree, telling children a story about creation; two men bragging about their sexual prowess; a woman speaking a silent prayer for the life growing within her: these may leave no traces in the archaeological record, though they are vitally important. But written history is no different; the written record is no more inclusive than the archaeological record. The lives of poor people, of slaves, and, for much of western history, of women get short shrift in the historical record, no matter how detailed that record may seem. Such deficiencies are not a reason to reject the study of history. Similarly, we can admit to the incomplete nature of the archaeological record while still asserting that, imperfect and challenging as it may be, the archaeological record is all we have for the vast amount of time human beings and our ancestors have been on this planet.

How Sites Are Preserved

Once material objects are laid on or in the earth, natural processes may cover, protect, and preserve them. Ash or lava spewed from a volcano, silt from a flooding river, sand blown by the wind, a collapsed cave roof, an avalanche—all may cover the objects left behind by people, preserving them until nature or archaeologists uncover them many years later. Some of the materials used by people, especially stone tools and pottery, preserve very well under most circumstances. Other materials, like bone and plant remains, require particular conditions for preservation. When archaeologists and paleoanthropologists are lucky, an archaeological site is itself like a fossil, a preserved physical representation of a past people and way of life.

In certain cases, the catastrophic agency of a community's destruction ironically acts, at least in part, to preserve the archaeological site left behind. There is no better example of this than what occurred at the beautiful Roman harbor town of Pompeii (Cooley 2003).

Nestled between the Bay of Naples and the foot of a towering volcanic mountain named Vesuvius, the residents of Pompeii had long been subject to the rumblings of their looming neighbor. We know that an enormous earthquake rocked Pompeii in A.D. 62, causing significant damage. In the years following this, numerous smaller tremors were felt by the city's residents, who likely became inured to the bad behavior of the volcano. Those tremors increased in frequency and amplitude in the early summer of A.D. 79 and then, on August 24, Vesuvius erupted catastrophically, hurling what is estimated to have been about 4 cubic km (a cubic mile) of ash into the atmosphere, some of it reaching an altitude of as much as 30 km (more than 18 mi; that's three times higher than the cruising altitude of a standard commercial jet). The prevailing wind, along with gravity, brought the plume of **ejecta** over the city, resulting in a shower of **pumice** that accumulated like an eerie, ashy snow on the streets and rooftops. Falling at an estimated rate of 15 cm (about 6 in) per hour (faster, by far, than any snowfall you have experienced), the weight of the accumulating pumice eventually collapsed roofs and filled the streets and houses of Pompeii, attaining a height of about 2.8 m (9 ft; Cooley 2003:40).

It is believed that the accumulating pumice killed only a few hundred residents of Pompeii, but it was a series of **pyroclastic** surges—what amounts to a sequence of devastatingly hot avalanches—on August 25 racing down the slopes of Vesuvius at speeds approaching 200 km (almost 125 mi) per hour that killed thousands more and, essentially, killed the city as well (Cooley 2003:42). If you were in Pompeii at the time and saw the surge coming, it was already too late for you to escape. Pompeii had succumbed to one of the most awesome forces in nature and lay as a great sepulcher, undisturbed, for more than 1,500 years.

After its destruction, Pompeii and the area surrounding the city were abandoned by any who had survived the eruption of Vesuvius, and no attempt was made to rebuild. Blanketed in ash, Pompeii slowly faded from memory until it was all but forgotten.

The initial fall of pumice had killed hundreds and destroyed most of the homes of Pompeii's residents, but it also protected the walls of those homes from the destructive force of the pyroclastic flow on the following day. Sealed in pumice, these walls—as well as the boulevards, avenues, and back alleys of Pompeii—were neither burned nor crushed but preserved, insulated from the elements and looters. Then, in A.D. 1595, a bit more than 1,500 years after its tragic destruction, the city was rediscovered by excavators. Researchers soon began the arduous task of removing the hardened ash and pumice layer, revealing the homes, theaters, and civic buildings of Pompeii, with their sometimes well-preserved wall paintings and tiled mosaics. Though the roofs are gone, today the

▶ **Figure 2.2**
Volcanic ash was long ago removed by archaeologists from around the columns, arches, walls, and stairways of Pompeii, here dramatically framed by the jagged caldera of Vesuvius, the volcano that destroyed the city and killed many of its residents. (K. L. Feder)

city is a strange place, a ghost town that appears to have been abandoned months or only a few years ago (Figure 2.2).

Even some of the inhabitants of Pompeii were preserved, in a way, when their bodies were entombed by the ash deposited by the pyroclastic surges on August 25. Entombed in a hard crust of ash, the bodies decayed away, leaving a hollow in the shape of the deceased (Dwyer 2010). When discovered, these hollows were filled with plaster and the ash chipped away, revealing a series of extraordinary phantasms—crudely cast, three-dimensional images of human tragedies (Figure 2.3).

How Sites Are Found

Archaeological sites are found in a number of ways. While some natural processes may preserve sites, other such processes may expose them. Rivers cutting into their banks, wind blowing sand away from an area, or waves eroding a beach may bring to light ancient, buried remains (Figure 2.4). Many of the sites related

◀ **Figure 2.3**
Eerie images of people, like this one of what appears to be a sleeping child, were made when archaeologists found gaps in the volcanic ash that covered Pompeii, which they then filled with plaster. The child depicted here was not sleeping, but dead, a victim of the eruption. The falling ash first killed the child and then hardened before the body decomposed, leaving a hollow, a perfect child-shaped mold of one of those unfortunate enough to have been caught in the catastrophic eruption of Vesuvius in A.D. 79. (K. L. Feder)

◀ **Figure 2.4**
Some archaeological
sites are revealed by
chance through the
agency of natural
processes. Here at Skara
Brae, at the Orkney
Mountains north of
Scotland, an ancient site
a few thousand years
old was exposed by the
winds and waves of a
North Atlantic storm.
(K. L. Feder)

to the earliest history of humanity have been exposed by these processes of erosion. Places such as Olduvai Gorge in Tanzania and the Hadar region of Ethiopia (see Chapters 3 and 4) present naturally exposed layers of ancient geological deposits (Figure 2.5). By walking over these places systematically in a procedure called **pedestrian survey**, paleoanthropologists and archaeologists found many of the important ancestral human fossils discussed in this book.

In other cases, archaeologists do not have the luxury of naturally exposed ancient layers in which to search for artifacts, ecofacts, or human skeletons. In these

◀ **Figure 2.5**
Researchers are shown
here at Olduvai Gorge,
searching for remnants of
early hominid occupation
of one of the most
important fossil localities
on Earth (see Chapter 3).
(Rick Ergenbright/Corbis)

◀ **Figure 2.6**
In areas of the world where natural processes have not exposed ancient sites, archaeologists must dig to reveal buried cultural deposits. Test pits are often excavated to explore an area for buried archaeological material. Here you are looking up a line of test pits—a test pit "transect." The pits are 10 meters apart and all soil is passed through ⅛-inch hardware cloth in the search for artifacts and ecofacts. (K. L. Feder)

areas, scientists search for sites through a process of sub-surface sampling, placing **test pits** at regular intervals in an attempt to locate ancient material buried by natural processes (Figure 2.6). In some cases aerial photography can help identify large-scale land modifications or buried remains that affect the growth of vegetation.

How Information Is Recovered

Once a site has been found, the arduous task of extracting the physical evidence from the ground begins. Paleoanthropological and archaeological evidence is rare, precious, and often fragile, so the methods used to unearth it have been designed accordingly.

We must recover our data with great care. Though we may use power equipment and picks and shovels to remove the culturally sterile overburden, once within the zone of a site we ordinarily rely on hand-held trowels, dental picks, and brushes to remove the soil enclosing site materials (Figure 2.7). Material may be left exactly where found in order to expose the possible **associations** among the remains. For example, a single stone, found

▶ **Figure 2.7**
Once a site has been found, it must be excavated in a regular and ordered way. Not only must artifacts and ecofacts be preserved, the spatial relationships among the materials found at a site must also be maintained. Excavation in square units by slowly peeling away soil layers aids in this task. (K. L. Feder)

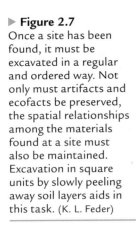

and then tossed in a bag, is not nearly as informative as a series of stones, each one left in place, that together denote an earth oven (Figure 2.8).

Context is the key here. A single artifact, devoid of any context—where it was found, what items it was found in proximity to—provides the archaeologist or paleoanthropologist with only a fraction of the information provided by an object for which context has been preserved and recorded. Consider the various possible contexts of a spearpoint in Figure 2.9. In 2.9b the spearpoint is found embedded in an animal bone. In 2.9c the same artifact is depicted as part of a **cache**, or collection, of other spearpoints. In 2.9d, again the same artifact is shown, this time stuck in the eye orbit of a human being. Finally, in 2.9e the

▲ **Figure 2.8**
The stones lining the bottom of a 4,000-year-old earth oven demarcate this archaeological feature. The stones were heated in a fire and then placed in the bottom of a pit, where the heat radiated by the stones was used for cooking.(K. L. Feder)

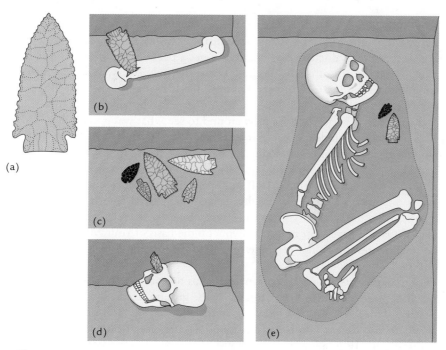

▲ **Figure 2.9**
An isolated artifact may tell us about an ancient technology, but to determine the use and meaning an object had to an ancient people, context is crucial. Consider the same artifact (a) recovered archaeologically from very different contexts: (b) embedded in an animal bone; (c) as one in a cluster of spearpoints found in an ancient hiding place; (d) stuck in the skull of a human being; (e) as a grave offering to a deceased hunter. In each case the artifact looks exactly the same, but its context—and, therefore, its deduced use and meaning—is different. (From Kenneth Feder and Michael Park, *Human Antiquity: An Introduction to Physical Anthropology and Archaeology*, Fourth Edition, Mayfield Publishing Company, 2001. Reprinted with permission from The McGraw-Hill Companies)

spearpoint is shown as one of two next to the skeletal remains of a person. In each case the spearpoint is exactly the same, but its setting and spatial associations differ, suggesting different uses or meanings of the object, respectively: a hunting weapon, part of a tool kit, a weapon of war, an offering to a deceased member of the group.

Though it might be an exaggeration to say that in archaeology spatial context is everything, it certainly is crucial. This should explain in part why archaeologists and paleoanthropologists are meticulous in excavating sites. A site is much more than just the sum of its individual parts (artifacts and ecofacts). Objects need to be carefully exposed, leaving them, at least initially, in place in order to preserve their spatial contexts and associations. This also explains why detailed and time-consuming record keeping is important before specimens are removed from the ground and returned to the lab for analysis. As careful as we are in excavating a site, we can miss small fragmentary remains. All excavated soil ordinarily is sifted through wire screening of ¼-inch, ⅛-inch, or even smaller mesh to ensure 100% recovery. In some cases the soil matrix may be taken to an on- or off-site lab, where standing water may be used to help in separating artifacts, ecofacts, or human bone from the surrounding soil.

Archaeology at a Distance: Noninvasive Methods of Data Collection

Beyond the ordinary probings that accompany regular health screenings, twice in my 60 or so years doctors have wanted to get a peek inside of me. Throughout most of the history of medicine there was really only one way for them to accomplish this: exploratory surgery. For example, if a patient experienced chronic pain at a particular spot—like the back—a doctor might have to anesthetize and then cut him or her open for a look around to see what was going on.

I am grateful, indeed, that this wasn't my fate. Doctors now have at their disposal all manner of technologies for examining the inside of a patient's body without recourse to the surgical knife. X-rays, computed tomography (CT) scans, magnetic resonance imaging (MRI), and the like allow a doctor to explore what's going on inside of you without the dangers of general anesthesia, the risk of infection, or the possibility of surgical error. It really is pretty great to avoid all that drama and have your doctor tell you, on the basis of your MRI, that "there's nothing interesting going on inside of you" and send you home with back exercises and a bottle of aspirin.

Archaeologists are in a situation analogous to your doctor. We are interested in what's going on inside a mummy, inside the ground, or inside a stone structure. While we are not nearly as far along as the modern medical profession in this regard, we do have a number of imaging technologies at our disposal that, like CT scans or MRIs, allow us to peer inside without digging holes or damaging precious remains.

For example, it seems obvious that human remains might present us with information concerning the health of ancient people. Avoiding a potentially damaging, invasive procedure by using the same kind of CT scanner available at your local hospital, researchers recently examined the hearts of 52 Egyptian mummies. The result: Though the average age of death was only 40, nearly half already exhibited evidence of atherosclerosis, in other words, hardening of the arteries (Pringle 2011a).

Monuments like earth mounds or stone pyramids present another challenge to the archaeologist. Perhaps there is a tomb secreted at the base of the mound, hidden chambers in the pyramid, or internal clues within that might enable us to determine how an edifice was constructed. Excavating to the base of a large mound can be a daunting and dangerous exercise, as well as potentially damaging to the monument. Peering into the internal structure of a stone building can be all but impossible without doing violence to its integrity. However, there are technologies that provide for ways to accomplish these tasks. For example, a microgravimetric study has been conducted on the Great Pyramid at Giza, in Egypt. Without drilling into any pyramid blocks or dismantling any elements of the structure, scientists were able to peer inside the pyramid. In a fascinating sequence of events, the study revealed evidence of the pyramid's construction that supported a hypothesis for how the pyramid had been built, long before the hypothesis had even been suggested (Brier and Houdin 2008). I'll reveal the particulars of this study in Chapter 10.

Finally, it is probably true that the most time-consuming element of archaeology—and the thing that led me to the MRI I mentioned earlier—is the literally back-breaking labor involved in moving enormous quantities of dirt in an attempt to reveal buried archaeological material. Here, too, there are emerging noninvasive technologies that allow us to look into the ground without moving any dirt.

For example, electrical resistivity survey involves sending an electrical current through the ground. The current is affected by the medium through which it passes. A buried brick wall, an in-filled irrigation canal, or a hollow tomb each has a different level of resistance to the current, and this can be read by the operator of the survey instrument, alerting archaeologists to the presence of hidden features invisible from the surface.

You've probably witnessed scenes in movies or documentaries where air traffic controllers or military personnel use radar to track commercial and private planes, enemy fighter jets, or incoming missiles. In this application of radar, an electromagnetic pulse is aimed at the sky, encounters objects (planes, a flock of birds, etc.), and then bounces back to be gathered by a receiving dish. The nature of the reflected signal indicates the kind of object the radar pulse encountered and its size, location, altitude, and speed.

In **ground-penetrating radar (GPR)**, an electromagnetic pulse is aimed, not at the sky, but into the ground (Conyers 2004). Just as in the aeronautical use of radar, the bounced-back signal can indicate something about the nature of whatever it has encountered. Lawrence Conyers (http://mysite.du.edu/~lconyer/) has used GPR very successfully to located ancient kivas in the American southwest (see Chapter 14); the remains of buried building foundations in Petra, Jordan; and the unmarked burials of a small group of African slaves killed in a shipwreck along Florida's Key West coast just before the Civil War. GPR and similar technologies can't replace the need to dig, but they certainly can help in determining where we ought to be digging.

In some cases, an ancient, large-scale monument may have been completely obscured by modern activity including agriculture and construction, but its magnetic ghost can still be seen by the application of remote sensing devices. For example, historical records indicated the approximate location of what was

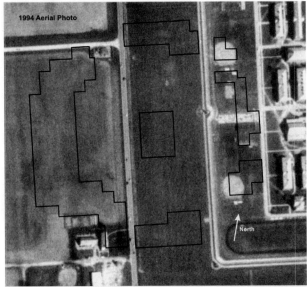

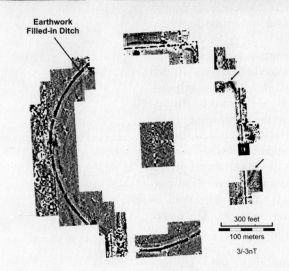

◀ **Figure 2.10**
Sometimes science produces magic. The top image is an aerial photograph of an area that is currently the location of an Ohio prison. There doesn't appear to be anything in the photo that suggests that this was the location of an ancient monument. The application of a remote sensing technique, proton magnetometry, produced the image on the bottom, clearly outlining the location of a buried soil signature marking the location of an enormous circular earthwork built by the aboriginal inhabitants of Ohio about 2,000 years ago. (Courtesy of Jarrod Burks)

historically labeled the Shriver Circle, an earthwork built by the indigenous people of Ohio—in this case, a circular mound of earth with an accompanying ditch circumscribing a vast space (Burks 2010; and see Chapter 14). All we have today is a sketch made in the early nineteenth century and a surveyor's map made in 1848. Though huge—the diameter of the circular embankment is about 400 m (1,300 ft), circumscribing an area of more than 20 acres—the entire area was leveled as a military camp during World War I. There is hardly any remaining surface indication of the earthwork. If you could walk over the entire site today—you can't because it's now on the grounds of a prison—you'd be hard pressed to recognize that there was a significant archaeological monument under your feet. Much of the site had, in essence, been erased, at least from the surface. Then, in 2008, by using a **proton magnetometer**, a device that measures minor fluctuations in the earth's magnetic field that may result from alterations in the soil, archaeologists Jarrod Burks (2010) and Robert Cook (Burks and Cook 2011) were able to identify the buried and mostly hidden remains of the 2,000-year-old earthwork. The magnetometer's readout is stunning, almost magical (Figure 2.10). The lost earthwork has been recovered, at least as a magnetometer image. Through remote sensing, a part of America's ancient legacy, long thought destroyed, was revealed.

Analyzing Archaeological Data

Like detectives at the scene of a crime, archaeologists collect physical evidence at the scene of a life. We can break this archaeological evidence down into the following categories: artifacts, ecofacts, and human skeletons. Each category requires its own forms of analysis.

How Artifacts Are Analyzed

In analyzing artifacts, at a minimum we want to know where the raw materials for the objects came from, how the items were manufactured, how they were used, and the social context in which they were made and used.

The Sources of Raw Materials

We can attempt to figure out where ancient people obtained their raw materials through a process called **trace element analysis**, in which impurities present in tiny or "trace" amounts are scanned for. Essentially, this involves a precise determination of the chemical makeup of artifacts and of potential geographic sources for the raw materials from which artifacts were made by any one of a number of procedures such as **neutron activation analysis** and **X-ray fluorescence**. The percentages of particular impurities often are unique and diagnostic of specific geographic sources and can serve as a fingerprint for place of origin. In other words, two pieces of turquoise (or obsidian or copper, etc.) may look entirely alike but have distinctive chemical compositions traceable to different sources. Artifacts are examined for their particular percentages of these trace elements. Possible sources for the raw material from which the artifact was made are also examined for their trace element percentages. If a raw material source and the artifact have matching trace element profiles, a scientist can suggest that the raw material for the artifact derived from that source.

For example, it has been conservatively estimated that a million turquoise artifacts have been found in Mesoamerica (E. Powell 2005), but there is an interesting problem; there aren't any known, extensive turquoise sources in central Mexico where most of the artifacts have been found. Archaeologists and geologists have long known, however, that there are significant sources of extremely high-quality turquoise in the American Southwest, in Arizona and New Mexico especially, not all that far away from central Mexico. Could the Southwest turquoise have been the raw material from which the artisans of ancient Mexico made their often spectacular works of art, and what might we conclude about trade and contact between the ancient inhabitants of the regions (Figure 2.11)? Archaeologist Phil Weigand has been testing that hypothesis for more than 30 years through the application of trace element chemistry, specifically through neutron activation analysis (NAA).

NAA produces a chemical signature for a raw material by bombarding it with neutrons. Weigand has collected samples of raw turquoise from 44 sources in the American Southwest and California. When I was an undergraduate anthropology major at the State University of New York at Stonybrook, I was one of several students who prepared turquoise samples from these sources for NAA, which established the chemical signatures of each of these sources. With Brookhaven Lab physicist Garman Harbottle, Weigand was able to determine the chemical composition of finished artifacts excavated from sites in Mexico whose trace element signatures matched those determined from

▼ **Figure 2.11**
The raw materials from which artifacts were made can sometimes be traced to their geographic sources through the analysis of their trace element chemistry. In this way, for example, archaeologist Phil Weigand has been able to show that much of the turquoise used to produce jewelry and other items of adornment in ancient Mexico was obtained by their artisans from sources in Arizona and New Mexico. (Werner Forman/Corbis)

▼ **Figure 2.12**
Archaeologists can gain insights about making and using tools by attempting to replicate their manufacture and use. Here, archaeology students are shown with some of their replicated tools: a bow and arrow, a fire-starting kit, a metate (grindstone), and a spear thrower or "atlatl" (see Chapter 6 for a detailed description of this weapon). (K. L. Feder)

sources in the Southwest. Many of the artifacts found in Mexico, thus, had been manufactured from turquoise that originated in the American Southwest.

Tool Manufacture and Use

Through **experimental replication**, the process of attempting to authentically re-create ancient artifacts, researchers can assess how an item was made (Figure 2.12). They also examine historically described groups that possessed a technology analogous to that of the ancient people being studied. Scientists can deduce the use an artifact served from its **morphology**—its form, what it looked like—and by the evidence of **wear patterns**. Different actions (piercing, cutting, scraping, engraving, chopping) performed by different tools on different raw materials (stone, wood, leather, bone, antler) leave distinctive and diagnostic wear traces, or "edge damage" (striations, polish, scars), that can be assessed through replication (Shea 1992). In an experiment conducted by archaeologist Lawrence Keeley

(1980), researchers used stone-tool replicas to perform different tasks on particular raw materials. For example, some tools were used to cut animal hide, some were used to saw wood, some were used to scrape meat off of bone, while others were used to drill in antler. Each tool used was then examined carefully under a microscope, and the particular kinds of resulting polish, damage, or wear on each were catalogued. This experiment essentially defined the damage or wear that accompanies each kind of use so that these tools and those from subsequent experiments and experimenters can serve as models for stone-tool wear patterns in the analysis of ancient specimens. If the ancient wear patterns match those seen on a particular experimental tool, researchers can conclude that the archaeological implement was used in much the same way.

Social Patterns

Along with providing insights into technology and use, artifacts can sometimes help illuminate less concrete aspects of ancient lifeways. The particular style of an artifact made by an individual may tell us something about who taught the maker. How people learn to make objects within a culture is a social decision. For example, they may learn from a parent who is passing down a family tradition of spearpoint or ceramic styles. The style seen in the archaeological remains, therefore, embodies this aspect of an ancient social system. Some archaeological features even more directly reveal the nonmaterial practices of a people. Most obvious here are burials, which often directly reflect a group's religious ideology as it relates to recognition of the significance of death as well as possible belief in an afterlife. Neandertals (see Chapter 5) interred their dead with tools and food 60,000 years ago, and what we uncover may tell us much about their perspective on life and death. Egyptian pharaohs were laid to rest in sumptuous splendor (see Chapter 10), and what we unearth in their pyramids informs us of their beliefs about the meaning of death.

How Ecofacts Are Analyzed

Animal bones, charred seeds, nut fragments, the shells of marine organisms, and fruit pits recovered at sites may represent the food remains of past people. Because diet is an important part of a culture, scientists would like to reconstruct the subsistence practices of prehistoric people. Because the skeletons of different animal species are usually distinctive, the kinds of animals present in an archaeological deposit can often be identified if remains are not too fragmented. Many archaeology labs possess **osteological comparative collections**, or bone libraries, where ancient specimens can be compared to known, labeled specimens to help identify the species recovered in excavation (Figure 2.13). The minimum number of animals represented in the **faunal assemblage** at a site can also be reconstructed. Because most animals exhibit two distinct forms on the basis of sex— that is, **sexual dimorphism**—scientists often can distinguish male from female animals. In addition, because animals go through a number of **osteological** developmental stages—changes in their bones as they grow and mature—it is also often possible to determine the age at death of an animal hunted, killed, cooked, and eaten by a prehistoric people. Furthermore, scientists can differentiate the bones of wild animals from those of domesticated animals: Domesticated animals frequently are smaller than their wild ancestors; the teeth of domesticated dogs

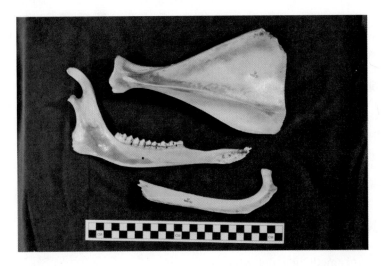

▲ **Figure 2.13**
Bones from an
osteological comparative
collection; from top to
bottom, the scapula
(shoulder blade), the
left side of the mandible
(lower jaw), and a
rib bone of a white-
tailed deer (*Odocoileus
virginianus*). (K. L. Feder)

are more crowded than those of their wolf progenitors; and the bones of wild animals are often denser than those of their domesticated descendants. We can learn much about the subsistence strategies of an ancient people if we can determine the species of an animal and its sex and age, whether the people hunted only older animals, and whether they avoided killing females or killed most of the young males but allowed females to survive to adulthood (a common pattern among domesticated animals).

Plant remains, including seeds, nuts, and wood, can be recovered and analyzed, and the contribution of plant foods to the diet can be assessed. Because plants are available seasonally, the yearly schedule of a people can be reconstructed based on which plant foods are present at a site and which are absent. We usually can differentiate the seeds, grains, or fruits of wild species from those that have been altered by humans through **artificial selection** (see Chapter 8) in the process of domestication.

Plant and animal communities often rely on a particular, sometimes rather narrow, range of climatic variables including amount of rainfall, length of the growing season, and high and low temperatures. By identifying the existence of particular plant and animal communities in the past, we can deduce the presence of climatic conditions such communities required for their survival. For example, caribou are not currently native to southern New York State, yet their remains have been found there—apparently they were on the menu—at the Dutchess Quarry Cave site, a more than 10,000-year-old occupation of the Hudson River valley near the modern town of Athens in Orange County. Today, caribou live far to the north in Canada and require a much colder climate than the one that currently characterizes southern New York. Their presence there 10,000 years ago implies a much colder climate then. This, in turn, provides archaeologists with important information about the environment to which human beings living in this same place adapted.

The human body is not entirely efficient when it comes to digestion. That is to say, not everything we swallow is digested and available to provide energy for our bodies. Some materials are exceptionally difficult for us to break down and digest and often are passed through our bodies and end up in our feces. When these fecal deposits preserve, as can happen, for example, in cave environments, they are called **coprolites**. When coprolites can be recovered, fragmentary remains of undigested food are collected and identified. Analysis of coprolites has aided in tracing the first Americans (Chapter 7) and the origins of agriculture (Chapter 8). Although it certainly would not be characterized by anyone as the most romantic part of archaeology—I'm guessing that the next installment of the Indiana Jones franchise, if there is one, will not have Indy tracking down the mystical coprolites of the Aztecs or whomever—coprolites are a valuable ecofact in the study of an ancient diet.

Palynology

One of the most important sources of information about past plant communities is **pollen**, the male gamete in plant sexual reproduction. Pollen grains tend to be rather durable and can preserve for thousands and even tens of thousands of years. Beyond this, pollen morphology is species specific: The pollen produced by each species is unique and distinguishable from the pollen produced by other kinds of plants. In other words, each spe-

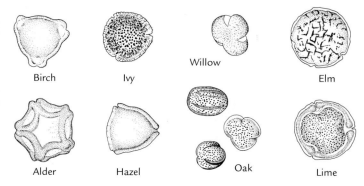

cies produces pollen that can serve in the manner of a fingerprint by which the presence of a species at a particular place in the past can be verified (Figure 2.14). Upon recovery of pollen from an ancient soil layer at or nearby an archaeological site, researchers can calculate the percentages of the various kinds of pollen falling on a site when it was occupied. Next, they attempt to locate modern locations where the **pollen rain**—the percentages of the pollen of different plant species that rains down in the spring today—is a close match for the percentages derived for an ancient time and place. When a good match can be found, it is reasonable to conclude that the ancient climate in which the site's inhabitants found themselves was similar to the climate of the modern location with a similar pollen rain.

The modern pollen profile of my own state of Connecticut, for example, contains an abundance of pollen from cold-loving trees like pine and birch, but there also is plenty from temperate-climate species like oak, maple, and hickory. Fourteen thousand years ago, however, the pollen falling on the state included only one of these species, pine; 60% of the pollen in that period came from bushes that don't even grow in Connecticut today but can be found thriving only in the Canadian Arctic (Davis 1969). The pollen species percentages as a whole falling on Connecticut 14,000 years ago look nothing like the modern breakdown but are a reasonably good match for what falls in northeastern Canada today (Figure 2.15). From this we can deduce that the climate of Connecticut 14,000 years ago was probably quite similar to what we find in the modern Canadian Arctic. **Palynology** provides a vital, direct link to the plant communities that characterized given places and times. This, in turn, allows us to suggest what the overall climate was like at those times and places.

Carbon Isotopes

All plants conduct photosynthesis, but not all photosynthesis is the same. In fact, there are a number of different **photosynthesis pathways**. For example, the **C3 pathway** characterizes most trees, and the **C4 pathway** typifies most grasses. These two pathways do essentially the same thing: They are the processes by which plants extract carbon from the carbon dioxide they respire and then use that carbon to produce leaves, stems, roots, bark, wood, and so on. These two pathways differ, however, in how they treat the different varieties (**isotopes**) of carbon in the atmosphere. We will see later in this chapter that one carbon variety, ^{14}C, is valuable in dating archaeological material. Here, an analysis of the concentration of another version of carbon, ^{13}C, provides data that can be useful

▲ **Figure 2.14**
Examples of the pollen grains of eight different plant species, magnified 5,000 times. Pollen grain form is species specific. By recovering pollen from archaeological levels, palynologists can identify the plants growing in an area when it was occupied in the past, reconstruct the makeup of a previous plant community, and deduce the nature of the environment that must have been in place for the reconstructed plant community to have survived. (From Kenneth Feder and Michael Park, *Human Antiquity: An Introduction to Physical Anthropology and Archaeology*, Fourth Edition, Mayfield Publishing Company, 2001. Reprinted with permission from The McGraw-Hill Companies)

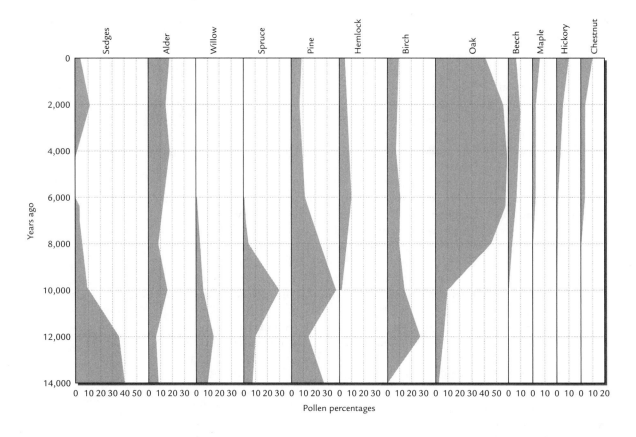

Sedges   Alder   Willow   Spruce   Pine   Hemlock   Birch   Oak   Beech   Maple   Hickory   Chestnut

Years ago

0

2,000

4,000

6,000

8,000

10,000

12,000

14,000

0 10 20 30 40 50 0 10 20 30 0 10 20 30 0 10 20 30 0 10 20 30 0 10 20 30 0 10 20 30 0 10 20 30 40 50 0 10 0 10 0 10 0 10 20

Pollen percentages

▲ **Figure 2.15**
The pollen profile from Rogers Lake, southeastern Connecticut, showing a dramatic change in plant communities over the last 14,000 years. (Based on Davis 1969)

in environmental reconstruction. C3 pathway plants, the trees, select against ^{13}C during photosynthesis. After trees extract carbon atoms from carbon dioxide, those atoms that happen to be ^{13}C are filtered out to a degree. C4 pathway plants, most grasses and sedges, have no such bias. They use whatever ^{13}C they take in and incorporate this carbon into their various parts. As a result, C4 pathway plants have a higher concentration of ^{13}C than do C3 pathway plants.

The soil in which plants grow and even the bones of the animals that ate the plants all reflect the concentration of ^{13}C in the preponderance of plants growing in an area at a particular time period. When and where **carbon isotope analysis** shows that concentration was relatively high, it means that grasses dominated the plant community. When the ^{13}C concentration was relatively low, it means that trees dominated.

As we will see in Chapter 3, an analysis of dramatic changes in ^{13}C concentrations over time suggests fundamental changes in the kinds of plant communities that characterized regions, continents, and even the entire planet. For example, ^{13}C measurements made at multiple locations indicates a worldwide contraction of forests and their replacement by grasslands beginning about 7 million years ago. The time of these shrinking forests is also characterized by a wave of extinction of forest-dwelling ape species and may have helped set the stage for the success of an apelike creature that could thrive in grasslands. That creature may very well have been our ancestor.

Phytoliths

Plants also produce a nonorganic residue consisting of microscopic mineral particles called **phytoliths** (Figure 2.16). Phytoliths are quite durable and can last in soil deposits or, when we are lucky, on the edges of tools used to process the plants that produced them. Phytolith form is unique to each plant species, so, when phytoliths are recovered at an archaeological site, specialists can determine the species of plants growing in the area when the site was occupied and might even be able to tell the species of plants cut, pounded, or ground with the tool. We'll see how important phytoliths have been in assessing the development of agricultural economies in Chapter 8.

Oxygen Isotopes

Planetwide changes in climate can also be read in the oxygen isotope record preserved in the fossil shells of ancient marine microorganisms called **foraminifera** ("forams" to those in the know). Foram shells reflect the ratio of two isotopes of oxygen, ^{16}O and ^{18}O, in seawater when these organisms were alive. Because ^{16}O is lighter than ^{18}O, water molecules (H_2O) with the lighter oxygen isotope evaporate more readily than do those with the heavier variety. Ordinarily, this makes little difference because the water that evaporates from the ocean returns as rain or as meltwater from frozen precipitation. However, during cold periods, water evaporates from the ocean and some of it falls as snow on land in higher elevations and upper latitudes. During periods of worldwide temperature decline, an increasing amount of that frozen precipitation remains locked in as ice, not returning to the ocean. As a result, a disproportionate amount of lighter oxygen water is removed from the evaporation-precipitation cycle during these cold periods. The oceans, therefore, become depleted of ^{16}O relative to ^{18}O. Foram shells reflect this depletion as they incorporate oxygen in the surrounding seawater into their shells. Therefore, when the proportion of ^{16}O in foram shells exhibits a drop, it's a good bet that worldwide temperature was experiencing a decline as well. When later foram shells show a return of higher ^{16}O levels, this indicates a change toward warmer temperatures. The oxygen isotope proportion curve (see Figure 4.11) has been worked out for the past 780,000 years or so based on ancient dated submarine strata in which foram shells have been recovered and analyzed (Shackleton and Opdyke 1973, 1976). Scientists have used this curve to figure out changes in worldwide temperature and glacial ice coverage during the Pleistocene epoch or the Ice Age.

Although the environment cannot cause a particular adaptation to develop, and a change in the environment does not guarantee any specific evolutionary change or behavioral adjustment, it does serve as the stage on which adaptations, evolutionary developments, and behavioral adjustments are played out. Clearly, to understand human adaptation, archaeologists and paleoanthropologists need to understand the nature of the ancient environments to which humans adapted.

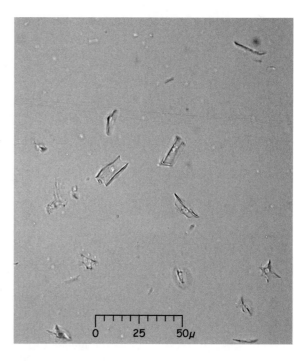

▲ **Figure 2.16**
Phytoliths are inorganic, silica bodies produced by plants. Phytoliths are useful to archaeologists because they are durable and each species produces distinct forms; specialists can identify the plant from the phytolith. Pictured here are maize phytoliths. (Courtesy Deborah Pearsall/ University of Missouri Paleoethnobotany Lab)

Reconstructing animal communities through the identification of their bones and reconstructing plant communities on the basis of their macroscopic remains, through palynology, and by carbon isotope analysis contribute to our understanding of the environments that played a crucial role in shaping the human story.

How Human and Prehuman Skeletal Remains Are Analyzed

The bones of human ancestors are an invaluable resource to paleoanthropologists and archaeologists. To begin with, the fact that archaic forms of human beings existed is shown most clearly by the presence of their bones, which are different from those of either apes or modern humans. (See the many photographs in Chapters 3 through 5 of creatures who were ancestral to us but, at the same time, were not quite us.) These bones can inform us about how human ancestors walked, the kinds of climates to which they were adapted, the foods they ate, their general level of nutrition, and the diseases and traumas from which they suffered. Comparing the bones of ancient human ancestors to those of modern people can help us place these specimens accurately in the human evolutionary line.

The Species Represented by a Bone

Ordinarily, the first question scientists ask about a bone concerns its species. When bones are complete, species identification is relatively straightforward because the precise form of each bone in an animal's body is unique to its species. For example, each of the 206 bones of the adult human body is uniquely human and cannot be mistaken for the bones of any other animal species. As a result, for the most part, the species of an intact bone found at an ancient archaeological site can be identified with great accuracy.

The identification of species can be tricky, however, when we deal with the remains of possible human ancestors. A first step is to compare the excavated bones with those of modern people. When the recovered bones exhibit features or landmarks that are uniquely human—for example, the position of the point of connection between the top of the spinal column and the base of the cranium reflecting the diagnostically human pattern of walking on two feet rather than four—we can confidently conclude at least that the bones being examined belonged to an individual in the human family. Also, very detailed and careful measurements can be taken of the bones and teeth of excavated specimens. Ordinarily, if those measurements—for example, the thickness of tooth enamel or the proportions of the bones in the hands—fall outside the range of those same measurements taken on human beings, we may conclude that the bones do not belong to a modern human being.

What happens when the bones being examined fall outside the range of variation of any living species, as do many of the bones discussed in Chapters 3 through 5? Sometimes, a new designation is created—for example, *Ardipithecus, Sahelanthropus,* or *Australopithecus*—to reflect the fact that the bones do not belong to any known, living creature but rather to an extinct variety that had not been recognized previously (Chapter 3). The next problem that may arise, however, concerns the interpretation of subsequent discoveries. Does a new fossil with features that indicate it did not belong to any living species belong to an already defined fossil species, or should we invent a new species designation for the newly discovered bones?

Remember, when judging whether or not a bone belonged to an animal of a known, living species, we need to determine whether its various measurements fall within the ranges of variation calculated for the living group. These ranges are very well known for modern human beings. A bone's identity as human or not can be determined. But how do we determine if a newly discovered bone whose measurements fall outside the human range belonged to an extinct species that has already been defined? Here we don't have nearly as good an idea of what the range of variation is for the bones of an extinct species. You cannot figure out a range of variation when there is only one specimen. The accuracy of a range cannot be meaningful when there are only a few examples. So it can be extremely difficult to figure out if the new bone's statistics fall within or outside that poorly known range. Beyond this, perhaps instead of placing a new specimen in a new species, we should expand the metrical definition of our own species to include it as well.

As a result, there is an element of subjectivity in inserting a fossil into a given extinct species or using the fossil to name a new species. Some paleoanthropologists are "lumpers," accepting a wide range of variation in ancient species and lumping most new finds into one of the already existing categories. Others are "splitters," assuming a narrow range of acceptable variation and naming new species with nearly every new discovery on the basis of rather small differences between the new find and already defined groups.

I admit this can be confusing, even to experienced researchers, but there is no right and wrong here. Naming new species and categorizing new finds cannot be absolutely objective, and there is much disagreement about the number of ancient, extinct species in the human evolutionary line. Keep this in mind when reading Chapters 3 through 5.

The Sex of a Skeleton

Many of the police dramas currently on television include forensic analysis of human remains (*Bones* is likely the most obvious example, but *CSI* and assorted versions of *Law and Order* also come to mind) with medical examiners attempting to identify people—their sex, age at death, geographic origin, and pathology—on the basis of incomplete skeletal remains. The techniques employed by these television scientists are based on those actually employed in the analysis of ancient skeletal remains.

For example, this book will refer to specific fossils as being male or female. This identification is possible because of the recognition of **sexual dimorphism**. Human and ape males, for example, have skeletons that often are readily distinguishable from those of females of the same species. Among humans and apes, males tend to be larger, with heavier, denser, and rougher bones than females. In addition, males tend to have larger, heavier skulls, with larger and rougher areas for muscle attachment. In some ape species, males have a bony crest on the top of their skulls, whereas females lack this feature. Also, in some species, males have a large ridge of bone above the eye orbits (sockets). Females either lack this feature or have a smaller bony ridge. Among human beings, all of the various angles of the pelvis that control the overall size of the birth canal are, of necessity, larger in the vast majority of females than in males. With enough skeletal elements recovered, modern forensic scientists as well as paleoanthropologists can correctly distinguish males and females more than 95% of the time (Krogman 1973).

The Age at Death

Our discussion of human skeletons will occasionally mention an individual's approximate age at death. The bones of human children go through a series of developmental changes during the course of their lives. For example, tooth eruption and replacement provide developmental time-posts in human maturation. The **deciduous dentition**—the baby teeth—erupt above the gum line in a regular order and at fairly well-established times (Figure 2.17). The permanent teeth then replace the baby teeth, also in a regular pattern, at reasonably well-fixed ages until, finally, the wisdom teeth—the 18-year molars—come in. Using a chart like that shown in Figure 2.17, one can estimate the age of a child under 18 based on which teeth have already erupted above the gum line and which teeth have yet to appear.

Another developmental time-post can be found on the long bones—the various bones of the arms, legs, hands, and feet. When we are born, each of the long bones is in three sections: a shaft, or **diaphysis**, and two endcaps, or **epiphyses** (*sing.*, epiphysis). In a process called **epiphyseal fusion**, the shafts and endcaps fuse to one another during growth at more or less set times during our teen years; this fusion reflects maturity and full growth (see Figure 2.17). Once again, by reference to the time range when each of the individual epiphyses fuses to its respective diaphysis, the age at death of an immature individual can be estimated fairly accurately.

Later in life, changes are less regularly timed, reflecting gradual deterioration of our bones rather than consistent time-posts. This deterioration, while inevitable, is subject to great variability depending on the life and work history of the individual, so determining a person's age based on his or her state of deterioration can be problematic. There are, however, some changes in the adult skeleton that are more consistently timed. For example, **cranial sutures**—the places where the different cranial plates come together—fuse through time. Young adults usually exhibit well-defined sutures, whereas aged people may have had their sutures disappear entirely. The region where the pubic bones come together—the **pubic symphysis**—can also be used to estimate the age at death of an individual. At their point of articulation, the faces of the left and right pubic bones go through a fairly regular, age-dependent sequence of changes.

Geographic Origin

We all recognize that people's physical features differ based on the geography of their origins; humans from different parts of the world possess a constellation of physical traits—skin color, nose shape, hair texture, body proportions—that tend to distinguish them from people from other parts of the world. Skeletal traits also vary geographically; so in some instances, the skeletal remains of individuals can be traced to the part of the world from which they came. For example, one reason we know that Native Americans originated in Asia is that the oldest skeletal remains in North America share a group of skeletal characteristics with Asian people (see Chapter 7).

In an episode of one of the programs in the *Law and Order* franchise, the bones of a small child were found. There was no obvious match between the child represented by the remnant skeletal elements and any child reported missing in the Greater New York City region. It became the job of the medical exam-

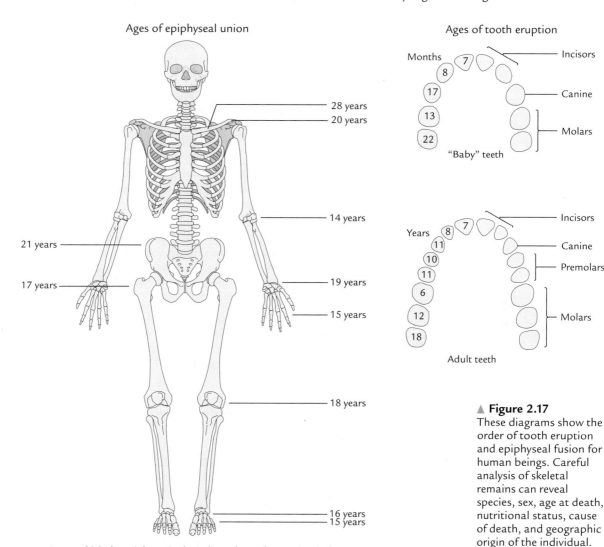

Ages of epiphyseal union

Ages of tooth eruption

28 years
20 years

14 years

21 years

17 years

19 years

15 years

18 years

16 years
15 years

Months

7
8
17
13
22

Incisors

Canine

Molars

"Baby" teeth

Years

8 7
11
10
11
6
12
18

Incisors

Canine

Premolars

Molars

Adult teeth

Age at which the epiphyses in the indicated area fuse to the shafts.

▲ **Figure 2.17**
These diagrams show the order of tooth eruption and epiphyseal fusion for human beings. Careful analysis of skeletal remains can reveal species, sex, age at death, nutritional status, cause of death, and geographic origin of the individual.

iner (ME) to try to coax out the child's biography as revealed by his bones. The ME performed what, even by the standards of television cop dramas, seemed to be magic; she told the investigating officers that the child had been born in Africa, as well as where he had been raised (which was different from his birthplace) and even how long he had been in the area of New York City.

It wasn't magic at all, but the application of a set of techniques useful to medical examiners and forensic anthropologists, as well as archaeologists and paleoanthropologists. Just as raw materials like turquoise or obsidian have diagnostic trace element signatures, so do a region's soils. Those signatures become enshrined in plants that grow in a region and then those same signatures become fixed in the bones of the animals and people who eat the plants that grow in that region.

The element strontium (chemical symbol Sr) is particularly useful in this kind of analysis. The ratio of the two isotopes of strontium varies between regions, and (here's the coolest part) the strontium becomes a part of your teeth as you are developing, and your tooth enamel reflects the ratio of those isotopes when they first developed (B. Fowler 2007). For example, the strontium isotope ratio in your adult tooth enamel right now reflects the ratio when the enamel developed when you were a little kid (the buds of your adult teeth were already in your upper and lower jaws when you were an infant). It doesn't change through time. So, if a forensic anthropologist were to examine the strontium in your teeth today, he or she could probably match it up with the geographic region in which you lived when you were a kid, showing where you were born and where you spent the beginning of your life. In an application of this form of analysis, for example, researchers were able to determine that some of those buried in high-status graves at the Bolivian sites of Tiwanaku and Chan Chan (see Chapter 13) were born locally, and some were outsiders (Knudson et al. 2004).

The strontium in your bones, on the other hand, does change through time, but very slowly, measured over the course of a decade. So, the strontium isotope ratio in your bones isn't necessarily a reflection of where you were born but, instead, where you've lived for the last decade or so. Strontium analysis of a bone from a man buried in a cave located at another Tiwanaku site in southern Bolivia, for example, revealed that he had lived in the general area for more than a decade. In other words, he was a local person and not someone from outside of the region (Knudson et al. 2005). The geographic origins of some of those buried at Stonehenge have been traced using their strontium signatures (Chapter 9).

Strontium isotope analysis, therefore, provides a useful way of measuring migration patterns and social patterns of movement across a landscape.

Pathology and Disease

The 206 bones in a human body are like a book on which some of that human's life experiences are written. Healed bone breaks, episodes of malnutrition during growth, specific dietary deficiencies, the ingestion of certain poisons, arthritis, tuberculosis, syphilis, cancers, and many other conditions leave recognizable traces on bones. These marks can be read by the specialist in **paleopathology**. The paleopathological evidence on the bones of European Neandertals is discussed in Chapter 5; the high level of malnutrition evident on their bones may explain why the Neandertals became extinct.

As mentioned previously in this chapter, two photosynthesis pathways, C3 and C4, differ in the degree to which they utilize one of the stable varieties of the element carbon (specifically, ^{13}C); C3 plants (mostly trees) tend to filter out ^{13}C, while C4 plants (mostly grasses and sedges) do not. As a result, as mentioned earlier, C3 plants tend to have a measurably lower ^{13}C "signal" or concentration than do C4 plants. The bones of animals, including those of people, who eat plant products reflect the ^{13}C levels of their foods. So, the bones of a people who subsisted on tree foods (fruits and nuts) will exhibit a lower ^{13}C signal than those bones of a people who relied to a greater extent on the seeds, leaves, or roots of grasses. When the bones of these two different peoples are studied, their ^{13}C signals can be determined, and the source of the bulk of their foods—C3 or C4 plants—can be deduced.

Determining the Age of a Site or Specimen

It may be the first question people ask about an archaeological site or artifact: "How old is it?" In fact, it is one of the key questions that archaeologists and paleoanthropologists hope to answer about the sites they excavate and the artifacts they uncover. In attempting to illuminate the chronology of human evolution, paleoanthropologists need to know the ages of the various fossils discussed in this book. In their efforts to produce a narrative of the lengthy history of the human race before there was writing and to expose the cultural processes at work that produced that narrative, archaeologists need to know when major developments—the earliest production and use of tools, the origins of hunting, the development of agriculture, the growth of class societies—took place.

Chronology has always been important in paleoanthropology and archaeology, but until fairly recently in the history of these disciplines, dating fossils and sites depended on sequences based on **stratigraphic** layering of the earth's surface—and a lot of guesswork. The fundamental technique had changed little since William Smith recognized its applicability in the late eighteenth and early nineteenth centuries (see Chapter 1). Dating was not absolute, but relative; scientists could determine whether a fossil or site was older or younger than another fossil or site depending on whether it was in a higher or lower stratigraphic layer. Fossil specimens and archaeological sites were assigned to particular stratigraphic layers. Though no certainty could be achieved, scientists derived dates based on assumed rates of formation of the layers above and below, on the guessed ages of fossils of extinct species found in association with human remains, and on a bit of intuition.

Dating Techniques Based on Radioactive Decay

Stratigraphic sequences, fossil associations, and even a bit of intuition are still used by paleoanthropologists and archaeologists in dating specimens, but these are no longer the only or primary methods of dating. Researchers can now rely on **radiometric** dating techniques based on the known rates of decay of several radioactive (unstable) isotopes (varieties) of common elements such as carbon (^{14}C dating), uranium (uranium series dating), and potassium (potassium/argon, or K/Ar, dating). These techniques provide **absolute dates** rather than **relative dates**. This does not necessarily mean they are accurate or precise, though we strive for both. The term *absolute* means only that we can associate a year or range of years with an object or site rather than place the sites or objects only in chronological order, as is the case in relative dating. Absolute dating is also referred to as *chronometric*, meaning, literally, that in its application we are attempting to measure time.

K/Ar Dating

One technique that has been particularly useful when applied to early human ancestors is **K/Ar dating** (Dalrymple and Lanphere 1969). A newer version of the technique, **argon/argon dating**, is more accurate and is now used more often than the older procedure, but it is still based on measuring the amount of argon 40 buildup in volcanic rock (Deino, Renne, and Swisher 1998). Argon/argon dates can be extremely accurate; a recent refinement of the technique produces dates that are within 0.25% of the date of an object of known age (Kuiper et al. 2008).

Potassium is a common element found in volcanic deposits. A radioactive variety of potassium decays into argon gas. When a volcanic layer is deposited, all of the argon already present from previous potassium decay bubbles off into the atmosphere. In a sense, the atomic clock in the ash or lava is set to zero and there is no argon left in the deposit. When the volcanic rock solidifies, the unstable potassium continues its slow decay to argon, which is trapped in the rock. Because we know the rate at which the radioactive variety of potassium decays to argon—its **half-life** is 1.25 billion years—by measuring how much argon has accumulated in the rock, we can determine how long the argon has been building up since the rock was last liquefied (that is, since the volcanic eruption deposited the lava) and, therefore, when that rock was deposited.

Potassium/argon and argon/argon dating provide an age for the rock itself. You can't use the technique directly to date an artifact made from the rock. For example, there is a volcanic deposit in my hometown that has been dated to about 180 million years ago. People living in the valley bordering the mountain where exposures of that volcanic rock can be found quarried some of it and made tools about 5,000 years ago. The tools are 5,000 years old, even though potassium/argon or argon/argon dating would still provide a date of 180 million years; that date indicates when the molten lava solidified and not when people made artifacts from that rock.

In most applications of potassium/argon and argon/argon dating, human fossils are found above or below a datable layer (Figure 2.18). When a fossil is found above a dated layer, the fossil must be younger than that layer; that is, the creature was alive at some point after the volcanic layer was deposited. The date on the layer below a fossil represents a maximum age for the fossils; they cannot be any older than the age of the volcanic flow that underlies them. When a fossil is found beneath a dated layer, we can be sure it is older than that deposit; that is, the creature was living in the area before the dated layer was deposited. The date on a layer above a fossil represents a minimum age; the fossils may date to any time before the volcanic layer that overlies them, but they cannot be any younger. Under the best of circumstances, the fossils can be associated with layers both above and below them, enabling us to bracket their age.

There is one notable exception to the indirect application of these dating procedures. The humanlike footprints found in hardened volcanic ash at Laetoli in Tanzania, to be discussed in more detail in Chapter 3, must be the same age as the rock itself; the ash fell and was moistened by a soft rain, and then two individuals walked across it, leaving their trails. The wet ash quickly hardened, was covered by additional ash, and, in this way, was preserved. Dating the rock therefore allows for a precise, direct determination of the age of the footprints.

^{14}C Dating

Carbon is an extremely abundant element and one of the building blocks of life on earth; every living thing contains carbon. The most common and stable variety of carbon is ^{12}C. The numeral 12 refers to the number of particles in the carbon atom's nucleus: 6 positively charged particles, or protons, and 6 neutral particles, or neutrons. A radioactive isotope of carbon is produced when free

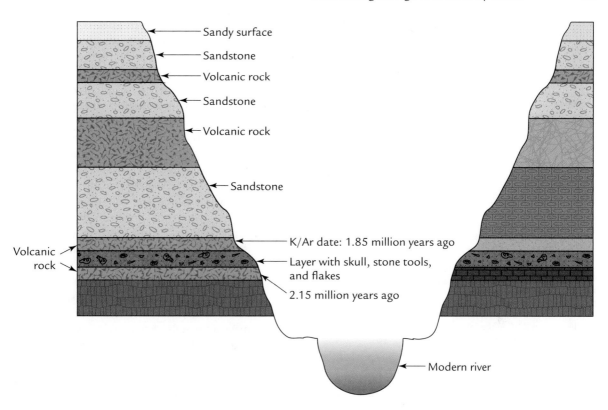

Sandy surface

Sandstone

Volcanic rock

Sandstone

Volcanic rock

Sandstone

K/Ar date: 1.85 million years ago

Layer with skull, stone tools, and flakes

2.15 million years ago

Volcanic rock

Modern river

neutrons originating in the sun stream toward earth and collide with nitrogen atoms in the earth's atmosphere. The resulting variety of the element is carbon 14 (^{14}C) for the 14 particles in its nucleus (6 protons and 8 neutrons).

Because ^{14}C and ^{12}C are nearly identical chemically, they combine equally with oxygen to produce carbon dioxide, which plants take in through respiration. Plants exhale oxygen and keep the carbon atoms—both ^{14}C and ^{12}C—which they then use in the production of leaves, branches, roots, nuts, seeds, or fruits. Again, because ^{12}C and ^{14}C are so similar chemically, the proportion of ^{12}C to ^{14}C in grasses, trees, and bushes is the same as it is in the atmosphere (one trillion ^{12}C atoms for every one ^{14}C atom). When animals eat the products of these plants and again when other animals eat these animals, the ratio of ^{12}C to ^{14}C across the food web remains the same. In fact, all living things on earth are part of the carbon cycle and maintain the same proportion of stable ^{12}C to unstable ^{14}C during their lifetimes—a proportion that is, in turn, the same proportion as is seen in the atmosphere.

As an unstable isotope, ^{14}C ultimately decays, reverting back to the nitrogen atom from which it was produced. Like radioactive potassium, ^{14}C decays at a regular, naturally fixed half-life—in its case, 5,730 years. Once an organism dies, no new carbon is respired or ingested, and so the constantly decaying ^{14}C is no longer replenished. When an organism has been out of this carbon cycle for a substantial amount of time—measured in the hundreds, thousands, or tens of thousands of years—it contains significantly less ^{14}C than it did when it was alive. How much less can be measured and the amount of time it must

▲ **Figure 2.18**
Combining stratigraphic analysis with potassium/argon dating has enabled scientists to bracket the ages of ancient hominid skeletons and artifacts. In this hypothetical example the remains of a human ancestor have been found in a layer overlying a lava flow dated through potassium/argon to 2.15 million years ago and underlying a subsequent flow dating to 1.85 million years. The hominid remains must date, therefore, to some time between 1.85 and 2.15 million years ago.

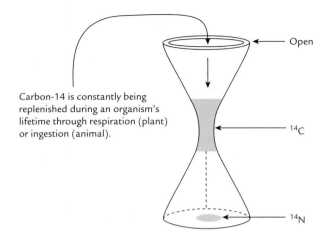

Carbon-14 is constantly being replenished during an organism's lifetime through respiration (plant) or ingestion (animal).

Once an organism dies, the top of the hourglass is shut and the Carbon-14 that decays is not replenished and the amount left (like the sand left in the top section of an hourglass) is a function of time. Measuring the amount of sand left at the top of a callibrated hourglass tells us how long ago the hourglass was turned over. Calculating the amount of Carbon-14 left in an organism tells us how long ago the organism died.

▲ **Figure 2.19**
The process of radioactive decay of ^{14}C can be likened to the sands pouring out of the top of an hourglass. In an hourglass, sand escapes the top chamber and accumulates on the bottom at a fixed rate; the amount of sand left on top can be used to calculate how long ago the hourglass was flipped over. In an analogous manner, ^{14}C decays to nitrogen at a fixed rate; the amount of radiocarbon left in the remains of an organism can be used to determine how long ago it died.

have taken based on its known, fixed rate of decay for that much loss to have occurred can be determined based on the known rate of decay.

So the decay of ^{14}C provides a natural clock, a kind of hourglass where the rate at which the sand pours into the bottom of the glass is known (Figure 2.19). One need only determine how much sand (^{14}C) was present initially in the hourglass (organism) and how much now remains to establish approximately when the glass was overturned (when the organism died). For the **radiocarbon dating** (**carbon dating**, ^{14}C dating) to produce accurate results, the item being dated needs to be at least a few hundred and ordinarily less than about 50,000 years old. **Accelerator mass spectrometry (AMS)**, another method of ^{14}C dating, may ultimately extend the viable dating range back beyond this. For now, AMS dating allows for much smaller samples to be radiocarbon-dated.

Fluctuations in solar radiation cause changes in the production of ^{14}C in the atmosphere over broad stretches of time, and this variation has an effect on the dates derived through radiocarbon dating. During periods when ^{14}C was being produced at a slightly higher rate, dated items will produce dates that are a little younger than their actual, or "calendar," age. On the other hand, during periods when ^{14}C was being produced at a lower rate, dated items produce dates that are a little older than their actual age. A partial solution to this complication is provided by **dendrochronology,** discussed next.

Dating Techniques Based on Biology
Dendrochronology
Dendrochronology, or tree-ring dating, is an extremely accurate biological dating technique. Its usefulness in dating archaeological sites results from four factors that apply in some areas of the world.

1. Trees add one growth ring every year.
2. The width of each year's tree ring is controlled by an environmental condition or set of conditions such as spring rainfall amount or temperature.
3. Any sequence of varying tree-ring widths over a long period of time is unique.
4. All trees in a given area reflect the same pattern of changes through time in tree-ring width.

By overlapping ring sequences of living trees with those of old dead trees, a **master sequence** of tree-ring width variation over many years has been developed. By analysis of bristlecone pine trees, a master sequence greater than 9,000 years has been produced for the American West. The master sequence constructed in England extends to 7,000 years ago; the master sequence developed in western Germany extends back even further to about 10,000 years ago. When an archaeological site is located that contains wood or even entire cross sections of logs, the succession of thick and thin rings in the ancient specimens can be compared to the master sequence. By determining where the individual sequence overlaps with the master sequence, the life span of the tree can be fixed in time (Figure 2.20). By seeing in what year these archaeological specimens were cut down—the actual year in which the tree's final ring was added—an exact date can be associated with the site.

Dendrochronological master sequences have been used to assess the accuracy of radiocarbon dating. Here's how that worked. First, individual tree rings were carbon-dated. Old rings are no longer growing and are, therefore, removed from the carbon cycle; ^{14}C is not being replenished in them. A ring laid down 1,000 years ago in a *living* redwood tree, for example, should produce a carbon date of about 1,000 years. A very large sample of carbon dates derived from old tree rings has been carefully compared to the age of each of those rings as determined by dendrochronology (those are called the calendar ages; since dendrochronological dates are actual, counted years, they are the equivalent of calendar years). The resulting **calibration curve**, now extending back to 12,593 years ago, allows a radiocarbon date within this period to be converted to a calendar year date (Reimer 2012; Figure 2.21). In general, the further back in time, the more a radiocarbon date will *underestimate* the actual age of whatever

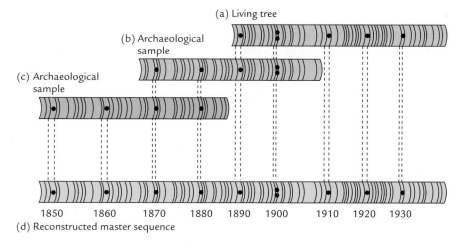

(a) Living tree
(b) Archaeological sample
(c) Archaeological sample

1850   1860   1870   1880   1890   1900   1910   1920   1930
(d) Reconstructed master sequence

▲ **Figure 2.20**
Cross section of tree rings from a living tree (a) overlaps the ring sequence from an archaeological sample (b), which, in turn, overlaps part of the sequence of another archaeological sample (c). The overlapping of many samples allows for the construction of a "master sequence" of tree-ring width patterns (d). (From Robert J. Sharer and Wendy Ashmore, *Archaeology: Discovering Our Past*, Mayfield Publishing Company, 1993. Reprinted with permission from The McGraw-Hill Companies)

▶ **Figure 2.21**
Calibration curve for radiocarbon dates. The vertical axis represents the radiocarbon dates derived for a large number of tree-ring samples, and the horizontal axis represents the actual dendrochronologically derived dates for those same tree rings. As you can see, for tree rings that are more than about 3,000 years old, radiocarbon dates generally understate the true age of a sample.

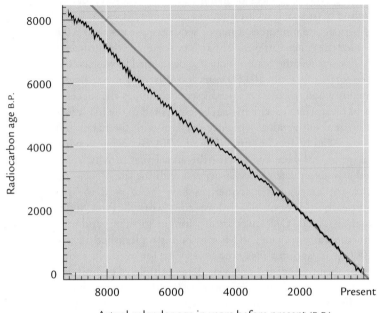

Actual calendar age in years before present (B.P.)
based on dendrochronology

is being dated; this underestimation can amount to several thousand years. The discovery of well-preserved remains of enormous Kauri trees in New Zealand may enable the extension of dendrochronological calibration back to 50,000 or even 60,000 years (Barry 2007).

The analysis of **varves**, layers of sediment that are deposited annually along lake and ocean shorelines and whose ages, therefore, can be calculated directly by counting back from the present, have been used to calibrate older radiocarbon dates in an approach conceptually similar to tree-ring dating. Radiocarbon dates derived from organic samples recovered from precisely dated varves have been compared to their respective varve "calendar" dates. The degree of error and the amount of correction needed to convert carbon dates to calendar dates for the period 11,200 to 52,800 years ago have been calculated in this way (Ramsey et al. 2012).

Dating Techniques Based on Radiation Damage

Luminescence Dating

Luminescence dating measures the amount of energy that is trapped in material recovered at archaeological sites as a result of natural radioactive decay in the surrounding soil. Again, such energy is released at a set rate in a given soil, so the amount captured in site materials reflects their age. The amount of energy captured by the archaeological material over time and, hence, its age can be measured after releasing the energy by heat (in the application called **thermolumines-cence**, or **TL**) or by laser light (in the application called **optically stimulated luminescence**, or **OSL**). Luminescence dating has been applied successfully to fired clay objects, especially pottery, as well as to stone that has been heated to a high temperature—for example, the rocks lining a fireplace. In both cases the application of heat—the firing of the pot or the heating of the stone in a fire—releases all of the energy previously trapped in the material. This effectively sets the trapped-charge clock to zero. Then once the pot or stone is returned to the earth, it again begins to accumulate energy at the set rate produced by the natural radioactivity of the surrounding soil. Knowing that rate allows calculation of how much time has elapsed since the object was heated and, therefore, when people were present at the site making pots or banking their hearths with stones.

Dating by Measuring Paleomagnetism

Paleomagnetic Dating

Paleomagnetic dating is based on the fact that the position of magnetic north is not a fixed point and continuously moves. In fact, the north magnetic pole of the earth is currently moving about 50 km (31 miles) each year in a northwesterly direction (Perkins 2007).

When heated sufficiently, ordinarily in excess of 500 or 600 degrees Celsius (930 to 1100 Fahrenheit), naturally magnetic particles on the earth's surface will align themselves with the current location of magnetic north. Once their temperature cools, for example, in a lava flow, that alignment is frozen in place and can be measured. If the material in which the magnetic particles are aligned can then be dated (for example, with the Ar/Ar method), we now know the direction and timing of the location of magnetic north. Dates can then be determined for other places when the alignment of magnetic particles found there matches the alignment of previously dated features. Using this procedure, scientists have produced a master map of North Pole locations for the last 7,000 years (Perkins 2007).

Just as the orientation of magnetic particles in an ancient lava flow may become fixed, in **archaeomagnetic dating** magnetic orientation can become "fossilized" in cultural features. For example, the magnetic particles in sediments that have infilled a canal may become lined up with the earth's magnetic field at the time of their deposition (Eighmy and Howard 1991). Similarly, the magnetic particles in clay making up the bricks of a kiln, like so many natural compass needles, may point to the location of magnetic north at the time they were heated. Careful study of dated sites with features exhibiting evidence of past magnetic orientation has provided data necessary for the production of a "master map" showing the location of magnetic north as it changed through time (Eighmy and Sternberg 1990). Figure 2.22 shows the deduced location of magnetic north based on archaeomagnetism between A.D. 600 and 1975. When the orientation

▼ **Figure 2.22**
Master map of the location of magnetic north from the period A.D. 600 to 1975 as determined at archaeological sites in the American Southwest (SWCV595). (Courtesy of Jeffrey Eighmy)

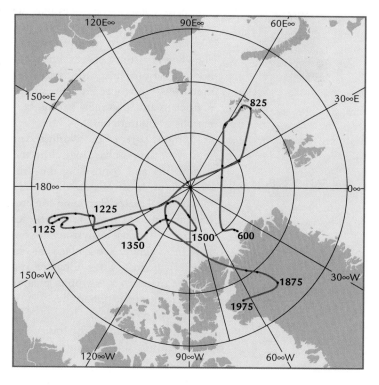

of the earth's magnetic field has been preserved in features found at an archaeological site dating to sometime in that period, a more precise estimate of the site's age can be deduced based on the dated location of magnetic north along this curve during the site's occupation.

The Ethics of Archaeological Research

Rather obviously I am a contemporary person, a product of the modern world, born in the middle of the twentieth century to an American family firmly ensconced in the middle class. I can add to this the fact that I am of European descent; my father's side of the family hails from Austria and my mother's from Poland, Germany, and Russia. Finally, I am university educated and trained as an archaeologist.

My personal identity and family bio are relevant here for the following reason: The vast majority of the archaeological fieldwork I have conducted during the course of my career has been at sites representing the villages, hunting camps, and quarries of Native Americans, people with whom I have no particular historical connection. This raises the following interesting ethical question: Since I am not ethnically Native American, what gives me the right to excavate the places where their ancestors lived?

This is not merely an issue of political correctness. For much of our discipline's history, archaeologists practiced what can best be described as archaeological colonialism. Europeans and Americans of European descent traveled the world looking for fabulous archaeological treasures, dug them up, and brought them home to sell or display in museums or, in some cases, just their own homes. The native peoples of places like Egypt, Peru, or China were rarely asked permission by foreign archaeologists to excavate in their countries, nor were they asked permission to remove the material evidences of their histories for display elsewhere. In some cases there were no local laws regulating archaeology and no real national institutions to oversee the archaeological activities of locals, much less foreigners. At best, archaeologists struck deals with local leaders or politicians and, like their natural resources, the archaeological heritage of many nations was plundered.

In most parts of the world today, governments have enacted laws that serve to protect their archaeological heritage by regulating the excavation of archaeological sites and controlling the disposition of artifacts recovered during those excavations. Most of these laws and regulations at least partially ensure that archaeological material remains the property of the government (or local university or museum) and is curated in the country of origin, though it may be loaned out for temporary analysis, exhibitions, or tours. In fact, in the last few years, I have been able to see artifacts and human body impressions from Pompeii (this chapter), the fossil Lucy (Chapter 3; and I have the *I Love Lucy* T-shirt to prove it), and the treasures of Egyptian pharaoh Tut Ankh Amen (Chapter 10), all during their national tours when they were on exhibit at the Discovery Center in Times Square, New York City.

In contrast, outside of Indian reservations, Native Americans in the United States are not able to control or regulate the vast majority of the archaeology conducted at the sites left behind by their ancestors, and most of that archaeology is conducted by people like me: non-Indians. It's easy to empathize with the discomfort some Native Americans feel about archaeology (Travis 2010); imagine a group of Native American scholars excavating the archaeological remains left behind by the U.S. cavalry during the Battle of the Little Bighorn (Custer's Last Stand) or the site left by the Pilgrims at Plimoth Plantation. It sounds fine to me, but I bet it might make a lot of people uncomfortable.

Indians do possess some control over one category of their cultural heritage: the burials of their ancestors. As a result of a U.S. law titled the Native American Graves Protection and Repatriation Act (NAGPRA), modern Indians are the legal stewards of burials that can be shown to contain the remains of their ancestors (http://www.nps.gov/nagpra/PUBLIC/INDEX.HTM).

NAGPRA is important, but far from perfect. A significant problem arises with ancient burials when it simply isn't possible to prove a direct historical connection between a living group and the ancient remains. It is simply impossible, for example, to prove that the 9,000-year-old bones found in San Diego, California, in 1976 are the remains of direct ancestors of the local Kumeyaay tribes who have claimed them in court (Gibbons 2011a). Scientists want to study the bones; the Kumeyaay want to rebury them. Problems arise as well when the very procedures that might help verify a direct connection between a specific group and an excavated skeleton (for example, a DNA study of the bones) are objectionable to the Native Americans who are claiming ownership. It can get particularly dicey when multiple claimants assert ownership, as is the case with Kennewick Man, where not just different Native American tribes claim a connection, but so does a group of Pacific Islanders as well as a group of people of Norse descent (Thomas 2000; Chapter 7). Needless to say, that case is a mess.

If you've been paying attention, you've noticed that I have cleverly avoided addressing the ethical conundrum I posed at the beginning of this section concerning my own fieldwork. Unfortunately, I don't have any easy answers or even any not-so-easy answers to the question raised by archaeologist and professor Bettina Arnold in the title of one of her courses: "Who owns the past?" Is it all of the people of the country in which the remains are found? Is it just the tribe or even just the family of the descendants? Do such questions even apply to the fossils of ancient hominids discussed in Chapters 3 through 5 of this book?

As vexing as this issue can be, the good news is that in some places native people are embracing archaeology as a tool for illuminating their own histories. For example, the Navajo tribe has its own archaeology department (Two-Bears 2006); their motto is "Learning from the past to build our future" (http://www.nnad.navajo-nsn.gov/). In Connecticut, the resurgent Pequot tribe has its own team of archaeologists (most of whom are not Indians) who conduct research both on the reservation and off the reservation at sites important in Pequot history. For example, Kevin McBride, the director of archaeology for the Pequot (hired by, but not a member of, the tribe and not a Native American), is currently conducting archaeological and historical research at sites related to the Pequot War of 1637. Though there may never be an answer to the question "Who owns the past?" that satisfies everyone, archaeologists today realize that we have a special ethical obligation to the people whose histories we study.

Summary

Archaeologists and paleoanthropologists apply a broad array of techniques in their investigation of the human past. This chapter has briefly surveyed some of the more important procedures for recovering and analyzing the data on which the rest of the book is based. How sites are formed, how they are preserved, and how they are discovered are key questions for archaeologists and paleoanthropologists. Once found, data can be analyzed to determine the age of the sites, how tools were made and used, the subsistence base of the people, and aspects of their social and even religious lives. Past peoples can also be investigated directly through analysis of their physical remains, which determines the age, sex, health status, and geographic origin of ancient individuals. The evolutionary relationship between a prehistoric person and modern human beings can therefore be determined. Using the general procedures outlined in this chapter and many other very specific analytical techniques mentioned throughout this book, archaeologists and paleoanthropologists can reveal the chronicle of the human past. We begin that chronicle in Chapter 3.

TO LEARN MORE

There are many fine textbooks that describe the way archaeologists and paleoanthropologists collect and interpret data about the human past. Any one of the following textbooks would be a good choice to continue your study of archaeological method: *Discovering Our Past: A Brief Introduction to Archaeology* by Wendy Ashmore and Robert J. Sharer (2009); *Archaeology: A Brief Introduction* (2005b) and *In the Beginning: An Introduction to Archaeology* (2008), both by Brian Fagan; *Archaeology: Down to Earth* (2010) by Robert L. Kelly and David Hurst Thomas; *Archaeology* (2012), by Robert Kelly and David Hurst Thomas; and *Linking to the Past: A Brief Introduction to Archaeology,* by Kenneth L. Feder (2008). For the analysis of human skeletal material, see Wilton Marion Krogman's *The Human Skeleton in Forensic Medicine* (1973) for a classical treatment. There is probably no better recent source than Tim White and Pieter Folkens' *Human Osteology* (1991).

Web links for this chapter can be found at www.oup.com/us/feder

3

African Roots

CHAPTER OVERVIEW

Ancient bones from Olduvai
Echoes of the very first cry
"Who made me, here and why?—
Beneath this copper sun."
—*Johnny Clegg*, from his song "Scatterlings of Africa" (Written by Johnny Clegg. Copyright 1982 Johnny Clegg/Rhythm Safari)

Though human beings are distinguished by large brains, great intelligence, and a reliance on culture, fossil evidence shows that large brains were not characteristic of our earliest ancestors. The first steps of the hominid family were literal first steps; walking on two, rather than four, feet was what first differentiated them from the apes.

The oldest members of the human family date to more than 6 million years ago, about the time our ancestors diverged from those of the modern apes. The different names we have assigned to these specimens—*Sahelanthropus*, *Ardipithecus*, *Orrorin*, and, after 4 million years ago, several varieties of *Australopithecus*—reflect actual physical differences as well as modern arguments about what those differences mean. These creatures share in common the fact that their brains were no larger than those of modern chimpanzees. What they all also seem to share is a skeletal anatomy suited to walking on two feet.

A fork in the hominid road appears about 2.5 million years ago, when a new form is seen in the fossil record. Along with an anatomy suited to upright walking, *Homo habilis* had a brain size beyond the range of the apes and exhibited a greater reliance on culture as seen in the production of stone tools. *Homo habilis* and some of the Australopithecines were contemporaries. While the latter were highly specialized and became extinct, the former are directly ancestral to modern humanity.

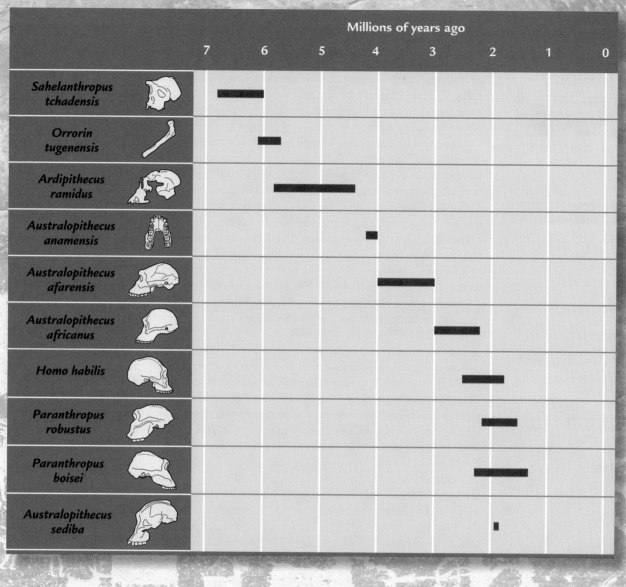

Millions of years ago

	7	6	5	4	3	2	1	0
Sahelanthropus tchadensis	▬							
Orrorin tugenensis		▬						
Ardipithecus ramidus			▬					
Australopithecus anamensis				▪				
Australopithecus afarensis				▬				
Australopithecus africanus					▬			
Homo habilis						▬		
Paranthropus robustus						▬		
Paranthropus boisei						▬		
Australopithecus sediba						▪		

BETWEEN RUNNING SHOES, FLIP-FLOPS, UGGS, HIKING boots, cowboy boots, tennis sneakers, Crocs, Clogs, and a host of other kinds of popular footwear, not many of us walk around in our bare feet all that much, at least not outside. We usually enclose our feet in footwear with hard soles, and we walk on even harder pavement. Walking barefoot on the soft sand of a beach, however, reminds us of the natural process of two-legged walking initiated by our ancestors beginning more than 6 million years ago.

Barefoot, walking is no longer a matter of two flat slabs of leather or rubber or some synthetic material, alternately clomping down on the pavement. Instead, we can sense our feet actually interacting with the earth, gripping into the soil beneath them, pushing us forward in our desire to get from here to there.

In the instant of each step, our heel strikes first, leaving deep impressions as the sand compresses beneath our weight, all of it focused on that small point at the heel. Then the foot rolls forward, the arch lightly curving over the sand, leaving a thin, sharp indentation with the side of the sole. Next, all in a fraction of a second, we rock up onto the balls of our feet, thrusting our center of gravity forward, as we push our alternate leg in front of us. Finally, our toes push down, gripping into the earth, with sand squishing up between and around them, as we propel our bodies forward, ready to catch ourselves in the next step with the other foot.

I remember in particular one time when I walked on a beach with my then 6-year-old son, Josh, and glanced back at our two sets of footprints, one big, one small, as the waves began the inevitable process of erasing them from the sand. Our disappearing trail of footprints reminded me of another such trail, made in a far distant time by two people who passed together across a landscape far different from the Cape Cod beach where my son and I walked. Those footprints, however, were not erased by the tide or blown away by the wind. Those prints, left in a fine volcanic ash on an East African plain in a place called Laetoli, in the modern nation of Tanzania, were preserved, allowing us in the present to examine the way our most ancient ancestors walked in the distant past (Hay and M. Leakey 1982; M. D. Leakey and Hay 1979; T. D. White and Suwa 1987).

That these footprints have been preserved is remarkable in itself. The conditions and sequence of events had to be perfect. First, a thin ash layer was deposited about 20 km (a little more than 12 mi) away from an erupting volcano. Soon after, a mild rain fell, turning the ash into the consistency of wet cement. Immediately following this, and before the ash had hardened, two people, and then a third, walked across its surface, leaving their footprints in the still-damp ash. Then the sun came out just in time to dry the ash bed to the hardness of rock before another rainfall might wash it all away. Finally, another ash layer fell, covering the footprint trail and protecting it from the natural erosion that might otherwise have destroyed it. Without any of these steps, the Laetoli footprints would have been as temporary as the footprints little Josh and I left on the beach at Cape Cod. Even ordinarily impassive scientists have characterized the 23-meter (about 75-ft) Laetoli trails as "miraculous" (Johanson and Edey 1981).

Those footprints were found more than 3.5 million years after the people, possibly a child and an adult, or perhaps a large adult male and a smaller adult female, strode across the surface (R. Leakey and Lewin 1992; Figure 3.1). We will never know their names or why they were walking, apparently in cadence

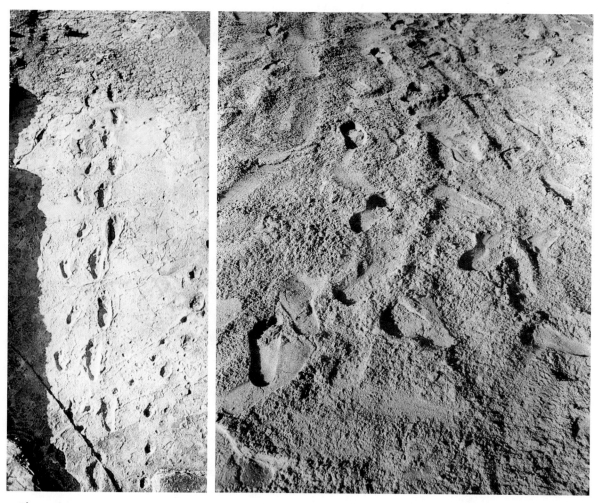

▲ **Figure 3.1**
On the left, the Laetoli trackway; the fossilized footprints of at least two human ancestors who walked in a remarkably modern fashion. On the right is the recent trackway of an anthropologist and his 6-year-old son. Though separated in time by more than 3.5 million years, the two sets of footprints clearly show the remarkable continuity of bipedal locomotion in the hominid family. (John Readers/SPL/Photo Researchers, Inc.; K. L. Feder)

and, perhaps, giving our imagination free rein, arm in arm across the ash bed (Figure 3.2). Yet, in taking those steps, they achieved a kind of immortality. Perhaps most remarkably, their footprints show that those anonymous folk, whose life journey occurred so many years ago, walked in a fashion that is nearly indistinguishable from the way modern humans walk (Charteris, Wall, and Nottrodt 1981; Day and Wickens 1980; T. White 1980; T. D. White and Suwa 1987). There are no impressions of the knuckles of a quadrupedal ape, no thumblike big toes. Their footprints are our footprints. Those people were among the earliest **hominids**, with whom all living people share a temporally distant but

▶ **Figure 3.2**
The dioramas at the American Museum of Natural History in New York City provide us with windows through which we can view other places and other times. Here, a diorama shows two hominids striding across the volcanic ash bed at Laetoli more than 3.5 million years ago.

biologically intimate connection. This chapter is about the first people and the world in which they lived.

YOU ARE SITTING DOWN IN A darkened movie theater. You've got your popcorn and soda, the ads and previews have just finished, and the main feature begins, a 2-hour movie representing the history of the universe. The very first moment of the film represents the first instant of the beginning of everything, the event cosmologists call "the Big Bang."

Here's the key to understanding the point of this exercise; in our imaginary movie, everything happens proportionally to when it actually happened in the history of the universe. Get it? In such a movie, the earth does not even form until more than 80 minutes after the first flash on the screen and the first living things—just single-celled organisms—don't make their appearance until about 90 minutes into the film. Dinosaurs briefly flash across the screen, and not until the 118-minute mark. The first of the apes do not appear until 119 minutes 50 seconds after the 120-minute-long movie began, and, finally, the earliest members of the human family do not appear until 1 hour 59 minutes 57 seconds into our metaphorical 2-hour movie. The entire human story, from our first upright walking ancestor to this moment, right now, is contained in just the final *3 seconds* of the film! Though this period may not seem very important from a universal perspective, in human terms we are talking about more than 6 million years, or 300,000 generations of human ancestors (at 20 years per generation). These metaphorical final 3 seconds of the film are the focus of paleoanthropologists and archaeologists.

Miocene Preface

Let's go back to look at the world at the 119-minute 50-second mark in the movie, when our nearest living nonhuman relatives first make their appearance. The world of this period, called the **Miocene** (from about 23 million to 5 million years ago; Figure 3.3), is one we can scarcely imagine. During this epoch, our planet was a matchless place for forest-dwelling creatures, and many ape species evolved to fill the varied **niches** offered by this rich world. Places that today are covered with grassland, prairie, and agricultural crops were then fertile forests, populated by an astounding bestiary of tree-loving species.

Fossil Apes of the Miocene

Primatologists now estimate that there were more than forty varieties—technically, **genera**—of apes living during the Miocene. Each genus (that's the singular for genera) encompassed multiple species; there are more than 100 ape species recognized and defined for this period of time spanning 18 million years (Begun 2003). Compare this situation to the present, with our paltry assemblage of only three genera of large or "great" apes divided into four species (chimp, bonobo, gorilla, and orangutan) and a single genus of the small or "lesser" apes divided into nine species of gibbons and siamangs (Figure 3.4).

During the early Miocene, the many and diverse ape species evolved primarily in Africa, but when the earth experienced a period of global warming between 16 and 15 million years ago, tropical and subtropical conditions expanded geographically and the ranges of some ape species expanded as well. Ape fossils dating to this period are found, not just in Africa, but also spread across Europe and Asia (Harrison 2010). The middle Miocene especially, between 13 and 9 million years

Era	Period	Epoch	Million years ago
Cenozoic	Quaternary	Holocene	0.01
		Pleistocene	2.6
	Tertiary	Pliocene	5
		Miocene	23
		Oligocene	38
		Eocene	55
		Paleocene	65
Mesozoic	Cretaceous		135
	Jurassic		190
	Triassic		225
Paleozoic	Permian		270
	Carboniferous		345
	Devonian		400
	Silurian		425
	Ordovician		500
	Cambrian		600
Precambrian	Proterozoic		1,000
	Archeozoic		3,000
	Azoic		4,600

◄ **Figure 3.3**
Humans appear extremely late on this standard time scale for earth history. The earliest hominids date to the end of the Miocene.

▲ **Figure 3.4**
A plethora of primates: a gibbon (upper left); a siamang (upper right); a contemplative
gorilla (lower left); a branch-wielding chimpanzee (lower right). (K. L. Feder)

ago, was a good time to be an ape and the number and diversity of ape species
expanded dramatically across much of the Old World.

Why the Study of Apes Is Relevant to the Study of Humanity

We are not descended from chimps, bonobos, gorillas, or orangutans. We did
not evolve from them. In fact, they have been evolving separately from us for as
long as we have been evolving separately from them. But we share with them a

common ancestor. Our evolutionary connection is apparent in our appearance and our behavior, as well as in our genes. Human and chimp DNA, in particular, are amazingly similar. In fact, a comparison of modern human, chimp, and gorilla DNA found that human beings and chimps are more similar to each other than either humans or chimps are to gorillas (Wildman, Grossman, and Goodman 2001). Figure 3.5, based in part on DNA evidence, presents a general **phylogeny** for the fossil and modern apes, showing how we currently conceive of their evolutionary relationships. The figure also shows how we view the human position on this phylogeny, and we focus our energies on that branch in the rest of this book.

By studying modern apes in a natural setting, primatologists hope to catch glimpses of behaviors the apes share with us: A chimp infant runs to its mother when it is frightened, and two adults embrace and pat each other's backs; chimps live in tightly knit social groups and make and use tools, and different geographic groups of chimps make different kinds of tools; and chimps occasionally walk on two feet while carrying objects in their hands. In these shared elements we likely are recognizing behaviors we have inherited from a common ancestor who lived more than 6 million years ago and from whom both chimpanzees and humans descended.

What Happened to the Apes at the End of the Miocene?

Today, the surviving ape species are threatened with extinction as a result of habitat destruction at the hands of humanity. As the tropical forests of Africa and Asia that are home to the apes are cleared for agriculture to support a burgeoning human population, the apes are pushed into smaller and smaller enclaves. Without a concerted effort by our species—the same species that is responsible for

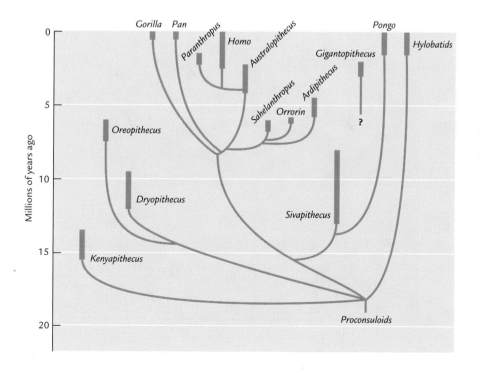

◀ **Figure 3.5**
A simplified phylogeny for apes and humans based on the fossil record. Human beings and our immediate evolutionary ancestors are located toward the top, after about 2.5 million years ago, and labeled "Homo."

their current precarious position—our nearest living evolutionary relatives may become extinct except in zoos and animal parks.

Beginning about 7 or 8 million years ago, toward the end of the Miocene, many species of apes that are represented in the fossil record also faced extinction, but not by any human agency; our direct ancestors had not yet evolved. Instead, a natural environmental change began to shrink the rich forest world. Large areas of the extensive forest lands began to contract sometime during the middle or late Miocene, to be replaced in part by grasslands, or **savannas**, by the beginning of the next epoch, the **Pliocene**, about 5 million years ago. And with the contraction of the forests, most of the ape species that had thrived there became extinct.

There is direct evidence to support this scenario. Remember the discussion in Chapter 2 about how most tree species are C3 photosynthesis pathway plants, which tend to select against the ^{13}C isoptope of carbon. As a result, when a region, continent, or even the world is dominated by the C3 photosynthesis pathway, ^{13}C levels in the soil, in the bones of animals that eat plant by-products, and in the bones of the animals that eat the animals that eat the plants all tend to have lower levels of ^{13}C than they do in times when C4 photosynthesis pathway plants—grasses and sedges—dominate. Simply put: Low levels of ^{13}C in the soil is a signature of a forested region; higher levels of ^{13}C is a signature of fewer trees and more grassland. Thure Cerling, Yang Wang, and Jay Quade (1993) have shown that soils and fossil teeth in south-central Asia (Pakistan) and North America (the western United States) exhibit a simultaneous, dramatic increase between 7 million and 5 million years ago in their concentration of the [13]C **isotope** (variety) of the element carbon (Figure 3.6). This dramatic increase in ^{13}C concentration at the end of the Miocene in soils and animal teeth is an indication of "a rapid expansion of C4 biomass [that is, grasses and sedges] in both the Old and the New World starting 7 to 5 million years ago" (Cerling et al. 1993:334). Recent research has only served to reinforce

▶ **Figure 3.6**
Graph showing the dramatic proportional increase of ^{13}C in fossil teeth and soils at the end of the Miocene. Reflecting an expansion of grasslands at the expense of the forests, this probably explains why an **arboreal** animal family like the apes experienced a wave of extinctions at the end of the Miocene. (From Cerling, Yang, and Quade 1993)

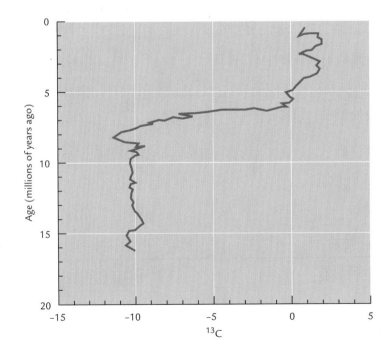

the apparent magnitude and rapidity of this shift from C3 to C4 plants at this time; it is characterized, for example, by biologist Erika Edwards and her colleagues (Edwards et al. 2010:588) as "explosive and broadly synchronous."

It might seem like magic to be able to go beyond a general description of ancient plant communities and actually estimate the percentage of tree cover in a region 7 or 8 million years after the fact. Thure Cerling and his colleagues (Cerling et al. 2011) have attempted to do precisely that based on their analysis of the carbon isotope signatures in soil samples taken in eastern Africa. By way of comparison, a typical modern "forest" is defined as having greater than 80% tree cover. Based on Cerling's interpretation of the carbon isotope ratios present in the 1,300 soil samples collected and analyzed by the team, there was less than 40% tree cover in much of eastern Africa 6 million years ago. In other words, by 6 million years ago, tropical forests hadn't disappeared, but they had substantially contracted, being replaced in many regions by an environmental **mosaic** characterized by patches of woodlands separated by expanses of grasslands. This is a very different world from the one in which the apes flourished during the Miocene, and it is not surprising under these environmental conditions that forest-dwelling species experienced increased competition for living room in a shrinking habitat, accompanied by the extinction of those who could not adapt to their new natural circumstances.

The Irony of Extinction

Almost certainly, those few ape species that survived the terminal Miocene possessed some characteristics that, by chance, gave them an advantage in the very different world that was establishing itself. Perhaps it was their remarkable ability for **brachiation** that ensured the survival of the ancestors of today's gibbons and siamangs when forests were shrinking and competition for remaining space was fierce. Maybe it was the strength, size, intelligence, and social systems of the ancestors of modern gorillas that allowed for their survival. The intelligence and behavioral flexibility of the ancestors of chimps and bonobos probably provided them with an advantage as the myriad Miocene ape species vied for space in the diminishing forests of 7 million years ago. The modern apes are the descendants of the survivors in this evolutionary struggle. The losers were those who, at the end of the Miocene, found themselves pushed into an alien habitat in which their physical and behavioral characteristics, honed by millions of years of evolution to life in a thick, humid forest, were useless.

The First Hominids

The first bipeds did not suddenly develop at the end of the Miocene, the product of evolutionary forcing as grasslands replaced forest habitat rendering **bipedal locomotion** beneficial. They didn't evolve bipedality because they needed to in the grasslands; evolution does not work that way. Novel features are not made to order. Instead, the paleoenvironmental record of carbon isotopes, as well as plant and animal remains dating to the times and places in which our first upright ancestors lived, shows that they were already thriving as bipeds in mosaic environments at the end of the Miocene (Figure 3.7).

It really was little more than luck that these apes already had the ability to efficiently and, perhaps, habitually walk on two legs. Perhaps because of their ability to walk upright, these apes were able to flourish at the end of the Miocene as the

▲ **Figure 3.7**
Whether accomplished by suspension from a branch (or, as depicted here, a rope), holding on to one another, or simply mastering the necessary balancing act, some modern apes possess the ability to walk on two feet. It is almost certain that some species of now-extinct Miocene apes were similarly able to walk on two feet. The ape suspended from the rope and the two hand-holders are siamangs. The ape succeeding at balancing on two feet without any help is an orangutan. (K. L. Feder)

grasslands expanded at the expense of the forests while most other ape species could not. It is the fossil record of this turning point in human evolution that commands our attention here (Figure 3.8).

Late Miocene Hominids

One of the most important discoveries related to the very early divergence of the hominid from the ape line is the fossil called *Sahelanthropus tchadensis*, found in the African nation of Chad. The original specimen consists of a spectacularly preserved **cranium.** Later, some mandibular and dental fragments from another, very similar individual were found nearby (Brunet et al. 2005; Gibbons 2002). This hominid was nicknamed "Toumai" by its discoverers, and the fossil dates to more than 6 million and as much as 7 million years ago about the time when, or soon after, the C3 forests were being replaced by C4 grasslands.

Toumai's nearly complete cranium is about the size of a chimpanzee's, indicating that it possessed a chimp-sized brain (Figure 3.9). However, in the shape of the face, *Sahelanthropus* was decidedly unlike that of a chimp. A bottom of a

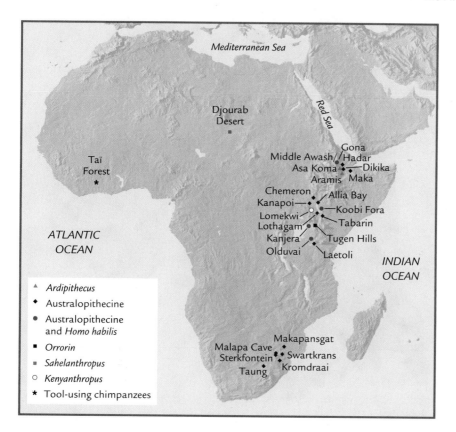

chimpanzee face, like that of all the great apes, thrusts forward, presenting a profile with, essentially, a snout. *Sahelanthropus* is quite different in this regard, with
a very flat face.

Though bones most directly reflective of locomotor patterns—those of the
hips and legs—were not recovered, there is a strong indicator of upright posture
in the well-preserved cranium. The position of its **foramen magnum** indicates
that *Sahelanthropus* was upright as well. It is positioned not at the back but at the
bottom of the cranium. This is another clear indication of upright posture and
bipedal locomotion.

So is Toumai our direct ancestor? We can't say because it was not the only
hominid living in Africa in the period between 7 and 4 million years ago. Another set of possible hominid bones, these from the Tugen Hills of northwestern
Kenya, have been dated to before 5.7 million years ago and may be as much as
6.1 million years old (Aiello and Collard 2001). Called *Orrorin tugenensis* by its
discoverers, its status as an early hominid is suggested by its teeth, but the primary
evidence used to support this claim is the fragments of three femurs recovered in
the excavation. The femurs were quite different from an ape's and, while not exactly like a modern human leg, it was very similar to that of later hominids where
the evidence of bipedality is more substantial (Richmond and Jungers 2008).

Dating to 4.4 million years ago (T. D. White et al. 2009), *Ardipithecus* or "Ardi"
(Figure 3.10) is literally "standing" before us; the shape and configuration of her
pelvis as well as the position of her foramen magnum prove that she was definitely

▶ **Figure 3.9**
Dating to more than 6 million years ago, the crucial period when genetic analysis suggests that the ape and human lines diverged, *Sahelanthropus tchadensis* may represent the oldest hominid specimen yet discovered. This cranium was discovered in 2001. (Courtesy of Michel Brunet, MPFT [Mission Paleoanthropologique Franco-Tchadienne])

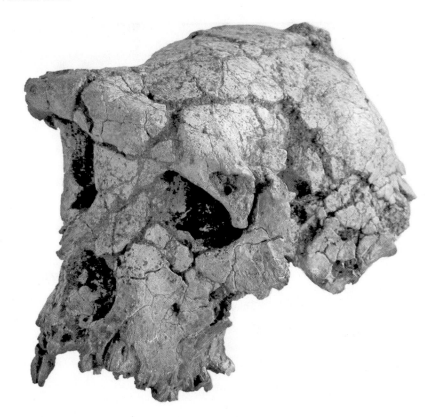

a biped, which positions her toward the base of the human line. But Ardi is a complicated specimen, and this can be seen especially in the following features. To begin with, Ardi does not have a humanlike hand; her thumbs are not positioned like ours, where we can easily touch the tip of our thumbs to each of our fingers. Ardi couldn't do that; she lacks the "opposability" that characterizes the human capacity for fine and precise manipulation. Even odder, however, is the configuration of Ardi's feet. Even though she was, like us and like our other hominid ancestors, bipedal, her feet look nothing at all like ours or those of *Australopithecus afarensis* who left the footprints at Laetoli mentioned in the prelude of this chapter. It really is pretty shocking to paleoanthropologists; Ardi's feet look like an ape's, with a large and divergent big toe, the characteristic that makes an ape's foot resemble the human hand rather than our foot. But however different Ardi's feet may have been from ours, she walked on two of them like we do, and not on all fours like the living apes.

A large team of researchers led by paleoanthropologist Tim White (White et al. 2009)—he was also one of the key investigators of the Laetoli footprints—has published a series of articles about *Ardipithecus* in a special October 2009 issue of *Science*. White and his colleagues believe that *Ardipithecus ramidus* is best explained as:

1. A creature at the base of the hominid line.
2. *Sahelanthropus* and *Orrorin* are probably other species of the same genus, *Ardipithecus*.

3. Ardi and her kind likely spent as much time in the trees as on the ground.
4. *Ardipithecus* did not live in a grassland habitat; its bipedal adaptation developed in an area characterized by woodland habitat.
5. *Ardipithecus* likely evolved into the earliest *Australopithecus* species.

In this scenario, chimps and gorillas diverged from the hominid line before the evolution of *Ardipithecus* and evolved quite separately from the hominids. This would mean that chimps and gorillas are not a very good model for what our human ancestors looked like; their high level of sexual dimorphism with large, aggressive males with substantial canine teeth used in competition with other males and their adaptation for quadrupedal knuckle walking were never a part of our hominid ancestry if *Ardipithecus* is at the base of our evolutionary line.

The period between 7 and 5 million years ago is still complicated with a host of hominids, any one of which might be directly ancestral to us. It is too early to determine the precise evolutionary relationships among the 7- to 5-million-year-old probable hominids discussed here. What is clear—and what is most important to understand—is that they all lived at a time soon after the human lineage diverged from that of the apes. Genetic analysis of human beings and chimps shows that we have been evolving separately for no more than about 7 million years. *Sahelanthropus, Orrorin,* and *Ardipithecus,* therefore, appear to be examples of what our ancestors looked like at the genesis of the human family.

The Genus *Australopithecus*

Dating to sometime between 4.17 and 4.07 million years ago are the exciting discoveries made in Kanapoi and Allia Bay, Kenya, between 1995 and 1997 (M. G. Leakey et al. 1998). The twelve specimens from Allia Bay and the nine from Kanapoi, including teeth, cranial fragments, and some bones below the skull, have been assigned the species name *Australopithecus anamensis*.

The *anamensis* jaw fragments and fossil teeth are apelike, but an upper arm bone exhibits many humanlike features. In addition, and more significant, both ends of a tibia (shin bone) that were recovered are very humanlike; its discoverers identify this bone as clearly indicating bipedal locomotion nearly half a million years before the Laetoli footprints. The environment in which *Australopithecus anamensis* lived was characterized by open woodland or bushland conditions.

Australopithecus afarensis

Far better known and with a far larger sample of remains is a later, somewhat less apelike form of the same genus, *Australopithecus afarensis*—most likely the creature that left the footprint trail described in this chapter's "Prelude." The great majority of these fossils date to the period from 4 million to 3 million years ago. The first *afarensis* fossils were found in the Afar geographical region of Ethiopia, at the site of Hadar (Figure 3.11), highlighted in this chapter's "Case Study Close-up" and the place where the famous *afarensis* fossil, Lucy, was found. Other *afarensis* specimens have been found including a very complete skeleton of a young child found in Dikika, Ethiopia (Alemseged et al. 2006), and a large adult male called "Big

▲ **Figure 3.10**
Artist's conception of *Ardipithecus*. (© 2008 Jay Matternes)

▲ **Figure 3.11**
Photograph of the 45% complete skeleton of the fossil known as Lucy: *Australopithecus afarensis*. Lucy and a series of thirteen other *afarensis* specimens have been dated to 3.18 million years ago. (© Alain Nogues/Sygma/Corbis)

Man" whose skeleton is about as complete as Lucy's (approximately 40%), dating to 3.6 million years ago (Gibbons 2010).

Among the key elements of the *afarensis* skeleton that have been found and used to define the species are the pelvis, vertebrae, a shoulder blade, leg bones, fingers, bones of the foot, jaws, skull fragments, a nearly complete cranium, and teeth. Together, these skeletal elements allow us to paint a reliable picture of a creature that was not becoming bipedal but already was fully upright (see this chapter's "Issues and Debates").

The **postcranial** skeleton (everything below the skull) of *afarensis* is diagnostic of a creature far more like a human than like an ape. For example, "Big Man" has a humanlike narrow chest, unlike the proportionally broad chests of apes, and an inwardly curving spine configured for standing on two legs, also far more like a modern human than a modern ape (Gibbons 2010). The feet of *afarensis* were also quite modern, lacking the divergent big toe of the apes and *Ardipithecus*. The ape's big toe is positioned on its foot just as our thumbs are positioned on our hands, allowing the ape to grasp objects with its feet (for example, to grasp tree branches when climbing) far better than we can. The recent discovery of an *afarensis* metatarsal shows clear evidence for an arched foot (Ward et al. 2011). Take off your shoes and socks, look at the tops of your feet, and press down in the space between your toes and your ankle to find the five long skinny bones in each foot that are your metatarsals. The shape and configuration of the metatarsals determine the degree to which an animal's foot is arched. The arch serves a valuable purpose for a biped. A quadruped disperses its weight across four feet, but when a human being walks or runs, all of his or her weight presses down on one foot and then the other. The human arch serves as a sort of shock absorber for all that weight concentrated on just one foot and is, therefore, part of the adaptation for bipedality. Apes do not have arched feet. You do. So did *afarensis*. Also, the pelvis was quite similar to ours and is easily distinguished from an ape's (see Figure 3.18); the configuration of the pelvis is an accurate indicator of a creature's mode of locomotion (see this chapter's "Issues and Debates"). Even in the case of the Dikika *afarensis* specimen, which is estimated to have been only 3 years old at the time of death, the bones of the legs and feet are quite humanlike and indicate that *afarensis* was bipedal.

Compared to human beings, the apes have proportionally very long arms in relation to their trunk and legs. Long, powerful arms allow the apes to climb or swing through trees as well as to walk quadrupedally on the ground. Human arms are, by comparison, short in relation to human legs; try walking on your hands and feet, and you will soon discover that it's pretty tedious; your legs are far too long and your arms are simply too short. Analysis of the proportions of upper and lower limbs in *afarensis* shows that in this respect as well the species was proportioned far more like modern humans than like apes (Shreeve 1996).

At the same time, the preserved scapula or shoulder blade of a specimen from the Dikika site in Ethiopia shows similarities with those of apes, implying that, while they certainly were bipedal, *afarensis* maintained an ape-like ability to climb trees and move among their branches (Gree and Alemseged 2012).

All of the essentially human qualities of the postcranial skeleton of *Australopithecus afarensis* must be contrasted with the almost entirely apelike features of its skull, as exhibited in the nearly complete cranium discovered at Hadar (Kimbel et al. 1994). This cranium, labeled A.L. 444-2 by its excavators, is the most complete *afarensis* skull yet found. It dates to about 3 million years ago, making this specimen one of the youngest yet identified in the *afarensis* fossil species. In its overall form, A.L. 444-2 is certainly more apelike than any subsequent human ancestor, including other, later versions of *Australopithecus* we will discuss. Cranial capacity is apelike, in the range of 380 cc to 430 cc—about the size of a modern chimpanzee and about one-third the human mean for brain size. The upper portion of the face is small when compared to the lower part (as in apes), which is the opposite of the pattern in modern human beings. The jaws jut out and are snoutlike—they are said to be **prognathous**—just like those in an adult ape and again quite different from the relatively flat face of a modern human.

The *afarensis* jaw presents a combination of apelike and humanlike features (Figure 3.12). Humans and apes have the same numbers and kinds of teeth: two incisors, one canine, two premolars, and three molars in each quadrant of the adult mouth. Human teeth, however, in both the upper jaw—the **maxilla**—and the lower jaw—the **mandible**—are positioned in a curving arch that expands to the rear of the mouth; ape teeth present a more boxlike appearance, with the premolars and molars set in nearly parallel rows perpendicular to the incisors. Also, apes have proportionally much larger canine teeth and a gap in the teeth of the opposing jaw to allow room for the large canines when the mouth is closed. This gap, or **diastema,** is not present in the human jaw; our canines are much smaller, and so no gap in the opposing jaw is needed. The *afarensis* jaw is not quite like an ape jaw but not quite like a human jaw either. The configuration of the teeth is more like a box than an arch; there is a small diastema, and tooth size, including that of the canines, that is more apelike than human.

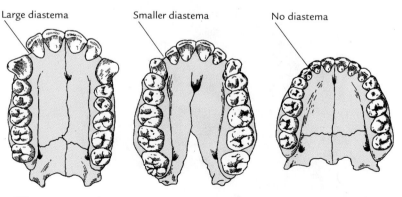

Large diastema   Smaller diastema   No diastema

Chimpanzee upper jaw   *Australopithecus* upper jaw   Human upper jaw

◄ **Figure 3.12**
Comparison of the maxillae (upper jaws) of chimps, *Australopithecus*, and modern human beings. The teeth in a chimp's mandible are arranged in a boxlike pattern, while those of a modern human being form a curve or arch. (From *Lucy: The Beginnings of Humankind.* © 1981 Donald C. Johanson & Mitland A. Edey. Drawings © Luba Dmytryk Gudz)

The evidence, then, is quite clear: *Australopithecus afarensis* seems to have been a bipedal ape living between 4 million and 3 million years ago. It looked like a chimpanzee standing on two short but otherwise humanlike legs, with no diverging big toe. What we share with *afarensis* is a mode of locomotion, but not a level of intelligence or a reliance on culture.

A Fork in the Hominid Road

At about 3 million years ago, there is evidence of the evolution of a somewhat different form of hominid. We call these new fossils by the name *Australopithecus africanus*. Like its evolutionary progenitors, *africanus* was bipedal and still walked in an essentially modern human fashion. It also retained a basically apelike skull and brain. There are a number of fairly well-preserved *africanus* crania, all apelike, with a sloping forehead and large ridges of bone above the eyes (Figure 3.13). On the other hand, the jaw and its teeth are a bit more humanlike and the face not so prognathous as that of *afarensis*, so in some ways it seems more human in appearance. Nevertheless, its brain size still falls into the range of that of the great apes.

Australopithecus africanus dates to no more than 3 million years ago and seems to fade out of the picture by about 2.2 million years ago. At that point, a larger bipedal form seems to have taken its place (Figure 3.14). Called *Paranthropus robustus*, it was a biped, and its brain size was a bit greater than in *africanus*. More significant is the difference in the cranial architecture of *robustus:* Where the top of the *africanus* skull is round and smooth, the top of the *robustus* skull sports a thin ridge of bone called a **sagittal crest**. Such a crest allows for a much larger, stronger temporalis muscle, which powers the movement of the mandible while chewing.

Interestingly, though the morphology of the *robustus* chewing apparatus appears to be specialized, analysis of the carbon isotopes in its teeth shows a varied diet of both C3 and C4 foods (Sponheimer et al. 2006; Ungar and Sponheimer 2011). In other words, though the teeth and jaws appear to be suited to chewing the tough seeds produced by tropical grasses (C4 plants), direct evidence of the carbon isotopes in the teeth indicate that soft leaves and fruits produced by trees

▶ **Figure 3.13**
Cranium of *Australopithecus africanus*, a lightly built or "gracile" australopithecine form that followed *afarensis* in southern Africa. *Africanus* flourished after 3 million years ago and appears to have become extinct by 2.2 million years ago. (Transvaal Museum, D. C. Panagos)

◀ **Figure 3.14**
Cranium and mandible of *Paranthropus robustus*. *Robustus* appears to have been a highly specialized hominid, with extremely powerful jaws adapted to processing a diet of hard, gritty foods. *Robustus* may have replaced *africanus*. It became extinct around 1 million years ago. (Transvaal Museum, D. C. Panagos)

and other C3 plants were an equally important part of the diet. The robust architecture of the chewing apparatus might have been an adaptation that allowed *robustus* to survive on only the tougher C4 plants when C3 foods were not available.

The *robustus* pattern of powerful cranial architecture is even more pronounced in another fossil hominid, *Paranthropus boisei*, whose specimens date from 2.3 million years ago to 1.2 million years ago, making it partially contemporaneous with *robustus* (Suwa et al. 1997). *Boisei* is different enough from *robustus* to warrant separate species status. In other words, there was more than one distinct hominid species living in Africa during the same period, a situation similar to the modern situation for **pongids**, in which there are two extant species of chimp (the common chimp and the bonobo).

When it comes to the period following *africanus*, it seems that the rule for hominid species is "the more, the merrier." For example, dating to just after 2 million years ago, two well-preserved specimens recovered in Malapa Cave in South Africa do not match either *africanus* or *Paranthropus* and have been designated as a new species: *Australopithecus sediba* (Berger et al. 2010; Pickering et al. 2011). These new fossils present us with a mosaic of traits, some humanlike, some apelike. For example, unlike in modern apes, the fingers and thumb in the preserved *sediba* hand suggest a humanlike ability to precisely manipulate objects. The bones of the pelvis clearly reflect a configuration adapted to bipedality. The feet, however, suggest a mode of upright walking far different from that seen in other ancient hominids or modern human beings, with an odd (from a modern human perspective) in-turning of the ankles, resulting in the creature's weight being balanced along the inside margin of the feet. A small cranium with a chimplike capacity of about 420 cc^3 rests on top of the *sediba* body.

I guess we're lucky that members of this species did not practice good dental hygiene. As a partial result of the fact that *Australopithecus sediba* individuals didn't brush or floss, we know something about their diets. Supported by the results of a carbon isotope study, an analysis of the wear on a few *sediba* teeth, and the recovery of phytoliths (see Chapter 2) from the 2-million-year-old tartar buildup on *sediba* teeth, researchers were able to determine that *sediba* diet consisted primarily of fruits, leaves, and tougher material such as bark, all from C3 plants, to the exclusion of C4 grasses, though soil analysis indicates that these grasses were locally available in the region where *sediba* lived (Henry et al. 2012). Such a diet is very similar to that of modern chimpanzees, who also selectively feast on local C3 plants, mainly ignoring tropical grasses.

Australopithecus sediba reflects the enormous complexity of the hominid story. It may reflect a descendant line of *africanus* and, therefore, a side branch of the line leading to us or, as the researchers of the specimen suggest, a line directly intermediate between the older *africanus* and the genus *Homo*.

A Different Path—*Homo habilis*

Soon after 2.5 million years ago, and just as the **australopithecines** were experiencing great changes in their evolutionary pathway, another hominid seems to have branched off from the main line of the *Australopithecus* genus. This breakaway group followed a different evolutionary route, one in which its survival on the African savanna was not the result of an increasingly specialized diet but, instead, was due to an increase in intelligence made possible by an expanding brain. This creature first appears in the fossil record about 2.4 million years ago (Bower 1993a, 1993b; Hill, Ward, and Brown 1992; Schrenk et al. 1993), a little before *africanus* became extinct, which makes it a contemporary of *Paranthropus robustus*. But this new form cannot be mistaken for any variety or form of *Australopithecus or Paranthropus*. With a much flatter face, a steeper forehead, and a larger brain—a mean size close to 700 cc, larger than any ape brain and just about one-half the modern human mean—this clearly is a new and different hominid (Figure 3.15). Specimens are few and there is a substantial amount of variation among these larger-brained hominids. Some see two different species dating to about 2.5 million years ago (M. G. Leakey et al. 2012). Others view the fossils as belonging to a single, diverse species called *Homo habilis*. We will take that approach here because, as paleoanthropologist Tim White (as cited in Gibbons 2012) maintains, we just don't know enough to clearly separate the specimens into different, contemporary species.

Assigning them to the same genus as modern humans means that *Homo habilis* was much more like us than were any of the australopithecines or paranthropines. Whereas taxonomically *Homo sapiens* might live in the same general neighborhood as *Australopithecus* and *Paranthropus*, we live on the same street as *Homo habilis*. The skull of *Homo habilis* was not just larger than that of the australopithecines but was shaped differently as well, with significantly less prognathism, a taller, steeper forehead, and a more rounded profile. All of these features seem to presage modern human beings.

The Ability to Make Tools

You might think that one of the key behavioral features that distinguishes people from other animals rests in our ability—and need—to use tools. In actuality, however, a number of animal species have been observed using tools in the wild. Sea otters will often grab a flat, smooth stone, rest it on their stomachs while they float on their backs in the water, and use the stone as a sort of anvil on which

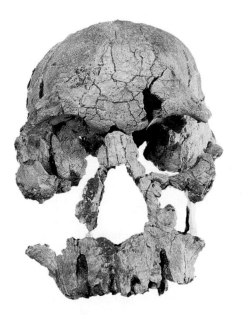
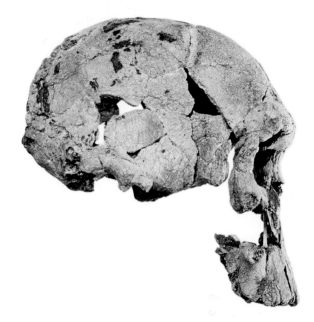

they smash open shells for the seafood within. Woodpecker finches have been seen using cactus spines held in their beaks to probe for insects in tree bark. Some chimps use stones to hammer open nutshells to get at the nutmeat within, even placing the nuts on stone anvils to magnify the effect.

Some chimpanzees go beyond this, not only using tools but also actually making them by physically modifying a raw material to a desired shape or form. For example, chimps will strip the bark off of twigs, which they then poke into termite mounds like fishing rods. The stripped twigs are wet and sticky, and termites will adhere to them. After pulling the twigs out of the mound, chimps eat the termites, which they apparently think are a delicious treat (Goodall 1986). Central African chimps have been seen crafting wooden clubs to crack open beehives from which they then collect honey using twigs, sometimes using a complex array of as many as five separate tools—pounder, perforator, enlarger, collector, and swab—in a precise sequence in order to extract the honey (Bower 2009a; McGrew 2010).

It isn't terribly surprising, therefore, that evidence indicates some tool use on the part of *Australopithecus afarensis*. Though the tools themselves have not been discovered, the results of their use have been at the Dikika site in Ethiopia. There, in a stratum dating to about 3.4 million years ago, researchers have discovered cut marks on a couple of animal bones that almost certainly were the result of butchering with the use of sharp-edged pieces of stone (McPherron et al. 2010). Without the tools themselves, it isn't possible to conclude that they were intentionally made stone flakes. It is entirely likely that these were merely "expedient" tools, naturally or, at least, unintentionally fractured pieces of rock whose size, shape, and configuration just happened to meet the needs of a hominid trying to cut meat off of a bone. None of the rock naturally occurring near the site could have produced a durable, sharp edge capable of making the marks seen on the bones. This may mean that *afarensis* had the ability to plan ahead, collecting the right kind of stone where it was available and then bringing it along on the hunt.

▲ **Figure 3.15**
The cranial capacity of this fragmentary cranium shows that *Homo habilis* possessed a brain larger than any ape's. Dated at 2.4 million years ago, *habilis* represents the first hominid with an expanded brain.
(© National Museums of Kenya)

Oldowan Technology

It's one thing to scrounge around for a rock and then use it as is to bang down on a bone to break it to extract the marrow, and it's another thing entirely to carefully alter a natural stone, intentionally sculpting it into a desired, specialized shape and form to render it suitable for carrying out a particular task. That requires enormous intelligence and skill. We see that level of forethought and skill in stone tools dating back to no more than about 2.6 million years ago at Gona, Ethiopia (Quade et al. 2004; Semaw et al. 1997). Tools like these were first recognized, defined, and described by the famous paleoanthropologist team of Louis and Mary Leakey (M. Leakey 1971). They called the tools **Oldowan,** after the place where they were first found and where the Leakeys had devoted so much of their research energy, Olduvai Gorge in Tanzania (Figure 3.16).

The maker of a stone tool, or the **knapper,** begins with a more or less spherical nodule of stone or **core.** Holding this **object piece** in one hand, the knapper strikes it with a **hammerstone,** usually a fortuitously shaped harder rock (or just one less likely to break as a result of its shape). Without much trouble, the knapper can knock a **flake** off the stone (Figure 3.17). Then the knapper turns the object piece around in his or her hand so the interior surface of the rock that was just exposed with the first hammerstone blow is facing up. Next, using that surface

▶ **Figure 3.16**
Homo habilis is also known to have been a tool producer. Here is a chopper from the Oldowan tradition of *Homo habilis*. (© Institute of Human Origins)

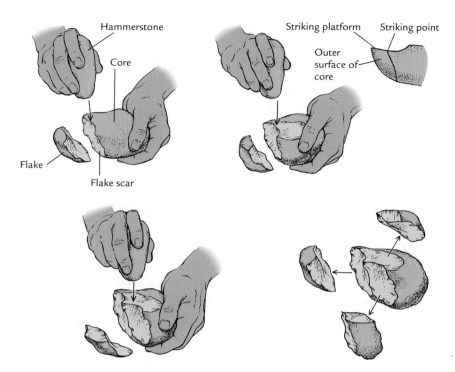

Hammerstone

Core

Flake

Flake scar

Striking platform   Striking point

Outer
surface of
core

as a **striking platform,** the knapper strikes down on it with the hammerstone, thereby removing a stone flake from the opposite side of the object piece. Repeating this several times can produce a number of sharp, relatively straight-edged flakes useful for cutting, scraping, sawing, chopping, and the like. Microscopic analysis of a large collection of Oldowan flakes shows that many were used for these purposes (Keeley and Toth 1981; Toth 1985). The flakes exhibit a polish on their edges that is typically caused by cutting plant material, butchering animals, and woodworking. Stone flakes are sharper, stronger, and more durable than the teeth or nails nature provided our ancestors. Although one doesn't need to be a genius to figure out how to make stone tools, it does take what researcher John Gowlett calls an "appreciation of the properties of stone" (1986:251). Try it yourself (be careful and always wear eye protection) and you'll see how challenging it can be. It takes a while even for modern people with our much larger brains to get a feel for how to break stone in a way that consistently results in the desired endproduct: sizeable, sharp-edged tool blanks. The production of Oldowan tools took some knowledge of the characteristics of different rocks, an understanding of their breakage patterns, forethought in planning the sequence of blows, a bit of hand–eye coordination, and flexibility to change the planned sequence when problems cropped up. More fundamentally, this process takes enough intelligence to recognize that a round, dull rock can be transformed into a large number of straight, thin, sharp pieces of rock suitable for many different uses. Clearly, this is the thought process of an intelligent being.

I am certain that most of us would not know what kinds of rock would be useful in toolmaking, and we wouldn't know where to find any of it even if we did know the kinds that work best. In the experimental archaeology course I teach in which students learn about stone-tool technology by attempting to actually replicate stone tools, I instruct them to go off into the wilds of Connecticut and collect stones from which they think they might be able to produce sharp-edged stone blades. We won't talk about the one student who actually bought rocks at a local rock shop (the price tag was still on one of them). Most students return to the class with sandstone and schist and other rock types common in our region but that shatter or crumble when struck, producing no usable tools. The point is, it takes knowledge and experience to recognize rocks with the best qualities for making tools. There is a lithic learning curve, and *Homo habilis* was pretty far along on that curve.

The hominids at Gona selected the best stone in their territory, rock that fractures readily, regularly, and predictably to produce sharp, thin flakes. At the Kanjera South site in Kenya, stone tools weren't made from the local limestone, from which sharp, durable tools cannot be made. Instead, the tools found at the site were made from far more durable raw materials from which sharp edges can be produced: quartzite and rhyolite. Those rock types were available no less than 13 kilometers distant from the site, implying quite a bit of planning and forethought by the tool makers, and not just a little bit of applied geological knowledge (Gibbons 2009c).

The Fate of *Homo habilis*

The existence of *Homo habilis* was rather short in evolutionary terms: Occurring first in deposits that are about 2.4 million years old, their remains disappear entirely sometime after about 1.8 million years ago. But the evidence does not imply that *Homo habilis* simply became extinct, leaving no evolutionary descendants. In fact, *habilis* appears to have evolved into another hominid species. This evolutionary jump and the new species that resulted are the focus of the next chapter.

What Were the First Steps in Hominid Evolution?

ISSUES AND DEBATES

The evidence regarding how the hominid family began is unequivocal. The first hominids were, fundamentally, bipedal apes; the first steps of our evolution were literally "first steps." The physical evidence shows that creatures dating to at least 6 million years ago had a skeletal anatomy, reflected in the morphology of their femurs as well as the positioning of their skulls on their vertebral columns, suitable for walking on two feet, in a manner similar to the way modern human beings walk. At the same time, these creatures possessed brains of a size and configuration virtually indistinguishable from those of some species of fossil and modern apes. The consensus on this is clear.

How Do We Know the Hominids Were Upright?

The configuration of the skeleton is quite different for creatures who walk quadrupedally and for those who are habitual bipeds. The most important part of the skeleton in this regard is the pelvis, made up of a left and a right **innominate** bone (Figure 3.18). The innominate bones of a primate quadruped—for example, a chimpanzee—have a long and narrow top blade (the **ilium**) that connects to the base of the pelvic bone (the **ischium**), creating a flat plane. A human innominate, on the other hand, has an ilium that is short and broad and, when compared

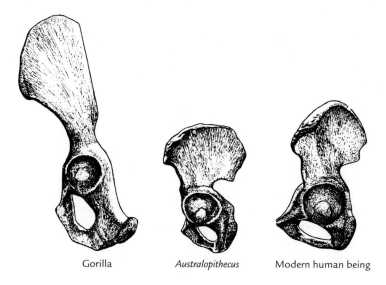

Gorilla   *Australopithecus*   Modern human being

◀ **Figure 3.18**
Comparison of the pelvis of a gorilla, *Australopithecus*, and a modern human. Though there certainly are some differences, the pelvises of the extinct and the modern hominid are far more similar than either is to that of the gorilla. This is true for the simple reason that pelvis determines the configuration of the muscles that attach to the upper leg, which, in turn, determines how an animal locomotes. Gorillas are quadrupeds. *Australopithecus* and modern human beings are bipeds. (From *The Antiquity of Human Walking* by John Napier. Copyright © April 1967 by Scientific American, Inc. All rights reserved; drawing copyright Enid Kotsching)

to a chimp's, flares out at the top and seems twisted to the side, producing a complex curve away from the plane of its ischium (Lovejoy 1988).

The configuration of the innominate bone in an animal determines the position of the large gluteal muscles, which in turn determines how the creature could most easily get around. Thus, the position of the ilium on the innominate bone of an extinct animal allows us, with some accuracy, to deduce how that creature walked—in other words, whether it got around on four legs or two.

There really is very little argument about the pelvis of *Australopithecus afarensis* as well as that of the other australopithecines with preserved pelvises; they have an innominate bone very similar to that of a modern human being (Lovejoy 1988; Lovejoy, Heiple, and Burnstein 1973; see Figure 3.18).

Is There Other Evidence for Bipedality?

Though the pelvis is the best place to look for evidence of locomotion, fossil discoveries are not made to order, and we don't always find this skeletal element. Other parts of early hominid anatomy, however, are also useful to assess a creature's locomotor pattern. For example, the femur of *Orrorin* has characteristics that indicate bipedality 6 million years ago. The Laetoli footprints (see Figure 3.1) are virtually indistinguishable from footprints of a modern human; individually they exhibit the typical pattern of a human foot, and together they match the human stride (Charteris, Wall, and Nottrodt 1981; Day and Wickens 1980; T. White 1980; T. D. White and Suwa 1987). The prints display a humanlike arch and lack any hint of the divergent big toe that characterizes the apes.

As we saw earlier, the location of the foramen magnum determines the position of the vertebral column, which in turn indicates whether a species is quadrupedal or bipedal. Fossil hominid crania as far back as *Sahelanthropus* possess a foramen magnum located at the base of the cranium, in nearly the same position as in modern human beings, who, of course, are bipedal.

Fragments of the **femur** (upper leg) and **tibia** (lower leg) of *afarensis* show clearly that its upper and lower leg joined at an angle more like that in modern human beings than that in apes (Johanson and Shreeve 1989). The preserved foot bones of *afarensis* are longer and more curved than the modern human form, but, like the footprints, they exhibit a modern arrangement of the big toe. In fact, when the large, well-preserved foot from the site of Hadar (see the "Case Study Close-up" in this chapter) is scaled down to the size of the Laetoli prints, it is a perfect match (Johanson and Shreeve 1989:197).

Why Bipedalism?

It's one thing to cite physical evidence to show that the earliest hominids walked on two feet. It's another thing to explain why bipedality evolved in the first place. If you are an ape, what is it about walking on two feet in the savanna or an environment marked by a mosaic of grassland and forest that increases your likelihood of survival and, in turn, the probability that you will reproduce and pass on the genetic disposition for bipedal locomotion to another generation, for whom greater proficiency for that mode can be further acted on by natural selection?

The Upright Provider

Consider the hypothesis proposed by Owen Lovejoy (1981, 1984, 2009), who suggests that the key advantage to bipedal locomotion, including that seen in *Ardipithecus*, was that it freed the hands to carry things, allowing males to carry food back to a camp or village where females and their offspring could be provisioned.

Among modern primates, chimp females raise their children alone. They are often good mothers, devoting much time and energy to the health and well-being of their offspring. Male chimps, on the other hand, generally have little to do with infants. Because chimp society is sexually promiscuous, the males don't know which, if any, infants they have sired. So, from an evolutionary perspective, why should they waste time providing for offspring that probably do not carry their genes?

Any help a chimp mother can get in providing for her offspring will improve the likelihood of survival of all of her children. It makes sense for her to solicit assistance from other chimps in her group, including adult males.

But how can a female chimp convince a male to do this? In Lovejoy's view, she must assure him that the offspring are his and that, by helping them, he ensures that half his genes get passed along as well. Only a pattern of sexual fidelity—in other words, monogamy—can do this. Basically, it's a trade: Females increase the likelihood their children will survive by remaining sexually faithful to one male. The male receives exclusive sexual access to a female and an increased probability that he will father offspring. All he has to do is faithfully provision the female and the children he has sired with her. This ability to bring food and other resources back to the female and the young is made feasible, in Lovejoy's view, by the freeing of the hands—which, in turn, is made possible by walking on two feet.

Remember, individual animals are not making a conscious choice to enhance their contribution to the evolutionary gene pool by the practice of monogamy. Females merely are choosing to associate with males who help them care for their children, and males help females who provide them with sex. These behaviors increase the probability that offspring survive to adulthood. In terms of natural selection, it should be apparent that those late Miocene apes who acted in a way that increased the likelihood of their offspring's survival were more successful than those who did not: Their population increased while other groups became extinct. Because the provisioning behavior was made possible by upright walking, that ability would be strongly selected for.

There is at least one glaring defect in Lovejoy's hypothesis (Tanner 1981; Zihlman and Tanner 1978): When a male is away gathering food, what is to prevent a female from having sex with other males? In fact, such behavior may be to her advantage because it would increase the number of males willing to provision her and her offspring. Sex is used in many of the social primates to make alliances and maintain friendships. In such a scenario, sexual fidelity might even be disadvantageous, particularly if the male doesn't do a good job of provisioning. Ultimately, it is difficult to understand how a more rigid pattern demanding sexual fidelity actually could have been maintained in ancient hominid societies.

The Upright Scavenger

Anthropologist Pat Shipman (1984, 1986) has proposed another hypothesis. Using the scanning electron microscope, Shipman has examined the remains of animal bones recovered at early hominid sites. She found microscopic evidence of tooth marks from predators and scavengers, as well as cut marks from stone tools, made when hominids removed the meat. In some instances she found carnivore and stone-tool marks on the same bones, either with the tool marks superimposed on the carnivore tooth marks or with the tool marks made first. In other words, sometimes carnivores had access to the bones only after the hominids had processed them (indicating hominid hunting behavior), and sometimes the hominids got at the bones after carnivores had already chewed on them, evidence that the hominids were scavenging the carcasses of animals killed by other carnivores.

Walking on two feet was likely advantageous to hominids who were opportunistic scavengers. Scavengers need to find their quarry, and that means walking great distances and scanning a broad territory for evidence of a predator kill. Bipedalism is highly energy-efficient, in part because it involves only two limbs and yields greater endurance for walking long distances. In addition, because scavengers always need to be wary of the return of the predator who did the killing in the first place, as well as of other large, aggressive scavengers—like hyenas or jackals, who might compete for the same kill—it is wise to get in and out quickly: Cut the meat off the bone as fast as possible and carry it back to a safe place to eat. The free hands of a bipedal hominid can carry both the tools for extracting the meat from the carcass and the meat.

The Efficient Walker

Primatologist Peter Rodman and anthropologist Henry McHenry (Johanson, Johanson, and Edgar 1994) have proposed what may be the simplest and most elegant hypothesis of all. After analyzing the energy expended by chimps when they walk quadrupedally and by humans with their upright gait, Rodman and McHenry determined that human locomotion was simply more efficient than chimp locomotion, meaning we expend less energy to accomplish the same task. Following on this hypothesis, researchers have recently calculated the actual difference in energy expenditure between quadrupeds and bipeds. It turns out that, while using half as many limbs, a human being walking on two legs expends only one-quarter the energy of a chimp walking on all fours (Sockol, Raichlen, and Pontzer 2007).

As the Miocene forest shrunk, some ape species may have thrived by exploiting the resources of the growing savanna, where food resources were more dispersed. An energetically efficient way of moving across increasing distances in the search for food became adaptively advantageous. The ability to walk efficiently on two feet may have provided that advantage.

The Endurance Runner

The Olympic marathon race (26 mi, 285 yd, 42.195 km) is run to commemorate a legendary marathon run by a Greek herald 2,500 years ago. A Greek herald named Phidippides ran the approximately 26-mile route from Marathon to Athens to announce the stunning victory of the Greeks over Persian invaders, and then promptly dropped dead.

In fact, human physiology seems supremely well adapted to running (Bramble and Lieberman 2004). Running is not just ramped-up walking; it is a very different manner of locomotion made possible by a unique combination of skeletal morphology, muscle configuration, and tendon placement (Zimmer 2004). For example, our tendons are arranged in a manner very different from those of chimps; they act like springs, allowing our legs to store energy with each stride. Our legs are proportionally much longer than those of the apes, allowing for longer strides and a faster pace, without expending the additional energy required to run faster by moving shorter legs more quickly. Running produces a pounding on our joints with each stride, but our skeletons are adapted to this as well. The surfaces where our leg bones meet—their **articular surfaces**—are proportionally broader in humans than in apes, allowing the great impacts of running to be dampened by spreading them out over a larger area. Bipedal running can be an unsteady way of moving about, and here too humans seem uniquely well adapted to maintain stability, especially with a pelvic configuration that allows for large and powerful gluteal muscles that work to keep us upright.

Bramble and Lieberman point out that the ability to run would have been highly advantageous both in hunting and in scavenging. Particularly before the development of long-distance weaponry—things like bows and arrows, developed much later—the need to catch up to prey, to get close enough to hurl rocks or other projectiles, provided good long-distance runners with a decided advantage (Carrier 1984). Scavengers, too, benefit from endurance running; based on clues provided by smell and the presence of circling vultures, wild dogs and hyenas regularly run great distances to exploit carcasses (Bramble and Lieberman 2004:351). Hominids who could run great distances would be able to better compete with these other scavengers for access to those carcasses.

So, the next time you compete in a marathon, or just watch one on TV, consider the possibility that the pounding, the agony, and the relentless pushing it takes to accomplish the run may be made possible because of evolutionary forces that enabled our ancestors on the plains of Africa more than 2 million years ago to successfully compete with animals larger, stronger, and faster than us.

Were the Early Hominids Hunters?

In all likelihood, hunting was not the dominant mode of subsistence among our most ancient ancestors. Dental morphology shows that *Ardipithecus* and *Orrorin* were browsers who consumed soft fruit and leaves, not carnivores who concentrated on animal flesh (Gibbons 2002). The preserved teeth of *Australopithecus afarensis* imply a diet of mostly fruits, leaves, roots, insects, and small mammals. In some cases they may have been able to scavenge the carcass of a larger animal, perhaps one killed by a lion. The 3.4-million-year-old bones mentioned previously on which tool marks were found at Dikika were from goat- and cow-sized animals (McPherron et al. 2010). The habitat in which *Australopithecus anamensis* lived implies a diet of fruit, insects, and small mammals.

Even for the toolmaking *Homo habilis*, there is no evidence that hunting dominated the subsistence quest. Neither the Oldowan choppers nor the used flakes would have been handy as spearpoints. Nevertheless, there is clear evidence of the processing of animal bone by *Homo habilis* to secure meat and marrow. Paleoanthropologist Pat Shipman (2011) pioneered studies that today enable researchers to distinguish marks left by gnawing carnivores from those produced by hominids using sharp-edged stone tools to cut meat from bone. Essentially, by experimentally replicating marks on bone, Shipman showed that carnivore teeth leave grooves that are U-shaped in microscopic profile, whereas stone tools leave V-shaped marks on bone. Shipman (2011:67) notes that at the 2.5-million-year-old *Homo habilis* sites of Gona and Bouri—the earliest sites that show the manufacture of stone tools—V-shaped cut marks have been found, indicating the use of stone tools to remove meat. At these same sites, some long bones show evidence of having been smashed open, almost certainly with stone hammers or choppers. The bones show diagnostic scarring that has been replicated experimentally by breaking fresh bones with a stone hammer. In all likelihood, this was done 2.5 million years ago in order to access the rich and nutrient-dense marrow located inside those bones.

We needn't be too concerned about the finer points of early hominid subsistence. All researchers would probably agree that hunting was not predominant in the subsistence base of the australopithecines or in *Homo habilis*. Though we have to be careful when generalizing from nonhuman primates, we do know that chimpanzees in the wild occasionally engage in cooperative hunts (Goodall 1986). As paleoanthropologist Daniel Stiles (1991) has pointed out, there is no reason to believe our hominid ancestors were less capable than chimps in their ability to plan, coordinate, and carry out a hunt. The first hominids were not born killers, but they probably did rely on meat to a certain degree, some of it scavenged, some from hunting. The early hominids probably were opportunistic foragers, taking whatever food they could, whenever the opportunity presented itself.

Where Did the Idea for Stone Tools Come From?

It is not intuitively obvious that a more or less spherical, relatively small, single nodule of stone can be transformed into a large number of consistently contoured stone flakes that cumulatively provide several feet of sharp tool edge. It takes some amount of reflection, study, and deliberation to figure out that stones with certain properties, when struck in the right way, at the right place, with just the right amount of force, and at the right angle can produce useful tools that can cut, pierce, or scrape far more effectively and efficiently than our teeth and nails. That *Homo habilis* was able to figure this all out is implied by the archaeological record of Oldowan tools. The question remains, then, "What might have inspired our first tool-using ancestors in this intellectual process?"

▶ **Figure 3.19**
Chimpanzees living in the Taï Forest of the African nation of Côte d'Ivoire use rock hammers and root and stone anvils to pound open nutshells to extract the rich and nutritious nutmeats. In this process, chimps may accidentally break the stones, producing, again accidentally, sharp-edged flakes of stone that litter the surroundings of the nut-processing stations. It is possible that our human ancestors used stones to perform the same task, producing flakes that they realized were, themselves, a valuable by-product of the activity, usable as tools. It may then have been a short intellectual leap for our ancestors to intentionally and directly produce stone tools. (Kennan Ward/Corbis)

Though chimps in the wild have never been observed intentionally modifying stone to make tools, as mentioned earlier in this chapter, they do use rocks to crack open hard-shelled nuts. Chimps in the Taï Forest of the African nation of Côte d'Ivoire, for example, use extremely hard igneous rocks that they have to collect from outcrops and then transport to the location of the nut-producing *Panda* trees (Mercader, Panger, and Boesch 2002). The chimps position the nuts on bedrock outcrops or exposed tree roots that serve as anvils and then crack the nuts open by striking them with the igneous hammers (Figure 3.19). Occasionally, slices of these hammers accidentally flake off, unintentionally producing sharp-edged stone flakes.

This got the researcher of the chimp behavior thinking. Nuts are a nutritious and abundant food source. When *Panda* nuts are in season in the Taï Forest, chimps have been calculated to obtain more than 3,000 calories of food per day from this food source (Mercader et al. 2002:1452). The researchers of chimp nut-cracking sensibly suggest the possibility that some Miocene apes and early hominids could have exploited the same or similar nut foods in their subsistence pursuit. The only viable way to access the rich meat of some species of nuts is to strike the nuts with a hard hammer. Certainly, Miocene hominids might have practiced the same nut-cracking behavior as the chimps in the Taï Forest. These same researchers have proposed that nut-cracking hominids might have been inspired by accidentally breaking their stone hammers and unintentionally producing sharp flakes that could be used as tools. Perhaps they recognized the utility of the sharp flakes and then set about the process of trying to figure out how to intentionally and consistently produce sharp stone flakes—for butchering an animal, cutting fiber, and so on. It is interesting to consider the possibility that the invention of stone tools ultimately was the by-product of an accident.

How Did Ancient Hominids Move About?

In chimp society, males tend to be homebodies, with females more likely to migrate out from the group into which they were born. In a remarkable bit of detective work, a team of researchers has determined that *Australopithecus africanus* and *Paranthropus robustus* may have followed a similar pattern. Using strontium analysis as discussed in Chapter 2, Sandi Copeland and her colleagues (Copeland et al. 2011) examined the strontium isotopes reflected in the teeth of male and female *africanus* and *robustus* individuals. Remember, the strontium isotope makeup in an individual's teeth reflects the strontium isotope proportions in the soil where they lived when they were young; the strontium pattern in the teeth is set during an individual's formative years. That rule still applies: The strontium isotope proportions in your teeth were set during your childhood and reflect the proportions in the environment in which you grew up. Copeland and her colleagues found that out of nine ancient hominids identified as males in the sample, eight had a strontium isotope composition that matched that from the immediate region in which their remains were found. In other words, they likely were born, matured, and died in the same limited geographic region where their bones were discovered. However, out of the ten females in the sample, fully half had a strontium isotope composition that differed dramatically from the local area in which their bones were found, suggesting that they had moved in from elsewhere upon reaching adulthood. This implies that *africanus* and *robustus* social groups consisted of related males who lived out their lives together into which they were born and unrelated females who migrated in from, perhaps, a number of other social groupings located in other regions. In this instance, strontium isotope analysis provides us with a sort of time machine for peering back at the ancient behavior of the hominids.

Why Is the Fossil Record of Human Evolution So Complicated?

It might seem to you that scientists love complexity. The more complicated the puzzle—whether it's about how stars evolved, how geological formations developed, or how our human line came into existence—the better we like it. As a scientist, I certainly can appreciate the complexity underlying the subjects I study, but I also understand that the lack of a simple story here can drive a student crazy.

Regarding the subject material of this book, I do recognize that a student's perspective and agenda might differ from mine. I mean, I hope you find the topics I delve into in this book of interest, but I realize that most of you aren't going to pursue a career in paleoanthropology or archaeology. I also recognize that, at least short term, most of you would like this book to provide you with a direct, comprehensible, even simple story that's easy to understand and even easier to remember for an exam or term paper. Unfortunately, I can't give that to you. I can, however, provide a chart that presents a general picture of the hypothesized relationships among the fossils discussed in this chapter (Figure 3.20).

I agree, if the ancient fossil hominids discussed here could be arrayed in a nice, neat sequence of firmly dated rungs on an evolutionary ladder representing progress from our genus's split from the apes on the first step, leading neatly and inexorably in a single line to us at the top, things would be so much easier to understand.

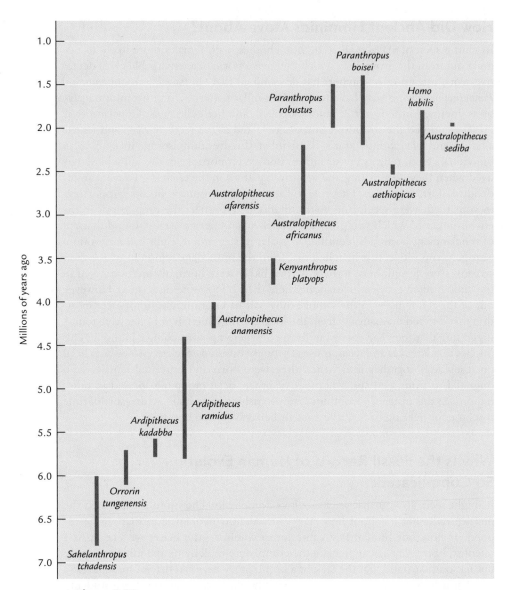

▲ **Figure 3.20**
This phylogeny shows the chronological relationships among the fossil hominids discussed in this chapter.

But if there's one thing evolutionary scientists have discovered, it is that nice, neat, simple, straight-line sequences are difficult to come by. Those evolutionary trees you may have seen in popular books with a single ancestral trunk leading to a series of easily distinguishable branches, each representing a separate evolutionary line leading finally to the twig that is the modern population of each discrete species, simply don't reflect the way things really work in biological evolution. A better analog than a tree is a densely branching bush with lots of thick growth, and many of its branches crossing other branches, leading nowhere in particular. As recent research has shown, there is a tremendous amount of diversity in our hominid ancestors (Leakey et al. 2012), and it may be excruciatingly difficult to tease out of the thicket a single evolutionary sequence, including our own.

I have listed a dizzying array of different fossils in this chapter, of which only some will turn out to be directly ancestral to us. Some of the fossils I discussed in this chapter were our evolutionary cousins, and some of these were dead ends in our evolutionary lineage. Some fossils represent entirely separate evolutionary lines only very distantly related to us, engaged in their own, separate, largely parallel pathway that included bipedality. And almost certainly, some of the fossils discussed here were our direct ancestors. Figuring which are which is one of the greatest challenges in paleoanthropology.

HADAR, LOCATED IN THE AFAR TRIANGLE of northeastern Ethiopia, is one of the most spectacular fossil hominid sites ever excavated. All by itself, the Hadar site disproves the notion that the pronouncements of paleontologists are based on a tiny handful of unrecognizable bone fragments or indistinguishable teeth. This one site produced 250 hominid fossil bones representing 14 individual members of the species *Australopithecus afarensis* (Johanson and Shreeve 1989:21). Perhaps most significantly, Hadar produced Lucy.

CASE STUDY
CLOSE-UP

The remains of the fossil that her discoverers named Lucy were found in 1974. Close to one-half of her skeleton was recovered, including parts of the skull, the lower jaw, ribs, vertebrae, arm bones, left innominate, left femur (upper leg), and parts of the lower right leg (see Figure 3.11). The following year, fragmentary remains of 13 more individuals were found, including 9 adults and 4 children. Dubbed "the First Family," all these individuals were deposited at the same time and seem to have died together.

The Hadar fossils provided the name for this hominid species, *Australopithecus afarensis*, after the Afar region of Ethiopia, where the site is located. Lucy and the First Family fossils constitute solid support for the interpretation presented in this chapter: Dating to more than 3.18 million years ago, these early hominids were, essentially, bipedal apes.

Lucy has received most of the attention as a result of her remarkable degree of preservation, but her size is not typical of the group found at Hadar. Lucy, an adult, was tiny by modern standards, standing only a little over 110 cm (3½ ft) tall, with an estimated weight of about 30 kg (65 lb), small even by *afarensis* standards. But Lucy is a female in a species that exhibits a large measure of **sexual dimorphism**—that is, a big difference between males and females. For example, among gorillas—a species with strong dimorphism—males are commonly twice the size of females. An analysis by Henry McHenry (1991) shows that sexual dimorphism among the known *afarensis* specimens is less than that exhibited by gorillas and orangutans but more than in chimpanzees and much more than in modern human beings where, on average, males are only about 10% to 15% larger than females. Lucy falls within the broad range of sizes represented in the First Family fossils. Though she is a small female, she is clearly a female.

The Hadar specimens show what these ancient hominids looked like: They were bipedal. Their arms were proportionally longer than those of modern humans, with hands quite modern in appearance except for fingers that curled more like an ape's fingers. Their jaws were an amalgam of ape and human. They had ape-sized brains housed in skulls that exhibited large, apelike bony ridges above the eyes and a highly prognathous profile.

I've admitted it previously on the pages of this book: I'm an antiquity dork. Perhaps that explains my emotional reaction that afternoon when I entered the dark exhibit room at the Discovery Times Square museum in New York City and first laid eyes on her. She was beautiful. Amazing. Transfixing.

It was Lucy. Not a reconstruction or a model: It was actually her, laid out in a climate-controlled, glass display case in the center of the exhibit hall. A number of people, all strangers to one another, had gathered around the case, peering in and gazing intently at each of her bones: her amazingly human-looking pelvis; the almost completely modern femur whose top can still articulate with that pelvis; her arching lower jaw; her tiny upper arm bones. So small, so delicate, so ancient, and yet so familiar.

Okay, maybe that sounds weird to you, getting all choked up about a handful of bones. Maybe you had to be there. Maybe you had to be me. But Lucy is a time traveler, speaking to us across more than 3 million years of human evolution. How can a person not be moved by that? Those of us there that day had each made a pilgrimage of sorts to visit our great-great-great- and beyond-great-grandmother, and it was incredibly difficult to say goodbye. A couple of us began laughing at our obvious inability to pull ourselves away. I'm not sure I learned anything about Lucy that day that I didn't already know, but the feelings engendered merely by being in her presence were more than worth the trip on so many levels.

Summary

Humanity began its evolutionary journey in Africa more than 6 million years ago as an "upright ape." Bipedal locomotion—not brain size or intelligence, the things that *most* distinguish us from the other animals—was what *first* differentiated us, the hominids, from the apes. *Sahelanthropus*, *Orrorin*, and *Ardipithecus* are among the candidates for the designation "oldest hominid," all dating to about 6 million years ago. By 4.2 million years ago, *Australopithecus anamensis* certainly was upright and may have been ancestral to all later forms of hominids. The ability to walk on two feet was advantageous in many ways: Hominids could travel with greater energy efficiency, which assisted in scavenging. Hominids seem uniquely adapted for long-distance running, and this ability to cover great distances may have been highly advantageous. With the hands freed, they could carry tools to where they were needed and bring back food to provision the young.

Around 2.5 million years ago, an environmental change in Africa, sparked by worldwide cooling, induced a burst of evolution in the hominid family. A number of varied species branched off from *Australopithecus afarensis* after this time. One branch, *Homo habilis*, had a brain size larger than any ape's. With its larger brain, *Homo habilis* was able to produce the first stone tools—simple but revealing a level of planning and forethought that reflects the great intelligence of this first member of our genus.

TO LEARN
MORE

As always, National Geographic presents a superbly illustrated and well-written piece on the exciting, new discoveries in paleoanthropology in an article in its July 2010 issue (Shreeve 2010). The article focuses on *Ardipithecus*. For very well-written, broad discussions of the paleoanthropology and archaeology of the first hominids, books written by some of the best-known scientists in the field are good choices: Donald Johanson and Kate Wong's (2009) *Lucy's Legacy* is a terrific, recent summary of the story of Lucy's discovery and her significance in human evolution. Also, see the beautiful coffee-table book written by Donald Johanson and Blake Edgar called *From Lucy to Language* (1996). There is no better source for artistic photographs of fossil hominid remains (taken by well-known photographer of paleoanthropological specimens David Brill).

For a broad summary of human evolution, take a look at *The Complete World of Human Evolution* by Chris Stringer and Peter Andrews (2012). It's a one-volume encyclopedia of sites, fossils, and concepts.

Web links for this chapter can be found at www.oup.com/us/feder

KEY TERMS

arboreal, 70	hominid, 65	Oldowan, 82
articular surfaces, 88	ilium, 84	phylogeny, 69
australopithecine, 80	innominate, 78	Pliocene, 70
bipedal locomotion, 71	ischium, 84	pongid, 79
brachiation, 71	isotope, 70	postcranial, 76
cranium, 72	knapper, 82	prognathous, 77
diastema, 77	mandible, 77	sagittal crest, 78
femur, 85	maxilla, 77	savanna, 70
flake, 82	Miocene, 67	sexual dimorphism, 93
foramen magnum, 73	mosaic, 71	striking platform, 83
genera, 67	niche, 67	tibia, 85
hammerstone, 82	object piece, 82	

4

The Human Lineage

CHAPTER OVERVIEW

Close to 1.8 million years ago, another great change is seen in the fossil record of Africa. A new hominid makes its appearance on the evolutionary stage—*Homo erectus*. *Homo erectus* possessed a brain larger than that of *Homo habilis* from which it evolved; the *Homo erectus* brain is two-thirds the size of modern humans.

Homo erectus exhibits increasing intelligence as well as an increasing reliance on cultural adaptations. Though born in an African nursery and possessing an anatomy best suited to life in the tropics, culture allowed *Homo erectus* to expand into other regions with very different climates soon after it first appeared in Africa. Tools found in Israel and bones found in the Republic of Georgia reflect the existence of a likely corridor of hominid expansion beyond Africa beginning soon after 1.8 million years ago. Remarkably, *Homo erectus* fossils have been found that date to nearly the same time far to the east, on the island of Java. They appear not to have entered into Europe until after 1 million years ago.

A sophisticated stone-tool technology, cooperative hunting, the controlled use of fire, clothing, and the possible construction of shelters were all a part of the *Homo erectus* adaptation. A reliance on culture is a hallmark of this human ancestor.

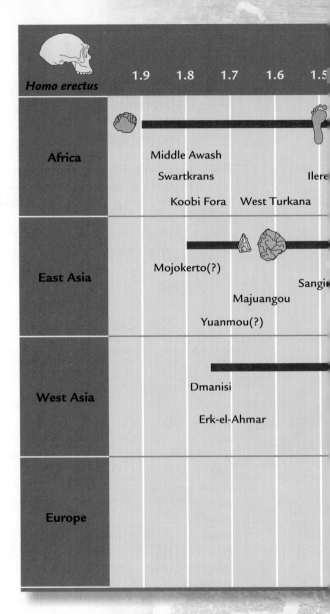

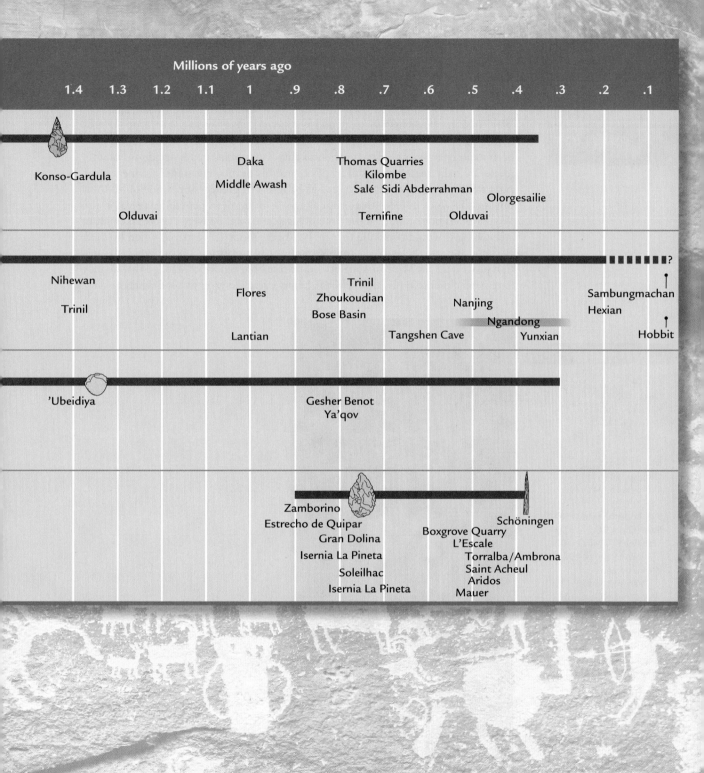

Millions of years ago

| 1.4 | 1.3 | 1.2 | 1.1 | 1 | .9 | .8 | .7 | .6 | .5 | .4 | .3 | .2 | .1 |

Konso-Gardula

Daka
Middle Awash

Thomas Quarries
Kilombe
Salé   Sidi Abderrahman
Olorgesailie

Olduvai

Ternifine   Olduvai

Nihewan

Trinil

Flores

Lantian

Trinil
Zhoukoudian
Bose Basin

Nanjing

Ngandong

Tangshen Cave   Yunxian

Sambungmachan
Hexian

Hobbit

'Ubeidiya

Gesher Benot
Ya'qov

Zamborino
Estrecho de Quipar
Gran Dolina
Isernia La Pineta
Soleilhac
Isernia La Pineta

Boxgrove Quarry
L'Escale
Torralba/Ambrona
Saint Acheul
Aridos
Mauer

Schöningen

PRELUDE

THE AGE AT DEATH OF THE West Turkana boy (Figure 4.1) is judged by paleoan-thropologists in much the same way that modern parents gauge the progress of their own children's physical development, by looking at his teeth (F. Brown et al. 1985:789; B. H. Smith 1993). As timeposted for a modern human child, all of the West Turkana boy's first (6-year) and second (12-year) molars had erupted; that is, they are above where the gum line would have been and, therefore, must have been exposed in his mouth when he was alive. Both of his upper deciduous canines (these are baby teeth) were still in place, and his permanent upper canine on the right side had been poised to replace its baby-tooth predecessor. None of his third molars (the wisdom teeth that erupt at age 18 in modern people) were yet in the West Turkana boy's mouth at the time of his death. So, if he were a modern child, an archaeologist would conclude that he had been about 12 years old when he died. Because of other skeletal development indicators suggesting a more rapid matura-tion process for the West Turkana boy, some researchers have concluded that he may have been closer to 8 (Gibbons 2008a). In any event, he was just a kid when he died.

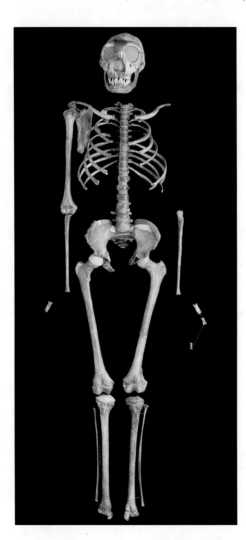

◀ **Figure 4.1**
One of the most complete fossil hominid skeletons ever found: KNM-WT-15000, the 12-year-old *Homo erectus* boy from Nariokotome.
(© David L. Brill)

The cause of death of the West Turkana boy is a sad mystery. His remarkably well-preserved, nearly complete skeleton shows great health and vigor. Alan Walker, one of the fossil's excavators, describes the Nariokotome boy as a "strapping youth" and estimates his height at between 5 feet 4 inches and 5 feet 8 inches (R. Leakey and Lewin 1992). That is considerably taller than a modern human boy of the same age in most populations.

The West Turkana boy died on the edge of a lagoon near a lake. The position of his bones indicates that his body floated face down in the shallow water after he died. Fortunately, no scavengers picked at his corpse as it decayed, so most of the body remained pretty much in place, if not intact. Animals coming to the lagoon for a drink may have walked on the body, breaking one of the legs and scattering the rest of the bones as the flesh, muscle, and tissue that had once been a boy were washed away. After the soft parts had decayed, a gentle current dispersed the bones across a linear distance of about 7 m (slightly more than 21 ft). The bones were then covered in the mucky lake bottom by waterborne silt and ash from a nearby volcano, where they rested for close to 1.55 million years.

In August 1984, Kenyan paleontologist Kamoya Kimeu was scouting for fossils in Nariokotome, in an area that is now a dry lake bed. Kimeu was looking for fossils on his day off before the camp of paleontologists moved to another locality as planned because so little of importance had been found in the area. Within a short time, he spotted a skull fragment, and an excavation was initiated. Soon the nearly complete skeletal remains of a boy were uncovered, revealing, with unprecedented clarity, an enormously ancient ancestor.

It is ironic that by dying in the right place at the right time, a young boy achieved an immortality that likely none of us will attain. Even 1.55 million years after he lived, in a time and world we can barely imagine, people still ponder his life. We place him in the taxonomic category *Homo erectus*, and his people are the focus of this chapter.

CHRONICLE

As INDICATED BY A SERIES OF fossil specimens, soon after 1.8 million B.P. in Africa, and nearly as long ago in Asia and somewhat later in Europe, an acceleration of human evolution took place. The new fossils are different enough from *Homo habilis* to warrant a new name or names for the reasons enumerated in our discussion of species designation in Chapter 3. The new specimens have skeletal anatomies so different from that of *habilis* that they cannot reasonably be placed in the same group. But what to name the new fossils, and should they all be placed together in the same group?

Many paleoanthropologists believe that all of the hominids that follow *Homo habilis* and predate *Homo sapiens*—from after 1.8 million B.P. until about 400,000 B.P. or even later—belong to a single species: *Homo erectus* (Potts et al. 2004). When the sample of specimens recovered for this group was small and anatomical variation seemed quite limited among those fossils found from Africa all the way to east Asia, this assumption was reasonable. A recent spate of discoveries has convinced others, however, based on highly technical analyses of the morphology of the various specimens, that this period of human evolution instead presents us with a number of related but more or less geographically separate species (Schwartz 2004): *Homo ergaster* in Africa, *Homo erectus* in central and east Asia, and *Homo antecessor* in Europe.

▶ **Figure 4.2**
Two competing models for the number of species, evolution, and spread of hominids after 2 million years ago (mya). In the more traditional model (left), *Homo habilis* gave rise to *Homo erectus* in Africa sometime after 2 mya. From there, *Homo erectus* populations quickly spread into Asia and, later, western Europe. In the competing model (right), *Homo habilis* gave rise to *Homo ergaster* in Africa sometime after 2 mya. *Homo habilis* or a descendant also spread into Asia soon after 2 mya, where it evolved into *Homo erectus*. *Homo ergaster* may have spread into Europe, where it gave rise to yet another hominid species, *Homo antecessor*, which later evolved into *Homo heidelbergensis*.

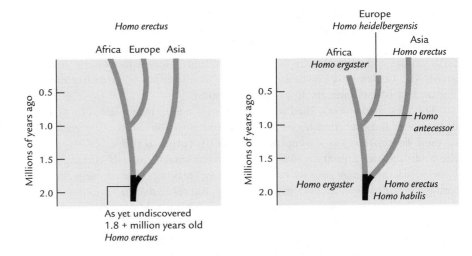

For the sake of clarity and to make this part of the human story more straightforward, we will take the simpler approach here, labeling all of the specimens to be discussed in this chapter *Homo erectus*. (Figure 4.2 presents two different phylogenies, one based on the simpler view followed here and one on the multispecies model.) Of course, the number of hominid species alive at any given time is of enormous importance. But for our purposes, it is not as important as understanding that—one species, two, three, or more—during the period from 1.8 million to after 400,000 B.P., populations of intelligent hominids, relying on cultural adaptations, spread throughout much of the Old World, using their intelligence to successfully adjust to a series of widely different environments.

Homo erectus

Potassium/argon dating has placed the oldest *Homo erectus* specimen—a skull labeled ER 3733 (Figure 4.3) from a rich fossil locality called Koobi Fora, east of Lake Turkana (R. Leakey and Walker 1985b)—at about 1.78 million years ago (Feibel, Brown, and McDougal 1989). Physically and culturally, *Homo erectus* is recognizably human, yet it is intriguingly different from us.

The cranium of this new member of the human lineage was quite different from that of its evolutionary antecedent, *Homo habilis* (Figure 4.4). To begin with, its skull, and by implication its brain, was significantly larger. Most specimens have cranial volumes in excess of 800 cc, and the species as a whole has a mean cranial capacity of about 960 cc (Table 4.1). This is an increase of more than 37% over *Homo habilis*, whose mean cranial capacity was only about 700 cc, and it's about two-thirds the volume of the modern human mean of 1,450 cc. The Nariokotome boy's cranial capacity was 880 cc; it is estimated that his brain size, had he lived to adulthood, would have been a little over 900 cc (Begun and Walker 1993:346). The largest members of the species have skulls with volumes of over 1,200 cc. This measurement places the brain size of the species far above that of *Homo habilis* and within the lower range of the size of the modern human brain.

The skull of *erectus* was not just larger than that of *habilis*, but it was also differently configured and differently proportioned in ways that signify a shift

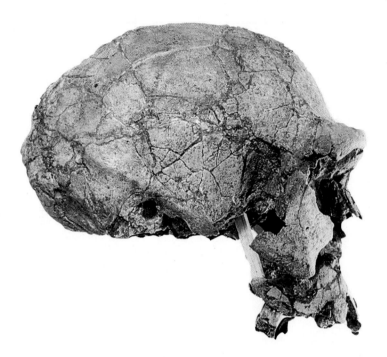

◀ **Figure 4.3**
The fossil cranium designated ER 3733. At nearly 1.8 million years of age, this is the oldest known specimen of the fossil species *Homo erectus*. (© National Museums of Kenya)

toward a more modern human appearance. For example, the forehead of *erectus* is somewhat flatter and less sloping than that of *habilis*, a bit more similar to the modern, virtually vertical human forehead. The back, or **occipital**, portion of the *erectus* skull is rounder than that of *habilis*, with a much larger area for muscle attachment. Larger and stronger muscles were needed to support its much larger, heavier skull.

Analysis of cranial endocasts of a number of *Homo erectus* specimens (Holloway 1980, 1981) shows intriguing similarities to the modern human brain. Most significantly, anthropologist Ralph Holloway discovered hemispheric asymmetry in the *erectus* brain, similar to that seen in modern human beings. The different halves, or hemispheres, of the human brain regulate different tasks; in particular, human speech is ordinarily controlled by the left hemisphere. As a result, the two halves of a human brain are of slightly different shape, proportion, and size. Whether the asymmetry in the endocasts of the *erectus* brain means they were capable of humanlike speech cannot be determined. But the configuration of the *erectus* brain was definitely more like that of modern human beings and different from that of the chimp, gorilla, orangutan, australopithecine, and *habilis* specimens to which Holloway compared them.

Beneath the intriguingly humanlike brain, the *erectus* face itself is somewhat flatter, projecting less than the *habilis* face, though it still

▼ Figure 4.4
Comparison of the skulls of *Homo habilis* and *Homo erectus*. The skull of *erectus* is larger and more modern (less apelike) than that of *habilis*.

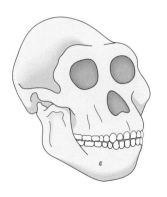

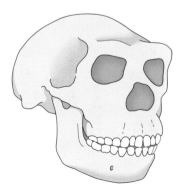

Homo habilis   *Homo erectus*

TABLE 4.1 Major *Homo erectus* Fossils Discussed in Chapter 4

Country	Locality	Fossils	Crania	Age	Brain size (cc, sub-adults in italics)
Kenya	East Turkana	Cranial and postcranial fragments including mandibles and pelvis and long bone fragments	KNM-ER 3733 KNM-ER 3883	1.78 million yrs 1.57 million yrs	850 800
	West Turkana	Nearly complete juvenile individual	KNM-WT 15000	1.6 million yrs	880
	Olorgesailie	Cranial fragments	KNM-OL 45500	0.97–0.90 million yrs	<800
Tanzania	Olduvai	Cranial and postcranial fragments including mandibles and pelvis and long bone fragments	OH 9 OH 12	1.25 million yrs 0.6–0.8 million yrs	1,060 800
Ethiopia	Daka	Cranium		1 million yrs	995
Algeria	Ternifine	Three mandibles and a skull fragment		0.5–0.7 million yrs	
Morocco	Thomas Quarries Sidi Abderrahman Salé	Mandible and skull fragments Two mandible fragments Skull fragments	Salé	0.5 million yrs 0.4 million yrs	880
Java	Trinil	Skull cap, femur	"Java Man"	<1 million yrs	940
	Sangiran	Cranial and postcranial fragments from ~40 individuals	S-2 S-4 S-10 S-12 S-17 1993 Cranium	0.7–1.6 million yrs 0.7–1.6 million yrs 0.7–1.6 million yrs 0.7–1.6 million yrs 0.7–1.6 million yrs 1.1–1.4 million yrs	800 900 850 1,050 1,000 856
	Ngandong	Cranial and postcranial fragments from >1 dozen individuals	N-1 N-6 N-11 N-12	<1 million yrs <1 million yrs <1 million yrs <1 million yrs	1,170 1,250 1,230 1,090
	Sambungmachan	Three partial crania	Sm3	<.5 million yrs	917
	Mojokerto	Child's cranium		1.8 million yrs?	663

(continued)

TABLE 4.1 Major *Homo erectus* Fossils Discussed in Chapter 4 *(continued)*

Country	Locality	Fossils	Crania	Age	Brain size (cc, sub-adults in italics)
Flores	Flores	Cranium, mandible, femur, tibia, pelvis, vertebrae, feet, hands	LB1 or "Hobbit"	18,000 yrs	*417*
China	Zhoukoudian	Cranial and postcranial remains of >40 individuals	II	<0.46 million yrs	1,030
			III	<0.46 million yrs	915
			VI	<0.46 million yrs	850
			X	<0.46 million yrs	1,225
			XI	<0.46 million yrs	1,015
			XII	<0.46 million yrs	1,030
			Locality 13	0.7 million yrs	
	Hexian (Lontandong)	Partial skull	"Hexian Man"	0.27 million yrs?	1,000
	Lantian (Gongwangling)	Cranial fragments and mandible	"Lantian Man"	1.15 million yrs	800
	Yunxian	Two crania		>0.35 million yrs	
	Tangshan Cave	Parts of two crania	"Nanjing Man"	>0.60 million yrs	
Georgia	Dmanisi	Three crania	Young male	1.75 million yrs	775
			Female teen	1.75 million yrs	*650*
			Young female	1.75 million yrs	*600*
		Mandible fragment and 16 teeth			
Spain	Gran Dolina	Remains of six individuals	Partial skull of child	0.8 million yrs	
England	Boxgrove Quarry	Tibia		0.48–0.51 million yrs	
				Mean (excluding sub-adults and "Hobbit")	960
				Mean (excluding sub-adults but including "Hobbit")	941
				Standard Deviation (excluding sub-adults and "Hobbit")	142
				Standard Deviation (excluding sub-adults but including "Hobbit")	268

Data from Asfaw et al. (2002); Gabunia et al. (2000); Holloway (1980, 1981); Rightmire (1990); Vekua et al. (2002).

is far more **prognathous** than that of a modern human. Above the eye orbits, *Homo erectus* crania display a ridge of bone called a **supraorbital torus.** This "brow ridge" is present in the skulls of all ape species and is generally absent in the modern human form, though some people, especially males, exhibit relatively smaller but discernible ridges above their eyes.

Below the skull, the bones of *Homo erectus* bear witness to a creature that indisputably walked upright, in a manner similar, if not identical, to that of modern human beings. Hominid footprints in Ileret, Kenya, dating to 1.5 million years ago clearly support this conclusion (Bennett et al. 2009). Preserved in two sedimentary layers at the site, the Ileret footprints are indistinguishable from those of a modern human being.

To be sure, the West Turkana boy and other, more fragmentary postcranial *Homo erectus* remains exhibit a skeletal architecture indicative of great muscularity and strength, probably outside the range of modern human beings. Nonetheless, as more than one paleoanthropologist has stated, you would not be alarmed if a *Homo erectus*, with a cap pulled down low over his or her forehead and face and appropriately dressed, were to sit down next to you in class.

▼ **Figure 4.5**
Fossil localities of *Homo erectus.*

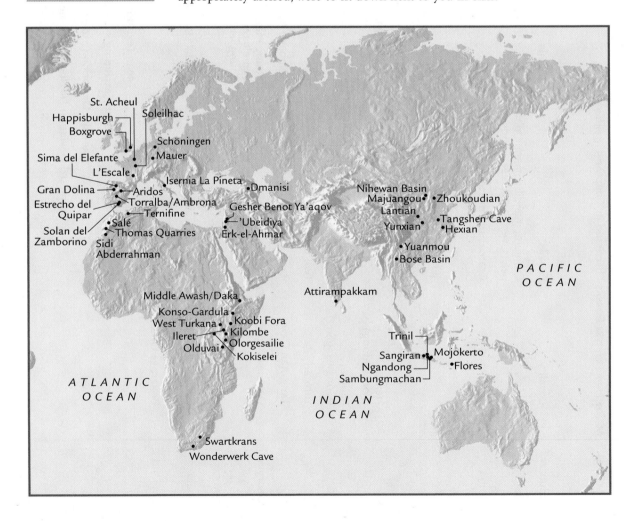

The Evolutionary Position of *Homo erectus*

The oldest *erectus* fossils are found in Africa, often in the same areas where *habilis* remains have been recovered (Figure 4.5). Current consensus, therefore, is that *Homo erectus* is the direct evolutionary descendant of the African hominid species *Homo habilis*, though not all agree on this point (see Issues and Debates).

Hominids Conquer the World

Homo erectus, like its hominid predecessors, evolved in Africa. Unlike its forebears, however, *Homo erectus*, or perhaps an immediate evolutionary descendant, was not restricted to that continent. Fossils similar to the *erectus* specimens found in Africa have been found in Asia and date to very soon after their initial appearance 1.8 million years ago.

If you look at a map or globe, it is easy to see that Africa is physically connected to the rest of its hemisphere only at its northeastern apex where it borders southwest Asia, the place we today call the Middle East. Not surprisingly, some of the oldest hominid sites outside of Africa have been found here in the broad zone where Europe and Asia come together (see Figure 4.5).

For example, at Erk-el-Ahmar in Israel an assemblage of choppers and flake tools have been excavated in a stratigraphic level bracketed between levels dated to 1.7 and 2.0 million years ago based on **paleomagnetism** (Holden 2002). Just a few kilometers north is another, somewhat younger, hominid site dating to 1.4 million years ago. Called 'Ubeidiya, it has produced a handful of choppers, picks, and flakes along with some very fragmentary remains of hominids (Belfer-Cohen and Goren-Inbar 1994).

Farther to the north, hominid fossils have been found in Dmanisi, near the shore of the Black Sea in the Republic of Georgia. Two mandibles, four relatively complete crania, and a number of elements of the postcranial skeleton (the bones below the head) including fragments of arm, leg, shoulder, vertebral column, and bones of the foot have now been unearthed there from a deposit that has been dated to about 1.77 million years ago (Figure 4.6; Gabunia et al. 2000; Holden 2003a; Lordkipanidze et al. 2007;Vekua et al. 2002).The four Dmanisi crania range in size from 600 to 775 cc (Figure 4.6;Vekua et al. 2002).

All four crania are small by African *Homo erectus* standards, but this may be explained by the fact that at Dmanisi we have the remains only of young individuals, whose heads had not reached their fully adult size; one of them is almost certainly a juvenile. Also, there is at least one small female—and possibly two—in the sample. Except for their size, the Dmanisi crania otherwise look remarkably like African *Homo erectus*

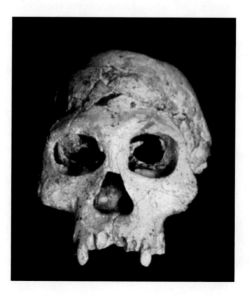

◀ **Figure 4.6**
Found near the intersection of three continents—Africa, Asia, and Europe—the Dmanisi specimens—one of the crania is shown here—found in the Republic of Georgia likely represent the remains of some of the earliest *Homo erectus* migrants out of Africa. (Photo by Gouram Tsibakhashvili. Courtesy Professor Dr. David Lordkipanidze, Deputy Director, Georgina State Museum)

crania dating to the same time period. When Pat Shipman, who had co-directed the excavation of the Nariokotome boy, first saw one of the Dmanisi mandibles, her reaction was one of amazement; the jaws were not just similar, but could have come from twins (Shipman 2000:491).

Below the skull, the Dmanisi hominids display an interesting mosaic of characteristics. Though the shape and probably positioning of their arm bones differ from those of a modern human being, resembling, instead, those of an *Australopithecus*, the overall proportions of the Dmanisi hominids are quite modern, with relatively long, humanlike legs and a distinctly human, arched foot.

The tool kit of the Dmanisi hominids is another piece of evidence that links them to an African hominid heritage. Only simple chopping and flake tools have been found at the site. These tools clearly belong to the Oldowan tradition seen at *Homo habilis* and early *Homo erectus* sites in Africa (Gibbons 2009b).

East Asia

It is a long way from Africa to the shore of the Black Sea, where the Dmanisi site is located, but it is not nearly the end of our journey or that of the hominid species *Homo erectus*. The next set of ancient sites we will visit are literally half a world away, at the other end of our planet's largest continent.

Dutch physician Eugene Dubois (1894) traveled to the island of Java in the western Pacific in the late nineteenth century expressly to seek out evidence of human origins in the Asian tropics. In 1891, along the Solo River in the vicinity of the town of Trinil, he came upon a **calvarium** that looked not quite human but not quite apelike (Figure 4.7). It possessed large brow ridges like those of apes. But the cranial capacity, as best as could be judged at the time, was far larger than an ape's while still smaller than a modern human's. Dubois labeled the find *Pithecanthropus erectus*, meaning "upright ape-man." Still popularly referred to as "Java Man," we now include Dubois's discovery in the *Homo erectus* species. Its estimated cranial capacity of 940 cc and its age (still uncertain but probably about 1 million years old) place it firmly in the *erectus* species. A number of other *Homo erectus* specimens have been found on Java (see Table 4.1 and Figure 4.8). Though Java today is an island, during periods of lowered sea level it was part of the mainland of Southeast Asia, enabling *Homo erectus* to arrive there on foot.

Application of the argon/argon technique has provided chronological dates for a number of the Java *Homo erectus* specimens. For example, several *Homo erectus* fossils found at the very rich Sangiran locality on Java have now been dated to more than 1.0 million and perhaps as much as 1.6 million years ago (Larick et al. 2001). Additionally, the skull of a juvenile *Homo erectus* found at the Mojokerto locality on Java is now estimated to be close to 1.75 million years old, about as old as the oldest specimens in Africa, thousands of miles away (Swisher et al. 1994).

On Java, *Homo erectus* appears to have been an extremely long-lived species,

▼ **Figure 4.7**
The first skull fragment found of *Homo erectus* was this skullcap found in Java in the late nineteenth century by the Dutch scientist Eugene Dubois. (© Naturalis Biodiversity Center, the Netherlands)

surviving long after it had become extinct in Africa, Europe, and the rest of Asia. *Homo erectus* fossils recovered at the Ngandong and Sambungmachan sites have recently been dated to sometime between just 27,000 and 53,000 years ago (Swisher et al., 1996).

Homo erectus: Ocean Explorer?

As distant as all other *Homo erectus* sites are from their ultimate source in Africa, all of these places are within "walking distance" of their point of origin—at least over many generations of wandering and expansion. Remember, when *Homo erectus* arrived, the island of Java was connected to the Southeast Asian mainland as the result of lowered sea level, so members of that species walked there over dry land. However, stone tools have been recovered on the island of Flores, located east of Java, just below a stratigraphic level dating to 1.02 million years ago (Brumm et al. 2010). Flores is separated from Java by a deep, natural underwater trench. Even during periods of lowered sea level, Flores would still have been separated from lands to the west by approximately 19 km (12 mi) of open sea. For *Homo erectus* to get to Flores, it must have been by floating there.

Robert G. Bednarik is so interested in the seafaring capability of *Homo erectus* that he has been willing to risk his reputation and even his life on its study. He has twice constructed bamboo rafts,

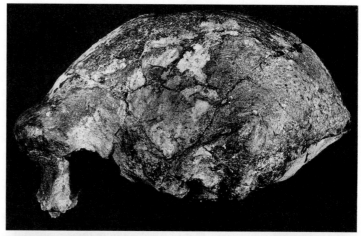

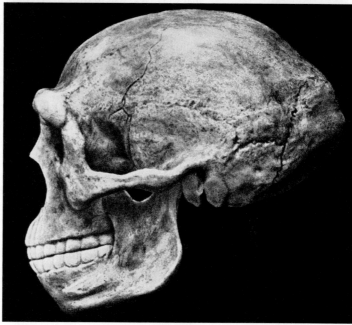

▲ **Figure 4.8**
Crania of *Homo erectus* from Sangiran, Java (top), and Zhoukoudian in China (bottom). (Top, courtesy of Ralph L. Holloway. Bottom, © Bettmann/CORBIS)

which he has then taken to sea with hardy crews, attempting to show the seaworthiness of watercraft so elementary that perhaps *Homo erectus* would have been capable of making and sailing them (Bower 2003). Through trial and error—his first attempt at crossing the 48-km (30-mi) sea gap between the Indonesian islands of Bali and Lombok (they are in the same chain of islands as Flores) was abandoned after 6 fruitless hours of rowing—in 2000 Bednarik and his crew barely, but safely, crossed between those two islands in about 12 hours. Like all replicative archaeological experiments, this proves only that such a trip is possible, not that *Homo erectus* had actually been capable of building and then sailing a similar craft. Nevertheless, we do know that *Homo erectus* made it to Flores, and Bednarik has provided and successfully tested one possible way in which this may have happened.

China and India

The oldest evidence for the presence of hominids in China has been found in the form of chert, sandstone, quartz, and andesite cores and flakes at the Majuangou site in the Nihewan River basin (Zhu et al. 2004). This site presents researchers with another example of how quickly *Homo erectus* must have spread across the face of Asia once expanding beyond its place of origin in Africa. The Nihewan is located in north-central China, and the lowest stratigraphic layer at the site that has produced stone artifacts has been dated to 1.66 million years ago. Remember that the oldest *Homo erectus* find outside of Africa dates to 1.78 million years ago at Dmanisi, located at the other side of the Asian continent from Majuangou. This implies that it took *Homo erectus* just a little more than 200,000 years to spread across several thousand miles of territory.

It is also important to point out that Majuangou is situated at 40° N latitude. Hominids living there would have been faced with a climate far different from that of Africa, where they evolved. Their ability to adapt to the very different environmental conditions of northern China is a testament to their reliance upon and the effectiveness of their cultural adaptation. The oldest hominid fossils in China with confirmed dates are all somewhat younger than this (see Table 4.1).

One of the most important *Homo erectus* sites ever discovered in China—and certainly the most widely known hominid locality—is in the village of Zhoukoudian, about 50 km (35 mi) southwest of Beijing. The cave at the site and the surrounding area produced the remains of about 45 *Homo erectus* individuals in a region possessing a continental climate (typified by hot summers and cold winters with ample precipitation spread more or less evenly throughout the year), then and now, not unlike that in the northern United States—obviously a far cry from the climate of tropical Africa, where the species originated. Occupation of the main site (Locality 1) by "Peking Man" has been dated to 770,000 years ago (Ciochon and Bettis 2009). Another site, located about 1 km south of the original Peking Man cave site, Locality 13, has been dated to 700,000 years ago (Jia and Huang 1990).

More details concerning the site, its discovery, and its significance—and the tragic mystery of the disappearance of the fossils more than 60 years ago—are provided in this chapter's "Case Study Close-up" (see Figure 4.8).

Moving further back to the African source of the species is the Attirampakkam site in southeast India. Here, dating to more than 1.5 million years ago, researchers excavated a broad array of tools including bifacially flaked axes made from coarse quartzite cobbles (Pappu et al. 2011).

The evidence for *Homo erectus* in east and south Asia presents an interesting puzzle. It seems pretty clear that *erectus* originated in Africa from *Homo habilis* roots and spread north and east from that continent. One might have expected, therefore, that *erectus* sites would be oldest in Africa, a bit younger close by in southwest Asia, and then successively younger as they expanded eastward. The archaeological record does not show that, suggesting a very quick migration east and then, later, an infilling of habitats in between Africa and East Asia.

Europe

The oldest hominid fossil in Europe was found in the Sima del Elefante cave in the mountains of northern Spain. Excavators discovered part of a humanlike lower jaw in a cave deposit dating to about 1.2 million years ago (Carbonell et al.

2008). Stone flakes and the cut bones of large mammalian species provide further evidence of a hominid presence in the cave at this time.

Though no indisputable *Homo erectus* remains have been found at the Solana del Zamborino and Estrecho del Quipar sites in southeastern Spain, they have produced the oldest evidence of **handaxe** production in Europe (see the discussion of handaxes later in this chapter). Researchers have found finely made specimens at both of these sites in stratigraphic layers dating to between 0.76 and 0.9 million years ago (Scott and Gibert 2009).

Gran Dolina in the Atapuerca Mountains in Spain is one of the most significant hominid sites in Europe (Carbonell et al. 1995). Dating to more than 800,000 and perhaps as much as 1 million years ago (Parés and Pérez-González 1995), the Gran Dolina hominid fossils include the remains of at least six individuals, including two adults, one teenager, and one 10- to 12-year-old child. The preserved lower portion of the child's body is entirely modern in its morphology and therefore quite different from that seen in *Homo erectus* fossils dating to the same period. As a result, the Gran Dolina researchers have assigned these fossils to a new species, *Homo antecessor* (Bermúdez de Castro et al. 1997). As a result of the mosaic of primitive and modern traits of the Gran Dolina fossils, the researchers suggest that *antecessor* represents a descendant of *Homo erectus* (see Figure 4.2). Whether *antecessor* possesses features sufficiently different from those of *erectus* to justify the naming of a new hominid species becomes an argument between the lumpers and the splitters again, and the details need not concern us here. Following the practice established at the beginning of this chapter, we will label these specimens as *Homo erectus*. Whatever we call them, it is reasonable to say that African hominids first entered Europe by about 1.2 million years ago. Why they arrived to colonize Europe so long after they had spread into Asia as far as the island of Java (1.75 million years ago) and northern China (1.66 million years ago) will be addressed in "Issues and Debates."

The Age of Ice

For reasons that are still uncertain, beginning at about 2.6 million years ago (Kerr 2009; Mascarelli 2009) the earth became a significantly colder place. Particularly after about 900,000 years ago, northern latitudes and higher elevations were covered by huge, expanding ice fields called **glaciers** (Shackleton and Opdyke 1973, 1976; Figures 4.9 and 4.10).

This colder period of time is called the **Pleistocene epoch** (see Figure 3.3 for a time chart placing the Pleistocene chronologically in the history of the earth). Researchers mark the end of the Pleistocene at 10,000 years ago, when worldwide temperature rose and glaciers shrank. The modern period is called the **Holocene epoch**. Many climate experts believe that the Holocene is simply a relatively warm period that is destined to end in only a few thousand years, with glacial conditions nearly certain to return. How gobal warming will affect this is, at this point, anybody's guess.

Though initially conceptualized and still commonly thought of as an "Ice Age" of unremitting cold, the Pleistocene actually was an epoch of fluctuating climate, with periods called **glacials** much colder than the present. These glacials were characterized by widespread ice and snow cover—imagine most of the central

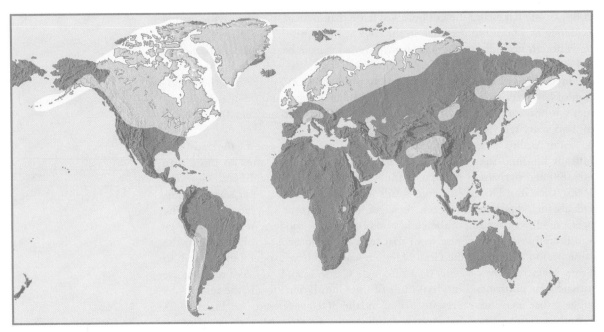

▲ **Figure 4.9**
Map of worldwide glacial coverage during the peak periods of glaciation during the
Pleistocene epoch.

▶ **Figure 4.10**
Greenland, shown here
from the air, serves as
a model for conditions
in much of the northern
hemisphere and higher
elevations during the
Pleistocene epoch.
(K. L. Feder)

and northern United States and Canada and much of northern Europe looking and feeling like Greenland. But within the glacials themselves were colder and warmer periods, with attendant glacial advances (**stadials**) and retreats (**interstadials**). Between the glacials were relatively long **interglacial** periods, during which temperatures often approached, sometimes equaled, and rarely may even have exceeded the modern level.

The pattern of temperature fluctuation and glacial advance and retreat can be studied in a number of ways. Glaciers leave significant and recognizable features as they cover the land. If you live in the northern third of the United States or virtually anywhere in Canada, then you can still see the effects of the huge, moving continental sheets and rivers of ice, some a few kilometers thick, as they rode over everything in their path. Glacial geologists can read a landscape for its glacial deposits, which can then be dated to develop a chronology of glaciation, as each subsequent expansion of ice overrode the previous one. (See Richard Foster Flint's *Glacial and Quaternary Geology*, 1971, for the classic work on the New World Pleistocene.)

The Oxygen Isotope Curve

Remember the discussion of the analysis of oxygen isotopes in Chapter 2. The ratio of two isotopes of oxygen, ^{16}O and ^{18}O, in oceanic water changes as a result of changes in worldwide temperature and in the amount of water tied up in long-lasting ice fields in the world's higher latitudes and higher elevations. Simply, the colder the world gets and the more ice builds up on land, the lower the proportion of ^{16}O in water and, concomitantly, in the shells of marine microorganisms. The shells of those organisms can be collected, dated, and measured for their isotope concentrations. Those concentrations can, in turn, be interpreted as a record of fluctuations in worldwide temperature.

The curve representing the relative worldwide proportion of $^{16}O:^{18}O$ through time has been determined by Shackleton and Opdyke (1973, 1976; and see Chapter 2). Their results are presented in Figure 4.11. Covering the last 780,000 years, the Shackleton and Opdyke chronology exhibits ten periods of drops in ^{16}O and therefore significantly colder temperatures and greater ice cover on the earth's surface. Further research has indicated at least ten additional such periods in the first half of the Pleistocene.

All of this climatic instability must have affected our hominid ancestors. Though *Homo erectus* did not penetrate into areas where there were large continental ice sheets, all of the earth was influenced during the Pleistocene. Sea level dropped substantially, perhaps by as much as 125 m (more than 400 ft), during glacial maxima. Such a drop altered the configuration of most of the world's coasts, exposing as dry land thousands of square kilometers that previously were and presently are under water. Lowered sea levels would have made the colonization of islands like Flores easier by lessening the distance between them and the nearest mainland. The climate of areas even far south of the farthest extent of the glaciers changed, as low-pressure systems altered their usual flow patterns. These changes certainly altered the conditions to which *Homo erectus* needed to adapt. Adaptive flexibility seems to have been a hallmark of the members of this species. Their ability to inhabit new regions with environmental conditions far different

▶ **Figure 4.11**
The Shackelton and Opdyke curve of ^{18}O concentration in fossil foraminifera. The curve is an indirect reflection of glacial expansion and contraction during the last 780,000 years.

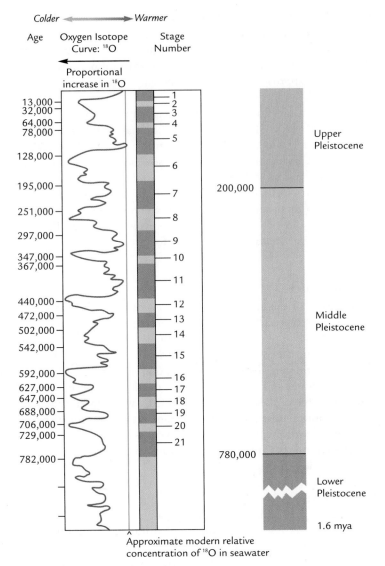

Odd-numbered stages (in orange) = warmer periods, less glacial ice cover
Even-numbered stages (in blue) = colder periods, more glacial ice cover

from their tropical source, as well as their ability to change as their surroundings altered, bear witness to their great intelligence and in fact their humanity (see "Issues and Debates").

Homo erectus: The Toolmaker

In a class I teach called "Experimental Archaeology," we spend a lot of time trying to replicate, as authentically as possible, various stone tools made by prehistoric people. We follow a chronological, evolutionary sequence, first replicating the Oldowan tools of *Homo habilis* and then making copies of the **Acheulean**

handaxe (named for the French site of Saint-Acheul, where they were first iden-tified) that typifies *Homo erectus*, at least in Africa and Europe.

Students generally have little trouble making impressive versions of Oldowan choppers and flake tools—with a little effort and after mastering the proper striking angle of hammerstone on core. This is not the case, however, for the *Homo erectus* handaxe, which is not that easy to make, at least not without lots of practice, knowledge, and time. Only a few of my students develop proficiency in handaxe production.

The oldest handaxes have been found at the Kokiselei 4 site, located on the western margin of Lake Turkana in Kenya and dating to 1.76 million years ago (Figure 4.12; Lepre et al. 2011). This date corresponds very closely with the age of the oldest *Homo erectus* specimens discussed earlier in this chapter. Even to an untrained eye, handaxes look much more tightly patterned and even more aesthetically pleasing than the Oldowan tools discussed in Chapter 3. In fact, when shown an Oldowan tool many think it just looks like a beat-up rock. Everyone, when shown an Acheulean handaxe, immediately recognizes it as a human-made tool.

In a truly amazing research project, well-known stone tool replicator Bruce Bradley was hooked up to a device (a positron emission tomography scanner) that tracked his brain activity while making an Oldowan chopper and a late-style Acheulean handaxe (Normille 2012). Researchers determined that while Bradley was making the Oldowan tool, the scanner showed brain activity normally associ-ated with hand gripping and coordination. That's not surprising. However, when Bradley was making the handaxe, the areas in his brain associated with abstract thought, hierarchical organization, and language lit up. In other words, all kind of stuff is going on in the brain of an individual making a complex stone tool like a handaxe; you can't accomplish that without a brain capable of such activity.

To be sure, as you might expect, the oldest examples of handaxes are fairly crude and simple, at least by the standards set by those made a half-million years later (Figure 4.13). The Kokiselei handaxes are less than perfectly symmetrical and are rather thick, and their edges are irregular, looking, in fact, like a fancied-up Oldowan

◀ **Figure 4.12**
Dating to 1.76 million years ago, the handaxes recovered at the Kokiselei 4 site on the western shore of Lake Turkana in the African nation of Kenya are the oldest yet discovered anywhere in the world. You can clearly see the symmetry—I would even call it beauty—its ancient maker incorporated into the design of this multipurpose tool. (Courtesy Pierre-Jean Texier)

▲ **Figure 4.13**
A finely chipped,
symmetrical Lower
Paleolithic handaxe.
(© Boltin Picture Library/
Bridgeman Art Library)

chopping tool (Chapter 3). In all honesty, they look sort of like what I produce when I attempt to replicate Acheulean handaxes for my classes. They're okay, and my students are marginally impressed, but I wouldn't display them in a museum.

Later **Acheulean tradition** handaxes especially are symmetrical, finely flaked, and often aesthetically exquisite (see Figure 4.13). Dozens of flakes are removed from the core, not just a few (Figure 4.14). Even quite simple handaxes can take 25 individual hammer strikes. The best-made examples, which date to after 1 million B.P., in Africa and more recently in Europe, took nearly three times that number (Constable 1973:128). Each flake blow must be located precisely in order to allow for the proper positioning of the next strike. The stone must be turned over again and again between hammer strikes to maintain symmetry and to keep the edge of the tool straight. All—or, at least, most—of the exterior rind, or **cortex**, of the object piece was removed in order to keep the tool relatively thin and light, so

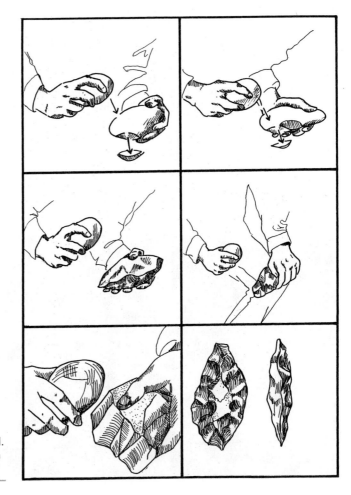

▶ **Figure 4.14**
Through a process of bifacial flaking, a symmetrical, finely made handaxe was produced. Compare this to the process of making Oldowan tools (see Figure 3.17). (Noel G. Coonce)

flakes needed to shoot across the face of the axe at the same time that the edge was being maintained. This takes great skill, precision, and strength.

Experimental archaeologist Mark Newcomer (1971) has replicated handaxes, determining that at least some were made in three separate steps. First, a blank, or **preform,** was roughed out with a stone hammer into the general shape of the desired end product. Then the preform was refined via a second stage of percussion with a softer stone or even a piece of antler used in thinning the tool. Finally, the edges were straightened and sharpened in one last application of percussion. All the work was worth it: For the same mass of stone, a handaxe produces about four times more cutting edge than an Oldowan chopper and, at the same time, yields far more usable, sharp flakes. During the production of a single handaxe, Newcomer produced more than 50 flakes usable for cutting or scraping. The handaxe appears to have been an all-purpose tool (a colleague of mine calls them the "Swiss Army rocks" of the Pleistocene). Its sharp tip was used for piercing, the thin edges for cutting, and the steeper-angled edges toward the butt of the tool for scraping or chopping.

Subsistence

Remember one major issue concerning the subsistence base of *Homo habilis:* Did the members of this species hunt big game or merely scavenge remnants of kills left by carnivores? As a whole, the evidence supports the view that *Homo habilis* had a broad and opportunistic subsistence strategy: Big-game hunting was probably not preeminent, but hunting, scavenging, and gathering wild plants together provided subsistence for *Homo habilis.*

Evidence for the importance of hunting in *Homo erectus* is more substantial. For example, the remains of four butchered rhinoceroses were found at the Boxgrove Quarry site in England. The 150 handaxes found at the site would have served well in butchering the thick-skinned rhinos (Pitts and Roberts 2000). The researchers at Boxgrove have demonstrated that butchering marks were made on the animals' vertebrae, just where you would expect for the most efficient dismembering of the animal. Beyond this, the excavators recovered a horse scapula at Boxgrove exhibiting a wound that appears to have been made with a spear (Pitts and Roberts 2000:260).

Three remarkably well-preserved wooden spears were recovered from a coal mine in Schöningen, Germany (Thieme 1997). Found in a well-understood stratigraphic sequence, the spears are approximately 400,000 years old and range in size from 1.82 to 2.30 m (about 6 to 7.5 ft) in length (Figure 4.15). These artifacts are thought to be spears, in part, on the basis of gross morphology (they have sharpened tips and certainly resemble more recent spears). Beyond this, all three spears were made the same way; each was produced from a spruce sapling with the harder, denser, and heavier wood from the base of the tree used for the spear tip, which was sharpened. The butt ends of the spears taper gently, and the balance point of each spear is located about one-third the spear length from the tip, just as it is in a modern javelin. Their form seems a clear indication that the spears were meant to be thrown, and their size implies that large game animals were the target.

There is clear evidence that *Homo erectus* butchered animals at Aridos 1 and 2, 18 km (11 mi) southeast of Madrid, Spain (Villa 1990). Both sites produced a

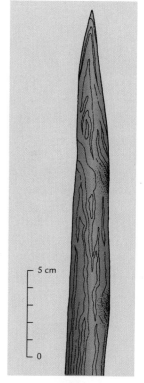

5 cm

0

▲ **Figure 4.15**
This 400,000-year-old throwing spear was one of three found at the Schöningen site in Germany. These spears are evidence of hunting on the part of their makers and represent a hint of the role organic materials—which preserve only under extraordinary circumstances—played in ancient tool technology. (Courtesy Harmut Thieme)

butchered elephant, dating to probably about 350,000 years ago. Mixed in with the bones were the tools used to cut off the meat, as well as the waste flakes produced in sharpening the cutting and scraping tools. While there is no evidence of hunting at either Aridos site—no spearpoints were found, for example—there also is no evidence that *Homo erectus* gained access to the carcasses after carnivores had their fill—there are no tooth or gnaw marks on the bones.

The facts that the flint serving as the raw material for the tools at Aridos came from deposits at a 3-km distance and that much of the toolmaking occurred away from the butchery site, with mostly sharpening conducted on-site, offer evidence for what researcher Paola Villa calls "planning depth." In other words, the hominids who butchered the elephant carcasses at Aridos knew that elephants roamed the area and that there was always a chance one or more of them might die at any given time—the Aridos 1 elephant was a juvenile and Aridos 2 was an old male, both part of subpopulations with high natural mortality rates. The *Homo erectus* population in the area seems to have planned for the lucky occasions when a carcass became available by collecting the raw material and making the tools in advance. Planning ahead for a future eventuality is a human behavior, and the evidence at Aridos suggests that *Homo erectus* was capable of such behavior.

That the *Homo erectus* diet consisted of much more than meat is shown at the 800,000-year-old Gesher Benot Ya'aqov site (GBY) in Israel (Goren-Inbar et al. 2002). Among the artifacts researchers recovered at the site were chunks of stone, including cores, blocks, slabs, and flakes of hard, volcanic rock. Fifty-four of these chunks exhibited a peculiar pitting. Experimental replication indicates that the pits on these stones (and on those found at other ancient sites) are produced by using them as hammers to break open nuts.

Remember our discussion in Chapter 3 of chimpanzee nut-cracking behavior in the Taï Forest of the African nation of Côte d'Ivoire. It seems that *Homo erectus* was exploiting a similar set of resources at GBY. Because of waterlogged conditions at the site, organic preservation was quite high. The site's researchers were able to recover the remains of seven separate species of plants that produce hard-shelled edible seeds or nuts that would have required hard hammering to break open to gain access to their nutritious kernels.

Is *Homo erectus* an Evolved *Homo habilis*?

ISSUES AND DEBATES

It has long been the consensus—and it would make the story considerably simpler if it were the case—that *Homo habilis* in Africa evolved into *Homo erectus*, also in Africa, in a nice, neat evolutionary line. There is, however, a problem with this scenario; some *Homo habilis* fossils appear to be considerably younger than the oldest fossils of what should be their descendants. The oldest *Homo erectus* fossils now date to about 1.8 million years ago, while a recently excavated partial *Homo habilis* jaw has been dated to 1.44 million years ago (Spoor et al. 2007). Beyond this, another recently discovered specimen of what otherwise presents the morphology of *Homo erectus* has a cranial capacity (691 cc) that more closely matches *Homo habilis* (Spoor et al. 2007).

These fossils complicate our otherwise neat evolutionary scenario. Some suggest that, instead of representing a single line, *Homo habilis* and *Homo erectus* were evolutionary cousins, descended from a third, older, and not yet discovered common ancestor. It is also possible that, while one population of *habilis* evolved into a larger-brained *Homo erectus*, other *habilis* populations continued as they always had, chronologically overlapping with their larger-brained relatives. It is not yet clear and, as is always the case in paleoanthropology, scientists need more fossils to solve this issue.

Did the Pleistocene Cause the Evolution of *Homo erectus?*

We saw in the case of the earliest split between pongid and hominid at the end of the Miocene, after 8 million and probably between 7 and 5 million years ago, that a significant change in climate predated and may have inspired the evolution of our ancestors. It is tempting to suggest that the changes produced by the Pleistocene are at the root of the apparently rapid divergence of *Homo erectus* from *Homo habilis* sometime soon after 2 million years ago. However, the timing of the climate changes during the Pleistocene seems to rule out this possibility.

Even if the Pleistocene is not at the root of the development of *erectus* as a new species of hominid, it remains an important consideration in our reconstruction of *Homo erectus's* intelligence and cultural capability. *Homo erectus* whose origin we can trace to the tropics was able to thrive and expand geographically despite the unsettled climatic and geographic conditions produced by the Pleistocene. Its adaptability and flexibility are hallmarks of the human cultural adaptation and show how similar to us members of this different species must have been.

What Enabled the Geographic Expansion of *Homo erectus?*

The spread of members of *Homo erectus* out of Africa into new habitats with different climates, resources, and challenges was not made possible by or accompanied by any change in their physical adaptation.

Intelligence

It seems clear that what enabled *Homo erectus* to survive where human ancestors had not previously been able to penetrate was intelligence and the ability to invent new adaptations as needed. Whereas *Homo habilis* certainly was a cultural creature, as shown by its invention, manufacture, and use of stone tools, *Homo erectus* seems to have been the first human ancestor to genuinely rely for survival on the invented, learned, and passed-down adaptations of culture. In the use of sophisticated tools and ultimately in the taming of fire (see the next section), *Homo erectus* exhibits how similar the species was to us.

Consider the diversity of environments with which this one hominid species was associated across its enormous geographic range. Certainly, *Homo erectus* began its evolutionary journey in the warm and humid tropics of Africa at least 1.8 million years ago and likely possessed physical adaptations for that environment. The rapid expansion of this species across much of southern Asia may indicate a natural affinity for a tropical or subtropical climate. But physical adaptations and natural affinities cannot explain *Homo erectus* thriving in northern China more than 1.6 million years ago where the climate was cold and dry (Zhu et al.

2001). In western Europe, artifacts attributable to *Homo erectus* have been found as far north as England. For example, the stratigraphic layer in which artifacts have been recovered at the Happisburgh site in Norfolk, United Kingdom, dates to 0.78 million years ago (Parfitt et al. 2010). Paleoenvironmental data (primarily pollen) from that same layer indicates that the hominids were living in a northern boreal forest dominated by pine and spruce trees. Imagine the forests and climate of northern New England and the northern Great Plains of the United States and Canada as an analog. That's a far cry from the tropical forests and grasslands that characterized the African homeland of *Homo erectus*. The vast extent of the longitudinal (east-west) range of *Homo erectus* evidences its ability to spread quickly from Africa to easternmost Asia. The vast extent of its latitudinal range (north-south) and the wide diversity of climates in which *Homo erectus* survived are indications of a flexibility and adaptability made possible by culture. Possession of the intelligence to invent new adaptations virtually instantaneously when the need presents itself is usually considered a uniquely human trait. This kind of intelligence and a reliance on the cultural adaptation define what it means to be a human being and are the most important things we modern humans share with our evolutionary kin, *Homo erectus*.

Control of Fire

There is something very compelling, even to twenty-first-century humans, about a simple open flame: the smell of wood smoke, the crackling and popping of dry tinder, the warmth of the fire. I grew up in a house without a fireplace, but a local television station would, on certain holidays, actually broadcast a film loop of a roaring flame. Imagine getting all cozy in front of a two-dimensional image of a fireplace on your TV. In black and white. Okay, it lacked much of the charm of a real fireplace, but we made do and it shows how drawn we are even to just the idea of a flaming hearth. For countless generations of our human ancestors, fire was more than just a diversion; it meant warmth and light, power and strength—in fact, survival itself. When did the first human ancestors make the great leap from fearing this elemental natural force to understanding and controlling it? We can now trace back the controlled use of fire by our hominid progenitors to about 1 million years ago. Researchers working in Wonderwerk Cave in Northern Cape Province in South Africa have found remains of burned bone and the ashes of burned plant material in a stratigraphic layer that also included Acheulean tools including handaxes (Berna et al. 2012). An earlier level of the same cave, dating to 1.4 million years ago, exhibited no evidence of the use of fire.

Though indisputable evidence of the use of fire by the *Homo erectus* inhabitants of Zhoukoudian in northern China is lacking, the new date derived for the cave's occupation—770,000 years—puts it right in the middle of an extremely cold glacial stadial (Guanjun et al. 2009). Without the ability to warm themselves by a controlled fire, it seems unlikely that *Homo erectus* could have survived the cold temperatures of a glacial period in northeast Asia. It seems reasonable to suggest that these hominids, in fact, had the use of fire more than three-quarters of a million years ago.

The controlled use of fire may have been the key cultural adaptation that enabled members of this tropically derived and adapted species to survive outside the tropics (Balter 2004b). Fire gives warmth and protection from animals. Fire also produces light and therefore probably played an important role in extending the usable part of the day for members of a species who, like us and most other primates, relied primarily on vision for their sensory input but who, also like us, did not see well in the dark.

Fire also enables cooking. As primatologist Richard Wrangham (2009) suggests, cooking, in a sense, helps predigest our food, decreasing the energy we might expend in actual digestion, freeing up those calories for other biological processes. Among the biological processes that would benefit from this includes those related to the brain. Our brains are consumers of energy far out of proportion to their mass: at about 1,350 grams (3 pounds), the brain constitutes less than 2% of our mass but consumes, even at rest, 25% of our energy. Cooking, therefore, is advantageous for a large-brained hominid, making more calories available for those big brains.

The "Art"of Making Tools

An important point should be made about the handaxes we discussed previously: They were better made than they had to be. That is to say, the Acheulean handaxes—at least many of the later ones—have a symmetry, balance, precision, and beauty that took a lot of work, but work that was not absolutely necessary from a utilitarian perspective (see Figure 4.13). A high level of consistency in handaxe form can be found within sites, as if the makers were adhering to a particular standard (Gowlett 1984).

That such extra care was taken in their production implies that their makers were interested in more than simple utility. *Homo erectus* toolmakers may have been producing beautiful objects for the sake of displaying their great skill or for the sheer pleasure of producing a thing of symmetry and beauty. Though the first true art is usually associated with anatomically modern humans of a much later period—the cave paintings of the European Upper Paleolithic (see Chapter 6) are clearly recognizable as art—for producing stone tools more artfully than they needed to, some of our much earlier ancestors may well deserve the credit, if not for being the first true artists, then at least for being the world's first craftspeople (Gowlett 1984). They produced useful tools in a manner so artful we recognize the "art" in their craft as much as 1.76 million years after they made them.

Who Were the Hobbit Hominids?

In an interesting bit of synchronicity, I saw the MSNBC report of the discovery of what researchers (P. Brown et al. 2004; Morwood et al. 2004) were calling *Homo floresiensis* soon after watching the DVD of the third movie in the *Lord of the Rings* trilogy. I suppose that is why it struck me as mildly hilarious that some were referring to the diminutive female hominid recovered on the Indonesian island of Flores as a "hobbit." With a tiny head, an adult height of not even 1 m (less than 3 ft), and a probable weight of about 20 kg (44 lb)—essentially the size of a 4-year-old modern human child—indeed it was hobbit-sized. Brain size has been computed to have been about 417 cc, about the mean size of a chimp and equivalent to the brain size of a newborn modern human baby (Figure 4.16). Small though their brains may have been, these hobbit-sized hominids appear

▲ **Figure 4.16**
The tiny skull of a
diminutive hominid,
found on the island of
Flores in the western
Pacific, caught the
attention of the public
when it was discovered
in 2004, not only for
the reason that it
immediately was likened
to a Hobbit. Called by
its discoverers *Homo
floresiensis*, the very
small-brained hominid
produced sophisticated
stone tools and lived
only just 18,000 years
ago, long after similar
creatures had become
extinct. (© STEPHEN
HIRD/Reuters/Corbis)

to have been quite intelligent; a variety of well-made stone flake tools were found alongside the fossil.

It isn't all that often that a paleoanthropological discovery is covered by the networks, every major cable news channel, and newspapers as well. The hobbit hook helped; and the Flores fossil—consisting of a cranium, mandible, the right half of the pelvis, the right femur and **tibia**, additional fragmented bones of the left leg, both hands and feet, and the vertebral column—was one of those rare instances that generated a tremendous amount of interest among scientists and nonscientists alike for a number of reasons beyond any *Lord of the Rings* allusions (Figure 4.17).

Though the discoverers applied a new species name to the fossil, in many ways it resembles a highly miniaturized *Homo erectus*. But how and why would an adult *Homo erectus* be so tiny? Some suggested that *Homo floresiensis* was, in fact, merely an exceptional *Homo erectus* individual, one afflicted by some rare genetic growth disorder, a sort of "*Little Hominid, Big World*" scenario. Others proposed that what the discoverers were calling *Homo floresiensis* was an anatomically modern human being, but one reflecting a pathology called **microcephaly,** a condition marked by a small head enclosing a small brain, usually resulting in severe mental retardation.

Others suggested that the small size might be an example of the well-known biological phenomenon of island dwarfing. As biologist Jared Diamond (2004) points out, there are many examples of nature selecting for smaller versions of animals who have colonized remote islands. So, conceivably, *Homo erectus* ancestors arrived on Flores by way of a very difficult and unlikely journey and managed to survive on the island for a long period. In this scenario, small individuals among those early arrivals were at an adaptive advantage, perhaps because they could survive on less food and water than their larger companions. Over time, natural selection for smaller individuals resulted in an entire population of very small hominids. Support for this hypothesis has been revealed in new excavations at the site. Along with the right arm bones from the original "Hobbit," researchers recovered another mandible, a vertebra, and a shoulder blade, as well as a mix of arm, leg, finger, and toe bones from as many as nine additional individuals, all about the same size as the first discovery (Morwood et al. 2004).

To assess the place of the Hobbit, researchers have analyzed the interior of the recovered cranium using **three-dimensional computed tomography,** a process by which they were able to produce what amounts to a "virtual brain," or, at least, a virtual image of the surface of the Hobbit's brain (Falk et al. 2005; Falk 2012). They compared their results to those obtained by applying the same technology to a sample of other crania, including those belonging to various hominid and pongid species, including *Australopithecus, Homo erectus, Homo sapiens* (including a modern human pygmy and a modern microcephalic), gorilla, and chimpanzee.

The results of this research indicate that the Flores cranium is not a perfect match for any of the specimens to which it was compared. However, it was absolutely clear that the Hobbit was neither an ape nor a modern human with microcephaly. Equally clearly, the Hobbit was not a modern human pygmy. In fact, though the ratio of its brain size to its body size is similar to what is seen for *Australopithecus*, the virtual brain of *Homo floresiensis* actually was a pretty good match for that of *Homo erectus*, leading some researchers to conclude that, though not of the same species, *Homo floresiensis* shares a common ancestor with *Homo erectus*. The tiny size of the brain and the association with complex stone tools astonishes everybody and is leading to a reassessment of the significance of overall brain size in the evolution of intelligence in the hominid family.

Though the opinion of the paleoanthropological community is far from unanimous, each form of analysis seems to support the hypothesis that Flores hominid fossils are a diminutive version of *Homo erectus*. The mandibles and shoulders are dissimilar to modern humans (Culotta 2008), and a recent examination by a team led by researcher Matthew Tocheri (Tocheri et al. 2007) has shown that the bones of the Hobbit wrist show a configuration more like ancient hominids. In keeping with the Hobbit reference, the fossil varieties seem to have had proportionally huge feet, though I can't vouch for their hairiness (Culotta 2008; Jungers et al. 2009). The fossil Hobbit's feet were differently configured from those of a modern human being and their length, proportional to their legs, is more like that seen in apes (Jungers et al. 2009).

Just as astonishing as the creature's small size and chimp-sized brain was the date researchers determined for the stratigraphic layer in which she was found. Luminescence dating bracketed the sediments above and below the skeleton to a period between 35,000 and 14,000 years ago, and charcoal from the layer of the bones produced a date of 18,000 years ago, suggesting that the Flores fossil is even younger than the remarkably young specimens from Ngandong and Sambungmachan on Java. All three sites have produced amazingly recent dates for an extinct version of a human ancestor, but there are precedents for the continued existence on an isolated island of a remnant population of a species extinct everywhere else. This supports the possibility already mentioned that even after the evolution of anatomically modern human beings, other, older versions of human beings, in this case, *Homo erectus* or, at least, something very similar to *Homo erectus*, continued to survive in some isolated places until fairly recently.

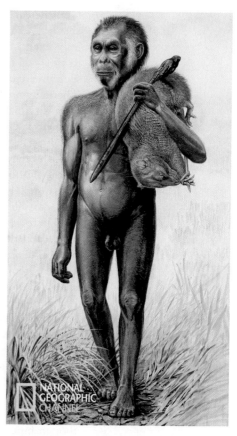

▲ **Figure 4.17**
An artist's conception of what a living example of *Homo floresiensis* might have looked like; or, if you prefer, what a real Hobbit looks like. (© AP/ Wide World Photo)

Raising *Homo erectus*

My understanding of the care necessary for raising human babies as compared to the young of other species has been forged on the anvil of experience: I've got two kids and have raised six cats, and there simply is no comparison. We adopted the various cats when they were between 7 and 15 weeks old and ready to leave their mothers. They all could walk, could feed themselves, were litter-box trained, and were fierce hunters of blowing leaves and dust bunnies. My kids, like all baby humans, are another story. Immediately following birth and for an extended period thereafter, my kids were capable of crying, filling their diapers, sleeping, and little else.

Whereas after just several weeks of life, animals such as cats attain a reasonable level of competence at moving around, eating, and defending themselves, at least against their litter mates, human children are utterly dependent on adults to satisfy all their needs for a very long time—usually years, even decades. Some specialists characterize even full-term human babies (9 months of gestation) as inherently premature and little more than embryos living outside the womb. The term **altricial** is used to characterize baby birds who are completely dependent on their parents for fulfilling their needs. Intellectually, human babies are anything but altricial; almost from birth they begin to gather and process sensory information, and they are quickly insatiably curious and experimental about their world. Physically, however, they are born at an earlier stage of development and remain immature for longer than the offspring of other species; human babies are said to be **secondarily altricial.**

There are a number of reasons why evolution would have selected for a seemingly dangerous situation in which human children are born at an early stage of physical development. A reconfiguration of the human pelvis was necessary to allow our first hominid ancestors to stand up. This change in pelvic form provided for a change in muscle positioning and shape necessary for bipedal locomotion. It also had an incidental effect: It greatly narrowed the pelvic outlet in females, making it far more difficult for a baby's body to pass through the birth canal. This difficulty can be shown by a simple statistic: Average birth labor time for a chimpanzee is about 2 hours; for a human mother it is more than 14 hours (Rosenberg 1992:99; see this study for an informative discussion of the evolution of human childbirth).

A detailed comparison by anthropologists Robert Tague and Owen Lovejoy (1986) of the reconstructed pelvis of the fossil Lucy (*Australopithecus afarensis*) with the pelvises of a chimpanzee and a modern human female indicates that, though bipedality probably complicated birth for *Australopithecus* females, it still was not as problematic as it is for modern human women (Figure 4.18). The brains of the various *Australopithecus* species were still quite small, so while there may have been a tighter fit at birth, this probably presented little problem because their heads were still no bigger than those of chimp babies. However, as natural selection began to favor greater intelligence in the hominids—made possible by an increase in brain and therefore head size—a problem did develop: A smaller pelvic outlet was forced to accommodate an increasingly large head at birth.

Nature's solution, still hardly perfect, as witnessed by the often difficult time women have in childbirth, was twofold. The first strategy was to maximize pelvic outlet size in females by fine-tuning the configuration of the pelvis. Male and female human pelvises became readily distinguishable because the pelvis exhibits sexual dimorphism. The second strategy of natural selection was timing the birth of human babies at an earlier stage in fetal development, when the head, though large, was still small enough to pass through the birth canal. Today this timing is reflected in the fact that the human newborn has a smaller head, proportional to its ultimate adult size, than do any of the living apes. A human newborn's brain is less than 25% of its ultimate adult size (Jordaan 1976:274). Compare this to the great apes, in whom a newborn's brain is more than 40% of its adult size or to a typical monkey, the macaque, whose brain at birth is 70% of its adult volume. Beyond this, a human child takes twice as long to reach adulthood than does a chimpanzee (Gibbons 2008b). Human beings are born at an immature stage of development and then mature much more slowly than our primate cousins.

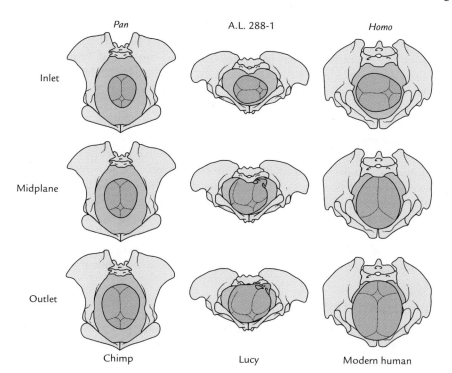

Inlet

Midplane

Outlet

Pan   A.L. 288-1   Homo

Chimp   Lucy   Modern human

◀ **Figure 4.18**
The birth canals of apes
and modern human
beings, and the fossil
pelvises of extinct
hominids allow for a
comparison in the birth
process of these three
kinds of creatures.
(Courtesy of Robert Tague)

Most human brain growth occurs outside the womb, after birth. This is fundamentally different from the situation for all the apes. For example, whereas the rate of brain growth declines dramatically in chimpanzees immediately after birth, human babies maintain what is essentially a relatively fast fetal rate of brain growth for an entire year after they are born (R. D. Martin 1989; Rosenberg 1992:106). The proportionally small size of the human baby's head at birth is what enables the baby to be born at all, given the constraints of pelvic outlet size necessitated by upright walking. But this situation presents problems, for the less developed a newborn of any species is, the more susceptible it is to trauma, infection, cold, and death.

Birth at an early stage of development for an organism with a large and complex brain has some advantages. Stimulation and learning begin earlier, while the brain is still experiencing rapid growth, and bonding between parents and children is, of necessity, stronger. This timing can be advantageous in a species that depends for its survival so thoroughly on learned behavior and social relations. It is beneficial for humans to be born at an immature stage of development and to have an extended childhood; the learning curve is simply a lot steeper and longer for us than it is for cows, cats, or even other primates.

An additional hypothesis holds that one of the key changes that characterized ancient hominids from *Homo habilis* onward is **neoteny**, or the "holding on" to features that are typical of newborn apes (Gould 1977). And modern human adults resemble baby chimps more than they resemble adult chimpanzees. Our lack of body hair, rounded skulls, flat faces, and even the point of articulation between the base of our skull and backbone are all things we share with fetal or newborn, but not adult, chimpanzees.

The pelvis of a female *Homo erectus* has been recovered from a fossil site in Gona, Ethiopia (Simpson et al. 2008). Dating to between 0.9 and 1.4 million years ago, the pelvis has a relatively large birth canal when compared to that of a modern human female. Researchers calculated that a baby with a cranial size of about 315 cc could have passed through the Gona birth canal. That's about 33% of the size of an adult *Homo erectus* cranium as calculated in Table 4.1. Compare that to the virtual reconstruction of a Neandertal newborn recovered in Mezmaiskaya Cave in Crimea, Russia. This newborn's brain size was calculated by researchers at somewhere between 381 and 416 cm (Gibbons 2008b), which is about the maximum size of a modern human newborn's brain size as well.

As stated previously, in the Great Apes, a newborn baby's brain is more developed, about 40% of its adult size. In modern humans, a newborn baby's brain is only about 25% of its adult size. In other words, *Homo erectus* babies were born at an earlier stage of development than a chimp but were not quite as immature, at least in terms of the growth of their brains, as Neandertals or human beings. So, at least based on this one *Homo erectus* pelvis (of course, we'd like to see more such pelvises in order to support this conclusion), it looks like *Homo erectus* was on the path to the modern pattern of giving birth to very immature newborns.

Where Are the Handaxes?

As we've seen in this chapter, there's a neat correspondence between the appearance of the first *Homo erectus* fossils in Africa at about 1.8 million years ago and the presence also in Africa of that species' earliest "signature" tool: the bifacial, teardrop-shaped, symmetrical handaxe. We have also seen how, very soon after their initial appearance in Africa, members of the species can be found in west Asia, east Asia, and finally Europe.

One might have expected that the *Homo erectus* individuals who spread north out of Africa and then so quickly east across the Old World would have brought their advanced tool kit, including handaxes, with them. Interestingly, this turns out not to be the case. For example, handaxes are not present in the 1.77-million-year-old assemblage at Dmanisi in Georgia. Instead, the Dmanisi hominids exhibit a stone-tool technology reminiscent of Oldowan. The similarly ancient hominids on Java didn't make handaxes. In China, handaxes are found in association with *Homo erectus* remains, but rarely and not until after 1 million years ago (in the Bose Basin in southern China; Yamei et al. 2000).

Homo erectus not bringing along handaxes as they expanded across Asia is the equivalent of modern Americans migrating without their cell phones or iPods. How can we explain this?

1. It is possible that *Homo erectus* first expanded out of Africa before they developed handaxe technology. Handaxes moved east with subsequent population movements (getting to India by 1.5 million years ago and China after 1 million years ago).
2. Maybe *Homo erectus* first expanded out of Africa before they developed handaxe technology and the handaxelike tools found later in east Asia were the product of an independent, parallel development.
3. Perhaps handaxes will be found in the future at the oldest sites in west and east Asia.
4. In the most extreme proposal, *Homo erectus* was actually an Asian species that developed handaxe technology only after arriving in Africa.

Right now, the data cannot definitively support any of these hypotheses, though I'd probably put money on the first explanation. As is often the case in paleoanthropology, only with additional data will we be able to determine which, if any, of these explanations is the correct one.

When Did *Homo erectus* Become Extinct?

It should be clear by this point that human evolution was not a simple, progressive process with each species thriving during its time and then giving way to the next in line, repeating this process as a series of steps leading directly to modern human beings. The human story is, instead, far more complex, characterized until fairly recently by geographically separated, multiple contemporary hominids (Figure 4.19).

We will begin the next chapter talking about a new, more modern-looking hominid species that can be dated to about 400,000 years ago. The appearance of this new species does not mean that all older species conveniently disappeared from the scene at that time. In fact, in the scenario presented in this book, only one of the *Homo erectus* populations—that in Africa—is directly ancestral to us. That African *Homo erectus* line evolved into another hominid that looked and behaved more like modern humans, while other branches of *Homo erectus*, particularly those in Europe and Asia, almost certainly continued on more or less

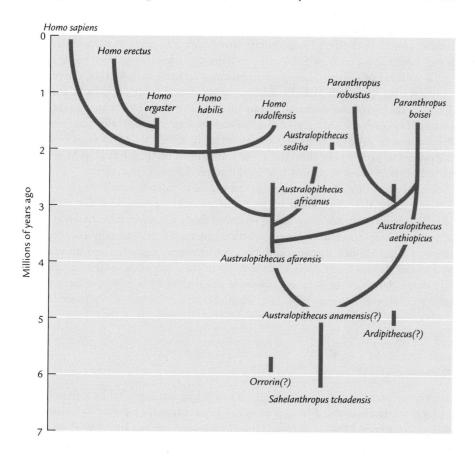

◀ **Figure 4.19**
One phylogeny proposed for the fossil hominids. (Based partially on Bernard Wood 1992a, 1992b)

the same as they always had perhaps into the very recent past as implied by the Ngandong, Sambungmachan, and Flores fossils.

CASE STUDY CLOSE-UP

IN 1918 A FOSSIL LOCALITY SOUTHWEST OF Beijing, China, was explored by Swedish geologist Johan Gunnar Andersson. Andersson took advantage of a local Chinese belief that fossil bones were actually the remnants of dragons and that powder made from ground-up "dragon bones" was a cure-all. Many local druggists collected such bones for use in their medicines. Even today, paleontologists rely on local druggists for leads in their search for fossil ("dragon") bones (Jian and Rice 1990).

In 1918 Andersson was directed by a druggist to a hill called Jigushan (Chicken Bone Hill) near the village of Zhoukoudian (Jia and Huang 1990). Convinced there was a rich array of fossil bones in the surrounding region, he began excavating on another hill, called Longgoshan—Dragon Bone Hill. In 1926 two humanlike teeth were recovered; in 1929, with the dig now led by British scientist Davidson Black, a nearly intact skull was encountered in a cave at the top of the hill (Locality 1). The fossil was recognizably different from almost everything that had been found previously, with the possible exception of Java Man. A new species was named and defined: *Sinanthropus pekinensis*. The specimens from Zhoukoudian are now included in the species *Homo erectus*, but in the popular mind both then and now, they may forever be known as "Peking Man" (see Figure 4.8, bottom).

The cave at Dragon Bone Hill was spectacularly productive by any standards. By the time excavations were finished at Zhoukoudian, the expedition had recovered, along with thousands of specimens of ancient animals, 15 fragmentary skulls, 6 more complete crania, 13 fragmentary mandibles, 3 upper jaws, some postcranial bones (including pieces of femur, upper arms, toe bones, numerous teeth), and a single vertebra of Peking Man (Jia and Huang 1990:161–62). All told, the remains of more than 40 hominid individuals were recovered from deposits in the cave. Though dating of the hominid occupation of the cave has been fraught with uncertainty, a recent redating of the site shows that the cave was first occupied approximately 770,000 years ago (Guanjun et al. 2009). Being so numerous and discovered so early in our thinking about human evolution, the Peking Man fossils played an important historical role in the scientific conceptualization of human evolution and in interpretations of the culture of ancient human beings.

Tragically, the Zhoukoudian hominid assemblage was lost during World War II when the fossils were being removed from China by U.S. Marines in an attempt to keep them away from Japanese invaders, coincidentally on the same day that Pearl Harbor was attacked. The Marines were captured and imprisoned, and to this day no one knows what became of their precious fossil cargo. (It may have been destroyed by Japanese troops or simply lost, or it may have been found later by Chinese druggists who ground the bones up for medicine. There is even a very slight possibility that some are still hidden away in China, Japan, or the United States.)

Summary

Sometime after 1.8 million years ago, *Homo habilis* was replaced by a new hominid species, *Homo erectus*. *Erectus* possessed a larger brain than *habilis*; its mean brain size of just under 1,000 cc is two-thirds the modern human mean. With its larger brain and attendant greater intelligence, *Homo erectus* was able to adapt to the changing environmental conditions posed by the Pleistocene epoch.

Homo erectus was the first ancestral human being to expand beyond the borders of our hominid family's African birthplace and nursery. Following the most reasonable trail beyond the borders of Africa, *Homo erectus* fossils and their tools are found in southwest Asia and Eurasia more than 1.7 million years ago, very soon after they first appeared in Africa. For reasons that are still debated, these African migrants did not enter into western Europe until later, perhaps about 1.2 million years ago.

It was intelligence and not any physical adaptation that enabled *Homo erectus* to adapt to the diversity of habitats offered throughout Asia. New and more sophisticated tools, new methods of hunting, and the use of fire were all part of the *Homo erectus* behavioral repertoire.

Homo erectus was a stable and long-lived species. Fossils from Africa to east Asia show a consistent morphology from close to 1.8 million to 400,000 years ago. After 400,000 years ago, brain size, relatively stable during the existence of *erectus*, exhibits a rapid increase, signifying the evolution of the first *Homo sapiens* from an *erectus* base.

Richard Leakey and Roger Lewin's (1992) *Origins Reconsidered: In Search of What Makes Us Human* discusses the discovery, excavation, and interpretation of the Nariokotome skeleton. Much information about *Homo erectus* is offered in *Ancestors: In Search of Human Origins* by Don and Lenora Johanson and Blake Edgar (1994). A very helpful, popular summary of evolution with quite a bit of information on the Lower Paleolithic is provided in Alan Walker and Pat Shipman's *The Wisdom of the Bones* (1996). Paleoanthropologist Harry Shapiro's *Peking Man* (1974) provides a riveting account of the discovery and loss of Peking Man.

For a summary of the discovery and interpretation of *Homo floresiensis*, take a look at a book co-authored by one of its discoverers, Mike Morwood (Morwood and van Oosterzee 2006), *The Discovery of the Hobbit: The Scientific Breakthrough that Changed the Face of Human History*.

TO LEARN MORE

Web links for this chapter can be found at www.oup.com/us/feder

KEY TERMS

altricial, 122	Holocene epoch, 109	preform, 115
Acheulean handaxe, 112	interglacial, 111	prognathous, 104
Acheulean tradition, 114	interstadial, 111	secondarily altricial, 122
calvarium, 106	microcephaly, 120	stadial, 111
cortex, 114	neoteny, 123	supraorbital torus, 104
glacial, 109	occipital, 101	three-dimensional computed
glacier, 109	paleomagnetism, 105	tomography, 120
handaxe, 109	Pleistocene epoch, 109	tibia, 120

5

The First Humans

The Evolution of *Homo sapiens*

CHAPTER OVERVIEW

Beginning about 500,000 years ago, a great change is seen in the fossil hominid record. Brain size expanded, and the fossils look so much more modern they are categorized as *Homo sapiens*, though of a type classified as "archaic" or "premodern."

The best known of the archaic *Homo sapiens* are the Neandertals. Represented by the skeletons of hundreds of individuals and the **mitochondrial DNA** of a handful of them, the Neandertals seem to have developed alongside the ancestors of modern-looking human beings. They appear to have been physically highly specialized to life in the arctic cold of Pleistocene (Ice Age) Europe and West Asia. Neandertal bones reflect an enormous level of physical strength, in many cases beyond that seen in modern human beings. Ultimately, they may have been too specialized for cold and strength; the last of the Neandertals died out soon after 30,000 years ago.

Anatomically modern human beings appear in the fossil record sometime between 200,000

and 100,000 years ago. The question must be posed: "How did these first anatomically modern human beings arise?" Two competing models—the multiregional approach and the replacement hypothesis—have been proposed. In the multiregional model, modern human beings evolved from their archaic antecedents—the premodern humans discussed in this chapter—in various world areas more or less simultaneously. In the replacement model, modern humans

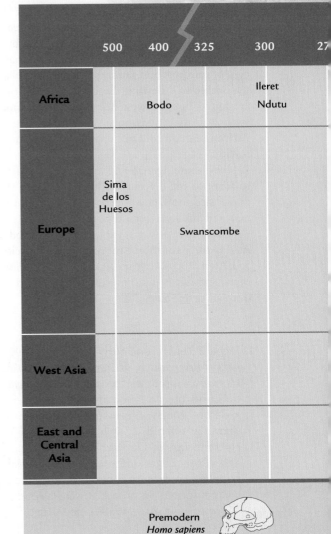

	500	400	325	300	27
Africa		Bodo		Ileret Ndutu	
Europe	Sima de los Huesos		Swanscombe		
West Asia					
East and Central Asia					

Premodern
Homo sapiens

Thousands of years ago

| 250 | 225 | 200 | 175 | 150 | 125 | 100 | 75 | 50 | 25 |

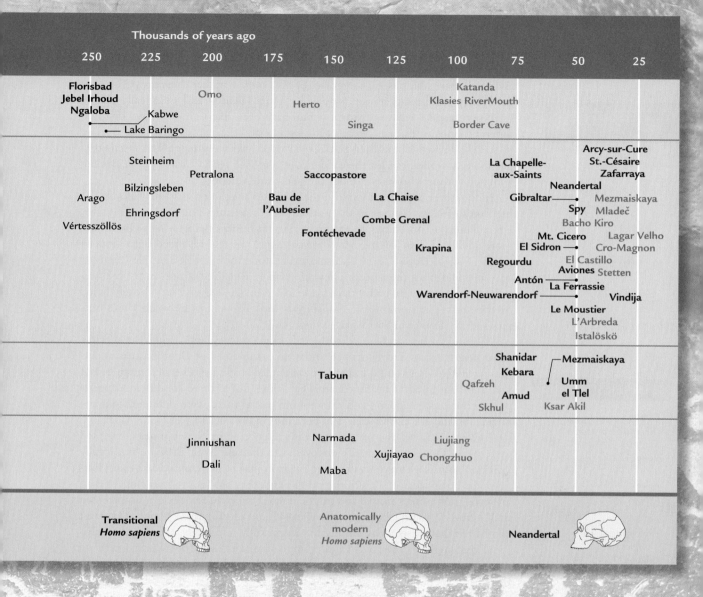

Florisbad
Jebel Irhoud
Ngaloba
Kabwe
Lake Baringo

Omo

Herto

Singa

Katanda
Klasies RiverMouth

Border Cave

Arago
Vértesszöllös

Steinheim
Bilzingsleben
Ehringsdorf

Petralona

Bau de
l'Aubesier

Saccopastore

La Chaise
Combe Grenal
Fontéchevade

Krapina

La Chapelle-
aux-Saints

Regourdu

Antón

Warendorf-Neuwarendorf

Neandertal

Gibraltar
Spy

Mt. Cicero
El Sidron

Aviones
La Ferrassie
Le Moustier

Arcy-sur-Cure
St.-Césaire
Zafarraya

Mezmaiskaya
Mladeč
Bacho Kiro
Lagar Velho
Cro-Magnon
El Castillo
Stetten
Vindija
L'Arbreda
Istalöskö

Tabun

Shanidar
Kebara
Qafzeh
Amud
Skhul

Mezmaiskaya
Umm
el Tlel
Ksar Akil

Jinniushan
Dali

Narmada
Maba

Xujiayao

Liujiang
Chongzhuo

Transitional
Homo sapiens

Anatomically
modern
Homo sapiens

Neandertal

---

evolved from a premodern variety just once, in one
place—probably southern Africa—and spread out
from there. In this scenario, anatomically modern
human beings replaced premodern humans wherever the two came in contact. A deductive test of
the evidence using skeletal, artifactual, and genetic
evidence is applied in this chapter. The result shows
something more complicated than either simple
model would predict.

SCIENCE CONSISTENTLY HAS SHOWN THAT, THOUGH *individual* human beings may differ in terms of their athletic propensities, math and writing skills, or musical and artistic talents, collectively all human *groups* share equally in these physical and intellectual abilities. All categories of humanity, whether these are defined by nationality or ethnicity, are in fact equally smart, talented, and athletically gifted.

Now imagine what the world would have been like if, instead, two or more different kinds of human beings with *unequal* abilities had evolved side by side in the ancient world and then actually survived into the present. This fascinating possibility was the basis for the 1953 novel *You Shall Know Them*, by Jean Bruller, a French author who wrote under the pen name Vercors.

In the novel, a group of explorers investigates a secluded, pristine valley in the highlands of New Guinea in the mid-twentieth century. The explorers discover a population of a presumedly extinct variety of human beings—*living* hominids, more advanced than Peking Man (*Homo erectus*) yet less advanced than modern people. Called "tropis," these creatures make stone tools, speak a simple language, have fire, and bury their dead. They are human. But they're not us. By the way, there was a stunningly bad movie made in 1970, *Skullduggery*, very loosely based on the book. The hominids in *Skullduggery* look like a cross between 1960s hippies and the Ewoks in Star Wars. Enough said.

All modern human beings belong to a single species (and a single subspecies), *Homo sapiens sapiens*, and all of us are more alike than different. But this situation was not inevitable. There could today be different, coexisting species of human beings with different physical and intellectual capacities, just as there are different species of bear, antelope, elephant, and camel—and just as there were different, contemporaneous, and coexisting species of hominids in the ancient past (see Chapter 3).

In Vercors's novel, the primitive people discovered in New Guinea are treated quite badly. They are essentially enslaved. On the one hand, they are not legally "people," so no law prevents their exploitation (just as there is no law against harnessing a horse to a plow). On the other hand, they are far more intelligent than any other nonhuman animal and can be trained to do things modern humans can do but find degrading, boring, or dangerous. Considering the amount of mistrust and hatred that exists today among the empirically minimally different individuals of our single species, it is frightening to consider what the world would be like if there were truly different, coexisting species of human beings. Remarkably, this nearly happened.

The Neandertals to be discussed in this chapter are an extinct variety of human beings that come chronologically closer to the modern era than do any other nonmodern hominid; they became extinct less than 30,000 years ago, a mere tick of the evolutionary clock. In fact, there was an overlap of tens of millennia during the waning years of the Neandertals and the ascendance of the earliest anatomically modern humans (AMHs). As we will see later in this chapter, there even is strong genetic evidence that at least some AMH populations in Europe and Asia interbred with Neandertals, producing hybrid offspring.

The Neandertals were not only similar to us in many ways but also quite different. Though often depicted as apelike or subhuman, they managed to survive for tens of thousands of years during an extremely harsh period of the Pleistocene, or Ice Age. They did so through their great intelligence, inventing sophisticated stone tools for hunting, producing clothing and shelter, and using fire. Neandertals are also noted for another behavior that contradicts their modern stereotype: They buried their dead. In recognizing the enormity of death and in ceremonially disposing of the mortal remains of their comrades, they exhibited a behavior that shows their close kinship to us.

Despite this, Neandertals were surely quite different from us both in how they looked and, most likely, in their intellectual capabilities. Considering how badly we humans treat one another—and that we are more similar to one another in how we look and how we think than we would be to living Neandertals—the Neandertals probably would have ended up like the primitive hominids in Vercors's book, doomed by us to lives of confinement, drudgery, and pain (Gould 1988).

CHRONICLE

As we saw in Chapter 4, after about 1 million B.P., the tapestry of human evolution seems to have been characterized by a single primary thread (*Homo erectus*) made up of three generally similar strands in Africa, Asia, and Europe. Then, beginning as far back as 600,000 years ago, there was a burst of change, with new hominid varieties appearing on the evolutionary stage. Though regional differences are maintained among the fossils seen in Africa, Asia, and Europe, these hominids share in common the fact that they are morphologically more modern in appearance than previous hominid species, so much more modern in cranial capacity and shape, in fact, that some researchers call these new hominids **premodern,** or **archaic,** *Homo sapiens* (Figure 5.1).

These premodern humans shared a bigger, more modern brain than previous hominids had. The mean cranial capacity of the premoderns (excluding the

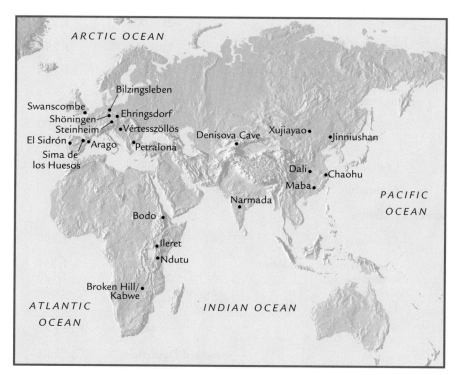

▲ **Figure 5.1**
Fossil localities of premodern *Homo sapiens*.

Neandertals, who will be treated separately) was a little over 1,200 cc—more than 20% larger than that of their evolutionary antecedents and about 80% of the modern human mean of about 1,450 cc (see Table 5.1). Most of the premodern fossil specimens still possess large brow ridges. But more like the modern form, they also exhibit steeper foreheads, generally (though not universally) thinner cranial bones, and flatter faces than *erectus*.

TABLE 5.1 Major Premodern *Homo sapiens* Fossils (Exclusive of the Neandertals) Discussed in Chapter 5

Country	Locality	Fossils	Age (years)	Brain size (cc)
Germany	Steinheim	Cranium	200,000–240,000	1,200
	Bilzingsleben	Cranial fragments	228,000	
	Ehringsdorf	Cranial fragments	225,000	
	Mauer	Mandible	<450,000	
England	Swanscombe	Occipital cranium	225,000	1,325
Greece	Petralona	Cranium	160,000–240,000	1,400
France	Arago	Cranium and fragmentary remains of 7 individuals	250,000	1,200
Spain	Atapuerca	Remains of at least 30 individuals	>300,000	1,125
			>300,000	1,390
			>300,000	1,220
Hungary	Vértesszöllös	Occipital fragments	200,000	1,250
Zambia	Kabwe (Broken Hill)	Cranium, additional cranial and postcranial remains of several individuals	>125,000	1,280
Tanzania	Ndutu (Olduvai)	Cranium	200,000–400,000	1,100
Kenya	Ileret	Cranium	300,000	1,400
Ethiopia	Bodo	Cranium	200,000–400,000	
South Africa	Elandsfontein	Cranium		
India	Narmada	Cranium	150,000?	1,300
China	Jinniushan	Nearly complete skeleton	200,000	1,350
	Dali	Cranium	200,000	1,120
	Maba	Cranium	130,000–170,000	
	Xujiayao	Fragments of 11 individuals	100,000–125,000	
			Mean	1,261.43
			Standard Deviation	87.86

Data from Arsuaga et al. (1993); Day (1986); Pope (1992); Rightmire (1991).

Premodern Humans: Fossil Evidence

Versions of premodern *Homo sapiens* are known from Africa, Asia, and Europe, where they appear to have evolved in place from previous indigenous populations of hominids. See Table 5.1 for a summary of the sites of the premodern human beings and see Figure 5.2 for a photographic sample of their crania.

▲ **Figure 5.2**
The Kabwe (formerly called Broken Hill) specimen from South African (top), the Steinheim cranium from Germany (bottom), and the cranium from Sima de los Huesos (The Pit of Bones) in the Atapuerca Mountains, Spain (middle), are among the best preserved of the premodern *Homo sapiens* crania. (© The Natural History Museum, London; © JAVIER TRUEBA/MSF/SCIENCE PHOTO LIBRARY; courtesy Milford Wolpoff)

Premodern Humans: Cultural Evidence

When we begin replicating stone tools in my experimental archaeology course, it is the tendency of many students simply to grab hold of a couple of random rocks, placing one in each hand. Next, they close their eyes (behind the required safety goggles), wind up with their dominant hand, say a prayer (well, some do), and viciously smash down on the rock they were hoping to break. This approach isn't particularly effective and involves a level of serendipity and knuckle smashing that our ancient ancestors left behind more than 2.5 million years ago. Sure, using my students' initial approach, you may produce, by sheer luck and determination, some usable, sharp-edged flakes. But this is a wasteful strategy, and much of the good stone my students worked so hard to find and transport back to the lab ends up as battered, shattered chunks of useless rock. Stone toolmaking, as my students soon learn, is not a random but a highly controlled, well-thought-out process, designed to get the most sharp-edged flakes of a consistent size and shape as is possible from a stone nodule.

The **Levallois** stone-tool industry that typifies premodern *Homo sapiens* allows the toolmaker to accurately predict the shape and size of a flake about

▶ **Figure 5.3**
In Europe and west Asia, the archaic humans developed a toolmaking technology called Levallois in which a stone core was prepared so as to allow the production of flakes of a consistent size and form. The steps of Levallois core preparation and blade production are presented here. (After J. Bordaz 1970)

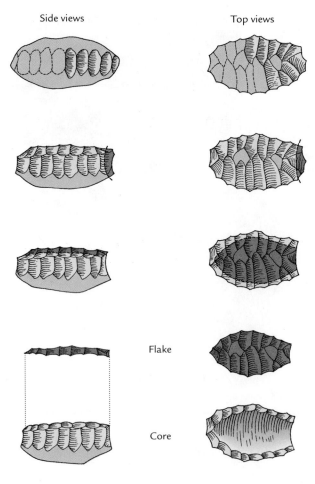

Side views   Top views

Flake

Core

to be removed from a stone core. This new industry involved a shift in emphasis from the production of core tools to the production of flake tools. Instead of sculpting a single, large, multipurpose tool (like the handaxe) from a stone nodule and using only the waste flakes that fortuitously fit a given need, emphasis now shifted to the flakes themselves, whose form and size were controlled by careful preparation of the core (Figure 5.3). The stone nodule, or core, was no longer the object to be shaped into a tool but instead became the source from which flakes of given sizes and shapes were produced. The flakes were used as blanks to be refined into tools intended for specific tasks. The Levallois technique enabled flakes of predetermined and consistent size and form to be produced (Figure 5.4).

The Levallois technique involves this kind of careful preparation of the stone core for patterned and predictable flake removal. Preparing the core allowed pre-modern humans finer control of flake removal than had previously been possible. By precisely controlling the size and form of a flake, each finished tool could be more highly specialized for a particular task. The right shape for tools with functions like cutting, piercing, or perforating could be ensured. The technique was also far more efficient in its use of stone than either Oldowan or Acheulean. A greater amount of sharp, usable edge is produced per unit weight of core. A

◀ **Figure 5.4**
Levallois flakes from sites in Israel. These triangular flakes may have been used as stone tips on wooden spear shafts. (Courtesy of John Shea)

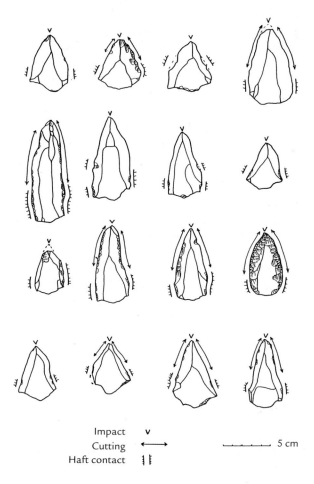

Impact   v
Cutting   ⟵⟶
Haft contact   ꠱ ꠵   ⌐____ 5 cm

replicative study by Bruce Bradley (Gamble 1986) showed that four or five consistently shaped flakes could be removed from a single Levallois core.

It now appears that as long as 500,000 years ago in southern Africa, hominids were producing stone points which they likely hafted onto shafts for use in hunting (Wilkens et al. 2012). The production of such multicomponent tools marks an enormous jump in toolmaking abilities by our ancestors.

The Neandertals

You know that an extinct variety of human being has become a cultural icon when it's used in a national television advertising campaign by a major corporation, the characters in the ad become (mercifully only for a short time) the stars of a sitcom, and one of them even turned up, in full makeup, for an in-depth interview by Barbara Walters on *The View*.

Almost certainly you have seen the commercials. The first in the series begins inside what appears to be a television studio where the crew is, in fact, filming a commercial. The mellifluously voiced spokesperson, commenting on the advantages of the product he is shilling for, states: "It's so easy to use GEICO.com, a caveman could do it." At that point, the camera swings rapidly to the crew member holding the boom mike. He is, rather stereotypically, a caveman, apparently a Neandertal,* with an extremely hairy body (he's shirtless and wearing shorts, and he is one furry dude), unkempt, and with huge brow ridges and a prognathous face. The Neandertal, clearly offended by the ad copy, throws down the mike, points an accusing finger at the actor and spits out, in perfect diction, "Not cool!" and storms out of the studio.

The ad campaign (http://www.youtube.com/watch?v=3F3qzfTCDG4&feature=related) wasn't breaking any new ground; Neandertal "cavemen" have always been caricatured as primitive and dumb. Look at the earliest artistic reconstruction of a Neandertal published in 1909 in the French magazine *L'Illustration* (Figure 5.5). The image is a laughable caricature of a scary-looking, hairy ape-man. Neandertals have been the archetype of "cavemen" ever since: ugly, apelike, violent, brutish, and stupid (Hager 1994). The television ad is funny precisely because it works against the stereotype, depicting Neandertals as just hairy and big-browed "regular guys" who, in fact, are quite sensitive about being pigeonholed in this way.

In reality the Neandertals were just another group of premodern human beings. They happen to be better known because of a number of historical accidents. For example, they were abundant in Europe (Figure 5.6), and most early paleoanthropological research was undertaken there because most of the world's

---

*You will sometimes find *Neandertal* spelled *Neanderthal*. The original German spelling included an *h*, though it was (and is) pronounced as if no *h* were present. Modern German spelling has removed the *h*, so it is not used in this text. To complicate matters further, according to the rules of biological nomenclature, under most circumstances the original name given to a species cannot be changed. Because the Neandertals were originally given the species name *neanderthalensis*, with the silent *h*, we are obliged to leave the *h* when using the taxonomic name.

◄ **Figure 5.5**
The first artist's
conception of a
Neandertal as it
appeared in the popular
press, first in the French
magazine *L'Illustration*
and soon thereafter
in the *Illustrated London
News* (March 6, 1909).
(*Illustrated London News*,
March 6, 1909. Artist:
Kupka)

paleoanthropologists have come from Europe. Also, Neandertals used caves extensively, and archaeological remains are better preserved in cave settings.

The Neandertal name comes from the Neander Valley in Germany, where, in 1856, not the first such fossil was found but the one that first caught the attention of the scientific community (see Chapter 1; Figure 5.7). Though it was big, indicating a brain size at least as large as that of a modern human being, the shape was all wrong, with protruding, apelike bony ridges above the eyes, a face that projected forward like that of an ape, and a flattened profile rather than the rounded profile of a modern human skull.

Researchers of the time had difficulty explaining the Neandertal skull. (One scholar even suggested that its peculiar appearance was the result of "stupendous blows" with a heavy instrument sustained during the individual's lifetime.) However, as more Neandertal specimens—as all such similar fossils were labeled—were discovered in Europe, it became clear that the Neandertal skull form represented a distinct and extinct variety of humanity.

In the attempt to assess the precise relationship between the Neandertals and modern humans, a major error crept into the discussion. In 1913 French scientist Marcellin Boule produced a reconstruction of the entire Neandertal skeleton that was rife with error (Boule and Vallois 1923). Assuming, on the basis of the form of the skull, that the Neandertals were apelike, Boule's reconstruction showed a bent-over, splayed-toe, apelike creature. It probably didn't help that the specimen Boule chose to focus on had had a bad case of arthritis that may have caused the individual to bend over when walking.

But who were the Neandertals, really? The evidence now is quite extensive that they were not club-toting caricatures. They were a distinctive, now-extinct variety of premodern human beings, in some ways like us and in some ways

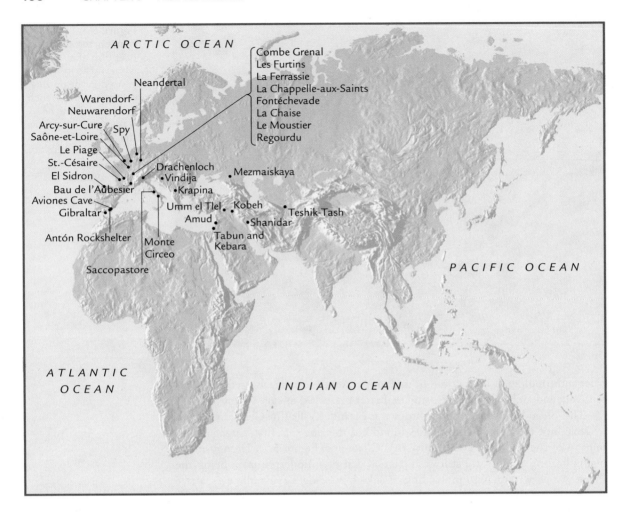

ARCTIC OCEAN

Combe Grenal
Les Furtins
La Ferrassie
La Chappelle-aux-Saints
Fontéchevade
La Chaise
Le Moustier
Regourdu

Neandertal

Warendorf-
Neuwarendorf
Arcy-sur-Cure   Spy
Saône-et-Loire
Le Piage
St.-Césaire
El Sidron
Bau de l'Aubesier
Aviones Cave
Gibraltar

Drachenloch
Vindija
Krapina

Mezmaiskaya

Umm el Tlel   Kobeh   Teshik-Tash
Amud
Shanidar
Tabun and
Kebara

Antón Rockshelter   Monte
Circeo

Saccopastore

PACIFIC OCEAN

ATLANTIC
OCEAN

INDIAN OCEAN

▲ **Figure 5.6**
Fossil localities of
Neandertals.

very different (Figure 5.8). Some paleoanthropologists apply the taxonomic label
Homo sapiens neanderthalensis to them, though others believe that they were sufficiently different from anatomically modern human beings that they are not
directly ancestral to us and warrant a separate species classification, *Homo neanderthalensis*. Their roots in Europe can now be traced back to more than 300,000
years ago, an age equivalent to that of some of the other European premoderns
listed in Table 5.1. However, true, or "classic," Neandertals possessing all the typical traits (to be discussed) were confined to Europe and west Asia and date from
about 130,000 to 30,000 years ago.

Morphological Evidence

Though we recognize the Neandertals were related to modern humanity, controversy persists over their precise place in the human family: Were they our
evolutionary grandparents or just distant cousins who followed a separate evolutionary pathway? (See Trinkaus 1983a, 1983b, 1986, 1989; Trinkaus and Shipman
1993; Wolpoff 1989b; and especially F. Smith 1991.)

◀ **Figure 5.7**
The skullcap of the specimen that gave this group of archaic humans their name, discovered in the Neander Valley in Germany in 1856. (© Landschaftsverband Rheinland)

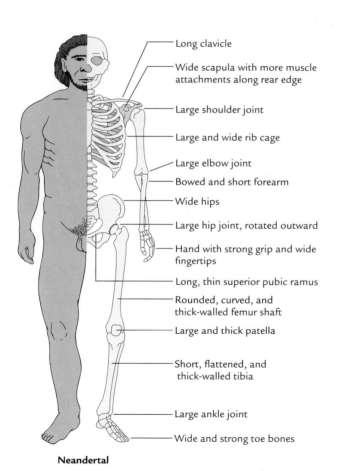

- Long clavicle
- Wide scapula with more muscle attachments along rear edge
- Large shoulder joint
- Large and wide rib cage
- Large elbow joint
- Bowed and short forearm
- Wide hips
- Large hip joint, rotated outward
- Hand with strong grip and wide fingertips
- Long, thin superior pubic ramus
- Rounded, curved, and thick-walled femur shaft
- Large and thick patella
- Short, flattened, and thick-walled tibia
- Large ankle joint
- Wide and strong toe bones

Neandertal

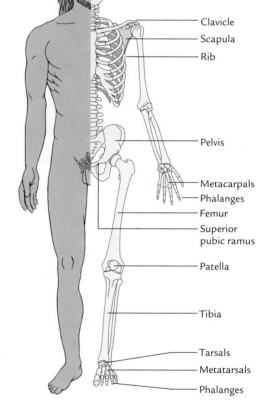

- Clavicle
- Scapula
- Rib
- Pelvis
- Metacarpals
- Phalanges
- Femur
- Superior pubic ramus
- Patella
- Tibia
- Tarsals
- Metatarsals
- Phalanges

Modern *Homo sapiens*

▲ **Figure 5.8**
In this comparison of the skeletons of a modern human being and a Neandertal, the so-called musculoskeletal hypertrophy of the Neandertals when compared to modern humans is readily apparent. (After Stringer and Gamble 1993)

Cranial Morphology

The Neandertals were not tiny-brained cavemen. In fact, Neandertal brain size often surpassed that of modern human beings. Cranial capacities range from about 1,300 cc to more than 1,600 cc, with a mean of nearly 1,480 cc (see Table 5.2); modern human mean cranial capacity is about 1,450 cc.

Though similar in size, the shape of the Neandertal cranium was different from ours. Viewed from the side, the modern human head presents a round profile while the Neandertal cranial profile is flatter. The configuration of the Neandertal brain, therefore, was different from ours, with less in the front and more to the rear. A recent investigation shows these differences developing in early childhood. Using a computed tomography (CT) scanner to trace brain expansion in human and chimp children during their years of development, researchers found a dramatic widening of the temporal lobes of the brain among humans but not chimps during the first year of life (Gunz et al. 2010). When the development of the Neandertal brain was compared to humans and chimps (by creating imprints called endocasts of Neandertal brains from four preserved crania), the

TABLE 5.2 Major Neandertal Specimens Discussed in Chapter 5

Country	Locality	Fossils	Crania	Age (years)	Brain size (cc)
Germany	Neandertal	Skullcap			1,250
France	La Chapelle	Skeleton	"Old Man"		1,620
	Fontéchevade	Cranial fragments of several individuals		100,000	1,500
	La Ferrassie	8 skeletons		>38,000	1,680
	La Chaise	Cranium		126,000	
	St.-Césaire	Skeleton		36,000	
Belgium	Spy	Cranium			
Italy	Mt. Circeo	Cranium			
	Saccopastore	Cranium			1,350
Yugoslavia	Krapina	Cranial and postcranial fragments of >45 individuals		Isotope stage 5	1,300
Israel	Tabun	Skeleton, mandible, postcranial fragments		60,000	1,270
	Amud	Skeleton		70,000	1,740
	Kebara	Postcranial skeleton		60,000	
Iraq	Shanidar	9 partial skeletons		70,000	1,600
				Mean	1,478.89
				Standard Deviation	165.68

Data from Day (1986).

researchers found no marked ballooning of the temporal lobe like that experienced during the development of modern human infants. This is significant since the temporal lobe is important in our ability to create abstract representations of our surroundings.

Further, Neandertal skulls were marked with huge brow ridges like those of older hominid species, their lower faces protruded in an apelike fashion, and there was an enormous mass of bone at the rear (occipital) portion of the skull, where large muscles were attached that enabled the Neandertals to balance their large, heavy heads. The Neandertal face was large, with the lower portion far forward of the eyes and brows. The Neandertal nasal bridge was wide and flaring, and Neandertals lacked the thin, pointy chin that typifies modern human beings. The robust features and flat profile of the Neandertal head can be seen even in young Neandertals, including a 3-year-old Neandertal child from Gibraltar (Dean, Stringer, and Bromage 1986), an infant possibly as young as 6 months old from Amud Cave in Israel (Ponce de Léon and Zollikofer 2001), and even a neonate estimated to have been no more than 4 months old when he or she died (Maureille 2002).

From the Neck Down: Designed for Cold

Contrary to Boule's reconstruction, below the head the Neandertal skeleton is essentially modern in appearance but with some crucial differences. One morphological pattern is consistent with a physical adaptation to cold: Neandertals were relatively wide with broad, squat torsos and short extremities (see Figure 5.8; Ruff et al. 1993; Trinkaus 1983a), a body form associated in modern humans with cold environments because it retains heat better than does a body with a small torso and long limbs. Anthropologist Christopher Ruff (1993) compares the Neandertal body to that of a modern Inuit (Eskimo). This adaptation probably reflects the fact that the Neandertals flourished during a glacial maxima in Ice Age Europe.

This biological adaptation to life under cold conditions may explain how the Neandertals were able to survive as far north as just shy of the Arctic Circle in Russia more than 30,000 years ago (Slimak et al. 2011).

From the Neck Down: Built for Strength

In about every area on the skeleton where researchers have looked, the Neandertals exhibit what is called **musculoskeletal hypertrophy**. For example, the Neandertals were generally short and stocky when compared to modern humans, and the bones of their lower legs reflect this build (Gibbons 1996). The breadth of their scapulae (shoulder blades) and the length of their clavicles (collar bones), along with the robustness of areas of muscle attachment on those bones, are indicative of broad, powerful shoulders (Churchill and Trinkaus 1990).

The great size and robustness of their upper arm bones (Ben-Itzhak, Smith, and Bloom 1988) and the large areas for muscle attachment on their forearms (Trinkaus 1983a) are clear indications that the Neandertals had tremendous upper-body strength. Also, in their ribs and vertebrae Neandertal bones show areas for muscle attachment far larger than what is seen in modern humans.

Researcher Wesley Niewoehner (2001) conducted an intensive analysis of Neandertal hand and finger bones, comparing them in detail to those of anatomically modern human beings. Niewoehner concludes that Neandertal hand anatomy indicates that they were capable of an enormously strong "power grip" in which objects are held in the palm with the fleshy part of the base of the thumb serving as a brace. In other words, if you were to shake a Neandertal's hand, you would need to be prepared to get yours crushed. Paleoanthropologist Fred Smith has succinctly summarized the anatomical data in this way: "Neandertals seem to represent the high-water mark for the genus *Homo* in favoring the brawn approach to environmental adaptation" (1991:225). Put another way, a spear-wielding Neandertal would have been an imposing adversary.

Fossil Evidence
Neandertal Origins
The hominids noted in Table 5.1 whose remains were recovered at Sima de los Huesos in the Atapuerca Mountains of northern Spain may be four times as old as the oldest of the so-called classic Neandertals. Recent dating (by uranium series methods; see Chapter 2) of the deposits in which the Sima de los Huesos were recovered suggests that they might actually be at least 500,000 years old (Balter 2009b). Nevertheless, the researchers characterize the morphology of the crania of the two adults and one child thus far recovered as "Neandertal-like" and as anticipating the Neandertal cranial form (Arsuaga et al. 1993:535).

"Classic" Neandertals
The great florescence of the Neandertals in Europe and southwest Asia occurred between 80,000 and 40,000 years ago. Sites that have produced important Neandertal remains that are closely similar in morphology include Le Moustier, La Chapelle-aux-Saints, and La Ferrassie in France; Spy in Belgium; Saccopastore and Mt. Circeo in Italy; Krapina in Yugoslavia; Amud, Kebara, and Tabun in Israel (Figure 5.9); and Shanidar in Iraq.

Neandertal Culture
Stone Tools
Named for the French Neandertal site of Le Moustier, the **Mousterian** tool-making tradition of the Neandertals represents not a replacement of the Levallois technique but rather a refinement. Mousterian flakes were smaller and more precisely made than the earlier Levallois flakes: The Neandertals were capable of

▶ **Figure 5.9**
These typical Neandertal skulls are from (left) Amud and (right) Tabun in Israel. (Left, © Israel Antiquities Authority; right, © The Natural History Museum, London)

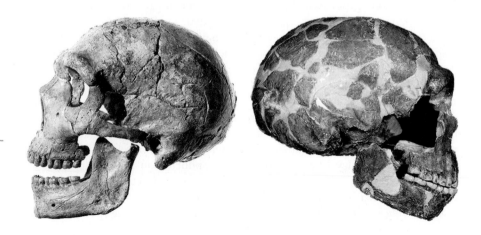

producing flakes whose size and shape matched more precisely the form needed for a predesignated purpose. Instead of a single all-purpose tool like a handaxe or a few particular kinds of tools as in the earlier Levallois industry, dozens of different task-specific, standardized Mousterian tool types are recognized. Archaeologist François Bordes (1972) defined 63 specific Mousterian tool types for cutting, slicing, piercing, scraping, sawing, and pounding (Figure 5.10). Each Mousterian flake received more precise treatment once it was removed from the core. Whereas an Acheulean handaxe may have required as many as 65 blows of a hammerstone, the production of a highly specialized Mousterian tool required an additional hundred or more blows to shape and sharpen the edge once the flake was removed from its core (Constable 1973). The complexity of the Neandertal stone-tool assemblage clearly is the result of the complexity of what the Neandertals were doing with those tools.

Subsistence

Though we cannot provide anything like a detailed breakdown of the Neandertal diet, there is some direct, if general, evidence of what items were on the menu. For example, investigators at Kebara Cave in Israel (Bar-Yosef et al. 1992) found evidence of an abundance of gazelle and fallow deer in the Neandertal diet. Evidence of burning and cut marks on their bones, as well as on those of elephant, horse, and several other mammalian species, shows the breadth of the animal subsistence base of the cave inhabitants. An abundance of carbonized seeds of wild peas found in the fireplaces is a direct indicator that the Kebara Neandertals also ate locally available vegetable foods.

Though a single kill may not give us a statistical measure of the contribution of hunting to the Neandertal diet, it can at least provide dramatic evidence that hunting was a part of the Neandertal behavioral repertoire. At the 50,000-year-old Umm el Tlel site in Syria, researchers found a shattered stone point still embedded in one of the cervical vertebrae (neck bones) of a wild ass (Boëda et al. 1999). Apparently, the stone had been hafted onto a shaft, likely of wood, and had been thrust so powerfully into the animal's neck that the stone weapon had shattered in two places, at its tip and base.

An isotope analysis of Neandertal bones further points to the importance of meat in their diet. The ratios of stable isotopes of carbon and nitrogen in the bones of carnivores and herbivores are demonstrably different and can be used as a relative measure of the proportion of meat and plant foods in the diet. When Neandertal bones recovered at the Vindija Cave site in Croatia were analyzed in this way, their carbon-to-nitrogen proportions were similar to those determined for contemporary carnivores, in particular, saber-toothed cats, and quite different from that same calculation performed on herbivores (Richards et al. 2000).

The extent of the faunal deposits at some Neandertal sites clearly indicates that these premodern human beings were proficient at obtaining meat for their diet. That they likely were successful hunters should not be surprising considering the enormous skeletal and muscular strength that would have provided Neandertal hunters the stamina necessary to walk great distances in tracking animals—and in Pleistocene Europe, in the snow and cold. Their ability to track down animals across great distances, their great physical strength, and their sophisticated **tool kit** would have made them formidable hunters indeed.

▲ **Figure 5.10**
Typical Mousterian tradition tools, a variety of core and flake technology practiced by the Neandertals. (From F. Bordes, Mousterian Cultures in France. *Science* 134:803. © 1961. Reprinted with permission from American Association for the Advancement of Science)

Compassion

It is often said that a society can be judged by how it treats its sick or injured. Ironically, evidence shows that the Neandertals, whose intelligence is so often maligned and who are so often used as a symbol for brutality, may actually have been compassionate and caring creatures. This suggestion stems from evidence of the survival of Neandertal individuals who had significant health problems or who had suffered severe trauma sometime during their lives. Some of these individuals had been in such bad shape that they probably could have survived only with the help of comrades.

For example, the Neandertal male who lived in Shanidar Cave in Iraq lived a rather eventful life, to judge by his skeleton, which showed several serious but healed bone fractures (Solecki 1971; Trinkaus 1983b). The bony ridge around his left eye had been fractured so badly that it is likely the blow blinded his eye. His right arm had been so severely smashed that the lower part had been amputated (perhaps by the blow, perhaps intentionally in an early example of surgical amputation). The right leg showed signs of disease and possible trauma.

It is clear this individual had sustained a series of heavy traumas at some time in his life and that rather remarkably he had survived. Such survival would have been impossible without the help and care of his companions, indicating a level of care, at least during the healing process, that is usually associated only with modern human beings. That the Neandertals may have cared for the sick and wounded merely shows how similar they may have been to us.

Ancient Family

Modern Family is a much loved and highly awarded television show about, obviously enough, a "modern family" with its diverse mixture of formats, ethnicities, sexual orientations, age differences, and so on. Though it might seem a trifle morbid, if all of the characters in that show were now anthropological specimens, we might still be able to identify, at least in a general sense, who these people were, where they came from, and who was biologically related to whom through the application of the types of analysis discussed in Chapter 2 and mentioned throughout this book.

Just such an analysis has been performed on the remains of a dozen Neandertals, an apparent ancient family, recovered at the El Sidrón site in Spain (Lalueza-Fox et al. 2010). Genetic analysis in particular showed that the three adult males were all closely related to one another, but the three adult females were not close blood relatives of any of the males or of each other. Two of the children are genetically similar to one of the females; the other young child appears to be directly related to one of the other females. Those females may very well have been the mothers of those respective kids.

Notice that this pattern of closely related males and unrelated females living together in a group matches what was seen in Chapter 3 where a strontium isotope analysis of the diets of *Australopithecus* and *Paranthropus* also indicated that males remained in their region of birth throughout their lives while the females in the group migrated in from elsewhere. Among modern groups this practice is called **patrilocality**—males stay in the village or community into which they are born, their sisters move to other villages to find mates—following a general pattern in which females move into communities to become the mates of males to whom they are not related. In a preliminary conclusion, the authors suggest that Neandertals practiced a version of patrilocality.

Symbolic Expression

The creative or artistic impulse and the desire to use symbols in expressing that impulse might seem to be uniquely human traits. Did the Neandertals have that same desire?

Although there is no evidence that, as is commonly claimed in popular reconstructions, the Neandertals worshipped cave bears (Kurtén 1976), they do appear to have produced works of art. Examples of grooved or perforated bones, perforated animal teeth, polished ivory, and even geometrically incised bone and ivory found at Neandertal sites are the closest things yet found that could reflect an artistic impulse on the part of the Neandertals (Bahn 1998; Chase and Dibble 1987; Simek 1992). At one site in France, Arcy-sur-Cure, there are more than 142 such objects (Hublin et al. 1996). Perforated and painted shells have been found at two Neandertal sites in southeast Spain, Aviones cave and Antón rockshelter; both sites date to close to 50,000 years ago (Balter 2010). Some of the perforated objects found at Neandertal sites may have been used in personal ornamentation—for example, as pendants (Figure 5.11).

What might the use of such possible ornamentation tell us about the Neandertals? Even today, along with simply providing beautiful decoration, our jewelry may be intended to convey messages to others concerning our marital status, our economic position, our membership in a particular social group, or even our religion. It is an intriguing possibility that in wearing items of personal adornment, Neandertals may also have been conveying messages like these in a symbolic way.

Burial of the Dead

In at least one essential area, Neandertals behaved as we do: They buried their dead. At sites such as Le Moustier, La Chapelle-aux-Saints, and La Ferrassie in France; Teshik-Tash in Uzbekistan; Shanidar in Iraq; and Amud, Tabun, and Kebara in Israel, the evidence indicates that Neandertals interred their dead in the ground, most often in an intentionally flexed position, knees drawn up toward

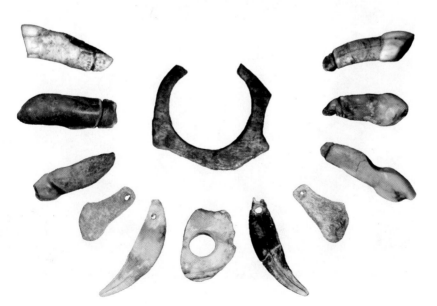

◀ **Figure 5.11**
Though commonly viewed as unintelligent brutes, the archaeological record of the Neandertals belies this mischaracterization. These artifacts from the French site of Arcy-sur-Cure are tiny works of art, carvings that may have served as items of adornment made and worn by these significantly different, but fully human creatures. (© Jean-Jacques Hublin)

the chest, and even with some simple items such as stone or bone implements, ochre, or unmodified animal bone (Figure 5.12; Harrold 1980).

Archaeologists Anna Belfer-Cohen and Erella Hovers (1992) surveyed burial data for the Middle Paleolithic period of the Neandertals and counted 59 intentional burials. They point out that these burials make no sense as a mere hygienic way to dispose of a dead body. Why put that much time into digging a hole if a dead body can be far more unceremoniously dumped in the woods, allowing scavengers to do the work? They conclude that the Neandertals were burying their dead in recognition of the significance of death.

We should not conclude that Neandertals were just like us—had funerals, memorial services, and formalized cemeteries—but the questions raised by the

▶ **Figure 5.12**
In burying their dead, the Neandertals were exhibiting a behavior that shows their affinity with modern humans. This photograph shows the Neandertal burial found at the site of La Ferrassie in France. (© Musée de l'Homme, Paris. M. Lucas, photographer)

intentional disposal of the dead practiced by the Neandertals may be more important than the answers we might suggest. Clearly, Neandertals understood the significance of death and recognized it through burial. Here again, these very different human ancestors exhibit their kinship to us.

Anatomically Modern *Homo sapiens*

Between 500,000 and 150,000 years ago, the hominid family appears to have been a complex tapestry with multiple threads represented by several significantly different regional variants of premodern humans. As we have just seen, by about 300,000 years ago, one of those threads began to differentiate, eventually evolving into the classic Neandertal form by about 125,000 years ago. It now appears that around the same time that the classical Neandertals were becoming established in Europe, and maybe a little before, another one of those hominid threads also had differentiated. This thread eventually developed a morphology that we can all examine directly, simply by looking in the mirror. It is us.

An African Source

Two crania, labeled Omo I and Omo II, were discovered along the Omo River in southern Ethiopia in 1967 (Figure 5.13; Day 1969). The crania were recovered from an ancient layer (specifically Member I) of what geologists call the **Kibish Formation**. Omo I was immediately recognized as anatomically modern, or nearly so, while Omo II appeared to retain a more archaic or premodern appearance (Day 1969).

Applying the argon/argon procedure (Chapter 2), Member I of the Kibish Formation and, by association, the Omo crania are now firmly dated to 195,000 years ago (McDougall, Brown, and Fleagle 2005). This represents the oldest date yet derived for a specimen, Omo I, that appears to have been anatomically modern.

◀ **Figure 5.13**
The Omo I cranium. Round in profile and lacking a major bony protuberance in the rear (the occipital region), the Omo I cranium indicates a modern morphology. Recent redating of the sediments in which Omo I was recovered indicate that, at an age of 195,000 years, it is the oldest anatomically modern human fossil remain yet discovered. (Courtesy of M. H. Day)

The Omo and slightly younger crania show that, just like the first hominids (Chapter 3), the first members of the genus *Homo* (Chapter 3), the first *Homo erectus* specimens (Chapter 4), and the earliest representatives of the premodern humans (this chapter), the earliest morphologically modern human beings have been found in Africa.

Following this, the paleoanthropological record in Africa shows the shift to the entirely modern form known as **anatomically modern *Homo sapiens.*** The Border Cave site, for example, produced the remains of four hominids from different layers in the cave deposit: a complete mandible, a partial mandible, a fragmentary infant skeleton, and a fairly complete cranium (Figure 5.14). The cranium looks quite modern (Rightmire 1979).

Electron spin resonance (ESR) dates on animal teeth found in association with the hominid remains indicate that the cranium and partial mandible are probably more than 70,000 to 80,000 and less than 90,000 years old; the complete mandible is 50,000 to 65,000 years old; and the infant skeleton is 70,000 to 80,000 years old (Grün, Beaumont, and Stringer 1990).

Klasies River Mouth (KRM; see Figure 5.27) was meticulously excavated in 1966–68 and then again between 1984 and 1989. Thousands of artifacts and several fragmentary human remains were recovered, including two upper jaws, teeth, a lower arm (ulna), and cranial and mandibular fragments (Bräuer, Deacon, and Zipfel 1992; Deacon and Shuurman 1992; Rightmire 1984, 1991; Singer and Wymer 1982).

The morphology of the KRM specimens is modern. A modern human chin was clearly apparent in at least one of the mandibles, and the cranial fragments show no evidence of large brow ridges. Finally, ESR dating of animal teeth found in the same layer as the hominid fossils places the age of the specimens at about 90,000 years (Grün, Shackleton, and Deacon 1990).

▶ **Figure 5.14**
A nearly complete skull from Border Cave in South Africa. The Border Cave hominid is an early anatomically modern human being. (Courtesy of Professor P. V. Tobias, University of the Witwatersrand, Johannesburg, South Africa)

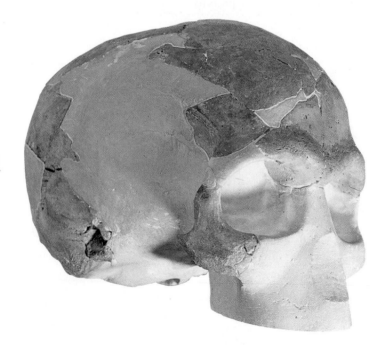

Explaining the Evolution of Us

Remember our discussion in Chapter 2 about how in the historical sciences we rely on a "convergence of evidence" to build a consensus about how things occurred in antiquity? Though there is a long-standing controversy about the origins of anatomically modern humans, there now seems to be an emerging convergence of archaeological, osteological, and genetic evidence. This convergence is leading to a consensus, though, to be sure, there's still plenty of controversy on this issue.

Until fairly recently, a line was firmly drawn between those who supported the so-called replacement model of human evolution and those who preferred a perspective called the multiregional model. Let's look at each of these models (Figure 5.15).

The Replacement Model

In the **replacement model**, whose chief proponent is British paleoanthropologist Christopher B. Stringer (1990, 1992a, 1992b, 1994, 2012a; Stringer and Andrews 1988), nearly all of the fossils of premodern humans listed in this chapter (at least those from Europe and Asia) represent extinct forms of human beings, dead ends that contributed very little to the evolution of modern humanity. Instead, the evolution of anatomically modern human beings is considered to have occurred just once, in one place—Africa—and fairly recently, between 100,000 and 200,000 years ago.

In this view, the first anatomically modern human beings spread out from their African homeland, first into southwest Asia and then east to the rest of Asia and north and west to Europe. There, these African-originating modern humans encountered populations of premodern humans—including remnant groups of *Homo erectus.* For a time they were contemporaries, perhaps living virtually next door to each other. The anatomically modern humans possessed some fundamental advantage, as yet poorly understood, over their premodern neighbors—perhaps they were smarter and could communicate more effectively, a result of

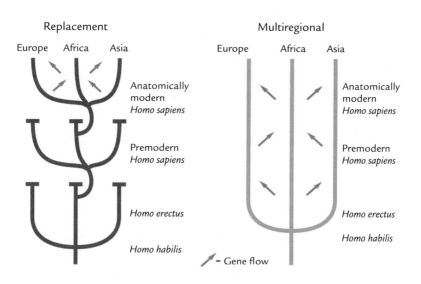

◀ **Figure 5.15**
Schematic depiction of the replacement and the multiregional models of the evolution of anatomically modern *Homo sapiens.*

their differently configured brains. The modern-looking humans replaced premoderns wherever they came into contact. Premoderns could not successfully compete for resources with the modern humans and so became extinct, leaving no genetic endowment to modern humanity.

The Multiregional Model

In the **multiregional** (or **regional continuity**) **model,** whose champion is American paleoanthropologist Milford Wolpoff (Frayer et al. 1993; Thorne and Wolpoff 1992; Wolpoff 1989a, 1992; Wolpoff and Caspari 1990; Wolpoff et al. 1994; Wolpoff, Wu, and Thorne 1984), the evolution of modern human beings was a geographically broad process, not an event restricted to a single region. Various geographically separated groups of premodern humans—representing many regions—together evolved toward the modern form. Enough contact between groups in Africa, Europe, and Asia was maintained to allow for **gene flow** among them. This gene flow was sufficient to keep the premoderns as a single, variable species. Through migration and intermarriage among the different groups, new, advantageous modern traits, originating in various places and among different archaic groups, rippled through the population of premodern humans (Wolpoff et al. 1994:178). Together and simultaneously, not separately and independently, all these groups evolved into the modern form while maintaining some relatively minor regional traits traceable to their premodern ancestors. Gene flow among groups was not so great as to wipe out such local, regional, or "racial" characteristics. So *Homo erectus* and premodern *Homo sapiens* in east Asia evolved into the modern people of Asia. In this view, the Neandertals of Europe and west Asia evolved into modern Europeans and west Asians and the premodern humans of Africa evolved into the modern people of Africa. All groups remained part of the human species, yet all maintained their own unique physical features.

Replacement, Multiregional, or Something Else? A Convergence of Evidence

What We Would Expect on the Basis of the Replacement Model

ISSUES AND DEBATES

If the replacement model is correct—if early anatomically modern humans evolved in Africa from earlier archaic roots and then spread from there, replacing indigenous hominids in Europe and Asia—then the fossil record should show the following:

1. The oldest anatomically modern human fossils should be found in Africa and nowhere else.
2. There should be anatomical continuity only in Africa. That is to say, fossil forms intermediate between premoderns and moderns should be found only in Africa.
3. Outside of Africa, the emigrant moderns should be contemporaries of indigenous premoderns until the nonmodern humans become extinct.
4. The first anatomically modern humans in Europe and Asia should look like the early anatomically modern humans in Africa, because that is where they originated.

5. The archaeological record is expected to show the sudden appearance of nonlocal, African-originating artifact types in Europe and Asia as the early anatomically modern African population spread from its place of origin.

6. Anatomically modern humans should be genetically distinct from premoderns. Modern human DNA should be quite similar to DNA recovered from the bones of ancient, anatomically modern-looking humans. DNA recovered from the bones of premodern humans should be significantly different from that of their anatomically modern-looking contemporaries as well as from the DNA of living people.

What We Would Expect on the Basis of the Multiregional Model

If the multiregional hypothesis is to be upheld, then the following, quite different predictions can be made about the fossil record:

1. Early versions of anatomically modern *Homo sapiens* should be found in many different regions. No one region should have anatomically modern fossils substantially older than any other region.

2. Intermediate forms—advanced premoderns—should be found in each region, because evolution from premodern to modern occurred everywhere.

3. Because local premoderns are everywhere ancestral to modern humans in their regions, there should be no or very little chronological overlap between the premodern and modern forms.

4. Local skeletal traits should show continuity between premodern and modern humans, because in each region local premoderns evolved into modern people.

5. The archaeological record should show a continuity in regional artifact types. As local premodern humans evolved physically into modern humans, their archaic toolmaking traditions evolved into more sophisticated modern traditions.

6. DNA recovered from the bones of ancient, archaic-looking human beings should be as similar to the DNA of modern humans as is the DNA recovered from the bones of ancient, modern-looking individuals.

Referring to the map in Figure 5.16, let's assess the evidence as it relates to the predictions made in each model.

Testing the Implications of Replacement and Continuity

1. Are the oldest anatomically modern human fossils found in Africa and nowhere else, or are early versions of anatomically modern Homo sapiens found in many different regions?

The oldest anatomically modern human skeletal remains yet found are those mentioned earlier in this chapter, found at the Omo site in Ethiopia (see Figure 5.13). At an age of 195,000 years, the Omo remains are older, by far, than any anatomically modern or near-modern remains found anywhere in Asia or Europe. We can then trace the subsequent expansion from Africa of anatomically modern humans across the face of the earth (Figure 5.17). The earliest skeletons of anatomically modern human beings outside of Africa have been found in Israel, at the Skhul and Qafzeh sites now dated to somewhere between 96,000 and 119,000 years ago. It is easy to imagine anatomically modern humans in east

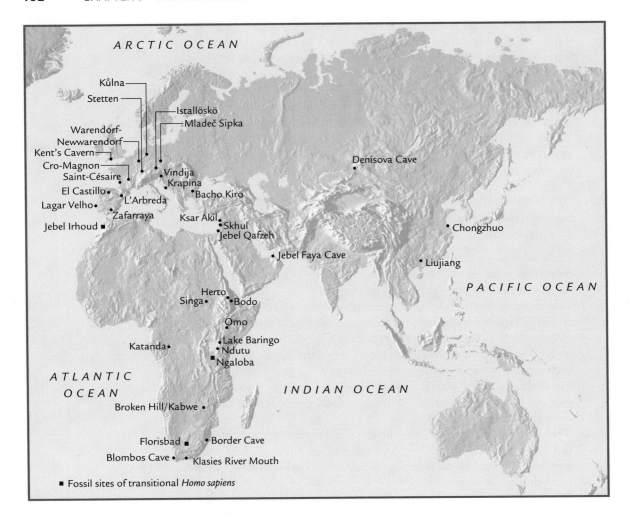

ARCTIC OCEAN

Kůlna
Stetten
Istallöskö
Mladeč Sipka
Warendorf-
Newwarendorf
Kent's Cavern
Cro-Magnon
Saint-Césaire
El Castillo
Lagar Velho
L'Arbreda
Zafarraya
Jebel Irhoud
Vindija
Krapina
Bacho Kiro
Ksar Akil
Skhul
Jebel Qafzeh
Jebel Faya Cave
Denisova Cave
Chongzhuo
Liujiang
PACIFIC OCEAN
Herto
Singa
Bodo
Omo
Katanda
Lake Baringo
Ndutu
Ngaloba
ATLANTIC OCEAN
INDIAN OCEAN
Broken Hill/Kabwe
Florisbad
Blombos Cave
Border Cave
Klasies River Mouth

■ Fossil sites of transitional *Homo sapiens*

▲ **Figure 5.16**
Fossil localities of early anatomically modern *Homo sapiens* and late, near-modern transitional forms.

Africa moving north as their population expanded, leading to their arrival at sites like Skhul and Qazeh at this time.

Though hominid skeletons have not been found, stone tools matching those seen at anatomically modern human sites in Africa have been found at the Jebel Faya site located on the eastern coast of Saudi Arabia dating to 123,000 years ago (Armitage et al. 2011). The people responsible for those tools may have followed a path north into Israel and then south and east into Arabia. Alternatively, ancient African moderns may have migrated directly into the Arabian peninsula over water, across the very narrow Bab al-Mandab Strait. The descendants of these people, probably crossing the Persian Gulf and then following the Indian Ocean coast, arrived in India perhaps a little before 60,000 years ago, after a major volcanic eruption (the Toba eruption) there dating to 74,000 years ago (though there is some intriguing evidence of their arrival stratigraphically below the volcanic deposit and, therefore, before the eruption; Appenzeller 2012). The earliest anatomically modern human remains in east Asia (specifically, in China) are represented by a mandible found at the Chongzhuo site in southwest China, dating

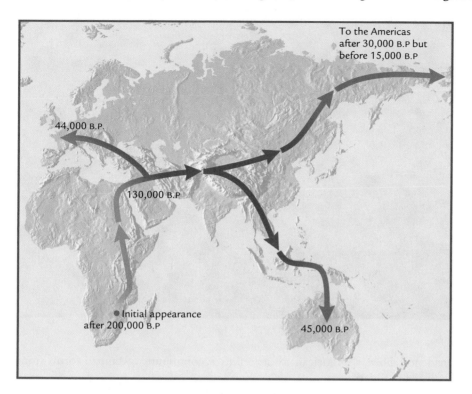

To the Americas
after 30,000 B.P but
before 15,000 B.P

44,000 B.P.

130,000 B.P

Initial appearance
after 200,000 B.P

45,000 B.P

◀ **Figure 5.17**
The geography of the
evolution of modern
humans as implied by
the replacement model.

to 110,000 years ago (Stone 2009). The earliest evidence of hominids in Greater Australia (including New Guinea) dates to about 50,000 years ago, and they are all anatomically modern (see Chapter 7). The oldest modern human remains found in Europe are younger, dating to no more than 44,000 years ago at Kent's Cavern in the United Kingdom (Higham et al. 2011). People, again anatomically modern, move into the New World sometime after 20,000 years ago, and across the islands of the Pacific just a few thousand years ago (see Chapter 7). Though there are many details to be worked out, including the precise timing of this population wave of anatomically modern people across the globe, the evidence converges on a scenario in which they originated in Africa where the sites are considerably older. This evidence in this case lends support to the replacement model.

2. Is there continuity only in Africa, or are forms intermediate between premodern and modern humans found in many regions?

African fossils like Bodo (600,000 years ago), Ileret (300,000 years ago), Ndutu (more than 200,000 years ago), and Kabwe possess a suite of archaic features, while the Omo I remains in Ethiopia, at 195,000 years ago, look modern or very nearly so. The replacement hypothesis predicts that there should be forms intermediate between the premodern and modern humans in one place, Africa, and that prediction seems to be borne out by the evidence. The Florisbad (South Africa), Ngaloba (Laetoli hominid 18, in Tanzania), and Jebel Irhoud (Morocco; Figure 5.18) crania all appear to represent forms transitional between the premoderns listed previously and the modern-looking Omo remains. Together this

▶ **Figure 5.18**
The cranium from Jebel Irhoud in north Africa has been interpreted as representing a form intermediate between archaic and modern *Homo sapiens*. Some researchers contend that intermediate forms such as this one are found only in Africa, lending support to one of the major predictions of the replacement hypothesis. (© Musée de l'Homme, Paris)

evidence shows that African fossils reflect a continuum of human forms from archaic to modern.

3. Were premodern and anatomically modern human beings contemporaries?

The replacement model predicts that outside of Africa fossil evidence will show the contemporaneity of locally evolved premodern humans and immigrant groups of African moderns; southwest Asia is pointed to as verification. There, in caves that are sometimes in close proximity to each other, the remains of Neandertals and anatomically modern humans have been found. Dating techniques place the premodern and modern humans in their respective caves during the same periods and may even indicate that the modern humans are *older* than some of the Neandertals. For example, classic Neandertals have been excavated at Kebara Cave, as well as at the sites of Amud and Tabun (see Figure 5.9), in Israel. With their large, heavy skulls, large brow ridges, flattened occipitals, sloping foreheads, and prognathism, their form is unmistakably Neandertal. The Kebara site dates to 60,000, Amud is closer to 70,000, and Tabun has now been dated to about 100,000 years ago (McDermott et al. 1993).

As previously mentioned, robust but otherwise rather modern-looking specimens have been excavated at the sites of Skhul and Qafzeh, also in Israel (Figure 5.19). Skhul, on Mount Carmel, is not even 100 m (300 ft) from Tabun, with its Neandertal fossils, and Qafzeh is less than 30 km (18 mi) east of those two cave sites. Kebara Cave is also close by, about 10 km (6 mi) south of Mount Carmel. It is remarkable that such different-looking, generally contemporaneous hominids have been found in such a restricted area (see Figure 5.6).

The Skhul and Qafzeh sites are now judged to date to as much as 119,000 and 96,000 years ago, respectively (Shea 2007), which is broadly contemporaneous with the Neandertals at Tabun. Combining the skeletal and archaeological

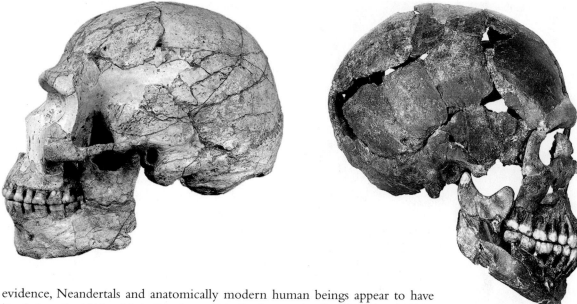

evidence, Neandertals and anatomically modern human beings appear to have lived virtually side by side in Southwest Asia for thousands of years (Balter 2009b).

The oldest of the classic Neandertals are found in Europe and date to 125,000 years ago. The last of the Neandertals again are found in Europe with remains at Saint Césaire (Figure 5.20) in France dating to 36,000 years ago (Mercier et al. 1991; Stringer and Grün 1991), Zafarraya in Spain dating to 33,400 years ago (Rose 1995), and the latest of the Vindija remains in Croatia dating to 28,000 years ago (F. Smith et al. 1999). The oldest of the anatomically modern human remains in Europe are older than these youngest Neandertals. This temporal overlap between Neandertals and anatomically modern humans in Europe is congruent with the replacement hypothesis.

4. Is there a break in the form of premodern and modern human fossils outside of Africa, or do local skeletal traits show continuity between premodern and modern humans in each region?

If anatomically modern humans evolved in Africa and spread from there, replacing premoderns in all regions, locally derived, region-specific anatomical traits should have disappeared in each area as the indigenous premoderns became extinct. The modern in-migrants in Europe and Asia should have looked like the earliest anatomically modern Africans and not at all like the local premoderns they were replacing. Local traits presently seen among modern people (skeletal features that are the equivalent of "racial" characteristics) would have evolved only very recently, after the replacement occurred. If, instead, there was regional continuity in Africa, Europe, and Asia, then region-specific traits of the skeleton might be expected to be maintained within populations evolving from premodern to modern. In other words, skeletal traits specific to a particular region would show continuity from *Homo erectus* through premodern *Homo sapiens*, through the earliest anatomically modern humans, right up to the population of human beings living in an area today (at least among those individuals who can trace their ancestry back deeply in the area).

▲ **Figure 5.19**
The Skhul (left) and Qafzeh (right) skulls from Israel are quite modern in appearance. Neandertals lived in Israel at the same time, supporting another of the major implications of the replacement hypothesis. (left, © Courtesy of the Peabody Museum of Archaeology and Ethnology, Harvard University, 2004.24.21754; right, Laboratory of Vertebrate and Human Paleontology, Paris, Bernard Vandermeersch)

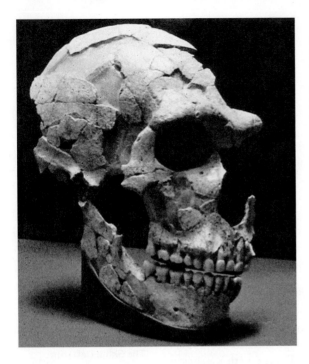

▲ Figure 5.20
The Neandertal skull from St. Césaire, France. The St. Césaire specimen is the most recent of the Neandertals, dating to about 36,000 years ago. This is long after anatomically modern *Homo sapiens* evolved, making problematic any hypothesis that modern humans evolved from the Neandertals. (Transparency #A11, courtesy of Department of Library Services, American Museum of Natural History)

Remember our discussion of Neandertal skeletal anatomy earlier in this chapter. There we said that the Neandertals were built for strength and for cold, with broad chests and short, thick arms and legs. The oldest skeletons of anatomically modern human beings found in Europe date to between 25,000 and 40,000 years ago and don't look anything like this. Tall and thin, with long extremities, they looked, as Christopher Stringer has said, "as if they walked straight out of Africa" (as quoted in P. E. Ross 1991:47).

5. Does the archaeological record show the sudden appearance of nonlocal, African-originating artifact types in Europe and Asia as the early anatomically modern African population spread out from its place of origin, or is there continuity in regional artifact types as local premodern humans evolved into modern ones?

Assessing the sophistication of a stone-tool technology can be a bit subjective. It may be difficult to state, categorically, that one technology is "more advanced" or "more sophisticated" than another. Ordinarily, a technology that (1) requires a greater number of steps and more forethought in preparing a stone core, (2) results in greater efficiency (producing a greater amount of usable edge), and (3) produces tools that simply do the job better because they are sharper or more aerodynamic is considered to be more advanced or sophisticated (Figure 5.21).

A technology that produces **blade** tools fits these criteria for increased sophistication. The production of long, thin, sharp blades of a consistent size and shape ordinarily requires more preparation of the stone core from which the blades are struck, results in a more efficient use of the stone, and produces proportionally more cutting edge from the same amount of stone than in the Mousterian technology. And, in fact, when we look to Africa, we see evidence of the production of blade tools long before they turn up in Europe or Asia.

The oldest stone blade tools have been found in Africa by researchers Cara Roure Johnson and Sally McBrearty, at five sites located in the Baringo Basin, in Kenya (Gibbons 2009d). The sites date to an amazing 500,000 years ago, ten times as old as the oldest blade tools found in Europe. McBrearty has also found stone blades in Africa that date to 240,000 years old (Gutin 1995). She found these stone blades at a site near Lake Baringo, and they show careful core preparation that resulted in consistently sized and shaped stone blades (Figure 5.22). There also is evidence for blade tools at Klasies River Mouth (Figure 5.23; see this chapter's "Case Study Close-up"). The tools are quite consistent in size and shape. KRM dates to about 90,000 years ago.

All of the stone tool technologies discussed so far in this book are based on percussion, removing a flake by striking one stone (the object piece) with another (the hammerstone). Percussion flaking certainly takes a tremendous amount of skill in knowing precisely where to strike the object piece with your hammerstone, at what angle, and with how much force. For greater precision and more

▶ **Figure 5.21**
Archaeologists, including me, often label a tool or a technology "sophisticated" without defining what they mean by that. These two figures reflect what I mean when I call the lithic technology of anatomically modern humans more sophisticated than the technologies of premodern humans. The top graph shows the number of applications of force needed to produce a finished tool in each labeled technology (from oldest to most recent, left to right on the horizontal axis). The bottom graph shows the number of inches of sharp edge produced from each pound of rock (in the same order). Simply put, the Aurignacian tool technology of anatomically modern human beings required more steps and produced more usable edge than previous technologies. That's what I mean when I call it more sophisticated than previous technologies.

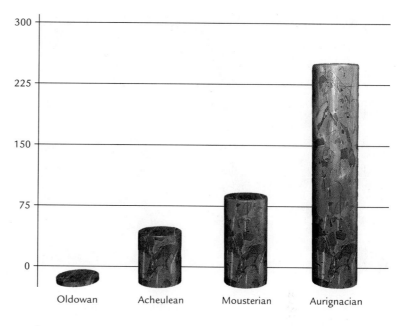

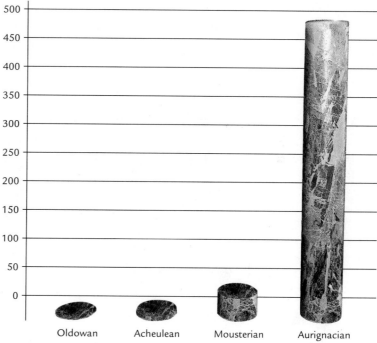

control of the exact placement of the force on the object piece, however, by 75,000 years ago the anatomically modern human residents of Blombos Cave in South Africa (we'll talk a lot about that site in Chapter 6) used another procedure (Mourre, Villa, and Henshilwood 2010). Called **pressure flaking**, it involves applying the force necessary to remove a flake, not by striking the object piece, but by carefully positioning the hard tip of, in all likelihood, an antler, pushing into the edge of a stone, and virtually peeling off a flake across the surface of the stone (Figure 5.24). Pushing at an edge with an antler does not produce as much force as striking it with a hard stone, but the precision and control in positioning and applying the force is far greater. Pressure flaking doesn't replace percussion, but it's a valuable addition to the methods of the toolmaker. Pressure flaking is seen first in Africa among anatomically modern humans. It is seen in Europe and Asia more than 30,000 years after it appears in South Africa, again supporting the replacement hypothesis.

◄ **Figure 5.22**
Blade tools represent a technological advance over flake tools, reflecting a more efficient use of lithic raw materials, producing more useable edges. Evidence of a blade technology has been found at Lake Baringo in Kenya, dating to 240,000 years ago. (Courtesy Sally McBrearty)

The Middle Stone Age African blade and bone tools do not appear to have accompanied their makers on their migration to Asia. In fact, there is no archaeological evidence in the form of an alien or invasive tool technology in Asia that might mark the arrival of immigrant, anatomically modern Africans. The earliest modern-looking hominids in southwest and east Asia practiced the same stone-toolmaking tradition as the local, indigenous archaic-looking people. The stone-tool assemblages from Skhul and Qafzeh, with their modern-looking fossils, and nearby Tabun, with its contemporary, archaic-looking fossils, exhibit the same stone-tool tradition: The people at these sites were all making Mousterian tools (Shea 1990; Thorne and Wolpoff 1992).

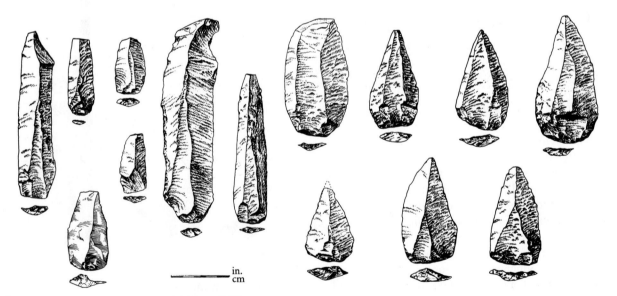

▲ **Figure 5.23**
Long blade tools dating to close to 100,000 years ago from the site of Klasies River Mouth, South Africa. These tools were associated with fragmentary remains of anatomically modern human beings. (From *The Middle Stone Age at Klasies River Mouth, South Africa*, by Ronald Singer and John Wymer, University of Chicago Press, 1982)

The earliest sites exhibiting the **Aurignacian** tradition in Europe include L'Arbreda Cave in eastern Spain, El Castillo Cave in northern Spain, Istállóskö in Hungary, and Bacho Kiro Cave in Bulgaria (Straus 1989). As mentioned previously, the Spanish sites date to about 38,000 years ago (Bischoff et al. 1989; Valdes and Bischoff 1989); the Hungarian and Bulgarian sites date to as much as 43,000 years ago. Archaeologist James Bischoff and his colleagues, who analyzed the Spanish sites, characterize the appearance of Aurignacian tools in the Spanish caves, as well as the other European sites mentioned, as "abrupt" (Bischoff et al. 1989:573). The Mousterian and Aurignacian technologies are quite different, and, in the case of the Spanish sites, the raw materials used are different: The Mousterian flakes are almost all made of locally available quartz and quartzite, whereas the Aurignacian tools are almost all made of a more distantly available flint. There is no evidence there of a slow, steady transition from a Mousterian to an Aurignacian tradition,

▲ **Figure 5.24**
Two beautifully flaked tools excavated at Blombos Cave in South Africa. The edges of the tools were precisely shaped and sharpened, not through the application of force by percussion but by precisely applying pressure with a pointed tool, probably the narrow tip of an antler. (From "Early Use of Pressure Flaking on Lithic Artifacts at Blombos Cave, South Africa," by Vincent Mourre, Paolo Villa, and Christopher S. Henshilwood, *Science* 330:6004. Reprinted with permission from AAAS.)

no sign of an evolution of the simpler Mousterian tradition of the Neandertals to the more sophisticated Aurignacian tradition of the first anatomically modern humans in Europe. Bischoff and his colleagues take this to support the replacement model; when a new toolmaking tradition appears abruptly in the archaeological record, with no evidence of its having evolved from an earlier way of doing things, it is often concluded that the new tradition arrived from the outside, the product of a new group's migration into the area. Researcher Paul Mellars (2004) also points out that the dates derived for Aurignacian sites across Europe imply a wave of population expansion from east to west. In other words, the first Aurignacian sites, generally, are oldest in the Middle East, a bit more recent in eastern Europe, and successively younger as one moves to the west. This is exactly the pattern we would expect if the bearers of that technology were migrants from the Middle East, expanding their territory westward across Europe through time.

Soon after the blade-based Aurignacian tradition arrived in Europe along with anatomically modern people, rather interestingly the Mousterian tradition of the resident Neandertals began to change. The Neandertals began to produce tools that look more like the blades being produced by the incoming anatomically modern humans. It appears as though the native Neandertals and the anatomically modern migrants were, at least, aware of each other, and the Neandertals appear to have been picking up some of the toolmaking practices of the newcomers.

The best known of these apparently hybridized technologies is the **Châtelperronian**, in France, seen at Neandertal sites like Saint-Césaire and Arcy-sur-Cure (Figure 5.25). This technological tradition has much in common with Mousterian and differs only in the addition of long, thin blade tools, exactly the kind of tools that characterize the Aurignacian tradition. Elsewhere in Europe the situation may have been repeated, and other "hybrid" tool traditions are suggested for Italy, Greece, and central Europe (Gibbons 2001). This suggests a fascinating

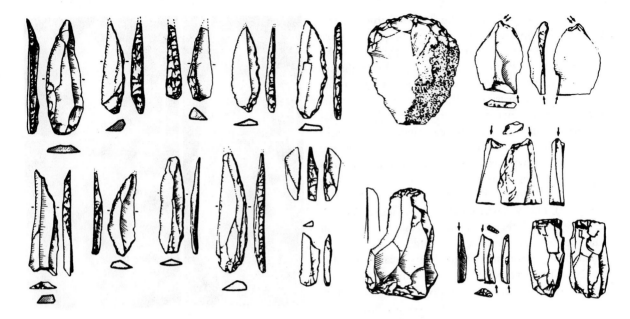

▲ **Figure 5.25**
Tools of the Châtelperronian tradition. Tools like these were found with the St. Césaire Neandertal. It has been suggested that this tradition represents a cultural blending of the Neandertal Mousterian and the anatomically modern human tradition called Aurignacian. (Adapted from Bordes and Labrot 1967)

scenario of contact between two fundamentally different kinds of human beings in Europe after 40,000 years ago.

A careful analysis of the Châtelperronian blades shows that their production was somewhat different from Aurignacian blades. In other words, Neandertals had not simply watched anatomically modern humans produce blade tools and then unquestioningly copied each of the steps (Bahn 1998). Châtelperronian is rather short-lived, dated between about 36,000 and 33,000 years ago. Châtelperronian artifacts are sometimes found in the same sites as Aurignacian but separated stratigraphically; they are sometimes even interdigitated, with Châtelperronian tools in layers sometimes above Aurignacian tools, sometimes below (and sometimes both), such as at Le Piage in France (Simek 1992). This indicates fairly clearly that they were produced by separate groups who inhabited these sites at different times. The Châtelperronian, therefore, can be interpreted as supporting the replacement model in Europe.

6. Are anatomically modern humans genetically distinct from premoderns? In the replacement model, modern human DNA should be quite similar to DNA recovered from the bones of ancient, anatomically modern humans. DNA recovered from the bones of premodern humans should be significantly different from that of contemporary, anatomically modern humans, as well as from the DNA of living people.

Working like crime scene investigators trying to determine the identity of the fragmentary remains of a murder victim, researchers have now reconstructed the full **nuclear DNA** sequence—the genome—of the Neandertals from the remains recovered at four sites (Green et al. 2010). This genome reconstruction was based on an analysis of remains from Vindija Cave in Croatia (dated to 38,000 B.P.), El Sidron in Spain (49,000 B.P.), the Neander Valley site in Germany (40,000 B.P.), and Mezmaiskaya in southern Russia (between 60,000 and 70,000 B.P.).

Overall, the derived Neandertal genome is quite similar to that of modern humans, showing that, though we may have looked quite different from each other, under the skin we shared a lot in common. There were, however, discernible and significant differences between the Neandertals, on the one hand, and the modern human beings, on the other. Importantly, in 212 specific regions of our genetic instructions, we modern humans exhibited forms not seen in any of the Neandertals (Green et al. 2010:717). Probably not coincidentally, one of those genetic discontinuities between the Neandertals and us controls certain morphological characteristics of our skulls, specifically a protruding forehead, seen in modern humans but not of Neandertals, whose foreheads sloped back at a sharp angle. So, the metaphor of the forensic investigator of a crime scene can be extended; with a DNA sample in hand, a crime scene investigator would be able to determine if the murder victim had been a modern human being, or a Neandertal.

One of the most fascinating results of the genome project was the discovery of small stretches within the genetic signatures of some modern human populations—specifically in Europe and Asia—not seen in other modern people, but that are the same as those seen in the Neandertal genome. Though it is possible that these similarities were inherited from a common ancestor, it seems more likely the result of ancient interbreeding between the groups. In other words, the genes of some modern people show that they have Neandertals in their ancestral lineage.

That finding was shocking to the supporters of replacement and generated not just a few high-fives among the supporters of multiregionalism. If modern humans carry Neandertal genes, then we did not replace them, at least not in their entirety. In fact, in a sense, we couldn't replace them; we are them. To be fair, however, the amount of Neandertal genetic intrusion into the anatomically modern human genome is quite small, representing only about 1%–4%, and reflects a pattern of strong though certainly imperfect separation between the groups when they coexisted. In other words, when Neandertals and anatomically modern humans came into contact, there cannot have been any biological barriers to their interbreeding, but likely there were culturally determined restrictions. I have this bizarre image of Neandertal parents flipping out because their daughter was dating one of those boys from the group with the long, lanky bodies and the tall, flat foreheads, you know, the people who talk too much and think they're so smart. As silly as that sounds, those kinds of cultural rules and restrictions might actually explain why there wasn't more genetic admixture.

The fascinating possibility of interbreeding between Neandertals and anatomically modern humans who lived in the same regions at the same time may also be borne out by skeletal evidence. The excavators of a 24,500-year-old fossil from the Lagar Velho site near Lisbon, Portugal, believe the specimen represents a Neandertal/human hybrid (Duarte et al. 1999; Zilhao and Trinkaus 2003).

The bones are those of a 4½-year-old boy. The cranium was crushed, but the mandible was only somewhat damaged and looks like the lower jaw of a modern human child, much as one might expect for the given date. Furthermore, the boy had been carefully buried in a manner typical of modern human beings in Spain and Portugal dating from the period around 25,000 years ago. However, a careful analysis of the postcranial skeleton revealed that the young boy had an extremely robust body, with a wide, barrel chest and proportionally short arms and legs. In other words, the bodily proportions, along with some detailed skeletal characteristics, of the Velho child were Neandertal-like. The paleoanthropologists who analyzed the remains describe the skeleton as a "morphological mosaic" and believe that the mixture of modern and Neandertal traits seen in the child's skeleton is the result of a long-term pattern of interbreeding between contemporary anatomically modern human beings and Neandertals (Duarte et al. 1999:7608).

We can summarize the implications of the reconstruction of the Neandertal genome and skeletal evidence of interbreeding in this way:

1. The majority of the modern human genome can be traced to our AMH ancestors who originated in Africa. Whatever human modern population you sample today, we all share a common genetic heritage and that heritage is traceable to anatomically modern human beings who appeared in Africa nearly 200,000 years ago.
2. A small but significant percentage (between 1% and 4%) of the genome of modern humans who can trace their ancestry to Europe and Asia originated in Neandertal populations.
3. Modern Africans do not possess any of the Neandertal DNA signature.

And there's more. There appears to be another example of the "make love, not war" approach on the part of anatomically modern and archaic humans in eastern Asia with a group now called the Denisovans.

In a discipline marked by some really interesting names for hominid fossils—"Neandertal," "Java Man," the "australpithecines"—the "Denisovans" doesn't quite seem to measure up. Denisovans, to me, sounds more like a name we might apply to members of a religious cult who revere their leader, you know, Dennis. They have a compound in Idaho. In reality, the Denisovans are named for Denisova Cave, located in southern Russia, near its border with Kazakhstan (Borat's home turf), where their so far rather meager remains have been found. It's not the number of remains that makes the inhabitants of Denisova Cave so interesting. It's the level of preservation of genetic material recovered from a finger bone that has caused most of the excitement.

Artifacts have been recovered in excavations in the cave in stratigraphic levels dated to between 30,000 and 48,000 years ago. Some of the artifacts are pretty typically Mousterian and, therefore, attributable to a Neandertal presence in the cave. Some of the artifacts have been labeled Upper Paleolithic and likely were made by anatomically modern humans. Researchers expected the DNA recovered from the finger bone to be diagnostic of either Neandertal or anatomically moderns. It turned out not to be diagnostic of either of these groups but, instead, reflected the genome of another type of human being altogether. A careful analysis of the Denisovan genome suggests that the bone belonged to an archaic human group, different both from modern human and Neandertal, but similar enough to the latter to suggest that they were "sister groups" who shared a common ancestor (Reich et al. 2010). In other words, based on a comparative analysis of the genomes of Neandertals and the Denisovans, it would appear that they diverged from a common root of premodern humans (Figure 5.26). That divergence occurred long ago enough to have resulted in the degree of their genetic difference. However, Neandertals and Denisovans are more similar to one another than either is to anatomically modern humans, meaning that the premodern line that led to anatomically modern humans branched before the Neandertal/Denisovan line went its not quite separate way.

Just as we saw in the comparison of the Neandertal and anatomically modern human genome reconstructions, geneticists have found that a snippet of Denisovan DNA is present in the modern human genome. Specifically, it represents about 5% of the genome of some modern human populations in East Asia, especially in Melanesians and the aboriginal people of Australia (Gibbons 2011c; Rasmussen et al. 2011). In fact, a recent study has pinpointed some of the functions of Denisovan DNA in modern human populations, suggesting that significant elements of the immune system were inherited from the Denisovans (Abi-Rached et al. 2011).

Replacement or Continuity?

At least as it now stands, the cumulative data in archaeology and genomic research seem to support the following scenario. Ancient human ancestors evolved in Africa and spread from there first to Asia and then to Europe about 1.8 million years ago (Chapter 4). Various forms of premodern human beings evolved in Africa, Europe (especially the Neandertals), and Asia. Anatomically modern human beings evolved in one place, Africa, by about 200,000 years ago and spread out from there. Their entry point to the rest of the world was the Middle East; they arrived there sometime before 100,000 years ago. While there, at about 80,000 years ago, they encountered a population of a different kind of human, Neandertals, who likely were migrating south, fleeing very tough glacial conditions in Europe. The AMH and Neandertal populations interacted and, in a few cases, actually interbred. The reason there is no Neandertal DNA among modern Africans is that the Neandertals didn't live in Africa, so only the AMH migrants to the Middle East encountered them. Interestingly, new genetic evidence seems to show that ancient AMH populations in Africa were contemporaries of non-Neandertal premodern humans and interacted and interbred with them as well (Hammer et al. 2011). Again, the influence of archaic DNA is small (the authors estimate that 2% of the modern African human genome can be traced to archaic intrusion about 35,000 years ago). As our anatomically modern ancestors expanded to the east, they encountered at least one other premodern group with whom they interacted and interbred: the Denisovans. All of us alive today can, ultimately, be traced to the first anatomically modern humans in Africa. We are all, appropriating the phrase of composer, singer, and anthropologist Johnny Clegg, "scatterlings of Africa."

So which view holds sway: replacement or multiregionalism? Okay, it's all Byzantine and complicated, but here we go: It appears that the replacement view, though supported by the archaeological evidence, has, in its pure form, been invalidated by genomic research. However, a modified replacement approach still works; geneticist Svante Pääbo characterizes the development of modern human beings as "leaky replacement" with the vast majority of what makes us human derived from an African source that evolved 200,000 years ago, but with a dose here and there of genetic material from possibly three different and now-extinct

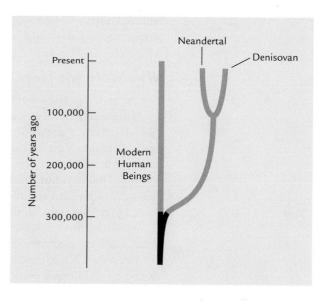

▲ **Figure 5.26**
One view of the chronological and genealogical relationships among anatomically modern human beings, the Neandertals, and the Denisovans.

archaic humans (Gibbons 2011b). We'll go with that for the time being until the always required additional, clarifying data is forthcoming.

Why Were the Neandertals Replaced?

The Neandertals and other premodern humans are extinct, having been replaced by anatomically modern human beings. In the view presented in this book, the Neandertals were not the immediate ancestors of modern people but rather a side branch of human evolution, at least partially overlapping in time with anatomically modern human beings. What significant advantages did the early anatomically modern humans have over the premoderns that led to the survival of the modern humans and the extinction of the premoderns? The European fossil record may shed light on this question.

As alluded to in Chapter 2, the human skeleton preserves a record of dietary deficiencies suffered during its developmental years. For example, **Harris lines,** cracks on the ends of long bones (arm and leg) that result from dietary deficiency during the developing years, and **enamel hypoplasia,** zones of thin tooth enamel that result from unmet nutritional needs during early childhood, are present to a far greater degree in Neandertal remains than in the remains of early anatomically modern human beings. Marsha Oglivie, Bryan Curran, and Erik Trinkaus (1989), for example, found evidence of hypoplasia in the enamel of 36% of 669 Neandertal teeth, reflecting an estimated incidence of 75% in the individuals represented. This is more than double the incidence in nutritionally stressed recent human samples (Oglivie, Curran, and Trinkaus 1989:30). Other studies have produced similar results (Brennan 1991; Molnar and Molnar 1985). As Olga Soffer (1994) points out, this paleopathological evidence indicates that Neandertal children suffered far more physical stress than did their anatomically modern contemporaries.

Archaeologist Mary Stiner (1994) has determined that anatomically modern humans were more adept than the Neandertals at wringing every last bit of nutrition out of those foods that were available in Pleistocene Europe. Neandertals broke open animal bones to extract the rich protein of the marrow, whereas anatomically modern humans boiled the bones to get at the same food source. Stiner estimates that you can extract twice as much fat out of a bone by boiling it (as cited in Balter 2001).

This superiority of the cultural adaptation of the early anatomically modern human beings appears to have been the key to their success. Even though the Neandertals appear to have been biologically better adapted than anatomically modern human beings to the cold, through the invention and application of a superior cultural buffer that may have included warmer, tailored clothing, superior hearths, and so on, anatomically modern humans were actually better able to survive the cold than the Neandertals. Through reconstruction of local climate conditions where the archaeological sites of Neandertals and anatomically moderns have been found in Europe, researchers Leslie Aiello and Peter Wheeler have shown that the locations where anatomically modern humans lived had median temperatures (specifically, windchills) that were between 4 and 7 degrees Celsius *colder* than the Neandertal sites (Balter 2004a).

However we explain it, the archaeological record clearly shows that while Neandertal populations were declining, the population of anatomically modern human beings was experiencing an explosion. Researchers Paul Mellars and Jennifer French (2011) performed a meta-analysis of the archaeological assemblages in western Europe. Specifically, they looked at the number of sites, the sizes of each site, and the density of tools at those sites dating to the Late Pleistocene. Though, of course, we don't have census data for this period, the authors used the variables of site count, size, and artifact density as proxy measures for population size. They then compared the numbers for late Neandertal and early AMH sites. The authors concluded that there was as much as a 10-fold increase in population between the time of Neandertal dominance and AMH replacement in Europe after 40,000 years ago. This would seem to represent another clear picture of Neandertals fading away into extinction while our anatomically modern direct ancestors thrived.

Our anatomically modern human ancestors were not precisely adapted to the environmental conditions of late Pleistocene Europe, as were the Neandertals, and this likely contributed to their survival. They were not locked into a particular set of environmental circumstances, and when those conditions changed dramatically, they simply were not affected as severely. The essence of the modern adaptation is cultural flexibility, the ability to respond, even to rapid and dramatic environmental changes, by inventing new technologies and approaches to subsistence, housing, clothing, heating, and so on. The key behavioral advantage of modern human beings is our flexibility, that is, our ability to adapt to a wide range of conditions, and this may have meant the difference between survival and extinction in the late Pleistocene.

CASE STUDY CLOSE-UP

THE CAVES NEAR WHERE THE KLASIES RIVER empties into the Indian Ocean may have been first explored scientifically in 1923 during a survey of caves and rock shelters along the South African coast (Figure 5.27: Singer and Wymer 1982). The human remains recovered at Klasies River Mouth (KRM) have already been discussed in this chapter, so the focus here is on the stone-tool assemblage and the faunal remains.

An extensive array of stone tools was recovered at KRM. The vast majority of the tools were made from locally available beach cobble quartzite. Cobbles used by the cave's inhabitants to make tools were available virtually at the doorstep of the Klasies River Mouth caves.

The technology represented at KRM is, in the vernacular of African archaeology, a Middle Stone Age (MSA) industry, which means that it is essentially Mousterian in its technology. For the duration of the Late Middle Stone Age occupation of the caves, the inhabitants were removing flakes of various shapes and sizes from carefully prepared nodules of stone in a manner not unlike that of their European contemporaries.

Compared to European Mousterian industries, however, KRM technology exhibits a number of more finely made long flakes, called blades, with parallel or slightly subparallel (gently converging) sides (see Figure 5.25). Some blades with converging edges had been further flaked, after removal from their cores, into apparent spearpoints. Some of these tools seem, in a general way, to anticipate later, more advanced Late Stone Age industries in Africa and even the Aurignacian industry of the European Upper Paleolithic, to be discussed in Chapter 6. It is probably not coincidental that these more advanced-looking tools are found associated with modern-looking humans. Faunal analysis of the bone assemblage at KRM

▶ **Figure 5.27**
The area around the caves at Klasies River Mouth, South Africa. (From *The Middle Stone Age at Klasies River Mouth, South Africa*, by Ronald Singer and John Wymer, University of Chicago Press, 1982)

supports the notion that hunting played a major role in the inhabitants' subsistence. We know that the inhabitants of KRM and other Middle Stone Age sites in coastal South Africa were among the first people in the world to exploit aquatic resources, including shellfish, seals, penguins, fish, and sea birds (Klein 1977).

A detailed analysis by Richard G. Milo of the Klasies River Mouth faunal assemblage shows that the inhabitants were active hunters of large game animals (Bower 1997). About 20% of the 5,400 animal bones examined showed signs of butchery, often in areas that indicate the humans at Klasies were extracting prime cuts of meat, not just scavenging what carnivores had left behind (there are few signs of carnivores gnawing on the bones). Beyond this, a stone spearpoint was found embedded in the cervical vertebrae of a giant buffalo. Milo's analysis indicates that anatomically modern human beings were hunting in a behaviorally modern way by 100,000 years ago in South Africa.

Summary

Beginning as much as 600,000 years ago, existing hominids gave way to more modern-looking hominid forms. With a mean cranial capacity exceeding 1,220 cc, the brain size of these premodern humans falls well within the modern human range. One sort of premodern human, the Neandertal, is the best known of these. Present in large numbers in Europe and southwest Asia, Neandertals were successful and intelligent hominids. There is evidence that they cared for their sick, buried their dead, and were the first human ancestor to produce art. The preponderance of evidence seems to indicate that the Neandertals were physically specialized to life in Ice Age Europe and represent an extinct side-branch of human evolution.

Two different models have been proposed to explain the evolution from premodern to anatomically modern human beings. The replacement model maintains that anatomically modern people evolved just once from a population of premodern *Homo sapiens* living in Africa, sometime between close to 200,000 years ago. After 100,000 years ago, these first anatomically modern humans expanded beyond the boundaries of Africa, encountering and replacing indigenous groups of premodern *Homo sapiens* and even, possibly, *Homo erectus*, which had reached Europe and Asia during a previous period of hominid expansion out of Africa. The multiregional model proposes that anatomically modern humans evolved as a group across all of Africa, Europe, and Asia, together and simultaneously. Gene flow resulting from mating was sufficient to move newly evolved modern traits throughout the many premodern populations but was not sufficient to swamp local physical features, which have been maintained into the present era as so-called racial characteristics. The data discussed in this chapter, consisting of skeletal evidence, artifacts, and genetics, seem to lend support to a "leaky replacement" model in which we owe most, but not all, of our genetic legacy to our African forebears.

TO LEARN MORE

Michael Balter's article in the October 9, 2009, issue of *Nature* provides a good summary of some of the complicated issues surrounding the nature of the relationship between Neandertal and anatomically modern human beings. Who the Neandertals were and what happened to them are mysteries that have captured the popular imagination. As a result, there is no shortage of popular articles and books focusing on these extinct members of the human lineage. Paul Jordan (2001b) has written a wonderful book on the Neandertal question titled, simply, *Neanderthal*. Another terrific recent book is *The Neanderthal's Necklace: In Search of the Fast Thinkers*, written by Juan Luis Arsuaga (2002), one of the excavators of the Atapuerca pre-Neandertals. Christopher Stringer's (2012b) *The Origins of Our Species* focuses on the topic of its title. Finally, if you're looking for a popular summary article that puts the story of human evolution together as we now understand it, there's no better source than the article by Alison Brooks (2010), "What Does It Mean to Be Human? A Behavioral Perspective," in the Spring issue of the newsletter *AnthroNotes*, published by the Smithsonian Institution.

Web links for this chapter can be found at www.oup.com/us/feder

KEY TERMS

anatomically modern
   Homo sapiens, 148
archaic *Homo sapiens*, 131
Aurignacian, 159
blade, 156
Châtelperronian, 159
enamel hypoplasia, 164
gene flow, 150

Harris lines, 164
Kibish Formation, 147
Levallois, 134
mitochondrial
   DNA, 128
Mousterian, 142
multiregional (regional
   continuity) model, 150

musculoskeletal
   hypertrophy, 141
nuclear DNA, 160
patrilocality, 144
premodern *Homo sapiens*, 131
pressure flaking, 157
replacement model, 149
tool kit, 143

6

Expanding Intellectual Horizons

Art and Ideas in the Upper Paleolithic and Late Stone Age

CHAPTER OVERVIEW

The Upper Paleolithic of Europe and Asia and the New Stone Age of Africa are marked by dramatic changes in human culture the world over. Some of these changes seem to be rooted in developments seen among the earliest anatomically modern human beings of Africa. The 77,000-year-old polished bone tools and incised ochre objects found in Blombos Cave, in South Africa, seem to presage an explosion in stone and bone technology and in the artistic impulse. After 50,000 years ago, we see a dramatic shift toward a lithic technology based on the production of blade tools; an expansion in the subsistence quest; an increase in site size; use of raw materials like bone, shell, and antler; the production of nonutilitarian objects; the use of exotic materials; the elaboration of burials; and the production of true art in the form of cave paintings and portable sculptures. The tools and art of the Upper Paleolithic and New Stone Age are, even to current members of the human family, recognizably the product of a modern level of human intelligence.

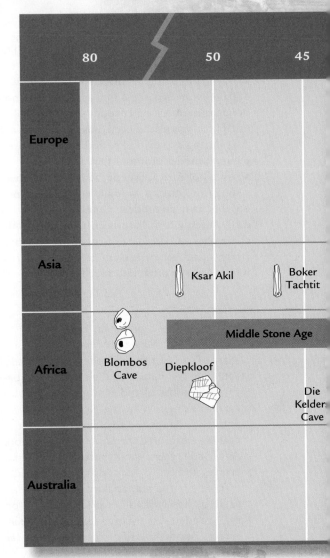

Thousands of years ago

| 40 | 35 | 30 | 25 | 20 | 15 | 10 |

Aurignacian Gravettian Solutrean Magdelanian

Fumane Cave

Hohle Fels Cave

Kent's Cavern
Arcy-sur-Cure
Chauvet

Cussac Cave

Abri Pataud

Dolni Vestonice I

Sungir'

Cosquer Cave

Peche-Merle,
Jouclas,
Sungir'

Cosquer

Lascaux

Altamira,
Niaux,
Fonte de Gaume,
Rouffignac,
Les Combarelles,
Les Trois-Frères
Rocher de la Peine

Mother Grundy's Parlour,
Gough's Cave,
Enlène Cave

Pavlov

Kostenki-Borshevo

Mal'ta

Amvrosievka

Late Stone Age

Haua Fteah

Apollo 11 Cave

Eland's Bay Cave

Panaramitee North

Wharton Hill

Koonalda Cave

IT'S ALMOST A CLICHÉ HERE IN North America that the broad, blank panels of our refrigerator doors serve as personal art galleries on which we display the creative work of our kids. On paper canvases their boldly colored images in crayon, pencil, ink, paint, chalk, and marker decorate our kitchen appliances.

Who could deny the obvious talent of these young artists? More to the point, who could deny their humanity? Although there have been entertaining attempts to get zoo animals to produce works of art (chimpanzees and elephants), which then sell for ridiculous sums (at least they raise money for financially strapped zoos), only human beings possess the desire, the ability, and perhaps even the *need* to produce art.

Educational psychologists have long pondered the significance of the universal and unique human behavior of producing art, which manifests itself even when we are quite young (DiLeo 1970; Gardner 1980; G. Thomas and Silk 1990). For the best-known child development researcher, Jean Piaget (Piaget and Inhelder 1969), drawings reflect the developmental stages a child's intellect passes through on the road to adulthood.

Some researchers have emphasized the sensory pleasure kids obtain (both motor and visual) from producing a picture; still others (Arnheim 1956) have suggested that drawing and painting are simply "universally satisfying." I'm not even sure what that means. Nevertheless, I am certain that most of you passed through the well-established stages of symbolic/artistic achievement, unaware of the arguments among psychologists over the significance of your accomplishments. Each of you has been a link in a long chain of human beings—first as children, later as adults—who have applied pigment to paper and, really quite astonishingly, produced something that was initially just in our heads but now resides outside of them. This chain begins perhaps more than 90,000 years ago with our anatomically modern ancestors and continues to the present. The periods when we see the explosion of uniquely modern human capacities like artistic, symbolic expression—the Upper Paleolithic and Late Stone Age—are the focus of this chapter.

WE LIVE IN A TIME WHEN we are constantly being bombarded by new technologies that, once introduced, progress at a dizzying pace. iPods, iPads, iPhones, and laptop computers didn't even exist two decades ago and now they're nearly ubiquitous. Buy one of those devices today and you can guarantee that, in 6 months, there will be a more advanced, faster, thinner, glossier, shinier, far more awesome, even more "insanely great" (a Steve Jobs term), and less expensive version.

New Ideas: Reflections of the Modern Human Mind

The temporally overlapping Late Stone Age of Africa and Upper Paleolithic of Europe and Asia were also times of invention and technological development when, as paleoanthropologist Lyn Wadley (2009) characterizes it, our ancestors first exhibited evidence of "complex cognition." This is reflected by a series of either brand new technologies or older technologies that experienced a great leap forward. Among these technologies or behaviors that characterize the Late Stone Age and Upper Paleolithic are: 1. the reliance on new and improved stone-tool technologies; 2. new hunting and weapons technologies; 3. a broadening of the subsistence quest; 4. branching out in raw materials; 5. new uses for plant materials; 6. the acquisition of raw materials from a great distance; 7. larger sites of population aggregation; 8. an abundance of nonutilitarian objects; 9. elaborate burials; and 10. symbolic expression through the production of art.

1. New and Improved Stone-Tool Technologies

I realize that in my discussion of stone-tool technology, I keep revisiting the lessons learned in my experimental archaeology course where students attempt to replicate ancient stone tools. As I mentioned in Chapter 3, almost everyone is capable of making replicas of 2.4-million-year-old Oldowan choppers and flake tools. As I went on to note in Chapter 4, 1.8-million-year-old Acheulean handaxes are a bit more challenging, but some students are capable of making pretty good replicas. When it comes to the Upper Paleolithic stone-tool technologies just mentioned, however, a far smaller proportion of my students become proficient at replicating the tools. Nonetheless, it is an interesting exercise, the most important lesson of which may be that the tools appear to be as much a reflection of art as craft. Upper Paleolithic blade tools, in their graceful symmetry, appear to be the result of an attempt to make something as beautiful as it is useful. Their manufacture, therefore, is an entirely human process.

Though in the previous chapter we saw that blade tools first appear in the African archaeological record about 500,000 years ago, and evidence for a blade-based stone-tool technology dates to 240,000 years ago in Kenya and 90,000 years ago in southern Africa, it wasn't until as recently as 52,000 years ago that blade making spread into Europe and Asia. For example, at Boker Tachtit in Israel (Marks 1990, 1993) and Ksar Akil in Lebanon (Ohnuma and Bergman 1990), the shift from Levallois technology to a stone-tool technology based on the production of elongated blades occurred by as much as 52,000 years ago at Ksar Akil and 45,000 years ago at Boker Tachtit (Figure 6.1; Marks 1993:12). South of this, in Africa, Late Stone Age sites like Haua Fteah Cave show this shift to have

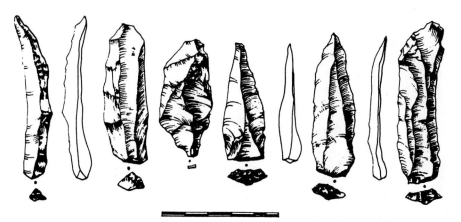

▲ **Figure 6.1**
Stone blades from the site of Ksar Akil in Lebanon. This technology, based on the production of stone blades, dates back to before 40,000 and may be as old as 52,000 years old at this site. (Reprinted from Paul Mellars, ed., *The Emergence of Modern Humans: An Archaeological Perspective*. Copyright © 1990 Edinburgh University Press. Used by permission of the publisher, Cornell University Press.)

occurred by about 40,000 B.P. (Van Peer and Vermeersch 1990). In central and southeastern Europe, the shift from Mousterian flake to Upper Paleolithic blade production occurred before 40,000 B.P. (Svoboda 1993); in western Europe, the shift seems to have occurred a bit later, about 38,000 B.P. (Allsworth-Jones 1990).

The blade technologies of the Upper Paleolithic are short-lived, and change is greatly accelerated. In western Europe, for example, the **Aurignacian** tradition consisted of a specific set of tools that included retouched blades, engraving tools called burins, and stone scrapers, and it is dated to between 34,000 B.P. and 27,000 B.P. From 27,000 B.P. to 21,000 B.P., the **Gravettian** tradition developed, with its emphasis on smaller blades and denticulate knives. The **Solutrean** tradition, dated from 21,000 B.P. to 16,000 B.P., is the most striking of all, characterized by finely made, bifacially flaked, symmetrical, leaf-shaped projectile points. Solutrean points are among the most finely made stone tools ever found (Figure 6.2). The Solutrean was followed by the **Magdelanian**, from 16,000 B.P. to 11,000 B.P., when the emphasis was not on stone tools at all but rather on bone and antler, with the attendant production of microblades.

Artifacts from the various industries of the Upper Paleolithic reveal two very important facts. First, lithic technology had become more complex and elaborate, with a number of different manufacturing techniques that used stone more efficiently; produced more effective tools for cutting, scraping, piercing, and so on; and yielded objects far more symmetrical, balanced, and aerodynamic than those of the Middle Paleolithic. From our twenty-first-century vantage point (or, perhaps, bias), Upper Paleolithic and Late Stone Age industries produced tools that are more aesthetically pleasing, more artfully rendered, than those of earlier traditions.

Second, and equally as important, the profusion of specific tool-tradition names points to one of the most salient differences between the Middle and Upper Paleolithic: Whereas Middle Paleolithic technology was marked by relative homogeneity temporally and geographically, Upper Paleolithic technology was characterized by an explosion of toolmaking diversity marked by relatively rapid change and far greater geographic variability.

2. New Hunting and Weapons Technologies

Based in part on a detailed analysis of the fracture patterns present on sharp-pointed stone tools recovered there, researchers believe that residents of Sibudu Cave, South Africa, may have developed an early version of the bow and arrow as much as 64,000 years ago (Lombard and Phillipson 2010). The bow and arrow is a complex tool whose production requires a series of inventions and skills—understanding the ability to store energy through the bending of a carefully carved piece of wood; the manufacture of a flexible, durable string to add to the stored energy and to release it suddenly; the creation of knots that can both hold tightly and be easily unhooked; and the manufacture of an aerodynamic projectile.

▼ **Figure 6.2**
The stone-tool technology of the Upper Paleolithic included the production of beautifully flaked, symmetrical spearpoints shaped like a willow leaf. Solutrean spearpoints like these, made more than 18,000 years ago, represent, in an aesthetic sense, some of the finest stone tools ever made. (K. L. Feder)

Also in Sibudu Cave, in a level dating to more than 70,000 years ago, scientists discovered on some of the stone-tool bases a residue consisting of a mixture of *Acacia* gum, beeswax, and ochre (Wadley, Hodgskiss, and Grant 2009). In a replicative experiment, those same scientists determined that the residue was a carefully crafted adhesive intended to firmly attach stone tools to handles. As they point out, the production of the adhesive was a "multilevel" operation (p. 9593), requiring a consistent and coordinated set of procedures done in the correct order, with ingredients mixed together in proper proportions and heated to the correct temperature for a successful outcome.

The **spear-thrower** was an innovation of the Upper Paleolithic and Late Stone Age. In a wonderful example of how words can move across temporal and cultural barriers, modern scholars often use the term "atlatl" instead of "spear-thrower." Atlatl is a word in the native language of the Aztecs of Mexico (see Chapter 12). So we now commonly apply a sixteenth-century Aztec word for devices developed in Europe more than 30,000 years ago. The atlatl is an elongated, hooked handle that attaches to the butt of a spear and effectively increases the length of the arm of the person throwing the spear. A longer arm increases the contact time between the inception of the throw and the release, allowing for greater accuracy, speed, and distance; it works for the same reason a baseball pitcher with a long arm can often throw the ball harder and faster than can someone with a shorter pitching arm. The spear-thrower is a remarkable example of applied physics practiced by ancient humans. By artificially extending the arm—and by exploiting the stored energy in the bending shaft of the dart as it is thrown—both ancient people and the Aztecs were able to dramatically increase the accuracy as well as the power with which they could launch a spear in the quest for food or in battle.

Experiments have compared the force of various methods of propelling a projectile. The force of a dart thrown with a spear-thrower far exceeds that generated by a hand-thrown spear, a traditional bow, or even a modern compound bow (Karl and Bruchert 1997). Spears propelled by a spear-throwing device have been clocked at more than 100 mph, and a computer-designed spear-thrower recently produced a record throw of 250 m (over 800 ft)!

Spear-throwers date back to as much as 30,000 years ago. The bearers of this technology certainly had an advantage in the hunt over those who needed to get much closer to large, dangerous animals in order to successfully spear them. A 13,000-year-old spear-thrower from Enlène Cave, France, was carved from reindeer antler (Dennell 1986). Along with being a useful tool, this spear-thrower is far more beautiful than it had to be; the handle was finely carved into the image of two ibexes (mountain goats) locked in combat (Figure 6.3).

Finally, there is circumstantial evidence for another hunting technology at Sibudu Cave in South Africa. Lyn Wadley (2010) suggests that the abundance of small, forest-dwelling animals among the food remains dating there to 65,000 years ago is an indication that the residents may have developed traps and snares, as these smaller creatures would have been extremely difficult to hunt with projectiles.

3. Broadening the Subsistence Base

Undeniably, the hunting of big game—**megafauna**—made a significant contribution to the subsistence of Upper Paleolithic people. In central and eastern Europe, for example, sites dating between 28,000 B.P. and 10,000 B.P. reflect the

▶ **Figure 6.3**
Two ibexes wrestle on this fragment of a spear-thrower. The fine carving of this artifact is diagnostic of the Upper Paleolithic, an example of the great skill and artistic abilities of this period. (Musée de l'Homme; photo by D. Destable)

major role of the woolly mammoth in the subsistence base of Upper Paleolithic people. At a single site, Dolni Vestonice I, researchers have identified the remains of more than 100 mammoths butchered by the inhabitants (Soffer 1993). At this same site, butchering marks have been located on the remains of horse and reindeer as well.

The situation is much the same in Africa and western Europe, where Upper Paleolithic and Late Stone Age inhabitants exploited local large game animals. In Siberia, the site of Mal'ta near Irkutsk shows extensive hunting of woolly mammoth and reindeer. In South Africa, at Late Stone Age sites such as Die Kelders Cave and Eland's Bay Cave, remains of eland (a large antelope) are abundant, and there is evidence of the hunting of the Cape buffalo, a far more dangerous animal and one avoided during the Middle Stone Age (Klein 1983). In the Upper Paleolithic of western Europe, at sites such as Abri Pataud in France, excavators found the bones of reindeer, elephant, horse, and wild cattle (R. White 1982). At Mother Grundy's Parlour, a cave occupation site in Great Britain dating to about 12,000 B.P., the remains of woolly rhinoceros and mammoth, reindeer, and wild horse were found (C. Smith 1992). Also in Great Britain, Gough's Cave shows extensive use of wild horse and red deer more than 12,200 years ago (C. Smith 1992).

Following the pattern established at a few Middle Stone Age sites of anatomically modern humans in Africa, most notably Klasies River Mouth, Die Kelders, and Blombos Cave, the remains of fish have been found at Late Stone Age sites. The same South African sites just mentioned, for example, show evidence of the extensive reliance on seals, penguins, dolphins, mollusks, and flying shorebirds (Henshilwood et al. 2002; Klein 1983:43). The bones or shells of these organisms have been found, along with grooved-stone net weights used in fishing and possible early fishhooks (called "gorges") that were baited and attached to lines.

Small mammals also contributed to the food quest. At Dolni Vestonice I and at the nearby site of Pavlov, there is indirect evidence of the use of nets in hunting small game (Pringle 1997). Fragments of netting made by the inhabitants of these sites, dating from between 29,000 and 22,000 years ago, had accidentally been pressed into the clay floors of the inhabitants' houses. In a few cases, those houses burned and the impressions of the netting were preserved in the baked clay. The nets were sophisticated, indicating a probable long tradition of net weaving (Adovasio, Soffer, and Klima 1996). The netting mesh was too fine to have been used to capture large animals, but there are plenty of bones of smaller creatures, including hare and fox, at these sites. A large hare can produce 6 pounds of meat and a pelt. Driving small mammals like hares into nets is an efficient hunting technique that all members of a social group can participate in—the very young and the aged, pregnant or nursing females, and, of course, young males in their prime. It seems likely, therefore, that net hunting played a substantial role in subsistence at these and other sites that date to the same period (Pringle 1998).

Plant foods also contributed to the diets of our anatomically modern human ancestors. Sarah Mason has found the burned residue of edible taproots in hearths at Dolni Vestonice I (Pringle 1998). And berries have been found in hearths at other Upper Paleolithic sites. It is highly unlikely that Upper Paleolithic people overlooked important sources of protein, carbohydrates, or vitamins available in their territories. Portrayals of ancient hunters fighting a daily duel to the death with huge, aggressive beasts may offer us a romantic image, but it seems an unlikely strategy for survival. It is far more likely that the people of the Upper Paleolithic subsisted on a broad spectrum of foods, including the meat from animals both large and small, birds, fish, seeds, nuts, berries, and starchy roots. Archaeological evidence is finally beginning to support this sensible reconstruction.

4. Branching Out in Raw Materials and Developing New Technologies

We begin to see a branching out in the use of raw materials by anatomically modern people in the African Middle Stone Age. In the same Middle Stone Age layers at Blombos Cave dating to 77,000 years ago in which incised ochre rods were recovered (see the beginning of this chapter), researchers found 28 precisely crafted bone tools (Henshilwood et al. 2001; Figure 6.4). Inhabitants of the cave made bone awls and apparent spearpoints in a way that implies a strict adherence to a sequence of steps throughout the toolmaking process. As the formal and consistent fashioning of bone tools is not seen at the sites of premodern humans, the Blombos researchers conclude that this is one indicator of the technological sophistication of the anatomically modern humans who inhabited the cave, more than 25,000 years before the inception of the Late Stone Age in Africa and the Upper Paleolithic in Europe and Asia.

In another example of early symbolic expression, French archaeologist Pierre-Jean Texier has reported the discovery of etched ostrich eggshells at Diepkloof Rock Shelter in South Africa (Bower 2010). The makers of the art scratched a series of parallel and perpendicular lines into the surfaces of the eggshells producing what appears to be, for all intents and purposes, a pattern of regular and consistent doodling.

▲ Figure 6.4
This finely sharpened
awl is one among
28 precisely crafted,
technologically
sophisticated bone
tools recovered at
Blombos Cave, South
Africa, dating to more
than 70,000 years ago.
(Photograph courtesy of
Chris Henshilwood, African
Heritage Institute, Cape
Town)

Although the use of bone tools after 50,000 years ago may not have been absolutely innovative, the use of bone, as well as ivory, antler, and shell for the production of tools used in sewing—for example, awls, punches, and needles—and for hunting equipment—for example, spear tips—is a virtual hallmark of the Upper Paleolithic. For example, along the Dnestr River in Russia, Upper Paleolithic sites have produced slotted daggers of reindeer antler. At the Kosoutsy site in this same region, reindeer antler was also used as a raw material to manufacture spearpoints for use in the hunt, and thin slivers of reindeer bone were used in the production of eyed needles (Borziyak 1993).

Eyed needles allowed for more precisely tailored and sewn clothing. The production of protective outergarments that were, at least to a degree, windproof and waterproof, with seams stitched tightly through the use of such needles, would have been extremely important as people spread into colder climates, fundamentally inhospitable to our tropically evolved and adapted ancestors. In no small measure, tight, weatherproof seams enabled by thin, eyed needles made expansion into places like the Arctic a more reasonable possibility for ancient humans. Direct evidence of the production of tailored clothing comes from the 22,000-year-old site of Sungir', just north of Moscow, in Russia as well as Jouclas, in France (Dennell 1986). Beads used for fastening were found in a pattern in the ground at Sungir', outlining what appears to have been pants, a shirt or jacket, a cap, and shoes (Klein 1989; R. White 1993).

When rock shatters on its own as a result of freezing and thawing, by skittering along in a flowing stream, or even just by gravity hurling a stone downhill into another one, it can accidently and coincidently produce sharp, sometimes useful edges. It has never seemed to me that it was that big of an intellectual leap for our ancestors to have figured out that one can take out of the equation the serendipity of natural, fortuitous breakage and, instead, intentionally shatter rock in a consistent way to make tools with specific uses in mind. It does not surprise me that our ancestors figured this out more than 2.6 million years ago (see Chapter 3).

This kind of obvious experiential evidence about what happens to rocks when you smash them, however, doesn't really apply to the development of ceramic technology. There simply aren't very many natural processes an individual regularly encounters in nature in which a high temperature is accidently applied to a mushy, kind of sticky dirt, producing a durable, waterproof, and largely fireproof material. There's no obvious pathway in nature to a "eureka" moment: "Hey, I bet I can intentionally shape a vessel from that mushy, sticky dirt, put it in a fire, and make a sweet pot or bowl for myself, suitable for cooking mammoth stew, serving salsa, or whatever."

Therefore, I am deeply impressed that our ancestors had figured exactly this out as much as 20,000 years ago. A number of Upper Paleolithic figurines found in Europe (some of the so-called Venus figurines discussed later in this chapter) were made from fired clay. Perhaps, in this case, the original intention was to produce a figurine from that mushy, sticky dirt and then, "oops," it was dropped in the fire by accident, and "wow," instead of melting or burning, which you might have expected, it maintained its shape and became hard and durable.

Perhaps of even greater significance than the accidental production of ceramic figurines was the manufacture of pottery vessels in China, at a site in Xianrendong Cave in Jiangxi Province. There, archaeologists have found ceramic sherds representing the oldest pottery discovered anywhere in the world so far. A series of radiocarbon dates derived from organic material collected from the lowest layer in the cave in which pottery sherds were also recovered produced dates in the range of 19,000 to 20,000 years ago (Wu et al. 2012). Certainly, this is impressive as an example of branching out in the use of raw materials and in the invention of a new technology. This is also significant in terms of what pottery vessels provide: efficient, durable, easily made cooking and storage vessels. Pottery is a game changer: Clay is abundant and easily obtained; a durable, waterproof cooking pot increases the ability to extract energy from various foods, including meats and starches (Carmody, Weintraub, and Wrangham 2011); sealable storage vessels can protect foods from rodents. The Chinese evidence indicates that this happened in the Upper Paleolithic/Late Stone Age and represents another significant technological achievement of the people who lived during this period.

5. New Uses for Plant Materials

There is evidence in Sibudu Cave for a particular kind of domestic practice using local plant material. Archaeology in the cave revealed that more than 70,000 years ago, residents lined the floor with plant material, including species that possess a natural insecticide (Wadley et al. 2011). Those who visit the cave today remark on the abundant presence of mosquitos in the area, so no doubt any natural way to keep these annoying and possibly disease-carrying insects away would have been helpful.

6. The Acquisition of Raw Materials from a Great Distance

The ability to obtain raw materials and manufactured goods from great distances might seem to be a feature strictly of modern societies. Look around your house and try counting the goods that originated in other countries—stereo equipment and cameras manufactured in Japan, clothing made in India, and so on. The last time I purchased an iPod, I was able to track it from the factory where it was manufactured in Shanghai, China, to my house in Connecticut; my iPod's trip from its place of manufacture to my house took all of about two days. Amazing.

Whereas Middle Paleolithic people relied on raw materials whose source was close to their habitations, in the Upper Paleolithic we see far more extensive use of raw materials available only at great distances from living sites. For example, at the Kostenki-Borshevo sites in Russia, inhabitants used local lithic materials (quartzite and brown and yellow flint) in making stone tools. Also used, however, was a black flint that possessed superior chipping qualities (it chipped more regularly) but was not available in the Kostenki-Borshevo region. Trace element analysis (see Chapter 2) of the raw materials recovered at the site suggests that the flint obtained by the inhabitants of the Kostenki-Borshevo region for their artifacts actually came from a source 300 km (186 mi) distant (Klein 1969:227).

The situation is much the same throughout the geographic extent of Upper Paleolithic cultures. For example, in Moravia, in south-central Europe, flint commonly was moved across distances of 100 km (62 mi) from its source (Oliva 1993:52). In rare instances, apparently highly valued material like obsidian (volcanic glass) from Hungary is found in Paleolithic sites up to 500 km (310 mi) away (Oliva 1993:52). Even where quite serviceable stone was available locally, material obtainable only from great distances was often used. Archaeologist Martin Oliva (1993) suggests that maintaining long-distance contacts through trade seems to have been more important than the specific qualities of the lithics themselves and that the stone and its trade took on more of a ritual meaning than just a utilitarian significance. The use of raw materials from great distances away by Upper Paleolithic peoples implies a greater reliance on trade with distant groups and perhaps also implies broader social networks (hypothetically maintained by seasonal get-togethers evidenced at the aggregation sites) than anything seen in Middle Paleolithic contexts.

7. Larger Sites of Population Aggregation

Middle Paleolithic sites tend to be small, representative of the encampments of nomadic, **opportunistic foragers,** who took whatever resources they could wherever they became available, without much planning in advance (Binford 1984). Though Upper Paleolithic sites include similarly small foraging camps, much larger sites also date to the Upper Paleolithic. Randall White (1982) interprets these as places of aggregation, localities where numerous small bands of people would come together seasonally. The site of Mal'ta, in Siberia, for example, covers an area of some 600 m² (about 6,500 ft²; Chard 1974:20); it includes the remains of numerous dwellings whose frames were made from the large bones of woolly mammoth (Figure 6.5). This size is far larger than that of the standard Middle Paleolithic site.

The **settlement pattern** of the Middle Paleolithic with its complement of small sites scattered across the landscape would seem to reflect a strategy

▶ **Figure 6.5**
In the Upper Paleolithic in Siberia, trees were not generally available for construction, but the bones of large game animals were. Shown here is a reconstruction of a dwelling made of mammoth bone (top) and a hide-covered structure with a superstructure of wood, bone, and antler from the site of Mal'ta. (Negative no. 69368fr15, courtesy of the Department of Library Services, American Museum of Natural History)

of **opportunistic foraging,** where people followed resources wherever they might become available. The pattern of subsistence in the Upper Paleolithic appears to be different, at least in part, as reflected by the existence of large sites where populations came together during a yearly cycle. People still lived in nomadic bands, but the movement of the band was no longer unrestricted, instead following a fixed yearly pattern where at least some seasonally occupied sites were returned to each year, perhaps by members of several bands.

During the Upper Paleolithic, therefore, the settlement pattern seems to indicate a shift to a fixed seasonal round as part of a strategy of **logistical collecting** (Binford 1984). Subsistence and movements were planned out in advance as people gained a detailed knowledge of their territory, seasonality, and the behavior and shifting locations of the plants and animals on which they subsisted.

Some sites were continually visited by aggregations of related people during fixed and known times of the year when resources may have been particularly abundant at these places—for example, at a topographic bottleneck on a migration route for large animals. Some of these sites, perhaps, became ritually sanctified through the use of artwork to denote the significance of a particular place to the members of the group. This possibility is discussed in the section on the appearance of artwork in the Upper Paleolithic and in "Issues and Debates."

8. Abundance of Nonutilitarian Objects

In my classes I see many students, men and women, wearing nonutilitarian items of personal adornment: necklaces, earrings, nose rings, tongue studs, ear cuffs, finger rings, bracelets, anklets, hairpins. Some have gold and silver draping every extremity and dangling from a multitude of pierced body parts. All our bodies look basically the same, built along one of two fundamental models: male or female. But we have invented numerous ways of decorating ourselves—defining, identifying, and distinguishing ourselves—with objects of adornment.

Artifacts interpretable as items of personal adornment are rare at the sites of premodern humans. The Neandertal site of Arcy-sur-Cure is one of the very few places where multiple objects of personal adornment have been found associated with premoderns (see Figure 5.11). For the most part, stone, bone, antler, shell, or ivory jewelry is restricted to the sites of anatomically modern human beings.

One of the oldest sites where such items of adornment have been found is the Grotte des Pigeons in Morocco, in northwestern Africa. Excavators recovered thirteen perforated mollusk shell ornaments there in a cave level dated to 82,000 years ago (Bower 2007). The perforations appear to have been made intentionally and wear along the margins of the perforations likely resulted when the shells rubbed against a cord from which they likely were suspended.

The same kind of perforated shells have been found in greater numbers at the previously mentioned Blombos Cave in South Africa. There, dating to 75,000 years ago in the same stratigraphic level in which the red ochre mentioned on page 181 was recovered, researchers have found 41 perforated mollusk shell beads (Henshilwood et al. 2004). The perforation appears at the same spot on 36 of the shells—on the back near the lip (Figure 6.6). As was true in the case of the Moroccan artifacts, the location of the holes in the Blombos shells is rarely seen in nature and clearly seems to have been intentional, perhaps to hang the beads in a necklace.

▲ **Figure 6.6**
These perforated shell beads found in Blombos Cave, South Africa, date to 75,000 years ago. They are among the earliest nonutilitarian artifacts yet found by archaeologists and reflect both the capacity and the desire to produce decorative art at this early date. (Courtesy of Chris Henshilwood and the Centre for Development Studies, University of Bergen)

The Grotte des Pigeons and Blombos Cave beads date to the African Middle Stone Age, but it is in the Late Stone Age and Upper Paleolithic when there appears to be an explosion in the production of items of personal adornment and other nonutilitarian objects. For example, a handful of 40,000-year-old sites in Africa, west Asia, and Europe have produced shell beads or perforated teeth, likely intended to be suspended from a necklace. Dating to 15,000 B.P., Mal'ta, in central Asia (Chard 1974), has produced a wealth of items of adornment. A small child was found buried at Mal'ta with a necklace made of bone and antler beads (Figure 6.7). Also found were schematic carvings of birds, a carved bone plaque with designs consisting of dots and wavy lines etched or punched into the surface of the bone, and depictions of human beings (Figure 6.8).

As Randall White (1982) points out, the appearance of items of personal adornment that were often painstakingly made, frequently out of exotic material that must have been difficult to obtain—and therefore "expensive" in terms of time and effort to obtain it—is significant. In White's view, such objects imply increasing awareness and importance of individual identity in Upper Paleolithic society. Whatever the specific significance of the development of items of personal adornment, it seems clear that people in the Upper Paleolithic were much like ourselves.

9. More Elaborate Burials

Whatever your philosophy or religion, the death of a loved one or the contemplation of one's own mortality is pretty momentous stuff. How we dispose of and memorialize our dead is a reflection of how we view death, and the archaeological record has much to tell us about how our ancestors dealt with the end of life.

If the modern folktale is true, a woman in California (sometimes the story has it in Florida) was buried in a nightgown, seated at the wheel of her brand new Jaguar (or Porsche, take your pick). That's certainly making a statement. More commonly, married people may be buried wearing their wedding bands. Devout Christians may be interred with a cross around their neck.

Burying the dead with treasured personal items is a long-standing human tradition. Egyptian pharaohs were buried with food, jewelry, furniture—even other people (see Chapter 10). The emperors of imperial China were buried with chariots and entire life-size ceramic armies of soldiers and horses (see Chapter 11). We see this pattern repeated over and over. Whether because it is believed that the deceased will need such items in the afterlife or simply because of the desire to place some items of personal identification with a departed friend, the practice of burying the dead with objects that were meaningful to them and their loved ones seems nearly universal. See the "Case Study Close-up" in this chapter for an example of elaborate ritual burials in the Upper Paleolithic.

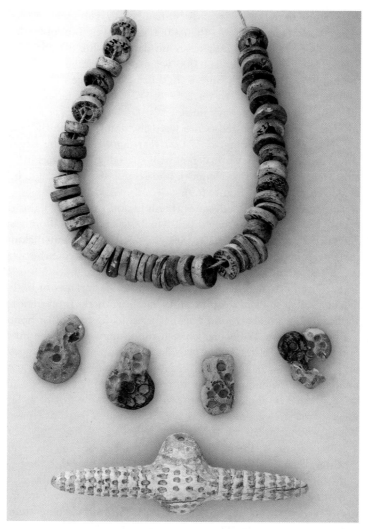

◀ **Figure 6.7**
This necklace, made of antler and bone beads, was found in Siberia at the Upper Paleolithic site of Mal'ta. The site has produced a wealth of beautifully made pieces of artwork including sculpted pieces of bone, antler, and ivory, dating to around 15,000 B.P. (Photograph © The State Hermitage Museum, St. Petersburg)

▲ **Figure 6.8**
This figurine is one of some 30 such artifacts carved from the bone of woolly mammoth found at the site of Mal'ta, in Siberia. (Musée de l'Homme, J. Oster)

10. Symbolic Expression Through the Production of Art

The first possible glimmerings of artistic expression by our anatomically modern human ancestors have now been traced back to about 164,000 years ago at Pinnacle Cave on the Cape of South Africa (Gibbons 2007a). There, archaeologists recovered pieces of the red ochre. Red ochre is a form of hematite, a soft mineral consisting of iron oxide, actually ranging in color from near black through various shades of red and orange. Ground up into a powder and mixed with a binder (animal grease, egg white, or even saliva), ochre has been used by people all over the world to produce red-hued paint.

The ochre pieces recovered at Pinnacle Cave had been worn down by the inhabitants. That may have resulted from the use of ochre powder in a glue used to make tools, but modern people also wear away ochre when they use the pieces like crayons for decorating their own bodies. It is at least possible that the inhabitants of Pinnacle Cave did the same thing.

The use of red ochre by early human beings is also seen at Blombos Cave, also in South Africa, where more than 8,000 pieces were brought in by the inhabitants (Henshilwood et al. 2002; there are no natural ochre deposits in the cave). There, in a layer dated to about 100,000 years ago, researchers found 13 fragments of the mineral, all of which bore unmistakable evidence of incising in the form of a series of parallel lines (Balter 2009a). There also are fan-shaped etchings, cross-hatching, and series of wavy lines.

Pieces of modified red ochre were also found by the Blombos excavators in a level of the cave dating to 77,000 years ago. Two of the larger chunks of the ochre found at this level had regularly spaced incised markings in the form of crosshatching across their lengths, intersected at a right angle by another set of incised, parallel lines (Figure 6.9).

Henshilwood and colleagues (Heshilwood et al. 2011) also discovered what appear to be two ochre-based paint-making stations at Blombos Cave in South Africa in a level dating to 101,000 years ago. Both paint-making kits consisted of an abalone shell and a quartzite cobble grinding stone the appropriate size to fit into the shell itself (in one case the cobble was, indeed, found nestled in the shell). Ground ochre was found on the interior surfaces of both shells, the surfaces of which showed scraping and scratching marks from their use as a grinding surface. The team also found traces of ground-up trabecular bone mixed in with the ground ochre. Trabecular bone is the spongy part of the inside of an animal bone. The spongy bone is rich in fat and the researchers suggest that the most likely reason the paint makers ground it up with the ochre was to supply the binder in the production of a liquid paint. Though we can't speculate about what the paint makers intended to do with the paint, the fact that they made it at all suggests the strong possibility that they intended to paint something and, in so doing, produce art.

The authors of the study admit that it is not possible to determine what the etching means, but they maintain that it is not simple doodling—though that, in and of itself, would be interesting evidence of another kind of modern human practice. They suggest that the markings follow convention; are abstract, unrelated to any real or natural images (the maker was not simply depicting something seen in nature); and may be symbolic—in other words, the markings are symbols that had a certain meaning that could have been "read" by anyone familiar with the

▶ **Figure 6.9**
Among the 8,000 fragments of ochre recovered at Blombos Cave, South Africa, from a habitation level dated to more than 70,000 years ago, was this intentionally incised piece with regular cross-hatching. The markings seem to reflect abstract thinking and symbolic notation by the ancient human beings who inhabited the cave. (Photograph courtesy of Chris Henshilwood. Photo by Francesco d'Errico)

arbitrary code on which the symbols were based. It is not surprising that human beings are capable of this. We do this all the time. What is surprising is that ancient humans may have been doing this as much as 100,000 years ago.

We can imagine many compelling scenes from the human past—for example, australopithecines walking side by side on an African ash bed (Chapter 3) or Neandertals mourning over the remains of a fallen comrade placed in a crudely dug grave. But perhaps none of these is more evocative than an imagined scene of two cave painters from the Upper Paleolithic.

In the dark and distant recesses of a cave's narrow passageway, a flickering oil lamp smears dancing shadows on a flat rock wall. A young woman, tall and muscular, her arms coated with a thin layer of grime and sweat, carefully places a dark slurry in her mouth. Next, she holds a hollow reed to her lips and places her other hand palm down on the rock face. Aiming the reed at the area around her hand, she begins puffing up her cheeks, spraying a fine mist of pigment out of the end of the reed. Some of the paint thinly coats her hand, but much of it covers the cave wall immediately around the area hidden by her palm and fingers. After a few puffs through the reed, she removes her hand from the cave wall, and we see in our mind's eye her remarkable artistic creation: a negative image of her own hand, a signature some 20,000 years old calling out across time.

By her side, a tall and broad young man with a deeply lined face belying his years dips a frayed twig into a thick red paste. Using skills of observation and artistry developed during his short life, he conjures up a vision held in a part of his memory as deep as where he now labors breathlessly in the cave: The horse, wild and free, runs across his mind, her legs leaving the ground as she gallops in her desperate but doomed attempt to flee from the hunters. A deep red gash on her belly where a stone-tipped spear pierced her hide leaks her lifeblood. Soon, he remembers, very soon, she falls, and his comrades are upon her, thrusting their spears deep into her viscera. Then, at last, she is quiet and still. He shudders, thinking of her spirit now returned to the sky. Then he remembers the taste of her flesh in his mouth. Her life lost, the life of his people maintained. It is the way of life and death in the world he knows.

Now long dead and no longer of this life but of another world, a world of stories and magic, the mare lives again in a creation of pigment, memory, awe, and sorcery. Once a creature of blood and bone, of sinew and muscle, she is now a creature of color and binder. No longer running across the plains of western Europe, she now runs and bellows on a flat sheet of rock, straining against her fate and bleeding eternally in the deep recesses of a dark cave. In this incarnation, she has lived for 20,000 years now; and in her life of pigment and memory and magic, she will live forever.

A Revolution of Intellect: The Meaning of Upper Paleolithic Art

As stated previously in this chapter, symbolic expression is a uniquely human ability. Only humans are capable of converting ideas into images that we then can recognize and understand as expressions of those specific ideas. Stick-figure renderings of animals and Michelangelo's paintings on the ceiling of the Sistine Chapel; crude tally marks on sticks of ochre and complex mathematical formulas;

geometric patterns etched into cave walls and the words printed on the pages of anthropology textbooks: All of these involve the use of symbols, some abstract, some realistic. The ability to create and then "read" symbols virtually defines the human mind.

The Earliest Art: Australia and Africa

Though we may not know what the images and objects mean, many artifacts dated to the period beginning about 40,000 years ago clearly denote the use of symbol and the production of art (Figure 6.10). For example, at Wharton Hill in Australia, more than 36,000 years ago, an ancient artist etched an oval shape into the abutting rock face (Bednarik 1993:5; see Chapter 7 for a discussion of the human presence in Australia). To derive a radiocarbon date, archaeologists recovered organic material from inside the groove. Encased in the rock varnish (a weathering rind of rock that builds up on an exposed surface) of the **petro-**

▼ **Figure 6.10**
Upper Paleolithic/ Late Stone Age sites in Australia, Europe, Asia, and Africa.

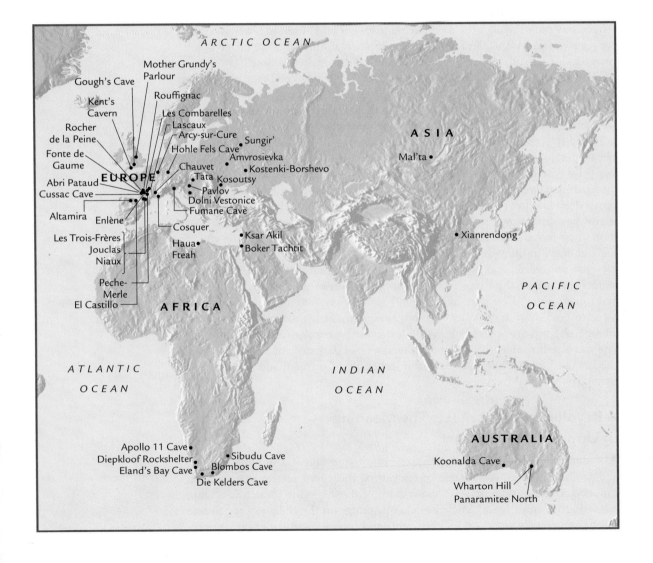

glyph (literally, "rock-writing"), the organic deposit could have gotten into the groove only after the groove was made, providing, therefore, a minimum possible age for the carved oval shape. At the nearby site of Panaramitee North, a curvilinear petroglyph has been dated via the same technique to 43,000 B.P. (Bednarik 1993:6).

The earliest known African art has been dated to as early as 30,000 B.P. (Phillipson 1993). Stone slabs with painted and engraved images of animals have been excavated from deposits dating to this time at the Apollo 11 Cave site in southern Namibia (Balter 2012). The images are naturalistic renderings of the fauna of southern Africa for the time period of their production.

Upper Paleolithic Art in Europe

The artwork of late Pleistocene Europe is far better known than the Australian or the African artwork, partly as a result of geography—it is found in an area where extensive archaeology has been conducted—and partly because of placement—its location in caves has kept it better preserved. In the cave paintings (**parietal art**) and in carved statues and inscribed bone, antler, and ivory (**mobiliary art**), Upper Paleolithic Europeans produced an astounding amount of art (see Figure 6.10). Some of the paintings and inscribed artifacts incorporate geometric designs and abstract images whose meanings are difficult to interpret. In many of the paintings and carvings, though we may never be certain of the artist's intent (see "Issues and Debates"), we cannot help but recognize the images they were producing. Cave walls in France and Spain especially, but also others scattered throughout Europe, are adorned with realistic depictions of the animals of the Upper Paleolithic. Images of prehistoric horse and bison, woolly mammoth and rhinoceros, reindeer and wild cattle flow across cave-wall canvases at places like Lascaux and Altamira, Les Combarelles, Niaux, Les Trois-Frères, Peche-Merle, and Fonte de Gaume (see Figures 6.11 and 6.12; Leroi-Gourhan 1982). Southwestern Europe alone has more than 300 caves with Paleolithic artwork, and more caves are found fairly regularly.

To assess the origins and evolution of cave paintings, it is important to obtain accurate dates for when Paleolithic artists created their truly timeless masterpieces. Unfortunately, this isn't often easy to do; cave paintings can be notoriously difficult to date accurately. When organic material was used in the production of the pigment or binder—for example, charcoal for creating a black paint or animal fat for making the binder to hold the pigment—samples can be retrieved for radiocarbon dating. This, however, involves damaging part of the artwork. Recently, researchers have used a workaround for dating some of the Paleolithic paintings in eleven caves in northwestern Spain.

If you've ever visited a solution cavern (for example, Luray Caverns in Virginia, Carlsbad in New Mexico, or Howe in New York), I'm sure you've seen the results of the development of calcite deposits called flowstone creating the phantasmagorical shapes that characterize these amazing places. In some cases, the slow drip of flowstone has created a thin veneer over cave art, and A. W. G. Pike and colleagues (Pike et al. 2012) have removed some of the calcite overlying paintings and used uranium series dating procedures to date those deposits (see Chapter 2 for a discussion of uranium series dating). Of course, the calcite can only develop over a painting after the painting was produced, so the procedure

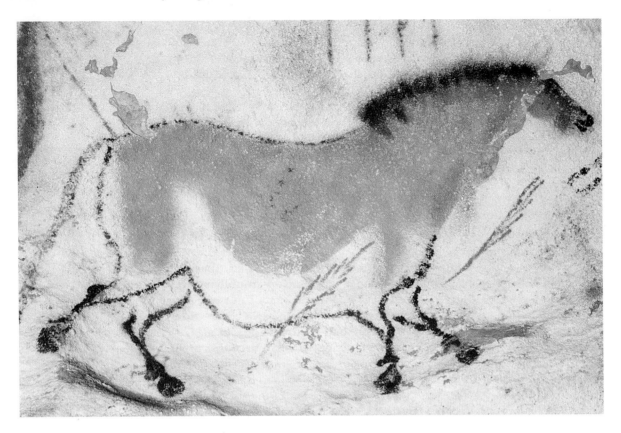

▲ **Figure 6.11**
The so-called Chinese Horse from Lascaux, France, is one of the best known and most beautiful of the Upper Paleolithic cave paintings. Viewing these pieces of art allows us at least in a small way to look at the Upper Paleolithic world through the eyes of those who lived it. (© Robert Harding/Robert Harding World Imagery/Corbis)

provides a date the painting must be greater than. In this way, the researchers determined that the painting of a red disk at El Castillo Cave was more than 40,000 years old, making it the oldest known example of cave art. At the even better-known cave of Altamira, club-shaped designs were coated by calcite dated to nearly 36,000 years ago.

The most exciting find in the last 15 years, Chauvet Cave (Hughes 1995), near Avignon, France, contains an amazing array of paintings. Most people who have seen them consider them some of the most beautiful examples of Paleolithic artwork ever discovered (see Figure 6.12). The dates derived for the artwork represented by the paintings of more than 400 individual animals at Chauvet are stunning: The two oldest dates of the eight derived from carbon samples taken from the organically based paint used to produce the images on the cave walls were close to 32,000 years old (Balter 2008b; Chauvet, Deschamps, and Hillaire 1996).

In their paintings, produced from 32,000 years ago to 10,000 years ago, the artists of the Upper Paleolithic have willed to us evocative images of their natural surroundings and, at the same time, whispered to us of their intellectual world. At Niaux, in France, a prehistoric bison with two spears still hanging from its belly lies dying on a cave wall, recalling for eternity a life and a death that transpired nearly 20,000 years ago. At Rouffignac, also in France, two woolly mammoths confront each other, frozen in an apparent dance for dominance that a human being likely witnessed and then, in art, immortalized. At Chauvet, a group of overlapping, stiff-maned horses, rendered with a degree of realism that can only be described as breathtaking, relax on the cave wall surface as they have for 30,000 years. At Lascaux, a badly injured bison, its viscera hanging from its wounded belly, is facing its human attacker in a final, defiant act of confrontation that can never end. It is a marvelous legacy of art and intellect, one that fascinates us today, tens of thousands of years after the drawings were produced.

Upper Paleolithic artists also depicted themselves, though commonly more schematically and less realistically. One of the oldest of these human portraits was found in 2000 at Cussac Cave, located in the Dordogne Valley in France. More than 100 incised, rather than painted, images of animals including mammoth, rhinoceros, deer, horse, and bison were found on the cave wall. Along with the animals drawn by the Paleolithic artists was the outline of a human female. The skeletal remains of seven people were found in the cave. Radiocarbon dating of their bones provided a date of more than 25,000 years ago, and it is assumed that this is also the date of the images in the cave (Balter 2001).

What might the human depictions mean? Researchers Patricia Rice and Ann Paterson (1988) analyzed more than 100 human images from 32 caves in western Europe. Their statistics are provocative: More than three-quarters of the images are men, who tend to be depicted singly, in an active mode—running, walking, throwing spears. Females tend to be portrayed at rest and in close proximity to other females. What does this mean in terms of the roles of males and females in Paleolithic society? This glimpse into the sexual division of labor in societies that existed more than 15,000 years ago simply is not based on a sample large enough to allow us to draw any conclusions. Though largely enigmatic in the meaning of their images, these caves were clearly not art galleries. In the more than 150 mostly western European caves where significant numbers of paintings have been found, some images overlap and the strange juxtapositioning of the animals—some floating above others, some upside down in relation to others—shows quite clearly that individual paintings and panels were not intended as part of a single tableau. The relative frequency of species depicted and their locations are not

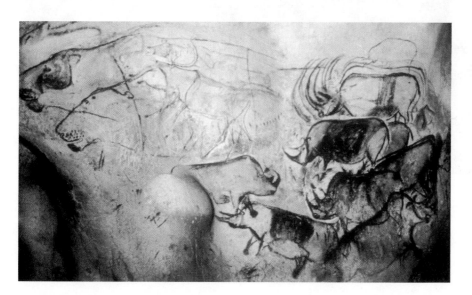

◀ **Figure 6.12**
Rock panel from Chauvet Cave in southern France. Dating to more than 20,000 years ago, Upper Paleolithic artists painted more than 300 animals on the cave wall, including these wonderful depictions of rhinoceroses and lions—animals that inhabited France during the Pleistocene Epoch. (AP/Wide World Photos)

random. Carnivores, for example, are often placed in the least accessible parts of the caves, and the herbivores seem to be depicted in proportion to their significance in the diet of the people who painted them (see "Issues and Debates"). Whereas at some caves animal species that served as food for Paleolithic hunters predominate, Chauvet Cave has quite a few paintings of carnivores: 3 cave lions, a panther, and 15 images of cave bears (the bones of almost 200 of which were also found at the cave, dated to the same period people were painting its walls). Chauvet also presents us with the single largest concentration of paintings of woolly rhinoceroses—50 of them.

Figurines

The art of the Late Stone Age and Upper Paleolithic includes sculptural as well as painted work. Hohle Fels Cave in southwestern Germany has been a proverbial treasure trove of such sculptures and has recently produced the oldest depiction of the human form, a female figurine with greatly exaggerated sexual features, dating to at least 35,000 years ago (Conrad 2009). This early "**Venus figurine**," as these carvings of the female form are generally called, was carved from woolly mammoth ivory and is about 60 mm (2.4 in) tall. There's a small knob where the head should be (likely used as a point of suspension, perhaps from a necklace), the breasts, belly, and thighs are proportionally quite large, and the vulva is explicit and pronounced (Figure 6.13).

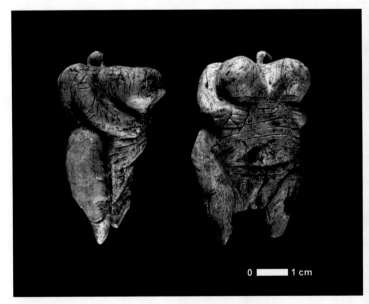

0 ▬▬ 1 cm

▲ **Figure 6.13**
Two so-called Venus figurines. The famous Venus of Willendorf (right) and two views of a recently discovered, 35,000-year-old Venus from Hohle Fels Cave in southwestern Germany fit the common stereotype of such figurines: broad hips, large breasts, fat bellies, and vague faces. (Left, Hilde Jensen, copyright © University of Tübingen; right © Ali Meyer/Corbis)

Most of the Venus figurines are younger, dating to the period between 27,000 and 20,000 years ago (Gamble 1986), and many mirror the appearance of the Hohle Fels specimen, lacking faces but with large breasts and buttocks. This particular variety of the female figurines has become the stereotype of this class of artifacts, perhaps, as archaeologist Patricia Rice (1981) points out, because these are the ones most often depicted in books on prehistoric art. Many researchers have suggested that they were fertility symbols, realistic depictions of pregnant females, or portrayals of women with various medical conditions.

However, these suggestions are difficult to support when large samples are examined. Rice (1981) looked at a group of 188 Venus figurines and found their shape, size, and form to be quite varied. There were depictions of thin and fat women, women with large breasts and women with small breasts, pregnant and not pregnant women, and women who were, by Rice's estimation, old, middle-aged, and young (based on the depiction of physical appearance, especially the presence or absence of lines in their faces and in how flat or saggy breasts, stomachs, hips, and buttocks looked).

Rice (1981:408) proposes that the deduced age spread of the Upper Paleolithic female figurines in her large sample was remarkably similar to the actual age distribution in historical hunter-gatherer populations. So in her view, the Venus figurines depict women of all shapes and sizes, all ages, and all states of fertility.

Also found in Hohle Fels Cave and dated to between 33,000 and 30,000 years ago are figurines depicting, respectively, a graceful waterfowl in flight and the head of what appears to be a wild horse (Conrad 2003). Another series of animal carvings in Germany includes depictions of bears, lions, and mammoths (Sinclair 2003).

It is not so surprising that people whose lives depended on an understanding of the animal life with which they shared the planet painted and carved their representations. Some of the animals depicted are the prey of ancient human hunters, but a preponderance are impressive, dangerous, aggressive predators, fierce and intelligent hunters who were likely viewed by ancient people with a mixture of fear and respect; they were creatures whose characteristics ancient humans might have hoped to emulate (Conrad 2003; Sinclair 2003).

As beautifully rendered as some of the ancient sculptures just discussed may have been, another set of figurines may be even more significant in terms of the insights they provide us into the intellectual and even spiritual lives of ancient people. These carvings are not depictions of animals or even of people but of strange chimeras, beasts that appear to be part human, part animal.

Two such sculptures excavated in Germany and dating to about 30,000 years ago appear to display the body of a human and the head of a lion (Sinclair 2003). Again from Hohle Fels Cave in Germany, along with the aforementioned water bird and horse, is an upright figure that seems to be a human being from the neck down, but a lion from the neck up. Another statue, the "Lion Man" from Hohlenstein-Stadel cave, may be a bit younger, but even more clearly shows a human, standing on two legs, although with a very obvious lion's head (Figure 6.14). The meaning of carvings like these is unclear, but perhaps we are seeing in them some element of the spiritual world of ancient people, a world inhabited by beasts hosting spirits of both people and the animals whose courage and ferocity they hoped to emulate.

◀ **Figure 6.14**
The so-called "Lion Man" from Hohlenstein-Stadel cave is a chimera, a mythical combination of two different kinds of animals, in this instance, a human being and a lion. Though its specific meaning is unclear, the Lion Man almost certainly reflects an element of the spiritual world of ancient people. (Thomas Stephan, © Ulmer Museum)

The precise meaning of the cave paintings, as well as of the figurines, is elusive. But what is key here is that in painting their images in caves, in engraving designs on antler, and in sculpting depictions of women, the artists of the Upper Paleolithic were doing something that we recognize as human behavior: They were creating images from their memory, filtered through the lens of their imagination. In doing this, they left us wonderful works to ponder.

The Sound of Music

The production and appreciation of music appears to be a human universal. Music excites and soothes (the old saying, usually misquoted, is "Music hath charms to soothe the savage breast" [a common misquote here replaces "breast" with "beast"]); in other words, music makes us feel better when we're upset or down. Indeed, music makes us laugh, cry, clap, dance, sway, snap our fingers, play air guitar, and headbang. And it now appears that music has been touching us, altering our moods, delighting and entertaining us for more than 40,000 years. The oldest musical instruments were flutes, dating to more than 40,000 years ago at Geissenklösterle Cave in Germany (Higham et al. 2012). Hohle Fels Cave, that same cave that has produced the earliest figurative representation of a human being and some of the oldest sculptures of animals, has also produced musical instruments, specifically bone and ivory flutes (Conrad, Malina, and Münzel 2009). The larger of the bone flutes was made from naturally hollow bone of a vulture and possesses five preserved finger holes (Figure 6.15); the smaller flute was made from the naturally hollow bone of a swan and has just three preserved holes. Fragments of two more flutes were found in the cave. These were made of ivory and were manufactured by first splitting the ivory along the long axis, hollowing out the shaft, and then gluing the pieces back together.

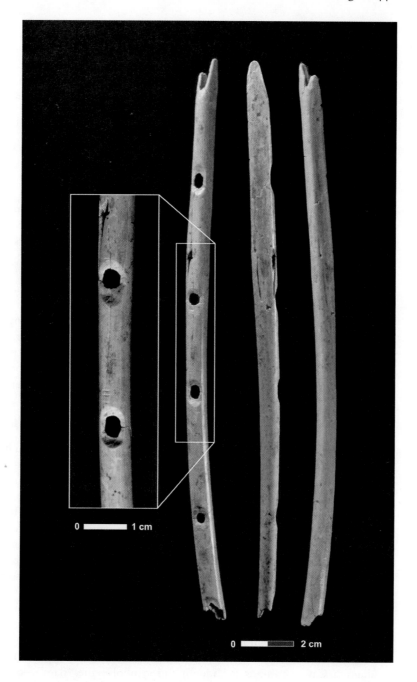

Among the oldest musical instruments ever found are these 35,000-year-old bone flutes from Germany. (Hilde Jensen, copyright © University of Tübingen)

There is no convincing evidence for music production—or appreciation—among other hominids, including the Neandertals, but in the flutes excavated in southwestern Germany we have clear proof of the existence of music in the cultural repertoire of anatomically modern human beings by at least 40,000 years ago.

What Does the Art of the Upper Paleolithic Mean?

It is difficult not to be moved by the images that adorn the cave walls of ancient Europe and elsewhere. With twenty-first-century-A.D. eyes, we can appreciate the glorious beauty and movement of the artwork. But what did these works mean to the twentieth- and thirtieth-millennium-B.P. eyes of their creators? And why did they create them?

There are as many answers to these questions as researchers who have contemplated them. Some have argued that the art of the Upper Paleolithic explains itself: It is (and was) beautiful and, just like modern art, was produced for the simple joy of creating something of beauty and power. It was "art for art's sake" (Halvorson 1987).

Many researchers have sought deeper meaning in the art. For example, it is often suggested that when a hunting people depict animals in their artwork, they are necessarily practicing what is called sympathetic magic. The hunters paint the animals and show them being speared or captured in the magical, symbolic realm to ensure their capture and slaughter in the real world.

Patricia Rice and Ann Paterson (1985, 1986) have attempted to quantify this hypothesis. Their statistical analysis of the numbers and kinds of animals seen on cave walls in the European Upper Paleolithic shows interesting correlations with the faunal assemblages of habitation sites in Spain and France. Small, non-aggressive animals such as reindeer and red deer were important in the diet of the cave painters and seem to have been depicted on cave walls in proportion to their economic importance. On the other hand, animals less often seen in faunal assemblages but impressive, dangerous, and productive of large quantities of meat when they were successfully procured also were commonly included in the artwork.

Other researchers have suggested that cave paintings depicted actual historical events, hunts symbolically and artistically recorded for posterity. And still others have likened the paintings to mounted animal-head trophies hung on walls by their modern hunters. A painstaking analysis of the animals depicted on the walls of Chauvet Cave has enabled analysts to determine the order in which overlapping images were painted. These same researchers have suggested that the sequential appearance of animals as they were being painted—in one panel, a herd of bison was painted first and then, as if appearing to hunt them, a pride of lions was painted next—reflects the sequence of either an actual hunt witnessed by the artists or a hunt imagined by them (Bower 2008b).

Some researchers interpret the artwork as part of a system of communication of ideas—a system that uses animals and geometric patterns as symbols, the specific meaning of which may be lost forever. For example, archaeologist Meg Conkey (1980) views the 1,200 bones engraved with abstract geometric patterns at Altamira Cave, Spain, as the identifying symbols—the "flags"—of different groups of people who came together at the cave during periods of population aggregation.

Anthropologist Michael Jochim (1983) views the cave paintings of northern Spain and southern France—the so-called Franco-Cantabrian region—as symbols marking territory. Social stresses that accompanied population influx into the region during the period after 25,000 B.P. may have resulted in the need to mark territory with symbols of ownership. Painting animals—probably the most important resources of a territory—within a sacred place in the territory like a cave might have served to announce to all interlopers the rightful ownership of the surrounding lands. Prehistorian Clive Gamble (1982, 1986) views the Venus figurines as a symbolic social glue, helping to maintain social connections between geographically distant groups through a common religion and art style.

A neuropsychological approach has been applied by researchers J. D. Lewis-Williams and T. A. Dowson (1988) to explain at least some of the less naturalistic cave art. They note that there are six basic geometric forms that people who are placed into an altered state of consciousness under experimental conditions report seeing: dots, wavy lines, zigzags, crosshatching or grids, concentric circles or U-shaped lines, and parallel lines (Bower 1996). Interestingly, these geometric forms are precisely those seen in some ancient cave art dating to more than 30,000 years ago.

Lewis-Williams and Dowson's approach is cross-cultural. In other words, they surveyed a wide variety of historical and archaeological cultures, finding common images in artwork all over the world. Lewis-Williams and Dowson point out ethnographic records of shamans or priests who, in an attempt to communicate with spirits or to see into other worlds, induce a trancelike state by fasting, dancing, hyperventilating, going into isolation in absolute darkness, undergoing sleep deprivation, even ingesting hallucinogens. When these shamans produce an artistic representation of what they have seen and experienced in their trances, they often include the geometric shapes induced in modern experimental subjects that also are seen in Upper Paleolithic artwork.

The trance-induced images are not culturally determined but result, in part, from the structure of the optic system itself and are, therefore, universal. Perhaps through sleep deprivation, staring at a flickering fire, or ingesting drugs, ancient shamans or priests induced these images in their own optic systems. They then translated these images to cave walls as part of religious rituals.

The art of the Upper Paleolithic has been depressingly resistant to any comprehensive explanation for its existence. That we cannot even fathom the reason for our own children's scribblings (see this chapter's "Prelude") does not bode well for our attempt to illuminate the motives for and meanings of the artwork of our Upper Paleolithic ancestors. Perhaps we are destined merely to enjoy the cave paintings and Venus figurines, much as we delight in those crayon, pencil, and paint images we attach with magnets to our refrigerators. That would not be so terrible, so great is the aesthetic enjoyment we might derive from them. Then again, there are insights yet to be extracted from these beautiful puzzles that when solved will tell us much about what it means to be a human being.

The Importance of Living Long: The Grandmother Effect

I grew up and even entered into my teen years in the enviable and not all that uncommon position of knowing all four of my grandparents. My father's parents lived not too far away, and I remember how much I enjoyed our frequent visits. My mother's parents lived even closer, just across the hall in the same multifamily house. They served as surrogate parents when my own were at work or away—

for example, when my mother was in the hospital giving birth to my sister. My two children have not been quite so lucky; my wife's father passed away several months before our second child was born. Nevertheless, our folks have always spent as much time as they could with their grandkids, doting on them, and they have always been generous with their advice, help, time, and resources.

Clearly my kids have benefited in ways both tangible and intangible by having grandparents around, and so have my wife and I. We especially appreciated the help our parents provided when our first child was born. We were pretty comfortable as parents of a newborn, but, admittedly, we were doing it all for the first time. I freely admit that, at least occasionally, I was concerned that I might break the kid. Grandparents can be and were for us a tremendous help—yes, sometimes that help can be a source of friction—but emotionally drained, physically exhausted, and psychically spent new parents can use all the help they can get.

Statistics show that the existence of grandparents and the help they can provide to their own children in raising their kids is more than simply a convenience; it actually increases the likelihood that the kids will survive and thrive. In a survey of mortality statistics in eighteenth- and nineteenth-century Finland and Canada, researchers showed that the presence of a grandmother in the household increased both the number of children born to her children and the proportion of those grandchildren who survived to adulthood (Lahdenpera et al. 2004). In other words, a surviving grandmother present in a household contributed a significant benefit to the reproductive success of her daughters and daughters-in-law as well as the longevity of her grandchildren.

It now appears that the the "grandmother effect" may be traced back to no more than about 30,000 years ago. Rachel Caspari and Sang-Hee Lee (2004) assessed the age at death of ancient hominids by examining teeth, including those that belonged to *Australopithecus, Homo erectus*, premodern human beings including Neandertals, and anatomically modern *Homo sapiens* from the European Upper Paleolithic. Caspari and Lee found that, within the context of a slight apparent increase through time in individual longevity among the hominids, there was a significant and substantial longevity leap between the premoderns and anatomically modern humans only in the Upper Paleolithic. In fact, within their sample, for the first time, at about 30,000 years ago, there was a major change in the human population pyramid; for the first time, there appear to have been a greater number of older adults than younger adults among the hominids.

So, the existence of doting, generous, helpful, and knowledgeable grandparents seems to have been a rather recent development in human evolution. The presence of grandparents, an older generation of people with experiences and memories that track back to a previous time—grandparents are, in fact, a living library—likely had a significant impact in the transmission of cultural memories and knowledge.

CASE STUDY CLOSE-UP

THE SITE OF SUNGIR' IS LOCATED about 150 km (93 mi) northeast of Moscow, in Russia (R. White 1993). To date, nine burials have been excavated at the 28,000-year-old site. The better-preserved remains have been identified as a 60-year-old male; a female skull; a headless adult; an adult, probably male; a 7- to 9-year-old girl; and a 13-year-old boy.

The Sungir' graves are loaded with **grave goods,** primarily items of adornment (all data on the Sungir' graves are taken from R. White 1993:287–296). The older male was adorned with nearly 3,000 finely worked ivory beads; some apparently were part of a beaded cap, and the rest were positioned in strands around his body (Figure 6.16). A flat stone pendant was located on his neck. On his arms were 25 finely carved bracelets made from the ivory of a woolly mammoth. The adolescent boy's body was surrounded with more than 4,900 ivory beads. A carved ivory pendant had been placed on his chest. He wore a belt decorated with 250 polar fox teeth. There was an ivory pin at his throat, an ivory lance and carved ivory disk at his side, an ivory sculpture of a woolly mammoth under his shoulder, and by his left side a human femur (not his own) whose cavity was filled with red ochre. Next to the adolescent boy lay the young girl, buried with more than 5,200 strung beads, an ivory pin at her throat (perhaps a clasp for a garment long since decayed away), small ivory lances, and three ivory disks carved with intricate latticework.

An enormous amount of time must have been invested in preparing these items for burial. Replication of the beads has indicated that 45 minutes to an hour was needed to make just *one* of the ivory beads in the Sungir' burials (R. White 1993:296). If this estimate is accurate, more than 2,000 hours of work were needed just for the beads in the older man's burial, and more than 3,500 hours per child were needed for their beadwork.

The children's burials at Sungir', therefore, actually took more time and effort than did those of the adults, and therein lies an interesting thought. Paleoanthropologist Randall White notes that in most hunting and gathering societies, status is earned and not ascribed. A lifetime of work and achievement results in elevated status, and this earns an individual respect that is eventually manifested in an elaborate burial with all the trappings—like the finely made objects that accompanied the 60-year-old male at Sungir'. But children have not lived long enough to achieve status or wealth. As White suggests, children buried with high-status goods must have been afforded their high status not because of what they had accomplished in life but rather on the basis of who they were related to. White goes on to suggest that the situation at Sungir' implies the existence of a complex social system in which status was passed down from one generation to the next.

Certainly, the burials imply that 28,000 years ago, the people at Sungir' were much like us, viewing their children as their most precious and beloved possessions. The tragedy of the early death of a child required significant symbols to mark her or his passing. Twenty-eight thousand years after they were secreted in their graves, the beads, pendants, pins, lances, and sculptures interred with the children of Sungir' resonate with what can only be interpreted as the love those left behind felt for the young ones who had died.

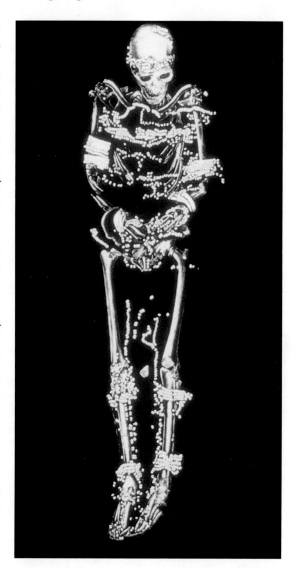

▲ **Figure 6.16**
This skeleton of an older man who lived more than 25,000 years ago is one of the nine burials excavated at the Upper Paleolithic site of Sungir' near Moscow. More than 3,000 ivory beads were sewn into his burial garments. (© Musée de l'Homme, O. Bader)

Summary

Glimmerings of enormous change emanate from the Middle Stone Age and the Middle Paleolithic. Incised ochre rods, shell beads, engraved ostrich shells, and simple pendants provide just a faint hint of what is to come in the explosion of change that transforms the intellectual landscape of a time called the Upper Paleolithic and Late Stone Age. The cultures of the period are characterized by the production of blade tools; a broadening of the subsistence base; an increase in the size of some sites (implying a practice of temporary population aggregation); the use of bone, antler, ivory, and shell in toolmaking; the production of nonutilitarian items, some of which served as items of personal adornment; the extensive use of nonlocal, exotic raw materials; the regular placement of elaborate grave goods in burials—including items of personal adornment; and the first appearance of artwork, in the form of naturalistic paintings, fanciful sculptures, and engraved bone and antler. In their use of symbol, whether realistic in the case of animals painted on cave walls or abstract in the form of geometric patterns etched into bone or carved into rock, the artists of the Upper Paleolithic and Late Stone Age were practicing a behavior that is one of the hallmarks of the modern human intellect.

TO LEARN MORE

Individually, paleoanthropologists Chris Stringer and Ian Tattersall have been prolific thinkers and authors on the topic of the evolution of anatomically modern humans. Check out their popularly oriented books for their insightful perspectives: *The Origin of Our Species* (Stringer 2012b), *Lone Survivors: How We Came to Be the Only Humans on Earth* (Stringer 2012a), and *Masters of the Planet: The Search for Our Human Origins* (Tattersall 2012).

Informative, densely illustrated coffee-table books have been published on several of the major cave painting sites. For Lascaux, there is Mario Ruspoli's *The Cave of Lascaux: The Final Photographs* (1986), a virtual encyclopedia of the major art panels in the cave, with the last photos taken before the cave was closed to ensure its preservation. Chauvet Cave has its own book as well, titled *Dawn of Art: The Chauvet Cave* (1996), by Jean-Marie Chauvet, Éliette Brunel Deschamps, and Christian Hillaire. On the Spanish cave Altamira, there is *The Cave of Altamira*, by Pedro A. Saura Ramos (1998). Finally, for Cosquer Cave there is *The Cave Beneath the Sea: Paleolithic Images at Cosquer*, by Jean Clottes and Jean Courtin (1996). The format of these books is pretty similar with detailed discussions of the discovery of the caves, their archaeological contexts, dating, and, of course, the art. The photographs are the primary draw of these books, and the imagery is truly mind-boggling.

There also are a number of books that cover the cave art more broadly, examining and comparing styles and methods at different sites, including but not limited to the major caves that are the focus of the books just listed. One of the best of these is *Journey Through the Ice Age*, by Paul Bahn and Jean Vertut (1997), a comprehensive guide to cave art. Another general book that attempts to explain the art as the result of shamanism is *The Shamans of Prehistory: Trance and Magic in the Painted Caves*, by Jean Clottes and David Lewis-Williams (1998). If all you do is look at the photographs in any of these books, it will have been time well spent, and you likely will want to read the text to learn more about humanity's first artistic explosion.

Web links for this chapter can be found at www.oup.com/us/feder

7

Expanding Geographic Horizons

New Worlds

	45	40
Sunda		Niah Cave Lang Rongrien
New Guinea		Huon Bobongara Hill
Australia	Panaramitee North	SwanRiver Carpenter's Gap Keilor Lake Mungo Ngarrabulgan Malakunanja
Tasmania		
Pacific Islands		
Northeast Asia		Mamontovaya Kurya

CHAPTER OVERVIEW

After 50,000 years ago, human population expanded beyond Africa, Europe, and Asia and into the rest of the habitable world. Sahul (Australia/New Guinea/Tasmania) exhibits clear evidence of human occupation by about 50,000 years ago. The islands of western Melanesia were populated beginning about 35,000 years ago. Micronesia and Polynesia also show evidence of occupation after 3,500 years ago as human population expanded eastward into the Pacific.

An enormous body of land called Beringia, joining northeast Asia and northwest North America, was exposed during periods of lowered sea level that accompanied the expansion of glacial ice during the Pleistocene. Inhabitants of northeast Asia expanded into the interior and along the coast of Beringia and, ultimately, into the New World, probably by about 20,000 years ago. Some migrants may have traveled along the coast reaching as far south as Chile by 13,000 years ago. Others seem to have migrated through the interior, reaching the American southeast perhaps as early as 18,000 years ago. Though the dates of the earliest sites in the New World are controversial, the archaeological record provides unequivocal evidence of a highly successful human adaptation to the Late Pleistocene world of the Western Hemisphere at least as early as about 12,000 years ago.

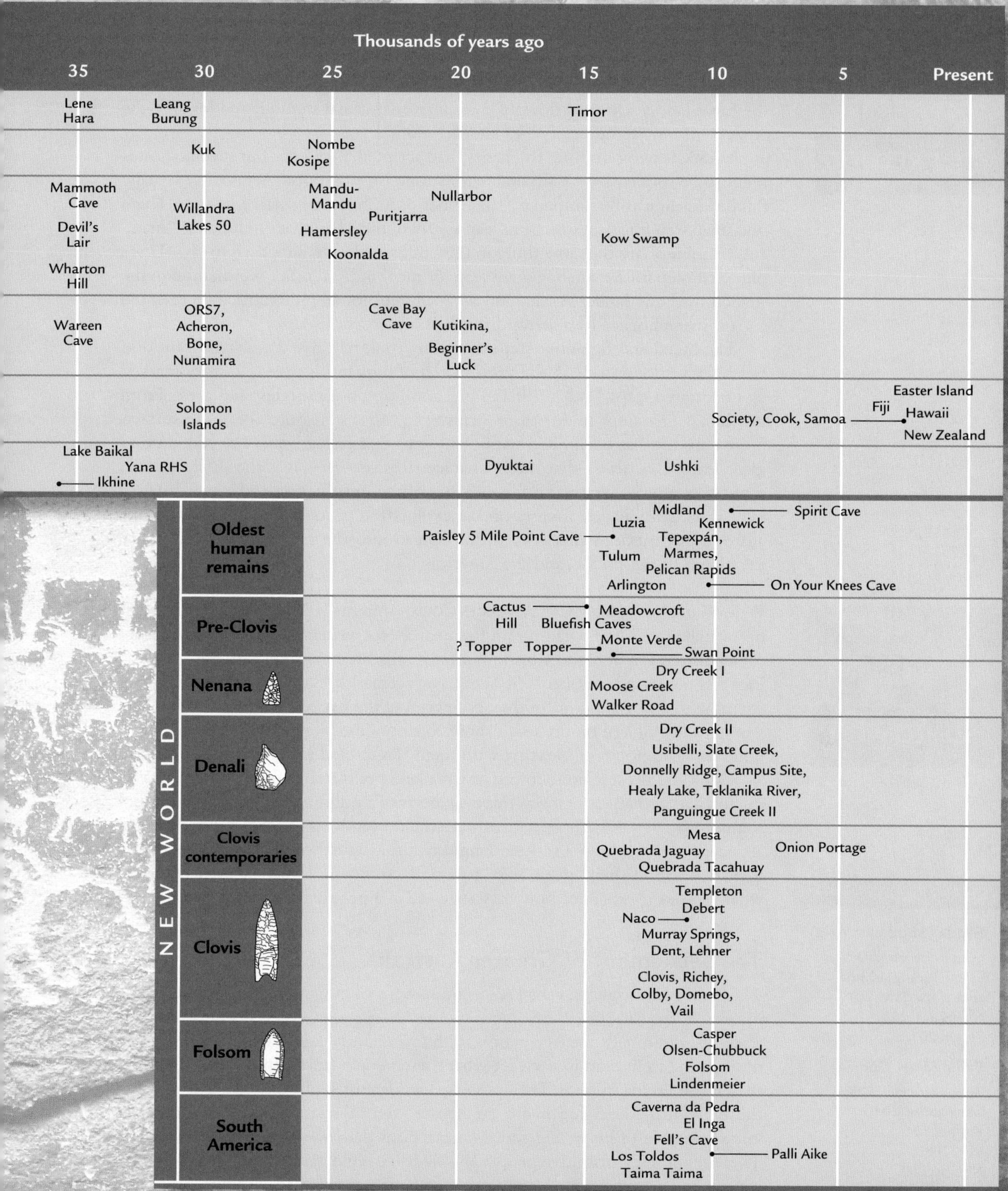

Thousands of years ago

35 30 25 20 15 10 5 Present

Lene Hara | Leang Burung | Timor

Kuk | Nombe / Kosipe

Mammoth Cave | Willandra Lakes 50 | Mandu-Mandu | Nullarbor
Devil's Lair | | Puritjarra | Kow Swamp
Wharton Hill | Hamersley
| Koonalda

Wareen Cave | ORS7, Acheron, Bone, Nunamira | Cave Bay Cave | Kutikina, Beginner's Luck

Solomon Islands | Society, Cook, Samoa — Fiji — Easter Island / Hawaii / New Zealand

Lake Baikal / Yana RHS | Dyuktai | Ushki
● — Ikhine

NEW WORLD

Oldest human remains
Paisley 5 Mile Point Cave ● — Luzia | Midland ● — Spirit Cave
Kennewick
Tepexpán,
Tulum | Marmes, Pelican Rapids
Arlington | On Your Knees Cave

Pre-Clovis
Cactus — Meadowcroft
Hill | Bluefish Caves
? Topper | Topper — Monte Verde
Swan Point

Nenana
Dry Creek I
Moose Creek
Walker Road

Denali
Dry Creek II
Usibelli, Slate Creek,
Donnelly Ridge, Campus Site,
Healy Lake, Teklanika River,
Panguingue Creek II

Clovis contemporaries
Mesa
Quebrada Jaguay | Onion Portage
Quebrada Tacahuay

Clovis
Templeton
Naco — Debert
Murray Springs,
Dent, Lehner
Clovis, Richey,
Colby, Domebo,
Vail

Folsom
Casper
Olsen-Chubbuck
Folsom
Lindenmeier

South America
Caverna da Pedra
El Inga
Fell's Cave
Los Toldos ● — Palli Aike
Taima Taima

PRELUDE

SUNDAY, JULY 20, 1969, WAS A momentous day in human history: For the first time in the existence of our species, a human being walked on the soil of another world. On that day, American astronaut Neil Armstrong left the relative safety of the lunar lander, climbed down the ladder, took a final step off, and became the citizen—if only temporarily—of another world.

NASA, leaving nothing to chance, had scripted a weighty but succinct statement to be spoken by the first human to walk on the moon. Armstrong actually flubbed his line as he jumped off the lander onto the lunar surface, saying: "That's one small step for man, one giant leap for mankind." But that's redundant; "man," and "mankind" are the same thing in this context. He was supposed to say, "That's one small step for *a* man, one giant leap for mankind." In other words, though the step off the lunar lander was literally a "small step" for an individual, it represented a giant metaphorical leap forward for the human species.

The literal and figurative step Armstrong took that day was a significant one, but really just one stride in the great march of human history—a history marked by uncounted steps, both small and big, and leaps, both modest and great. From our literal first steps in Africa to Armstrong's first step onto the lunar surface, human history has been filled with small steps that collectively have added up to giant leaps. One thing that surely characterizes our species is the desire to take those steps and to explore both new vistas of the imagination and actual vistas of new lands. This chapter focuses on the exploration of such new horizons by our anatomically modern ancestors as they spread into the new worlds of Australia, the islands of the Pacific, and the Americas.

CHRONICLE

WHEN BRITISH EXPLORER CAPTAIN JAMES COOK'S ship made landfall on the east coast of Australia in 1770, he had no professional speechwriters to help commemorate the occasion. The record of his first impressions on encountering native Australians is more mundane than Neil Armstrong's remarks: "Sunday 29th April. Saw as we came in on both points of the bay Several of the natives and a few hutts. Men, women and children on the south shore abreast of the Ship, to which place I went in the boats in hopes of speaking with them" (as quoted in A. G. Price 1971:65).

Cook and those who followed found a land populated by more than a quarter million and perhaps as many as three-quarters of a million people (Mulvaney and Kamminga 1999:69). Those natives were the descendants of settlers who had also arrived by sea. Lacking a written language, the original settlers left no record of their reaction to their "giant leap" to a new continent. Only the archaeological record speaks to us about how they survived as a people in their new world.

The Settlement of Greater Australia

The original Australians, called Aborigines, were an enigma to the European colonizers. In the Europeans' myopic view, the Aborigines seemed primitive in their material culture, a Stone Age people with few material advances, throwbacks to a distant time in human history. Yet what these people lacked in things, they more than made up for in ideas. They possessed a range of sophisticated social systems; the individual Aborigine had a far denser web of relations and was far more knowledgeable of his or her social connections than was the average European. These supposedly primitive people also had a richly detailed mythology and oral history and a sophisticated knowledge of their natural surroundings. Australian

Aborigines also produced a deeply textured artistic tradition, painting fantastical images of the animals they encountered in their environment, as well as the ancestors, heroes, and spirits that inhabited their spirit world (Gray 1996; Mulvaney and Kamminga 1999). As different as they were from the European settlers, these native Australians shared at least one thing with the newcomers; as already mentioned, they had arrived by watercraft (Birdsell 1977; Jones 1989, 1992; J. P. White and O'Connell 1982). Their voyages of exploration and migration—a series of small steps adding up to one giant leap to a new world—occurred at least 40,000 years before the arrival of the Europeans.

Paleogeography in the Western Pacific

As discussed in Chapter 4, during the height of the Pleistocene sea level was lowered by at least 100 m (about 325 ft) and perhaps as much as 135 m (about 440 ft). This means that during glacial maxima, the islands of Java, Sumatra, Bali, and Borneo were connected to each other in a single landmass called **Sunda** (or **Sundaland**; Figure 7.1). Sunda, in turn, was connected to mainland southeast Asia. The oceans separating these islands from one another, as well as from Asia proper, are not as deep as the amount by which sea level was depressed during glacial maxima. Wide swaths of land connecting these territories, now many meters under the ocean's surface, were exposed during periods of lowered sea level.

During these same periods of depressed sea levels, Australia, New Guinea, and Tasmania were similarly connected as a single landmass, called **Sahul**, or "Greater Australia" (see Figure 7.1). Unlike Sunda, however, Sahul was never connected to mainland Asia. Even when the Pleistocene glaciers were at their most extensive and sea level was at its lowest, Sahul was still separated from Asia by a water barrier. In fact, Greater Australia has been separated from Asia since the two were separated through continental drift more than 100 million years ago. This

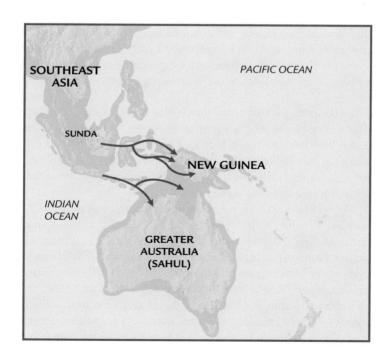

◀ **Figure 7.1**
Map showing the current coastlines of Australia, New Guinea, and southeast Asia as well as the coastline during glacial maxima. Arrows show proposed migration routes from Sunda (the combined land mass of the islands of southeast Asia) to Sahul (Greater Australia).

long-standing isolation of Australia has resulted in that continent's unique native fauna of kangaroos, wallabies, wombats, and koala bears—which are marsupials (primitive mammals that give birth to very immature young that complete their gestation in pouches)—and platypuses, echidnas, and spiny anteaters—which are monotremes (egg-laying mammals).

The **Wallace Trench**, located between New Guinea–Australia and Java–Borneo, is an enormous undersea chasm, nearly 7,500 m (25,000 ft) deep. Though the distance between the shores of Sunda and Sahul lessened as sea level became depressed during glacial maxima at 65,000 years ago, then 53,000 years ago, and again at 35,000 years ago, the islands never coalesced, kept apart by the deep waters of **Wallacea**, the sea over the Wallace Trench (Glover 1993).

The Road to Sahul

Oceanic islands in Wallacea, like Timor and Sulawesi, would have served as stepping stones between Asia and Australia during the Pleistocene. Anthropologist Joseph Birdsell (1977) has suggested a series of possible routes from Sunda to Sahul during periods of lowered sea level (see Figure 7.1). During glacial maxima and the concomitant lowering of sea level, one viable route starts on the eastern shore of contemporary Borneo, continues east through Sulawesi, and includes several island hops to northwest New Guinea. The longest interisland gap would be about 70 km (43 mi); the mean of the eight gaps in this route is only about 28 km (17 mi; Birdsell 1977:127). An alternate route suggested by Birdsell is more southerly, beginning in Java, traversing the Indonesian archipelago, crossing south to Timor and then south to Australia proper. This route also contains eight ocean crossings, with a maximum of 87 km (54 mi) and a mean of a little more than 19 km (12 mi) between landfalls (Birdsell 1977:127). When sea level is not as low as the proposed maximum, the distances become greater and the trip more difficult.

As Birdsell points out, this voyage likely did not take place all at once but transpired, perhaps, over several generations, as people with a marine adaptation explored the islands in their vicinity and discovered more distant islands perhaps by intentional voyages of exploration and accidentally by being blown off course during storms. These people might then have settled on some of the islands, and the process would have been repeated, pushing the limits of their world ever farther out along its edges.

The Discovery of Greater Australia

The timing of the original human discovery and settlement of Greater Australia has long been disputed. It cannot have preceded a human presence on coastal southeast Asia (which is the most logical source for the native Australian population), and it must have followed the development of a coastal adaptation and the invention of seaworthy watercraft.

As we saw in Chapter 4, stone tools dating to as much as 900,000 years ago have been found on the island of Flores, located at the eastern end of the Indonesian archipelago (Morwood et al. 1998). With the lowered sea level of that time period, Flores was separated from the mainland by only about 19 km (12 mi) of open water. Nevertheless, this indicates that even at this early date, hominids were capable of surviving at least short deepwater crossings.

It should come as no surprise, therefore, that anatomically modern humans were capable of crossing the wide stretches of open ocean separating Greater Australia from Sunda by about 50,000 years ago. Unfortunately, however, only a very few archaeological sites have been found thus far at the most logical points along the presumed island pathway (Figure 7.2).

One of the older sites in southeast Asia is located in Niah Cave on the island of Borneo. Newly derived radiocarbon dates firmly place the earliest human occupation of Niah Cave at around 46,000 years ago. The site was occupied until about 34,000 years ago, and a fully modern, lightly constructed human skull recovered at the site has produced a uranium series date of 37,000 years ago (Holden 2007).

The oldest evidence for the occupation of the island of Timor, located east of Flores in the Indonesian archipelago, was found in Lene Hara Cave. More than 400 pieces of chipped stone as well as shell beads were found by excavators in association with charcoal that has been radiocarbon-dated to at least 35,000 B.P. (Holden 2001).

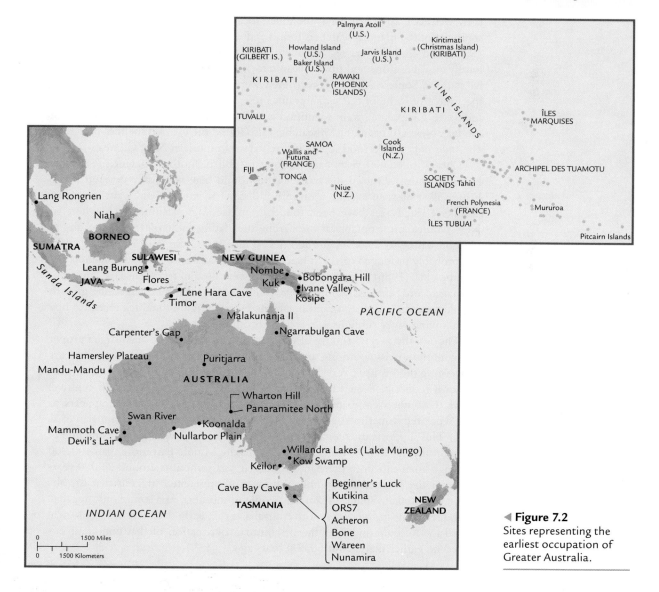

◀ **Figure 7.2**
Sites representing the earliest occupation of Greater Australia.

The archaeological evidence found on these Indonesian islands supports the idea that they served as stepping-stones in a wave of human population east from southeast Asia into the western Pacific. Even farther east and toward the north lay the planet's largest ocean, with widely scattered, fertile bits of land, many of which would also be settled in antiquity by human voyagers (see the discussion later in this chapter). To the east and south, however, lay the biggest real-estate prize of all: the landmass of Greater Australia. It is on the settlement of this region that we next focus our attention.

The Earliest Occupation of Greater Australia

The Archaeology of Sahul

The earliest settlement of New Guinea, an island a little larger in area than the state of California, can now be traced back to just after 50,000 years ago (Summerhayes et al. 2010). In the Ivane Valley, located on the Huon Peninsula on the southeast of the island, researchers found and excavated seven sites dating between 49,000 and 43,000 years ago. Residents of the sites made stone tools, both from locally available stone and from volcanic rock located about 20 km away from the habitations. Some of the tools recovered were used in processing plant material; the source of some of the starch grains preserved on the working edges of some tools (see Chapter 8) were identified as yam, an important food in the diet of modern New Guineans. The researchers also found the charred shells of processed *Pandanus* nuts, a wild food source still relied on in modern New Guinea.

Dating to 40,000 years ago, Bobongara Hill is another ancient site on the Huon Peninsula. One of the artifact types found here was also recovered at the Ivane Valley sites: an axelike tool with a distinct narrowing or "waist" along its middle. Waisted axes have been found in archaeological contexts elsewhere in New Guinea, most notably at the Kosipe site, dating to 26,000 years ago, and at Nombe, dating to 25,000 years ago (J. P. White and O'Connell 1982). The waist was probably produced to aid in hafting the stone axe onto a wooden handle. Les Groube et al. (1986) suggest that these axes were used in forest clearing, an activity that, according to Rhys Jones (1989:764), would have encouraged the growth of wild foods like yams, taro, and sugarcane by opening up the thick forest canopy and allowing more sunlight to reach the ground.

Though the precise timing of the first human settlement of Australia proper is a contentious issue among archaeologists, geologists, and geneticists data are converging on this issue. A recent analysis of the genome of an aboriginal Australian man (conducted on a lock of hair collected in the early twentieth century) shows that, when compared to other Eurasians, the Australian line appears to have separated sometime between 62,000 and 75,000 years ago (Rasmussen et al. 2011). This supports the scenario proposed in Chapter 5 with an ancestral line of anatomically modern Africans spreading into the Middle East more than 100,000 years ago, then east from there into southern Asia sometime around 74,000 years ago, after the Toba eruption. The genome study just cited suggests that the aboriginal Australians split off from the people in southern Asia sometime after that. That doesn't mean they made it to Australia at that early date. The archaeological record for Australia indicates the first human occupation of that continent occurred no earlier than about 50,000 years ago.

Crucial in the debate about the timing of the earliest human settlement of Australia is the Lake Mungo 3 skeleton, the remains of an anatomically modern human being. Lake Mungo is one of a number of dry lake beds located in the Willandra Lakes region of western New South Wales in southeastern Australia. Found in 1974, the geological deposit in which the burial was encountered indicates that the skeleton is about 40,000 years old (Bowler et al. 2003).

Though the dating of Lake Mungo 3 places the remains at a time period of not more than 40,000 years ago, the story does not end there. Lake Mungo 3 burial does not represent the earliest human occupation of the area around the lake. Bowler and his colleagues also reported the discovery of 11 chipped stone tools found in a stratigraphic layer at Lake Mungo that was above a separate level dated to about 50,000 years ago and below another level dated to 46,000 years ago (Bowler et al. 2003:839). The stratigraphic bracketing of these artifacts indicates a date of between 46,000 and 50,000 years ago.

While the precise dating of sites in Australia older than 40,000 years continues to be debated, there is broad agreement among Australian archaeologists that there are many sites on the Australian continent that date to soon after 40,000 years ago (O'Connell and Allen 1998).

For example, the Upper Swan Bridge site in the southwestern part of the country has produced radiocarbon dates of 39,500 B.P., 37,100 B.P., and 35,000 B.P. in association with about 200 artifacts, including stone chips, worked flakes, and flakes with edges exhibiting wear patterns (Jones 1992). Also in southwest Australia is Devil's Lair, with a series of hearths, stone and bone artifacts, and the remains of kangaroos that had been killed, butchered, and eaten by the cave's human inhabitants. Radiocarbon dates place occupation of the cave at before 32,000 years ago and perhaps as much as 38,000 years ago (Jones 1992). Eleven kilometers (7 mi) northwest of Devil's Lair is Mammoth Cave, where burned bones, possible stone artifacts, and charcoal have been dated to between 31,000 years ago and 37,000 years ago. The Keilor site, near the city of Melbourne in southeastern Australia, has produced some quartzite flakes that were intentionally struck off a core. The soil layer in which the artifacts were recovered is estimated to be between 36,000 and 45,000 years old (J. P. White and O'Connell 1982). Radiocarbon and OSL procedures mutually support a date of about 37,000 B.P. for the earliest artifact-bearing strata at Ngarrabulgan Cave in north Queensland in eastern Australia (David et al. 1997).

Willandra Lakes

A second burial at Lake Mungo, Lake Mungo 1 (a cremated female), was located just 450 m (about 500 yd) away from Lake Mungo 3 (Bowler, Thorne, and Polach 1972). After her death, her body was burned, her bones were pulverized, and then she was interred. About 25% of the Lake Mungo 1 skeleton was recovered, and enough recognizable cranial fragments were found to partially reconstruct the skull. Much like the Lake Mungo 3 remains, the young woman was fully anatomically modern and rather **gracile** physiologically, lacking the large brow ridges or heavy buttressing bone typical of modern Australian natives (Bowler et al. 1970). Lake Mungo 1 has dated by radiocarbon to 24,710 years ago.

The Willandra Lakes skeleton was recovered just north of Lake Mungo. Dating to between 20,000 and 30,000 years ago, Willandra Lakes 50 (as the skeletal remains are designated) is far different in appearance from the Lake Mungo remains, exhibiting enormously thick cranial bones (some seven times thicker than the Lake Mungo specimens). As Australian archaeologist Rhys Jones (1992) has pointed out, in these three specimens (Mungo 1 and 3 and the Willandra Lakes 50 cranium) from sites just a few miles apart, there is a greater difference in cranial bone thickness than within and among modern human populations! For Jones, such a difference is not possible within a single population. He sees two biologically distinct populations inhabiting the same region of Australia at different times. However, as archaeologists J. Peter White and James O'Connell (1982) point out, this conclusion is difficult to support with such a small sample of crania for an entire continent and with so many differing habitats that people adapted to over such an extensive period of time. In their view, variations in cranial form merely reflect regional differentiation among native Australians, who can be derived from a single population wave from Asia more than 40,000 years ago.

The Spread Through Australia

The Australian sites discussed so far are located in a ring around the perimeter of the continent (see Figure 7.2). As archaeologist Sandra Bowdler (1977, 1990) points out, the initial human population entered Australia from the north and then spread primarily east and to a lesser degree west along the coast, focusing on those areas with tropical coastal environments most like those of the source areas from which it migrated. When the migrants moved inland, they always did so along major river systems, enabling a shift in their subsistence foods from marine to riverine resources.

This pattern makes sense when you consider that the first inhabitants of Australia were almost certainly a coastally adapted people. This coastal adaptation, including the use of watercraft, enabled their discovery of Sahul and their migration onto its landmass in the first place. People with a history of coastal subsistence would have been wise to spread along the coast of their newly found home. And, as shown, the oldest human sites in Australia are located along the modern coastal rim or in formerly wetter interiors drained by rivers or dotted with lakes.

The Australian Interior

The earliest inhabitants of Australia seem to have avoided, at least initially, the vast, harsh, dry interior of the continent (J. P. White 1993). Not until 20,000 to 25,000 years ago did human groups begin to penetrate the dry core of central Australia. For example, evidence from the Puritjarra Rockshelter in the Cleland Hills of central Australia shows that the cave was first occupied 22,000 years ago and then intermittently until 12,000 years ago (M. A. Smith 1987). The stone-tool assemblage included primarily large flake tools but also some small flakes and cores. Other interior sites of similar antiquity include two rockshelter sites from the Hamersley Plateau in western Australia—dated at 21,000 B.P. and 26,000 B.P., respectively—and evidence of flint mining in the Nullarbor Plain dated to 20,000 years ago (Jones 1987).

Tasmania

Located to the south of Australia's southeast coast, Tasmania is the last "new world" in Sahul to be occupied by human beings. A human population first entered what is today the island of Tasmania when it was still connected to the Australian continent. The earliest people of Tasmania lived farther south and closer to Antarctica than did any other human group to that point. The environment was entirely different from any faced previously by Australian Aborigines—a frozen tundra not unlike that of Upper Paleolithic Europe (see Chapter 6).

Tasmania shows archaeological evidence of occupation as early as 35,000 years ago at Wareen Cave and 30,000 years ago at the ORS7 site as well as at Acheron, Bone, Bluff, and Nunamira Caves in south-central Tasmania (Cosgrove, Allen, and Marshall 1990). Archaeologists Richard Cosgrove, Jim Allen, and Brendan Marshall (1990) conducted a survey of south-central Tasmania, locating 41 sites occupied between 30,000 and 11,000 years ago. Sites like Cave Bay Cave, located on Hunter Island off the northwest coast of Tasmania, date to about 23,000 B.P. (Bowdler 1974). On Tasmania proper there is Beginner's Luck Cave and Kutikina Cave (formerly Fraser Cave), both initially occupied at 20,000 years ago. Kutikina is extraordinarily rich, with over 75,000 stone flakes and tools recovered from less than a 1% sample of the site (Kiernan, Jones, and Ranson 1983). Most of the tools are steep-edged scrapers, similar in appearance to those recovered at Lake Mungo. The faunal assemblage is dominated by the remains of the large wallaby, which is a member of the kangaroo family, and the wombat, a sizable, heavyset, burrowing marsupial (Kiernan et al. 1983:30). Interestingly, there are no remains of the larger, now extinct animals that typified the Pleistocene of Australia. This Australian Pleistocene megafauna probably was already extinct by the time humans first penetrated Tasmania.

Greater Australia: A Broad Range of Adaptations

In the stereotype, the Australian Aborigines were a homogeneous group, possessed of a simple technology, barely eking out a living in the great arid desert of central Australia. In this view, they had become stuck in time, holdovers from a primitive Stone Age society, forever limited by their harsh environment. But the archaeological record shows clearly that such a stereotype is inadequate to characterize Aboriginal culture. Rather, the ancestors of the native people of Australia arrived by watercraft by at least 40,000 years ago in what had to have been, at least in part, a planned, intentional migration. Beginning with an adaptation to a tropical, coastal environment, they managed by 20,000 years ago to have adapted to the myriad habitats of Greater Australia. Coastal people maintained many of their original maritime adaptations, but others adjusted to the temperate regions of the interior, and some even developed cultural strategies for coping with environments as diverse as the Great Sandy Desert in the interior—one of the hottest, driest places on earth—and the sub-Antarctic tundra of south-central Tasmania.

And the lives of these people extended far beyond the quest for subsistence. In Koonalda Cave, located near Australia's south-central coast, is some fascinating, ancient artwork, a series of meandering lines made by human fingers as much as 24,000 years ago—a sort of finger painting in the soft limestone of the cave's ceiling (Johanson, Johanson, and Edgar 1994). As mentioned in Chapter 6, potentially even older art has been dated at Wharton Hill and Panaramitee North, where microscopic vegetable matter recovered from within the grooves of petroglyphs of geometric figures has been dated to 36,000 B.P. and 43,000 B.P., respectively (Bednarik 1993).

The lesson of the earliest settlement of Australia is not one of the persistence of a primitive, backward people but of the nearly infinite capacity of human groups for adaptive flexibility. It is a lesson we will see repeated in the initial discovery of and migration to the Americas.

East Into the Pacific

As mentioned earlier in this chapter, as population expanded from southeast Asia to the east, a more southerly route brought human beings to the enormous landmass of Greater Australia. A more northerly route brought migrants out into the vast unexplored world of the Pacific Ocean. Covering more than one-third of the earth's surface, the Pacific stretches 15,500 km (9,600 mi) from north to south and 20,000 km (more than 12,000 mi) from east to west (Figure 7.3). Its total area is about 180 million km^2 (70 million mi^2). Europeans, considered relative latecomers, did not cross the Pacific until Ferdinand Magellan's circumnavigation of the globe in A.D. 1519–1522. Close to 1,000 of the 25,000 islands scattered across the ocean were already inhabited by people—and had been for a few thousand years—by the time of Magellan's voyage.

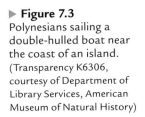

▶ **Figure 7.3**
Polynesians sailing a double-hulled boat near the coast of an island. (Transparency K6306, courtesy of Department of Library Services, American Museum of Natural History)

A Pacific Islander "Age of Exploration"

The fascinating story of the initial exploration and settlement of the Pacific belies the cultural conceit that the "age of exploration" began and ended in the European Renaissance. The successful exploration and colonization of Pacific islands by a people long before and without some of the technological advantages of European explorers (such as quadrants, sextants, compasses) is all the more remarkable when you consider the following: The total landmass of the 25,000 Pacific islands represents only 0.7% of the total area of the ocean, and average island size is only about 10 km by 6 km (6 mi by 4 mi; Terrell 1986:14). Some of the inhabited islands are far smaller. Though many of these islands are geographically clustered and "intervisible" (visible one from the other), the individual clusters are often separated by hundreds, even thousands, of kilometers. Simply finding such island clusters while sailing a small canoe required great skill and not just a little luck. Finding one's way home and then returning to settle the newly discovered island was nothing short of miraculous.

Yet, discover, explore, and colonize many of those islands is precisely what settlers from southeast Asia and New Guinea did. And they accomplished this largely as the result of intentional geographic expansion. Certainly, serendipity played a role in the peopling of the Pacific. Though countless sailors must have been blown off course and died before making it to safe haven, some lucky ones may have made accidental landfall on uninhabited islands and become their permanent settlers. But this cannot be the primary way in which Pacific islands were colonized. Just as Europeans in the fifteenth century began deliberately to explore the oceans, the southeast Asians and New Guineans must have been doing the same many years before. As archaeologist Geoffrey Irwin (1993:7) points out, "We know colonisation was deliberate, because explorers took with them the plants and animals, women and men necessary to establish viable settlements." Computer simulations conducted by anthropologist John Moore support this assertion. Moore shows pretty clearly that for a colonization to be successful there need to be at least five to ten men and five to ten women in the founding group (Balter 2007b). In other words, colonization of the Pacific was largely planned, and colonists brought with them the people and things necessary for the successful establishment of new communities.

Pacific Geography

The Pacific islands are usually divided into three groupings: **Melanesia**—the so-called black islands of New Guinea and smaller islands to the east, including the Solomon Islands, the Bismarck Archipelago, Santa Cruz, New Caledonia, Vanuatu, and Fiji; **Micronesia**—the "small islands" north of Melanesia; and **Polynesia**—"many islands," including a broad triangle of islands demarcated at its points by Hawaii to the north, Easter Island to the southeast, and New Zealand to the southwest.

Pacific Archaeology

Some of the larger islands of Melanesia, including New Britain and New Ireland in the Bismarck Archipelago, were settled by seafaring explorers from Australia by at least 35,000 years ago, not that long after the initial settlement of the island continent (O'Connell and Allen 1998). Even farther to the east, Buka, in the Solomon Island chain, was discovered and settled no less than 28,000 years ago. At a distance of 180 km (110 mi) from the Bismarck Archipelago, the initial settlement of the Solomons is proof of sophisticated navigational skills on the part of the settlers. The Melanesian islands farther to the east and in deeper water, as well as all the islands of Micronesia and Polynesia, were settled much later in a second wave of exploration and migration beginning probably little more than 3,500 years ago (Irwin 1993).

If you draw a line connecting Hawaii to Rapa Nui (Easter Island) to the southeast, from Rapa Nui west to New Zealand, and then northeast back to Hawaii, you've delineated a triangular swath of the Pacific with about the same surface area as North America within which there are about 500 islands whose combined land area is only a tiny fraction of that continent. As Janet Wilmshurst and her colleagues characterize Polynesia, it represents the "last prehistoric expansion of modern humans" (Wilmshurst et al. 2008:1815).

The spread of people through Polynesia was accompanied by a common culture. Because they were a maritime people, fishing played a significant role in their food quest. They also were food producers, who brought non-native agricultural staples with them as they colonized islands, including pig, as a major source of animal protein, and domesticated root crops, especially yams. They also brought a common pottery style, called **Lapita** (Figure 7.4). In fact, the earliest

▶ **Figure 7.4**
Lapita pottery is found virtually everywhere Polynesians explored and settled after 3500 B.P. (Courtesy of Dr. Richard Shutler, Jr., and Dr. Mary Elizabeth Shutler)

occurrence of a human population on the inhabited islands of Polynesia is invariably marked by the appearance of Lapita pottery. The Lapita designation is now applied to the entire cultural complex of Polynesia and includes a maritime adaptation, the raising of pigs, the growing of certain root crops and fruit trees, the use of shell in producing tools and ornaments, and the manufacture of Lapita pottery.

The Lapita complex is absent from Australia or the islands of Micronesia. It appears first in the archaeological record of the Bismarck Archipelago and, perhaps, Fiji a little more than 3,500 years ago (Irwin 1993:39). Expansion proceeded eastward, with large island groups like Tonga at 2,800 years ago (Burley and Dickinson 2001) and Samoa and the Cook Islands (2,500 years ago).

The rest of the islands of Polynesia were inhabited much more recently, less than 1,000 years ago. The results of a detailed examination of more than 1,400 radiocarbon dates conducted by Janet Wilmshurst and her colleagues are presented in Table 7.1 (taken from Wilmshurst et al. 2010 and Wilmshurst et al. 2008; and see Figure 7.2).

The dating of the earliest human settlement of New Zealand is an interesting case. Most people carry a lot of baggage when they travel, walk about, or migrate, packing the stuff they're going to need. However, not everything in that baggage is intentionally packed; wherever we go, we bring along accidental hitchhikers in the form of bacteria, viruses, insects, and even animals.

In a visual cliché of maritime shipping, a rat scurries up the ropes attaching a ship to the dock in order to enter the hold, not because it desires a sea voyage, but to feast on the food stored within. If the rat stays too long, it finds itself hours, days, weeks, or even months later alighting on a foreign shore. If it's lucky, it will find that others of its kind have previously made the same accidental voyage, it will find mates, and bouncing baby rats will result in this new world.

Archaeologists can take advantage of this common scenario and attempt to trace the movement of human groups who have unintentionally packed rats and other species in their baggage as they traveled the world. Janet Wilmshurst and her colleagues (Wilmshurst et al. 2008) have done just this to determine the timing of the earliest human settlement of New Zealand. Rats are not indigenous to New Zealand, but arrived there when people, almost certainly unintentionally, brought

---

TABLE 7.1 Earliest Dates for the Settlement of Central and Eastern Polynesia and New Zealand

Island Group	Oldest Radiocarbon Date Range (all dates A.D.)
Society	1025–1121
Rapa Nui	1200–1253
Marquesas	1200–1277
Hawaii	1219–1266
New Zealand	1230–1280
Southern Cook	1250–1281

them there. Radiocarbon dating of rat bones at archaeological sites and sites where owls killed and ate them clearly shows that New Zealand was first settled by stow-away rats—and, therefore, by the sailors on whose craft they stowed away—no earlier than the middle of the thirteenth century A.D. That's a very good estimate for the first human settlement of New Zealand.

We know from the ethnographic record that the native peoples of the Pacific were brilliant navigators. They built up a substantial reservoir of knowledge about currents and wind patterns. Even without navigational devices, the native navigators of the Pacific could reckon by the stars, were familiar with cloud patterns indicating that land was nearby, possessed a detailed knowledge of bird flight paths from island to island, and constructed seaworthy ships capable of journeys across wide stretches of open ocean.

Coming to America

On Thursday, October 11, 1492, a sea voyager had an encounter that forever affected the trajectory of human history—another one of those small steps that resulted in a giant leap in the march of human history. Documenting the ship's arrival, the journal of the captain of that momentous voyage reads: "When we stepped ashore we saw fine green trees, streams everywhere and different kinds of fruit. . . . Soon many of the islanders gathered around us. I could see that they were people who would be more easily converted to our Holy Faith by love than by coercion" (Cummins 1992:94). Though it didn't quite work out that way, thus begins Christopher Columbus's narrative of the first contact between Europeans and American natives since the series of short-lived, brutal incidents on Newfoundland in Canada that were recorded in the Viking sagas about 1,000 years ago (Magnusson and Paulsson 1965).

Thinking he had discovered a series of islands off the coast of Asia, Columbus called the people he encountered *los Indios*, or Indians. After his initial voyage, Columbus returned three more times, always expecting that the Asian continent lay just beyond the limits of his previous exploration.

Though Columbus never accepted it, most European scholars concluded that he had happened on not a cluster of islands immediately off the coast of south Asia but, as Amerigo Vespucci was to characterize it in 1503, a "new world," populated by peoples unknown to and not even conceived of by Europeans. This New World consisted of two entire continents that make up almost 28.5% of the world's land surface, with a native population estimated to have been in the tens of millions and speaking more than 1,500 different languages and dialects. Over centuries and millennia, descendants of the small bands of hunters and gatherers who initially entered into the New World developed successful adaptations to nearly all of the countless habitats of the Western Hemisphere, from frigid arctic tundra to arid sandy deserts, from luxuriant tropical rain forests to temperate woodlands, from seacoasts to mountains, from river valleys to plateaus. And they lived ways of life as varied as did people inhabiting the "known" continents: hunters and gatherers in small, nomadic bands foraging for food in a seasonal round; fisherfolk in established villages, harvesting the plentiful natural resources of river and shore; farmers in huge adobe apartment complexes, tending the kinds of crops that even today feed the population of the planet. There were great kingdoms with impressive cities, splendid monuments of pyramids and palaces, and powerful hereditary rulers, not unlike King Ferdinand and Queen Isabella of Spain, the monarchs who had funded Columbus's expedition.

The Source of *los Indios*

Modern biological evidence is unequivocal; the source for the native population of the New World is Asia. Evidence in the form of mitochondrial DNA and comparison of the Y-chromosomes of living northeast Asians and Native Americans shows conclusively that they share a genetic heritage. All five mtDNA groupings (**haplogroups** A, B, C, D, and X) found among the native people of the New World can be traced to populations living in northeast Asia (Bolnick et al. 2012); in fact, all five variants are found among a group of Asian natives living along the shores of Lake Baikal in central Siberia (Derenko et al. 2001). Further, two specific mutations seen on the Y-chromosome of Native American males are also found only among human populations found in central Siberia (Bolnick and Smith 2007; Bortolini et al. 2003).

When first encountered by Europeans, however, there was broad speculation concerning the source of the Native American population (Feder 2013), and quite early on some scholars recognized a connection between the natives of the New World and the people of Asia. For example, Giovanni de Verrazzano, an Italian navigator sailing for France, made landfall at what is today the border of North and South Carolina. Sailing north along the coast, he entered Delaware Bay and the mouth of the Hudson River, sailed along Connecticut's coast, entered and explored Narragansett Bay in Rhode Island, and followed the shore of Cape Cod on his way home. In the report he prepared for his benefactors, Verrazzano noted that, in the color and texture of their hair and in the shape of their eyes, the people he encountered looked like the people of Asia.

But how close was Asia to North America, and where was the most plausible point of entry for Asians to enter the New World? In 1732 two Russian traders, Ivan Fyodorov and Mikhail Gvozdev, discovered what the native people of northeast Asia and northwest America already knew, that Asia and America were separated by only about 85 km (53 mi) of sea, a geographical feature now called the Bering Strait (Figure 7.5).

Today the Bering Strait is only 30 m to 50 m (100 ft–165 ft) deep. But during periods of glacial maxima in the Pleistocene, sea level was depressed by far more than this, by as much as 135 m (440 ft), exposing a platform of land connecting Russia and Alaska that was as wide, perhaps, as 1,500 km (1,000 mi) from north to south, a land area of more than 2 million km² (770,000 mi²). During long periods in the Pleistocene, people in northeast Asia could have walked into the New World across the body of land today called **Beringia**, or the **Bering Land Bridge** (see Figure 7.5).

▼ **Figure 7.5**
Map of the modern coastlines of northeast Asia and northwest North America as well as the projected coastline of Beringia during glacial maxima.

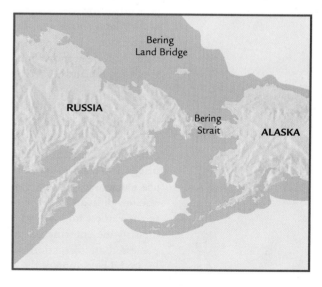

When Did the First Migrants Arrive?

Though most anthropologists accept a Beringian route for America's first human settlers, there is still great controversy over the timing of their arrival. To find out when people first entered the Americas from Siberia, we need to know three things:

1. When was Beringia exposed and open for travel?
2. When was eastern Siberia first inhabited (the source population for New World migrants)?
3. What is the age of the earliest New World sites?

When Was Beringia Exposed and Open for Travel?

If Australia's first settlers could have populated their "new world" more than 40,000 years ago (remember, there was no land bridge between Sunda and Sahul; they had no choice but to arrive by boat), then northeast Asians might have done the same thing during periods when no land bridge was present between Asia and North America. And even without a land bridge, during periods of extreme cold, the Bering Strait would have frozen, producing an ice bridge between the two hemispheres.

Nonetheless, a 1,500-km-wide land connection between the two continents certainly would have been very convenient, facilitating the movement of animals and people either through the interior of northeast Asia, then through the middle of the exposed land bridge, and then into the interior of Alaska, or else along the Pacific coast of northeast Asia, then along the southern Beringian coast, and finally south along the coast of northwest North America (see Figure 7.5).

Beringia was exposed several times during the Pleistocene and was above water more or less continuously from the period beginning about 35,000 until about 11,000 years ago. Analysis of submarine sediments in the area where the land bridge was located indicates a peak in glacial conditions between 22,000 and 19,000 years ago (Yokoyama et al. 2000). Sea level was at a low point for a few hundred years sometime during this period, and Beringia would have been at its most extensive, providing a broad pathway to the New World from the Old for both animals and the people who hunted them. Radiocarbon dating of peat deposits that now reside beneath the Bering Sea but that must have been produced on dry land shows that the land bridge was still exposed, at least in part, until shortly after 11,000 years ago (Elias et al. 1996). So, in fact, the land bridge was available for the movement of animal and people for much of the time between about 35,000 and 11,000 years ago.

When Was Eastern Siberia First Inhabited?

Just as the most likely source area for the original migration of people into Australia is poorly known archaeologically, so too is the most likely source area for the original migration of people into the New World. Eastern Siberia is a difficult place to do archaeology, and relatively little work has been done there. Archaeologist David Meltzer (2009) points out that even after decades of work in Siberia it remains difficult to say with any certainty which site or culture may be ancestral to the earliest migrants to America.

Anyone entering the New World from the Old through Beringia must have possessed an adaptation to the extreme climate of the region in which it was located. The timing of the earliest human adaptation to the Arctic and sub-Arctic, therefore, serves as a limiting factor in our discussion of the timing of human movement into and across Beringia. This cannot have occurred before humans had developed the highly specialized adaptation necessary to survive the rigors of life in the far north (Figure 7.6).

The oldest archaeological evidence of a human presence in the Arctic has been found far from Beringia, at the Mamontovaya Kurya site in the northeasternmost section of European Russia (Pavlov, Svendsen, and Indrelid 2001). Here, at a latitude of 66° 34′, humans subsisted in the harsh climate of the Arctic by hunting mammoth, horse, reindeer, and wolf close to 40,000 years ago. Moving east, sites in the Arctic are younger than this. The Yana RHS site provides the oldest evidence of human occupation of the Arctic in eastern Siberia (Pitulko et al. 2004). Here, people living along the banks of the Yana River at 70° N latitude subsisted primarily by hunting large game animals like reindeer, bison, woolly mammoth, and musk-ox at least 32,000 years ago. Farther south, radiocarbon dates indicate that central Siberia, for example, around the area of Lake Baikal, was occupied no earlier than about 34,000 years ago. Dyuktai Cave, located near the Aldan River in central Siberia, was occupied 14,000 years ago (Figure 7.7 and Table 7.2). The **wedge-shaped cores** from which the inhabitants produced blades there are similar in appearance to cores found in Denali Complex sites in Alaska dating to 10,700 years ago and discussed later in this chapter. (See Figure 7.12 and compare it to Figure 7.7.)

In far eastern Siberia, the lowest stratigraphic levels at sites like those around Ushki Lake on the Kamchatka Peninsula have now been dated to about 11,300 B.P. (Goebel, Waters, and Dikova, 2003). The stone-tool industry seen in the oldest Ushki Lake component included small, finely made, stemmed, bifacially flaked spearpoints. Bifacial points are also a hallmark of the **Clovis** culture found in the New World, discussed later in this chapter. One point form found at Ushki is a small, rounded triangle, sort of tear-dropped in shape, highly reminiscent of a

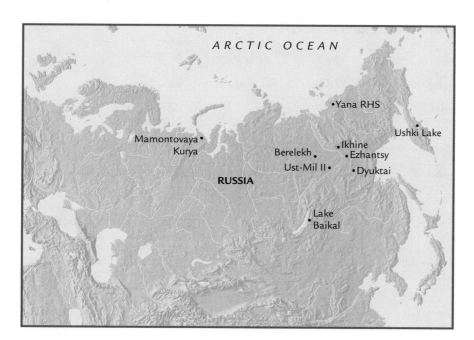

◀ **Figure 7.6**
Map showing the locations of a number of important localities in Russia mentioned in the text that may provide important information related to the migration of human beings from the Old World to the New in the Late Pleistocene.

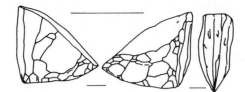
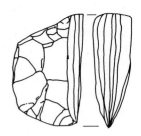

0   5 cm

▲ **Figure 7.7**
Stone tools from the Dyuktai culture, eastern Russia, at about 18,000 B.P. Note the preponderance of so-called wedge-shaped cores. These are small stone cores of the implied shape from which sharp microblades were removed. (From "The Dyuktai Culture and New World Origins" by Seon-bonk Yi and Geoffrey Clark, University of Chicago Press, 0005)

point type called **Chindadn** found in Nenana Complex sites in Alaska (Meltzer 2009; discussed later in this chapter).

It is clear that people were living in Siberia, on the western edge of Beringia, practicing stone-tool technologies that at least could be ancestral to those first technologies seen at the other end of the land bridge between Asia and the New World. Considering the age of the oldest Siberian sites, it seems likely that the movement of people into the New World from Siberia occurred probably no more than about 20,000 years ago. This time period, you will remember, represents a glacial maximum, with attendant maximum sea-level decline, during which the land bridge was at its largest.

What Is the Age of the Earliest New World Sites?

When Beringia became exposed as sea level fell, people adapted to the interior habitats of northeast Asia would have been able to expand their territories by moving east through the interior of the land bridge and then into the interior of

TABLE 7.2 Sample of Sites in Russia Occupied at Times of Possible Human Population Movement into North America

Site Name	Location	Age	Artifacts
Berelekh	Lower Indigirka Valley	12,000–13,000 years ago	Bifaces
Ushki Lake	Kamchatka	11,300 years ago	Bifaces, burins, micro-blades, unifaces
Ust'-Mil II	Central Siberia	11,500–35,000 years ago	Wedge-shaped cores
Dyuktai Cave	Central Siberia	After 18,000 years ago	Wedge-shaped cores, bifaces
Ikhine	Southern Siberia	31,000–34,000 years ago	Burins, cores
Ezhantsy	Central Siberia	35,000 years ago	Wedge-shaped cores, biface fragments
Mamontovaya Kurya	Arctic Russia, Ural Mountains	40,000 years ago	Mammoth, horse, reindeer, and wolf bones; unmodified flakes; bifaces
Yana RHS	Yana River	32,000 years ago	Stone flakes, rhino horn

northwestern North America. At the same time, people living along the Pacific coast of northeast Asia could have moved along the coast of the land bridge as it became exposed. As sea level continued to fall, the growing coasts of northeast Asia and northwest North America finally coalesced, creating a single coast from northeast Asia, across the newly exposed land bridge coast, and then along the coast of northwestern North America. Over several generations, northeast Asians expanding east along this coast would have found themselves in the New World, where they might have continued the process of expansion south along its coast. These migrants, moving through the interior as well as along the coast, would have had no sense that they were moving into a "new world": They merely would have been taking advantage of additional, newly accessible territory (Figure 7.8).

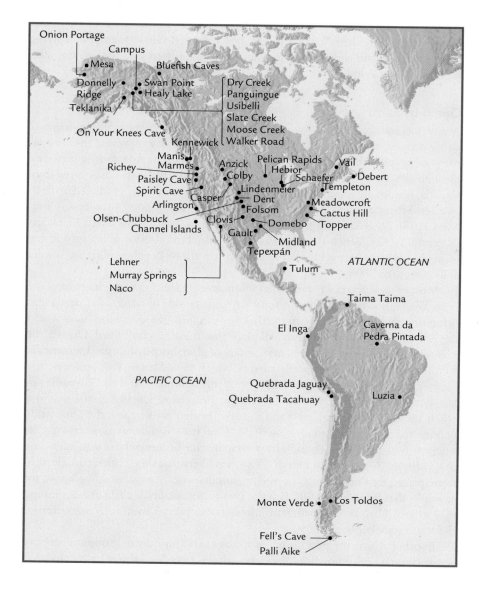

◀ **Figure 7.8**
Sites representing the earliest occupation of North and South America.

The First Human Settlement of America

The legend of the midnight ride of Paul Revere tells us that one or two lamplights placed in the window of the Old North Church steeple would signal the mode of the British attack on Boston: "One if by land, and two if by sea." Regarding the first "invasion" of America by human beings, there also are two possible modes of movement: The first migrants may have been an interior-adapted people taking an interior land route, or they may have been a coastally adapted people taking a sea route along the coast. Obviously, to assess which of these is correct—or whether both routes were used simultaneously by different groups—we need to locate the oldest sites in the New World.

It would be convenient if the oldest sites in the New World were located near the point of entry, either in the interior of Alaska for a group arriving by land or along the Alaskan coast for a group arriving by sea. Unfortunately, the Alaskan interior can be a very inhospitable place to conduct archaeology, and many places along the coast that might have provided shelter for a people living and moving within sight of the sea have been inundated by sea-level rise after the last glacial period.

One If by Land

A few ancient sites in northwestern North America have provided evidence of an interior adaptation. The inhabitants of these sites may represent the descendants of people who came from the interior of northeast Asia and then crossed through the interior of the land bridge. For example, Bluefish Caves in western Canada, reasonably close to the Beringian point of entry, has produced artifacts in a level that has been dated to between 15,000 and 12,000 years ago (Cinq-Mars 1978). The oldest firmly dated occupation of Alaska is the Swan Point Site in central Alaska. When the site was occupied (about 14,000 years ago) it was located in what, effectively, was the eastern margin of Beringia (Goebel, Waters, and O'Rourke 2008).

Most of the evidence for the late Pleistocene occupation of the interior of the New World, however, has been found far to the south of Alaska. Before we can bring the transplanted Asians from Alaska, south into the rest of the New World, there is an additional environmental issue that must be considered. During the Pleistocene, there were two primary centers of glacial expansion: the **Laurentide** ice sheet in northeastern North America, which spread south, east, and west and covered much of the northern latitudes of this continent, and the **Cordilleran** ice sheet, whose center was in the Rocky Mountains. During glacial maxima, when sea level was at its lowest and the land bridge at its largest, the Laurentide continental glacier reached its western limit and the Cordilleran mountain glacier reached its eastern limit. Though the two major ice bodies did not wax and wane in synchrony (Catto and Mandryk 1990), it is likely that they coalesced, at least in some places, for periods of time as they simultaneously expanded. We know, for example, that by about 24,000 B.P. the two major ice fields coalesced beginning in northern Canada, producing an impenetrable barrier to human migration to the south (Goebel et al. 2008).

In other words, the periods when it was easiest for human groups to migrate across Beringia from northeast Asia into what is now Alaska may have coincided with the periods when it was difficult and maybe impossible for them to spread farther south because their way was blocked by an impenetrable ice barrier a few kilometers high. That being the case, people may have migrated into the New World—specifically, the interior of Alaska—only to be stuck there until the merged ice sheets to the south split apart. Retraction of the glaciers and the opening of an **ice-free corridor** (sometimes called the **McKenzie corridor**) is now dated to 14,000 years ago (Figure 7.9).

The lowest cultural levels at the Debra L. Friedkin site in central Texas have produced more than 15,500 artifacts, the vast majority of which are **debitage** flakes, broken bits of stone produced when tools are being made (Waters, Forman, Jennings et al. 2011). Among the 56 actual stone tools recovered in what researchers are calling the Buttermilk Creek Complex are bifacially flaked tools including one that is "lanceolate" (oval shape and pointed on both ends, like a lance), a discoidal core, sharpened flakes, and blades, all made of locally available chert (Figure 7.10). Analysis of the shape of the tools, the configuration of their working edges, and an examination of the wear patterns left behind on those edges as the result of use suggest that the folks at the site were hunting and butchering animals, and perhaps processing hides and cutting wood.

Along with being an artifactually rich site, the occupation levels are clearly delineated by stratigraphy. The primary layer in which the Buttermilk Creek Complex artifacts were recovered has been dated to 15,500 years ago by optically stimulated luminescence (see Chapter 2), making Debra L. Friedkin perhaps the oldest firmly dated site in North America. Far south of where migrants

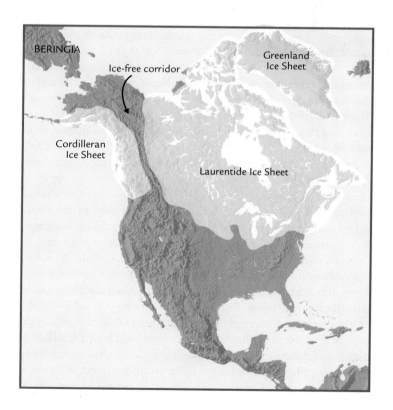

◀ **Figure 7.9**
Map showing the proposed boundaries of the Cordilleran and Laurentide ice sheets of North America. Though the two ice sheets may have coalesced in some localized areas during glacial maxima, it is suggested that an ice-free corridor existed for long periods. Such a corridor might have allowed the migration of people south of Alaska into North America south of the ice sheets. (Courtesy of David Meltzer)

0 1 2 cm

▲ **Figure 7.10**
An assortment of
stone tools that reflect
the Buttermilk Creek
Complex defined at the
Debra L. Friedkin site in
central Texas including
part of a spearpoint, an
adze, and lots of flakes
and blades likely used to
perform tasks involving
cutting and scraping.
The tools were recovered
from a stratigraphic
level dated to 15,500
years ago. (From "The
Buttermilk Creek Complex
and the Origins of Clovis at
the Debra L. Friedkin Site,
Texas" by Michael R. Waters
et al., *Science* 331:6024.
Reprinted with permission
from AAAS.)

would have emerged from an ice-free corridor, this
site implies that even older sites should yet be found
to the north.

Though stone artifacts may be the most common
data available to answer questions about the timing
and nature of the earliest human settlement of the
New World, they are not the only source of information.
In a number of cases, the osteological remains
of now-extinct animals exhibiting apparent butchery
marks made by stone tools have contributed to the
discussion. For example, the remains of apparently
hunted and butchered woolly mammoth have been
excavated in Wisconsin at the Schaefer and Hebior
sites. Schaefer is dated to 14,200 years ago (Joyce
2006). Hebior is somewhat older, producing a date of
14,800 years ago.

The Manis site, in the state of Washington, also
provides us with the remains of a killed animal, in this
case a mastodon (another form of extinct elephant;
based on their tooth surfaces, it looks like mammoths
were browsers of leaves while mastodons were graz-
ers). The Manis site mastodon revealed something else;
embedded in one of the animal's ribs is the weapon
that may have killed it: a sharpened bone spear tip
(Figure 7.11; Waters et al. 2011). A radiocarbon date
of the mastodon's remains indicates that it lived and
died about 13,800 years ago.

Located in western Pennsylvania, south of the ice
sheets and thousands of miles from Beringia, is Meadowcroft Rockshelter, one of
the oldest and most deeply stratified archaeological sites ever excavated in North
America. Within the natural rock enclosure, human beings made tools, cooked
food, and threw away trash, taking advantage of the natural protection the small
cave afforded.

Moving back in time, the excavators of Meadowcroft have chronicled the
human occupation of western Pennsylvania, covering a time span of thousands of
years (Adovasio et al. 1979–80a, 1979–80b; Adovasio, Donahue, and Stuckenrath
1990; Carlisle and Adovasio 1982). And at the base of the sequence brought to
light by these researchers is one of the oldest radiocarbon dates associated with
human-made material south of Alaska. Six dates earlier than 12,800 B.P. have
been associated with stone tools near the base of the Meadowcroft sequence.
Sealed beneath a rockfall from the roof of the shelter dated to 13,400 B.P. were
some 400 lithic artifacts, including blades, knives with retouched edges, and a
bifacial projectile point (Figure 7.12).

The stratigraphy at the Cactus Hill site in Virginia indicates the presence of an
ancient settlement of the American southeast. Here, a stone-scraping tool, stone
blades, and the core from which the blades were struck were found by archaeologist Joseph McAvoy and his group in an undisturbed soil layer. When specialists
have examined the Cactus Hill blades, they note substantial similarities with the

tools recovered at the oldest levels at Meadowcroft Rockshelter (Bonnichsen and Schneider 2001–02).

At Cactus Hill researchers were able to recover enough organic material for a date. The remarkable result: The **pre-Clovis** layer has been radiocarbon dated to about 15,000 years ago (Bower 2000; though there is some question whether the date was derived from older charcoal that had mixed with a younger archaeological deposit).

As you certainly realize, Texas, Wisconsin, Pennsylvania, and Virginia aren't anywhere close to Beringia. Because the inhabitants of these sites could not have parachuted into their habitation, the necessary implication is that we should be able to find an extensive archaeological trail of sites successively older still, leading from their locations back to Beringia, reflecting the movement of people through an ice-free corridor, south of the glaciers, and then east. This archaeological trail does not yet exist, but it's fair to say that we are seeing the evidence converging on a scenario of human migration from northeast Asia into the New World sometime after about 16,000 years ago.

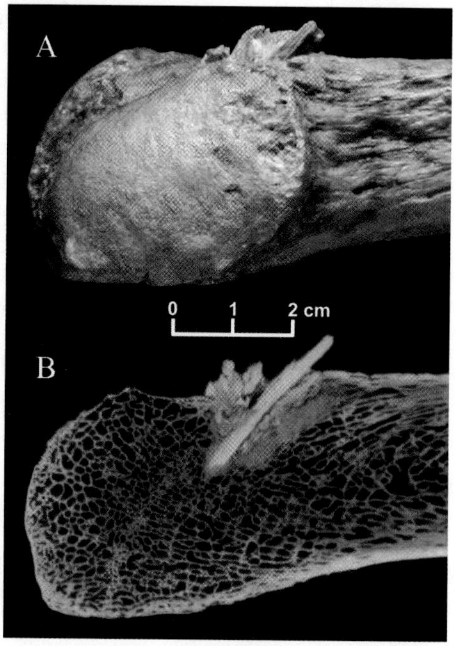

Two If by Sea

Though not located on the coast, the Paisley 5 Mile Point Caves in Oregon may represent an interior settlement of early Beringian coastal migrants (Gilbert et al. 2008). There, researchers found what they have identified as 65 coprolites—deposits of preserved feces in the caves. I'll spare you jokes about "endangered

▲ **Figure 7.11**
It's not often that an archaeologist can claim that he or she found what amounts to a "smoking gun." Just such a discovery was made at the Manis site in Washington State. Shown here in both a regular photograph and in a radiograph is one of the ribs of an ancient mastodon that had been pierced by a bone spearpoint. Radiocarbon dates the mastodon to 13,800 years ago. (From "Pre-Clovis Mastodon Hunting 13,800 Years Ago at the Manis Site, Washington" by Michael R. Waters et al., *Science* 334:6054. Reprinted with permission from AAAS.)

▲ **Figure 7.12**
Stone tools from the earliest indisputable cultural layer at the Meadowcroft Rockshelter in western Pennsylvania. The layer in which the tools were found dates to more than 12,800 years ago. Meadowcroft is considered by many to pose a good case for a pre-Clovis settlement of the New World. (Courtesy of James Adovasio, Mercyhurst Archaeological Institute)

feces." Although there was some contamination (DNA most likely from the excavators was found in the coprolites along with DNA from a wolf or fox), the coprolites definitely contained human DNA that has been identified as belonging to the Native American haplogroup A (Jenkins et al. 2012). Researchers obtained 190 radiocarbon dates on organic material in the cave including some of the coprolites. The oldest of these dates suggest an age of about 14,300 years for the earliest settlement of the caves (Jenkins et al. 2012). Spearpoints made of a style called the Western Stemmed Tradition were found in the caves in strata dated to as much as about 13,250 years ago. This makes this style of spearpoint contemporary with the Clovis points found all across North America as discussed later in this chapter.

At a site that more directly relates to a coastal route into the New World from Beringia, paleontologist Timothy Heaton found substantial evidence of plant and animal life in the ancient layers of On Your Knees Cave, specifically in strata that dated to the late Pleistocene (Dixon 1999). This discovery indicates that even with glaciers all around it, there were places where human beings could have found sufficient resources for survival. And, in fact, at On Your Knees Cave there is direct evidence for that, at least late in this story. A human skeleton was found in the cave and dated to about 10,500 years ago. Isotope analysis of the bones indicated the individual's diet consisted almost entirely of marine foods; in fact, the isotope calculations performed on this person's bones were similar to the same calculations performed on the bones of marine mammal carnivores like ringed seal and sea otter (Dixon 1999:118). The point is, even in Alaska, it seems that there were havens for a maritime people and that the coastal route may have offered a feasible pathway into the New World.

Farther south along the coast, archaeologist Jon Erlandson and his colleagues have reported the results of their excavation of three sites located on the Channel Islands, just off the coast of southern California near Santa Barbara (Erlandson et al. 2011). Radiocarbon dating places the earliest occupation of the islands at between 12,200 and 11,200 years ago. Erlandson recovered finely made stone tools including stemmed points somewhat similar to those at Paisley 5 Mile Point Caves and interesting crescent-shaped knives (Figure 7.13). Most were made of locally available chert, but the source for an obsidian (volcanic glass) artifact found there is more than 300 km away, in eastern California.

There was excellent organic preservation at the island sites and a clear maritime focus is exhibited in the faunal assemblage. The Channel Island residents caught myriad species of fish (rock fish, greenling, sculpin, surfperch, and herring); they collected several different kinds of shellfish (abalone and mussel, as well as crab); they caught sea birds (albatross and cormorant) and migrating fowl (Canada goose and snow goose); and they hunted marine mammals. This kind of subsistence focus matches our expectations for a people adapted to and migrating along a coastal route.

If we skip ahead far to the south we come to the Monte Verde site, located on Chinchihuapa Creek in Chile (Dillehay 1987, 1989, 1996, 1997; Dillehay and Collins 1988). In addition to finding hundreds of stone artifacts, including long, slender spearpoints and cutting and scraping tools, the excavators of the site, led by archaeologist Tom Dillehay, found wooden lances and stakes that likely held down the bases of the inhabitants' hide-covered tents. The wet peat that covered

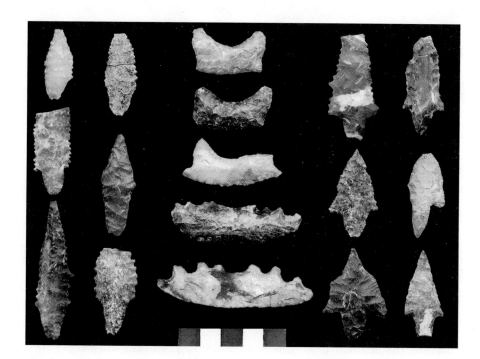

◀ **Figure 7.13**
An array of spearpoints and knives found on the Channel Islands off the coast of southern California near Santa Barbara. Mostly made of locally available raw materials, the tools were found in strata that date back as much as 12,200 years, showing that a maritime adaptation has deep roots in North America. (From "Paleoindian Seafaring, Maritime Technologies, and Coastal Foraging on California's Channel Island" by Jon M. Erlandson et al., *Science* 331:6021. Reprinted with permission from AAAS.)

the site produced an environment in which the bones of animals killed and butchered at the site, and even pieces of meat and skin tissue (identified as mastodon) and fragments of almost 70 different plant species, were preserved. Thirty radiocarbon dates firmly date the site to at least 12,500 years ago. Recent analysis of marine algae and seaweed adhering to the working edges of stone tools found at Monte Verde pushes the dating back even a little further, producing radiocarbon dates close to 14,600 B.P. (Dillehay et al. 2008).

Located near the coast, Monte Verde might best be explained as the remains of a community whose distant ancestors had entered the New World along the Beringian coast, obviously before 14,600 B.P. Archaeologist David Meltzer suggests that the age of the Monte Verde site implies a time of entry into the New World along the Beringian coast before 20,000 B.P. (1997:755). These coastal migrants traveled south along the Pacific coast of the New World—virtually all of their sites would have been submerged by rising sea level and cannot be found. Eventually, these people reached the southern coast of South America, fully 16,000 kilometers (nearly 10,000 miles) from the Bering Land Bridge entrypoint, where they then moved into the interior, leaving the remains at Monte Verde.

Alaska

Back in Alaska, close to the Beringian point of entry, are a number of sites dating to before 11,000 B.P. As archaeologists William Powers and John Hoffecker (1989) point out, it is now clear that there was a widespread tradition of producing small blades from wedge-shaped cores in northeast Asia and northwest North America at the end of the Pleistocene. Sites with wedge-shaped cores and **microblades** have been excavated in Siberia, China, Japan, and Mongolia, as well as in Alaska and northwestern Canada (Morlan 1970). These sites are older in the Old World than in the New World, and a "genetic" connection between the industries of western and eastern Beringia seems clear. Conceivably, these sites may represent a separate wave of population movement from the Old World to the New.

Denali and Nenana

Sites exhibiting tools of the locally designated **Denali Complex** of wedge-shaped cores, microblades, bifacial knives, and **burins** have been excavated in the Nenana Valley, about 100 km (62.5 mi) southwest of Fairbanks, in east-central Alaska (Figure 7.14; Powers and Hoffecker 1989). Sites such as Dry Creek (Component II), Panguingue Creek (Component II), Usibelli, and Slate Creek in the Nenana Valley are assigned to the Denali Complex; Dry Creek has produced a radiocarbon date of about 10,700 B.P. (Powers and Hamilton 1978). Denali Complex sites outside of the Nenana Valley include Donnelly Ridge in central Alaska, the Campus site near Fairbanks, the Teklanika River sites in Mt. McKinley National Park, and Healy Lake (West 1967). These all date to around 10,000 years ago (West 1975). A very different-looking industry of microblades and cores has been found in the earliest levels at the Onion Portage site (Akmak) in western Alaska, also dating to around 10,000 B.P. (D. D. Anderson 1968, 1970).

All of this seems to provide a very neat and simple answer to questions surrounding the first human settlement of the Americas: Beginning some 18,000 years ago, microblade-making northeast Asians like those at the Dyuktai site slowly made their way across Beringia, ending up in Alaska by about 10,700 years ago or a few hundred years earlier. The problem is that Denali Complex sites are not

▶ **Figure 7.14**
Stone tools from the Denali Complex of Alaska dating to after 11,000 B.P. Note the presence of wedge-shaped cores here (g and h), suggesting a derivation from the older wedge-shaped cores in Asia. (Courtesy of William Powers)

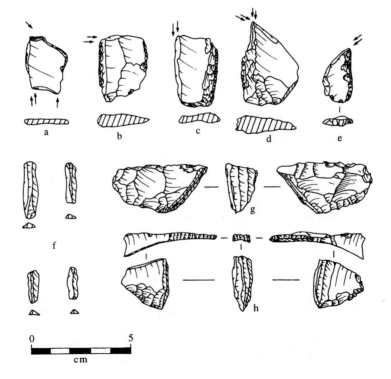

the oldest in the New World; they're not even the oldest in Alaska. There is a cultural level at Dry Creek (Component I) earlier than the Denali level at the same site, and the Moose Creek and Walker Road sites have produced radiocarbon dates ranging between 11,000 B.P. and 11,800 B.P. in their lowest levels. The stone-tool assemblages at these sites—classified as the **Nenana Complex**—show no evidence of Denali Complex wedge-shaped cores and look very little like the stone-tool assemblage at Dyuktai. Instead, these assemblages include bifacially flaked spearpoints (Figure 7.15).

The stone tools representative of the Nenana Complex bear a general resemblance to those found in the lowest stratigraphic level at Ushki Lake, in Kamchatka, mentioned previously. Both the Nenana and Ushki Lake (Component 7) industries consist of small, bifacially worked knives and unifacially retouched flakes and blades; both lack microblades (Dikov 1978; Goebel et al. 2003). As previously mentioned, the teardrop shape of the Neanana Chindadn point is similar in form to a spearpoint found at Ushki. Interestingly, Component 6 at Ushki Lake, dating to 10,000 B.P., has a stone-tool industry quite similar to Denali; both are characterized by the presence of microblades (Goebel et al. 2003).

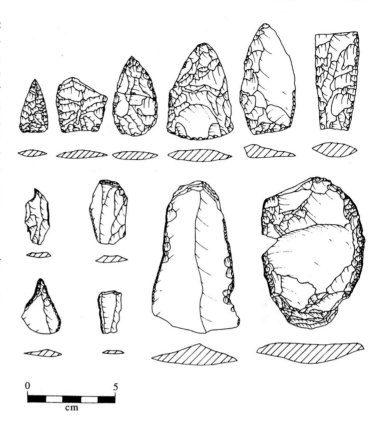

▲ **Figure 7.15**
Stone tools from the Nenana Complex of Alaska, dating to 11,800 B.P. The lack of wedge-shaped cores, the presence of bifacially flaked tools, and dates that are older than those associated with the Denali Complex suggest a different and older migration of northeast Asians into the New World. (Courtesy of William Powers)

The Nenana Complex may be derived from the industry seen at Ushki in Kamchatka, representing an early movement of Asians (about 12,000 B.P.) across the Bering Land Bridge into the New World. Following the hypothesis of West (1981), Powers and Hoffecker (1989) suggest that the Siberian microblade industry seen at sites like Dyuktai and Ushki Component 6 may be at least indirectly ancestral to the later Denali Complex (dated to about 11,000 B.P.) and other early New World microblade industries. Denali, in this view, represents a migration subsequent to an earlier movement of Siberians with a bifacial industry like that seen at the Ushki and Nenana Complex sites.

As Powers and Hoffecker see it, the Denali Complex was restricted to the far north. However, in their view, possessors of the earlier Nenana stone-tool tradition were able to expand to the south. Archaeologists Ted Goebel, Roger Powers, and Nancy Bigelow (1991) point out that, with the exception of fluted spearpoints (to be discussed shortly), the Nenana stone-tool assemblage is virtually identical to that seen to the south and associated with these points. Descendants of these people, Powers and Hoffecker argue, made a small technological step in spearpoint form—the so-called **fluted point**—that allowed for an enormous adaptive leap and the successful occupation of two continents.

Settlement of the Americas

It would be great if all of the data concerning the earliest human movement into the Americas fit into a nice, comprehensible package, telling a clear and unambiguous story giving us a straight line of the sites of migrants, starting in eastern Asia as they initially entered into and then spread through the New World. Unfortunately, that's not the case. Archaeologists continue to argue about contamination of material used to produce radiocarbon dates, the integrity of stratigraphy, and even the identification of some specimens as artifacts. With that in mind, researchers Ted Goebel, Michael Waters, and Dennis O'Rourke (2008) have made a nobel effort to summarize glacial, genetic, and archaeological data from northeast Asia and the Americas that might solve the puzzles that surround the earliest settlement of the New World. By their account:

1. Archaeological evidence indicates that the earliest human settlement of eastern Siberia dates to about 40,000 years ago. In other words, people were in western Beringia by about that time.
2. Based on rates of change in mtDNA, northeast Asian natives and the population that became Native Americans appear to have separated sometime between 25,000 and 20,000 years ago. This suggests that the inhabitants of western Beringia moved into eastern Beringia, most of which is now underwater but this includes interior Alaska and the Canadian Yukon, by about 20,000 years ago.
3. Analysis of the Y-chromosomes of modern northeast Asians and Native Americans suggests a separation date at about the same time, sometime between 22,500 and 20,000 years ago.
4. Variability within Native American mtDNA suggests a dispersal through North and South America south of Beringia sometime around 16,000 years ago. In other words, the genetic evidence indicates that the inhabitants of eastern Beringia in the Late Pleistocene did not themselves geographically separate until this time. A recent mathematical simulation based on an analysis of mutations in the mitochondria of 77 people led researchers to suggest that, perhaps, a few thousand people left northeast Asia and entered into the interior of Alaska about 40,000 years ago, and spread south only about 16,000 years ago (Kitchen, Miyamoto, and Mulligan 2008).
5. As glaciers waxed and waned at the end of the Pleistocene, a possible migration route along the Pacific coast of North America became available south of Beringia by about 15,000 years ago.
6. Archaeological evidence far to the south of Beringia, in Monte Verde, Chile, supports an initial migration along the coast route soon after 15,000 years ago.
7. An interior route from eastern Beringia (interior Alaska and northwestern Canada) south of the glaciers, through an ice-free corridor between the Laurentide and Cordilleran ice fields into the American Great Plains became available for animal and human movement no earlier than about 14,000 years ago.
8. Archaeological evidence recovered at Meadowcroft Rockshelter in Pennsylvania may reflect a habitation by migrants who passed through the ice-

free corridor into the interior of North America at this time. Cactus Hill and Topper may be too old to fit this model, but in some interpretations of their dates, these too could be less than 14,000 years old and supportive of the scenario presented here.

Geneticist David Reich and his colleagues (Reich et al. 2012) conducted an analysis of the DNA of a sample of living Native Americans representing 34 different populations or tribal groupings spread across North and South America. A statistical analysis showed that the people in the sample could be broken down into three distinct genetic clusters: Most could be grouped into what the researchers called "First American" and these people were spread across much of the New World. Modern Eskimos (in Alaska, Canada, and Greenland) and Aleuts (people from the Aleutian Islands of Alaska) formed a second genetic cluster, and the Chipewyan people of Canada constituted a third group. The researchers believe that the three modern genetic groupings are different enough and distinct enough to suggest three different population sources in northeast Asia for the native population of the New World. They further concluded from this that the movement of people into the New World occurred in three separate waves, each represented by a modern genetic cluster. Archaeologists would be convinced of this conclusion if similar results could be extracted from the oldest human skeletons in the New World.

Clovis

Called **Clovis** for the site in New Mexico where the distinctive spearpoints that characterize the tool assemblage were first recognized, **Paleoindian** sites number in the hundreds and are found throughout the continental United States. Where dates have been derived through ^{14}C, almost all Clovis sites fit into a narrow range, between 13,200 B.P. and 11,900 B.P., appearing virtually simultaneously across much of the New World (Haynes 1982, 1987, 1992).

Clovis Technology

Clovis spearpoints are distinctive in having a channel, or flute, on both faces (Figure 7.16). The channel, made by removing (usually) a single broad flake from both faces of the point, originating at the base and ordinarily extending one-quarter to one-third of the way toward the tip, is assumed to have been an aid in hafting the stone point onto a wooden shaft. As mentioned previously, this small technological step seems to have resulted in an adaptive leap that allowed for the rapid expansion of human groups across the New World. This great leap forward is strictly an American invention. **Fluted points** are never found in Siberia or anywhere else in eastern Asia, nor are they present in the Nenana Complex in Alaska. Clovis points are, in fact, rare in Alaska altogether and when found there are dated to the late stage of Clovis culture. In other words, Clovis did not originate in the north but developed somewhere else and moved north only later.

It is, as yet, unclear where Clovis originated, though most archaeologists point to somewhere in the American Midwest or Midsouth. For example, some of the specific chipping patterns seen at the 15,500-year-old Debra L. Friedkin site mentioned earlier in this chapter seem to presage some of the technical aspects of Clovis technology and, in fact, a Clovis component overlies the ancient layer

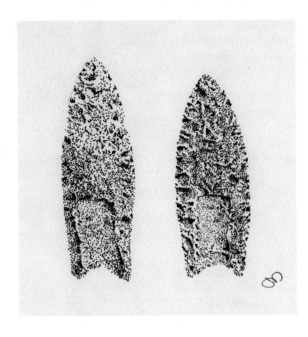

▲ **Figure 7.16**
Fluted points are characterized by channels or "flutes"—as in "fluted columns"—on both faces. The flutes likely aided in hafting the spearpoints onto wooden shafts. Fluted points are a New World invention; they are not found in northeast Asia or, for that matter, anywhere else in the world. The two points depicted here are the Clovis variety. (Illustration by Jennifer Davis)

(Waters, Forman, et al. 2011). The Debra L. Friedkin site may be the solution to the question of where Clovis came from.

The rapid, almost simultaneous appearance of fluted points throughout much of the New World is striking. Whereas there are relatively few sites in America dated to before 13,000 years ago (see "Issues and Debates"), there is a virtual explosion of Clovis sites in the American Southwest and beyond dating to after this (Haynes 1992). Stratified sites such as Clovis, Lehner, Murray Springs, Dent, Colby, and Domebo, all in the Southwest, produced fluted spearpoints and dates in that time range (Haynes 1982).

Clovis points are also found throughout Canada, the continental United States, and Mexico. In the Northwest, the spectacular Richey Clovis Cache in central Washington State, an apparent ceremonial interment of huge fluted points as much as 23.25 cm (a bit more than 9 in) in length, has been dated at 11,200 B.P. (Gramly 1993; Mehringer and Foit 1990). In the American Northeast and Southeast, thousands of fluted points have been recovered from hundreds of sites (D. Anderson 1990). Sites may be younger in the East—but not much: The Vail site in Maine has produced radiocarbon dates of 10,300 B.P. and 11,120 B.P. (Gramly 1982); the mean radiocarbon age of the Debert fluted-point site in Nova Scotia is 10,600 B.P. (MacDonald 1985); and Templeton (6LF21) in Connecticut has been dated to 10,190 B.P. (Moeller 1980).

Even at the most distant New World spot imaginable from Beringia, Fell's Cave at the southern tip of South America (Tierra del Fuego), a fluted point in association with the bones of extinct horse and sloth has been recovered from a site dated to 10,000 years ago (Bruhns 1994). Nonfluted fishtail points were also found in Fell's Cave and in other sites dating to this time in South America at sites such as Palli Aike, also in Tierra del Fuego, Los Toldos in Patagonia, and El Inga in northern Ecuador. Long, leaf-shaped El Jobo points were found at Taima Taima in Venezuela, also dating to the late Pleistocene.

Clovis Subsistence

Though the image of Paleoindians risking life and limb to track down and kill a two-ton, hairy elephant is romantic, they most probably relied on root grubbing, seed gathering, and small-mammal trapping, at least some of the time (Johnson 1991; Meltzer 1993a). Certainly, during some parts of the year, most Paleoindian groups relied on hunting for survival. But once past the glacial and periglacial north and onto the American plains, they could find and exploit many other foods, including seeds, nuts, berries, fish, and small mammals. Away from the glacial front, where animals may have been the only consistent source of food—for example, in the woodlands of eastern North America—Paleoindians were probably "generalist foragers" who not only took big game when the opportunity presented itself but also exploited smaller game and plant foods in their territories (Dincauze 1993).

Geologist C. Vance Haynes points out that the remains of the two varieties of extinct North American elephants, the woolly mammoth and the mastodon, have been recovered from the majority of Clovis sites in the American West, where animal bones have been preserved (1982:390). There are, in fact, a dozen known Clovis sites where the butchered remains of mammoths or mastodons have been excavated. When these elephants became extinct around 11,000 years ago, the Paleoindians in the western United States shifted their hunting focus to bison. The technology changed, producing shorter spearpoints, but with channels extending almost to the tip. These so-called **Folsom** points (Figures 7.17) are of the culture that bears the same name.

First Skeletons

The oldest human skeletons yet found in the New World date to no more than about 13,000 years ago. A skeleton found in an underwater cave near the town of Tulum, on the east coast of the Yucatan Peninsula in Mexico, has been radio-carbon dated to 13,600 years ago (Barclay 2008). The Arlington Spring bones from Santa Rosa Island in California (Owen 1984) have produced a date of 13,000 B.P., making them among the oldest human remains in the New World. The cranium called "Luzia" was found in Brazil, north of Rio De Janeiro, and has a proposed age of slightly more than 13,000 years. The female skeleton from Midland, Texas (originally called "Midland Man" but now known to have been a female), has been dated by uranium series to 11,600 years ago (Hoppe 1992). The remains of a cremated child buried beneath a house floor have been found at the Upward Sun River site in central Alaska. The burial has been dated to 11,500 years ago (Potter et al. 2011). A small number of other human remains have been dated, with varying degrees of certainty, to the period between about 11,500 and 10,500 years ago: the Tepexpán skeleton from Mexico; the Pelican Rapids find (known as "Minnesota Man," another misidentified female); the Marmes skull from Washington State; and Wilsall (Anzick) skeleton in Montana. Somewhat more recent are the remains of Spirit Cave Man in Nevada, dating to about 9,400 years ago, and the remains of Kennewick Man in Washington State, dating to about 9,300 years ago.

Much has been made of the fact that these oldest human remains found in the New World do not match the morphology of modern Native Americans. Modern Native Americans tend to have short, broad skulls with tall, wide faces and broad cheekbones. The oldest crania in the New World simply look different: Their crania exhibit a longer and narrower cranial vault. The overall look is less robust or rugged than modern Indians, and their faces aren't as broad.

For example, before a radiocarbon date was obtained, Kennewick Man was initially identified as a white settler, largely because of the shape of his skull. The female Luzia appears to have more in common morphologically with the crania of native Africans or even Australians than she does with modern Native Americans (Parfit 2000).

Does this mean that the people who left behind the oldest skeletal remains in the New World are not the ancestors of modern Native Americans and that the ancestors of modern natives represent a different, later migration to the New World? Not really. In fact, head shape simply seems not to matter all that much in tracing populations. Skeletal morphology, including cranial shape, can change from one generation to the next as a result of changes in diet and behavior. DNA is the key, and DNA supports the model of a migration to the New World from northeast Asia through Beringia.

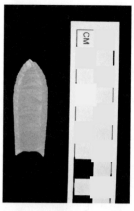

▲ **Figure 7.17**
Paleoindian fluted Folsom point from the Johnson site, Colorado. Folsom points are younger than Clovis points, they are generally smaller than Clovis, and the flute extends nearly the entire length of the point. Where animal bones are found in association with Folsom points, bison clearly was the ancient hunters' choice. (Courtesy R. M. Gramly)

People have been in the New World for more than 15,000 years. They have been adapting to the many habitats of the Americas during this entire time. It is expected that the processes of evolution would have altered their appearance to varying degrees in that lengthy period. Though the research is still in its initial stages, and though the sample size is quite small, skeletal morphology still indicates that, indeed, the first human migrants to the New World came from Asia, but at a time before the entire stereotypical suite of modern Asian skeletal features had developed on the west side of Beringia.

Why Were the Pacific Islands Settled?

Geoffrey Irwin (1993:211–212) lists some of the possible motives for the expansion into the vast and previously uncharted Pacific: curiosity about what lay beyond the horizon, a desire to find areas suitable for habitation and rich in resources, and the need to find new land as a result of overpopulation or warfare. As Irwin points out, motives are not testable archaeologically. And, as John Terrell (1986) indicates, the motives to move out into the Pacific were likely as mixed and as varied as those of Europeans in their own age of exploration.

Whatever the reasons, the many inhabited islands of the Pacific, populated initially by people possessing very few, rather homogeneous cultures, produced a wide array of adaptations once they were settled. Settlers exploited the most valuable resources, developing their own unique adaptations to each island or island chain. On New Zealand, the moa—a large flightless bird unique to that nation—became a major component in the diet of a hunting society. Powerful and complex agricultural societies arose on Hawaii and Tonga (Kirch 1984). The fascinating people of Easter Island arrived there sometime after A.D. 800 and developed great skills at organizing their own labor, which enabled the quarrying, carving, transportation, and erection of about 900 enormous stone sculptures that have generated such interest and speculation (Figure 7.18). All of today's enormous diversity developed from those first courageous voyages across the vast Pacific Ocean a few thousand years ago.

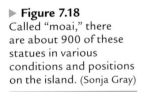

▶ **Figure 7.18**
Called "moai," there are about 900 of these statues in various conditions and positions on the island. (Sonja Gray)

Could Native Americans Really Have Come from Europe Instead of Asia?

It can often be a good thing to step back from the "facts" that we all know to be true and consider, at least the possibility, that everything we know is instead wrong. This happened recently when it was proposed that the native people of the New World may have arrived during the late Pleistocene, not from Asia through Beringia but instead by boat from Europe along the margin of the ice-covered waters of the northern Atlantic. This scenario fundamentally calls into question all of our current models of the settlement of the New World based on archaeology, linguistics, biological anthropology, and genetics, but it's still worth a look.

The argument presented by archaeologists Dennis Stanford and Bruce Bradley (2012) is based on perceived detailed and deep technological and morphological similarities between Clovis technology and that of the Solutrean tradition of the European Upper Paleolithic (see Chapter 6). Stanford is an archaeologist at the Smithsonian, and I don't think there is a human being on the planet who knows more about lithic technology than Bradley. Nevertheless, the hypothesis has little to recommend it.

Archaeologist Lawrence Guy Straus (2000) has provided a detailed response to Stanford and Bradley's proposal, providing the perspective of an expert on the Solutrean. Straus rejects the suggestion of a Solutrean/Clovis connection completely, calling the Solutrean an "impossible candidate" as the source for Clovis. As Straus points out, perhaps the biggest problem in attempting to trace Clovis technology to the Solutrean lies in timing. On the one hand, the Solutrean is a short-lived technological tradition that essentially disappeared from Europe by 17,000 years ago. Clovis, on the other hand, didn't develop in North America until nearly 4,000 years later. Attempting to prove a connection between the makers of stone-tool technologies whose homelands are separated by 5,000 km (about 3,100 mi) of ocean is difficult enough. Connecting two peoples separated by 4,000 years seems quite impossible.

Straus also points out the lack of any evidence of maritime abilities on the part of the Solutrean toolmakers that might have made a trans-Atlantic crossing by them feasible, even through a series of island-to-island hops. Furthermore, the Solutrean toolmakers didn't live in the far north of Europe, where movement along the ice-covered Atlantic might have been an option for a maritime people.

Straus's argument against a connection between Solutrean and Clovis seems definitive. The hypothesis of a European source for the indigenous people of the Americas, at least those responsible for Clovis, is not supported by the evidence at hand.

Who—or What—Killed the American and Australian Megafauna?

Archaeologists, historians, and paleoecologists have long been aware of the curious, apparent correlation between the first arrival of human groups in Australia and in the New World and the massive extinction of large game animals that occurred in these two regions. In Australia, 23 of the 24 animal genera whose individual members weighed more than 45 kg (about 100 lb) became extinct between 51,000 and 40,000 years ago (Roberts and Brook 2010). On the island of Tasmania, seven large animal species including a kangaroo weighing in at more than 150 kg (330 lb) became extinct soon after 43,000 years ago (Turney et al. 2008), and in North America, 34 large mammalian genera disappeared soon after 11,000 years ago (Grayson 1987:8).

Maybe these extinctions had been the result of something very big and very bad happening to our planet. It certainly sounds pretty scary yet cool: Maybe the Late Pleistocene megafauna of North America was wiped out 12,900 years ago by a radiation burst from a nearby supernova explosion or by an enormous asteroid crashing to earth or by our planet's close encounter with a killer comet. Maybe, whatever the ultimate source of the cataclysm, it precipitated the 1,000-year-long, worldwide cold snap called the Younger Dryas period by geologists and paleoclimatologists (see Chapter 8) and this killed off the megafauna (Firestone et al. 2007). It screams screenplay, doesn't it? It should star Bruce Willis. I mean, he's saved us from an asteroid impact already, in *Armageddon*, didn't he? Well, sure, he ended up dead at the end of that movie. But we can bring him back.

Well, the cosmic catastrophe just described was seriously suggested as a possible explanation for Late Pleistocene megafauna extinction, a smaller version of the impact 65 million years ago that is believed to have plunged our planet into a prolonged winter that, in turn, killed off the dinosaurs. There were hints in the geological record that something like that might have happened 12,900 years ago: the presence of tiny magnetic spheres that could have resulted from a cosmic impact; strata displaying charcoal deposits from widespread fires from that period; tiny diamond crystals that could have resulted from a crushing impact.

It cannot be denied that it was an interesting hypothesis. Like all scientific hypotheses, it was held up to careful scrutiny by other scientists who were skeptical. That's how scientists should respond to a new hypothesis.

The conclusion and consensus: no dice. None of the proposed markers of the catastrophe have been verified (Kerr 2010). There was no Late Pleistocene, catastrophic cosmic impact. Bruce Willis can relax. There must be some other cause for Late Pleistocene extinctions.

Interestingly, the dates for Late Pleistocene megafauna extinctions are close enough to the timing of both the first appearance of human beings in Australia and Tasmania and the age of the first widespread and successful adaptation to North America (Clovis) to raise the obvious question: Were the human migrants in some way responsible for these events?

Ecologist Paul S. Martin's "Pleistocene overkill" hypothesis (P. S. Martin 1967; and see P. S. Martin and Wright 1967) involves a compelling scenario: The first human migrants to the American heartland find a flourishing bestiary that would put any modern African game park to shame. The seemingly limitless food source allows these paleohunters to expand their population at a rapid rate, ultimately filling two continents. Yet the seeds of their destruction are planted in the magnitude of their success. Large game animals, their populations already stressed by the changing climate at the end of the Pleistocene, are overhunted and ultimately suffer extinction. The human hunters at the root cause of this disaster go on to shift their adaptive strategies to other resources, having little choice but to drastically restructure their subsistence and their culture.

In an exciting piece of research, Jacquelyn Gill and her colleagues discovered that a kind of fungus—*Sporomiella*—that thrives on herbivore dung was abundant in North America up until about 14,800 years ago (Gill et al. 2009). After that, the spores produced by the fungus (and, by implication, the fungus itself) declined dramatically. This signifies either that the herbivores happily depositing solid wastes upon which *Sporomiella* thrived became totally constipated 14,800 years ago, or, more likely, they suffered a massive die-off at that point leading, rather obviously, to a decline in the main food source of *Sporomiella* (and making it a lot more pleasant to walk around without your shoes on). Though it's not possible at this point to prove what caused that die-off, it is clear, based on the fungal spore data, that the die-off happened at least a couple of thousand years *before* pollen analysis indicates that climate changed dramatically. In other words, the Pleistocene megafauna of North America—50% of all mammal species more than 32 kg (70 pounds) and 100% of all species more than 1000 kg (2,200 pounds) (Gill et al. 2009:1100)—had already either become extinct or were on the verge of extinction before they experienced a dramatic climate change. Human beings (bearers of a pre-Clovis culture), however, likely were in North America at about the time of the fungal spore decline, not proving but at least conforming with the notion that it was human activity that led to the extinction of the megafaua.

Many scholars continue to support this scenario. For example, geologist Larry Agenbroad (1988) has mapped the locations of dated Clovis sites alongside the distribution of dated sites where the remains of woolly mammoths have been found (in both archaeological and purely paleontological contexts). These distributions show remarkable synchrony (Agenbroad 1988:71). The species hardest hit in the extinction wave were large animals who would have been precisely those preferred by hunters, slow breeders who would have been most affected by overhunting. At the same time, animal species that survived the extinction wave tended to be nocturnal and/or tree, mountain, or deep forest dwellers, precisely the kinds of animals that might not be on the human menu because they are difficult to find (Barnosky et al. 2004).

In Australia, as in North America, the data are in the dung. There, too, *Sporomiella* has shown a very rapid decline, dropping off virtually to zero at 41,000 years ago (Rule et al. 2012). This timing does not coincide with Late Pleistocene climate change, nor did Rule and her colleagues find a correspondence with other environmental factors, like wide-scale burning. The only thing the drop-off in *Sporomiella* and the deduced disappearance of large animals correlate with is the appearance of human hunters in Australia. The situation on Tasmania was quite the same. For example, the latest dates derived on bones of three species of giant kangaroos on Tasmania correspond precisely with the earliest dates for the human settlement on the island (Turney et al. 2008). Was this a coincidence or did the presence of humans contribute to this extinction?

As of this moment, which factors were key and which were incidental in the extinction of megafauna at the end of the Pleistocene is unclear. As most researchers admit, it will take years of research to solve this puzzle.

THROUGHOUT HUMAN HISTORY—AND THAT INCLUDES the part before there was writing—people often have elected to locate their settlements with practical considerations in mind. Folks concerned about aggressive, nasty neighbors may choose to place their communities in secluded, out-of-the-way spots that are hidden and readily defendable. A maritime people might decide to situate

CASE STUDY CLOSE-UP

a

b

c

◄ Figure 7.19
People, both ancient and modern, choose to settle in certain locations as a result of a constellation of factors including the ready availability of important and valuable natural resources. It is almost certainly the case that the Paleoindians who settled at the Gault site based their decision at least in part on the presence of accessible seams of a very high-quality chert, perfect for making durable and sharp-edged stone tools. (Courtesy Michael R. Waters)

their villages along the shores of a protected bay for the gentle harbors such places provide for their boats. A people who rely on long-distance trade can settle near the convergence of a number of streams whose watercourses provide convenient avenues for canoes used to access the distant regions in multiple directions. People may also choose to live near places where useful and valuable resources are readily available, both for convenient access and, perhaps, to be able to control the access of folks who live elsewhere. For example, in recent history towns may grow up around coal seams, oil fields, or gold deposits.

The location of the Gault site in south-central Texas is an example of this kind of practical decision making on the part of Paleoindians 13,000 years ago. The site, one of the oldest in the United States and just 250 meters upstream from the even older Debra L. Friedkin site discussed earlier in this chapter, clearly was situated by its inhabitants to most conveniently exploit a local rock source—Edwards chert—that can be readily and predictably flaked into sharp-edged and durable tools (Figure 7.19; Waters, Pevny, and Carlson 2011).

The artifact assemblage at Gault clearly shows that quarrying the local stone and then manufacturing tools from it were the primary activities conducted at the site. The site was, in fact, as its excavators label it, a "quarry workshop." Lithics were the most abundant remains found during the excavation in 2000, totaling more than 66,500 fragments. The vast majority of these bits of chipped stone was debitage, the waste flakes discarded during quarrying and toolmaking. Stone toolmaking is a reductive process; essentially, the knapper is sculpting a tool from a larger chunk of rock. In the process, lots of very small flakes are produced (microdebitage) that are of no use because of their size. I see this all the time in my experimental archaeology course where, even after a few hours of work by a dozen students, the floor of the lab is littered with tiny flakes of unusable stone.

It's just the nature of the process. Of the 66,502 flakes recovered in the 2000 dig at Gault, about 62,874 (almost 95%) were microdebitage and most of the rest (3,487 pieces) were larger waste flakes (macrodebitage).

Broken or complete tools and cores and core fragments were also recovered at the site, including fifty-one generic bifaces (tools chipped on both faces in order to produce a straight, sharp edge), forty-four cores and core fragments (these were chert nodules from which blades and flakes were removed), five projectile points, one knife, ten scraping tools, and three preforms (unfinished tools) (Figure 7.20; Waters, Pevny, and Carlson 2011:8). Excavators even found a single quartzite hammerstone, its end battered from striking flakes from the chert cores found at the site. We often use quartzite hammerstones in my experimental archaeology course; the rock is hard and dense and very well suited for peeling sharp flakes from stone cores.

By closely examining the lithics, researchers identified essentially two reductive pathways taken in toolmaking at the site. Both pathways began with the selection of vaguely rectangular blocks of chert from the quarry. In one pathway, these blocks were reduced to conical or wedge-shaped cores from which blade tools then were produced. In the other manufacturing pathway, rectangular chert blocks were collected from which large flakes were struck. From these flakes the Gault knappers produced bifaces and, ultimately, tools like the projectile points and knives.

Though organic preservation wasn't great at Gault, among the 5,700 mostly small bone fragments recovered, a few species could be identified and at least a part of the Gault residents' diet discerned. Among the species found at Gault were bison, white-tailed deer, rabbit, bear, and turtle. This broad spectrum of animals in the Gault diet reflects a diverse subsistence base and belies the stereotype of Paleoindians existing solely by hunting large game animals. This makes a great deal of sense. The overreliance on one or a very few food sources can be a recipe for disaster if conditions change and those few sources decline in numbers or even become extinct. The broad subsistence base seen at Gault provided options for its residents when environmental conditions changed.

A single hearth was identified at the site. One can imagine a group of knappers gathered around that hearth, cooking food as they made tools, telling stories of yesterday's hunt, and laughing as one of the toolmakers curses after being cut

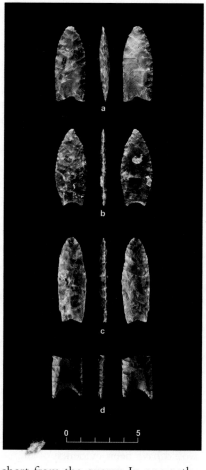
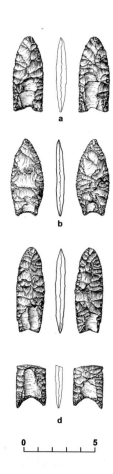

▲ **Figure 7.20**
Within the extensive lithic assemblage of more than 66,000 artifacts at the 13,000-year-old Gault site in central Texas were finished, bifacially flaked tools. Among the bifaces were these exquisitely made fluted points. (Courtesy Michael R. Waters)

by a sharp stone blade. It is an evocative image and it dates to a time deep in the history of North America.

Summary

In the late Pleistocene, expanding human populations intruded into new territories and ultimately migrated into three previously uninhabited continents: Australia, North America, and South America. Australia was populated by coastally adapted southeast Asians. Using watercraft, by accident and perhaps through intentional exploration, they moved out into the western Pacific; inhabited the oceanic islands of Borneo, Sulawesi, and Timor; and eventually made landfall on Greater Australia: New Guinea, Tasmania, and Australia proper. Archaeological evidence offers a date for this habitation of 50,000 years ago—during a period of lowered sea level, when the trip by watercraft would have been easier than it is today. The first settlers maintained a tropical/coastal orientation to their economy, initially turning inland only along major rivers. The dry interior of the continent was settled about 20,000 years later. During the Pleistocene, the New World was intermittently connected to the Old World by a vast land bridge, making it possible for interior-dwelling people in northeast Asia to travel through the interior of the land bridge into the interior of northwest America and for coastal people in northeast Asia to travel along the southern Beringian coast onto the coast of northwestern North America and from there south.

Sites as distant from the land bridge as Monte Verde in Chile (dated to 14,600 B.P.), Meadowcroft Rockshelter in western Pennsylvania (dated to 13,400 B.P.), Cactus Hill in Virginia (dated to 15,000 B.P.), and the Debra L. Friedkin site in Texas (dated to 15,500 B.P.) imply a much earlier time of entry onto the land bridge—20,000 years ago or possibly more—but no definitive archaeological evidence of sites this old in the New World has yet been found. Many sites that would have been evidence of migrants taking a coastal route to the south were long ago inundated by rising sea level at the end of the Pleistocene. Interior sites may be so ephemeral that finding them could be almost impossible. Several early sites in Alaska and the Canadian Yukon date to the period immediately after 12,000 years ago and bear lithic industries analogous to those in Siberia. Some of the early settlers moved south, perhaps through an ice-free corridor, into the American West, where they invented a new projectile point technology. These fluted projectile points allowed these settlers to expand across two continents. These Clovis people may not have been the first arrivals; some sites in both North and South America may be older. But Clovis represents the first broadly successful occupation of the New World.

TO LEARN
MORE

For a detailed overview of Australia's past, see John Mulvaney and Johan Kamminga's *Prehistory of Australia* (1999). Two excellent sources on the colonization of the Pacific are John Terrell's *Prehistory in the Pacific Islands* (1986) and Geoffrey Irwin's *The Prehistoric Exploration and Colonisation of the Pacific* (1993).

For the most current popular summary of the issue of who first populated the New World and when, see archaeologist David Meltzer's (2009) *First Peoples in a New World*. For a succinct summary of the earliest settlement of the Americas, read "Coming to America" by Andrew Curry in the May 3, 2012, issue of *Nature*. For a review of the data concerning the role played by human hunters in the extinction of megafauna at the end of the Pleistocene, read the article by Barnosky et al. titled "Assessing the Causes of Late Pleistocene Extinctions on the Continents," in the October 1, 2004, issue of *Science*. For a splendid summary of the archaeology of the Gault site, see *Clovis Lithic Technology: Investigation of a Stratified Workshop at Gault, Texas* (Waters, Pevny, and Carlson 2011).

A well-written and predictably wonderfully illustrated article written by Michael Parfit, "The Hunt for the First Americans," was published in the December 2000 issue of *National Geographic*. That issue contained a spectacular map showing the locations of the many ancient sites so far discovered in this search in North and South America.

Web links for this chapter can be found at www.oup.com/us/feder

KEY TERMS

Beringia (or Bering Land Bridge), 213
burin, 224
Chindadn, 216
Clovis, 215
Cordilleran, 218
debitage, 219
Denali Complex, 224
fluted point, 221
Folsom, 229

gracile, 205
haplogroup, 213
ice-free corridor (or McKenzie corridor), 219
Lapita, 210
Laurentide, 218
Melanesia, 209
microblade, 223
Micronesia, 209
Nenana Complex, 209

Paleoindian, 225
Polynesia, 227
pre-Clovis, 209
Sunda (or Sundaland), 221
Sahul, 201
Wallacea, 202
Wallace Trench, 202
wedge-shaped core, 215

8

After the Ice

The Food-Producing Revolution

CHAPTER OVERVIEW

As the post-Pleistocene environment became more diverse, many areas are marked by increasing cultural diversity during what is called the Mesolithic period in the Old World and the Archaic in the New World. Different societies responded in different ways to post-Pleistocene changes. Some human groups expanded their resource base and practiced a broad subsistence strategy. Others intensified the subsistence quest, focusing on a small number of particularly rich resources. Some groups continued a nomadic pattern, moving to exploit the seasonal shift in resource availability. Other groups became more sedentary, investing their subsistence labors in a particular place.

	13	12.5	12	11.5
Europe	Franchthi Cave	Younger Dryas		
North America				
Asia			Djalai-nor	
Australia				
South America				Caverna da Pedra Pintada
				Quebrada Tacahuay
				Quebrada Jaguay
Africa				

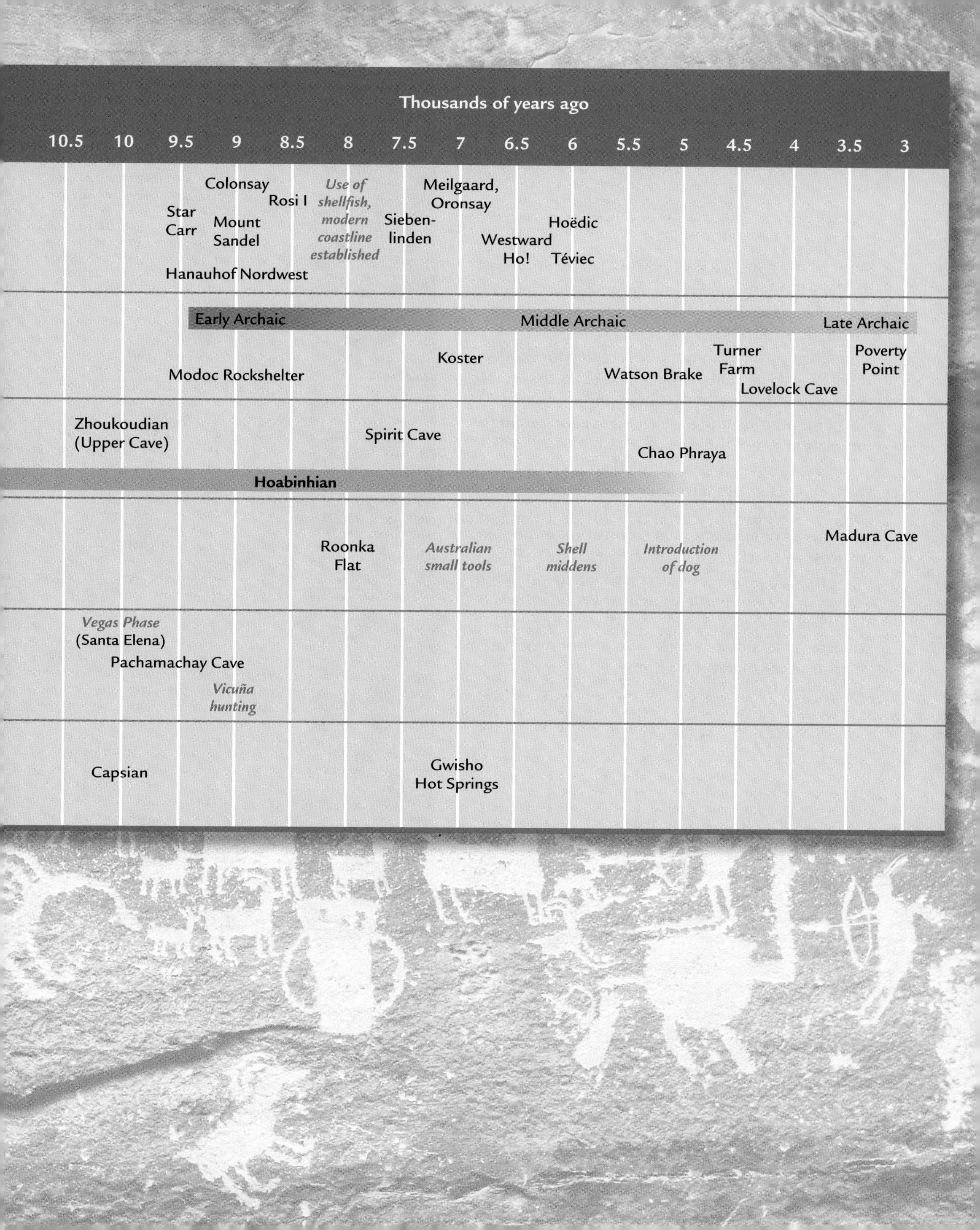

Thousands of years ago

| 10.5 | 10 | 9.5 | 9 | 8.5 | 8 | 7.5 | 7 | 6.5 | 6 | 5.5 | 5 | 4.5 | 4 | 3.5 | 3 |

Colonsay
Rosi I
Use of shellfish, modern coastline established
Meilgaard, Oronsay
Star Carr
Mount Sandel
Sieben-linden
Hoëdic
Westward Ho!
Téviec
Hanauhof Nordwest

Early Archaic   Middle Archaic   Late Archaic

Koster
Turner Farm
Poverty Point
Modoc Rockshelter
Watson Brake
Lovelock Cave

Zhoukoudian (Upper Cave)
Spirit Cave
Chao Phraya

Hoabinhian

Roonka Flat
Australian small tools
Shell middens
Introduction of dog
Madura Cave

Vegas Phase (Santa Elena)
Pachamachay Cave
Vicuña hunting

Capsian
Gwisho Hot Springs

The food-producing revolution of the Neolithic period represents one response to the changes wrought by the end of the Pleistocene. Some human groups began not just foraging for food—hunting wild animals, fishing, and collecting edible plants found in nature—but actually producing it. By concentrating and tending plants and taming animals that were of economic importance, and by allowing only those individual animals or plants with characteristics desirable from a human sub-sistence standpoint to survive and propagate, a number of different human groups began the slow process referred to as "artificial selection." This shift to food production occurred independently in several places in the New and Old Worlds. Today, our diets reflect a vast and varied array of foods, the great majority of which were first domesticated by people many millennia ago.

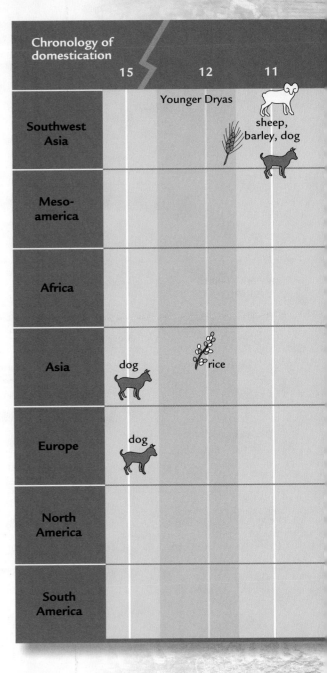

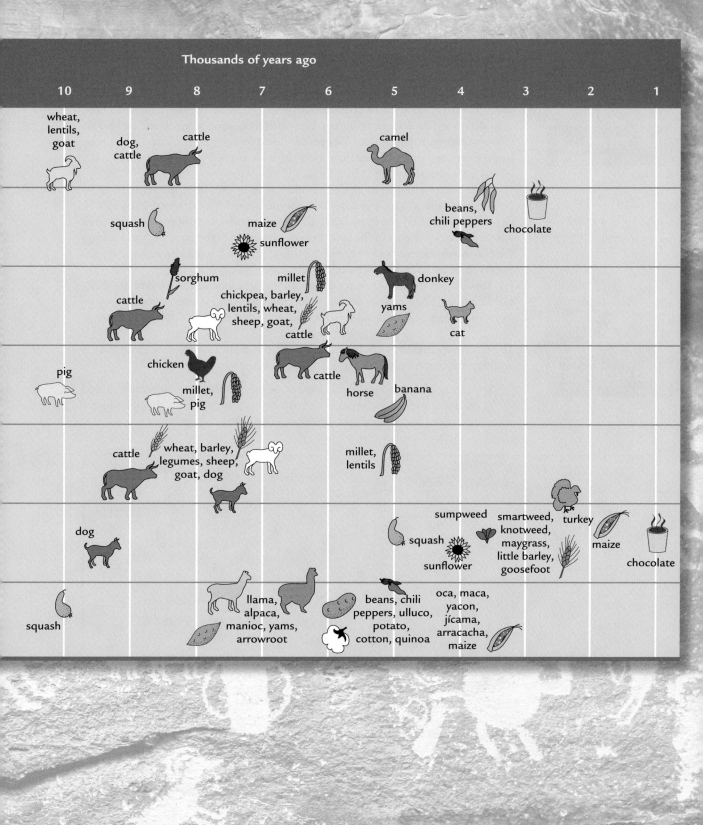

Thousands of years ago

10 9 8 7 6 5 4 3 2 1

wheat, lentils, goat

dog, cattle

cattle

camel

beans, chili peppers

chocolate

squash

maize

sunflower

sorghum

millet

donkey

cattle

chickpea, barley, lentils, wheat, sheep, goat, cattle

yams

cat

pig

chicken

millet, pig

cattle

horse

banana

cattle

wheat, barley, legumes, sheep, goat, dog

millet, lentils

dog

sumpweed

squash

sunflower

smartweed, knotweed, maygrass, little barley, goosefoot

turkey

maize

chocolate

squash

llama, alpaca, manioc, yams, arrowroot

beans, chili peppers, ulluco, potato, cotton, quinoa

oca, maca, yacon, jícama, arracacha, maize

PRELUDE

You have probably tasted and maybe regularly eat the traditional foods of a number of different ethnic groups. Virtually every city in North America has restaurants specializing in Chinese, Japanese, or Korean food with their rice-based dishes; Italian food with its pasta-based meals; Mexican cuisine with beans and corn flour tortillas and tacos; Indian food with its unique blend of spices; Middle Eastern food with wheat flour pita bread, chickpeas, and lentils; Greek food with lamb; German food with beef and pork; as well as the Native American turkey we eat on Thanksgiving.

What's interesting from our perspective here is that all of the ingredients in these foods—plants and animals—were domesticated thousands of years ago. In fact, it is difficult to come up with any economically significant modern food source that was not part of the food base in some part of the ancient world during the **Neolithic**. Even chocolate, without which life itself would be impossible, was the result of an ancient process of domestication.

This chapter focuses on cultural changes that accompanied the end of the Pleistocene and the beginning of the Holocene, the epoch that continues to the present, including a shift in human subsistence from food gathering to food production.

CHRONICLE

THE KEY CHARACTERISTIC OF THE CULTURES of the early Holocene (Figure 8.1) is adaptive change, reflected in the following features:

1. In most places, the archaeological record shows that human groups shifted their subsistence focus as the animals and plants on which they previously had relied became extinct or unavailable in their home regions.

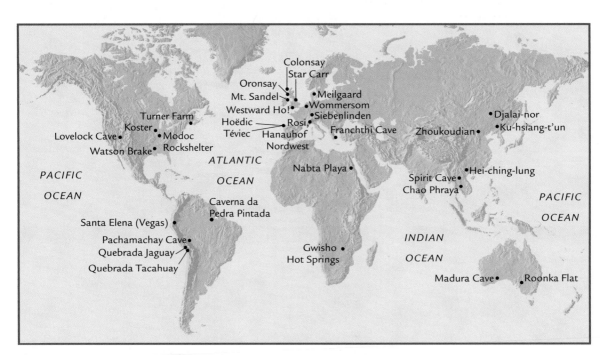

▲ **Figure 8.1**
Sites of the early post-Pleistocene.

2. A broad and rich diversity characterizes the cultural adaptations developed by people all over the world in response to the new, modern climatic regimes that are ultimately established in the Holocene. This diversity is reflected in a proliferation of subsistence strategies, artifact assemblages, and settlement patterns as seen in the archaeological record.

3. In some regions, the post-Pleistocene subsistence base changed from mega-fauna to smaller animals, fish, shellfish, and birds and included a greater reliance on plant foods previously absent or rare during glacial conditions.

4. In some areas, the focus on certain abundant resources encouraged a shift from a nomadic existence to a more sedentary one.

In some regions the subsistence shift involved more intensive exploitation of some uniquely productive elements in the food quest. In these regions, people focused on a small number of highly productive resources.

Europe

A warming trend can be deduced from the pollen record of Europe for the period after 16,000 B.P. This trend was sufficient to render even Scandinavia ice free just 3,000 years later, by about 13,000 B.P. This warming was interrupted at least once by a rapid and severe shift back to glacial conditions. This so-called **Younger Dryas** interval began soon after 12,900 years ago and appears to have lasted for about 1,300 years, until about 11,600 years ago (Lowell and Kelly 2008; Severinghaus et al. 1998). I mentioned the Younger Dryas cold interval in Chapter 7; some suggested that it was the result of a cosmic impact (with a meteor or a comet), but geological evidence simply does not support this scenario.

Whatever its cause, Younger Dryas was a relatively minor deviation from a trend that would result in near-modern conditions across much of Europe by 8500 B.P. (Gamble 1986; T. D. Price 1991; C. Smith 1992). The return to colder and drier conditions at the end of the Younger Dryas had a significant worldwide impact on hunters and gatherers and may have contributed to subsistence changes with vast implications for the modern world. Sea level was rising, too, breaking the connection between Great Britain and the continent by 8,000 years ago and establishing modern coastlines relatively soon thereafter (Figure 8.2; Megaw and Simpson 1979; C. Smith 1992).

The assemblage of large game animals, including woolly mammoth and rhinoceros, wild cattle, horse, and reindeer, that characterized the Pleistocene was gone throughout most of Europe after 9000 B.P. The cold-loving grasses and sedges of the tundra on which those large herbivores subsisted were replaced first by birch and pine trees and later by elm and oak to the south. The big-game animals that had subsisted on those grasses and sedges were replaced by smaller, less mobile, forest-dwelling animal species, including red deer, roe deer, and wild pig, along with even smaller fur-bearing animals such as marten, beaver, otter, and wolf (T. D. Price 1991). As archaeologist T. Douglas Price (1991:190) points out, the key characteristic of the environment of Holocene Europe when compared to that of the Pleistocene was the vast array of plants and animals available for exploitation. Thus, the most salient feature of the food resource base of post-Pleistocene Europe was its diversity.

▶ **Figure 8.2**
As this map of the coastline of Europe during the early Holocene shows, broad areas that were dry land 9,500 years ago are today under the sea. (Courtesy of T. Douglas Price)

It was to the extremely diverse mixture of plants and animals establishing themselves in post-Pleistocene Europe that human groups adapted. This diversity, both within and between regions, helps explain the cultural record of Europe after the ice. The European **Mesolithic**—the cultural period that follows the Paleolithic in Europe and precedes the appearance of farming cultures—was marked by many of the features of post-Pleistocene cultures.

Mesolithic Subsistence Patterns

While Upper Paleolithic sites in northern Europe commonly have only a single large mammal species represented, archaeologist Christopher Meiklejohn (1978:67) points out that in a survey of seven Mesolithic sites of the **Maglemosian** culture in Great Britain and France, 11 different large-animal species were reported, with an average of 4 different species at each site. In the cold climate of post-Pleistocene northern Europe, hunting was a significant element in the subsistence quest. Mesolithic sites ordinarily produce a wide array of animal food species, including red deer, roe deer, elk, wild ox, wild sheep, goat, pig, and rabbit. Small fur-bearing mammals such as wolf, fox, badger, beaver, marten, squirrel, and hare were used by these Mesolithic people, almost certainly for their warm pelts.

Charred seeds provide evidence for the significance of plant foods in the Mesolithic diet. Hazelnut shells are commonly found in Mesolithic sites in northern

Europe, and the hazelnut and other nut foods, along with water lily and wild apple, probably made a significant seasonal contribution to the diet (T. D. Price 1987). For example, near Scotland, on the island of Colonsay, in the Hebrides, an enormous pit was found containing thousands of roasted hazelnut shells (Denison 1995). The hazelnuts likely were being processed in the pit, perhaps to render the nutmeats suitable for grinding into a flour. Radiocarbon dates on the shells indicate that this occurred close to 9,000 years ago.

Although rising post-Pleistocene sea levels have inundated most Mesolithic coastal sites and many ancient lakes have become dry land (see Figure 8.2), where local topography has preserved the ancient coast, Mesolithic sites are numerous. Excavation of such sites has shown, predictably, an extensive reliance on coastal resources. Of greatest significance was the pike, a saltwater fish that enters inland channels and inlets to spawn.

The bones of marine mammals are also found in Mesolithic contexts. Species that were hunted include ringed, harp, and gray seals. The remains of hunted or beached whales and porpoises are also found. Birds also contributed to the subsistence quest; 55 different species have been found in Mesolithic sites. For example, at Mount Sandel in Ireland, the remains of duck, pigeon, dove, grouse, goshawk, and capercaillie were excavated (T. D. Price 1987:248).

Shellfish also made an important contribution to the diet in coastal localities. For example, at the Danish site of Meilgaard, a shell **midden** with a volume of 2,000 m³ (21,000 ft³) was made up of millions of mollusk shells (Bailey 1978). In Portugal, coastal middens consisting primarily of mollusk shell are common for the period after 7400 B.P. Mesolithic shell middens dot the island of Oronsay, 30 km (20 mi) off the west coast of Scotland (Mellars 1978). Crab and limpet shells, along with the bones of seal, fish, and 30 species of birds, were found among the food remains (T. D. Price 1987). At Westward Ho! in north Devon, England, Mesolithic kitchen middens of oyster, winkle, mussel, and limpet shells have been dated to more than 6,500 years ago (T. D. Price 1987).

Diversity and Regionalization

Whereas a single lithic tradition characterized the Middle Paleolithic across much of Europe, and only a few geographically demarcated, different, but related traditions were present there in the Upper Paleolithic, the Mesolithic period in Europe was marked by a far more diverse cultural pattern. For example, throughout northern Europe archaeologist T. Douglas Price (1991:199) counts at least 15 different regional stone-toolmaking patterns by the end of the Mesolithic.

Cultural regions of the European Upper Paleolithic—as determined by the geographic extent of archaeological sites where similar tool styles and types are found—have been estimated to encompass as much as 100,000 km² (38,610 mi²). During the Mesolithic, defining cultural regions or territories the same way results in a far greater number of much smaller territories, more on the order of 1,000 km² (386 mi²) each (T. D. Price 1991:200). Trading networks show much the same pattern (T. D. Price 1987). Whereas trading networks actually extended over longer distances in the Upper Paleolithic (see Chapter 6), trade during the Mesolithic was more intraregional. Trade materials didn't move as far as they had in the Upper Paleolithic, but more of them were moving through the more geographically restricted regional systems.

The subsistence patterns of Mesolithic people also appear to reflect regionalization, even on a very small scale. For example, when the isotope signatures of human bones recovered from two Mesolithic sites located only about 30 kilometers (18.6 miles) apart in Brittany, along the northwest coast of France, were compared by archaeologist Rick Schulting, the diets of the inhabitants appear to have been quite different. At one site, Hoëdic, much of the food base consisted of fish and marine mammals while at Téviec, subsistence focused on terrestrial food sources (Spinney 2008).

The most important thing all that information shows is this: Various groups settled into their own distinct regions in Europe after the Pleistocene, evolved their own adaptations to their unique set of local postglacial environmental conditions, and developed their own tool assemblages and their own distinctive patterns of subsistence and settlement.

Asia

In the north, Chang (1986) recognizes two major Mesolithic groupings on the basis of stone tools: a blade-and-flake industry in the forests of Manchuria and a microblade industry in the riverine and lake habitats that constituted oases in the deserts of Mongolia (Figure 8.3).

The regions of Mongolia inhabited by the **microblade** manufacturers are characterized by dry, shallow depressions that were small lakes during early post-

▶ **Figure 8.3**
Artifacts from the post-Pleistocene culture in Manchuria, northern China. (From *The Archaeology of Ancient China*, by K. C. Chang, © 1987, Yale University Press, with permission)

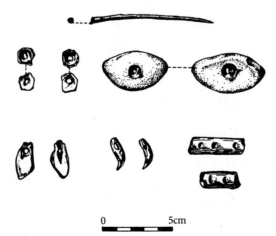

0   5cm

Pleistocene times. Spearpoints and arrow points are few at these sites, probably indicating the marginality of hunting. The most common faunal remain is ostrich shell fragments, and people almost certainly relied on the fish available in the lakes around which they settled.

Evidence at sites like Djalai-nor and Ku-hsiang-t'un, in the woodlands of Manchuria, indicates that hunting was more important than in the lakeside habitations. Spearpoints are more common, as are bone and antler tools. At sites like the Upper Cave at Zhoukoudian, a Mesolithic occupation of north China near where *Homo erectus* remains were discovered (see Chapter 4), the faunal remains of wapiti (elk) and ostrich have been found. Whereas these were hunted for food, smaller mammals such as badger, fox, wildcat, and tiger were hunted for their thick, warm fur and their teeth, which the Mesolithic occupants of the Upper Cave site perforated to make items of personal adornment. Zhoukoudian is located some distance from the Chinese coast, yet also found in abundance in the Upper Cave Mesolithic deposits were the remains of marine shellfish, which were traded for and then used to manufacture beads and other nonutilitarian items found at the site.

In southern China, another distinct set of Mesolithic adaptations evolved in response to the end-of-Pleistocene conditions. Environmental change was not as dramatic here, and there is great continuity with the Upper Paleolithic cultures of the region. The tradition of making stone tools from chipped pebbles is called **Hoabinhian** and marks the southern Chinese Mesolithic. Sites such as Hei-ching-lung imply a subsistence base that included wapiti, wild cattle, other small game, mollusks, and wild plant foods. However, a diversity of tools and adaptations can be seen in the south as well with some industries characterized by large flake tools and others featuring much smaller stone tools (Wenming and Youping 2005).

A similar pattern of regionalization can be seen farther south in mainland southeast Asia (Higham 1989). Along with a great diversity of archaeological cultures dated to the Mesolithic, an increasingly sedentary way of life is also seen in some particularly rich areas. The broad range of foods available in Thailand at the Spirit Cave site, occupied more than 7,500 years ago, apparently allowed for a settling into and focusing on the territory immediately surrounding the cave. The Khong stream at the base of the cliff face where the cave was located provided fish and freshwater crab. The surrounding forest provided otter, several monkey species (including langur and macaque), bamboo rat, badger, porcupine, and the sambar and pig deer, the bones of which have all been found in the Spirit Cave excavations (Gorman 1972). Along with animal foods, the remains of 22 genera of plants have been recovered in the cave, including bamboo, betel nut (a stimulant), butternut, and assorted tropical fruits (Higham 1989:53).

Spirit Cave and other upland sites in north Thailand not only share their own unique set of adaptations but also exhibit the same pattern seen in many other ecologically distinct regions of southeast Asia: the Red River Delta region of northern Vietnam, the Vietnamese coast, the Chao Phraya plains of southern Thailand, and the Gulf of Siam coast. Each region has produced vastly different yet contemporaneous archaeological cultures dating to the Mesolithic.

Africa

Like Australia, the African continent was not affected as severely by climate change at the end of the Pleistocene as were Europe, Asia, and the Americas. Africa was not glaciated and suffered much less extinction of large mammals. The kind of regionalization seen on the other continents in the early post-Pleistocene is seen in Africa in an earlier period. As indicated by archaeologist David W. Phillipson in his synthesis of African prehistory, the period of 100,000 to 8,000 years ago is characterized by the movement away from "broad cultural uniformity" and "towards the establishment of distinct regional traditions" (1993:60).

Typical among the regional cultures was that of the **Iberomaurusians** of northwest Africa (Klein 1993). At about 16,000 B.P., they inhabited the coastal plain and interior of what is today Tunisia and Morocco. They made small stone blade artifacts and used them as scraping and piercing tools—the former for scraping animal hides in clothing manufacture and the latter as arrow points or spearpoints for hunting. The animals that were the core of their subsistence strategy included wild cattle, gazelle, hartebeest, and Barbary sheep. Also important in their coastal habitat were marine mollusks, including snails. Though no plant food remains have been found in Iberomaurusian sites, grinding stones and digging-stick weights indicate some reliance on seeds, nuts, and roots.

Change accompanies the end of the Pleistocene, but there is no great cultural upheaval in Africa. After 10,000 B.P. in northwest Africa, the Iberomaurusian culture is replaced by another, called **Capsian**; as paleoanthropologist Richard Klein (1993) points out, this may have involved an actual migration of new people into the area, where they replaced the older inhabitants. Capsian subsistence is not very different from that of the preceding Iberomaurusians. The inhabitants continued to hunt wild sheep, collect shellfish and snails, dig for roots, and grind seeds and nuts. The Capsians set very small **microlith** blades into wooden or bone handles. These tools appear to have been used to harvest wild stands of grains; the microliths themselves exhibit a diagnostic kind of wear, or polish, called "sickle sheen" from repeated use in cutting the stalks of tall, grasslike plants.

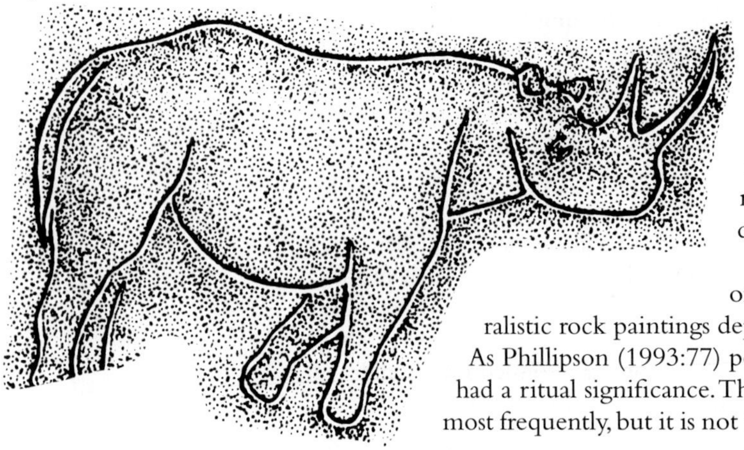

The use of microlithic **backed blades** is all but ubiquitous in Holocene Africa. During the early post-Pleistocene of southern Africa, microlithic industries predominate at coastal locales where preservation is high; in dry caves and waterlogged sites such as Gwisho Hot Springs in Zambia, a broad array of artifacts was recovered, including bows and arrows, digging sticks, bark trays, and bags and clothing of leather. Plant foods were important in the diet within a seasonal round that saw winter settlement of the coast and summers spent inland.

South Africa also saw a proliferation of artwork, with an abundance of naturalistic rock paintings depicting animals and people (Figure 8.4). As Phillipson (1993:77) points out, the paintings almost certainly had a ritual significance. The eland—a large antelope—is depicted most frequently, but it is not the animal most commonly represented

▼ **Figure 8.4**
Naturalistic engraving of a rhinoceros found in southern Africa and dating to the post-Pleistocene. (From *African Archaeology*, by David W. Phillipson, 1993, p. 76, Fig. 4.8, Cambridge University Press, with permission)

in the faunal assemblage at archaeological sites dated to the same period. Historically, however, the eland played an important role in the religions of some southern African people, and its abundance in ancient rock paintings may indicate that the ritual importance of the eland has a long history.

As seen in Europe and Asia, Africa, too, is marked by an explosion of cultural diversity as people became more specifically adapted to their own particular regions in the early Holocene. The stage is now set, here as elsewhere, for a revolution in human subsistence.

Australia

Though climate change in Australia at the end of the Pleistocene was not as dramatic as that seen in the higher latitudes of Europe and America, conditions did alter significantly. Mean temperatures rose beginning about 8,700 years ago in the period called the **Holocene Warm Maximum**. Depending on your location in Australia, temperatures were between 0.5°C (0.9°F) and 3°C (5.4°F) higher than they are currently (Mulvaney and Kamminga 1999:226). Outside of the drier southeast, rainfall appears to have increased during this period by 20% to 50%; lakes were full, and even the dry interior of the continent was a bit wetter (Mulvaney and Kamminga 1999:226). The Holocene Warm Maximum ended, and the cooler and drier conditions of modern Australia were established by about 4,500 years ago.

Aboriginal culture changed during this period; for example, ground stone hatchets and flaked stone adzes make their appearance during the Holocene Warm Maximum (Figure 8.5). Also, archaeologists have identified what they have labeled the **Australian Small Tool Phase**, which began around 6,000 years ago and became widespread within about a thousand years. The phase is marked by the production of blade tools, reflecting a more efficient use of stone than in earlier technologies. The Small Tool Phase also included the production of extremely finely made, unifacially and bifacially retouched spearpoints, the aesthetic equal to anything seen in the European Upper Paleolithic or among the Paleoindians of the New World (Figure 8.6).

The inhabitants of Australia seem to have maintained a relatively stable subsistence adaptation through the late Pleistocene and Holocene and even into the modern era. Marine shellfish became a major component of the diet of Australia's coastal people only after 8,000 years ago, around the time that the modern coastal configuration was established. Large shell middens dating especially to after 6000 B.P. are common along the temperate southeast coast and to a lesser degree on the tropical north coast. Shellfish seems not to have been a significant food source along the southwest coast at any time in Australia's history; there are no shell middens, and ethnographic groups in the area were not reported to have been much interested in shellfish (J. P. White and O'Connell 1982).

▶ **Figure 8.5**
Stone hatchets and flaked adzes from the post-Pleistocene culture of Australia.
(From *A Prehistory of Australia, New Guinea, and Sahul*, by J. Peter White and James F. O'Connell, Academic Press, with permission)

▶ **Figure 8.6**
Beautifully flaked,
precisely sharpened,
leaf-shaped weapons—
unifacially retouched
points on the left and
symmetrically bifacial
points (in the box on the
right)—of the Small Tool
Phase in Australia.
(From Mulvaney and
Kamminga 1999)

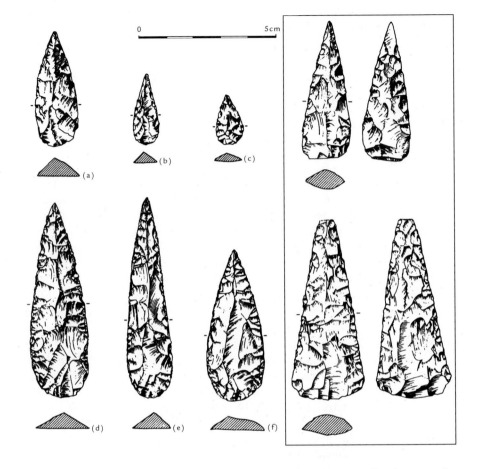

The major period of cultural change in Holocene Australia dates to the period beginning about 5,000 years ago. In their synthesis of Australian prehistory, J. Peter White and James F. O'Connell (1982:104–105) point out that in this period the dingo is seen in archaeological contexts for the first time. The dingo is nearly as emblematic of the wildlife of Australia as the kangaroo and the koala. A feral dog, the dingo is a nonmarsupial migrant, a descendant of domesticated dogs likely brought to Australia by travelers ultimately from southeast Asia who journeyed through the islands of the western Pacific (dog remains have been found on Borneo dating to 4,500 years ago) and who made landfall on Australia's northern coast.

By intention or by accident, some of these travelers' dogs ended up stranded in Australia, where they managed to survive in the wild. Dingoes became a fixture around human settlements, reverting to their tame condition, likely maintaining some degree of independence but accompanying people on hunts, serving as guard dogs and companions. The earliest evidence for the presence of dingoes in Australia has been found at the Madura Cave site on the Nullarbor Plain in Western Australia, with a radiocarbon date of 3450 B.P. (Mulvaney and Kamminga 1999:259). Dingoes are intelligent, sturdy, and resilient animals and spread quickly across the continent. After 3,000 years ago, their remains are common at archaeological sites in Australia.

A few sites, Roonka Flat being the most impressive, exhibit evidence of an elaboration of the burial ritual in Holocene Australia. Of the 82 burials located at this site, most date to recent times, but 12 can be assigned to the period between 4,000 and 7,000 years ago. A few of these were shaft tombs, vertical interments of the deceased. Most of the Roonka Flat burials contained grave goods, including the lower jaws of animals (with drilled holes for suspension), drilled shells, and bone pins. A few adults were buried with the bones of human infants.

A number of changes in the archaeological record of Australia, including an apparent increase in **sedentism** in some locations, a concomitant increase in site size, and evidence of social differentiation in burials, has led at least one researcher, Harry Lourandos (1997), to suggest that native Australians underwent a process of economic intensification and an increase in social complexity in the period after about 5,000 years ago. Lourandos notes the existence of an intricate and extensive cluster of ancient channels dug by native Australians in the south-west section of Victoria, the southeasternmost province of the island continent. Lourandos maintains that the channels were the product of communal labor, dug in order to connect a series of lakes and wetlands to enable the inhabitants to collect large quantities of seasonally migrating eels (Mulvaney and Kamminga 1999). The excavation of these channels would have required a cooperative effort on the part of a large cohort of people at a level not evidenced in older Australian sites. The resulting production of a food surplus allowed for an increase in sedentism, population growth, and, perhaps, social differentiation, with some individuals or families able to concentrate wealth and increase social status.

Some researchers have suggested that the increase in regional diversity of art styles seen in Holocene rock paintings (Figure 8.7) resulted from economic

◀ **Figure 8.7**
The ancient people of Australia produced beautiful and artistically distinctive rock paintings across nearly their entire history. (© Theo Allofs/ Corbis)

regionalization as geographically separated groups intensified the food quest, focusing on particularly rich resources in their own areas, as the native people did by intensifying their exploitation of eels in southwest Victoria (Mulvaney and Kamminga 1999). Whatever the cause, this diversity of styles is a clear indication of cultural heterogeneity in prehistoric Australia. A growth in cultural diversity is precisely what we have seen in the rest of the world during the Holocene epoch.

North America

As in Europe, the archaeological record bears witness to a dramatic shift in culture in North America after 10,000 B.P. New World prehistorians have recognized the great cultural changes that accompanied the end of the Pleistocene by bestowing a different name on the cultures of this period. In Europe, the Upper Paleolithic is followed by the Mesolithic; in America the Paleoindian period is followed by the **Archaic**, lasting from about 9,000 to 3,000 years ago. The Archaic represents a complex era when specific adaptations to the different climatic and environmental regimes became established across North America.

Regionalism in the New World Archaic

Archaic cultures of North America traditionally have been divided geographically, reflecting adaptations to the post-Pleistocene habitats that characterized the continent. Post-Pleistocene cultures named for the regions to which people adapted include the Desert Archaic of the Great Basin, the Southwestern Archaic, the **Shell Mound Archaic** of the Southeast, the Eastern Archaic, the Central Archaic, and the Western Archaic, as well as the **Paleo–Arctic tradition** (Willey 1966). In other words, various prehistoric people in North America began following their own regionally focused adaptive pathways in the face of the new conditions being established at the end of the Pleistocene.

Even this geographic breakdown masks the diversity within these regions. As in Europe, regionalization is the hallmark of the post-Pleistocene of North America. For example, archaeologist Dean Snow (1980), in his synthesis work on the archaeology of New England and New York State, further breaks down the Archaic cultures based on region, subsistence focus, and other behavioral characteristics. Snow describes a **Lake Forest Archaic** tradition (northern New England west of Maine and western New York), which apparently developed as a response to the unique conditions of the areas adjacent to the Great Lakes and the lake region of western New England. The material culture shows a heavy reliance on **lacustrine** (lake) resources, with a settlement pattern of home bases on lakeshores occupied in the spring and seasonal winter and summer hunting in the uplands surrounding the lakes (Figure 8.8).

Snow's **Maritime Archaic** is situated on New England's North Atlantic coast—primarily in Maine but also extending north into New Brunswick. Sites such as Turner Farm in Maine, dating to 4,600 years ago, show a clear subsistence focus on sea resources. Bone fishhooks, net weights and plummets, and faunal remains indicate that fish was a major component of the diet; even **pelagic** (open ocean as opposed to coastal) creatures like swordfish were hunted from open boats in the deep sea. Human burials were filled with finely crafted objects such as long slate knives and carvings of whales and dolphins (Figure 8.9). The human

▲ **Figure 8.8**
Lake Forest Archaic
people exploited the
shores of the Great
Lakes and other large,
inland bodies of water
(Lake Michigan is shown
here). Chipped stone
artifacts depicted are
typical spearpoints
of this culture. (Photo
by K. L. Feder; artifact
drawings from *A Typology
and Nomenclature for New
York State Projectile Points*,
by William A. Ritchie,
1971; reprinted with the
permission of the New York
State Museum and Science
Service)

remains were powdered with red ochre (a mineral), giving the name "the Red Paint People" to these Archaic inhabitants of coastal Maine. The rich maritime resources allowed for sedentary coastal home bases. Snow also defines a **Mast Forest Archaic** for most of southern New England. The term "mast" refers to the acorns and other nut foods from trees (hickory, beechnut, chestnut, walnut) that accumulate on the ground of the forest and serve as food for animals. These Mast Forest Indians focused on the rich resources of the river-drained woodlands of New England. They hunted deer and trapped small animals, fished in the rivers using nets and weirs as well as hooks and lines, and collected acorn, hickory, walnut, and chestnut in the fall and the seeds, leaves, and roots of wild plants in the spring (Figure 8.10).

Although deep-sea fishing and marine mammal hunting in New England seem to have been the exclusive province of the Maritime Archaic tradition, the use of shore resources was not confined to them. The Mast Forest Archaic also has a coastal component, with a heavy reliance on shellfish such as oyster, scallop, soft-shell clam, and quahog.

The same pattern of cultural regionalization in the Archaic is repeated elsewhere in North America. Piñon nuts were a major component of the diet throughout much of the desert West. The Archaic occupation of the desert shows a subsistence focus on desert lakes that are now dry, low-lying areas called sinks. For example, at Lovelock Cave, in Nevada, paleofeces provide direct evidence for the diet of its Archaic inhabitants. The cave was located near a desert lake (now the dry Humboldt Sink). Virtually all of the food remains retrieved from the preserved human feces in the cave came from the lake and its immediate environs (Heizer and Napton 1970) and included duck, mudhen, chub fish, and plant foods like cattail and wetland grasses.

In the Midwest is Modoc Rockshelter, located less than 15 km (9.3 mi) from the Mississippi River in Illinois. Modoc was successively occupied from

▲ **Figure 8.9**
The Maritime Archaic
people developed an
adaptation that focused
on resources of the
Atlantic coast (the
southern coast of Maine
is shown here). Ground
stone artifacts like
those shown here are
typical of this culture.
(Artifact drawing from
C. C. Willoughby's
*Antiquities of the New England
Indians,* 1935; photo by
K. L. Feder)

the early Holocene, beginning close to 9000 B.P. and continuing through the
Archaic period and into the subsequent Woodland period (Ahler 1993; M. L.
Fowler 1959). Melvin Fowler, the principal investigator of the site, was able to
trace the evolution of subsistence strategies on the part of the inhabitants of
the rockshelter from the Early through the Middle and into the Late Archaic.
Fowler deduced that the initial occupants of Modoc were generalists, subsist-
ing on whatever foods were available in their early Holocene environment in
the broad region of the rockshelter. Later, the site's inhabitants began to tighten
their subsistence approach, intensifying the food quest by focusing on a smaller
number of productive, locally available food resources. In the Arctic, the resources
of the coast were heavily exploited by the Holocene inhabitants, with evidence
of seal, sea lion, walrus, and puffin as major elements in the diet. In the far West,
nut foods became key elements in the diet, establishing a subsistence pattern that
would continue into the historic period.

In yet another example of regionalism, the Shell Mound Archaic has been defined for the American Southeast, in particular at sites marked by extensive and deep
piles of freshwater shells located along the Tennessee River in Tennessee and the
Green River in Kentucky. Sites located in South Carolina, Georgia, West Virginia,
and Florida, similarly characterized by substantial accumulations of freshwater—
particularly mussel—shells, are also included in the Shell Mound Archaic.

Koster: Emblem of the Archaic
The Archaic people of Koster, in Illinois, hunted deer, small mammals, and migra-
tory fowl, including ducks and geese (Figure 8.11). The carbonized seeds of wild
smartweed, sunflower, goosefoot, pigweed, and marsh elder were found at the site

▲ **Figure 8.10**
The Mast Forest
Archaic cultural
pattern is centered in
the thickly wooded
valleys of southern New
England (a Connecticut
woodland is shown
here). Chipped stone
artifacts depicted are
typical of Mast Forest
Archaic spearpoints.
(Photo by K. L. Feder;
artifact drawings from *A
Typology and Nomenclature
for New York State Projectile
Points*, by William A.
Ritchie, 1971, reprinted
with the permission of the
New York State Museum
and Science Service)

and were major contributors to the diet (see the discussion of the domestication of these crops later in this chapter). Fish and freshwater shellfish were collected in the river, and nut foods such as hickory, hazelnut, and acorn were harvested seasonally in the uplands around the river valley. Groundnuts, wild duck potatoes, cattail shoots, pecans, pawpaws, persimmons, and sassafras root rounded out the broad subsistence base at Koster.

Three human burials dating to nearly 6000 B.P. were recovered at Koster and, like those seen in the Shell Mound Archaic farther to the south and east, there were differences in the amounts and kinds of grave goods interred with the deceased, implying at least the beginning of some degree of social differentiation. Also at Koster, there was another type of burial, not of people, but of dogs. These interments appear to be not the mere hygienic disposal of dead animals but the ritual entombment of creatures important to those interring them (Figure 8.12).

▶ **Figure 8.11**
The Koster site excavation in Illinois revealed a series of overlapping habitations dating from the early post-Pleistocene, illuminating the evolving adaptations to the area around the Illinois River during the Archaic period of North American Prehistory. (Courtesy of Northwestern University)

The three buried dogs excavated at Koster were consistently laid out in shallow pits with their legs turned in and their heads set in toward their bodies, affecting the appearance of animals merely asleep. The dogs did not look like their wild ancestor, the wolf, but had proportionally large heads and short legs. At a calculated height of 45 to 50 cm (18–20 in), the Koster dogs were the approximate height of modern fox terriers (Struever and Holton 2000:38). In fact, they likely looked very much like the *techichi*, a domesticated breed described by chroniclers of the Native Americans separated from the Koster dogs by more than 5,000 years.

The presence of domesticated dogs at Koster is highly significant and likely resulted from the intentional breeding of wild animals with characteristics deemed advantageous by those who controlled them; perhaps they were less aggressive, more submissive to humans, loyal, strong, and more willing to help their human masters in exchange for food and affection than were their wild cousins. The domestication of plants and animals is the major focus of the next chapter,

and the taming and domestication of the dog by people in the post-Pleistocene provides a model for the revolution to come in the relationship between human beings and plants and animals.

South America

The end of the Pleistocene wrought changes of climate in South America and attendant changes in the subsistence focus of the people living there. In some areas with a restricted community of edible plants and animals, human groups became highly specialized in exploiting individual species or a small number of species. For example, with the extinction of mastodon, horse, glyptodont (giant armadillo), megatherium (giant ground sloth), and many other Pleistocene species, some human groups who previously had at least partially relied on the hunting of these animals shifted focus to the single set of large game animals remaining after the Pleistocene—**camelids**. The South American camels included the wild guanaco and vicuña (llamas and alpacas are the domesticated versions of South American camels). For example, at Pachamachay Cave in the Peruvian Andes, a subsistence focus on vicuña hunting developed after 9000 B.P. (Bruhns 1994).

Elsewhere, a broadening of the subsistence quest is apparent. The Vegas complex, located in the Santa Elena Peninsula of Ecuador, shows an early (late Paleoindian) evolution of a maritime subsistence focus. This shift is ultimately seen in the coastal desert from northern Peru to southern Chile, where archaeological evidence shows early post-Pleistocene groups heavily exploiting resources like mollusks. This maritime, or **littoral**, tradition is seen, if a bit later, in coastal Colombia and Venezuela and also along the Caribbean Atlantic coasts of South

America. Hunting remained important in some areas; some of the coastal sites are located near tar pits, natural traps where animals could have been killed once mired in the thick natural petroleum deposits.

But maritime resources seem to have become most important to people living near the coast in post-Pleistocene South America. Some places even show signs of a population movement away from the interior and toward the coast. These post-Pleistocene coastal sites tend to be larger than earlier sites, more permanent, and with more elaborate burials. A sedentary way of life on the coast, made possible by the rich and reliable resources of the sea, seems to have set the stage, at least in part, for the great cultural changes that were to occur in South America (see Chapters 9 and 13).

The Shift from Food Collection to Food Production

During the Mesolithic as well as the Paleolithic that preceded it—in fact, for more than 99% of human history—people have relied exclusively on the wild foods that nature provided. It is only very recently, within the past 12,000 years or so, that human groups began actively controlling their food sources by artificially producing conditions under which these sources could thrive and then, by manipulating them, altering them from a natural state. The rest of this chapter focuses on this ultimately momentous change in how people feed themselves.

Humans Taking the Place of Nature: Artificial Selection

Though we refer to the shift from foraging to farming as a revolution, that term may be misleading. In fact, settled agricultural life represents not so much a rapid revolution as a point in a process stretched out along a lengthy continuum of change. The transition from Paleolithic and Mesolithic food gathering to the Neolithic reliance on agriculture took thousands of years.

As archaeologist Naomi Miller (1992) lays out the continuum from foraging to farming, it begins with collecting wild foods and continues through a lengthy period of actively tending wild plants and animals. In some instances, this may lead to manipulation of the reproduction of economically important plants or animals through **artificial selection**—that is, the directed breeding of plants and animals possessing characteristics deemed beneficial to human beings. At this stage, human beings (in a manner analogous to natural selection as defined by Charles Darwin—see Chapter 1) select for propagation only those individuals within a plant or animal species that possess some natural endowments useful to people. In describing the "art" of artificial selection, Darwin pointed out: "One of the most remarkable features in our domesticated races is that we see in them adaptations, not indeed to the animal's or plant's own good, but to man's use or fancy" (1859:47).

So both at the origins of agriculture and in our modern systems, humans protect and encourage only those individual plants that produce more, larger, or more readily digested seeds; only those individual animals within a species that exhibit less aggression and produce the most meat, milk, or wool; or only those trees that bear larger fruits. Selected animals in a wild species may be corralled, fed, and protected from predators. Certain individual plants within a wild species may be watered or weeded or planted near the village and then fenced in to prevent animals from eating them.

After many generations of such treatment, and as people have an increased opportunity to even more carefully select for propagation plants or animals with desirable characteristics, the cultivated plants and animals no longer resemble their wild ancestors or neighbors. They have been so altered through artificial selection that, again in a manner analogous to natural selection, they can no longer be considered the same species. They have, in essence, co-evolved with their human overseers, no longer adapting to natural conditions but changing under the conditions established by people (Rindos 1984).

Such plants and animals are said to be **domesticated.** Under extreme conditions of **domestication**, they cannot survive without human beings to attend to their needs and to propagate them. They are no longer adapted to a natural world but, rather, to a culturally constructed world of agriculture and animal husbandry. And in every case, the prehistoric record is clear: Wherever such a "revolution" occurred, it transpired over thousands of years. This chapter documents such a process for the Near East, Mesoamerica, Asia, Africa, Europe, North America, and South America.

Archaeological Evidence of Human Control of Plant and Animal Species

Because the shift from food gathering to food production was a process rather than an event, there really is no single point along that continuum of subsistence change marking a definitive or absolute break between foraging and food production. We can, however, recognize aspects of that continuum of change in the archaeological record and thereby reveal the nature of the process that resulted ultimately in the development of an agricultural way of life.

Geography

For example, in the early steps in the path leading to full-blown agriculture, the plants and animals tended or encouraged by people in order to increase their yields will look just like their wild predecessors. Their remains as recovered in the archaeological record—seeds, nutshells, bones—will be indistinguishable from those of their truly wild forebears. However, as noted previously, in this early step in food production human beings tend to take care of, protect, oversee, and encourage populations of wild plants or animals. As a strategy to increase the production of food, humans may attempt to expand the territory where economically important species grow by moving these plants and animals to habitats or regions where they do not thrive naturally. In fact, in many cases, these plants and animals brought into new territories will survive only through human care. For example, as we will see later in this chapter, food plants native to and first domesticated more than 10,000 years ago in the Middle East including wheat, barley, lentils, peas, and chickpeas turn up in archaeological sites in Pakistan and Greece (by 9,000 years ago), the Balkans (by 8,000 years ago), and Italy, Spain, and Portugal (at around 7,500 years ago; Purugganan and Fuller 2009:846). None of those crops grew wild outside of the Middle East so their presence across a broad swath of west Asia and southern Europe is clear evidence of their having been brought there—and tended—by human beings.

When plant and animal remains appear abruptly in the archaeological record at sites located in territories where the plant and animal species represented are not known to have grown or lived naturally, it suggests human propagation or control. Even if the bones of the animals look just like those of wild members of their species, even if the seeds seem no different from those produced by wild plants, their appearance in locations where the wild versions of those plants and animals can't live implies that human beings were actively producing conditions—by watering plants, protecting seedlings from frost, providing food for animals—that allowed for the survival of these plants and animals. This level of human involvement can be a first step toward ultimate control of a species.

Size

Seeds produce the next generation of a plant species, and it may be advantageous in nature for a plant to produce lots of little seeds that ripen over a long period of time to ensure that at least some of the seeds will end up in the ground when conditions are appropriate for their survival through the winter and growth the following spring. However, for humans, seeds are not just the way a plant produces the next generation; they are a harvestable, nutritious commodity. It may be better, from a human perspective, to have a plant produce fewer but larger seeds—and therefore seeds with more food—and seeds that ripen all at once so that they can be efficiently harvested at the same time.

Humans tending wild plants may intentionally kill off those individuals that produce the smaller seeds and then care for and encourage those plants left that have bigger ones that ripen at the same time. Where seed remains recovered at an archaeological site are significantly larger than seed size in the wild, it may be evidence of this level of human involvement in the plants (Figure 8.13).

The size of animals exploited by human beings may also be an indicator of human activity. To make use of a population of animals more convenient, human beings may capture a group of them and corral them or otherwise impede their movement. Larger, more aggressive animals that might thrive in the wild as dominant members of a herd now may be a liability, dangerous to their human captors, and these animals may be killed off. Only the less dangerous, perhaps smaller and less aggressive members of a population may be allowed to survive, and, in turn, these become the only members of the animal group that produce offspring that may also be smaller and less aggressive. Here again, though their individual bones found in an archaeological context may be no different in their form from those of wild members of their species, a significant decrease in size may be another early indication of human control by selection and breeding.

Seed Morphology

Along with size, other characteristics of seeds may be selected for differently by nature and people. For example, in many plant species, especially in temperate zones, the thickness of the protective, exterior seed coat may be important in determining whether or not the seed survives long enough to produce another plant. A thick seed coat may delay germination, protecting the enclosed seed during the winter and from late spring frosts. More of these thick-coated seeds survive, producing more thick-coated seeds when they grow into plants and mature. Thus, natural selection acts to produce more plants producing thick-coated seeds. However, where human beings plant the seeds and tend the seedlings, the delay in germination caused by a thick seed coat is no longer an advantage—people may be

▲ **Figure 8.13**
Through artificial selection, people may encourage the survival of early germinating and quick-growing plants produced by larger seeds. Archaeologists recognize that selection when the seeds recovered in archaeological contexts are larger than those found in the wild and untended versions of the same species. See the three examples here: on the left, from top to bottom, are the wild seeds of marsh elder, sunflower, and squash; on the right, from top to bottom, are seeds from the domesticated versions of these crops. (© Chip Clark 1995)

protecting seedlings from the cold—and may actually become disadvantageous. When a bunch of seeds are planted in a seed bed, the early germinators have a head start when it comes time to thin out the garden. Late germinators will be smaller and likely the first plants culled and discarded. Where people are consistently thinning out the seedlings growing from thick-coated seeds, only those members of a species that produce thin-coated seeds will grow. Where archaeological remains of seeds are recovered exhibiting seed coats significantly thinner than those produced by the same plant species in the wild, human control may be the cause.

There comes a point in the life cycle of a plant when the seeds it produces need to detach. All plants have developed mechanisms for the detachment and dispersal of seeds on the ground to produce the next generation of plants. The point of connection between a seed and its plant needs to become rather brittle at just the right time of ripening to allow a passing wind, a wandering animal, or a burst of rainfall to detach the seed.

This perfectly sensible feature of plants, however, produces a problem for human harvesters. The sharp blow of a sickle can harvest a plant but at the same time is more than adequate to detach and disperse on the ground most of the seeds that the sickle wielder is attempting to harvest. In fact, in what may at least initially be an entirely accidental result of harvesting practices, a disproportionate percentage of seeds that remain stubbornly attached to a plant stalk may make it back to the village, the seeds with a brittle attachment having already been detached in harvesting and transport. As a result, only the seeds ill-equipped to survive and that end up in the ground in the wild will be returned to the village where they may be planted nearby. In this way, subsequent generations of the plants near a settlement may produce a greater proportion of seed attachments that don't become brittle in the fall but, instead, will end up in the ground for propagation by their human overseers. Where the archaeological record shows the development of a predominance of nonbrittle attachments of seeds in plants harvested by an ancient people, this kind of unconscious selection may be at work.

Osteological Changes

It is as true in animals as it is in people: Degree and strenuousness of physical activity sculpts our bodies—our bones as well as our muscles. The bones of animals that are penned or corralled will not be as dense or as strongly built as the bones of their wild counterparts who roam freely where they experience strenuous physical challenges on a regular basis. These differences between the bones of free-roaming and penned animals are apparent in zoo inhabitants and can be seen in bones recovered in the archaeological record. Lightly constructed bones of otherwise wild animals found in archaeological contexts may be interpreted as resulting from the animals having been penned by human controllers and protectors throughout their lives.

Population Characteristics

Bones found in an ancient fireplace or trash pile may not always indicate whether the animal was truly wild or instead was tended by human overseers. However, sometimes the age and sex profile of an animal population can be used to determine the relationship between the people and the animals they utilized.

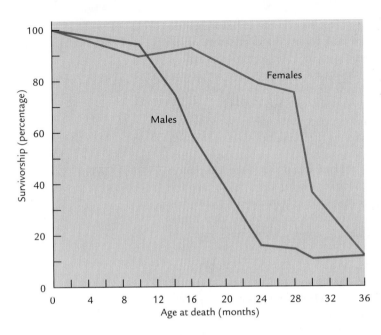

▲ Figure 8.14
Sex and survivorship curves for male and female goats from Ganj Dareh in Iran. The graph shows that male goats were slaughtered at an earlier age than females. That pattern is typical in tended or domesticated animals; females are valuable for their production of milk and baby goats and so are kept alive longer than males. (From Zeder and Hesse 2000)

This occurs because human hunters of wild animals have significantly less control over the age and sex of the animal they successfully harvest than does the human overseer of a captive population. A hungry hunter will kill whatever animal he or she has in his or her sights—young or old, male or female, it makes little difference. But in the case of a captive population, a human overseer can be far more selective. Knowing that adult males tend to be more dangerous and aggressive than adult females—and also aware that only a very few adult males are needed to impregnate a large herd of females—most males may be killed and eaten while they are still juveniles. It may make sense to keep females alive through their reproductive years as they are worth more as breeders and perhaps milk or wool producers than as food—they will be eaten anyway but only when they become too old to produce offspring.

With a sufficiently large population represented by bones at an archaeological site, researchers can determine the age and sex profile of the animals being used by people. When an overabundance of the bones of subadult males is found at an archaeological site, this may indicate that people had a level of control over the population greater than what would be expected if they merely had been hunting free-roaming wild animals. This population characteristic implies that the people had corralled or penned the population of animals. This can lead to control of breeding by allowing only smaller, less aggressive, compliant males to live long enough to become breeders, which, in turn, may change the characteristics of the population animals under human control (Figure 8.14).

With all of these considerations in mind, it's time to examine the archaeological record to see where the kinds of evidence of tending and selection can be found.

The Near East

The name of the region in which many of the sites to be described here are located—the **Fertile Crescent**—is doubly descriptive. It is, indeed, shaped like a crescent, and it encompasses some of the richest and most fertile agricultural land in the Middle East. Beginning in Israel along the Mediterranean coast, the territory arcs to the northeast until it reaches its geographic apex—the top of the crescent—in Turkey and then bends to the south and east toward the Persian Gulf in Iran and Iraq (Figure 8.15). The late Pleistocene inhabitants of this region that now makes up parts of the nations of Israel, Jordan, Lebanon, Syria, Turkey, Iraq, and Iran long exploited wild varieties of **cereal** grasses, especially wheat and barley, that grow abundantly there.

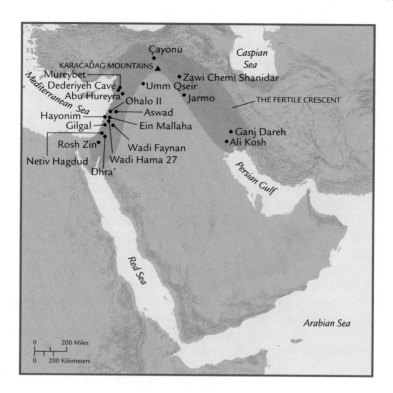

Late Pleistocene Foragers in the Near East

Paleoclimatological data indicate that much of the Middle East was cold and dry during the late Pleistocene, but the hilly Mediterranean coast was wetter and thickly forested. People living in the region relied on hunting for part of their subsistence; the bones of wild boar, fallow deer, gazelle, and ibex have been found in sites dating to the period 20,000 to 14,500 B.P. (Bar-Yosef 1998). During this same period, wild plant foods were a significant part of the diet. At the 19,000-year-old Ohalo II site in Israel, a large number of the seeds and fruits of several different plant species have been found (Kislev and Carmi 1992).

At the 19,000-year-old occupation of the Ohalo II site in Israel, a team led by paleobotanist Dolores Piperno (Piperno et al. 2004) found evidence of the diet of the inhabitants. Along with the remains of gazelles, birds, fish, mollusks, and rats, the team also recovered charred seed remains of wild barley and emmer wheat. Also, **starch grains** identifiable as wild barley were recovered from the surface of a large basalt grinding stone found at the site. As Piperno and her colleagues point out, stone tools for grinding or pounding seeds are first seen in the archaeological record of the Middle East at about 45,000 years ago and are abundant by 20,000 years ago.

The period from 14,500 to 12,900 years ago is technically called the Bølling-Allerød Interstadial. Remember from Chapter 4 that an interstadial represents a respite from glacial conditions. In the Middle East, the Bølling-Allerød Interstadial was marked by increasing temperatures and precipitation (Balter 2010b). A number of cultures have been defined for this period of climatic improvement. Among the best known of these is the **Natufian** culture, dating from 14,000 to 9,800 years ago.

Natufian sites are located in the Mediterranean woodland zone. Along with the hunting of a broad array of animals, it is during the Natufian, at about 14,000 years ago, that we see a dramatic shift in subsistence from simple to **complex foraging** based on plant foods. In complex foraging, subsistence is focused on a few rich resources. These are collected intensively and stored, both requiring and allowing for more sedentary, denser human populations. This pattern is reflected in the archaeological record of the Natufian by the increasing number of grinding stones, large bedrock mortars and smaller, more portable mortars and pestles, food-storage pits, pits for roasting plant foods, and microblades of flint exhibiting sickle polish. The remnants of an actual sickle have been found at a Natufian site by archaeologist Phillip C. Edwards. The handle was made from goat horn, and its maker had incised channels where sharp flint blades had been inset (Holden 2008). Natufian stone blades exhibit a sheen or polish that has been shown through replicative experiment to be the result of their use in cutting cereal plant stalks such as those of wheat, barley, millet, and sorghum (Unger-Hamilton 1989).

The Natufian culture homeland was located in the belt of woodland in the **Levant**. Here, wild cereal grasses offering human foragers protein and carbohydrate-rich seeds would have grown abundantly in open areas and as forest underbrush (Bar-Yosef 1998). Kernels and stalks of wild wheat and barley have been found at several Natufian sites. For example, at Mureybet and Abu Hureyra, in Syria, wild einkorn wheat and vetch (a **legume**—a plant that produces pods with seeds) have been found in roasting pits dated to more than 11,000 years ago and as much as 13,000 years ago. These sites are located about 100 km (62 mi) from where wheat grows wild today. This may be an indication of intentional movement of the wild plant into a new territory by people consciously attempting to increase its geographic range.

The intensive collection and storage of wild cereals like wheat necessitates a more sedentary way of life because the food source stays put and needs to be monitored regularly for the best time to harvest. At the same time, the abundant and dependable wild cereals, legumes, and nut foods allow for a sedentary life. For example, at Ein Mallaha, Hayonim Cave, and Rosh Zin in Israel, the remains of substantial houses with stone foundations ranging in diameter from 2 to 9 m (about 6–30 ft) have been found (Henry 1989:211–212). Similarly substantial and permanent structures are known from Mureybet in Syria, where the preferred building materials were clay and wood, and Abu Hureyra, also in Syria, where the houses were built down into the earth. The amount of labor needed to build such domiciles is a clear indication that they were intended for long-term use.

With the intensive, seasonal collection of cereals comes the need to store those foods for subsequent processing. For example, archaeologists have found a series of large circular structures at the 11,300-year-old Dhra' site in Jordan. The buildings appear to have had wooden floors raised above the ground in which especially wild barley was stored (Holden 2009).

Bone, tooth, and shell beads and pendants are commonly found in Natufian burials. Dentalium shells, which were a favorite raw material, were available— often at great distances from the Natufian sites where they were found. Along with such items of personal adornment, other works of art have been recovered from Natufian sites, primarily carved stone statuettes of animals and people (Figure 8.16).

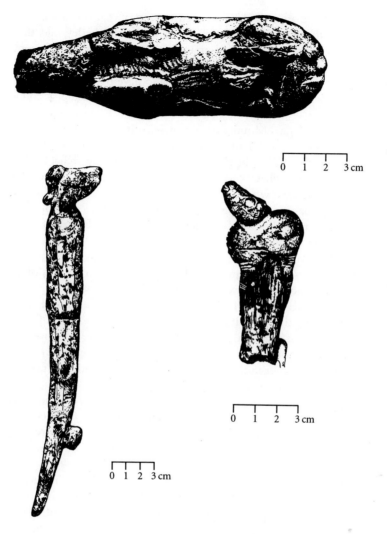

◀ **Figure 8.16**
Natufian artwork
including a carved animal
(top) and two carved
sickle hafts. (From *From
Foraging to Agriculture: The
Levant at the End of the Ice Age*,
by Donald O. Henry, 1989,
University of Pennsylvania
Press, with permission)

The First Agriculturalists

A return to colder and drier conditions in the Middle East between 12,900 and 11,600 years ago (during the Younger Dryas period mentioned previously in this chapter) in all likelihood resulted in a decrease in the abundance of wild cereal crops there. Archaeologist Ofer Bar-Yosef (1998) suggests that it is during this period that Natufians initiated an attempt to artificially increase the abundance of these cereals, perhaps by planting and then tending them. In this scenario, as people gained some measure of control over these wild plants, selection shifted from natural to artificial. As people began imposing their will by encouraging those individual plants that possessed useful characteristics (they had larger seeds and were hardier), the population of tended plants changed from a wild pattern to a pattern determined by human selection.

At Netiv Hagdud and Gilgal in Israel and at Ganj Dareh in Iran, in levels dating to 11,000 years ago, researchers recovered barley kernels that have been identified as an early domesticated version of that cereal. The size and morphology of the kernels distinguish them from wild barley, and they show features present in the domesticated grain. At Aswad in Syria and Çayönü in Turkey, domesticated wheats known as **emmer** and **einkorn** have been dated to more than 10,000 B.P. At both sites, lentils may also have been cultivated: At Aswad, 55% of the seeds of food plants recovered were from cultivated peas and lentils (N. Miller 1992:48).

In the Zagros Mountains, in northern Iraq, the site of Zawi Chemi Shanidar has produced a substantial faunal assemblage of sheep bones dated to 10,600 B.P. (Wright 1971). The population structure of the archaeological sample of the sheep is unlike what would be derived from a group of hunted animals. Almost all were slaughtered when young. This kind of consistency in the population profile of an animal species implies a level of control over the animals usually possible only under conditions of corralling. The animals, though genetically the same as those roaming wild, were kept, controlled, and tended by people.

The bones of goats discarded by the inhabitants of Ganj Dareh in Iran 10,000 years ago look just like the bones of wild members of their species. The key difference lies, however, not in their morphology but in their population profile (see Figure 8.14). Researchers Melinda Zeder and Brian Hesse (2000) have shown that the site's inhabitants exhibited a level of population control over the goats that is unlikely the result of hunting wild, free-roaming animals. A disproportionate number of the goat remains are those of subadult males. As mentioned earlier in this chapter, when humans control a population of animals by penning or corralling them, they often kill off young males, allowing females and only a sufficient number of males to live to ensure the survival of the captive population. It is interesting to note that this level of herd management occurred 10,000 years ago in the Middle East. Genetic diversity in goats from this region suggests that domestication of the species occurred 10,000 years ago (Luikart et al. 2001).

A bit farther to the west, in Turkey, there is fascinating evidence for the domestication of cattle as much as 8,500 years ago. There, at a number of sites, researchers have found, in association with an abundance of cow bones, hundreds of pottery sherds in which they found the residue of fatty acids diagnostic of cow milk (Evershed 2008). Though it is not entirely clear whether the cows were technically wild or domestic, certainly milked animals must be tended and tame animals. At the very least, these sites in Turkey allow us to trace back the origins of dairying to the middle of the ninth millennium B.P.

Genetic evidence points to the Middle East as a source for domestication of another animal, one not exploited as a food source, but for its abilities at hunting and defending its "pack": the dog. A recent, detailed genetic analysis of wolves and domesticated dogs indicates that, at least in terms of dogs domesticated in the Old World, the Middle Eastern gray wolf appears to have been the most significant source, suggesting that the dog was first domesticated there, in the home territory of the gray wolf (vonHoldt et al. 2010). Osteological evidence for the remains of wolflike animals exhibiting small jaws and tooth crowding has been found at archaeological sites in the Middle East dating to about 12,000 years ago; these remains may represent some of the earliest examples in the Old World of the transition of wild wolf to domesticated dog.

Mesoamerica

Mesoamerica includes the modern nations located south of the United States and north of South America (including Mexico, Guatemala, Belize, El Salvador, the western regions of Honduras and Nicaragua, and northwestern Costa Rica; Figure 8.17). This area contributed many valuable agricultural crops to the world, none more important than maize (corn), beans, and squash, the triumvirate of plants that provided the subsistence base for indigenous New World civilizations (see Chapter 12). The shift to an agricultural mode of subsistence has been documented in only a few sites: Guilá Naquitz Cave (Flannery 1986), Tamaulipas, and Tehuacán (MacNeish 1964, 1967). The Western Hemisphere's earliest evidence for the domestication of plants has been found in Mesoamerica.

The First Agriculturalists in the New World

Though maize (corn) is probably the first crop most people think of when asked to name the key agricultural crops domesticated by Native Americans, it was not the first wild plant they domesticated. The oldest evidence for domestication in the New World comes from Guilá Naquitz Cave in Oaxaca, Mexico, where squash seeds, rind fragments, and stems that are demonstrably different from those of wild squash have been recovered and dated to the period between 10,000 and 8,000 years ago (B. Smith 1997).

The seeds of the Guilá Naquitz squash are larger, the rinds thicker, and the stems bigger (likely implying larger fruits) than in wild specimens. Archaeologist Bruce Smith maintains that such increases result automatically when people plant and tend initially wild crops as they thin out later-germinating, slower-growing individual sprouts in a process called **seedbed selection**.

Though they may have domesticated squash first, when you think of the contribution made by the native people of the Americas to the diet of the modern world, maize is likely the first crop that springs to mind. Early steps in the transition of the small spikes of seeds on the wild **teosinte** plant from which the domesticated crop we call maize was derived, to the well-known, multirowed, large-kerneled cobs without which a summer barbeque would be incomplete, have now been traced to more than 7,000 years ago in Mexico. Evidence of the early domestication of maize has been found at the San Andrés site located in

◀ **Figure 8.17**
Archaeological sites in Mesoamerica where evidence of early food production has been found.

Mexico's tropical Gulf of Mexico wetlands in the province of Tabasco (K. O. Pope et al. 2001). Here, pollen grains whose form and size allow their identification as teosinte have been found in levels dating to 7,100 years ago. Though teosinte is a wild crop, its occurrence in the region where the site is located is telling. As the authors of the study point out, teosinte is not native to the coastal wetlands of Tabasco (K. O. Pope et al. 2001:1373). The appearance of teosinte pollen at the site at the same time that evidence indicates the inhabitants were intentionally clearing off parts of the forest by burning may indicate that the residents of San Andrés were attempting to increase the productivity of what was still a wild crop by artificially extending its territory. As we have discussed, this sort of behavior may represent one of the preliminary steps taken by a people along the continuum toward domestication and a subsistence system based on agriculture.

It is not until about 7,000 years ago at San Andrés that at least some of the recovered pollen is recognizable as domesticated maize. Another three centuries passed here before the archaeological record indicates a substantial shift toward an agricultural way of life with a fundamental reliance on maize and large-scale clearing to produce agricultural fields. The San Andrés site also produced evidence of the earliest domestication of sunflowers in the Western Hemisphere dating to about 4,500 years ago (K. O. Pope et al. 2001). Two multirowed mini-cobs producing tiny kernels of domesticated corn, looking quite different not only from the wild plant, teosinte, but also from the corn with which we are now familiar, have been found dating to 6,250 years ago at Guilá Naquitz Cave in the Oaxaca Valley in the southern highlands of Mexico. There is no evidence from earlier levels of this site of either teosinte or even more primitive early maize, so it is likely that earlier steps in maize domestication are yet to be found in the region.

Although it is likely that archaeologists at San Andrés and Guilá Naquitz Cave have revealed some of the early steps in maize domestication, researchers have not yet reached far enough back in time nor far enough back in the sequence to have revealed truly the first steps taken by the native people of the New World in their conversion of a wild crop into one of the domesticated pillars that support modern subsistence the world over, and so their work continues.

The Shift to Domesticated Foods Among the People of the Tehuacán Valley

The **Tehuacán** Valley project, conducted in 1961–64 in Mexico by archaeologist Richard MacNeish and an international team of 50 scholars from many disciplines (MacNeish 1964, 1967), provided archaeologists with our most detailed picture of the process of maize domestication (Figure 8.18). The project also resulted in a sequence of archaeological cultures spanning the period from 12,000 to 500 years ago, from the late Pleistocene to the period of initial European contact (De Tapia 1992).

An analysis of carbon isotopes has been conducted on bones from 12 of the human skeletons recovered at Tehuacán, allowing for the reconstruction of the general diet of the inhabitants (Farnsworth et al. 1985). As discussed in Chapter 3, uptake of the ^{13}C isotope differs among plant groups. Those following the C4 photosynthesis pathway—chiefly grasses and sedges—use proportionally more

◀ **Figure 8.18**
Sample of some of the prehistoric maize cobs recovered in excavations in the Tehuacán Valley. The chronology proceeds from left to right; the tiny cob on the far left is the oldest maize now AMS dated to about 5000 B.P. and on the right is a modern variety. (From *Prehistory of the Tehuacan Valley*, Volume 1, 1967, © Robert S. Peabody Museum of Archaeology, Phillips Academy, Andover, MA. All rights reserved)

^{13}C than those following the C3 pathway—most trees, herbs, and shrubs. Animals (this includes people) incorporate into their bones proportions of ^{13}C that reflect the proportions in the plant foods they eat (or the proportions in the animals they eat, which reflect the proportions in the plant foods the animals eat).

The isotope analysis of the Tehuacán material shows a clear jump in the reliance on C4 plants early in the Tehuacán sequence and then little change thereafter. Therefore, tropical grasses—of which teosinte is one—must have been mainstays of the diet of the people who produced the archaeological sites in the Tehuacán Valley.

Combining MacNeish's reconstruction with the isotope data, it appears that the inhabitants of the valley went through a long period of increasing sedentism before adopting an agricultural way of life. This lengthy period of dietary reliance on C4-pathway tropical grasses—including, perhaps, the wild progenitor of maize, teosinte—is similar to the situation seen in the Near East. Archaeologist Paul Farnsworth and colleagues (1985:112) suggest that an extended period of reliance on wild plants and increasing sedentism in Tehuacán was "a Mesoamerican equivalent of the Natufian."

The Greatest Native American Contribution to Food

Okay, maybe the heading of this section exaggerates things just a little. The native people of Mesoamerica domesticated the cacao plant and, in so doing, gave the rest of the world, eventually, the gift of chocolate. Residue analysis of early Maya ceramic vessels recovered at the more than 3,000-year-old Puerto Escondido site in Honduras in Central America displayed evidence of theobromine, a chemical that occurs only in the cacao plant (Henderson et al. 2007).

The ancient chocolate likely was consumed in liquid form but, oh well, the researchers did not report the discovery of marshmallow residue.

A Model of the Shift to a Food-Producing Way of Life in Mesoamerica

Archaeologist Kent Flannery (1968) maintains that the subsistence systems of late Pleistocene Mesoamerica were inherently stable. The seasonally restricted availability of certain resources and scheduling preferences for some resources over others available at the same time of year maintained this stable system in which no one resource was so intensively exploited that its abundance was threatened. Such a system can be said to be in "equilibrium."

In Flannery's view, however stable such a system might have been, it was susceptible to even a minor change in general conditions. For example, a mutation in teosinte that produced more easily harvested plants (see this chapter's "Issues and Debates) might have rendered this previously minor wild food more attractive. To take advantage of this more desirable form of teosinte, inhabitants of the region may have shifted other elements in the intricately balanced system. To encourage the growth of the new teosinte/wild maize, they may have changed their settlement pattern to allow more time in those places where teosinte grew, to encourage the new form. But this could have been accomplished only by changing the entire system of seasonal movement and scheduling. A pattern of larger and more sedentary groups may have developed to take advantage of the new teosinte. Overall population would have increased, necessitating a continual refinement through artificial selection of the new crop, to feed more mouths. **Microband**s would have become **macroband**s, and seasonal encampments semipermanent and then permanent villages.

In this way, the initial, casual, and almost accidental step of intensifying the exploitation of a crop could have thrown the entire system out of balance. The initial minor deviation from the established equilibrium would have become amplified as the culture tried to reestablish a new status quo. Other resources would have had to be granted less attention, resulting in the need to intensify further the use of the new crop. But intensification would have required a greater degree of sedentism, which would have meant even less time or opportunity for other resources. In Flannery's view, the intensification of the use of a particular food species can be the first step toward the inevitable destruction of a foraging subsistence system and the establishment of an entirely new equilibrium based on agriculture.

Africa

It cannot be said that there was a single agricultural revolution in Africa or even that there was a single point of origin for the African shift to a domesticated food base. Africa is enormous and has a broad range of climates and environments and a wide range of plant and animal communities. Myriad hunting-and-gathering cultures developed in Africa during postglacial times, each adapting in its own way to its region. And many different food-producing cultures developed in the African Neolithic, each devising its own adaptation through food production of the available plants and animals (Figure 8.19).

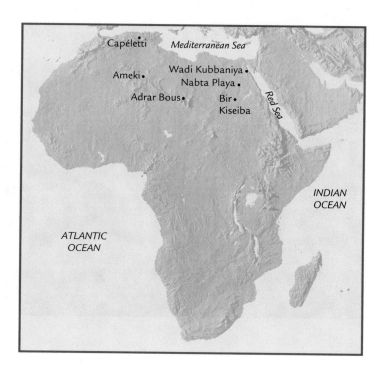

◀ **Figure 8.19**
Archaeological sites in
Africa where evidence of
early food production
has been found.

A Chronology of Food Production

The African reliance on wild plants extends well back into the late Pleistocene. At the Egyptian site of Wadi Kubbaniya, charred tubers of wild nutgrass have been dated to the period 18,000 to 17,000 years ago (Wendorf, Schild, and Close 1989; Wendorf et al. 1979). Heavily worn grindstones at the site were probably used to process the fat, starchy roots into flour. Stone blades inset into wooden or bone handles that served as sickles used in harvesting wild grains and the grinding stones necessary to process the grains into flour are both dated to 15,000 to 11,000 years ago in southern Egypt in a culture called the **Qadan** (Phillipson 1993).

An 8,000-year-old site in the Sahara Desert of southern Egypt, Nabta Playa, supplies further evidence of early Holocene subsistence in Africa. Researchers excavated 1 storage pit, 14 hearths, and 122 cooking features (Wendorf et al. 1992). They recovered thousands of seeds, representing 40 different species of wild plants. Among the plants represented in the archaeological sample were sorghum and a number of varieties of millet. There are hundreds of varieties of sorghum; many produce edible grains, and others produce a sweet molasses or syrup. Millet and sorghum are commonly grown in modern, indigenous African agricultural systems (Figure 8.20). In fact, though not well known outside the semiarid tropics, millet and sorghum are the primary sources of protein in certain regions of the world.

Also found in the storage and cooking features at Nabta Playa were the remains of various legumes, fruits, tubers, and nut foods. There is even some suggestion that the sorghum at least was in an incipient stage of domestication at this site (Figure 8.21). To the eye, the sorghum looks like the wild plant, but the

▶ **Figure 8.20**
Used primarily in the United States to produce animal feed, sorghum has historically been an important food crop, particularly in Africa where it was domesticated as much as 8,000 years ago. (© Philip Gould/Corbis)

▼ **Figure 8.21**
Charred seeds recovered from Nabta Playa. Among the 40 or so plants identified in the archaeological sample were those of sorghum, in what has been identified chemically as an incipient stage of domestication. (Courtesy of Krystyna Wasylikowa)

chemistry of the fats within the seeds is more like that of the modern domesticate. The identification of the sorghum from the site as a domesticate on this basis, however, is still far from clear. Nevertheless, as the site researchers point out, it is a "short step" (Wendorf et al. 1992:724) from the intensive use of sorghum and other wild plants to their domestication.

By 7000 B.P., early agriculturalists were living along the Nile River in Egypt, raising sheep, goats, and cattle and planting barley, emmer, lentil, and chickpea for food and flax for linen. The wild ancestors of domesticated sheep and goats are not native to Africa. These animals can be traced to the Middle East and Europe, where they lived in the wild and where domesticated versions appeared earlier than in Africa. Some of the crops were likewise introduced from the outside, but some may have been the result of indigenous experimentation.

To sort out the origins of domestic cattle in Africa, researchers have examined the genes of 50 separate breeds with long histories on the African continent (Bradley et al. 1998; Hanotte et al. 2002). For example, zebu cattle (*Bos indicus*), a common breed found in modern Africa, possess a hump on their backs directly behind the neck. Archaeological and genetic evidence allows us to trace the source of this breed to about 6,000 years ago in the Indus Valley in what is today Pakistan. It likely was introduced into eastern Africa sometime thereafter through trade and migration. However, the paleontological record along with early rock art shows that the oldest cattle in Africa were without the distinctive zebu hump. Humpless "taurine" cattle (*Bos taurus*) are also common in modern Africa, especially north of the Sahara Desert, and a humpless variety was first domesticated in the Middle East by about 8,000 years ago. Archaeological evidence suggests that this humpless variety was introduced into Africa by 6,500 years ago through trade and migration across a wide swath at the north of the continent.

According to animal researcher Olivier Hanotte et al.'s (2002) genetic analysis, along with the south Asian humped cattle and the Middle Eastern humpless varieties, there is a third, genetically distinct group of domesticated bovines in Africa. This third cluster, today most commonly found in southern Africa, represents a group of cattle breeds whose most likely source is the indigenous African species *Bos primigenius*. This species was almost certainly domesticated by Africans in their own, independent episode of animal domestication that may have occurred as much as 10,000 years ago.

The next time you get chastised for not washing the dishes or, at least, not doing a thorough enough job, make sure to mention how future archaeologists will benefit from your less than stellar performance in the kitchen. For example, researcher Julie Dunne and her colleagues (Dunne et al. 2012) have been able to determine that cows, almost certainly domesticated animals, were being used for milk production in Saharan Africa by as much as 5,200 years ago. They showed this through recovery and analysis of fat residues called lipids on the surfaces of 81 ceramic fragments. Cow milk was identified as the source of those lipids. Combined with the abundance of cow bones found in archaeological sites dating to this period in Saharan Africa, it seems clear that domesticated cattle had become an important element in subsistence at this early date.

Another animal domesticated in Africa, likely not for food but as a beast of burden, was the donkey. Archaeological evidence suggests that this occurred by about 5,000 years ago. Recently, researchers have compared the mtDNA of modern donkeys located in 52 separate countries across Asia, Africa, and Europe to that of wild asses in Africa and Asia (Beja-Pereira et al. 2004). All of the domesticated donkeys fell into two distinct mitochondrial groups, each of which was similar to one of two varieties of African wild asses. Neither of the two modern mitochondrial donkey groups was similar to Asian wild asses. Based on this, the authors of the study suggest that there may have been two independent domestications of donkeys from wild asses, both in Africa, with donkeys only later spreading from an African source into Asia and Europe.

Neolithic Cultures South of the Sahara

In Africa south of the Sahara, another set of largely independent agricultural revolutions took place, focusing on entirely indigenous tropical crops. Various millets (pearl, foxtail, finger, bullrush, broomcorn) were domesticated in tropical Africa. Domesticated pearl millet has been found dating to as early as 6,500 years ago—for example, at the Ameki site (Harlan 1992). Early sorghum domestication is seen at the Adrar Bous site dating to 4000 B.P. Yams, African rice, teff, fonio, groundnuts, enset, and noog are among other, entirely indigenous crops that were domesticated in sub-Saharan Africa in antiquity—all of which are unknown in the rest of the Neolithic world.

East and Central Asia

Most of us in the Western world think of rice as the agricultural food base of Asian peoples (Figure 8.22). As pointed out by archaeologist Gary Crawford (1992:8), however, there actually are 284 separate taxa of domesticated plants and animals known to have been used in east Asia.

Chronology of Food Production in China

The earliest evidence of plant or animal domestication in China from the Zeng-piyan Cave site in Guilan dates to the period after 10,300 B.P. (Figure 8.23). A large proportion (85%) of the animal bones are those of young pigs, less than 2 years of age (Chang 1986:102–103). As was the case at Ganj Dareh in Iran, this may indicate that the animals were not being hunted in the wild but instead were kept and tended. That the canine teeth are smaller than in a wild pig population may be explained by the artificial selection for the propagation of less dangerous animals with smaller teeth.

An analysis of a spate of radiocarbon dates associated with the remains of rice grains, husks, and other rice-plant remains, as well as the impressions of rice grains on ceramics, shows that very early varieties of domesticated rice date back to as much as 12,000 years ago along the middle Yangtze River in central China (Jones and Liu 2009). Ancient sites where early rice has been found both upstream and downstream of the middle Yangtze are younger, indicating that researcher Syuichi Toyama may have identified an early hearth for rice domestication in east Asia.

In northern China, the earliest Neolithic culture currently recognized is the **Peiligang**, as represented by sites such as Cishan, Peiligang, Laoguantai, Dadiwan, and Lixiatsun (Wenming 2005). Dating to between 8,500 and 7,000 years ago, the Peiligang culture is centered in the deciduous forest zone of northern China. The evidence shows clearly that Peiligang sites do not represent the first steps toward settled life based on agriculture; Peiligang sites are already well-established farming villages, with hunting, fishing, and the gathering of wild plants also contributing to the food quest. Cultigens include foxtail millet, broomcorn millet, and Chinese cabbage. Domesticated animals include pig, dog, and chicken. The foxtail millet may be the earliest domesticated variety in the world, having been radiocarbon dated to 10,000 years ago (Lawler 2009c). Genetic analysis indicates that Chinese millet may have been the ultimate source for later European millet.

The better-known, later Neolithic culture of China is called the **Yang-shao**. Typified by the Banpo site near Xian, Yang-shao sites are five times larger than Peiligang sites, and the villages are not arranged as haphazardly; they appear to have been planned out before construction. Crops of the Yang-shao include foxtail millet, Chinese cabbage, and rice, though rice was a relatively minor com-

▼ **Figure 8.22**
Rice, the mainstay of agriculture in Asia, was not the first crop domesticated on that continent. In fact, even after its domestication about 7,000 years ago, rice long remained a minor component in the diet. Today it is, along with wheat and corn, one of humanity's primary foods. (© Davide Erbetta/Grand Tour/Corbis)

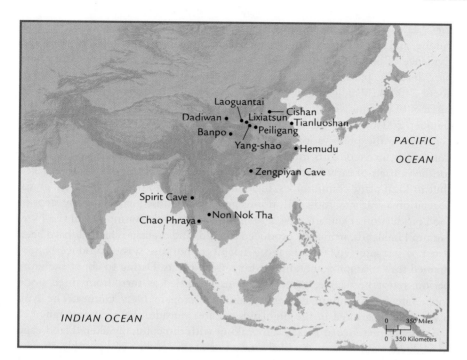

◀ **Figure 8.23**
Archaeological sites in
east Asia where evidence
of early food production
has been found.

ponent of the diet. Domesticated rice has been identified at the Hemudu site on
the Yangtze River just south of Shanghai, with a radiocarbon date of 7000 B.P.
(G. W. Crawford 1992:25).

Food Production in Southeast and Northeast Asia

The situation is not as clear in the rest of east Asia. Spirit Cave in northeast Thailand (mentioned earlier in this chapter) shows a clear reliance by about 12,000
B.P. on foods that were to become an integral part of the agricultural economies of later Neolithic peoples, including soybean, almond, cucumber, and water
chestnut (Gorman 1972). A possibly early form of domesticated rice—at least
rice that has been altered only slightly from its wild form—has been identified at Non Nok Tha in Thailand, dating to 5500 B.P. (Chang 1986). Indisputable evidence for domesticates in southeast Asia comes from excavations in the
Chao Phraya Valley in northeast Thailand at sites dated to about 5,000 years ago
(Higham 1989:80). The hunting and gathering of wild foods, along with the cultivation of rice, was the basis of this economy.

Data for Korea are sparse. Soils are very acidic, and few organic remains have
been recovered in early archaeological contexts. We know that by 3000 B.P.
domesticated millet was used in a mixed economy that included hunting, fishing,
gathering, and agriculture (Nelson 1993). Some archaeological evidence, in the
form of increased sedentism, suggests that farming may have begun a couple of
thousand years earlier.

There is far more information for Japan, but the sequence is not clear. The
late Pleistocene/early Holocene **Jomon** culture had a foraging subsistence base,
with an emphasis on resources of the sea. This productive resource base allowed

for a sedentary settlement pattern, with dense populations, elaborate material culture, and some large, semipermanent villages at more than 10,000 years ago. Evidence of domesticates, including rice, soybean, adzuki bean, buckwheat, and pear, does not appear at Jomon sites but appears in the later Yayoi culture, dated to about 2400 B.P. Radiocarbon dating of food residue recovered from the interior surfaces of ceramic vessels in Japan may push that date back to about 3000 B.P. (Holden 2003b).

Because the preservation of organic remains is often quite low in tropical rain forests, archaeologists focus on subtle changes in local ecology in the search for the impacts of early food production. In New Guinea, for example, a marked shift in local plant communities, including a change from forest to open, grassy vegetation as early as 7800 B.P., is interpreted as a consequence of early steps in food production (Denham et al. 2003). Also, at the Kuk Swamp site in the New Guinea Highlands, artificially produced mounds and drainage channels have been dated to just after 7,000 years ago. Their likely purpose was to produce better-drained soils to improve conditions for tended plants. Dating to about the same period, researchers collected starch grains identified as **taro** from three stone tools. Taro is a common modern subsistence crop in New Guinea. The Kuk Swamp site is located in the highlands, an area outside of the current range of the crop. Its presence at Kuk Swamp, along with the culturally altered landscape to facilitate plant growth, is a likely indicator of the tending and possible domestication of plants soon after 7,000 years ago. Additional direct evidence of food production and the domestication of local crops at Kuk Swamp comes in the form of preserved pollen grains and **phytoliths**, microscopic chunks of minerals that form in plants and that, ultimately, are released into the soil. Like pollen, phytolith morphology is species-specific; that is, each species of plant produces a unique suite of phytolith forms, recognizable and distinguishable from the phytoliths produced by other plant species. A high percentage at Kuk Swamp of phytoliths produced by banana trees in the period 4840 to 4440 B.P., found in an ecological context where researchers expected an abundance of grass phytoliths, is interpreted as evidence of the planting and domestication of banana at this time (Denham et al. 2003).

Domestication in Central Asia

Though central Asia is not usually thought of as a Neolithic center, the earliest evidence for the domestication of one kind of animal—the horse—has been found there. In a series of sites located in Kazakhstan (the not-so-fictional home of Sasha Baron Cohen's fictional character, Borat), archaeologists have found three lines of evidence for horse domestication or, at least, their tending and taming as much as 5,500 years ago (Outram et al. 2009): The horse leg bones recovered at these sites are not as robust as those of wild horses. Their size and proportions are far closer to domestic breeds than wild horses. Wear patterns seen on the jaws of the horses excavated are similar to what is seen in domesticated bridled horses. So, the Kazakhstan horses appear to have, at the least, been tame enough for people to ride.

Just as we saw in the case of the oldest domesticated cattle in Turkey, in ceramic sherds found in association with these horse bones, the residue of fatty acids was recovered. Analysis of the fatty acids identified their source as mare's milk. As a number of researchers familiar with wild horses have pointed out, no one in their right mind would attempt to milk a wild equine, so the evidence of milking here is a good indication that the Kazakhstan horses likely were domesticated or, at least, very tame animals used to direct contact with human beings.

Europe

Europe is a diverse continent with a complex prehistory. Regarding the shift to an agricultural mode of subsistence, it can be argued that, as for Africa, there was not one revolution but several (Whittle 1985). Archaeologist Robin Dennell (1992) indicates that a series of parallel shifts to domesticated plants and animals occurred in southeast Europe, in central Europe, along the northern Mediterranean coast, in the Alps, along the Atlantic coast, and in eastern and northeastern Europe. These agricultural revolutions, though not entirely independent of one another, occurred at different times, involved different crop and animal species, and had varying degrees of success (Figure 8.24).

For the most part, the Neolithic of Europe appears to have been imported from the south and east. Virtually all of the crops important in the European Neolithic, including einkorn, barley, bean, vetch, and lentils, are demonstrably Near Eastern in origin; there is little or no evidence for the existence of wild forms in Europe. The first appearance of these crops is in their domesticated form in the cultural contexts of archaeological sites dating to after 8000 B.P. Often these domesticated food sources seem to have been superimposed on an earlier, indigenous Mesolithic subsistence pattern (see the discussion earlier in this chapter) based on hunting animals and gathering acorns and hazelnuts (Dennell 1992). Certain crops—oats and some legumes—were probably domesticated independently by Europeans, but evidence so far indicates that the domestication occurred rather late in the Neolithic, after Near Eastern domesticates had already entered (via migrating farmers) and become important parts of the food base.

Domesticated plants don't sprout legs and migrate by themselves. How did southwest Asian domesticates make it into Europe in the first place? It turns out

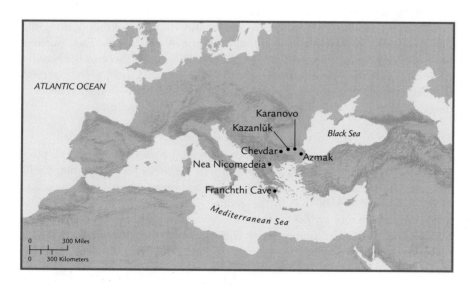

◀ **Figure 8.24**
Archaeological sites in Europe where evidence of early food production has been found.

that the crops moved into Europe as people from the Middle East physically moved there. Several recent analyses of DNA extracted from the bones of Europe's first agriculturalists show that they were not local people, not the descendants of hunters and gatherers who lived in Europe previously, but immigrants. For example, DNA has been extracted from the skeletons of 22 individuals from a graveyard associated with a Neolithic agricultural community in central Germany dating between 7,500 and 6,900 years ago. When comparing the recovered mitochondrial DNA with sequences in 55 different modern human populations, the closest match was found, not to local Germans, but to people in Turkey and the Near East (Haak et al. 2010). That's a strong indication that these early German farmers weren't locals, but immigrants from the south and east.

The same pattern has been seen as far north as Sweden. There, DNA was extracted from three skeletons recovered from burials at a village site of hunter-gatherers and DNA was recovered from a skeleton found in a burial at a nearby ancient farming site (Skoglund et al. 2012). Both sites date to around 5,000 years ago. The hunter-gatherer DNA was a close match for that of modern, northern Europeans. The farmer's strontium isotopes showed that she was born and raised within 100 km of where she was buried, but her DNA was a much closer match to that of people from southern Europe, specifically Greece and Cyprus. In other words, she herself was not an immigrant, but her ancestors were.

As was the case in southern Asia and Africa, domesticated cattle became an important element in the subsistence base of the European Neolithic. Unlike the situation in the Fertile Crescent, the Indus Valley, and Africa, however, Europeans seem not to have independently domesticated the cattle on which they came to rely. Genetic analysis of 392 living animals from the Middle East, Africa, and Europe and data derived from the bones of four members of an extinct wild European cattle species indicate that there was no in-place domestication of a native cattle breed in Europe. Instead, it seems that domestic cattle were brought into Europe primarily from the Middle East (Troy et al. 2001). None of the living cattle tested, including those in Europe, were genetically similar to the wild European samples. In fact, the modern domesticated European cattle were all quite similar in their genetic makeup to the Middle Eastern *Bos taurus* individuals in the sample. The predominant mitochondrial haplogroup among the European cattle represents a variety also present in the Middle East. Further, the European cattle reflected the least genetic diversity of those in the sample, suggesting that they are the most recent of the breeds. Cattle, then, represent another example of a species initially domesticated elsewhere and then brought into Europe as part of the shift from foraging to food production.

The Shift to Agriculture in Western Europe

Throughout the rest of Europe, the shift to agriculture seems to have taken place later than in the southeast. For example, sites in the Swiss Alps exhibiting a reliance on domesticated crops, including emmer and bread wheat, lentils, peas, and millet, date to after 5500 B.P. In the central European, early Neolithic culture known for its pottery whose surfaces are covered with linear bands of incised lines or dots and called, appropriately enough, **Linearbandkeramik (LBK)**, a subsistence base that included emmer, barley, and pulses (grainlike legumes) has been traced back to about 6500 B.P. Along the Atlantic coast, in Great Britain, France, and Spain, evidence of the use of domesticates (a similar mixture of cereals and legumes) dates to no more than about 6,000 years ago.

As noted in Chapter 2, a person's life history, including—especially—trauma, disease, and diet, is encoded in his or her bones. Recognizing that fact, researchers in Great Britain have examined the skeletal remains of 183 individuals, 19 dating to the Mesolithic (between 9,000 and 5,200 years ago) and the other 164 to the early Neolithic (between 5,200 and 4,500 years ago; Richards, Schulting, and Hedges 2003), looking at their proportions of the stable isotopes of carbon. A diet rich in fish and marine mammals is also rich in ^{13}C and, not surprisingly, the bones of the great majority of the Mesolithic people represented in the bone sample, many of whom lived along the coast, had a high concentration of ^{13}C relative to ^{12}C. All of the Neolithic skeletal remains, however, reflected a proportionally much lower concentration or signal of ^{13}C, which implies a rapid change in diet beginning at about 5200 B.P. Though most grasses follow the C4 photosynthesis pathway with higher ^{13}C concentrations, wheat and oats are C3 pathway plants with a low concentration of the ^{13}C isotope. The authors of the study conclude that C3 pathway plants abruptly replaced marine resources in the diet of Britons beginning 5,200 years ago, marking the beginning of food production as the primary mode of subsistence there.

North America

One of the most enduring images of the Indians of eastern North America is that of the natives helping the Pilgrims of seventeenth-century Plymouth, in Massachusetts, to survive their first winter in the New World. They brought the European settlers corn, beans, and squash and taught them how to plant and prepare these native agricultural foods.

Indeed, most historical native cultures in North America that were agricultural were dependent on these three crops. As we have seen earlier in this chapter, however, the wild ancestors of two of these crops—maize and beans—were tropically adapted plants, certainly not native to New England or the rest of North America. These crops were introduced into those areas north of Mexico in some unknown way—by trade, migration, indirect contact?

It is clear, however, that when maize penetrated the eastern woodlands of native America sometime after 1800 B.P., it did not replace an indigenous system of foraging for wild foods. Instead, maize initially supplemented an aboriginal pattern of hunting, collecting wild plants, and cultivating native squash and locally available seed plants (Figure 8.25). An independent, "pristine" pattern of indigenous domestication was established at about 4000 B.P., more than 2,000 years *before* the initial appearance of maize in the East (B. D. Smith 1989, 1992, 1995).

Indigenous Domestication North of Mexico

The primary native crops domesticated by the Indians of the eastern woodlands were squash, sunflower, marsh elder, goosefoot, and lamb's quarters (pigweed)—all producers of starchy or oil-rich seeds (Figure 8.26). At Napoleon Hollow in Illinois, for example, charred marsh elder seeds retrieved from a 4,000-year-old

▶ **Figure 8.25**
Archaeological sites in
North America where
evidence of early food
production has been
found.

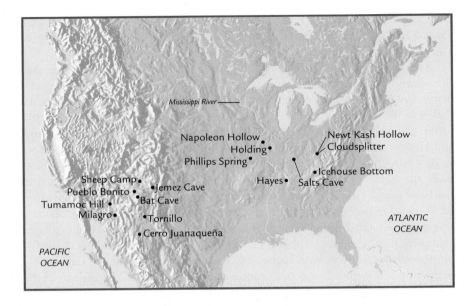

▶ **Figure 8.25**
Archaeological sites in
North America where
evidence of early food
production has been
found.

archaeological deposit are uniformly larger (by almost a third) than the seeds of
wild marsh elder (Ford 1985). The oldest evidence of domesticated sunflower in
North America has been dated to 4265 B.P., at the Hayes site in central Tennessee,
where the seeds are substantially larger than those of wild varieties (B. D. Smith
1995:191). Goosefoot seeds from Newt Kash Hollow and Cloudsplitter Rockshelter in Kentucky, though not larger, do have significantly thinner seed coats
than do wild plants. These thinner coats are most likely the result of intentional
human selection for plants that produced seeds with inedible coverings that were
thinner and therefore easier to penetrate and remove. Both sites have been dated
to about 3400 B.P.

Though squash was long thought to have moved into North America from
Mexico, archaeological evidence now indicates that it was domesticated independently in eastern North America as well. Squash seeds recovered at the Phillips
Spring site in Missouri, dating to 4500 to 4300 B.P., are significantly larger than
their modern wild counterparts (B. D. Smith 1995). The date for the site places
squash domestication in eastern North America at about the time of the domestication of some of the seed crops mentioned earlier, further supporting a picture
of a broad indigenous agricultural revolution in the East two millennia before the
introduction of maize.

Farming communities based on these native domesticates proliferated in the
eastern woodlands, specifically in the American Midwest and Midsouth, between
3,000 and 1,700 years ago. Along with goosefoot, pigweed, marsh elder, and sunflower, other crops that were used included knotweed, maygrass, squash, and a
little barley. As archaeologist Bruce D. Smith (1992) indicates, the representation
of the remains of these plants varies across the Midwest and Midsouth during
this period. Their overall significance varied in different times and places as these
domesticates became incorporated into a "mosaic of regionally variable . . . food
production systems" (B. D. Smith 1992:109).

The Appearance of Maize in the Eastern Woodlands

Maize begins to turn up in the archaeological record by about 1800 B.P.; some of the earliest evidence in North America for use of this most significant New World domesticate has been found at the Icehouse Bottom site in eastern Tennessee, with a radiocarbon date of 1775 B.P. (Chapman and Crites 1987). The Holding site, east of St. Louis, also has produced maize and may be slightly older (B. D. Smith 1995:191). For close to 1,000 years, however, maize continued to be a minor component of a broad subsistence system that still included hunting, fishing, collecting wild plants, and cultivating native seed crops. All of the indigenously domesticated crops of eastern North America are treelike in following the C3 photosynthesis pathway; maize, however, is a C4-pathway plant. Analysis of the carbon-isotope chemistry of human bones recovered at archaeological sites in this region shows a shift away from C3- and toward C4-pathway plants just before A.D. 1000, preserving a chronicle in bone of the adoption of maize-based agriculture by the native peoples of eastern North America (Figure 8.27). This shift to maize enabled the evolution of the most complex archaeological culture north of Mexico, the Mississippian temple mound builders of the Midwest and Southeast (see Chapter 14).

The American Southwest

Unlike the situation in eastern North America, there is little evidence in the Southwest for the development of agricultural economies before the introduction of the Mesoamerican domesticates of maize, beans, and squash. These crops moved in and became part of the subsistence base of people who had not practiced agriculture previously.

The route taken by maize agriculture as it expanded north from its Mexican source can, in some measure, be traced archaeologically. For example, maize has been found at the Cerro Juanaqueña site in northern Mexico, very close to the border with New Mexico.

▲ **Figure 8.26**
The sunflower (a), pigweed (b), and lamb's quarter (c) were three plants significant to their subsistence, domesticated by the native inhabitants of eastern North America beginning at about 4,200 years ago, at least 2,000 years before the introduction of Mesoamerican cultigens. (K. L. Feder)

▶ **Figure 8.27**
Graph showing the
dramatic jump in the level
of ^{13}C concentration in
the bones of prehistoric
Native Americans around
A.D. 1000. All of the
indigenous plant foods,
wild and domesticated,
of the native peoples
were C3-pathway plants
with relatively lower
^{13}C levels. Maize is a
C4-pathway plant with
relatively higher ^{13}C
levels. This jump in ^{13}C
levels, therefore, is taken
to mean an increase in
the reliance of maize
agriculture in eastern
North America. (From
The Emergence of Agriculture,
by Bruce Smith. © 1995 by
Scientific American Library.
Used with permission of
W. H. Freeman and
Company)

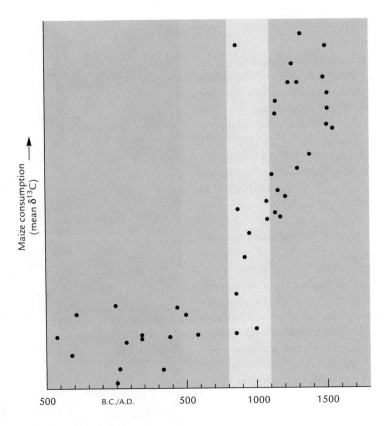

The site is large, with a substantial commitment to agriculture; it dates to sometime soon after 3500 B.P. (Hard and Roney 1998).

On the U.S. side of the border, **accelerator mass spectrometry (AMS)
dates** on maize from Bat Cave in western New Mexico and Tornillo Rockshelter in the southern part of that state show the crop to have been present by about
3200 B.P. (B. D. Smith 1995:202–203). A growing list of other sites shows the appearance of maize by 3,000 years ago or soon thereafter—for example, Milagro
in Arizona and Tumamoc Hill and Jemez Cave in New Mexico (Minnis 1992).
As Bruce Smith (1995) points out, it was during the four-century span between
3200 and 2800 B.P. that maize fully penetrated the American Southwest. Domesticated squash has been dated to about the same period at Sheep Camp Shelter
(Simmons 1986), and beans appear to have come in 200 or 300 years later.

Though maize, squash, and beans originated as Mesoamerican crops, there
was no movement of Mexican farmers northward, just the movement of the idea
of domestication and the crops themselves, perhaps through trade. Most everything else in Southwest culture—tools, pots, habitations—remained more or less
the same. Mesoamerican crops simply were grafted onto already existing lifeways.
These new foods required only minor cultural adjustments, and the native people
continued to exploit the wild plants and animals they always had.

The next time you sit down to your Thanksgiving turkey dinner, remember
that it was Native Americans who domesticated the bird. Conducted by molecular anthropologist Brian Kemp, DNA analysis of modern and archaeological

turkey bones from sites scattered across the United States and Mexico indicates that the native people of the American Southwest domesticated their own wild turkeys beginning about 2,200 years ago (Holden 2010).

Recent analysis of the interior surfaces of ceramic drinking cups found at Pueblo Bonito has revealed the remnants of a chocolate beverage (Crown and Hurst 2009). The Pueblo Bonito chocolate isn't nearly as old as the Mexican evidence noted previously in this chapter, dating to sometime between A.D. 1000 and A.D. 1125, but the similar, cylindrical cup forms used in both regions suggest a similar, ceremonial use. As cacao cannot be successfully grown in the American Southwest, the source of the chocolate found in the Pueblo Bonito cups likely was in the cacao plantations of Mesoamerica, about 1,600 km (1,000 mi) to the south.

South America

South America, like Africa, is enormous and contains a broad range of habitats with their attendant diverse plant and animal communities. As in Africa, geographic expanse and biological diversity mean human groups evolved many different regional cultural adaptations. And again, there was not just a single agricultural revolution in South America but several (Figure 8.28).

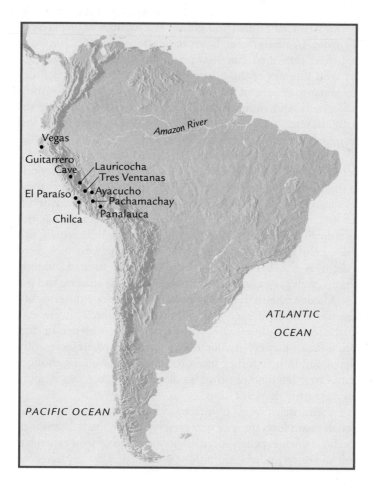

◀ **Figure 8.28**
Archaeological sites in South America where evidence of early food production has been found.

Three Regional Neolithics

Archaeologist Deborah Pearsall (1992) divides the South American Neolithic into three physiographic areas: low altitude, mid-altitude, and high altitude. Different plants growing wild in each of these divisions became the basis for distinct agricultural revolutions, with some crops from individual areas expanding into the others.

Sometime before 10,000 years ago in South America, the system of foraging for wild foods developed by Paleoindians was replaced by a more diverse and regionally specialized series of subsistence systems. In the Andes, hunters shifted from megafauna to small post-Pleistocene game such as deer and camelids (guanaco and vicuña). Elsewhere, subsistence shifted to a reliance on the abundant root crops of both the lowlands and the highlands; there is evidence in Chile for the use of a wild species of potato at Monte Verde by about 10,000 years ago (see Chapter 7 for a discussion of the earliest occupation of that site).

The earliest evidence for domesticated crops in South America appears not as seed fragments, rinds, or pollen but in the form of phytoliths. Researchers Dolores Piperno and Karen Stothert (2003) have determined that the phytoliths produced by wild and domesticated versions of the same plant type are distinguishable; the phytoliths of the domesticated varieties are significantly larger than those produced by their wild relatives.

Piperno and Stothert (2003) have recovered the phytoliths produced by the genus *Cucurbita* (squash and gourd) at a number of archaeological sites in coastal Ecuador. In stratigraphic layers dating to more than 10,000 years ago, these researchers recovered *Cucurbita* phytoliths already far larger than those produced by wild varieties of the plant. Piperno and Stothert conclude from this that the inhabitants of coastal Ecuador were exploiting the nutritious seeds of squash and gourds and, more than 10,000 years ago, were altering these plants through artificial selection. In other words, they were domesticating these plants and were engaged in a food-producing revolution.

Much of South America can be characterized as tropical as characterized by the region called Amazonia, the lowlands drained by the Amazon River. The Amazon is the second longest river in the world (the Nile is longer) and the largest in terms of the volume of water that courses through its channels and tributaries. Making up 40% of the land area of South America, Amazonia was densely populated and it is estimated that by the time Europeans entered the region, its indigenous people were cultivating more than 135 different crops, of which 83 were native species (Clement et al. 2010). Among the earliest domesticated and most significant indigenous crops grown in Amazonia were (and are) manioc and pineapple.

Manioc (the sixth most important domesticate in terms of yearly tons of production worldwide; see Table 8.1) is a root crop. This presents a great challenge to researchers interested in identifying early evidence of domestication. Roots are soft, not particularly durable, and unlikely to preserve in the wet, biologically active soil in which they grow. Researchers have long thought, in fact, that root crops have left little or no archaeological evidence that would enable the analysis of their early domestication.

Fortunately, however, when roots have been processed by use of a stone grinder, starch grains from the root may preserve in crevices in the stone. The shape and size of the grains are species-specific, and the grains of wild varieties of a plant are different and distinguishable from those produced by domesticated versions. And, in fact, the earliest definitive evidence of the use of domesticated plants south of Mexico has been found at the Aguadulce Shelter site in Panama by the recovery and analysis of starch grains on milling stones (Piperno et al. 2000). Dolores Piperno and her co-workers have identified the grains of domesticated manioc, yams, and arrowroot dating to nearly 7,000 years ago. Evidence shows that manioc domestication in South America is even older, dating to at least 8,000 years ago (Clement et al. 2010).

There is evidence of the domestication of common beans and chili peppers by 5,000 years ago at Guitarrero Cave in highland Peru, located in Pearsall's mid-altitude division (Kaplan, Lynch, and Smith 1973; Lynch et al. 1985). Also interpreted as an early domesticate at this site is the root crop ulluco, a source of brightly colored, carbohydrate-rich **tubers.** Ulluco is still popular as a delicacy in parts of South America.

On the east coast, phytoliths and starch grains from domesticated varieties of squash (4190 B.P.) and beans (3050 B.P.) have been recovered from grinding stones found in the La Plata Basin of southeastern Uruguay (Iriarte et al. 2004).

Domesticated squash and gourds were recovered at Ayacucho Cave in the central Peruvian Highlands. Also at this site is some of the earliest evidence for the domestication of an extremely important crop in the agriculture of South America: quinoa (Figure 8.29). Quinoa is a species of the genus *Chenopodium*. North American lamb's quarters (see Figure 8.26c) is another species in this genus. The earliest evidence of domesticated quinoa comes from Panalauca Cave in Peru. Quinoa seeds with thinner seed coats than in wild specimens have been dated there to between 4000 and 5000 B.P. (B. D. Smith 1995:173). Quinoa plants produce particularly nutritious seeds, with a mix of amino acids superior to that of the better-known grains (see "Issues and Debates"). In some areas of South America, particularly the higher altitudes, quinoa exceeded maize in agricultural importance (McCamant 1992). Only the potato was more important in the diet of the inhabitants of high-altitude South America.

Cold-loving, high-altitude-adapted domesticated root crops, especially the potato, were the staples of much of upland South America. Beyond this, it's fair to say that the potato was South America's most significant agricultural contribution to the world; today, it represents the fourth largest carbohydrate source in the human diet (Knapp 2008). Other important root crops, today unknown to most North Americans, also played important roles in the diet of ancient South America (Vietmeyer 1992). Oca, second in importance only to the potato, produced nutritious tubers at altitudes of up to 4,100 m (13,500 ft). The turnip-like maca was cultivated at elevations of 4,300 m (14,000 ft), making it the only domesticated food crop able to be grown at that altitude. Other high-altitude roots domesticated and relied on as sources of food in the South American uplands were yacon, the legume jícama, ulluco, and arracacha. The 500-year-old Inca

▼ **Figure 8.29**
Stand of quinoa, a significant food crop in ancient South America. In higher altitudes, it surpassed maize as a staple in the native diet. Quinoa has a better mix of amino acids than do most better-known crops. (Courtesy of John F. McCamant)

culture (to be discussed in Chapter 13), which occupied large portions of the western highlands of South America, relied more heavily on root crops than did any other of the world's ancient civilizations.

At the previously mentioned Aguadulce Shelter site in Panama, starch remains from domesticated maize were recovered from grindstones dating to close to 7,000 years ago, about the time of maize's earliest appearance in Mexico (Piperno et al. 2000). The earliest appearance of maize in South America postdates this by more than two millennia. Evidence of maize in the form of phytoliths has been found adhering to the surfaces of pottery sherds recovered at sites dating to 4,200 years ago in coastal Ecuador (K. Brown 2001). Luckily, along with not thoroughly scrubbing their dishes, the inhabitants of these sites did not floss their teeth; maize remains have been found in the tartar of the teeth of two human skeletons excavated there. In the La Plata Basin of Uruguay, maize kernels have been found dating to 3600 B.P. and maize phytoliths and starch grains have been found adhering to grinding stones associated with a date of 3460 B.P. (Iriarte et al. 2004). Clearly, the advantages of maize were as apparent to ancient people in the New World as they were to become to Old World visitors who brought maize back to their hemisphere where it became an important food crop. Once domesticated in Mesoamerica, maize spread into North and South America, where it became a food staple for agricultural people.

Animal Domestication in South America

Unlike in the Old World, where domesticated animals were a major part of human diets, animal husbandry played a relatively minor role in the New World. Among the few New World species that were successfully domesticated were the guinea pig (used as a food), the turkey, the dog, and the Muscovy duck. By far the most significant animal domestication in the New World was in South America (Kent 1987).

As mentioned earlier, the wild camelid species, the guanaco and vicuña, were exploited by post-Pleistocene hunters in western South America. In the central Andes, camelids became increasingly important in the diet, replacing deer as the subsistence focus sometime after 8000 B.P. Though why this shift occurred remains unclear, the ratio of camelid to deer bones at archaeological sites increases dramatically as wild camels were exploited more intensively. Vicuñas and guanacos are herd animals, with rigid dominance hierarchies. Their pattern of living in social groups and adhering to social hierarchies, along with their territoriality, rendered them attractive candidates for herding, controlling, taming, and then domesticating. Humans, placing themselves in the position of the most dominant members of the herd, could have exerted control over herds of wild camelids within their defined territory. Through artificial selection for animals more amenable to carrying heavy burdens and for animals that produced more meat and thicker wool, ancient South Americans produced domesticated llamas (as beasts of burden and for meat) and alpacas (for their wool and meat; Figure 8.30). Earliest evidence for this domestication has been found at Pachamachay and Lauricocha Caves in Peru, dating to as early as 6500 B.P. (Wing 1977).

Cotton

As was the case in the Near East, where flax was domesticated for use as a fiber at about 7000 B.P., a nonfood domesticate became an important element in the agricultural complex of South America. Domesticated cotton has been re-

▶ **Figure 8.30**
Llamas and alpacas were the only large animal species domesticated in the New World. Llamas were used as beasts of burden and for food. Alpacas were eaten as well; they also served as a source of wool. Pictured here is a group of guanacos (a), the wild ancestors of the llama (b). (K. L. Feder)

covered at Ayacucho Cave dating to just after 5000 B.P.

Cotton has also been recovered at the El Paraíso site on the Peruvian coast, a large and permanent settlement that has been dated to between 3800 and 3500 B.P. (Quilter et al. 1991). Eight or nine large complexes of rooms, covering a broad area, demarcate the site. Evidence found there suggests a mixed and broad subsistence base. Remains of domesticated food crops were recovered, including squash, chili pepper, common and lima bean, jícama root, and fruits, especially guava. At least of equal importance in the food quest were the rich natural resources of the coast, including anchovies, mussels, and clams. Wild plant foods also contributed to the subsistence base. Remains of domesticated cotton were far more abundant at the site than any of the domesticated foods. Cotton fiber was a major raw material for the production of fishing nets and lines as well as cloth. The authors of the El Paraíso Report maintain that the growth of this site is attributable to its location, perfect for the growing of cotton. Later, cotton became a major fiber for use in textiles of many cultures in South America.

How Was Domestication Accomplished?

In the domestication of plants and animals, human beings take the place of nature in the selection process. We can examine how this may have occurred for a number of different crops: wheat, maize, and beans.

ISSUES AND DEBATES

The Domestication of Wheat

The **rachis** of wild wheat—the area of attachment of the individual kernels of wheat—becomes quite brittle when the wheat ripens. A brittle rachis is a distinct advantage in nature. It promotes seed dispersal, which, in turn, promotes the growth

EINKORN   EMMER

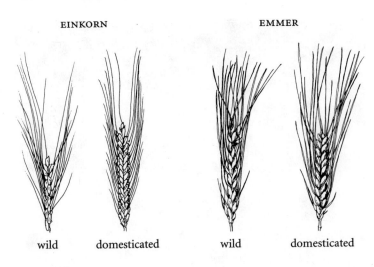

wild   domesticated   wild   domesticated

▲ **Figure 8.31**
Comparison of seed
heads of wild and
domesticated varieties
of einkorn and emmer
wheat.

of more wheat plants in the following growing season. When the kernels are ripe, a brittle rachis can be shattered by the wind, a rainstorm, or even an animal walking through a field (Figure 8.31).

Within any community of wild wheat plants today are individual plants that possess a combination of mutant genes for rachis form that results in a tougher, less brittle seed spike. Under conditions of natural selection, such forms are always in the minority, and they are at a clear disadvantage in terms of propagation: Their seeds are far less likely to disperse into the surrounding soil.

When humans enter the picture, however, the nature of selection changes drastically. Though preferred under wild conditions, a brittle rachis is *disadvantageous* for humans harvesting a wild crop, especially for those using a sickle to cut the plants off at the base. The impact of the tool is likely to shatter a brittle rachis, widely disperse the seeds, and make harvesting quite time-consuming.

Either by accident or by design—and likely a combination of the two—when humans harvested wild wheat, a greater proportion of the mutant plants with a tough rachis were brought back to the village. Most of the seeds of the more abundant plants with brittle connections simply fell off and did not make it back to the settlement. Again, either by accident or by design, more of the seeds of tough-rachis plants carrying the genetic instructions for that tough rachis became planted near human habitations. In this way, human beings fundamentally changed the process of selection, replacing a natural context with a human context to which the plants adapted.

Genetic evidence indicates that this process may first have occurred in southeast Turkey in the area of the Karacadağ Mountains. Researchers examined the DNA of 261 lines of wild wheat (einkorn), including 11 lines that grow abundantly in the Karacadağ Mountain region (Heun et al. 1997). Next, they compared the DNA of these strands of wild wheat to that of 68 lines of modern, domesticated einkorn wheat. They found that not only were the 11 lines of wheat from the Karacadağ Mountains the most genetically distinct of all the wild wheats, but of all the wild varieties sampled, the Karacadağ wheat was also the most genetically similar to the modern domesticated varieties examined. The presence of archaeological sites in the same region with evidence of the very early domestication of einkorn (for example, Abu Hureyra and Çayönü mentioned earlier in this chapter) lends further support to the hypothesis that the Karacadağ wild wheat was the ultimate source for the einkorn domesticated more than 10,000 years ago in southwest Asia.

From Teosinte to Maize

The wild maize, or teosinte plant, in some respects resembles the corn plant with which we are familiar. In fact, primitive varieties of maize are nearly identical to teosinte in cell form and genetic structure (Galinat 1992). However, teosinte produces not large cobs with rows of plump kernels but small seed spikes, each with a brittle rachis and tiny, thickly encased seeds (Figure 8.32). Teosinte seeds are nutritious and were exploited by ancient Mesoamericans. With their brittle rachis, however, they must have been difficult to harvest effectively. With their thick cases, teosinte seeds are well adapted for survival in the gut of an animal that has ingested them, to be "planted" somewhere else when they pass through the creature's digestive system intact (Federoff 2003). As mentioned earlier in this chapter, however, this feature renders the seeds at least less convenient for people who need to process them in order to make them nutritionally more accessible.

Luckily, just a few genes control those features. Genetic analysis has shown that probably only about five genetic loci control the physical characteristics that distinguish maize from teosinte (Doebley, Stec, and Hubbard 1997; Jaenicke-Després et al. 2003; Raloff 1993), and maizelike teosinte mutants are produced in wild populations (Beadle 1977). For example, a mutation in a single gene changes the extremely tough and stony fruitcase that encapsulates each teosinte kernel into a far more easily processed, and much more readily digestible, exposed or naked kernel (Wang et al. 2005). In other words, a single genetic mistake can transform a nutritious but challenging plant food into a nutritious and far more easily used plant food. Other mutations produce a plant with a tougher rachis, a feature that is not advantageous in the wild but is preferred by humans. We also know that a single mutation on one teosinte chromosome doubles the number of rows of kernels, and another alters the standard pattern of single spikelets to paired, again greatly increasing seed yield (Galinat 1992). Still another mutation enlarges the individual kernels.

As maize researcher Walton C. Galinat (1992) points out, ancient users of teosinte would have recognized the desirable characteristics of some of the mutant forms of that plant. In the wild, these rare forms would remain rare because cross-pollination would be occurring with the overwhelming abundance of nonmutant forms. By isolating the mutants, however, ancient Mesoamericans could have ensured that plants with rare features, maladaptive in nature but desirable for humans, cross-bred only with mutants with the same or other desirable

▼ **Figure 8.32**
Comparison of teosinte plant, spike, and seeds with maize plant, cob, and kernels.

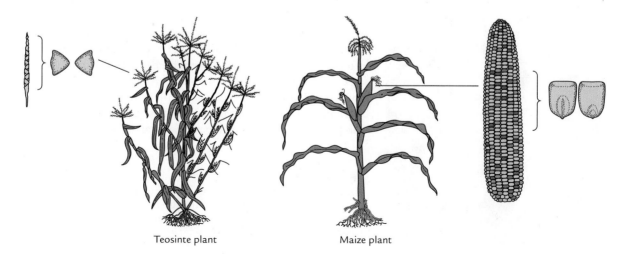

Teosinte plant   Maize plant

characteristics. As Galinat indicates, though ancient people lacked our knowledge of genetics, their powers of observation of the world around them were probably far better than our own—including, perhaps especially, their observation of the plant life on which they depended for survival. Applying the knowledge derived from such observation, they could have domesticated maize rather quickly. Once under human control, paleobotanical evidence shows consistent selection for larger cobs, which exhibit a steady pattern of growth from 6250 B.P. to 4400 B.P. (Jaenicke-Deprés et al. 2003).

Genetic analysis of the hundreds of varieties of maize and the many different kinds of wild teosinte has been conducted by plant biologist John Doebley. He has identified one particular teosinte subgroup that, based on its genetic makeup, could be the common ancestor of the many varieties of the domesticated crop: a race of teosinte that grows along the Balsas River in Mexico (Raloff 1993; Figure 8.33).

A recent genetic analysis of 193 maize and 67 teosinte samples shows that all of the extremely diverse current maize varieties originated from a single domestication "event" (Matsuoka et al. 2002). In other words, native people of the New World appear to have, through artificial selection, domesticated teosinte just once, and all the myriad modern varieties of maize have resulted from subsequent selection that enabled the use of the crop across an incredibly broad and climatically diverse geographic region, from the southern reaches of South America to the northern reaches of North America. This same genetic analysis confirms Doebley's hypothesis that maize is descended from a single variety of teosinte (*Zea mays* spp *parviglumis*), specifically one that grows in the uplands of southwest Mexico, in the Balsas River drainage. Based on mutation rates known for maize, it has been estimated that teosinte was first genetically modified by ancient Americans as much as 9,000 years ago (Matsuoka et al. 2002:6083). Remember that the oldest archaeological maize specimens are close to 7,000 years old, making the domestication of maize another example of the evolutionary nature of the process that led to a revolution in subsistence and society.

Beans

Wild beans grow in twisted pods that become brittle when ripe, and the beans themselves are rather impermeable. People selected for mutant beans with straight, limp, nonshattering pods for easier harvesting and for more permeable varieties, which reduced the time needed for soaking in water before they could be cooked (De Tapia 1992; Kaplan 1981; Kaplan and Kaplan 1992). This process may have been repeated several times in Mesoamerica

◀ **Figure 8.33**
Teosinte is the wild ancestor of maize. Pictured here is a modern variety (*Zea mays parviglumis*) from the Rio Balsas in Mexico that may be the form from which domesticated maize is descended. (Courtesy of Dolores Piperno, Smithsonian Tropical Research Institute)

and South America, ultimately providing the world with four separate domesticated bean species: common, lima and sievas, scarlet runner, and tepary beans, and the many varieties of these various species, including kidney, lima, pinto, wax, and navy (Kaplan and Kaplan 1992:61; another commonly eaten bean, fava, is an Old World domesticate).

The Remarkably Modern Cuisine of the Ancient World

As mentioned in this chapter's Prelude, you have probably tried the "ethnic" foods of different cultures that are widely available in the modern world. Chinese and Japanese food, Mexican cuisine, Middle Eastern food, Greek food, German food, Native American dishes, African, Spanish, French, Indian, Thai, Mongolian, and myriad other cuisines are all part of our modern diet. The essential ingredients of all of these ethnic or national cuisines including rice, wheat, corn, potatoes, beans, chickpeas, lentils, beef, pork, lamb, chicken, turkey, and the rest form the basis for the diet of the world's burgeoning human population at the turn of the twenty-first century. And all were domesticated in antiquity. In fact, it is difficult to come up with any economically significant modern food sources that were not part of the food base thousands of years ago, during the Neolithic. Two exceptions are strawberries, which were not domesticated until the Middle Ages, and pecans, which were not domesticated until 1846 (Diamond 1994). And remember, as mentioned earlier (but it can't be said enough), even chocolate was the result of an ancient process of domestication. Residue analysis of early Maya ceramic vessels recovered at the Rio Azul site in northeastern Guatemala, dating from A.D. 460 to 480, revealed the presence of a cacao-based beverage (Hurst et al. 2002). The researchers do not report the discovery of marshmallow residue.

So although we may think of ancient people as primitive, we have them to thank for virtually all the foods we rely on today. We have refined the work of the ancients by improving yield, increasing drought resistance, and accelerating ripening. But we have not added significantly to the inventory of domesticates.

Table 8.1 lists the top 47 domesticated crops worldwide as listed by the Food and Agriculture Organization of the United Nations in order of the number of tons of production yearly. I have added a column with our current best estimate for how long ago each of those crops was first domesticated. You can readily see that modern people rely absolutely on crops domesticated in antiquity.

Why Agriculture?

Many hypotheses have been put forth to explain why, more or less simultaneously, people all over the world adopted an agricultural subsistence system. Researchers Purugganan and Fuller (2009) count no fewer than 24 world regions where hunter-gatherers began tending and then domesticating crops after the end of the Pleistocene.

In other words, rather obviously, a revolution occurred across the face of the globe beginning as much as 13,000 years ago and lasting over 9,000 years, a revolution in which the pattern of foraging that had been successful for the hominid family for more than 6 million years was supplanted by a pattern of food production. What is not obvious, however, is *why* this shift took place at all.

TABLE 8.1 Modern Agricultural Crops in Order of Worldwide Production
and Approximate Dates of Earliest Domestication

	Crop	Domestication Date: Years Ago		Crop	Domestication Date: Years Ago
1	Sugar cane	5,000	25	Cucumbers and gherkins	3,000
2	Maize	7,000	26	Groundnuts, with shell	?
3	Wheat	10,000	27	Millet	8,500
4	Rice, paddy	12,000	28	Sunflower seed	7,500
5	Potatoes	5,000	29	Plantains	4,800
6	Cassava (manioc)	8,000	30	Mangoes, mangosteens, guavas	4,000
7	Soybeans	5,000	31	Eggplants (aubergines)	2,000
8	Sugar beet	4,000	32	Tangerines, mandarins, clementines	?
9	Oil palm fruit	2,800	33	Other melons (incl. cantaloupes)	?
10	Barley	11,000	34	Peppers, chili and green	5,000
11	Tomatoes	?	35	Carrots and turnips	5,000
12	Sweet potatoes	5,000	36	Oats	4,000
13	Watermelons	3,500	37	Lettuce and chicory	4,000
14	Bananas	4,800	38	Pears	2,300
15	Cabbages and other brassicas	?	39	Pumpkins, squash, and gourds	10,000
16	Apples	6,500	40	Beans, dry	5,000
17	Grapes	5,000	41	Pineapples	6,000
18	Oranges	?	42	Olives	7,000
19	Onions, dry	3,000	43	Cauliflowers and broccoli	2,000
20	Seed cotton	5,000	44	Peaches and nectarines	4,000
21	Sorghum	8,500	45	Rye	9,000
22	Coconuts	2,000	46	Garlic	3,500
23	Rapeseed	600	47	Spinach	?
24	Yams	7,000			

Niche Construction

As archaeologist Bruce D. Smith (2007) points out, a number of animal species, *Homo sapiens* among them, work intentionally—and diligently—to alter their surroundings to their own specifications. In essence they create or construct ecological niches in which they as well as plants and other animals can live. Smith uses the example of beavers who change their areas dramatically by clearing out trees and then using the downed trees to create ponds. Humans may do the same kind of habitat alteration and niche construction through, for example, controlled burns. By burning off forests, people can create or maintain habitats attractive to seed-bearing plants as well as, in turn, the grassland animals on which human beings may rely for their subsistence.

These kinds of habitat alterations obviously change conditions and create niches for animals living in an area. When you change or alter natural conditions you change or alter the course of natural selection; at least you change the conditions under which natural selection takes place. Beavers don't take it past changing general conditions and, then, in essence, letting the chips fall where they may. As Smith points out, human beings take this process of niche construction quite a few steps further by, for example, penning wild animals and taking over their control, planting seeds in beds of soil expressly produced by people to encourage their growth and productivity, and so on. By controlling the conditions in which plants grow and animals thrive, human beings control those plants and animals and replace nature in the process of selection. When that happens, domestication is a possible result.

Climate Change

Remember, all this is happening at the same time the earth is experiencing a brief return to colder conditions during the period called the Younger Dryas. In other words, between 12,900 and 11,600 years ago, human beings were faced with their own version of climate change. It seems clear in the Middle East, for example, that groups like the Natufians had experienced a population increase during the good times but were then faced with a shrinking carrying capacity when climate shifted.

One possible response to climate change—not necessarily a wise one—is denial. Keep playing the same game even though the cards have changed. Sit around with your fingers crossed that you're only experiencing a normal downturn, a short-lived blip, a minor bump in the road. Another possible response to significant change is to develop and implement new strategies for survival. The latter approach seems to apply to the Natufians and their descendants. Rather than simply wait hopefully for the climate to ameliorate and for the wild foods on which they subsisted to flourish again, they shifted their strategy from foraging wild foods to tending, encouraging, artificially selecting, and, ultimately, domesticating plants and animals in order to expand and render more reliable their subsistence base. In their response to climate change, perhaps we can learn a lesson from the Natufians.

A Multitude of Reasons

There probably was no single "prime cause" for the development of agriculture in all the places that it occurred. Perhaps there was no one "**Agricultural Revolution**" but many, each with its own explanation. As archaeologist Donald O. Henry (1989:236) points out, "given the complex ecological relationships that governed the transition from forager to food-producer," complexity and diversity in explaining these transitions is to be expected.

However, significant patterns do exist in the record. A sedentary settlement pattern (evidenced by substantial and permanent architectural forms) *preceded* the appearance of domesticated foods. In other words, in the late Pleistocene/early Holocene, some human groups began to settle into regions so plentiful in food resources that people could stay in one place for much of the year and collect enough food to survive and even thrive. Population might have grown exponentially as the sedentary life may have lowered infant mortality and extended the length of life. During a long period of population growth, the food quest would have been intensified to feed the growing number of mouths. One step in this intensification would have been to artificially raise the productivity of the nearby wild plants by creating conditions that increased the yield of food: clearing forest, planting seedbeds, weeding, fencing in. At this point, the plant selection process changed: Whereas before plants were adapting to natural conditions, now they were adapting to conditions produced by the cultural manipulation of the environment. This was the first step toward domestication and, ultimately, a way of life dependent entirely on food production.

Was Agriculture the "Worst Mistake in the History of the Human Race"?

Scientist Jared Diamond (1987) labeled agriculture the "worst mistake in the history of the human race" in the title of a provocative essay. His interesting idea is backed up by some impressive archaeological evidence. Clearly, agriculture can provide more food than can most foraging systems, and it can do so in a wide variety of habitats. In terms of caloric output, when agriculture works, it wins, hands down. Unfortunately, however, agriculture comes with some heavy baggage.

Biological anthropologists Mark Cohen and George Armelagos (1984) have summarized the evidence for the prevalence of paleopathology—ancient disease—coincident with the origins of agriculture in North, Central, and South America; the eastern Mediterranean; western Europe; the Middle East; southern Asia; and Nubia. When comparing parameters of health as revealed by prehistoric skeletons, in most instances older hunter-gatherer groups exhibited higher levels of health and nutrition than did the farmers who succeeded them. Specifically, there were higher levels of infection in farmers than in previous foragers in the same regions. Some early farming populations show increases in tubercular infections (Buikstra 1984); others show higher levels of gastrointestinal infections (seen in a survey of mummified humans in South America; Allison 1984). Many more farming groups show higher rates of infections of uncertain origin. Of course, agriculture itself doesn't cause disease; it merely establishes the conditions conducive for disease to spread: large, dense, sedentary populations.

Ironically, chronic malnutrition seems to be another major problem that accompanied the shift to an agricultural way of life. Although many people may stereotype hunter-gatherers as living hand-to-mouth, where every meal might be their last for some time, in most of the studies Cohen and Armelagos summarize, farmers show more evidence of malnutrition than do their foraging forebears.

Nutritionally based anemia (as evidenced by porosity of the skull) was found to be severe in a number of farming groups in the American Midwest. Other evidence for poorer nutrition among some farming groups included an overall decline in stature. Episodes of severe malnutrition among farmers was further indicated by more incidences of enamel hypoplasia (see the discussion in Chapter 5 regarding the Neandertals and this condition).

If you were a dentist during the Paleolithic or Mesolithic, you didn't have much to do. The analysis of human teeth dating to those periods shows little evidence of dental disease: very few cavities, little evidence of excessive crowding or gum disease. For example, Peter Ungar estimates that in a sample of human teeth dating to 20,000 years ago, fewer than 2% exhibit evidence of cavities (as cited in Gibbons 2012b). That low rate of decay begins to change dramatically with the advent of the Neolithic and the host of carbohydrate-rich foods made widely available by the agricultural revolution. Ungar estimates that the first farmers in the Middle East have a much higher cavity rate of about 9% (Gibbons 2012b:974). Of course, even that pales in comparison to modern levels. In the middle of the twentieth century, with the wide availability of refined sugar and before the advent of fluoridated water, between 50% and 90% of people living in the United States and Europe had cavities.

Perhaps most remarkable of all, for the majority of cases reported in a symposium Cohen and Armelagos organized on this issue, where age at death was calculated for the archaeological samples, hunter-gatherers lived longer than did the farmers in the same regions. They conclude: "Taken as a whole, these indicators fairly clearly suggest an overall decline in the quality—and probably in the length—of human life associated with the adoption of agriculture" (1984:594).

The results were depressingly similar for a sample of about 11,000 Europeans in the period after 3,000 years ago when agriculture became widespread on the continent (Gibbons 2009a). There is clear evidence following the establishment of an agriculture-reliant economy of diminishing stature, an increase in diseases that result from crowding, and an increase in dental pathologies as a result of a poor diet.

Implications of the Neolithic: The Roots of Social Complexity

For most of human history, we have foraged for food. Small nomadic groups could easily supply the necessities for their families. No one needed more, and providing for more than one's needs made little sense. The organization of such societies could be rather simple, revolving around age and sex categories. Such societies likely were largely **egalitarian;** beyond the usual distinctions based on age and sex, virtually all people had equivalent rights, status, and access to resources.

Archaeologist Donald Henry (1989) suggests that the combination of a rich habitat and sedentism led to a dramatic increase in human population. Given sufficient time, even in very rich habitats, human population size can reach **carrying capacity**: the maximum population an area can sustain within the context of a given subsistence system. And human population growth is like a runaway train: Once it picks up speed, it is difficult to control. So even after reaching an area's carrying capacity, Holocene human populations probably continued to grow in food-rich regions, overshooting the ability of the territory to feed the population, again within the context of the same subsistence strategy. In some areas, small changes in climate or minor changes in plant characteristics may have further destabilized local economies.

One possible response to surpassing the carrying capacity of a region is for a group to exploit adjoining land. However, good land may itself be limited—for example, to within the confines of a river valley. Where neighbors are in the same position, having filled up all the available desirable habitat in their home territories, expansion also is problematic. Impinging on the neighbors' territory can lead to conflict, especially when they too are up against the capacity of the land to provide enough food.

Another option is to stay put but shift and intensify the food quest in the same territory. The impulse to produce more food to feed a growing population was satisfied in some areas by the development of more complex subsistence strategies involving intensive labor and requiring more cooperation and greater coordination of increasing numbers of people. This development resulted in a change in the social and economic equations that defined those societies. Hierarchies that did not exist in earlier foraging groups but were helpful in structuring cooperative labor and in organizing more complex technologies probably became entrenched even before domestication and agriculture as pre-Neolithic societies reacted to population increase. The results of this strategy of intensification of the exploitation of wild foods were, at least in some regions, even better than the participants could have anticipated. Not only were people able to increase their wild food base enough to feed a larger population, but also they actually were able to produce a food surplus by artificially selecting for propagation the most productive individuals in their wild food species.

Though agriculture may have initially solved the problem of feeding an increasing population, it may have, ironically, worked too well, contributing to the rate at which that population increased subsequently. By providing an abundance of high-calorie foods, the food production revolution established conditions that actually accelerated the rate at which population increased (Bocquet-Appel 2011). As Jean-Pierre Bocquet-Appel shows, an analysis of the archaeological record indicates an abrupt demographic change beginning 11,000 years ago, a worldwide population explosion called the **Neolithic Demographic Transition (NDT)** that almost certainly contributed to the development of the economic, social, and political complexity to be discussed in the rest of this book.

CASE STUDY CLOSE-UP

THE REVOLUTION THAT IS THE FOCUS of this chapter was not an event but rather a slow process that only gradually changed the fundamental way people made a living. Analysis of this shift in the Khabur Basin in northeastern Syria is a perfect example (Zeder 1994a, 1994b). The area had been only sparsely occupied before 12,000 B.P. Beginning about 10,000 years ago, villages began turning up in the archaeological record with a subsistence base that included a variety of early domesticates, including wheat, lentils, peas, and beans. The bones of domesticated sheep and goats were found in early levels of these settlements, with pig and cattle remains showing up later.

A detailed analysis of one site in the Khabur Basin, Umm Qseir, clearly shows the evolutionary nature of the shift from foraging to farming. For example, after

8000 B.P., domesticated sheep, goat, and pig contributed to the diet in the settlement. But the Neolithic residents of Umm Qseir had not abandoned their earlier pattern of hunting and gathering. More than half the animal remains recovered at the site were of wild animals—gazelle, deer, wild cattle, hare, turtles, wild ass, birds, and freshwater clams (Zeder 1994b:5). The use of both wild and domesticated sources of food seems to reflect a seasonal rhythm at Umm Qseir. Most animal species have a particular mating season and a fairly consistent gestational period, so most of the offspring are born within a narrow period of time during the year. Because the age of death of a juvenile animal can be estimated based on tooth eruption and bone development, archaeologists can often determine the time of year an animal was killed. In other words, if the young of a particular species tend to be born in the early spring and many of the younger animals at a site were slaughtered in their 15th month of life, just count 15 months from early spring to determine when they were slaughtered. In this hypothetical example, they were killed in the summer.

Pigs were slaughtered most commonly at Umm Qseir between August and October. The ages of sheep and goats killed at the site correspond to this same period, which actually extended until January. This is the arid summer and early rainy season, precisely when wild resources would have been at their leanest. So domestication did not supplant foraging in the subsistence system at Umm Qseir. Instead, domestication allowed for the permanent occupation of an area rich with seasonally available wild foods, even during seasons when those wild foods were not plentiful.

As archaeologist Melinda Zeder (1994b) points out, here and elsewhere the Neolithic was not a period during which all people marched down the path to a purely agricultural mode of subsistence. For a long time, domestication complemented foraging but did not replace it. Only much later did agriculture and animal husbandry become the primary sources of food for most of the world's people, setting the stage for the period of time to be described in Chapters 10 to 15.

Summary

The common thread running through this chapter has been post-Pleistocene adaptation. Wherever we have looked in Europe, Asia, North and South America, Australia, and Africa, we have seen the same trends: intensification of food collection, increasing economic and social complexity, and a marked jump in regional, cultural diversity. After about 12,000 B.P., human beings were faced with fundamental changes in the Pleistocene environments to which they had become adapted. Land covered in ice became exposed, temperatures rose, and some areas became drier, others wetter. Land connections were breached, and coastal configurations rapidly changed. Animals on which some humans subsisted became extinct, and new, different animals took their place. Plants became available that were useful for food, in the form of nuts, seeds, fruits, leaves, or roots. People were faced with many options in the rapidly changing post-Pleistocene world. Some broadened the subsistence quest to include a wide variety of plant and animal resources. Others intensified the subsistence quest, focusing on a single resource or very few particularly productive resources. Other human groups became increasingly sedentary as they adapted to rich Holocene environments. As a result of the diversity of the post-Pleistocene resource base, cultural diversity increased exponentially, with myriad cultures proliferating, each thriving in its own territory. Some settlements became more permanent, and population grew. In a number of cases, the food quest was intensified further still as groups attempted to increase the productivity of the resources on which they depended.

TO LEARN MORE

For a summary of the European Mesolithic, T. Douglas Price's 1987 article titled "The Mesolithic of Western Europe" in the *Journal of World Prehistory* is a good source. For North America, see Brian Fagan's *Ancient North America* (2005) for a detailed textbook treatment of post-Pleistocene adaptations. For an excellent source on this and other periods of South America's prehistory, see Karen Olsen Bruhns's *Ancient South America* (1994). Several chapters of John Mulvaney and Johan Kamminga's (1999) excellent overview, *Prehistory of Australia*, are devoted to a detailed discussion and analysis of post-Pleistocene adaptations to the island continent. For Asia, the general works by Kwang-Chih Chang—including *The Archaeology of Ancient China* (4th ed., 1986)—as well as Charles Higham's *The Archaeology of Mainland Southeast Asia* (1989) include considerable discussions of the post-Pleistocene. For Africa, see David W. Phillipson's *African Archaeology* (2nd ed., 1993).

An extremely helpful source on the food-producing revolution is *Domestication of Plants in the Old World: The Origin and Spread of Cultivated Plants in West Asia, Europe, and the Nile Valley*, by Daniel Zohary and Maria Hopf (2001). Useful works discussing the food production revolution in individual regions or habitats are *Europe's First Farmers*, edited by T. Douglas Price (2000); *The Origins of Agriculture in the Lowland Neotropics*, by Dolores R. Piperno and Deborah M. Pearsall (1998); and *The Exploitation of Plant Resources in Ancient Africa*, edited by Marijke Van Der Veen (1999). An extremely detailed treatment of the origins of agriculture in the Near East is Donald O. Henry's *From Foraging to Agriculture: The Levant at the End of the Ice Age* (1989).

Archaeologist Bruce D. Smith's excellent synthesis titled *The Emergence of Agriculture* (1995) presents a broad, comparative survey of the origins of food production. His is the best detailed discussion of domestication written not just for other scientists but also for everybody interested in the topic.

Web links for this chapter can be found at www.oup.com/us/feder

accelerator mass
    spectrometry (AMS)
    dating, 282
Agricultural Revolution, 293
Archaic, 252
artificial selection, 258
Australian Small Tool
    Phase, 249
backed blade, 248
camelid, 257
Capsian, 248
carrying capacity, 295
cereal, 262
complex foraging, 264
domesticated, 259
domestication, 259
egalitarian, 295
einkorn, 266
emmer, 266
Fertile Crescent, 262

Hoabinhian, 247
Holocene Warm
    Maximum, 249
Iberomaurusian, 248
Jomon, 275
lacustrine, 252
Lake Forest Archaic, 252
legume, 264
Levant, 264
Linearbandkeramik, 278
littoral, 257
macroband, 270
Maglemosian, 244
Maritime Archaic, 252
Mast Forest Archaic, 253
Mesolithic, 244
microband, 270
microblade, 246
microlith, 248
midden, 243

Natufian, 263
Neolithic, 242
Neolithic Demographic
    Transition (NDT), 296
Paleo-Arctic tradition, 252
Peiligang, 276
pelagic, 252
phytolith, 276
Qadan, 271
rachis, 287
sedentism, 251
seedbed selection, 267
Shell Mound Archaic, 252
starch grains, 263
taro, 276
Tehuacán, 268
teosinte, 267
tuber, 285
Yang-shao, 274
Younger Dryas, 243

9

Roots of Complexity

The Origins of Civilization

CHAPTER OVERVIEW

For nearly all of the human past, societies were largely egalitarian with most decisions made at the level of the household, the family, or the local community. Populations were small and disbursed and decisions were made; labor was divided, distributed, and organized; and wealth was apportioned on the basis of family relationships. Beginning in the Holocene, however, some societies in the Old and New Worlds became socially, politically, and economically more complex. In these complex societies, authority, work, and decision making were organized beyond simply the household or family, on the basis of a larger social group. It is likely that complex social and political systems developed where the coordinated labor of a large group of people was needed to meet some immediate challenge or was beneficial in exploiting a unique opportunity. The great monuments that now dominate the archaeological record of some ancient cultures and, therefore, occupy the time of so many archaeologists are one result of the evolution of complex social, political, and economic systems where the labor of the many can be harnessed, organized, and controlled.

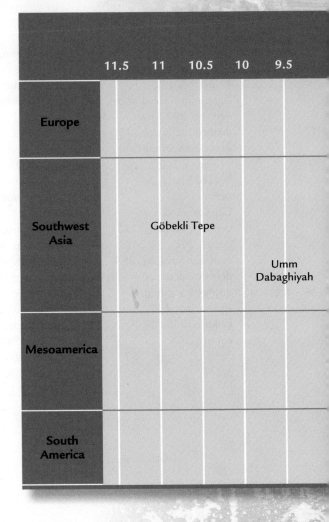

	11.5	11	10.5	10	9.5
Europe					
Southwest Asia		Göbekli Tepe			Umm Dabaghiyah
Mesoamerica					
South America					

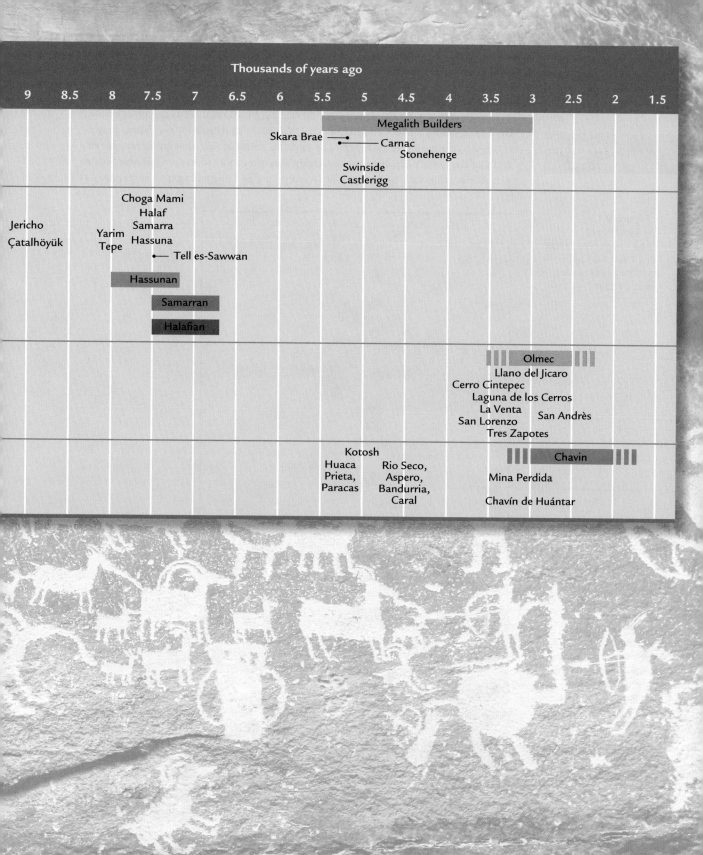

Thousands of years ago

9   8.5   8   7.5   7   6.5   6   5.5   5   4.5   4   3.5   3   2.5   2   1.5

Megalith Builders

Skara Brae ——•   —— Carnac
                                    Stonehenge
                        Swinside
                        Castlerigg

Choga Mami
Halaf
Jericho   Samarra
Çatalhöyük   Yarim   Hassuna
             Tepe
             •—— Tell es-Sawwan

Hassunan

Samarran

Halafian

Olmec
                              Llano del Jicaro
                        Cerro Cintepec
                              Laguna de los Cerros
                              La Venta
                        San Andrès
                        San Lorenzo
                              Tres Zapotes

Kotosh   Chavin
Huaca   Rio Seco,
Prieta,   Aspero,   Mina Perdida
Paracas   Bandurria,
             Caral   Chavín de Huántar

PRELUDE

EVEN IN RUIN AND ADJACENT TO a modern highway, Stonehenge is an ancient monument of uncommon beauty, majesty, and even mystery (Figures 9.1 and 9.2; Chippindale 2004). Though the tombs of the ancient rulers of Mesopotamia may reflect greater wealth (Chapter 10), and the pyramids of ancient Egypt were built on a far grander scale (see Chapter 10), the painted murals of the Maya may be more visually arresting (Chapter 12), and the stone blocks that make up the city walls of the Inca were cut with much greater precision (Chapter 13), the Stonehenge ruin that can be seen today is every bit as compelling and impressive as

▶ **Figure 9.1**
The location of Stonehenge, which was constructed by an early, chiefdom-level society in Great Britain.

▶ **Figure 9.2**
Stonehenge is both massive and marvelous; a remarkable monument made possible by the development of a society in which the labor of many could be commanded by the few. (K. L. Feder)

these other works of the ancient world (Ruggles 1996). In his book *The Martian Chronicles*, science fiction author Ray Bradbury (2006:110) described the remnants of an ancient Martian city in this way: "Perfect, faultless, in ruins, yes, but perfect, nonetheless." I think that's a compelling and appropriate description of Stonehenge as well (Figure 9.2).

The Construction of Stonehenge

In 2008, for the first time in 40 years, archaeologists were given the opportunity to excavate right in the middle of Stonehenge. Charcoal was discovered within the holes dug by the builders into which they placed the earliest circle of stones—the so-called bluestones—and, as a result, we have a much better idea of when the monument's construction was: 4,600 years ago (J. Morgan 2008).

A new analysis of radiocarbon dates reveals the following sequence for the construction of Stonehenge (Darvill, Marshall, Pearson, and Wainwright 2012; see Figure 9.3). About 5,000 years ago, people living in the south of England in an

▶ **Figure 9.3**
Phases in the construction of Stonehenge. (Jennifer Davis)

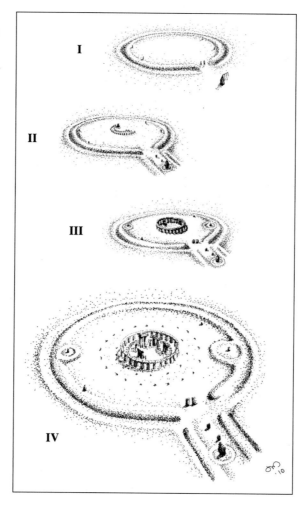

▲ Figure 9.4
Artist's conception of the raising of the stone lintels that topped the sarsens and trilithons of Stonehenge. Quarrying, shaping, moving, and erecting the uprights followed by the construction of staging to raise the lintels required the organized labor of a large number of people over an extended period of time. (© English Heritage)

area of low, undulating hills called the Salisbury Plain excavated a nearly perfectly circular ditch about 110 m (361 ft) in diameter. At first, this ditch was all that constituted Stonehenge. Then, about 400 hundred years later, a little before 4,600 years ago, the Stonehenge builders began transporting between 50 and 80 volcanic stones (called bluestones for their slightly blue hue) from the Preseli Mountains in southwest Wales, where weathering of the local rock produces naturally freestanding monoliths, perhaps inspiring the artificial construction of patterns of upright stone. The original bluestones were arranged in a double half-circle located in the center of the area circumscribed by the circular ditch.

The Stonehenge bluestones are a heavy, dense rock, each one weighing as much as 4,000 kg (more than 4.4 tons) and standing a little less than 2 meters (6 ft) high. The most direct route by which the stones can be transported from the Preseli Mountains to Stonehenge (by river and coastal routes) is still about 385 kilometers (240 miles; Alexander 2008). Transporting stones weighing more than 8,800 lb more than 200 miles and then erecting them was no mean feat for an otherwise technologically unremarkable farming people with no machines or even draft animals.

As impressive as the bluestone construction was, also at about 4,600 years ago, the builders did something even more remarkable. They quarried, transported, shaped, and erected the largest stones in the monument: the **trilithons**, made of a silicified sandstone called **sarsen** found in the area around the village of Avebury, located about 30 km (18.6 mi) north of Stonehenge. They are called trilithons because each of the five sets consisted of three stones: two uprights and one capstone. Arranged in a giant horseshoe shape, the trilithon uprights even individually are monumental. Each stands about 8 m (more than 26 ft) above the surface, with an additional 2 m (6.6 ft) of stone nestled in the chalky ground underlying the monument. The largest of the trilithon uprights weighs 45,000 kg (nearly 50 tons), and the associated **lintel** weighs 9,000 kg (10 tons)—and remember, this 10-ton block had to be raised up to and perched precisely on the top of its 26-ft-high trilithon upright pair.

And there's more. At about the same time, Stonehenge's builders began shaping and transporting 30 additional sarsens to be used as uprights and 30 more to be used as capstones or lintels joining the uprights. Smaller than the trilithon uprights, each stone in the second set of sarsen uprights is still over 3 m (nearly 10 ft) tall and weighs 25,000 kg (55,000 lb). The 30 sarsen uprights were erected in a continuous circle 29.6 m (97 ft) across, concentric with the older circular ditch. Each of the 30 uprights in the circle was connected to the adjacent stone by the sarsen lintels.

The tops of all of sarsen uprights were precisely carved to produce two knobs, or tenons. The builders of Stonehenge then prepared the 30 lintels, each weighing about 5,500 kg (more than 12,000 lb), for placement by sculpting two hollows, or mortises, on the bottom of each. Then, in an absolutely remarkable feat, they raised up these lintels and perched them on top, fitting the mortises on each lintel onto the tenons of two adjacent uprights (Figure 9.4). In other words, the Stonehenge builders employed in stone as hard as iron a joinery practice usually applied only to wood. Each lintel had to be shaped precisely, curved on the exterior and interior surfaces to match the arc of the circle of the sarsens. Even a slight deviation in shape and size of any of the 30 lintels and any slight misalignment of the tenons on the sarsens or of the mortises on the lintels would have made completion of the monument impossible. What resulted was a smooth ring of massive stones, precisely positioned and joined together (Figure 9.5). Imagine a project that involved a set of giant, many-tonned stone Lego blocks and you have a pretty good idea of the process of building the sarsen circle at Stonehenge.

▲ **Figure 9.5**
Depiction of an intact Stonehenge upon its completion 4,000 years ago. Note the precision with which the enormous sarsens and trilithon uprights were assembled, each connected to each other by their associated lintels. (From Kenneth L. Feder, *Frauds, Myths, and Mysteries,* Fourth Edition, Mayfield Publishing Company, 2001. Reprinted with permission from The McGraw-Hill Companies)

Imagining Stonehenge

In a project replicating ancient technology sponsored by the PBS science series *Nova* (Page and Cort 1997), a series of experiments were conducted in an attempt to determine how Stonehenge and other ancient monuments could have been built. Two parallel sets of squared-off log beams were placed in the ground, producing a wooden trackway, and a cement trilithon upright weighing 50 tons was attached to a wooden sled that fit onto the trackway. After a bit of trial and error, a crew of about 200 volunteers was able to move the enormously heavy replica. With the help of some fundamental engineering principles reasonably within the capability of ancient people, the volunteers were able to erect the trilithon upright, setting it into a 6-ft-deep socket they had excavated in the chalky subsoil. Then, using staging, levers, counterweights, and human muscle power, they raised the 10-ton trilithon lintel up above a trilithon upright pair and positioned it firmly on top of them, attaching it by using the same mortise and tenon joinery employed by the builders of Stonehenge. Many mistakes were made along the way, but the participants in this experiment showed that a group of people willing to work hard, a sensible division of labor, and an effective organization of that labor force could produce truly remarkable results in a relatively short period of time.

It could have been no different for the builders of Stonehenge and the hundreds of other stone monuments that can be found across much of Europe (Burl 1995), monuments whose primary features—being built of stone and tending to be massive—provide the name we apply to them: the **megaliths** (Figure 9.6). Consider Carnac, a less-well-known but equally impressive megalithic site located in Britanny, in northwestern France (Figure 9.7). As impressive as Stonehenge is, it consists of a total of a bit more than just 100 upright stones encompassed within a circle whose diameter is about 100 m. More than 5,000 years ago, the builders of Carnac, in contrast, constructed a far more expansive monument, positioning more than 3,000 upright stones in a series of about a dozen parallel rows, whose four primary segments together span a distance of more than 3 km (1.9 mi).

The labor involved in building Carnac is just as impressive as that which was needed in the case of Stonehenge and implies the existence of a social and political structure that could provide the organizational capacity to produce

▲ **Figure 9.6**
Stonehenge may be the best known, but it is only one of literally thousands of megalithic monuments located in western Europe. Two of the better preserved are shown here: Swinside stone circle (top) and the Chun Quoit dolmen (a burial chamber) in the west of England. (K. L. Feder)

monumentally scaled construction projects and, at the same time, demanded that such projects were undertaken.

The study of cattle bones recovered at a site located just 3 kilometers (1.9 miles) from Stonehenge may indicate the geographic extent of the reach of those who organized the labor to build the monument. An analysis of strontium isotopes found in the cows' teeth reveals ratios that are diagnostic of the types of soils in which the grasses consumed by those cows grazed. One of the cows could be traced to Scotland and one to Wales. The four other cows represented by the dental remains could not be traced precisely to a region in England but, at least, it was determined that they had not lived in any area nearby to Stonehenge. It would appear that the builders of Stonehenge came from all over Great Britain, bringing their cattle with them. This implies, as stated by archaeologist Mike Pitts, "an unusually large social and political network" behind the monument's construction (Balter 2008a:1704).

Stonehenge was a place of enormous ritual significance as shown, at least in part, by the number of burials found there, perhaps as many as 240 (Schmid 2008). Some of these burials are filled with elaborate and impressive grave goods. Perhaps most impressive of the graves is that of a man, between the ages of 35 to 45 (as determined by the techniques discussed in Chapter 2). Called the Amesbury Archer because of the presence, along with gold jewelry, copper knives, and flint tools, of polished stone wrist guards used for protecting an archer's wrist from being hurt by the bow string, the Amesbury Archer is significant for reasons beyond the impressive grave goods with which he was buried. Just as we saw for the cows at Stonehenge, an analysis of the strontium isotopes in his teeth shows a ratio completely different from what is present in the surrounding region and what is expected in remains of anyone born near Stonehenge. In fact, the strontium isotope ratio in the Archer's tooth enamel indicates that he was born not in the British Isles at all but in the foothills of the Alps, likely in an area that is today Germany and Switzerland (Alexander 2008:38). The Archer had been badly wounded—one of his legs was badly damaged—and some researchers now suggest that Stonehenge may have been a pilgramage spot where sick and wounded came to be healed (J. Morgan 2008).

Stonehenge was a sacred place and a pilgrimage destination where rituals were carried out and important people were buried. More than 4,000 years ago, people living across much of western Europe knew about Stonehenge. Some traveled there to participate in rituals. Some came, perhaps, to be healed. And a few made their

◀ **Figure 9.7**
The megalithic site of Carnac is located on the southern coast of Brittany, in northwestern France. The site consists of three primary clusters of nearly 3,000 stones, some enormous, set in neatly parallel rows stretching across nearly 3 km (1.9 miles) of the French countryside. Clearly the Carnac alignments required a large, coordinated, and willing labor force far beyond what an individual family could achieve. (K. L. Feder)

final journey there, to be buried in sight of the monument. Stonehenge, however, was not a village where people lived. The spheres of the sacred and the mundane were separated by its builders. About 3 kilometers (2 miles) away from Stonehenge, at a place called Durrington Walls, archaeologists have found dozens of fireplaces; the remains of hundreds, perhaps thousands of animals killed, butchered, and consumed by the inhabitants; and indicators of between 300 and 1,000 residences (Schmid 2008). There is clear evidence of a direct connection between Durrington Walls and the Stonehenge monument: Archaeologists discovered the remnants of a stone-surfaced road leading from the village to the River Avon located nearby. A short distance upstream along the river leads to another ancient stone-surfaced roadway, which, in turn, leads the traveler directly to Stonehenge. Durrington Walls appears to have been the place where, perhaps, Stonehenge's builders lived and where, almost certainly, the monument's ancient visitors feasted (Olding-Smee 2007). Think the Vatican, Mecca, or Jerusalem; Stonehenge appears to have been the equivalent of these sacred locations to the ancient people of Neolithic western Europe.

The builders of Stonehenge, Carnac, and the rest of the megalithic monuments are emblematic of a pattern we see throughout much of the world beginning more than 11,000 years ago. The roots of this new revolution in economic, social, and political complexity, evidenced in the archaeological record as monumental works, are the focus of this chapter.

EARLIER IN THIS BOOK, ARCHAEOLOGY WAS defined as the study of the material remains of human behavior. Most archaeologists focus on the material record—the stuff that people made and used—because these material remains are the only direct evidence we have of how people lived and what they accomplished during their lifetimes in the time before the invention of writing and the keeping of historical records. Ancient monuments such as Stonehenge and Carnac engage the archaeologist, at least in part, in the same way they engage everybody else: Very simply, they are beautiful and fascinating. To be frank, their enormous size and the

CHRONICLE

precision with which they were made are entirely unexpected in monuments so ancient. Beyond this, however, anthropologists are drawn to ancient monuments not just because of their visual magnificence or enchantment but also for what they imply about the abilities of past peoples to conscript and organize the labor necessary to produce them.

Simplicity and Complexity

Most hunting-and-gathering societies organize their social, political, and economic lives at the level of the household or the family. Populations tend to be small and dispersed. Decisions are made; labor is divided, distributed, and organized; and wealth is apportioned on the basis of family relationships.

Many of you probably have been involved in a family or local community project. Perhaps you helped your parents build a storage shed for gardening tools, or maybe it was a deck added on to the back of your house; some of you may have helped set up a community garden in your neighborhood, or you assisted in cleaning up and renovating an abandoned house. The number of people involved in the project likely was small, the number of distinctly different chores or jobs in the overall project relatively few, and the task of coordinating the labor fairly straightforward. After all, organizing a labor party can be pretty simple when all the folks involved in the project are related to one another; it's usually pretty clear who the head or heads of a family are, and the task of organizing and overseeing the project usually falls to these elders.

The project becomes a little more complicated when the labor party consists of a small number of friends, acquaintances, close neighbors, or merely people who happen to live in the same community. Obviously, what's needed is some consensus about who will direct the project and which jobs will be done by whom and when. But consensus can be reached relatively easily when the group is small, the abilities of each individual are readily apparent, and there is a direct, tangible, and obvious benefit for each person involved.

The project becomes far more complicated, however, when the group is large and there is no overall family or accepted community structure on which to base the coordination of a task. Remember the group of 200 volunteers who moved the single Stonehenge trilithon replica and who then raised the one lintel? They were not members of the same family or community. Of necessity, for the short period of time they participated, they had to accept the dictates of the people who organized the project. The project's organizers at least seemed to know what they were doing, and, therefore, their orders were followed. Now imagine the hundreds and even thousands of ancient farmers who built the real Stonehenge, Carnac, and the rest in fits and starts over the course of hundreds of years. In all likelihood, at any one time, many of the builders did not even know one another. There could have been no agreed upon family head to coordinate the project, no clear sense of obligation based on kinship that convinced people to participate or follow the dictates of the family head; and there probably was not even an expectation of reciprocity, no prospect that one would get something tangible in return for participating in the project.

Think about it. If the people in my extended family clear a patch of forest land for agricultural fields, I likely participate because, after all, I am obliged to help my family and, at the same time, it likely is my expectation that a piece of that cleared land will be for my use. But what possible material benefit would accrue to me if I donate my efforts to a vast pool of labor made up by lots of people to whom I am not related and likely don't even know, in the construction of an enormous stone monument?

For the decision to be made to build the monument in the first place and to conscript the labor force, to delegate tasks and coordinate all the many jobs that needed doing, there had to have been someone or, perhaps, a small group in charge. At the same time, there had to have been a social and political structure of command and an attendant process of decision making that transcended the individual household, family, or local community and that applied to the larger social group needed to accomplish the monumental task. Without such a structure, there likely would have been chaos. Chaos is the last thing needed when a large number of people are involved in a difficult and dangerous task requiring a great deal of precision.

The Development of Complexity: Before Agriculture

Scientists love it when new evidence is found that supports a long-cherished perspective about how the universe, the world, or human antiquity can be explained. In truth, I think scientists love it even more when new evidence is found that upends and causes us to totally consider those cherished perspectives. Göbekli Tepe, an archaeological site in Turkey, is exactly that kind of a game changer. In light of the discoveries made there by a team led by archaeologist Klaus Schmidt, we have needed to "rewrite the textbooks" (including this one) and, in essence, reassess our views concerning a crucial aspect of the human past (Curry 2008a, 2008b; Mann 2011).

Archaeologists usually interpret the production of monumental, ritually inspired structures as both reflecting and contingent upon the development of complex, agriculturally based economies. In other words, it has long been assumed that a stable and highly productive agricultural economy (like those discussed in Chapter 8) capable of producing a large food surplus was a prerequisite for the evolution of a multitiered social structure and hierarchical political system. It was further assumed that such social and political complexity—neither of which, it was thought, could develop in a hunting-and-gathering society—was required in order for the few to command the labors of the many. Big, elaborate monuments built by ancient people, in this vision, were the result and the most obvious and visible manifestation of this development. Essentially, as the assumption went, only agriculturalists could create a food surplus big enough to enable large numbers of people to spend their time and energy in nonsubsistence pursuits like building temples and pyramids or making splendid works of art to place in the tombs of great leaders.

It's a great hypothesis, but Göbekli Tepe contradicts it entirely. There's no evidence at all of agriculture or any kind of food production there. Subsistence at Göbekli Tepe clearly was based on hunting wild animals and gathering wild plants. Abundant food remains have been recovered at the site, but it's all been wild game including the bones of gazelle, wild sheep, wild boar, and red deer. Nevertheless, people there produced an incredible site characterized by monumentally scaled carved stones beginning 11,600 years ago (Curry 2008a; Mann 2011).

On the top of a high hill (the "tepe" in Göbekli Tepe), ancient people erected a series of rings of upright, monumentally scaled, precisely carved stones. In a way, it sort of presages the layout of Stonehenge. Twenty such rings have been identified so far, and only about 10% of the site has been excavated. The largest of the rings is about 20 m (65 ft) across. Each ring is demarcated by a number of limestone pillars, each carved into the shape of an upright, giant letter "T." The tallest pillar is nearly 5.5 m (18 ft) tall and weighs more than 14,500 kilograms (16 tons). Each pillar in a ring is a few feet from its adjacent one and a circular stone wall fills the gaps between them (Figure 9.8). One or two concentric rings of additional T-shaped pillars and walls were added over time inside of each initial ring, and at the center are two pillars taller than those demarcating the rings.

Many of the pillars have elaborately carved, fantastic, even phantasmagorical bas-reliefs of animals on their faces—not food animals or creatures we might assume were of economic value but, instead, mostly dangerous creatures like lions or scorpions. There also is a beautifully carved fox and a series of vultures (Figure 9.9).

Göbekli Tepe was purely a ceremonial, ritual site. Nobody lived there. The hill wouldn't have been a particularly good place to settle in any event; there's no water source, no spring or stream nearby. There are no house remains, no cooking hearths, no food storage areas, and no toolmaking loci. The only tools found at the site are those that were used for carving the monumentally scaled monoliths out of the limestone that makes up the hill. The makers of the Göbekli Tepe stone rings may have labored intensively to carve and erect the huge stones, but they didn't have to move them very far, perhaps no more than about 30 m (100 ft). Researchers have even found one limestone pillar still in the ground nearby where it was being extracted.

▶ **Figure 9.8**
One of the 20 well-preserved, excavated rings of monumental, decorated stones at Göbekli Tepe in Turkey. Dating to 11,600 years ago, the site is a clear reflection of complexity as represented in the social and political infrastructure necessary for construction of its monuments, among a people whose subsistence was based on hunting and gathering wild animals and plants. (© Vincent J. Musi/Corbis)

The reason Göbekli Tepe so intrigues and excites archaeologists is that the kind of labor force needed to produce the stone rings, the kind of coordination and cooperation implied by their construction, the ability to conscript and organize that much of a labor force, is unexpected among hunter-gatherers. As noted, it's usually assumed that the need to organize labor for agriculture sets the stage for the use of that social behavior in other, nonsubsistence pursuits. Schmidt (as cited in Mann 2011), however, suggests that the common archaeological construct has it exactly backward. He suggests that the desire, or even the need, to organize and coordinate labor for a nonutilitarian, ritual purpose is at the root of social complexity, and that this sets the stage for food production. In fact, Schmidt points out that by 10,500 years ago, a little more than 1,000 years after the beginning of construction at Göbekli Tepe, at a site just 32 km (20 mi) away, there's evidence of domesticated wheat, and 500 years later, by 10,000 years ago, residents of the region were well on their way to domesticating animals, with direct evidence of the corralling of sheep, cattle, and pigs (Curry 2008a). It's an interesting notion that the development of sociocultural complexity wasn't a result of the food-producing revolution but a product of the development of ritual complexity and the need to produce a food surplus to support large-scale, ritually focused construction. Additional research and the discovery of other places like Göbekli Tepe will enable us to test that hypothesis.

▲ **Figure 9.9**
One of the substantial, upright, T-shaped stones in the Göbekli Tepe stone circles, showing elaborate bas-relief carvings. (© Vincent J. Musi/Corbis)

More than 5,000 years later and a world away, similar evidence of monumental construction is found among a hunting-and-gathering people. In the American Southeast, during the Archaic period (see Chapter 8), we see indisputable evidence of this in the form of large-scale projects of mound building at the Watson Brake site in Louisiana (Russo 1996; J. W. Saunders et al. 1997). Beginning soon after 5,200 years ago, the inhabitants of the site constructed 11 distinct earth mounds and connecting ridges that together form an oval enclosure of mounded soil about 280 m (more than 900 ft) along its long axis (Frink 1997). The tallest of the mounds at Watson Brake is about 7.5 m (25 ft) high. As seen at Göbekli Tepe, hunter-gatherers in Louisiana were able to muster the labor of a large group of people to produce impressive monuments. Agriculture, apparently, was not a prerequisite for the development of the complex organizational skills needed to accomplish this.

The much larger and more impressive mound complex at the Poverty Point site, also in Louisiana, dates to before 3500 B.P. (Gibson 2001). Located adjacent to the Macon Bayou and the broad, rich floodplain of the Mississippi River, the Poverty Point earthworks are truly monumental in scale (Figure 9.10). The site consists of a series of six segmented, concentric earth ridges, enclosing a rough semicircle with a radius of 0.65 km (0.4 mi; the distance from its center to the edge of the outermost ridge). The ridge tops were living surfaces; archaeologists have found evidence of construction along their tops, along with hearths and trash pits. Each of the six segmented ridges is about 24 m (80 ft) wide, 3.5 m (10 ft) tall, and separated from adjacent ridges by about 45 m (150 ft). The outermost ridge is about 2 km (1.25 mi) long; altogether there are 9.7 km (6 mi) of these ridges in the Poverty Point earthwork surrounding a flat central plaza of 37 acres. If the soil to produce Poverty Point had been mounded up in 23-kg (50-lb) basket loads, it would have taken 30 million such loads to complete the monument (Kopper 1986).

Also part of the complex, outside of the ridge enclosure, was another monumental earthwork labeled Mound A, an earth monument about 21 m (about 70 ft) high, built in the shape of what appears to be a bird, covering an area of nearly 13 acres (Figure 9.11). I've climbed to the top of this mound on the modern steps built by the National Park Service; it's huge and its birdlike shape with open wings to both sides of the apex is clear from on top. A recent soil analysis by Tristram Kidder shows Mound A was built in a hurry, in perhaps no more than 90 days, which would suggest an extremely well-organized, substantially sized, not to mention highly motivated workforce (Kidder 2010:43). Detailed analysis of the extensive mound rings at Poverty Point suggests the place also was constructed over a relatively short period of time. Based on experiments in

▶ **Figure 9.10**
Depiction of the massive, partially octagonal earthworks at Poverty Point, Louisiana. An enormous amount of labor, perhaps coordinated by some central authority, was needed for the construction of this earthwork. (© Jon Gibson, State of Louisiana Division of Archaeology)

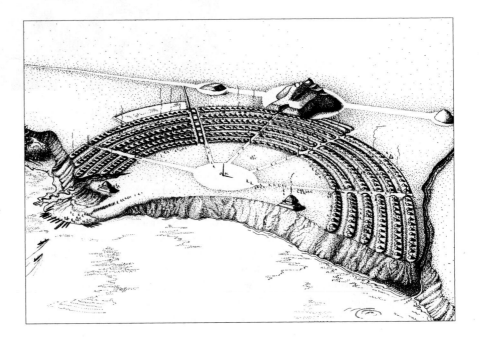

◀ **Figure 9.11**
The tallest mound at Poverty Point, in Louisiana, is about 70 feet high and covers about 13 acres (over 550,000 square feet). From the air, the mound appears to be in the shape of a bird, its wings spread. (K. L. Feder)

mound construction, Jon Gibson (2001) estimated that a thousand laborers could have constructed the Poverty Point earthworks in 2.5 years, if they worked every day during that period (no time off for holidays, I am afraid). The influence of Poverty Point was so geographically widespread, from the Gulf of Mexico to as far north as the Great Lakes, archaeologists refer to the Poverty Point interaction sphere or the Poverty Point culture to label the region and societies affected by it.

Just as at Göbekli Tepe and Watson Brake, the construction of the Poverty Point earthworks implies the existence of a large labor force coordinated through a complex social and political structure. The inhabitants of Poverty Point also were engaged in a broad trading network that enabled them to obtain raw materials, including hematite, slate, and lead ore, as well as good stone for making sharp-edged tools. The presence of these materials also implies that some people were freed from subsistence pursuits to obtain these precious resources not available in their local territory. All this should be understood within the context of the subsistence system of the builders of Poverty Point. They were hunter-gatherers living in an environment in which wild foods were abundant enough to allow for people to spend large quantities of their time in activities other than food gathering. Wild foods, especially fish and other aquatic resources, again seem to have been the mainstays of the Poverty Point diet. As archaeologist Jon Gibson (2001) maintains, these were people with a strong attachment to place, an ability to marshal the labors of a large group of people, and an ability to work communally for long stretches of time.

What we see in the case of Göbekli Tepe, Watson Brake, and Poverty Point were habitats so rich in resources that a surplus could be produced sufficient to feed a large force of workers while those workers were building monumental structures of stone or earth. The ancient people responsible for these sites weren't agricultural but can be called, instead, **affluent foragers**. Most of the civilizations we will discuss in Chapters 10 to 13—societies you've likely all heard about and that generate lots of documentaries on cable—relied on the enormous productivity of agriculturally based subsistence systems to render complexity possible, leading to the creation of an economic surplus and its concentration in an elite class. The social and political prerequisites for the production of large-scale communal works, however, can also arise among affluent foragers, and this may represent a parallel track toward the development of social and political complexity.

A Revolution in Subsistence, a Revolution in Society

In some post-Pleistocene settings, the extra work involved in applying new, more intensive subsistence strategies, as organized by these newly developed leaders, substantially increased the food base. The additional labor invested in planting seedbeds, tending wild plants, or corralling wild animals created a new cultural environment in which natural selection was supplanted by artificial selection. The result was domesticated plants and animals that eventually produced far more food than was actually needed to feed even the growing Holocene human population in some areas.

Those who could control this new food surplus—redistribute it, save it for times of need, or even own it—possessed, for perhaps the first time in human history, wealth and power. To be able to redistribute excess food, reward some people and punish others, accumulate precious materials in trade, and distribute other resources—or withhold them—during lean times is to have power.

A food surplus poses the challenge of what to do with it until it's used. To begin with, it needs to be stored. Village granaries are one solution, and their construction requires more communal labor. Once granaries are built and the grain is stored, the surplus must be protected from hungry animals, insects, and rot—not to mention greedy humans. So more communal projects are needed, more jobs are created for leaders to oversee, and there is more reinforcement for their position as leaders, as long as they are successful. Initially temporary, intended to last only until the task they were overseeing was complete, in some cases their leadership positions became permanent and even magnified. It is expensive to build storage facilities and to protect the food. So why bother? The most obvious reason is that a surplus can help tide people over during lean times—during non-growing seasons or during slim harvests. Plus, a food surplus can be distributed to individuals or families who have contributed significantly to the group, as a reward for hard work. Also, a food surplus can be used as wealth to obtain other valuable goods—or traded with the inhabitants of other regions for stone, metal, or other resources not locally available or accessible.

From Rank Societies to Chiefdoms

As long as such societies remain small, with leaders managing only individual villages, the potential for complexity ordinarily is limited. As population grows, however, and as more importance is vested in the leaders, that role may change. Anthropologist Elman Service (1975:71) refers to this as "the institutionalization of power": As the system expands geographically, group labor projects and the broader redistribution of food and other goods have a "politically integrative effect" (Service 1975:94). Social strata may develop, with the leader, or chief, and the chief's family at the top of the social pyramid. Chieftainship may be handed down from parent to child, further solidifying the position of the chief's family in the upper echelon of a stratified social system. A cadre of subordinate regional chiefs may also develop, each responsible for a local area and all reporting to the head chief. Most everyone else makes up the broad base of the social pyramid of these **chiefdoms**, giving at least some of the surplus they produce to the chiefs.

Complexity's Traces in the Old World

Jericho

After Göbekli Tepe, additional evidence of early large-scale communal construction can be seen deep in the sequence at a few sites in western Asia (Figure 9.12). For example, the archaeological site of Jericho, in Israel, was a village with a number of distinct features that at more than 9,000 years ago imply a movement away from the egalitarian pattern seen at other Neolithic sites (see Chapter 8). At about this time, the inhabitants of Jericho—later memorialized in the Old Testament of the Bible—built a massive stone wall around their community (Kenyon 1954). Made of drylaid stone, the wall was 2 m (6½ ft) thick at the base and nearly 7 m (23 ft) high in places, with ramparts up to 9 m (nearly 30 ft) high (Figure 9.13). The construction of this wall required a level of coordination of labor not previously seen in the world. Trade was an important element in the economy of early Jericho. Exotic raw materials, including Turkish obsidian, turquoise from the Sinai Peninsula, and cowrie shells from the Red Sea, are found at early levels of the site. The distribution of some of these exotic materials in human interments indicates a certain degree of social differentiation at Jericho: Whereas most burials were rather plain and undistinguished, one group of interments was set apart— the skulls were coated with a mask of clay, and the exotic cowrie shells were set into the eye sockets.

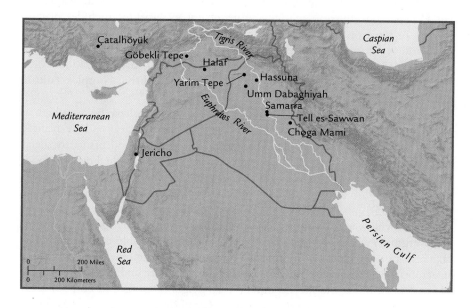

◀ **Figure 9.12**
Archaeological sites in western Asia where evidence of the evolution of chiefdom and early state-level societies has been found.

▲ Figure 9.13
The wall at Jericho is
among the earliest
archaeological
evidence in the world
for construction on a
monumental scale. The
builders of the wall likely
were members of an
ancient chiefdom society
beginning some 9,000
years ago. (© Bettmann/
Corbis)

Çatalhöyük

Located in central Turkey, near the town of Çumra, the site of Çatalhöyük presents a fascinating enigma to archaeologists (Balter 1998; Hodder 2005; Mellaart 1965). The oldest of the 18 occupation levels at the site dates to about 9,000 years ago, and the settlement persisted for 1,200 years. The site itself is about three times the size of Jericho, covering approximately 26 acres, and consists of what researchers have estimated to be about 2,000 densely compacted, interconnected homes within a huge, continuous structure (Figure 9.14). As Ian Hodder (2005), the director of archaeological research at the site, points out, there were no streets or avenues at Çatalhöyük, and most of the houses had no ground-level entrances. Çatalhöyük's residents moved around in their community across the rooftops, and it was through openings in the roof that individuals gained entrance into their own and their neighbors' dwellings. First excavated between 1961 and 1965 by archaeologist James Mellaart, the site immediately drew worldwide attention, in part because of its scale and in part because of the fantastic works of art in the form of painted murals found on the walls of some of the excavated rooms.

Archaeology at the site recommenced in 1993, led by British archaeologist Ian Hodder. The mission of these more recent excavations includes placing the site in a regional context, examining the changes in the natural environment and the domestication of plants and animals during the period between 13,000 and 7,000 years ago, investigating the ceremonial nature of the so-called shrines, and explaining the reasons why an early Neolithic complex culture developed here in the shadow of the Konya Mountains.

The site itself is substantial; population is estimated to have been as high as 8,000 at its peak of occupation. Though the inhabitants appear to have planted domesticated varieties of wheat and barley, and while they raised, primarily, sheep, goats, and to a lesser extent cattle, much of their food was supplied by wild foods including assorted wild grasses and tubers, lentils, hackberries, acorns, and pistachios (Balter 1998) as well as wild animals including wild cattle, pigs, and horses (Hodder, 2005).

Çatalhöyük was not a city but, as archaeologist Guillermo Algaze describes it, an "overgrown village" (as quoted in Balter 1998). For example, there is no public architecture, no evidence of municipal buildings, palaces, temples, or government structures. The community was, effectively, architecturally undifferentiated. There were no mansions at the site, no middle-class neighborhoods, and no poor areas. In fact, all of the houses excavated to date at Çatalhöyük show very similar living

◀ **Figure 9.14**
Çatalhöyük was a large, complex settlement of more than 5,000 people by about 8,000 years ago. Its location near an important obsidian source may explain the size and complexity of the community at this early date. (Times Books, 1988, reproduced with permission)

quarters. Most of the rooms at the site are of a standard size: about 25 m² (269 ft²). Ian Hodder suggests that the social unit at Çatalhöyük was the extended family living in four or five clusters of these rooms (Balter 1998:1443).

One of the most interesting elements at Çatalhöyük are rooms that were within family residences and in which ordinary activities like stone and bone toolmaking, food preparation and consumption, and also rituals were carried out (Hodder and Cessford 2004). These rooms were decorated to varying degrees with paintings, often of men in leopard-skin pelts hunting animals, usually wild bulls and stags, as well as with images of leopards and vultures. Along with two-dimensional works of art, these ritual rooms were also decorated with three-dimensional sculptures affixed to the walls. These sculptures also depicted animals, most often rams and bulls. The fixation on images of wild bulls is so apparent, archaeologist Ian Hodder (2005:40) jokingly states that "in many dwellings one seems hardly able to move without facing a bull's head or painting." The bones of animals, again, especially wild bulls, are found in concentrations at Çatalhöyük, out of proportion to their likely overall contribution to the diet. These concentrations may be the remains of special, ritual feasts (Hodder 2005:40).

There is little evidence of labor specialization at the site. For example, though many of the obsidian artifacts excavated at Çatalhöyük were very skillfully made, these seem to have been the widespread work of families and not the products of specialist craftspeople. Hodder and his crew have found waste flakes that result from the manufacture of obsidian tools fairly evenly spread throughout the site in what they are interpreting as the family compounds represented by the clusters they have excavated (Balter 1998). This is likely an indication that lots of people, not just a handful of specialists, were making tools from the volcanic glass available locally in the Konya Mountains.

There is no separate burial ground at the site. Instead, men and women, boys and girls, were all buried beneath the floors of rooms in the village. In an extreme case, under the floor of one room located in Building 1, excavators uncovered the remains of more than 60 people. It seems likely that the inclusive demographic structure of those buried under the houses reflects a profile similar to that of those living in the houses. In other words, it seems likely that the burials were the equivalent of family plots where people related to the family who lived in the home were buried (Hodder and Cessford 2004).

Though no evidence of economic or social inequality is reflected in the burials—no large tombs or rich arrays of grave goods—one class of people was adorned to a slightly greater degree with jewelry in the form of bracelets, anklets, and necklaces of stone and bone beads. This "privileged class" was not a wealthy elite but rather babies and infants. Room burials tended to be spatially concentrated, and the wall nearest the burials was often decorated with a mural. These murals depicted various scenes: an erupting volcano, people hunting deer, headless men, leopards with women riding on their backs.

▼ **Figure 9.15**
Called a mother goddess by some, the actual meaning of this sculpture of an obese, probably pregnant woman to the people of Çatalhöyük is unknown. (© Vincent J. Musi/ National Geographic Society/Corbis)

A few small sculptures have been found at Çatalhöyük. Probably the ones that have generated the most popular interest are those of what appear to be obese women, some apparently greatly pregnant and even in the process of childbirth (Figure 9.15). The original excavator, James Mellaart, labeled these fertility or mother goddesses, and though more recent analysts question this interpretation, the site has been embraced by some who believe that much of humanity went through a period in which people worshipped this goddess.

Çatalhöyük was, by all measures, a very successful village. It was home to thousands of people and endured for more than a millennium. It has long been thought that a large, dense, and long-lived community can survive only under a regime of social complexity, where there are people with the prestige, power, and position to regulate, rule, and control. But there is no archaeological evidence at Çatalhöyük for this kind of social, political, or economic differentiation: no wealthy people, no powerful individuals, no controlling group of folks who have bigger homes, who own better stuff, or who are treated differently in death. How does a very densely packed population of up to 8,000 people organize, coordinate, and regulate their activities; how does it deal with crowding, sanitation, economic necessities, and social realities without, apparently, any centralized authority, without a stratified social system with power invested in the few to maintain the orderly workings of the many? Ian Hodder and Craig Cessford (2004) recognize that this is one of the key issues that needs to be addressed at Çatalhöyük.

Mesopotamia: Land Between the Rivers

The waters of the Tigris and Euphrates Rivers begin their journey to the Persian Gulf as a series of small streams in the modern nations of Turkey, Syria, Iraq, and Iran. Flowing southeast, the twin rivers are separated across their lengths by no more than about 200 km (125 mi) and commonly by less than 100 km (62 mi) until they meet and jointly flow into the Persian Gulf. Together their valleys demarcate the boundaries of the region called **Mesopotamia**—Greek for "the land between the rivers" (see Figure 9.12). These rivers played a fundamental role in producing the flat expanse of fertile soil in which the seeds of the world's first civilization were planted (see Chapter 10).

The Roots of Complexity in Southwest Asia

Beginning from this simple Neolithic base, by about 8,000 years ago, a subtle transformation toward social, political, and economic complexity is evident in the archaeological record of northern Mesopotamia. The sites of Hassuna, Samarra, and Halaf, each exhibiting distinctive pottery and architecture, lend their names to a chronological succession of three distinctive farming cultures (with substantial temporal overlap): **Hassunan, Samarran**, and **Halafian.**

Dating from 8000 to 7200 B.P., Hassunan sites are small, typically about 100 m (328 ft) in diameter, with populations estimated at a few hundred (Lamberg-Karlovsky and Sabloff 1995:96). These sites show clear evidence of the primacy of agriculture in the subsistence base. At the Hassunan site of Yarim Tepe, for example, there is evidence of the planting of einkorn, emmer, bread, and club wheat as well as barley, peas, and lentils (Merpert and Munchaev 1987). Although the hunting of wild animals persisted at Yarim Tepe, as evidenced by the appearance of the remains of fallow deer, gazelle, and onager, some 82% of the bones recovered archaeologically were from domesticated animals, including sheep, goat, pig, and especially cattle (Maisels 1990:112).

Though in most ways unremarkable Neolithic villages, Hassunan sites do exhibit just a few hints of what was to come in Mesopotamia in the form of architectural sophistication. There are multiroomed houses with courtyards, for example, at Yarim Tepe. But as archaeologists C. C. Lamberg-Karlovsky and Jeremy Sabloff (1995:97–98) point out, overall, Hassunan sites reflect a pattern of "rustic simplicity"; architecture was simple and homogeneous, there is no evidence of temples or palaces, few precious or luxurious items have been found, and there is no evidence of high-status burials reflective of status differentiation.

The site of Samarra and others included in the Samarran culture are located farther south, deep into the floodplain of the Tigris. These sites date to after 7500 B.P. The diets of the inhabitants of Samarran sites included the resources offered by the river, with archaeological evidence for the heavy use of fish and mussels.

The inhabitants of the Samarran site of Tell es-Sawwan supplemented their diets by hunting gazelle and fallow deer, while they planted emmer and bread wheat, barley, and caper (a fruit-producing shrub; Helbaek 1965).

The fact that agriculture was a significant part of the subsistence system at Samarra and related sites is itself informative. As pointed out by archaeologist Joan Oates (1973), here, in the central section of Mesopotamia, rainfall is meager, and an agricultural way of life would have been generally difficult and in some places impossible without the construction of irrigation canals. Direct evidence of this canal building has been found at the Samarran site of Choga Mami. Remember earlier in this chapter, when we discussed the reasons for the evolution of social, political, and economic complexity, one factor cited was the need, under certain conditions, to develop an organizational structure to conscript and coordinate labor at a level above the household, family, or local community. Control of water resources needed to expand agricultural production can be a powerful incentive for such an organizational structure to develop and an important factor in its perpetuation. There is evidence for developing complexity in Samarran sites, including non-subsistence-related large-scale works that would have required a level of cooperation and coordination of labor not previously seen. Tell es-Sawwan, for example, was surrounded by an enormous wall and a ditch that would have required the pooled labor of a large number of workers. Samarra has a large, buttressed fortification wall that similarly would have required a large regulated workforce.

At the same time, there is telling archaeological evidence at Samarran sites that differences in status between leaders and followers, between those giving the orders in large-scale construction projects and those following the orders, were being ritually legitimized. Some of the graves at Tell es-Sawwan are far more elaborate than those at Hassunan sites, and the differences among the burials are much greater. Although most Samarran burials are rather plain, some are filled with luxurious goods made of alabaster, turquoise, copper, greenstone, obsidian, carnelian (a lustrous, reddish-brown stone), and shell-bead necklaces and bracelets. Differences in grave wealth imply an increasing economic and social gulf among members of the society (Lamberg-Karlovsky and Sabloff 1995). Some of these raw materials must have been valuable because they were rare; required a great amount of work to locate, quarry, or work; or were available only at a great distance. Turquoise, carnelian, and obsidian, for example, are not locally available in the Samarran territory and must have been traded for by the inhabitants of Tell es-Sawwan.

Perhaps these more elaborate burials are the graves of a developing elite or upper class whose special treatment in death was made possible—or, perhaps, necessary—by their differentiation in life. These individuals may have been singled out to organize, coordinate, and lead large-scale construction projects such as the canals at Choga Mami or the walls at Samarra and Tell es-Sawwan. Socially, politically, and, perhaps, economically elevated in life because of the special and powerful role they played in the society, these people seem to have then been exalted in death as well through the elaboration of their graves.

A new architectural feature is also seen at Samarran sites. After about 7400 B.P., the inhabitants constructed T-shaped buildings that were used to house the community's grain. As Lamberg-Karlovsky and Sabloff (1995:100–101) point out, the communal storage of grain suggests a pooling of labor in both farming and the construction of the building where the grain was stored. Again, to accomplish the construction of communal granaries and to ensure the maintenance of the stored grain at the scale suggested by the archaeological data for Samarran sites, people needed to be organized beyond the level of the household or family, and a more complex social and political structure evolved to accomplish these tasks. This process portends what will happen a few centuries later, farther south into Mesopotamia.

Halafian sites, dating from 7500 to 6700 B.P., are not as well known as those of Hassuna or Samarra. Almost certainly the inhabitants were farmers. The residential architecture was simple, but in Halafian villages, a new architectural form is seen in nonresidential, round buildings (sometimes called **tholoi**). They seem initially to have served as communal storage buildings, like the T-shaped buildings of the Samarran culture. The round buildings at some sites contained human burials along with ceremonial objects, leading some researchers to suggest that these structures also served as burial places for important people.

These archaeological discoveries dated to the Mesopotamian Neolithic show a clearly evolutionary pattern of increasing sophistication and complexity in architecture and material culture. Communal projects and high-status burials imply the existence of chiefdoms at this point in the development of these societies. The existence of communal storage/ceremonial structures by the middle of the eighth millennium B.P. is intriguing, perhaps foreshadowing the key role of the temple in the first true civilization, the Sumerian city-states (see Chapter 10).

Complexity's Traces in the New World

We have seen in this chapter how archaeological evidence shows that social and political complexity preceded the development of an agricultural subsistence base in both the Old (Göbekli Tepe) and New Worlds (Watson Brake and Poverty Point). Clearly, the affluent foragers at those sites were capable of conscripting and organizing substantial labor forces for the construction of elaborate monuments. It must be recognized that, however impressive their achievements were, when a stable and highly productive agricultural economy is added to the equation, there is a quantum leap in the monumentality and technological elaboration produced by some ancient societies. This can clearly be seen in both Mesoamerica (Figure 9.16) and South America (see Figure 9.21).

The Olmec

Small agricultural communities had been developing in Mesoamerica since about 5,000 years ago (see Chapter 8). It seems as though a geographically expansive pattern of small, egalitarian, and independent farming villages located along the Gulf Coast tropical lowlands, particularly in the Mexican states of Tabasco and Veracruz, evolved into a pattern of more closely interconnected and complexly structured communities sometime after 3,400 years ago (Diehl 1989, 2004; Pool 2007).

The complexity of the social, political, and economic order, as well as a pattern of a shared religious expression seen across a fairly broad geographic expanse, is reflected in the archaeological record by a constellation of common art motifs and monumental architectural patterns not previously seen in the New World.

► **Figure 9.16**
Archaeological sites
in Mesoamerica
where evidence of the
development of cultural
complexity has been
found.

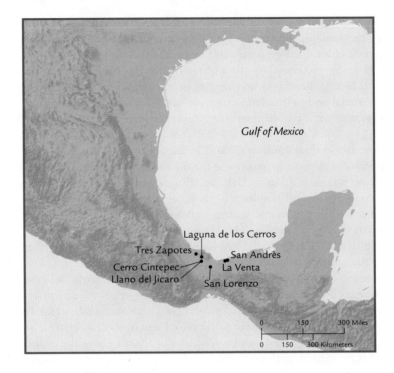

Gulf of Mexico

Laguna de los Cerros
Tres Zapotes
Cerro Cintepec
Llano del Jicaro
San Andrès
La Venta
San Lorenzo

0   150   300 Miles

0   150   300 Kilometers

The motifs and patterns constitute what archaeologists label **Olmec** (Pool 2007). The Olmec pattern includes several elements: depictions of a half-human, half-jaguar god; the production of jade sculptures; iron-ore mirrors; the construction of expansive platforms of earth; the construction of earthen pyramids; and the carving of huge basalt boulders into the form of human heads—perhaps actual depictions of some of the regional chiefs.

The Evolution of Complexity

The Olmec heartland, located between the Tuxtla Mountains to the west and the tropical lowlands of the Chontalpa to the east, is a vast and richly varied region of uplands, estuaries, and floodplains. Population growth facilitated by the abundant and diverse habitats of the Olmec region may be part of the explanation for how and why complex societies developed here. Some places in the lowlands offered particularly rich farmland. In the tropical lowlands of the Mexican Gulf Coast, the richest agricultural lands can be found along the natural levees produced by rivers that flow through it. Archaeologist Richard Diehl (2004:29) characterizes the location of San Lorenzo, the earliest Olmec city, as "one of the best pieces of real estate in the Olmec world." As he points out, the main portion of the settlement is located on a high, dry terrace that would have remained so even during times of severe flooding in its flood-prone, tropical rainforest habitat. While protected from the ravages of flooding, the presence of freshwater springs high up on the terrace meant the residents would never be lacking for drinking water. At the same time, San Lorenzo is positioned close to extremely fertile, agriculturally productive river levee soils and a host of important resources including sandstone and limestone for construction. Furthermore, the location of the community in close proximity to the confluences of a number of watercourses would have allowed its residents to monitor and, perhaps, control the flow of traffic and attendant commerce throughout the central area of the Olmec heartland.

The richness of the farmland and the wealth of food sources available to the Olmec within their home territory is made clear in the archaeological record of the San Andrés site in the eastern portion of the Olmec realm. There, remains of agricultural produce, including maize, manioc, beans, sunflower, corozo palm nuts, and cacao, have been found (Diehl 2004:85). The diet of the inhabitants at San Andrés was further supplemented with wild foods, including clam, turtle, catfish, gar, snapper, crocodile, and deer.

Perhaps, as archaeologist Richard Diehl (1989) suggests, population grew in particularly rich areas like San Lorenzo and San Andrés, and an increasingly complex pattern of social organization and political control, of necessity, evolved to maintain order. An elite class that could control people, organize their labor, and dominate trade was the result. These developing elites—perhaps initially Big Men and then chiefs—could mobilize the large regional populations to produce monumental works that might further legitimize their elevated social and economic status (Lowe 1989).

At the same time, the patchiness of resource distribution rendered other areas of the Olmec heartland uniquely attractive and valuable as well (Pool 2007). The estuarine region provided rich coastal resources, while the mountains provided a valuable source of volcanic rock for toolmaking and monument construction (D. Grove 1996). Natural asphalt, also used for making ceremonial items, was available only in a number of discrete locations (Pool 2007). Archaeologist Christopher Pool (2007:288) enumerates the valuable raw materials with uneven distribution throughout Olmec territory: basalt, red ochre, kaolin pottery clay, bitumen, cacao, marine shell, and salt. In Pool's view, the fact that these resources were available only in certain parts of the Olmec realm "encouraged the development of social networks by aspiring leaders to acquire locally unavailable prestige goods as well as critical materials for utilitarian artifacts" (2007:288).

Olmec Regal-Ritual Cities

Those initially small farming villages that were located on the best farmlands or in those areas most accessible to valuable resources became regionally significant as the residences of a developing elite class of people. Two such communities, La Venta in Tabasco and San Lorenzo in Veracruz, were settled initially nearly 3,650 years ago. A third, Laguna de los Cerros, also in Veracruz, was settled soon thereafter. These three villages became more than just farming settlements. Beginning first at San Lorenzo at about 3,400 years ago, by 2800 B.P. at La Venta, and then at Laguna de los Cerros and Tres Zapotes, they became political, economic, social, and religious focal points and, in turn, the most powerful settlements in the realm of the Olmec. San Lorenzo and La Venta have been characterized as **Regal–Ritual Centers** (Diehl 2004). At its peak, the center of San Lorenzo covered an area of about 7 km² (2.7 mi²); La Venta was less than 30% the size of San Lorenzo, covering about 2 km² (a little more than 0.75 mi²). Though often called "cities," the large Olmec population centers differed from our modern concept of an urban center primarily because they appear to have been only modestly populated. It is very difficult to suggest an actual size, but, in all likelihood, the populations of most Olmec centers did not exceed a thousand, including the ruler and his family, an elite class likely related to the ruler, artisans who served the elite, and a cohort of farmers. San Lorenzo, the largest Regal-Ritual Center, may have had a population of a few thousand. Most of what transpired in these Regal-Ritual Centers concerned the religious and political functions of the local polity.

The ability of the Olmec rulers to conscript and control the labor of a large population is evident in the archaeological record. For example, the Olmec moved enormous amounts of earth to construct platforms and pyramids and even to modify the landscape of their settlements. San Lorenzo is situated on a natural topographic eminence that had been added to and flattened by the inhabitants. It is estimated that the top 9 m (30 ft) of the plateau on which the community is located is artificial (Figure 9.17).

Perhaps the most striking of the Olmec sculpted works are the colossal boulders of basalt they carved into the representations of the heads of their rulers (Figure 9.18). Altogether, 17 of these enormous basalt sculptures have been found throughout the Olmec heartland. Ten of the heads were found at San Lorenzo and four at La Venta. Additionally, two were located at Tres Zapotes and one, the largest yet found, was found at La Cobata. They range in height from a little less than 1.47 m (4.8 ft) to more than 3.4 m (11.15 ft); they range in weight from 5,440 kg (6 tons) to a truly massive 45,000 kg (50 tons; Pool 2007:106). As David Grove indicates, these individualized depictions "glorified the rulers while they were alive, and commemorated them as revered ancestors after their death" (1996).

Monumental undertakings reflect the Olmec's growing ability to command and organize the labor of a large number of people, a characteristic typical of chiefdom societies. The artificial platform constructed at La Venta, for example, contained more than 2 million m³ (70 million ft³) of earth and is more than 32 m (105 ft) high. Many tons of basalt slabs were used to construct an elaborate water-supply system, now shown by excavations at San Lorenzo to have served as part of an aqueduct, providing drinking water to residents (D. Grove 1996). As indicated, the volcanic rock used to build the aqueduct as well as the raw material for the carved heads was obtained from the Tuxtla Mountains. A large quarry found at Llano del Jicaro, only about 7 km (4 mi) from Laguna de los Cerros, almost certainly was controlled by the elite at this Olmec center. This quarry is more than 80 km (50 mi) from San Lorenzo, yet large amounts of basalt were transported there, much of it by river. The movement of large quantities of this stone—and

▼ **Figure 9.17**
Layout of the Olmec capital of San Lorenzo with its major earthen mound and associated earthworks.

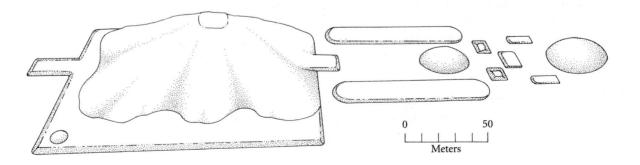

0   50
Meters

◄ Figure 9.18
This enormous basalt sculpture presents a portrait of an individual presumed to have been a ruler of the Olmec Regal-Ritual Center of La Venta. One of the larger of the 17 such sculptures found within the Olmec homeland, this example is a little less than 2 m (about 6 ft) tall, and about 1.5 m (5 ft) across. The source for the basalt from which this sculpture was produced is located more than 80 km (50 mi) from La Venta. (Danny Lehman/Corbis)

the enormous size of the boulders intended for the stone head sculptures—over such a great distance is another indicator of the ability of the Olmec chiefs to mobilize and manage the labor of a great mass of people.

Pool (2007:282) estimates that the mean size of the territories controlled by these four large Olmec centers was probably in the neighborhood of 2,000 km² (about 750 mi²; an area roughly half the size of Rhode Island, the smallest of the states). The people living in those territories likely provided labor (for building pyramids, moving the enormous basalt blocks, etc.) and at least a part of their food surplus, and, essentially, owed their allegience to the center. They received, in return, protection, order, ritual sanctification, access to exotic raw materials, and the promise of a pipeline to the gods.

Archaeologists attempt to reveal the interconnectedness of communities in a region by tracing common artifact styles, shared ways of making things, raw materials, and collective patterns of behavior that translate into the material, archaeological record. The widespread appearance of ceramic types that originated at San Lorenzo suggests that it was the dominant player in an extensive network of dozens of communities within an area of more than 600 km² (more than 230 mi²; Figure 9.19). San Lorenzo was surrounded by and closely related to what appears to have been four smaller, secondary centers, each of which also contained ritual objects similar to, though not nearly as many nor as impressive as, those found at San Lorenzo. Within the aforementioned 600-km² area were an additional 50 farming villages of various sizes, all of which appear to have been tied to San Lorenzo by a common pottery style and thus were also likely in the San Lorenzo orbit. Finally, in this same area, about 150 smaller-still agricultural hamlets and isolated farming homesteads have been located. The large, dispersed population in the villages and hamlets must have supplied most of the food for the political and religious elites living at San Lorenzo. This same population provided the labor necessary to construct the pyramids and platforms that mark the site, as well as

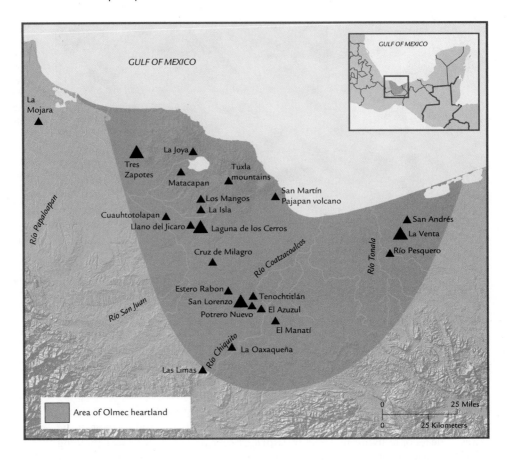

▲ **Figure 9.19**
Locations of major
Olmec sites, including
the four recognized
Regal-Ritual Centers:
La Venta, Tres Zapotes,
San Lorenzo, and
Laguna de los Cerros.
Sixteen of the 17 known
large basalt head ruler
portraits (see Figure
9.18) were found in these
Regal-Ritual Centers.

the strong backs to transport the heavy building and sculptural raw material that
so characterize San Lorenzo.

San Lorenzo is characterized by a large number of deeply impressive works
of art on a monumental as well as a smaller scale. Archaeologists have recovered
124 massive stone sculptures at the site, ranging in mass from a few hundred to a
stupendous 25,000 kg (about 28 tons).

Ninety smaller stone sculptures of various semiprecious stones have been
found at La Venta. Each one is, by itself, a splendid work of art but, even more
impressively, they were commonly found in clusters, ritual offerings depicting
scenes of Olmec life. In one of the most famous such caches, the jade and serpentine sculptures of 16 men were found standing in a vaguely circular configuration, all facing toward a center point with six additional polished upright
stones in a semicircle around them (Figure 9.20). The San Lorenzo and La Venta
sculptures of whatever scale were certainly the works of true artists, specialists
who produced them at the behest of the religious and ruling elite. As seen with
the evolution of complex societies in Mesopotamia, the growing authority of
leaders in Olmec society is reflected in the archaeological record of their burials. At La Venta, for example, one ruler or chief was buried in a sandstone sarcophagus carved into an elaborate depiction of a caiman (a Central and South
American crocodile).

◄ **Figure 9.20**
These splendid Olmec figurines at La Venta were made of jade and serpentine. They were discovered just as displayed here, with a central figure carved in stone encircled by the other individuals. The figurines are between 15 cm and 25 cm (6 in and 10 in) in height.
(© Boltin Picture Library/ Bridgeman Art Library)

What Was Olmec?

Olmec can be interpreted as a common religious iconography—a standardized set of visual images—that provided ideological and symbolic support for the sociopolitical system. The shared elements of Olmec religious iconography may have served to unify the large populations living around each of the ceremonial centers into politically unified chiefdoms. This commonality of religious expression and artistic depiction integrating large populations into individual Olmec chiefdoms, however, apparently did not lead to the geographically broader political integration among the various Olmec centers (Diehl 1989). There is no evidence for a single, overarching Olmec "nation" or political unit. It appears, instead, that each of the largest and most elaborate Olmec sites, especially San Lorenzo and La Venta, represents the center of a separate chiefdom, politically autonomous but linked by a common iconography.

The spread of Olmec iconography across a wide swath of Mesoamerica can be seen between 3,000 and 2,800 years ago. At this time, Olmec-like imagery appeared in El Salvador, Honduras, Costa Rica, and Guatemala, as well as the highlands of Mexico (the Valley of Mexico and Oaxaca).

What does this spread imply about the impact of Olmec on the development of civilization in Mesoamerica as a whole? Michael Coe (1968) has referred to Olmec as the "mother culture" of Mesoamerica, and in his synthesis of the Olmec Diehl (2004) largely agrees. Analysis of the primacy and subsequent spread of Olmec-style artifacts lends support to this notion. For example, San Lorenzo ceramics have been traced far beyond the confines of its local, 600-km² sphere of influence. Neutron activation analysis, a technique discussed in Chapter 2 that is useful in identifying the sources of raw materials from which artifacts were made, was applied to 725 Mesoamerican archaeological ceramics samples (Blomster, Neff, and Glascock 2005). The researchers collected more than 600 raw clay samples from San Lorenzo, Oaxaca, and the Basin of Mexico and compared their elemental composition to the archaeological ceramics. The results were absolute and definitive; pottery bearing typical San Lorenzo Olmec motifs and made from clay traceable to San Lorenzo has been found throughout Mesoamerica, including ancient sites in the Basin of Mexico, Guerrero, the Valley of Oaxaca, and Chiapas, as well as the Pacific coast. None of the ceramics from San Lorenzo were made from the clays found outside of its local area. The movement of clay and ideas about ceramic design all seem to have moved out from San Lorenzo. This lends strong support for Coe's and Diehl's view of Olmec as the original source of Mesoamerican civilization, to be discussed in more detail in Chapter 12.

South America

Until recently, the Norte Chico region of coastal Peru was not thought to have been a terribly fruitful place to investigate the origins of complexity in the New World (Mann 2005). After all, the oldest cities and first evidence of what is commonly called "civilization" in the Old World (Chapters 10 and 11) have been found in association with the extraordinarily productive habitats provided by major river valleys —the Nile, the Tigris and Euphrates, the Indus, and the Yangtse. Norte Chico is marked by only a handful of relatively small rivers—Rio Fortaleza, Rio Pativilca, Rio Huaura, and Rio Supe—and, furthermore, is one of the driest places on earth, with a mean annual rainfall of no more than about 5 cm (2 in). Agriculture is exceptionally difficult under these conditions, and Old World evidence—as well as evidence from elsewhere in the New World—has long supported the idea that complexity develops where the environment allows for a rich agricultural subsistence base capable of producing an enormous food surplus. Nevertheless, a series of archaeological surveys have shown that Norte Chico river valleys produced what some are calling the oldest evidence of the development of complexity in the New World (Haas, Creamer, and Ruiz 2004; Mann 2005). Located along the Rio Supe, Caral is an example of the early development of complex societies in Norte Chico (see Figure 9.21 for a map of the location of the South American sites discussed in this chapter).

Caral

Seen from the air, Caral appears ancient and alien, a forbidden, almost extraterrestrial landscape of weathered pyramidal mounds, decayed house remains, and sunken circular plazas (Figure 9.22). Yet here, archaeologists have found the earliest material remnants in South America, and, in fact, in the New World, of cultural complexity—a complexity characterized by social stratification, economic inequality, and a level of monumental architecture possible only by the organization and coordination of a substantial labor force (Solis, Haas, and Creamer 2001).

Located in the Supe River Valley, about 23 km (14 mi) from the Pacific coast and 200 km (about 124 mi) north of Lima, the modern capital of Peru, Caral was the capital of a complex society that developed in western South America more than 4,500 years ago. The site covers more than 160 acres and includes an enormous earth and stone "truncated," or flat-topped, pyramid— the Pirámide Mayor—which stands more than 18 m (60 ft) tall, covers an area of about 24,000 m^2 (6 acres), and contains 200,000 m^3 (7 million ft^3) of river cobbles and cut stone fill, all moved and mounded up by human effort,

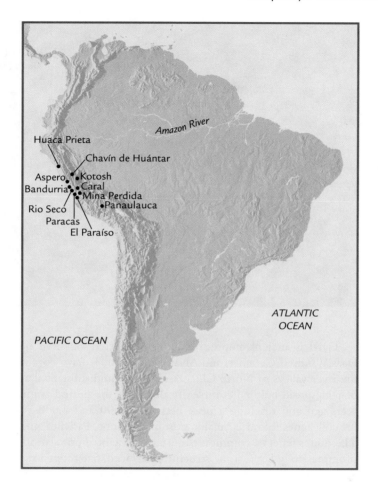

one basket load at a time (Solis et al. 2001:723). Imagine a structure 265 feet long, 265 feet wide, and nearly 100 feet tall, produced entirely by human effort, without mechanical assistance, and you have an idea of the monumental size of Pirámide Mayor at Caral.

Pirámide Mayor looms over the site, but it is not the only monumental structure produced by the inhabitants. Five other smaller pyramids demarcate the margins of a rectangular plaza, perhaps the social and spiritual center of the community. Alignments of numerous other smaller mounds and two large, circular plazas were also built by the site's inhabitants. Residential complexes in which the individuals of the community lived provide evidence for a substantial population segregated by economic distinctions.

The site's excavators have noted that each of the six major pyramids at the site are associated with elaborate complexes of finely constructed rooms made with substantial stone walls covered in plaster. Elsewhere at the site were other residential areas characterized by less substantially made structures of wooden poles, cane, and mud. The more elaborately made buildings were likely the residences of Caral's elite class; the wood and mud structures were the homes of the community's commoners (Pringle 2001).

▶ **Figure 9.22**
This aerial view of Caral in Peru shows the monumental scale of pyramid construction undertaken by the inhabitants. The site's age of more than 4,500 years places it at the very beginning in the New World of monumental architecture and the complex society necessary for its construction. (© George Steinmetz/Corbis)

Caral is ancient, impressive, and unexpected, but it is not alone. Jonathan Haas, Winifred Creamer, and Alvaro Ruiz (2004) have continued to investigate the river valleys of Norte Chico and have found substantial additional evidence of widespread cultural complexity dating to the period beginning about 5,200 years ago and reaching a peak between 4,500 and 4,000 years ago. Hass and his colleagues found 20 major sites in the Supe, Pativilca, and Fortaleza valleys. These sites reflect a common pattern of substantial populations; the construction of impressively large, stone structures; terraced, flat-topped pyramids that served as the bases for buildings; and expansive, sunken circular plazas as large as 40 m (131 ft) across. Though Pirámide Mayor at Caral is the largest of the Norte Chico structures, it is not the only monumentally scaled pyramid; the next largest has a volume of more than 100,000 m³ (3 million ft³).

The diet of the Norte Chico inhabitants was diverse and eclectic. Not surprisingly, agriculture made a significant contribution to subsistence. Excavators found evidence of a broad mix of domesticated plant foods including squash, beans, chili peppers, guava, lucuma (a round, green fruit), pacay (a sweet and smooth-textured legume), and camote (sweet potato; Haas et al. 2004:1022). With no domesticated animals, Norte Chico residents obtained large quantities of shellfish, notably mussels and clams, from the coast, indicating that Norte Chico was not alone in its development but relied on contact and trade with populations on the coast who themselves would be developing increasingly complex social and political structures soon after.

To produce the monumental structures seen at Caral and the other Norte Chico sites, there must have been a large resident population, a complex social organization to coordinate and control the labor needed to produce the monuments, and a productive subsistence base to put food on the tables of those too involved in construction to produce food on their own. But the dry desert that has long characterized Norte Chico was not at all conducive to agriculture. There is no substantial plain subject to annual flooding and natural rejuvenation that would have rendered agriculture feasible at the scale necessary to feed a population large enough to have constructed the monuments at Caral. The site's researchers recognize that it would have been possible to produce enough food to feed all of Norte Chico residents only by the application of irrigation technology. Certainly, a labor force capable of building the pyramids seen in the Norte Chico sites would have been able to dig and maintain canals. In fact, the necessity of canal construction to expand the subsistence base to feed a growing population might have served as the overriding rationale for people to have worked cooperatively in the first place, subjugating themselves to an organizing authority and resulting, ultimately, in the social distinctions and economic inequality evidenced at Norte Chico.

The Push Toward Complexity

West of Caral, on the Pacific coast, complex societies were also developing. Between 5500 and 5000 B.P., coastal villages that had increased in size and subsistence expanded to include domesticates such as gourds, squash, and kidney and lima beans (Pineda 1988). At this time at sites like Huaca Prieta and Paracas, there is some evidence of increasing social complexity. While most residential buildings at these sites are quite similar in size and form, other structures are a bit larger and more ambitious. Small pyramids and platforms are included in this category.

After 5000 B.P., these specialized structures became increasingly large and sophisticated. Large pyramids were built, dominating the sites of Bandurria, Rio Seco, and Aspero (Pineda 1988:76). At these sites, there also is evidence of a developing pattern of social stratification in the form of differing house sizes. Aspero, for example, is a large site, covering 30 acres. There are seven large and six smaller ceremonial mounds at Aspero, on top of which were constructed small temples that contained human burials. Around the mounds were open plazas and artificial terraces. A large resident population exploited the rich resources of the coast.

The first evidence of the use of metals in South America dates to about 3100 B.P. Among a series of six early ceremonial centers with earthen pyramids and mounds located in Peru's Lurin Valley, Mina Perdida has produced gold and copper artifacts (Burger and Gordon 1998). No smelting or casting was done at this early date. Both the gold and copper had been found in a natural, nearly pure or "native" state and then hammered into thin foils. The existence of substantial earthworks along with fine metalwork at Mina Perdida is clear evidence of increasing complexity in the Andean region at this time. There is no obvious archaeological evidence before 3000 B.P. at these Lurin Valley sites for social stratification or wealth differentiation. The construction of large earthworks implies the existence of chiefs, but these chiefs were treated no differently—their residences were no larger and their graves no more elaborate—than those who followed them.

Though the precise process is not at all clear, it seems that the development of irrigation technology, population growth, and movement into the interior was accompanied by social differentiation. Some villages, like Kotosh and Chavín de Huántar, were strategically located along natural trade routes between the coast to the west and the uplands to the east, and trade seems to have played an important role in the developing social complexity at these sites. The focus on monumental architecture associated with ceremonial structures like pyramids is a good indication that the newly evolved social and economic power, perhaps as a result of trade, was focused on a religious elite class who could control the increasingly complex economy.

As long as this pattern of development was restricted to the rather small, individual river valley systems that cross Peru, sociopolitical differentiation could not become too marked. There simply were not enough resources and wealth for the developing elites to monopolize to enable them to attain the status of Egyptian pharaohs or Mesopotamian city-state kings (see Chapter 10). But sometime after 3000 B.P., populations started growing and their needs expanded beyond the narrow confines of their own particular river valleys. In the view of archaeologist Tom Patterson (1993), contact and competition among the political entities within individual valleys was a significant factor in the development of Andean civilization.

Cultural Convergence: Chavin

About 3,000 years ago, an apparently unifying religion with a distinct and striking art style began to spread across the previously highly regionalized valleys (Figure 9.23). Called **Chavin** and initially centered at the site of Chavín de Huántar, like Olmec it seems to have served to bring together a large and geographically broad population under the banner of a single religious, if not political, entity. Archaeologist Richard Burger (1988:111) calls Chavin an empire, but a "religious," not a political, one. The Chavin art style that accompanied the religion included

▶ **Figure 9.23**
This quite whimsical effigy bowl—it's in the shape of an animal, perhaps a dog—is a typical representation of the clearly recognizable Chavin art style. (Heritage Images/Corbis)

▶ **Figure 9.24**
Some of the distinctive iconography of the Chavin art style is shown here. Like Olmec to the north, Chavin seems to have functioned as a unifying element in the establishment of complex society in South America. (Courtesy of Gordon Willey)

the depiction of felines (possibly jaguars), raptorial birds, snakes, the caiman (a South American crocodile), and the so-called Staff God—a presumed deity holding two rods or staffs (Figure 9.24). Accompanying Chavin artistic and religious expression were several technological innovations that further served as unifying elements during this period of Peruvian prehistory. Beautiful and intricately woven textiles displaying common Chavin motifs were woven with the hairs of domesticated camelids. Across the broad and expanding region where Chavin motifs spread, hammered gold objects and three-dimensional objects made from joined sheets of gold are also found. Metallurgists producing Chavin motifs also used such production techniques as soldering and sweat welding as well as the decoration technique of repoussé. Silver-gold alloys, a hallmark of South American metallurgy, are first seen in Chavin artifacts.

Chavín de Huántar itself was strategically placed along a natural route of trade and transportation between the highland valleys, the Peruvian coast, and the interior tropical forest (Burger 1995). As a result, it likely was a magnet for excess wealth generated by trade. A unifying art-religion would certainly have served to encourage this trade among previously very diverse groups. As archaeologist Karen Olsen Bruhns (1994) indicates, the site began about 3,000 years ago as a ceremonial center with a small population of residents, serving at least in part to facilitate trade between disparate groups living in different habitats, newly combined through a common mode of religious expression. By a little after 2500 B.P., however, this ceremonial center had grown to become one of the earliest urban centers in South America: a bustling town, with a large, dense population spread out across about 100 acres. Houses and neighborhoods were constructed according to a plan, a drainage system was in place, and temples and huge food-storage facilities served the residents. Perhaps as river valleys filled up with population, the need to obtain resources from outside these valleys increased. Places like Chavín de Huántar that were propitiously placed took advantage of this increased need by regulating the trade that had to pass through their territories. The Chavin art style spreading a common and unifying religion initially simply served to facilitate trade among various groups, but it ultimately brought people closer together in all spheres, spreading technological innovations as well as new social patterns. Those in a position to control trade and information as it flowed through this coalescing system became the first members of a differentiated class of people who lived in larger houses, spent their time propitiating the Chavin gods, and monopolized certain key symbols of power in the developing civilization.

Why Does Complexity Develop in the First Place?

ISSUES AND DEBATES

Why might a group of people take the road toward complexity? Why might individuals surrender some of their social, political, and economic independence and volunteer their labor to participate in a community project like the construction of a Stonehenge or a Carnac? If Klaus Schmidt, the excavator of Göbekli Tepe is correct, then social and political complexity developed, at least initially, not as a result of practical considerations in order to increase the subsistence base but rather, as Charles Mann (2011:57) characterizes it, the "human impulse to gather for sacred rituals." When such rituals included the desire to show the ability to control or dominate the natural world, perhaps people organized themselves to produce monuments like those at Göbekli Tepe and Watson Brake and Poverty Point. Even if this view is correct, it seems likely that Neolithic people also developed complex social and political structures to respond to more practical challenges where individuals gave up some of their personal sovereignty and donated their labor, at least initially, to reap individual and practical benefits.

For example, large-scale labor projects requiring coordination of the work of many people may have been made necessary by the need to increase agricultural output. The production of seedbeds or the construction of water control structures (dams, canals, reservoirs) may have required complex social, political, and economic organization, at least more complex than what had sufficed previously. An external military threat may have required the organization of an army or of a construction gang to build defensive works—for example, a wall around a settlement. Even the discovery of an abundant source of an important raw material—for example, clay, stone, or metal—may have been seen as an opportunity to generate wealth or concentrate power if people organized their labor to quarry the raw material or devise ways of monopolizing it.

The notion here is that once a complex social or political structure develops to meet an immediate and practical need, that structure might not simply disappear once the threat is eliminated, the challenge answered, or the opportunity exploited. Such a structure might find other projects, not always practical ones, to devote its time to. The great monuments that dominate the archaeological record of some ancient cultures and therefore occupy the time of so many archaeologists are, in this interpretation, merely the incidental effects of the evolution of complex social, political, and economic structures that developed in response to more concrete challenges, threats, or opportunities.

Is Complexity Inevitable?

This chapter has focused on the development of social, political, and economic complexity in the Neolithic. Remember that the evolution of complex societies, though certainly facilitated by the development of food-producing economies, was not the inevitable outcome of this shift in subsistence. The capacity to produce a surplus of food and the attendant ability to free a proportion of the population from subsistence activities in no way guarantees that a society will elect to do so.

In some cases, the first steps along a pathway toward intensifying the food quest, organizing labor beyond the family or local community, and subjugating individual needs for the perceived needs of the group lead to an ever intensifying spiral of escalating economic differentiation and inequality, increasing and solidifying social stratification, and growing distinctions in terms of the power wielded by individuals or families over everyone else. But this is not an inevitable trajectory. Food production and the surplus it makes possible merely open a door; other factors come into play in a society's determination whether or not to pass through that portal and follow a pathway that leads to a fundamental change in how the society is organized. In some cases, the decision to do so may be born of necessity. The need to produce more food to feed a burgeoning population or to respond to an external military threat may require the development of a new kind of societal structure in response. In other instances, the opportunity offered by a locally available resource may provide a source of wealth that can be more efficiently exploited by a complex social and political structure. The point is, the shift to complexity was neither universal nor inevitable.

CASE STUDY CLOSE-UP

IT MUST HAVE BEEN AN IMPOSING sight for pilgrims visiting Chavín de Huántar—and that almost certainly was the intention. The two major trails that led to the site along the Huachecsa and Mosna Rivers led not to the front entrance of the Old Temple but rather to the back sides of the monumental, U-shaped structure. At the end of either trail, visitors found themselves at the base of a massive, towering four-story wall of stone. Its setting and appearance were almost certainly intended as a message to all who saw it: Here is the seat of our power, the center of our might (Burger 1995). The Old Temple was a mammoth construction project, with thousands upon thousands of granite, sandstone, and limestone blocks laid on each other in thin courses. The temple spread out across a broad area, covering more than 7,100 m^2 (nearly 77,000 ft^2; more than 1.75 acres). Different segments of the temple differed somewhat in height; the top platform stood between 14 and 16 m (about 46 and 53 ft) above the surface. At about 10 m (33 ft) above the ground, at 3-m (10-ft) intervals, the builders of the Old Temple had inserted a series of striking, carved anthropomorphic (humanlike) and zoomorphic (animal-like) stone heads (Figure 9.25). At the back of each of the heads, carvers had made tenons that fit into sockets made in the wall behind them. Twice the size of actual human heads, snarling, with exposed fangs and contorted faces, these stone heads seem to float in the air, gazing down on visitors, expressing the power and authority of the Chavin gods. At the center of the Old Temple, ensconced in a tall chamber at the end of a dark corridor, stands a 4.5-m (almost

▶ **Figure 9.25**
A ghoulish figure set into the wall of the Old Temple at the site of Chavín de Huántar, one of several that gaze down upon visitors to the site. To the rear of the heads were carved tenons that fit into sockets in the wall of the temple. (© Ric Ergenbright/Corbis)

15-ft) tall upright monolith of granite today called the Lanzón. Onto the shaft of granite has been carved the shape of an anthropomorphic deity (Figure 9.26). The size and setting of the Lanzón have led scholars to the conclusion that this is the chief god in the Chavin pantheon of powerful supernatural beings, the god that the pilgrims may have come to worship. The precise meaning of the Old Temple has been lost to us. Perhaps its alignment has astronomical significance, the open section of the U facing the rising or setting of an important set of stars. Maybe the shape and setting of the building conveyed some symbolic message to those who followed the Chavin religion, a message we may never be able to comprehend. But this much is clear: The Old Temple was made possible by the social and political structures that characterize complex societies; and at the same time, it communicated to all who saw it the power of the Chavin gods as well as those upon whom they looked down with favor. It must have been a powerful message indeed.

Summary

Even before the shift to agriculture, the archaeological record bears witness to monumental manifestations of the development of social and political complexity. At sites like Göbekli Tepe in the Old World and Watson Brake and Poverty Point in the New, people relying on hunting and gathering for their subsistence appear to have developed complex ways of organizing labor that allowed them to construct enormous monuments.

Later, and in a more geographically broad pattern, following the shift from a subsistence strategy based on wild, collected foods to one at least partially reliant on domesticated, produced foods, numerous societies began to shift from a simple social and political organization based on the household or family to a more complex framework. In some cases, the shift to complexity was fueled by the need to

◀ **Figure 9.26**
Deep within the Old Temple at the site of Chavín de Huántar is the famous Lanzón carving, a fantastic creature—perhaps the chief god of the Chavin pantheon—carved from a single piece of granite. (From G. Willey. 1971. *Introduction to American Archaeology: South America*. Englewood Cliffs, NJ: Prentice Hall. Reprinted with permission of the author)

organize the labor of a large group of people to increase food production—for instance, to construct water-control facilities. In other instances, the development of a social and political structure to organize and coordinate monumental projects was necessitated by some external threat—for example, the construction of a defensive wall around a community. In still other cases, the evolution of an organizational framework beyond the household or family may have come about as the result of the unique opportunities offered by a particularly rich habitat or proximity to and monopolization of a valued resource. Whatever the particular case, the results of this shift to more complex social, political, and economic life and the shift to rank societies and chiefdoms are evidenced in the archaeological record by the monumental works made possible by large groups of organized people—Stonehenge is but one example. In some cases, the shift to complexity and the creation of ranks or classes are also evidenced in the archaeological record by the appearance of burials differentiated by the inclusion of precious raw materials and finely made works of art. Examples of the development of complexity in the Old World following the adoption of an agricultural subsistence base are seen at Jericho in Israel and Çatalhöyük in Turkey. Soon thereafter, this complexity can be seen developing in Mesopotamia. The earliest example in Mesoamerica is seen along the Mexican Gulf Coast among the people called Olmec. The earliest archaeological evidence for the development of complexity in South America is seen at about 4,500 years ago in Peru at the site of Caral, characterized by a cluster of enormous, flat-topped pyramids, plazas, and substantial residential complexes. By 3,000 years ago, the Chavin style developed as a regional iconography, a religious and artistic approach that served to unify a broad array of societies, setting the stage for the later development of regional states.

TO LEARN MORE

For an inclusive summary of how people through the centuries have viewed Stonehenge—and how they have been confused by the obvious sophistication exhibited by the monument in the context of an otherwise seemingly simple farming society—there is no better source than Christopher Chippindale's *Stonehenge Complete* (2004). Another wonderful book is Anthony Johnson's (2008) *Solving Stonehenge*, which attempts to do precisely what the title suggests. For a summary of the latest archaeological work at Stonehenge with, as always, great photographs, take a look at Caroline Alexander's *National Geographic* article, "If the Stones Could Speak," in its June 2008 issue. For a broad look at the megaliths, see Aubrey Burl's (2005) handsome book, *Great Stone Circles*. For a beautifully photographed, eclectic, and just plain fun book on the stone monuments of Great Britain, don't miss musician Julian Cope's (1998) *The Modern Antiquarian* chronicling his odyssey across the British landscape and his atlas of more than 300 sites.

Both for the photographs and for the fascinating summary, you should check out Charles C. Mann's *National Geographic* article on Göbekli Tepe ("Birth of Religion") in the June 2011 issue. Çatalhöyük now has its own "biographer," science writer Michael Balter (2005), who has written a terrific summary of the work done at the site: *The Goddess and the Bull: Çatalhöyük: An Archaeological Journey to the Dawn of Civilization*. For a thorough and thoroughly enjoyable discussion of the archaeology of the Olmec, there is no better source than Richard Diehl's (2004) book, *The Olmecs: America's First Civilization*.

Web links for this chapter can be found at www.oup.com/us/feder

KEY TERMS

affluent foragers, 313	lintel, 304	Regal-Ritual Centers, 323
Chavin, 332	megalith, 305	Samarran, 319
chiefdom, 315	Mesopotamia, 319	sarsen, 304
Halafian, 319	Olmec, 322	tholoi, 321
Hassunan, 319	Poverty Point culture, 313	trilithon, 304

10

An Explosion of Complexity

Mesopotamia, Africa, and Europe

CHAPTER OVERVIEW

A food surplus made possible by the agricultural revolution set the stage for the development of differential access to wealth, and with the concentration of wealth came the concentration of social and political power.

"Civilization," characterized by the existence of a formal government, social stratification, large and dense settlements, monumental edifices, elaborate burials, large armies, full-time artisans, and a system of record keeping, developed in several regions in the Old World as fewer people were needed in the subsistence quest and as rulers attempted to legitimize, reinforce, and magnify their position of power and their levels of wealth. This chapter focuses on four regions where complex societies developed: Mesopotamia, Egypt, southern Africa, and Crete.

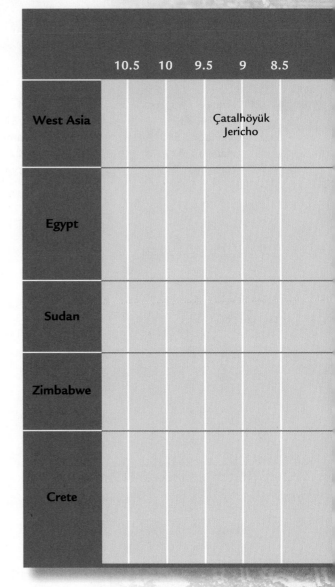

	10.5	10	9.5	9	8.5
West Asia				Çatalhöyük Jericho	
Egypt					
Sudan					
Zimbabwe					
Crete					

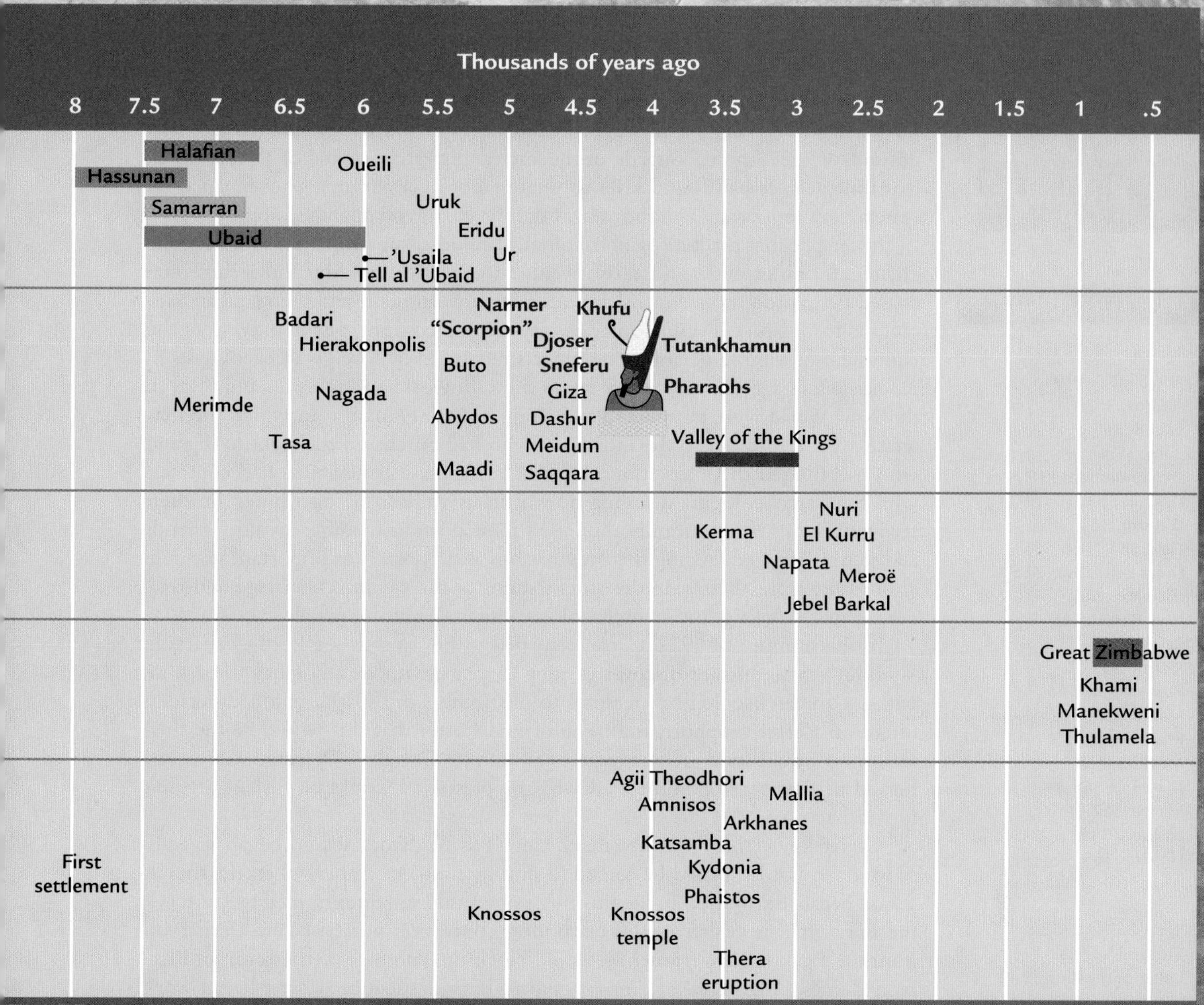

Thousands of years ago

8	7.5	7	6.5	6	5.5	5	4.5	4	3.5	3	2.5	2	1.5	1	.5

Halafian

Hassunan

Samarran

Ubaid

Oueili

Uruk

Eridu

Ur

'Usaila

Tell al 'Ubaid

Badari

Hierakonpolis

Merimde

Nagada

Tasa

Narmer

"Scorpion"

Buto

Abydos

Maadi

Djoser

Sneferu

Giza

Dashur

Meidum

Saqqara

Khufu

Tutankhamun

Pharaohs

Valley of the Kings

Kerma

Nuri

El Kurru

Napata

Jebel Barkal

Meroë

Great Zimbabwe

Khami

Manekweni

Thulamela

Agii Theodhori

Amnisos

Katsamba

Kydonia

Phaistos

Mallia

Arkhanes

First
settlement

Knossos

Knossos
temple

Thera
eruption

PRELUDE

BY THE SUMMER OF 1922, THE wealthy British nobleman George Herbert, whose official title was the Earl of Carnarvon, had all but run out of patience. For 15 years he had provided financial support for the work of archaeologist Howard Carter, who was digging in Egypt in the Valley of the Kings—the royal burial ground, or "necropolis," outside of the ancient Egyptian capital of Thebes. In all that time, Carter had found little to interest Lord Carnarvon or to enhance his benefactor's reputation as a sponsor of significant Egyptian archaeology.

In the peculiar practice of archaeological colonialism rampant throughout the eighteenth, nineteenth, and early twentieth centuries, wealthy Europeans purchased excavation "concessions" from foreign governments and then paid archaeologists to conduct investigations. Excavation concessions, put bluntly, were the equivalent of mining permits. The objects recovered by foreign archaeologists in places such as Egypt, Iraq, and Syria in the Old World and Mexico and Peru in the New World were considered to belong not to the nation in which the materials were found but to the individual who had purchased the right to dig and who had funded the excavations. In most cases, these benefactors had contracts with their archaeologists detailing how artifacts were to be distributed on their recovery. Sponsors commonly dispensed their portion to other wealthy friends and to museums, enhancing their reputations as supporters of important research; at the same time, they were divesting nations of their cultural heritage and rendering analysis of significant archaeological sites all but impossible.

In the summer of 1922, Carter returned to England to see Lord Carnarvon. Without any significant discoveries after 15 years, without any glory to bask in, without any archaeological treasures to distribute, Lord Carnarvon had decided to cut off Carter's support, and he informed Carter that this would be the final season he would fund archaeological research in the valley. Dejected, Carter returned to Egypt and commenced what he presumed would be his last digging for Carnarvon.

Carter knew there was not much time. His fieldwork season began in early November, and he would be forced to quit by mid-December, when the tourist season began. Excavation in the tiny piece of ground still unexamined by Carter—the only such piece left in the excavation concession purchased by Carnarvon from the Egyptian government—would block the entrance to the tomb of Pharaoh Rameses VI, the valley's most popular visitor destination. Carter began work on November 1, 1922, and within three days his Egyptian workers had discovered the beginning of a staircase leading down into the ground. The staircase was slowly cleared of rock; at the bottom was a sealed door bearing the official symbol of the royal burial ground: jackals, symbolically protecting the king's tomb. It seemed possible that Carter at last had found a sealed tomb of an Egyptian king.

Carter was cautiously optimistic, but there had been false starts and false hopes before. Believing that this was his last chance, Carter took a gamble and telegrammed Lord Carnarvon in England: "At last have made wonderful discovery in the Valley. A magnificent tomb with seals intact. Recovered same for your arrival: congratulations" (Fagan 1994:205). Carter suggested that the earl travel to Egypt to witness the opening of what Carter fervently hoped was an unplundered tomb.

After a difficult trip, Lord Carnarvon arrived, with his daughter, Lady Evelyn Herbert. Carter provided a viewing area for Carnarvon and Lady Evelyn where, protected from the relentless Egyptian sun by an umbrella, they watched while workers opened the door at the bottom of the staircase. But instead of the hoped-for tomb, beyond the door was a rubble-filled corridor carved in the rock. Disappointed but intrigued, the workers began the laborious process of removing the rock and debris from the corridor, which extended an excruciating 25 feet. At the end lay yet another door (above which, in case you were interested, there was no inscribed curse of any kind). For a great read about Tut, including a detailed deconstruction of the curse, see Joyce Tyldesley's book *Tutankhamen: The Search for an Egyptian King* (2012).

The cleared second doorway stood before Carter and Carnarvon on November 26, a little more than two weeks before Carnarvon's patience and money—and Carter's time—were to run out. Carter drilled a hole through the door. Beyond was clearly an open space, a subterranean room. Carter widened the drilled hole just enough so he could put his head, one arm, and a candle through. Carter's own words to describe what he saw are some of the most famous in all archaeology:

> "At first I could see nothing, the hot air escaping from the chamber causing the candle flame to flicker. But presently, as my eyes grew accustomed to the light, details of the room within emerged slowly from the mist, strange animals, statues, and gold—everywhere the glint of gold. For the moment— an eternity it must have seemed to the others standing by—I was struck dumb with amazement, and when Lord Carnarvon, unable to stand the suspense any longer, inquired anxiously, "Can you see anything?" it was all I could do to get out the words, "Yes, wonderful things!" (Buckley 1976:13)

Thus began the excavation of the fabulous tomb of the Egyptian "boy king," Tutankhamun (Figure 10.1). Though a relatively minor figure in Egyptian history, having served as pharaoh as a child from 1334 B.C. to 1325 B.C., Tutankhamun was to become the most famous of all ancient Egypt's rulers. His tomb had gone largely untouched since his death, and the spectacular array of burial goods in the tomb were to excite people everywhere (Figure 10.2).

▶ **Figure 10.1**
An iconic moment of discovery; this photograph captures the opening of the tomb of Egyptian pharaoh Tutankhamun. Archaeologist Howard Carter (kneeling) points to objects in the tomb as co-workers look in wonderment. (Hulton-Deutsch Collection/Corbis)

CHRONICLE

WE SAW IN CHAPTER 9 HOW in both the Old and New Worlds a very few hunting-and-gathering societies and several food-producing societies followed a pathway that led them to organize their social, political, and economic lives in ways that were more complex than in other Neolithic and hunter-gatherer societies. The resulting cultures—called rank societies or chiefdoms—provide material evidence for the elevation of a proportion of a population to higher social, political, and often economic status. These elevated individuals achieved authority and accumulated wealth by becoming the heads of new social and political structures that developed out of a need to organize labor at a level beyond the household or the family. We see in the archaeological record the material manifestation of the end products of that organized labor—megalithic monuments like Göbekli Tepe and Stonehenge, Jericho's wall, Çatalhöyük's architecture, the Olmec heads, and Caral's pyramids—and in the ritual sanctification of the higher status of the leaders by their elevated treatment in death—in other words, their entombment in elaborate burials with precious grave goods.

In a few areas, the elaboration of social, political, and economic systems did not end here but continued to intensify, producing societies where the authority of a chief to *convince* others to follow his lead became the power of a pharaoh or king to *demand* obedience. With an exponentially greater degree of control combined with improved technology and a larger population, we see the development of a new kind of social order: the **state**.

The far greater concentration of power and control that characterizes and even defines the state allowed for the production of far larger and more impressive monuments and artwork, albeit made possible by the subjugation of a large class of people whose labor was devoted to the dictates of the ruler or rulers. Perhaps because in the present only the admittedly impressive material manifestations of these early state societies are immediately apparent—and the toil and servitude of the workers and peasants whose backbreaking work produced them is hidden from our view—we refer to the evolution of state societies as the development of "civilization." The material achievements of these societies are impressive indeed, and we will devote much of this chapter to discussing them. As we do so, however, we should always bear in mind that great pyramids, ziggurats, temples, and palaces come at a human price. For every King Tut buried in great splendor, there must have been hundreds and even thousands of peasants whose labor made possible the life the Boy King lived and whose toil provided Tut and his cohorts with an eternity surrounded by grandeur.

▼ **Figure 10.2**
The gold mask that covered the face of the boy king Tutankhamun as it was found by Howard Carter. (© The Gallery Collection/Corbis)

The Evolution of the State

Civilization is easier to recognize than to define. We know it when we see it, but find it a challenge to articulate what makes it so. Certainly, when we visit or see images of Egyptian pyramids or Mesopotamian temples (in this chapter), the cites of the Harappan civilization (Chapter 11), or ancient Maya cities or the palaces of the Inca (in Chapters 12 and 13), we know we are in the presence of the complex phenomenon called "civilization." But how can we formally define what we recognize intuitively?

A state is both quantitatively and qualitatively different from a chiefdom. States ordinarily are bigger and their material accomplishments more impressive. But they are more than simply big, impressive chiefdoms; states are true **class societies**, often rigidly stratified into social levels. The ruling class controls the populace not by consensus but by coercion and force. A state possesses a true government with formal laws and regulations—and formal penalties for those who disobey—and the ruling class in a state society runs the government. "Civilization" is most often used to characterize the recognizable material results of the development of state societies. Because archaeologists deal most directly with such material consequences, this discussion will use the terms "state" and "civilization" interchangeably.

The Character of Civilization

The most obvious material symbols of state societies are **monumental works**. The ruins of huge public buildings, tombs, temples, palaces, pyramids, and such are all the spoor of ancient civilizations. Works such as the Egyptian Sphinx, the Pyramid of the Sun at Teotihuacán in Mexico, the Citadel at Mohenjodaro in Pakistan, and the great ziggurat at Ur in Iraq are the features by which we recognize ancient civilizations. However, while these monuments may represent the most obvious manifestation of state societies, they do not necessarily define them. How ancient people were able to coalesce their labor to build impressive monuments—and why they felt compelled to participate in their construction—are the key puzzles in our attempt to understand the evolution of ancient civilizations.

Food Surplus

Look around any of your classrooms and conduct a silent census of the distribution of the declared majors of your classmates. I'm sure there are some who are aiming for a degree in business, or perhaps in education, in one of the sciences, in computers, engineering, psychology, social work, maybe even anthropology. How many of your cohorts, do you think, are majoring in agriculture; how many hope to be farmers? I'll bet that, at least at most universities or colleges, that number will be very small. That fact is indicative of complex societies, ancient ones as well as our modern one (Figure 10.3). Civilizations rely absolutely on an agricultural base in which the few are able to feed the many, where only a relatively small proportion of the population needs to be engaged in full-time agricultural pursuits. Their production of a food surplus that then is distributed by a coordinating, overseeing authority allows for other members of the society to engage in other activities: to be soldiers, craftspeople, astronomers, traders, teachers, engineers, doctors, and even archaeologists.

Large, Dense Populations

Increasingly efficient agricultural systems, along with the capacity to distribute food to nonproducers, allow for increasingly large and dense communities, sometimes culminating in the development of urban centers—in other words, the city.

▶ **Figure 10.3**
This graph reflects a pattern commonly seen in civilizations: a decrease in the number of people needed to engage full time in subsistence pursuits. Between 1920 and 2010, the average farmer went from producing enough food to feed eight people beyond his or her immediate family to 210. With fewer people needed on the farm, as a result of greater agricultural productivity and efficiency, more people are free to spend their time in the military, the temple, the factory, and the marketplace.

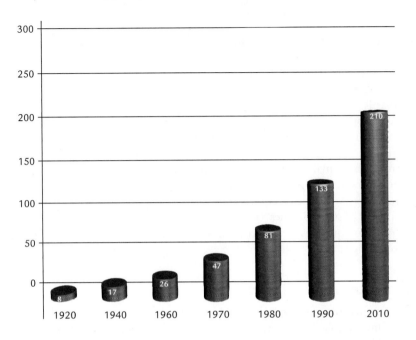

As a local population increases in size and density—that is, as a growing population becomes packed into a relatively restricted area in the process of urbanization—a host of challenges are presented: How is order to be maintained among the many people now living virtually next door to each other? How are disputes among neighbors to be resolved? How are necessities—including food—produced outside of the urban area to be distributed among the populace? Issues of property ownership, transportation, and even practical concerns such as the disposal of human waste become greatly magnified when a large number of people are living in close proximity to one another, leading to a spiral of change amplifying the social and economic complexity of a group of people. Social and political structures need to be developed to deal with these and other problems. These structures fundamentally change the social and political lives of people living in urban centers by restricting behaviors that might be detrimental to the larger group.

Social Stratification

Great pyramids, walls, palaces, irrigation networks, temples, and roads, as well as beautiful paintings, exquisite ceramics, gold statues, and fine linen—the "wonderful things" that Howard Carter saw in Tut's tomb—are the result of an increasingly complex, layered, or "stratified," socioeconomic system. Such a system enables the production of monuments and great art and, at the same time, demands their production. **Social stratification** in a complex civilization is a division of society into levels, or strata, that one does not achieve but into which one is born (Figure 10.4). One's social level defines one's role in life, one's status, one's material wealth, one's power (or degree of powerlessness)—in essence, one's destiny. Monuments and great art are only the material symbols of the powerful position of members of the elite social strata in these societies.

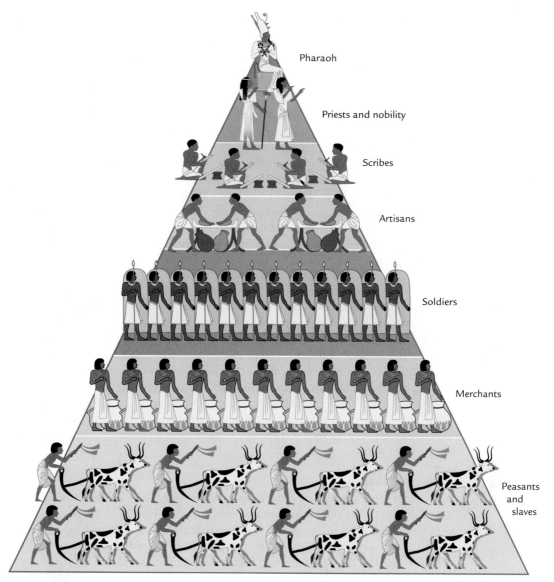

Pharaoh

Priests and nobility

Scribes

Artisans

Soldiers

Merchants

Peasants
and
slaves

▲ **Figure 10.4**
The metaphor of a social pyramid is particularly apt when discussing ancient
civilizations, including that of ancient Egypt. At the pinnacle rests the god-king;
beneath him there is a small coterie of powerful priests and nobles, below whom rest
larger and less powerful groups of important people including scribes and artisans.
These people are, in turn, supported by a phalanx of soldiers and a population
of merchants. The entire framework of the pyramid is supported by the largest
group of all, workers, peasants, and slaves without whose toil the pyramid—both
the metaphorical social pyramid and actual pyramid monuments—could not be
constructed and maintained.

A Formal Government

Along with social stratification, a state possesses a true "government," defined by archaeologist Joseph Tainter (1988:26) as a "specialized decision-making organization with a monopoly of force, and with the power to draft for work, levy and collect taxes, and decree and enforce laws." The power of the state provided by its formal government is wielded by members of the upper social classes. Pharaohs, emperors, and kings, along with the nobles serving under them, are members of a permanently circumscribed social class of people ruling the great masses of people who make up a state society.

The kings, pharaohs, or emperors of state societies have much more than authority; they rule by more than simply the consensus of the populace. Instead, they have true power: the ability to make decisions, give commands, and then make sure those commands are carried out. Jail, enforced labor, banishment, and even the gallows await those who fail to heed the dictates of the ruler of a state society. The rulers of state societies sit atop a formal government with fixed laws. Leaders in such societies possess the ability to enforce those laws.

Labor Specialization

With the **specialization of labor**, certain individuals can devote all their time to perfecting skills in sophisticated and time-consuming specialties, such as technology, engineering, the arts, and crafts. Without the devotion of a lifetime's work, the level of skill exhibited in the great works associated with early civilizations, like the "wonderful things" in King Tut's tomb, could not have been achieved. Specialists can exist only in a society where enough food can be produced to feed all those people engaged in full-time specialist pursuits and where the social system provides a rationale for their existence. Such specialists are needed only in a society that demands their work by and for certain powerful people of an even higher class.

Record Keeping

Without some **system of record keeping** by which the elite could keep track of food surpluses and labor and, in essence, dictate history by recording it in a manner beneficial to them, it is unlikely that the entire system supporting the civilization could ever have developed. In modern America, for instance, how well would the Internal Revenue Service function if there were no way to keep track of individual income and yearly tax contribution? On the other hand, a system of keeping records that can reinforce the legitimacy of the rule of the king—for instance, by demonstrating descent from previous rulers or even from the gods—is another important way the system justifies and maintains itself. As a result of the record keeping of civilizations, in this chapter and Chapter 11 we begin to breach the edge of history, reaching the end of the human story that is the focus of this book—that part of the human saga from the period before history.

Monumental Works

Finally, let us return to where we began this discussion, with the most obvious symbols of civilizations, the monumental works by which we recognize them in the archaeological record. Those monuments are made possible by the characteristics of the state just enumerated. A food surplus freeing the labor of a large labor force; a large, dense population; a stratified social system in which the many serve the dictates of the few; a formal government that enforces that social inequality; specialization; and a system of record keeping together make possible the production of the monumental works and great art that first command our attention when we are confronted by the remains of an ancient civilization.

Great monuments and art, therefore, are enabled by the social and political system of the state. The rulers in state societies have the power to cause the construction of fabulous tombs filled with splendid works of art. They can conscript armies, collect taxes, and call up workforces.

In a feedback process, such power, at the same time, adds compelling support for the existence of the state. In complex civilizations, the great mass of people must believe that there are individuals who can rightfully require their labor, time, and wealth. As archaeologist Joseph Tainter (1988) puts it, the early elites had to convince the great mass of society that their rule was legitimate—in other words, "proper and valid"—and that the political world with a powerful elite commanding from on high and accumulating great wealth was "as it should be" (Tainter 1988:27). And, as the old saying goes, "nothing succeeds like success"; an awe-inspiring pyramid or temple may go a long way toward convincing the populace that the ruler who commanded that such a thing be built actually is as powerful as he is purported to be, and commands the attention of the gods, and that allegiance is due to him. Monumental works also serve as a warning to neighboring groups: "See what we are capable of? Don't mess with us." Almost certainly, the great Egyptian monument of Abu Simbel, located along the Nile, at the southern threshold of ancient Egyptian territory, conveyed a powerful message (Figure 10.5): "If we can build this, imagine how powerful our army must be."

Pyramids, great tombs, huge palaces, and the like are the material symbols of the power of the state, both for those living within such systems and for those of us in the modern world who study them. In addition to being literal monuments to kings, gods, or generals, they also stand as symbolic monuments to the power of the state. They serve the role of providing, as Tainter characterizes it (1988:28), "sacred legitimization" for the power of the elite, and they reflect "the need to establish and constantly reinforce legitimacy" (Tainter 1988:27).

▼ **Figure 10.5**
Built along the Nile at the southern margin of ancient Egyptian civilization, the gargantuan statues (look at the size of the people in the photograph) presented a message to anyone traveling downstream, into their territory: "We are powerful. Don't mess with us." (M. H. Feder)

The Geography of Civilizations

Perhaps most remarkably, these features of the world's first civilizations evolved not once but several times, in both the Old and New Worlds: in southwest Asia and Egypt (this chapter); the Indus Valley of Pakistan, eastern China, and the island of Crete (Chapter 11); and Mesoamerica (Chapter 12) and Peru (Chapter 13). These primary civilizations developed more or less independently, each following its own path. The next sections will present brief synopses of the evolution of each of the centers of early civilization in the Old World.

Mesopotamia

In Chapter 9, we discussed the origins of one of the world's earliest complex societies in the land between the Tigris and Euphrates Rivers. We saw the evidence for complexity reflected in large-scale communal works such as granaries and defensive walls that surrounded entire villages. Southern Mesopotamia is also the place where archaeological evidence indicates that the world's first civilization developed.

Accelerating Change: The Ubaid

By about 6300 B.P., the area of southern Mesopotamia shows substantial movement toward what we are here calling civilization. The culture of southern Mesopotamia during this period is called **Ubaid** and is reflected at the sites of Tell al 'Ubaid, Tell Oueili, Eridu, 'Usaila, and Ur (Figure 10.6). Beyond its rich floodplain soil, Mesopotamia proper has few other resources. As archaeologist Harriet Crawford (1991) points out, there are no sources for stone or metal in Mesopotamia and few areas with enough trees to provide wood for construction. It is not surprising, therefore, that Ubaid sites appear rather suddenly in this area, with no evidence of previous development. Much of the area simply was not immediately attractive to Neolithic farmers in the Middle East. Southern Mesopotamia was populated only after 6,300 years ago, when population growth, made possible by the settled life of the Neolithic, forced people to expand out onto the floodplain. Similarly, this area was populated only when the construction of a system of water control became technologically—and socially—feasible.

The Role of Irrigation

The floodplain of the Tigris–Euphrates system is not an easy habitat to exploit, but with the construction of irrigation canals to bring water to fields in the summer and to drain them after the spring floods, it becomes enormously pro-

▶ **Figure 10.6**
Archaeological sites in western Asia where evidence of the evolution of chiefdom and early state-level societies has been found.

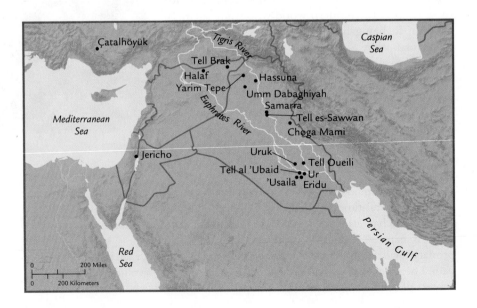

ductive farmland. Canal construction requires a large population whose labor can be organized. At the same time, an effective irrigation system allows for the production of even more food to support a larger and denser population. Archaeologist Charles Maisels (1990) proposes that the deciding factors in the development of Mesopotamia's complex societies were (1) the need to concentrate population along the arable lands near the rivers, thereby increasing population locally, (2) the need to develop a complex social system that would allow the construction of canals, and (3) the ability of irrigation to produce a food surplus. In other words, the development of civilization was the result of dynamic feedback among population growth, the development of complex irrigation systems, and the attendant new social order necessary to organize and ultimately command the labor of the growing population.

Power Invested in the Temple

In early Mesopotamia, as elsewhere, no political or military structure was in place that could provide designers, builders, supervisors, maintainers, and controllers of the irrigation networks. Early Neolithic cultures were likely largely egalitarian or rank societies. But in Mesopotamia, again as elsewhere, one institution in society was set apart, and extraordinary powers resided there even before social complexity increased. That institution was the temple (Figure 10.7). As seen in Chapter 9, religious shrines or temples date back to well before the Ubaid period in Mesopotamia. In the view of archaeologists C. C. Lamberg-Karlovsky and Jeremy Sabloff (1995), when population grew and expanded onto the floodplain and when irrigation works became a necessity, a need developed for the evolution of an institution that could organize the labor necessary to build and maintain these works. In their view, the religious elite quickly filled the power vacuum and became the dominant political and social as well as religious force in Mesopotamian society. In other words, priests became chiefs. Control of the irrigation networks led to power, and with power came the ability to control the enormous food surplus that the evolving system produced.

Mesopotamia's First Cities: The Uruk Period

With the large and complex settlements of the Ubaid as a base, after 6000 B.P., dramatic changes occurred in southern Mesopotamia, and a number of communities became much larger. Between 5500 and 5200 B.P., the settlement at Uruk (also called Warka) became so large, with a population estimated to be more than 10,000, that we can reasonably call it a city—in fact, the world's first.

The growth of Uruk occurred, at least in part, through a process of population concentration. Archaeological evidence indicates that many of the smaller farming communities around Uruk were abandoned, with their populations congregating in the growing urban center.

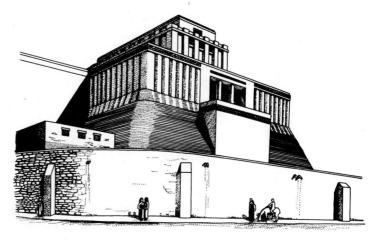

▼ **Figure 10.7**
Artist's conception of the temple at the early Mesopotamian city of Eridu at around 5000 B.P. when the population of this early urban settlement is estimated to have been about 5,000 people. (From *The Art of the Ancient Near East* by Seton Lloyd, published by Thames & Hudson, Ltd., London, 1961)

▲ **Figure 10.8**
The impressive ziggurat at the Mesopotomian city of Ur. Built more than 4,000 years ago, the ziggurat is a testament to the ability of early state societies to conscript the labor of a large population to produce monumental public works. (© Michael S. Yamashita/Corbis)

That this movement of population may have resulted from widespread warfare is supported by evidence at Uruk itself, where defensive fortifications were built at this time.

Another site, Eridu, became an urban center soon after Uruk, with an estimated population of 5,000; a large, finely built temple; and a neighborhood of larger houses with more impressive material culture, belonging to the newly evolved elite. By the Early Dynastic Period of the Sumerian civilization, dated from 4850 to 4600 B.P., there were more than 20 urban centers, or **city-states**—each with its own temple and territory consisting of a four-tiered hierarchy of settlement types, including the city and its associated towns, villages, and hamlets (Adams and Nissen 1972; Figure 10.8).

Along with monumental works such as great temples, palaces, and pyramids, state societies express in symbolic ways the social and political stratification that defines them. There is no more obvious example of this than in how the rulers of these societies are treated in death. The elite classes in state society are buried in a splendor that symbolizes their superior economic, social, and political positions in life.

Consider, for example, the cemetery at the Mesopotamian city of Ur; it contains more than 2,000 graves, only 16 of which were the interments of members of the elite class. The vast majority of the graves are simple, the final resting places of ordinary people. They are little more than holes in the ground with a few personal effects placed in the graves. The burials of the elite are far different, placed in stone chambers with vaulted roofs—one even possessed a dome. One of the tombs, that of a queen called Pu-abi, is emblematic of the royal interments at Ur.

A headdress of gold, festooned with semiprecious stones, was placed on Pu-abi's head. Around her were gold and silver containers, an intricately designed harp, a gaming table, and another 250 or so objects (Figure 10.9). In the Royal Cemetery, many of those interred were sacrifices, people dispatched to the afterlife to accompany the deceased noblemen or -women. These common people did not die of grief or by suicide. They were killed. For example, when examining closely 2 of the skulls of the 63 retainers interred at the Royal Cemetery of Ur, researchers noted the presence of radial fractures, caused by deadly blows to the head (Baadsgaard et al. 2011). After they were killed, the sacrificial victims had been dressed up in their best outfits, their bodies were preserved with mercury, and then they were lined up like wax figures in a morbid Halloween haunted house, destined to forever guard the passageway to a king's tomb.

I guess if you were a member of an elite class, you simply couldn't be happy in death without the help, protection, and company provided by soldiers and servants. Pu-abi was no different. Just outside the royal chamber were 10 more women (one with a harp—musical accompaniment for the journey), 5 soldiers, and 2 oxen. Beneath Queen Pu-abi's chamber was another tomb—a man's, possibly her husband's. This king was accompanied by 6 soldiers, 19 females wearing gold headpieces, 6 oxen, 2 chariots, a lyre, a gaming table, and an exquisite silver model of a boat. Such were the death settings of Ur nobility. Pu-abi's interment is emblematic of the wealth, power, and social position of the nobility of ancient Mesopotamia and, in fact, all of the other civilizations discussed in this text.

The Beginning of the Written Record

The research of archaeologist Denise Schmandt-Besserat (1992, 1996, 2002) has revealed the most likely scenario for how the use of recorded symbols evolved in Mesopotamia, proposing what is essentially a five-step process. The first step involved the use of so-called clay **tokens** that, beginning more than 9,000 years ago, litter sites in the Middle East (Lawler 2001). The tokens initially were made in 16 basic shapes, mostly geometric forms like cones, disks, spheres, and cylinders but also stylized animals and some that resemble pottery storage jars (Figure 10.10). Schmandt-Besserat has examined more than 8,000 of these tokens during more than 25 years of research. Some of these artifacts have been found at Hassuna, Samarra, and Halaf, all sites mentioned in Chapter 9

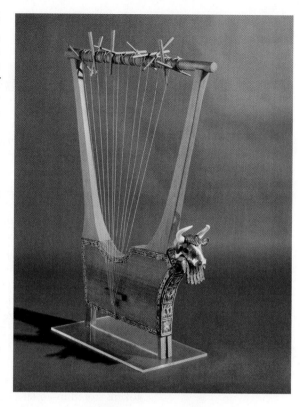

▲ **Figure 10.9**
From the 4,000-year-old tomb of Pu-abi in ancient Sumeria, this gold bull-head harp exemplifies a number of elements unique to state societies. Clearly the product of a specialist, this object, made from rare and precious materials, served to symbolize the standing of a member of the ruling class of a stratified society. Full-time specialists and social stratification are hallmarks of the state. (© The Gallery Collection/Corbis)

as part of our discussion of early evidence for an agricultural way of life. The tokens appear to have been used as counters for particular goods, symbols of specific products, and, just as important, specific quantities of these items. Schmandt-Besserat (2002) argues, for example, that a cone-shaped token was a counter for recording a small quantity of grain, while a sphere stood for a larger portion of the same material. Tokens have been found primarily in public buildings rather than private residences. Their presence in temples especially suggests their public function as well as the early connection between religion, the religious elite, and control of a food surplus. It would seem that the tokens were used to keep track of food flowing into communal grain-storage facilities or surplus food provided to the temple, perhaps as a tax or tithe.

The second step in Schmandt-Besserat's sequence began about 6,000 years ago when the tokens appear to have experienced an explosion of elaboration, jumping from 16 basic forms to about 300, with various markings etched onto their surfaces to further differentiate their meaning. More forms and the elaboration of marking them meant that more specific and precise record keeping was possible. Instead of simply recording a quantity of a material or product, the increased number and greater complexity of tokens allowed for more detailed records and for distinctions made between raw materials and goods manufactured from those materials.

By about 5,500 years ago, Schmandt-Besserat sees a third step in the development of record keeping in Mesopotamia. The tokens are no longer found as separate, individual counters but, rather, are found stored together in clay containers called

▲ **Figure 10.10**
Clay tokens with impressed or incised symbols from the Middle East. The tokens may represent the first evidence for a system of record keeping anywhere in the world. (Courtesy of Département des Antiquités Orientales, Musée du Louvre, Paris. Photograph courtesy of Denise Schmandt-Besserat)

▼ **Figure 10.11**
The cuneiform writing of Mesopotamia is the world's first written language. (© Gianni Dagli Orti/Corbis)

envelopes. Rather mysteriously, the envelopes were sealed shut, which would seem to negate the purpose of the tokens in record keeping. After all, if the appearance and number of tokens symbolically recorded the quantity of a set of objects, how could tokens still serve this useful function if they were removed from sight, stored in opaque clay containers? The Mesopotamians got around this by first impressing the tokens on the exterior surface of the clay envelope in which they were to be stored when that envelope clay was still moist and soft. So anyone who understood the token code could simply examine the surface of the clay envelope in which the tokens were stored to figure out which tokens and how many were housed therein in order to "read" the accounting information inside the container.

It took very little time for the fourth step to occur. No later than 5,200 years ago, record keepers realized that they didn't have to have a large number of individual sets of tokens stored in clay envelopes to represent and record quantities of goods. Instead, they could use a single set of tokens to directly press the information they symbolized onto a flattened piece of clay. The impressed marks on clay were no longer an indirect record of materials, recording the number and kinds of the tokens stored in an envelope, which in turn directly recorded quantities of goods. The impressed marks on slabs of clay now themselves became the direct record of the goods. As Schmandt-Besserat (2002) points out, by eliminating the use of physical objects, the tokens, as counters and by replacing them with marks impressed on soft clay surfaces, the Mesopotamians were producing the world's first texts.

There is one final, fifth step in Schmandt-Besserat's sequence. By 5,100 years ago, the tokens, which originally were the records themselves, and which had then transformed into the tools used to record the information they represented on clay tablets, were dispensed with entirely. Scribes now began impressing symbols directly onto soft clay tablets using a pointed tool, a stylus or pen, in a process of free-hand drawing. These markings, called **cuneiform**, allowed for an elaboration of the symbols marked on clay and the creation of a true system of writing (Figure 10.11).

Schmandt-Besserat's view of the origins of a system of record keeping, and, ultimately, record keeping through writing, meshes quite well with the reason why such a system was required by civilized societies. Knowledge is power, and the ability to possess and control knowledge through a system of coded, permanent records gave those who knew the code and kept the records an enormous advantage in their ability to control first the economic system and ultimately the political and social systems. Such a system allows those who keep the records to know precisely which individuals have contributed in the form of food or wealth to the temple or the king—and to know how much more is owed. Originating as a method for keeping track of mundane information, record keeping became a powerful tool for those who controlled it, a way of solidifying the power of the state. A system of record keeping, usually but not universally through writing (see the discussion of the Inca in Chapter 13), played a major role in Mesopotamia and elsewhere in allowing the state to maintain its level of control.

Egypt of the Pharaohs

Ancient Egypt is, for most people, uniquely illustrative of the mystery and allure of ancient civilization: the great pyramids at Giza, the enigmatic half-human, half-lion that is the Sphinx, and fabulous tombs filled with remarkable treasure. These monuments are all emblematic of the Egypt of the pharaohs and symbolic of the remarkable achievements of ancient Egyptian civilization at its peak. The roots of Egyptian civilization lie in the earliest Neolithic cultures that developed in the Nile Valley (Figure 10.12).

The Egyptian Neolithic

The Greek philosopher Herodotus characterized Egypt as "the gift of the Nile." By this he meant that in a vast, dead desert, the Nile is a vein of life-giving water, its valley a corridor of rich soil fertile enough to nurture the roots of one of humanity's most ancient civilizations.

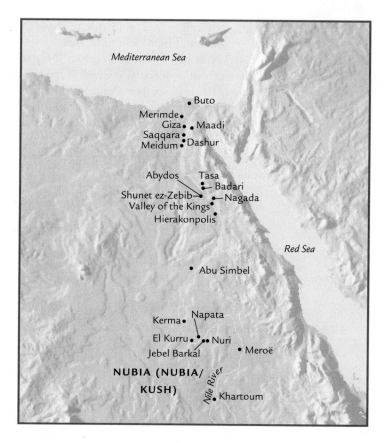

◀ **Figure 10.12**
Archaeological sites in northern Africa where evidence of early chiefdom and state-level societies has been found.

▲ **Figure 10.13**
This stunning image from space makes the point clear; the Nile Valley and delta represent a clearly delineated fertile landscape surrounded by an enormous desert. (Jacques Descloitres, MODIS Land Rapid Response Team, NASA/GSFC)

Scholars have long recognized that Egypt consists of two primary regions: Upper Egypt, which consists of the majority of the length of the Nile Valley ("upper" here refers to the flow of the river and signifies upstream and, therefore, is to the *south* because the Nile flows northward) and Lower Egypt (in the north), which is demarcated by the Nile delta, a broad, flat plain spanning about 400 km (248 mi) from east to west and 200 km (124 mi) from the mouth of the river to the south (Figure 10.13). The delta contains more than 60% of the inhabited area of ancient Egypt; the lengthy, narrow valley makes up the remaining 40%. The histories of these two regions are somewhat different and have been divided into a number of sequential components, shown in Table 10.1.

At about 5,750 years ago, compared to earlier sites in the Egyptian Neolithic, sites belonging to the **Amratian/Nagada I** culture in the south and **Omari A** culture in the north show a distinct shift in the subsistence focus, with an increasing concentration and reliance on domesticated animals, specifically sheep, goats, and cattle. These sites are larger; their occupation layers are thicker, indicating greater permanence; and their houses are more substantial: No longer oval and made of thatch, they are rectangular and made of mud-brick.

Beginning about 5,400 years ago, by **Late Gerzean** (**Nagada II** and **Maadian**) times, the first clear evidence of social inequality appears in Egypt in the form of differentiated burials. It appears that wealth in the form of finely made objects, often made of raw materials not locally available, is becoming concentrated in a nascent elite class who inter these objects with their dead (Bard 2000).

TABLE 10.1 Chronology of Predynastic Egypt

Years Ago	Upper Egypt	Lower Egypt
5,100	Protodynastic	Protodynastic
5,300	Nagada III	Nagada III
5,400	Late Gerzean (Nagada II)	Late Gerzean (Maadian)
5,650	Early Gerzean (Nagada II)	Omari B
5,750	Amratian (Nagada I)	Omari A
6,400	Badarian	
6,800		Merimden
7,200		Fayum A

Once wealth, social status, and, perhaps, political influence become concentrated in the hands of a few in a community, jockeying for even greater wealth, status, and influence occurs among the elite; and a single family under a supreme leader may come to dominate. This appears to have happened in Egypt about 5,300 years ago. At this time, in the period labeled **Nagada III** in both the north and the south, true centers of wealth and power developed as characterized by sites like Abydos, Nagada, Maadi, Buto, and, especially, Hierakonpolis. Brewer and Teeter (1999:32–33) liken these communities to city-states, small fiefdoms led by individuals they label "chieftain-kings."

Though the history of the development of the equivalent of city-states along the Nile seems clear, we are left with vexing questions: Why did power and wealth become concentrated in such places? How did individuals and their families manage to accumulate wealth, obtain power, and achieve a position in society superior to that of the rest of a community's inhabitants? The answers to these questions may be illuminated by the archaeology of one of these communities: Hierakonpolis.

Hierakonpolis

Hierakonpolis began its history nearly 6,000 years ago as a small Neolithic village on the west bank of the Nile (Hoffman 1979, 1983). Pottery manufacture became a booming business at Hierakonpolis, and ceramics manufactured in that town's kilns are found up and down the Nile. Though pottery likely originated as a small-scale, family-run affair, here it developed into a specialized craft, and a class of "pottery barons" developed. The burials of these people were larger and far more elaborate than were the interments of the rest of society. Brick-lined tombs cut into the bedrock mark the final resting places of the growing class of pottery makers.

After 5500 B.P., during Nagada II, or late Gerzean, times, irrigation canals were constructed, likely in response to a change in the local climate. A dry period that began at this time possibly resulted from local deforestation, which in turn resulted from the need to fuel the pottery kilns. The tombs of a developing elite became larger; some include a square stone building called a **mastaba** built on top of a subterranean, brick-lined or rock-cut tomb.

As population along the Nile grew and as competition for resources increased, previously small arguments or perceived injustices among and between neighboring towns grew into full-scale battles for control of the precious land base. Interestingly, the period after 5100 B.P. was marked by the abandonment of small villages located around the central places of Nagada and Hierakonpolis. The populations of the small towns seem to have moved into the larger settlements, making them substantially larger and more complex. Fortifications around Nagada and Hierakonpolis were built and expanded at this time, and the burials of the growing elite became increasingly elaborate (Kemp 1977).

First Writing

As discussed earlier in this chapter, large, complex, state societies—what we commonly call "civilizations"—need a way to keep track of wealth, goods, kinship, population, and even history. The Egyptian system of **hieroglyphic** writing is one of the best-known early systems of keeping track of these very things. The earliest evidence for Egyptian writing dates to about 5,200 years ago (Mitchell 1999; Wilkinson 2003a).

The system developed by the ancient Egyptians for recording information is a variety of picture writing. In the Egyptian system, some of the individual pictures represent entire words, others represent particular spoken sounds, and other symbols specify the meaning of the signs that precede them.

Unlike Mesopotamian writing with its long archaeological sequence beginning with clay tokens and culminating in a richly detailed and fully formed script, the origins of Egyptian writing have been difficult to trace. A team led by Egyptologist Gunter Dreyer discovered the oldest evidence of Egyptian hieroglyphics about 400 km (250 mi) south of Cairo at Abydos. Excavating a tomb the team labeled U-j, the final resting place of a leader called "Scorpion I," who ruled 5,200 years ago, Dreyer found about 200 small bone and ivory tags that were attached to containers holding linen and oil (Figure 10.14). The tags were small squares, measuring about 2 to 3 cm (0.8–1.2 in) on each side and bearing inscriptions that appear to be symbols documenting the goods, and perhaps indicating their geographic sources (Lawler 2001).

As Egyptologist Toby Wilkinson (2003a) points out, the writing on the tags is purely practical, not lauding the life of the leader with whom they were entombed, not telling great tales of the achievements of the king, of battles won or temples built. The writing on the tags simply represents an accounting of commodities, records of the materials accumulated for placement in the royal grave: how much of what provided by whom and from where.

This early writing served as the foundation for the hieroglyphic language of Egypt of the pharaohs (Figure 10.15). As noted previously, the development of a comprehensive system of record keeping like hieroglyphics is crucial in the evolution of state societies. Record keeping—usually, but not always, in the form of a written language—provides a powerful tool by which rulers can control and even monopolize information, especially related to the economy, labor, and even history itself. Winston Churchill is credited with the phrase, "History will be kind to me, for I intend to write it," and the pharaohs exploited this power, molding the story for their own benefit.

The discovery of the **Rosetta Stone** in Egypt was the key to deciphering Egyptian hieroglyphs (Figure 10.16). Carved in 196 B.C., the Rosetta Stone bore

▶ **Figure 10.14**
These inscribed bone tokens are just a few of the 200 found in the tomb labeled U-j at Abydos, the final resting place of a great leader known as "Scorpion I" who ruled more than 5,200 years ago. The tags were found attached to containers and the carved images are a form of writing, the earliest hieroglyphs yet found in Egypt, and appear to represent an accounting of goods donated to the king's burial. (© Gunter Dreyer/ Deutsches Archäologisches Institut, Kairo)

◀ **Figure 10.15**
Like our own monuments in Washington, D.C., covered with messages about our nation, its history, and political philosophy, Egyptian obelisks also were festooned with messages—in their hieroglyphic language. At the top of the photograph, you can see a supplicant on his knees in front of the pharaoh. (K. L. Feder)

▲ **Figure 10.16**
Discovered by the French military in 1799, the Rosetta Stone conveys a rather mundane message about the pharaoh Ptolemy V. More important than the narrative it presents is the fact that it presents it in three different languages including Greek and ancient Egyptian hieroglyphs. Since Greek was a known language, the Rosetta Stone provided a tool for cracking the code of the ancient hieroglyphic language of the Egyptians. (J. M. Feder)

a message consisting mostly of boilerplate establishing a cult worshipping the new pharaoh Ptolemy V. The message itself was of marginal importance; what was key is that it bore the same wording in three forms of writing: Greek and two versions of the written language of ancient Egypt, demotic and hieroglyphic. The Greek on the stone was well known when the stone was discovered in 1799 and could be read, serving, therefore, as a key to the meaning of the hieroglyphs. Through study of the Rosetta Stone, the Egyptian written language became decipherable and comprehensible.

First Pharaoh

Late in the sixth millennium B.P., a number of rulers, notably the locally powerful leaders of the city-states of Abydos, Hierakonpolis, and Nagada, appear to have attempted to unify all of the communities located along the Nile and bring them under their sway as the citizens of a single, enormously powerful nation (Wilkinson 2003b). Abydos, Hierakonpolis, and Nagada each dominated their own segments of territory along the Nile in Upper Egypt and competed amongst each other in the apparent attempt to unify the people in their cities as well as everyone else living up and down the river and to rule over them all (Figure 10.17).

▶ **Figure 10.17**
Abydos, Nagada, and Hierakonpolis were competing political and economic entities in the centuries before all Egypt was unified under a single pharaoh. This map depicts the probable geographic reaches of each of these pre-dynastic powers.

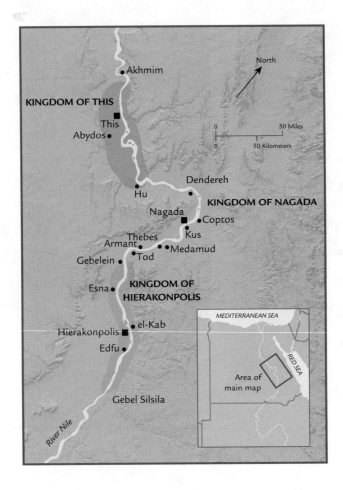

The leaders of these Egyptian city-states had become increasingly powerful and wealthy, and this growing power and wealth are reflected in their treatment upon death. For example, one burial—Tomb U-j, mentioned previously and dating to approximately 5,200 years ago—located in what appears to have been a royal cemetery at the site of Abydos, consists of eight chambers and seems to have been constructed to provide the deceased king with a small-scale model for his afterlife of the royal palace in which he lived in life (Wilkinson 2003b). Though the name of the leader interred in Tomb U-j is not known, some of the pots he was buried with bear the inscription of a scorpion. Some have, as a result, called him King Scorpion and list him among the first of the rulers over all of Egypt.

A scorpion image was also associated with an important ruler of Hierakonpolis. On a ceremonial macehead, the king is depicted in the act of ritually opening an irrigation canal. He is shown on a much larger scale than the other people on the mace head, a virtual giant, and he is wearing a crown that is seen in other depictions of kings in Upper Egypt. And there, directly in front of the great ruler's face, is the clear image of a scorpion (Figure 10.18). Some suggest that this depiction indicates that the Abydos leader buried in Tomb U-j—perhaps called King Scorpion—was considered by the people of Hierakonpolis to be their leader as well.

Egyptologists divide Egyptian history into 31 dynasties, which are, in turn, clustered into a number of periods. For a complete enumeration of the dynasties and reigns of all of Egypt's pharaohs, see http://www.touregypt.net/kings.htm. Narmer, sometimes also called Menes, is listed as the first true pharaoh, the ruler of the First Dynasty of ancient Egypt. Because King Scorpion predates Narmer, he is sometimes labeled the pharaoh of Dynasty 0.

A plaque celebrating the unification of Egypt and the ascension of the first pharaoh was discovered at Hierakonpolis. One side depicts a man with a mace or baton raised as if about to strike a kneeling enemy soldier (Figure 10.19). The standing man is wearing a crown that we know from later writing is the symbol of leadership of Upper Egypt. On the obverse of the plaque, the same man is depicted wearing a crown that includes the symbol of kingship of Lower Egypt. We can read his name on the object; it is Narmer. Narmer's ascension to the throne of Egypt occurred about 5100 B.P., about 100 years after the reign of King Scorpion.

▼ **Figure 10.18**
Found at the pre-dynastic city-state of Hierakonpolis, the Narmer Macehead shows an oversized king carrying out what appears to be an irrigation rite. Directly in front of the king's face is a scorpion. This has been interpreted as representing the name of the king—King Scorpion—who ruled Hierakonpolis. (© Werner Foreman/Art Resource, NY)

▲ Figure 10.19
The Narmer Palette
of Hierakonpolis.
The palette depicts
symbolically the
unification of Upper and
Lower Egypt under the
leadership of Narmer,
the first pharaoh in
about 5100 B.P.
(© Sandro Vannini/Corbis)

The Flowering of Egypt

After unification under Narmer, the early dynasties of ancient Egypt continued to consolidate their power as they unified the population living along the Nile within an increasingly centralized political and economic entity, the Egyptian state. The ruler, whom we can now legitimately call "pharaoh," was an all-powerful king who presided over a complex and multitiered organization. Individuals who previously had been rulers of autonomous villages or cities now were merely local administrators who owed their allegiance—and likely their continued good health—to the pharaoh. With the labor, agricultural surplus, soldiers, and wealth of not just a local community but all of the communities along the Nile at his disposal, pharaoh could conscript a vast and powerful army and a huge workforce to dig irrigation canals, construct palaces, and even build huge tombs to house his spirit in the afterlife. Pharaoh fed those thousands of laborers and warriors with the food reserves he accumulated through taxation of the enormous food surplus produced by thousands upon thousands of Egyptian farmers who, it is estimated, made up 75% of the Egyptian population of as many as 3 million people (Brewer and Teeter 1999:34).

The Egyptians continued the precedent they established in their earliest writing in the Abydos tombs of recording through their hieroglyphic writing system many of the mundane aspects of their economic lives, so we know quite a bit about how the system worked. Based on the amount of Nile flooding—those floodwaters irrigated and replenished farmland—state officials estimated regional agricultural productivity. Based on these estimates, they assessed a tax on local farmers, which they paid in bushels of grain. In return for their contribution to the state in terms of the food surplus they produced, in terms of labor and time contributed to work on state projects, and in terms of sons they provided to the army, local people were members in good standing in what was arguably the single most powerful political entity of the ancient world. Construction of irrigation canals enabled farmers to produce more food and, therefore, greater wealth. A powerful army provided secure borders that led to lengthy periods of peace and security. Participation in the rituals, rites, and obligations commanded by the gods—including working on the eternal resting place of the pharaoh, who was, himself, a god on earth—ensured a place for the individual in eternity.

A religious hierarchy developed to attend to the otherworldly affairs of ancient Egypt. For a vastly polytheistic religion, enormous bureaucracies developed to serve the needs of the gods and the needs of the bureaucracies. Though they had enormous landholdings, temples were exempt from taxation and became powerful and, in a sense, autonomous fiefdoms with agendas often different from that of the pharaoh. It is estimated that, during the Twentieth Dynasty, for example, the priesthood that served Amun, the most powerful god in the Egyptian pantheon, had at their disposal more than 40,000 laborers to tend to their lands, raising their own food and keeping cattle, goats, and fowl (Brewer and Teeter 1999:41).

During Egypt's 31 dynasties, we see a clear pattern marked by a succession of periods of political and economic domination of the rulers' world interspersed with periods of decline when power flowed back into the hands of local administrators or even foreigners.

The Pyramid Age

Egypt's Third and Fourth Dynasties mark two successive periods of power and domination. This can be seen in the frenzy of construction projects that characterize the period 2686–2498 B.C. (My dates for the pharaohs are taken from Shaw [2000], which are based on historical documents. Shaw's dates have recently been largely confirmed by precise radiocarbon dating [Ramsey et al. 2010].) Though Egypt continued as a major force in the ancient world for more than a thousand years after this, Egypt's most famous burial monuments were built during this short period of time.

Consider the first truly mammoth pharaonic burial monument, the stepped pyramid of the first pharaoh of the Third Dynasty, Djoser (Figure 10.20). Located at Saqqara and built of clay and stone, Djoser's pyramid rises through six steps to a height of roughly 60 m (197 ft). The base of the stepped pyramid covers a rectangular area exceeding 13,200 m^2 (more than 142,000 ft^2 or about 3.25 acres), and it is the primary element of a gargantuan mortuary complex of structures all built for the pharaoh.

It is in the Fourth Dynasty that an explosion of pyramid building occurs; in fact, the Fourth Dynasty is called "the pyramid age." The Fourth Dynasty's first pharaoh, Sneferu, was responsible for no fewer than three pyramids.

Sneferu was succeeded by his son, Khufu, whose pyramid has become emblematic of the technological and architectural accomplishments of ancient Egypt (see Figure 10.21). Located north of Dashur, at Giza, Khufu's burial monument

◀ **Figure 10.20**
The form of the stepped pyramid at Saqqara, built to memorialize the Egyptian pharaoh Djoser in about 4650 B.P., was based on earlier mastaba tombs of Egypt's elite. (M. H. Feder)

▶ **Figure 10.21**
The craft of pyramid building reached its apogee in the Fourth Dynasty at Giza with construction of the truly monumental burial chambers of Khufu, his son Khafre, and his grandson Menkaure. (Photo by M. H. Feder)

was finished in 2566 B.C. Consisting of more than 2.5 million stone blocks, Khufu's is the largest pyramid built in Egypt, a virtual mountain of stone rising to a dizzying height of 146.6 m (481 ft); in fact, it was the tallest human-made structure in the world until the construction of the Eiffel Tower in 1889. Khufu's pyramid is one of the iconic Giza triad of monuments (the other two are the pyramids of Khufu's son Khafre [Figure 10.22] and grandson Menkaure).

Altogether, the Egyptians constructed a little more than 100 pyramids. These final resting places of the pharaohs were not built by slaves but by Egyptian citi-

▶ **Figure 10.22**
Though by far the largest, the Great Sphinx is one of many hybrid human/lion depictions in ancient Egypt. Based on its position as part of his funerary compound, the face of the Great Sphinx is believed to depict the pharaoh Khafre. Khafre's nearby pyramid is one of the three that make up the Giza complex, including his father Khufu's (the largest pyramid in Egypt) and Khafre's son, Menkaure's. (M. H. Feder)

zens who were housed and fed, sometimes better than they were at home (see the Case Study Close-up in this chapter).

In the Eighteenth Dynasty, after the period of pyramid construction had long passed, a young boy ascended to the throne during a period of great turbulence. He ruled for approximately 10 years; he became pharaoh at the age of 9 and died when he was only 19. His name was Tutankhamun, and his splendid burial, which served as a metaphor for ancient civilization in the "Prelude" of this chapter, will likely forever stand as a symbol of ancient Egypt (see Figure 10.2).

Other African Civilizations

Ancient Egypt's influence reached far from its center in northeasternmost Africa. To the south, the ancient people of **Nubia**, initially inspired by the colossus to the north, developed their own uniquely African early civilization. The Egyptians called the land to the south **Kush**. If you travel south past the so-called first cataract near Aswan in modern Egypt (the first extensive rapids encountered moving along the Nile from north to south) into the modern nation of Sudan, continuing to the sixth cataract, north of the Sudanese city of Khartoum, you have traversed the territory of ancient Nubia (O'Connor 1993).

Dating to more than 3,500 years ago, the civilization of Kerma represents the first indigenous complex civilization in Africa south of the ancient Egyptian nation (Connah 1987). The site of Kerma itself is located on the east bank of the Nile, south of the third cataract in Sudan. The site has been called "the earliest city in Africa outside of Egypt" (O'Connor 1993:50). The center of Kerma covered 15 to 25 acres and was surrounded by a huge wall about 10 m (33 ft) high. Its fortifications included monumental towers called **deffufa**, constructed of mud-brick; the Western Deffufa is an enormous, solid mass of brick some 52 m (170 ft) long and 27 m (88 ft) wide. Today it still stands more than 19 m (62 ft) high, and it was even taller in antiquity.

To the east of the city was a large cemetery, marked by enormous **tumuli**—earth mounds marking the graves of the elite—averaging 88 m (288 ft) in diameter (O'Connor 1993:54). These graves bear witness to the degree of social stratification present in that society. The elite were placed on finely made wooden beds, some encased in gold, and well-crafted items were entombed with them for their enjoyment in the afterlife: bronze swords, bronze razors, fine clothing of leather, fans made of ostrich feathers, and large quantities of pottery. The most impressive grave in the cemetery, Tumulus X, represents the final resting place of an obviously important ruler of Kerma, surrounded by the remains of close to 400 sacrificed people (322 actual remains were found, but the burial was disturbed, and there likely were more burials interred with the primary grave).

After 2800 B.P., the influence of Kerma faded and another Nubian kingdom rose to take its place. Called Napata, it was centered just downstream of the fourth cataract. It likely developed when Egypt's long reach to the south weakened. Social stratification is evident at the cemeteries of El Kurru, Jebel Barkal, and Nuri, where the elite were buried in tombs topped with small pyramids reminiscent of those in ancient Egypt yet clearly of local construction. The main population center of the Napata polity was the very large town of Sanam.

Perhaps the best known of the ancient Nubian cultures is that of Meroë. The Meroitic civilization dates from about 2500 to 2200 B.P. and is clearly the

▲ Figure 10.23
The pyramids of the rulers of Meroë, an African civilization located to the south of pharaonic Egypt dating to between 2500 and 2200 B.P. (© Jonathan Blair/Corbis)

most complex and the most urban of the ancient civilizations south of Egypt (Connah 1987). The city of Meroë was a large settlement covering an area of about 0.75 km² (0.3 mi²). The center of the settlement consisted of a maze of monumental structures made of mud-brick and faced with fired brick. These buildings appear to have been palaces, meeting halls, temples, and residences for nobility and their workers. The central area of Meroë was surrounded by a monumental wall of mud-brick.

In an enormous graveyard excavated to the east of the city were about 600 simple interments of common people. Even farther to the east, in a graveyard called North Cemetery, the tombs of Meroitic nobility were found with small, stone pyramids built on top (Figure 10.23).

Clearly the civilizations of Nubia were at least partially indigenous developments with a heavy dose of influence from the north. Contact with Egypt may have been the catalyst that set local people on the road to great social complexity and technological sophistication. Once the process was initiated, however, Nubians evolved their own, distinct version of civilization.

Great Zimbabwe

For Europeans convinced that cultural complexity and civilization in Africa were restricted chronologically to that continent's antiquity and geographically to north of the Sahara, the ruins of Great Zimbabwe posed an intellectual dilemma. Its name was taken from the local Shona people who called the ruin, appropriately, *dzimbabwe*, "houses of stone." Indeed, these first European visitors were impressed by the immensity of its stone construction—the huge number of carefully shaped granite bricks used to build the walls that enclosed parts of the site and the majestic beauty of its dry-laid masonry (Figure 10.24). Clearly, the people who had built the great walls and enclosures of Zimbabwe had been a technologically and architecturally sophisticated people. Equally clearly, a complex social system must have been necessary to organize and oversee the labor needed to construct the very impressive remains.

The first Europeans to investigate Zimbabwe found it inconceivable that local Africans had been responsible for building the site. Their racist assumption was that sub-Saharan Africans were incapable of such a complex undertaking. As archaeologist Graham Connah (1987:183) points out, the European colonizers of Africa sought to deny the indigenous people of that continent their rightful cultural heritage. Some went so far as to suggest that Zimbabwe was associated with Solomon's Temple in Jerusalem, implying that Zimbabwe had been built not by native Africans but by interlopers from the Middle East. Such nonsense persisted for more than a century. Even into the 1960s and 1970s, attempts were made to disassociate ancient Zimbabwe from the modern inhabitants of sub-Saharan Africa (see the discussion in Garlake 1973). But the archaeological record is quite clear on this point. The builders of Great Zimbabwe and a large number of smaller sites of the same cultural tradition were the ancestors of the contemporary people of south-central Africa. More than 700 years ago, the people of Great Zimbabwe had produced their own indigenous complex society, inspired primarily by their own ability.

The Glory of Zimbabwe

Great Zimbabwe itself consists of an impressive set of stone-brick structures demarcating the central or elite precinct of a large town that likely also served as a ceremonial center for a widespread rural population, a residence for their gods as well as their chiefs. Massive and impressive, Great Zimbabwe grew by accretion as its population expanded and as its role as the central place of a developing complex society changed through time (Figure 10.25; Ndoro 1997).

Great Zimbabwe is the largest of close to 200 settlements built in the same style in an area known geologically as the Zimbabwe Plateau. A greater number of smaller sites in Botswana and South Africa without impressive stonework—for example, Danamombe, Khami, Manekweni, and Thulamela—likely represent the remains of villages that were part of a large and impressive chiefdom with Great Zimbabwe as its focal point, dating to A.D. 1100–1600 (Ndoro 1997; Figure 10.26). While these secondary sites cover tens or even hundreds of acres, Zimbabwe is larger by at least an order of magnitude, with its stone structures spread out over more than 7 km^2 (close to 3 mi^2, or nearly 1,800 acres).

Zimbabwe-style architecture includes large, dry-laid stone walls made of rectangular granite "bricks." Zimbabwe-style walls are massive and broad, with bastions, stepped platforms, towers, and large monoliths (massive, upright, single stones) incorporated into their construction (Figure 10.27). Some wall sections are ornately designed with the granite bricks laid in chevron and herringbone patterns. The monumental granite brick walls served as enclosures for a small part of the population, likely the elite of Zimbabwe society. Their homes were constructed of an extremely high-quality clay locally called **dagga**.

The two main structures at Great Zimbabwe—the "Hill Ruin" and the "Great Enclosure"—are the most imposing of the monuments built by these people. The

▲ **Figure 10.24**
Made of thousands of precisely cut granite bricks, the monumental stonework at Great Zimbabwe reflects a level of labor organization and coordination that is the hallmark of a complex society. (© Robert Holmes/ Corbis)

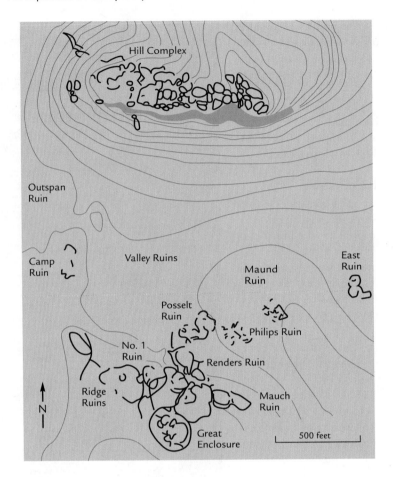

Hill Ruin is the smaller of the two, yet its walls stand some 11 m (about 36 ft) high. The Hill Ruin actually consists of two separate enclosures connected by a narrow passageway walled in with granite bricks. Altogether, the long axis of the Hill Ruin is more than the length of a football field, about 100 m (328 ft) long and 45 m (148 ft) wide. The Great Enclosure is larger still, an elliptical wall some 244 m (nearly 800 ft) in circumference, 5 m (16 ft) thick, and 10 m (33 ft) tall, enclosing a space with a maximum diameter of nearly 90 m (almost 300 ft). This truly monumental construction project required nearly 1 million granite bricks for its completion. More than simply massive, the masonry of the Great Enclosure is the finest in ancient Africa outside of Egypt. The bricks fit together virtually seamlessly; the walls are imposing yet, in places, delicately graceful. Interior walls demarcate space within the Great Enclosure, and there is, again, extensive evidence of dagga huts throughout. It has been suggested by some researchers that the Great Enclosure housed the elite of Zimbabwe society and that it was, in fact, a palace (Ndoro 1997).

Early archaeology at Great Zimbabwe centered on the great enclosures. Only recently have archaeologists turned their attention to the zone surrounding the enclosures. There they have found the remains of extensive settlements of dagga

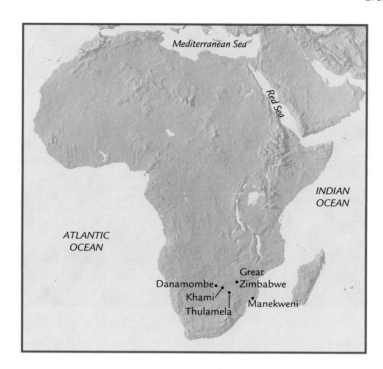

◀ **Figure 10.26**
Archaeological sites
in southern Africa
associated with Great
Zimbabwe.

huts, likely the houses of people of lower status than those residing within the walled compounds. The community had a dense, near–urban character; even the most conservative estimate puts Zimbabwe's population at its peak at about 2,000 adults (Ndoro 1997). Some have gauged the total population of Great Zimbabwe to have been as high as 18,000 at its peak (Connah 1987:184).

By one interpretation, Great Zimbabwe was the capital of a far-reaching chiefdom, sitting atop a hierarchy that included a middle level of smaller towns; there, secondary, regional elites lived within stone enclosures. A third level included small peasant villages without monumental stonework. Those living outside of the enclosures and those living in smaller villages provided the necessary economic support for the sociopolitical system by growing surpluses of sorghum and millet and by raising sheep, goats, and cattle.

The peasants provided food for the elite living in the enclosures. Archaeological faunal evidence implies that the elite had a diet different from that of the masses. For example, at the Zimbabwe site of Manekweni, it is apparent that those living outside of the enclosure were limited in their diet, with sheep and goat providing the bulk of their meat, whereas those living inside the enclosure, though they produced no food, were provided with beef for their subsistence (Barker 1978).

Zimbabwe's location may have been the key to its growth and complexity. Its location took strategic advantage of a number of trade routes, including those along which valuable ivory moved during the occupation of the site. Also, like the inhabitants of Çatalhöyük (Chapter 9), who were located near a precious and valuable resource (obsidian) and who could amass wealth as a result of controlling that resource, Great Zimbabwe was located near a significant natural source

▶ **Figure 10.27**
Example of the beautiful
masonry used in
Zimbabwe construction.
This stone tower is
located within one of the
enormous granite brick
enclosures at the site.
(© J. Laure)

of gold and likely came to dominate in its trade. The Zimbabwe elite may have derived and maintained their position as a class above the masses on the basis of the wealth they were able to accumulate through all manner of trade but, perhaps, especially this gold. That trade was widespread is evidenced in the archaeological record. Glass from Syria, faience (tin-glazed earthenware) bowls from Persia, and even Chinese celadon dishes (finely made ceramics with an olive, gray, or blue glazing) have been found at Zimbabwe (Ndoro 1997).

The walls of Great Zimbabwe and related settlements today are the most conspicuous evidence of the power of the elite in that society. It is likely that as trade in gold and other commodities served to enrich some families on the Zimbabwe Plateau, these families became economically and socially distinguished from everybody else. These elites were able to have the enclosures constructed, setting them physically apart from the great mass of people and reinforcing the fact that they were economically and socially apart from these people as well. Today the silent walls speak volumes to the archaeologist and historian, telling us that enormous power was invested in the elite of this society to direct and control the labor of the great mass of people.

Minoan Crete

The island of Crete is a tiny jewel in the eastern Mediterranean (Figure 10.28). It is long and narrow, less than 250 km (152 mi) from east to west and not more than 56 km (35 mi) from north to south. Its entire area is barely 8,260 km² (3,189 mi²), equaling, approximately, the combined area of the two smallest states in the United States: Rhode Island and Delaware. Along with being small, Crete is located a great distance from the mainland. Hominids may have occupied the island 130,000 years ago, but Crete became readily accessible only once the people of the Mediterranean developed seaworthy boats and navigational skills.

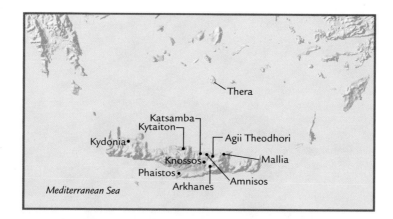

◀ **Figure 10.28**
Archaeological sites on
the island of Crete where
evidence of chiefdoms
and early state-level
societies has been found.

The oldest occupation of the island dates only to around 8000 B.P.; it was unin-habited by human beings before this time. Yet on this small island, occupied only relatively recently, Europe's first civilization was to develop.

The Rediscovery of Minoan Crete

In the 1890s, archaeologist Sir Arthur Evans discovered the remains of what he labeled the **Minoan** civilization on Crete (S. A. Evans 1921–1936). Evans had been inspired in his search by the Greek myth of King Minos of Crete, who kept a half-human, half-bull monster called the Minotaur deep in the recesses of a tortuous labyrinth. Until the twentieth century, King Minos and his civilization were assumed by many to be mythological, entirely the product of the imagi-nations of the myth- and legend-makers of ancient Greece. But some thinkers felt that the Greek myths reflected, in at least some of their particulars, historical truths. In perhaps the best-known example, archaeologist Heinrich Schliemann found the real Troy—assumed by many to be the product of the ancient Greek poet Homer's imagination—by taking Homer literally in his description of that ancient city and its location. In turn, Evans took seriously the core of the story of King Minos and a great civilization on Crete contemporary with or even older than that of ancient Greece.

Evans first visited Crete in 1894, and almost immediately recognized the great archaeological potential of a hillside at **Knossos** on the north-central part of the island. Eventually, Evans was able to purchase the site. In 1900, he initi-ated excavations and quickly discovered the spectacular remains of a great palace or temple (Figure 10.29; see the chapter titled "Arthur Evans and the Minoans" in Brian Fagan's 1994 book, *Quest for the Past: Great Discoveries in Archaeology*). This seemed to be the remains of King Minos's city, as described by the ancient Greeks. The temple was built up on an artificial mound some 7 m (almost 22 ft) high, composed of the piled-up remains of 10 successive building levels of Neo-lithic housing dating back to 8000 B.P. (J. D. Evans 1968).

Who Were the Minoans?

The settlers of Crete were people from the mainland of southeastern Europe and southwestern Asia, likely from Greece and Anatolia (Renfrew 1972:1979). Though probably initially discovered by chance, Crete soon was intentionally

▶ **Figure 10.29**
The temple at Knossos on Crete is the most impressive, though by no means the only material evidence of the monumental architecture of the ancient Minoan civilization. (M. H. Feder)

settled, in the ninth millennium B.P., by people who brought their Neolithic food base with them. Archaeological excavation of Neolithic Crete reveals the presence of emmer and bread wheat, along with sheep, goats, pigs, and cattle, none of which are native to the island (Warren 1987). The Neolithic population grew, and a number of farming villages dotted the island in the millennia following its initial settlement.

Crete was positioned geographically, at a crossroads for people sailing between southeastern Europe and the ancient civilizations of the Middle East and ancient Egypt. An influx of wealth from ancient trade between the peoples of three continents seems to have spurred a period of increasing complexity on Crete. The island itself provided perfect conditions for growing olives, and the olive oil produced on Crete and traded throughout the Mediterranean provided even more wealth to the island. A burst of development, centered on the site of Knossos, occurred at about 5000 B.P., beginning with the importation of bronze from the mainland. By about 3880 B.P., the first monumental edifice, the temple discovered and initially excavated by Evans, was constructed at the site of Knossos. The building consisted of a mazelike jumble of rooms, chambers, halls, and corridors. This main temple at Knossos is sometimes called, in fact, the "Labyrinth," a reference to the myth of King Minos's labyrinth with the Minotaur at its core (Castleden 1990a). Though fueled by trade and contact with older, established civilizations in Africa and the Middle East, civilization on Minoan Crete does not represent the transplantation of an alien culture. Crete benefited from its location, and the ideas and wealth that passed through the island certainly acted as a catalyst in the development of Minoan civilization. But as archaeologist Colin Renfrew (1979) points out, Minoan Crete by and large reflects an indigenous European development of civilized life, traceable to evolving complexity that had been going on in the Aegean for 1,000 years.

The Temple at Knossos

The temple at Knossos would at its peak ultimately cover an area of some 20,000 m² (more than 210,000 ft², or about 5 acres) and would contain about 1,000 separate rooms. The temple included a central courtyard with a pillar-lined hallway, a huge number of storage rooms, a ceremonial bath, and grand staircases leading to upper levels—some parts of the temple possessed three or even four stories. The walls of some of the living quarters and large halls were covered with magnificent fresco paintings of dolphins and especially bulls. The artistic depiction of bulls in ceremonial settings may be connected to the Greek story of the Minotaur (Figure 10.30).

One set of rooms has been interpreted as being the living quarters of the nobility of Knossos, replete with thrones, bathrooms, and a sophisticated drainage system for wastewater. The monumental proportions and complexity of the temple at Knossos are a clear indication of developing complexity in social, political, and economic spheres of the community. Further evidence of Minoan civilization is seen in the form of writing—so-called Linear A, as yet undeciphered.

Developments on Crete were halted, if only temporarily, by a catastrophic earthquake that all but destroyed the temple at Knossos in 3650 B.P. Another impressive temple on Crete at the site of Phaistos was also damaged at this time. That temple later was destroyed utterly in a fire. Remarkably, however, this catastrophe served only to spur further subsequent development on Crete in what is called the **New Temple Period**. Apparently, the wealth still pouring into the island was sufficient to overcome the impact of this natural disaster.

This peak in Minoan civilization occurred during the period 3650 to 3420 B.P. The temple of Knossos was rebuilt and became even larger and more impressive. Paintings and statuettes indicate a developing religion focused on goddesses and priestesses. Though the temple reflects a monumental level of labor on the part of

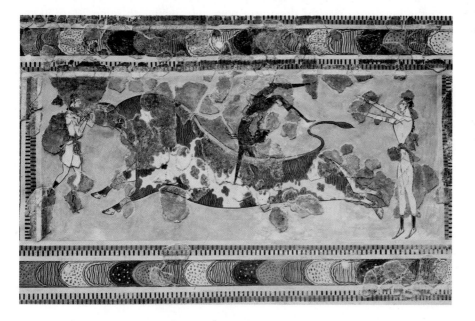

◀ **Figure 10.30**
This refurbished fresco at Knossos shows a daring gymnast performing a handstand on the back of a charging Bull. Bulls are a common theme at Knossos. (© Gustavo Tomsich/Corbis)

the island's inhabitants and would have been possible only in a socially stratified society, there is little evidence of the kind of personal conspicuous consumption on the part of the societies that marks ancient Egypt, Mesopotamia, or ancient China; there are no overwhelmingly ornate burials of an elite at Knossos or elsewhere on Crete. Small rural farming villages continued to supply their food surplus to support the temples located at Knossos and elsewhere. Large towns developed, each with its own temple and residential areas; Knossos was the largest and most impressive of these, but it was not the only one. At its peak, the population of Knossos and its surrounding "suburbs" may have been close to 100,000 people (Marinatos 1972:709), making it the largest concentration of people anywhere in the ancient world to that point in time.

The Eruption on Thera

This pattern of evolving complexity was brought to a halt by another, even more devastating natural catastrophe. Sometime around 3420 B.P. (perhaps a bit earlier) there was a cataclysmic volcanic eruption on the island today called Santorini (the ancient Greeks called it Thera, and before that it was Kalliste), 116 km (72 mi) north of Crete. The eruption itself, accompanied by severe earthquakes, badly damaged many settlements on Crete. The explosive force of the eruption of Thera has been judged to have been some four times as powerful as the volcanic conflagration of Krakatoa, a historically witnessed eruption in the Dutch East Indies in 1883 (Marinatos 1972:718). That catastrophe killed 36,000 people.

Certainly the damage to Knossos and other communities and the destruction of so many ports were devastating blows to the Minoan polity. The Minoan civilization developed and flourished, at least in part, as a result of trade; the loss of ports through which trade items passed and the probable destruction of the Minoan fleet of trading vessels must have had a tremendous impact on the Minoan economy. Perhaps of even greater significance, however, for the Minoans over the long term was the deposit of poisonous white ash some 20 to 30 cm (8–12 in) thick that fell from the sky following the explosive eruption on Thera. This rain of volcanic ash all but destroyed the agricultural economy on Crete for a time. The effects of the volcanic eruption on Thera were so widespread and catastrophic that it may have become the stuff of legend later on in the Mediterranean world; some have argued that Thera was the model for Plato's description of the Lost Continent of Atlantis (Feder 2013).

The Minoans were able to survive after Thera's eruption, but it is clear that they never fully recovered from the devastation delivered up by the eruption on Thera. It weakened them sufficiently so that soon after they were conquered by a developing civilization on mainland Greece, the **Mycenaeans**, the precursors to the ancient, historical Greeks. From there the Minoans passed into the stuff of myth and legend until Sir Arthur Evans conducted his archaeological investigation at Knossos at the outset of the twentieth century.

ISSUES AND DEBATES

MANY ISSUES AND DEBATES CONCERNING THE evolution of the world's earliest civilizations revolve around two broad questions: (1) Why did state societies develop? and (2) Why do civilized societies collapse? Why states develop is the focus of this chapter's "Issues and Debates" discussion. Why they collapse will be the focus of "Issues and Debates" in Chapters 12 and 13.

Why Did State Societies Develop?

At least initially, complex state societies offer to only a relatively small proportion of the population the "perks" so many of us expect. Especially in the world's earliest civilizations, most people worked harder than did people who lived in simpler Neolithic villages, and they gave up much of the control they had over their lives. Most people were needed to produce a surplus, part of which they turned over to the temple or the army or the state bureaucracy. Remember the estimate quoted earlier in this chapter: Perhaps as much as 75% of the population of Egypt worked as farmers, providing the state with their agricultural surplus. The peasants, who made up the greatest proportion of the population in all such societies, also provided labor for the state and often sons for military service—and possible death in foreign wars. Finally, as mentioned earlier in this chapter, simpler Neolithic societies probably were largely egalitarian, and most people had the same amount of wealth and about as much control over their lives as everyone else. With social stratification and the attendant evolution of an elite class or classes of kings, nobles, generals, and specialists, most people became second- or third-class citizens of a much larger political entity; archaeologist Thomas Patterson (1993:ix) characterizes the rulers of state societies as "bullies." Considering these factors, it seems reasonable to ask why civilization developed.

Conflict Models

Archaeologist Jonathan Haas (1982) divides explanations for the evolution of the complex civilization into the categories "conflict" and "integration." Conflict-based explanations, which Joseph Tainter (1988) calls "internal conflict" models, propose that complex civilizations evolved as a way to reduce, control, and mediate conflict among people living in a society.

Conflict theories, though diverse, have a number of fundamental propositions in common: Civilization is viewed as the outcome of a series of steps that began with the development of an agricultural economy by Neolithic people. In certain areas during the Neolithic, a substantial food surplus was possible. The production of a surplus by an individual or a family resulted in surplus, privately owned wealth. Some people got richer than others as a result of their larger surpluses. This, in turn, led to differences in status and ultimately to conflict between developing social classes. According to Joseph Tainter (1988:33), conflict theorists view the evolution of civilization and the state as the result of "divided interests" leading to domination and exploitation. An organizational solution to these conflicts arose in the form of a bureaucracy that served to validate the existence of social classes and at the same time served to mediate conflicts that arose between them.

Thus, according to the various conflict theories, agriculture led to surplus, which led to wealth, which produced different socioeconomic classes within Neolithic societies. With socioeconomic differentiation came the need to develop institutions that suppressed or mediated conflict between the newborn socioeconomic classes, often by sanctifying and legitimizing the newly evolved nonegalitarian social system. Symbols were needed to justify this new system ritually, and great works of art and architecture were produced. Thus do the social and material trappings of the state appear in the cultural evolutionary record.

Integration Models

Theories of state development that rely on models of integration rather than conflict have been proposed by thinkers as diverse as sociologist Herbert Spencer (1967), anthropologists Elman Service (1975) and Robert Carniero (1970), and historian Karl Wittfogel (1957). Integration theories, also, have a set of core propositions: Integration theories, which Joseph Tainter (1988:32) divides into "managerial" and "external conflict" models, see civilization as evolving from the need for increasingly complex integrative mechanisms in increasingly complex situations (Haas 1982:73). As Tainter (1988) points out, from the integrationist perspective, as the need developed to mobilize large and diverse populations to work together for the good of society, social institutions developed to expedite and at the same time justify, rationalize, codify, legitimize, and sanctify these activities.

From the integrationist perspective, though only a few can inhabit the top of the social, economic, and political pile, most members of civilizations do reap some benefits both directly and indirectly from the complex, stratified social system. The greatest benefits that accrue to the few—great palaces, spectacular tombs, luxurious lifestyles—are viewed as the price paid by society as a whole for the practical benefits that accrue to everyone as a result of the key social roles played by the elite.

For example, in the view of historian Karl Wittfogel (1957) in his "hydraulic hypothesis," irrigation works played a pivotal role in the development of civilization. The sedentary and secure lifeway made possible by agriculture fostered the growth of human population, and the size of some local populations increased significantly. With growth came the need to produce even greater amounts of food to feed an increasing number of mouths. This need then stimulated the need to increase the productivity of existing farmland and to expand the acreage under cultivation. Along the floodplains of large rivers, this expansion was made possible by the construction of sometimes enormous, complex, and costly (in labor investment) irrigation networks. Such waterworks required not just new technology but also new social and political institutions to organize and coordinate the labor necessary for their construction and maintenance.

Surplus labor could also be used to construct great homes and tombs for the members of the developing elite class; these material trappings of power developed as powerful symbols that served to legitimize the role of the elite class, further increasing the ability of these people to control the peasants.

Anthropologist Robert Carniero (1970) has suggested another avenue by which Neolithic societies may have crossed the threshold to civilization. Carniero cites the evidence for warfare commonly, though not universally, found in the world's early civilizations. He views this common thread as significant in the development of complex societies.

Though Carniero's use of warfare might seem to imply that his is a conflict-based model for the evolution of the state, in fact his model fits under Tainter's (1988:32) "external conflict" subset of the integrative model. In Carniero's view, in certain areas agricultural communities developed where their territories were inherently "circumscribed"—that is, geographically or socially restricted, surrounded either by unproductive farmland or productive land already inhabited by another group or groups of people. In such a scenario, once a group's home territory is filled up with a growing population, a rational option is to expand into the surrounding viable farmland or into the next group's territory by taking over their land through wars of conquest. The conquered group then becomes integrated into a larger political entity as second-class citizens. In this way, a system of social stratification develops. Social and political institutions develop to incorporate these people into a growing political unit; symbols of power evolve, legitimizing the control of the victors over the vanquished; and the seeds of civilized life are sown.

Was the Development of Civilization a Good Thing?

No matter how we formally define "civilization," I think the term inspires in most of us an image of progress, advancement, and refinement. Most, admittedly not all, perceive the development of civilization as beneficial and feel that our lives are better because of it. We live longer, in greater comfort, and have access to all kinds of toys and opportunities and choices we would not otherwise have. Maybe. At the same time, however, it's also clear in the archaeological record that the appearance of civilizations in the ancient world marks the development of some pretty unappealing behaviors resulting apparently from the need for civilizations to compete for land, natural resources, and labor (in other words, people, either as citizens or as slaves) and for the elites to more or less constantly attempt to express and reinforce their power. Organized, large-scale, intercultural violence—in other words, war—is one of the dark results of the development of civilization.

For example, archaeologists have found evidence for the slaughter of several hundred people more than 5,800 years ago, at a place called Tell Brak, 500 km (310 mi) from Damascus in modern Syria (McMahon, Soltysiak, and Weber 2011). Most of those killed were between the ages of 20 and 35. The dead were not ritually or reverentially buried; they were discovered in a disarticulated mess, in a mass grave that, according to the researchers, displayed "an extraordinary disregard" for the dead (as cited in Lawler 2012b:832). More than this, some of the bones of the deceased had been scraped down to make tools, which most likely were then used to remove the skin from the skulls, in all likelihood to make trophies for the victors of what appears to have been a vicious battle. Further evidence at the site indicates that, once having defiled the bodies of those killed, the winning side celebrated with a huge feast, dining on sheep, goats, and cattle.

Mind you, complex societies did not have a monopoly on violence. The archaeological record shows that ancient people before the development of state societies weren't living in some peaceful version of the Garden of Eden. Archaeologist Lawrence Keeley (1997) argued that almost all human groups have engaged in warfare on some level. That may be true. But the ability of complex societies to conscript and organize large numbers of people, whether to construct a canal, build an impressive burial chamber for the king, or conduct a military attack against an enemy, is several orders of magnitude higher than it is for societies that have not followed a pathway to complexity. As archaeologist Glenn Schwartz states it (as cited in Lawler 2012b:833): "Early complex societies were able to organize much more effective killing machines, given their administrative and technological capabilities and large populations." It is, perhaps, the ultimate paradox that the evolution of civilization has led to the most "uncivilized" behavior our species is capable of.

Archaeology and the Arab Spring

There was revolution in the air in the Arab world in 2012. From Morocco to Syria, dictators were being deposed, elections were held, and the voice of the people was being heard. In some cases, those dictators pushed back, resulting in the tragic deaths of thousands and even tens of thousands of people.

In the face of such political and social turmoil and in view of the human tragedy now being played out in Syria, I hope it doesn't sound too small of me to point out that the events occurring across northern Africa and the Middle East are having a negative impact on the archaeology of the region, but war and revolution have always had an effect on the study of antiquity. In Desert Storm, the first Iraq war, Saddam Hussein actually parked fighter jets adjacent to the Ziggurat at Ur (see Figure 10.8) in a cynical attempt to save them from destruction, assuming that the allied forces wouldn't dare bomb so close to one of the world's most ancient archaeological monuments (Figure 10.31). More recently, during the second Iraq War museums were looted and precious archaeological artifacts were lost. Even more recently, during a period of lawlessness, the Egyptian Museum in Cairo was looted, as were a number of archaeological sites. Zahi Hawass, the longtime director of Egypt's Supreme Council of Antiquities until Hosni Mubarak was deposed, and for many years the internationally recognized "face" of Egyptology (it was impossible in recent years to see a cable documentary about ancient Egypt in which Hawass wasn't interviewed, and he even starred in his own reality show), was removed from his position. Hawass was viewed as being too close to Egypt's deposed and imprisoned ruler, Hosni Mubarak.

▶ **Figure 10.31**
A declassified image from the first Gulf War (Desert Storm) showing two Iraqi fighter jets parked adjacent to the Ziggurat at Ur. Saddam Hussein hid them there in plain sight, apparently, in an attempt to prevent their destruction by the forces allied against him and his regime. (National Security Archive Electronic Briefing Book No. 88, "Eyes on Saddam, U.S. Overhead Imagery of Iraq," edited by Jeffrey T. Richelson. April 30, 2003. Image #42: Military Aircraft dispersed during Operation Desert Storm to Historical Site Near Tallil, Iraq. National Security Archive, Washington, D.C. www.nsarchive.org.)

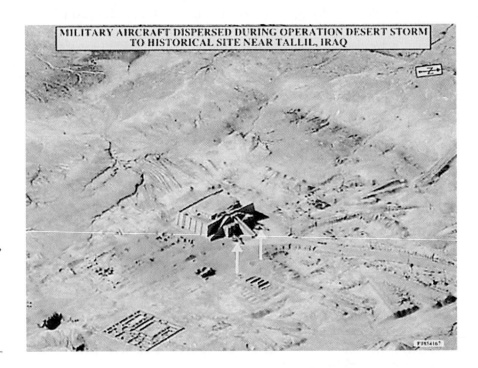

MILITARY AIRCRAFT DISPERSED DURING OPERATION DESERT STORM TO HISTORICAL SITE NEAR TALLIL, IRAQ

Though undoubtedly many foreigners conducting research in the Middle East found themselves in philosophical agreement with the goals of the Arab Spring, those foreigners also recognized that conditions were far too dangerous to continue their research (Marchant 2011). It is estimated that 120 teams of archaeologists left Syria (Lawler 2012c). We can only hope that democratically elected governments will successfully replace the dictatorships, that tyranny will be deposed, that peace will be restored, and that then archaeology can resume.

Many Paths to Civilization

None of the hypotheses proposed to explain the evolution of the world's first civilizations can be applied universally. There was no unilinear sequence of development reflected in all the cases discussed in this chapter. Not all civilizations responded to the same pressures; not all societies passed through the same sequence of steps.

In some cases (Egypt and the Indus Valley here and lowland Mesoamerica in Chapter 12), rich farmland coupled with the lack of other important resources was key to the evolution of civilization. Social complexity developed in these regions partly because society could produce a food surplus and because they needed to create an effective system of trade. In other regions (early developments at Çatalhöyük and Chavín de Huántar, discussed in Chapter 9, and places like Cerros in the Yucatán, to be discussed in Chapter 12), a rich resource base may have produced nodes of great surplus wealth and a developing social complexity. In some regions, the need to create enormous irrigation networks may have stimulated the growth of social institutions that led to social stratification. In some cases, social stratification and early state institutions may have already existed, but a quantum leap in their power may have occurred with the kind of social control made possible by the reliance on irrigation technology. In other regions, the need for large-scale defensive works may have resulted in the same kinds of changes in society (for example, in Mesopotamia, discussed here, and China, discussed in Chapter 11).

It seems there were many different pathways leading to societies we today recognize archaeologically as possessing the requisite features of what we have defined as civilization. Many cultural evolutionary roads have led to essentially the same place, and it is likely that not one but some—possibly all—of the explanations offered here can help us understand the process in each of the areas discussed. It also is likely that quite different combinations of these explanations can be differentially useful in explaining what transpired in the world's first civilizations.

IF YOU HAVE EVER SEEN THE Hollywood epic motion picture *The Ten Commandments*, with Charlton Heston in the role of the biblical Moses, you are familiar with the notion that the Egyptians relied on slave labor in the construction of their temples and tombs. In this view, under the crack of the overseer's whip, foreigners like the Hebrew immigrants to Egypt mentioned in the Old Testament, large numbers of war captives, and an assortment of criminals serving out their sentences together toiled under the ferocious Egyptian sun, literally worked to death in the service of the state.

**CASE STUDY
CLOSE-UP**

The archaeological record, however, is beginning to show something quite different. Remember, thousands, even tens of thousands of people, worked on construction projects like the pyramids; and these workers needed to be housed and fed. An enormous infrastructure needed to be established to provide all of the support services such a large workforce required. Virtual worker cities must have sprung up around these construction sites, and the archaeology of these communities shows a picture very different from the common conception of the lives of those who built the pyramids and palaces of ancient Egypt. For example, in 1999, Egyptologist Mark Lehner initiated a major project to excavate one of these worker cities on the Giza Plateau located in the shadow of the three great pyramids of the pharaoh Khufu, his son Khafre, and grandson Menkaure (Figure 10.32). If the workers who built these pyramids had been slaves, one might have expected that their overseers viewed them as largely expendable—with a strategy of treating them just well enough to keep them alive and working, but not expending a substantial amount of effort to keep them comfortable and healthy. Lehner interprets his archaeological research in the city as strongly contradicting this perspective. For example, he has found the remains of food provided to the pyramid workers; and, contrary to what one might expect of a slave class, they were eating better than nearly everybody else in Egypt. Lehner's crew has found and identified in the worker city a prodigious quantity of animal bones, especially of cattle, sheep, and goat, enough

▼ **Figure 10.32**
Excavation by Egyptologist Mark Lehner of the remains of the community of pyramid builders belies the common misconception that the tombs of the pharaohs were built by slaves. Lehner has found that the people who worked on the pyramids were well housed and ate better than most other Egyptians of their social class. (© Kenneth Garrett)

to support a crew of several thousand people eating meat every day, something not seen in the average Egyptian community (Shaw 2003:49). Further, Richard Redding, a faunal analyst examining the bones recovered by Lehner's crew, has determined that the animals being used to feed the pyramid workers had not been old and sick castoffs, as might be expected had the workers been slaves. Instead, the bones indicate that the animals used to feed the workers had been in their prime; much of the cattle bone came from young male animals, under two years of age (Shaw 2003:49). The archaeological evidence at Giza shows no prison camp or slave compound, but comfortable barracks, looking like over-sized Egyptian homes; an abundance of bakeries; and even cemeteries where the dead workers were accorded a level of respect and care in death that would be highly unlikely had they been slaves. In fact, recently a cluster of the tombs of pyramid workers has been found right alongside the Giza pyramids. Zahi Hawass points out that no slave tombs would have been built so near the pharaoh's burial site. Only highly esteemed workers, not slaves, would have been allowed such an honor.

Make no mistake, projects like constructing Khufu's pyramid were back-breaking and dangerous, but Lehner and others are confident that the labor, while likely not entirely voluntary, was, in large measure, considered a sacred duty by the citizens of Egypt. Today, people may complain about paying their taxes and, in the recent past of the United States, they may have worried about their sons being drafted into the Army; but citizens comply, viewing taxation and conscription as the price to be paid for living in a nation that builds roads and schools, protects its citizens and their property from criminals, and guards the borders from the attacks of enemies.

In a few instances, the pyramid workers of ancient Egypt left us messages in their own words, written on the enormous blocks of stone it had been their responsibility to move into place. These messages, perhaps more than anything else, provide us a unique insight into their own perspective of the nature of their labor for the state. Deep within Khufu's pyramid is a stone bearing this message: "We did this with pride in the name of our great King Khnum-Khuf," the formal name of the Pharaoh Khufu (Jackson and Stamp 2003:78). Those are not the words of slaves, but a message of pride by a group of pyramid workers who perceived their labor as the meaningful and necessary contribution of citizens serving their state.

Summary

The Neolithic set the stage for the development of sedentary farming villages in various places in the Old World. In a select few regions, an acceleration of cultural complexity led to the development of a stratified social system that controlled the excess wealth made possible through the ability to produce an agricultural food surplus. Social elites developed as part of a reorganization of society that allowed for orderly and systematic trade, the construction of irrigation canals to increase the food base, and the construction of monumental defensive fortifications. In these same regions, the new way of organizing and controlling human labor was utilized by the developing elite to construct less practical monumental works—temples, palaces, and mortuary features such as pyramids. This kind of monumental construction, today diagnostic of ancient civilizations, was both cause and effect of the new social dynamic of the world's first civilizations. Large, impressive monuments served as dramatic evidence of the power of the elite and symbolized and reified this power at the same time that it magnified it. In the Old World, the processes that led to the kinds of societies we are calling civilization occurred in Mesopotamia in the Middle East, in the Nile Valley of Egypt, in Sudan, in southern Africa, and on the island of Crete in the Mediterranean, all discussed in this chapter, and in the Indus Valley in Pakistan and in China, to be discussed in Chapter 11.

TO LEARN MORE

To learn more about the development of Mesopotamian civilization, see Harriet Crawford's *Sumer and the Sumerians* (1991). A thorough and detailed exposition of the history of ancient Egypt, beginning in its earliest prehistory, with chapters on each of the important kingdoms and dynasties can be found in *The Oxford History of Ancient Egypt*, edited by Ian Shaw (2000). For a detailed chronology of the reigns of each of the pharaohs, see Peter A. Clayton's *Chronicle of the Pharaohs* (1994). If you've ever wondered about how the ancient Egyptians accomplished their heroic feats of engineering and architecture, don't miss Dieter Arnold's *Building in Egypt* (1991). For a fascinating account of the engineering behind pyramid building, see Bob Brier and Jean-Pierre Houdin's *The Secret of the Great Pyramid* (2008). For a wonderful chronological treatment of ancient Egypt, see Mark Lehner's *The Complete Pyramids* (1997). For a broad-ranging book on the most popular—and yes, sometimes mysterious—topics surrounding the ancient Egyptian civilization, with articles written by an array of experts, *The Seventy Great Mysteries of Ancient Egypt* (2003), edited by Bill Manley, is informative, well written, and great fun.

Webber Ndoro's *Scientific American* article, "Great Zimbabwe" (1997), is a terrific source of information about this southern African kingdom. Rodney Castleden (1990b) is a terrific writer on topics related to the ancient world, and his book *Minoans: Life in Bronze Age Crete* is one of the best summaries of Europe's first civilization.

Web links for this chapter can be found at www.oup.com/us/feder

KEY TERMS

Amratian/Nagada I, 356
city-state, 352
civilization, 344
class society, 345
cuneiform, 354
dagga, 367
deffufa, 365
envelope, 354
hieroglyphic, 357
Knossos, 371

Kush, 365
Late Gerzean (Nagada II, Maadian), 356
mastaba, 357
Minoan, 371
monumental work, 345
Mycenaeans, 374
Nagada III, 357
New Temple Period, 373
Nubia, 365

Omari A, 356
Rosetta Stone, 358
social stratification, 346
specialization of labor, 348
state, 344
system of record keeping, 348
token, 353
tumuli, 365
Ubaid, 350

11

An Explosion of Complexity

The Indus Valley and China

CHAPTER OVERVIEW

"Civilization," characterized by the existence of a formal government, social stratification, large and dense settlements, monumental edifices, elaborate burials, large armies, full-time artisans, and a system of record keeping, developed in some parts of the Old World as fewer people were needed in the subsistence quest and as rulers attempted to legitimize, reinforce, and magnify their position of power and their level of wealth. This chapter focuses on two of the earliest examples of these complex societies: the Indus Valley and China.

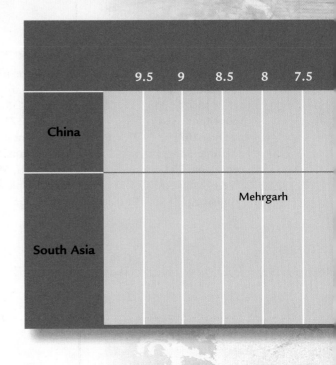

	9.5	9	8.5	8	7.5
China					
South Asia			Mehrgarh		

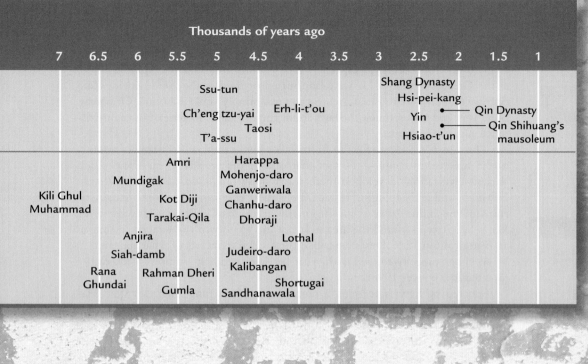

Thousands of years ago

7	6.5	6	5.5	5	4.5	4	3.5	3	2.5	2	1.5	1

Ssu-tun

Ch'eng tzu-yai

T'a-ssu

Taosi

Erh-li-t'ou

Shang Dynasty
Hsi-pei-kang
Yin
Hsiao-t'un

Qin Dynasty
Qin Shihuang's mausoleum

Amri

Mundigak

Kili Ghul
Muhammad

Kot Diji

Tarakai-Qila

Anjira

Siah-damb

Rana
Ghundai

Rahman Dheri

Gumla

Harappa
Mohenjo-daro
Ganweriwala
Chanhu-daro
Dhoraji

Lothal
Judeiro-daro
Kalibangan
Shortugai
Sandhanawala

PRELUDE

CHRONICLE

IN A SENSE, THERE WAS NO need for modern scholars to "discover" the ancient civilizations of Egypt and Mesopotamia. Both were historically well recorded by subsequent cultures and both were discussed in the Old Testament of the Bible. Many of the ruins of Egypt, especially the pyramids and the Great Sphinx, as well as the Great Ziggurat of Ur were not buried or hidden; they were obvious and obtrusive to any who visited their locales and simply walked around. Of course, there was, and still is, much to learn about these ancient societies, but their existence surprised no one.

This was not the case for the Indus Valley civilization of Pakistan. As recently as the nineteenth century, the fact that one of the world's greatest and oldest ancient civilizations developed there was wholly unknown, at least to Western historians and archaeologists. In fact, the earliest reference we have to enigmatic ruins in the Indus Valley comes from the account of a British Army deserter, James Lewis, who visited the area near the modern town of Harappa (posing as an American) in 1826. Lewis described the eroded remnants of what appeared to be an enormous city topped with what he described as a "ruinous brick castle" (as cited in Kenoyer 1998:20).

Spurred by Lewis's account, a number of British functionaries visited Harappa in the mid-1850s, but little came of it. Some assumed that what Lewis had described were the remains of a short-lived Buddhist community that dated to A.D. 625 to A.D. 645. When no obvious Buddhist artifacts were found there, scholars largely lost interest in the site and they looked no further and, it turns out, no deeper.

What happened next to reveal the extent of the ancient city of Harappa is ironic in the extreme. The British began building a rail system in the nineteenth century between the cities of Lahore and Multan. As there was a dearth of suitable stone to use to line the railway bed, the engineers of the project decided, instead, to collect and grind up ancient bricks found abundantly in mounds up and down the Indus, including the vast quantities available in the large mounds at Harappa. The sad fact is that much of what turned out to be the upper layers of the ancient city of Harappa were destroyed by the collection of the bricks with which its buildings were constructed.

It wasn't until the late nineteenth century that archaeologists rooting around in the devastated site began finding stone seals with inscriptions never before seen. If the site was not a historical Buddhist community, what was it and when did it date to? These questions inspired additional archaeological work in the 1920s, both at Harappa and at another enormous, enigmatic series of brick mounds 570 km (350 mi) to the south at a place called Mohenjo-daro. It was only through careful archaeological work in the early twentieth century that researchers realized that what appeared to be nothing more than giant, amorphous mounds of bricks were, in fact, the remains of two extraordinary, planned-out ancient cities filled with spectacular art, including bronze sculptures and gold jewelry, and also seals inscribed in an unrecognized language. And all of this was revealed through the report of an army deserter and the mining of the site for the construction of a railway bed.

SCHOLARS WERE STUNNED AND FACED WITH a fundamental question: Who were the people who built these marvelous cities along the Indus? It is a question archaeologists are still in the process of answering.

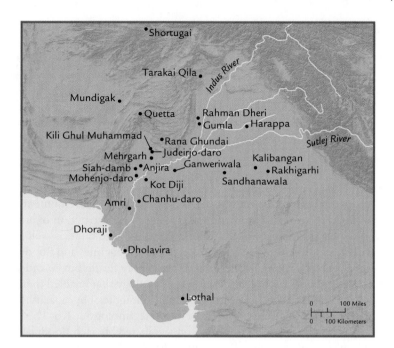

◀ **Figure 11.1**
Archaeological sites in India, Pakistan, and Afghanistan where evidence of the evolution of chiefdoms and early state-level societies has been found.

The Indus Valley Civilization

The roots of the Indus civilization are revealed in a series of archaeological sites located to the west (Figure 11.1). For example, the site of Mehrgarh is located along the course of the Bolan River as it exits the foothills of the mountainous region called Baluchistan. First occupied more than 8,500 years ago, the residents of Mehrgarh survived, in part, by hunting wild animals, especially deer, gazelle, and wild pig, but even in the earliest levels of the site there is evidence that people living at Mehrgarh raised domesticated goats and planted some wheat and primarily barley (Kenoyer 1998). Both the goats and the wheat had been brought in from the west; it would seem that the site's residents borrowed the idea of food production from their neighbors on the western Iranian plateau.

The village grew in size and complexity, and by 8,000 years ago Mehrgarh's residents were building large and compartmentalized facilities of mud-brick in which they appear to have been communally storing their grain (McIntosh 2002). The village included a number of residential units containing between six and nine rooms, probably the homes of individual families.

Around this time we also see the elaboration of burial practices, with people being interred with stone tools, bead and shell jewelry, and baby goats. Some of the shell objects found adorning the deceased were produced from conch, whose nearest source would have been the Arabian Sea, about 500 km (310 mi) to the south of the village. Jewelry made from lapis lazuli from Badakshan in northeastern Afghanistan and turquoise from Turkmenia, north of Afghanistan, was found in the burials as well; the sources of these stones are as much as 500 km (310 mi) distant from Mehrgarh. We also see at this time and accelerating after 7,500 years ago a decreased reliance on the hunting of wild animals; the frequencies of their bones in hearths and middens drop sharply as those of domesticated goats and cattle dramatically increase, signifying their expanded importance in subsistence at Mehrgarh.

Mehrgarh's location at the zone of transition between the uplands to the west and the floodplain to the east is important in our investigation of the Indus Valley civilization. The Indus is a treacherous river characterized by devastating and unpredictable flooding. Unlike the situation seen in Egypt or Mesopotamia, early Neolithic sites are not found along the river. As archaeologists Bridget Allchin and Raymond Allchin (1982:105) point out, local inhabitants' realization that the Indus system offered incredibly rich agricultural soil, coupled with their development of flood control and protection technology, allowed for the evolution of "an entirely new way of life."

Flood Control and Civilization in the Indus Valley

This shift to the floodplain was the key to the development of civilization in this part of the world. It was made possible by the development of technology for flood control and protection, including the construction of artificial mounds, on which at least a portion of the settlements were built, as well as monumental walls around entire villages for protection from enemies and floodwaters. In other words, the floodplain of the Indus is incredibly fertile but in order to exploit its rich soil, people needed to develop a technology that enabled them to control or, at least, mitigate the river's powerful and unpredictable capacity for destruction. We see the development of flood-control technology at Kot Diji.

The site of Kot Diji is located on the incredibly rich floodplain about 32 km (20 mi) east of the Indus River, immediately adjacent to one of its ancient flood channels (Figure 11.2). The village is surrounded by a huge wall with a limestone rubble foundation and a mud-brick superstructure with bastions upward of 5 m (more than 16 ft) high. This wall almost certainly served as defense not only against human enemies but also against a natural enemy—the floodwaters of the Indus. To the northeast is another large village called Kalibangan. Here, too, a massive mud-brick wall surrounds the settlement. Other substantial walled villages on the Indus floodplain, dating to the period after 5500 B.P., include the sites of Amri, Gumla, Rahman Dheri, and Tarakai Qila.

▼ **Figure 11.2**
The site of Kot Diji is located on an ancient channel of the Indus River in Pakistan. Kot Diji was surrounded by a monumental wall whose purpose likely was to keep its residents secure from human enemies as well as the floodwaters of the Indus. (Department of Archaeology and Museums, Karachi)

Cultural Convergence

An interesting feature of these settlements is the degree of what Jane McIntosh (2002:48) calls "cultural homogenization." Where previous Neolithic sites in Baluchistan all exhibit their own artifact styles in pottery and items of adornment, as people began moving out onto the floodplain of the Indus, a certain degree of uniformity appears, indicating a greater level of cultural and perhaps political unification. Most significantly, a common image of a horned water buffalo head begins appearing on pottery throughout the area at many of the sites mentioned. Also, terra-cotta statues of women, following a standardized style, appear at many of the sites dating to this period; some archaeologists have dubbed these "mother goddesses," implying a degree of religious unification as well (Allchin and Allchin 1982:163).

The spread of a shared religious iconography typifies the consolidation of ancient civilizations. We saw it in Chapter 9 in relation to the Olmec of Mesoamerica and the Chavin of South America. We are seeing it here, in the Indus Valley. We will see it again.

A few of these floodplain settlements began undergoing an exponential increase in size sometime after 4800 B.P., culminating in their crossing the boundary between town and true city. Five of these communities expanded in physical size as their populations grew, coming to dominate the physical and cultural landscapes of the Indus Valley. The initially small villages of Ganweriwala and Rakhigarhi each grew to cover more than 0.8 km^2 (about 200 acres or 0.3 mi^2). Another small village, Dholavira, expanded until it extended across an area of 1 km^2 (0.39 mi^2 or 247 acres); located on a now dry channel of the Ravi River, tributary to the Indus, the urban center of Harappa expanded over more than 1.5 km^2 (0.58 mi^2 or 370 acres); and, located along the southern reaches of the Indus River, the truly gargantuan Mohenjo-daro is estimated to have sprawled out across more than 250 hectares (about 1 mi^2 or 617 acres; all data were taken from Kenoyer 1998:49). Remember, these figures reflect the physical extent only of the urban centers themselves on the basis of the spread of archaeological evidence of houses, temples, streets, industrial zones, and the like. The surrounding hinterlands, populated by farmers whose produce literally fed the growth of the Indus Valley urban centers, were far larger. Kenoyer (1998:50) estimates that each of the five Indus cities just listed dominated an area of between 100,000 km^2 (38,000 mi^2, or an area greater than the state of Indiana, in the case of Ganweriwala) and nearly 170,000 km^2 (66,000 mi^2, or about the size of Washington State, in the case of Mohenjo-daro).

Cities of the Indus

During what archaeologists refer to as the "Mature Harappan period," lasting for 500 years, from 4500 to 4000 B.P. (Possehl 1980:5), Mohenjo-daro and Harappa developed into complex urban centers, with planned neighborhoods following a rectangular grid pattern, a sophisticated drainage system, communal granaries, bathhouses, and "citadels" consisting of great structures (palaces, temples, or even granaries; their function is not clearly known) built atop artificial mounds (Figure 11.3).

There are no census records for Harappa and Mohenjo-daro, so their populations, of course, can only be estimated. Certainly they were in the tens of

▲ **Figure 11.3**
The citadel of Mohenjo-daro (background) looms over the remnants of neatly gridded outstreets lined with the houses of the Indus Valley civilization's elite social class. (© Paul Almasy/Corbis)

thousands. Kenoyer (2005:29) suggests that the population of Harappa likely exceeded 40,000 and at its peak (both seasonally and in terms of its overall growth through time) may have been as high as 80,000. Estimates for the more expansive Mohenjo-daro are commensurately larger. Remember again, these estimates apply only to the urban centers themselves. Each Indus city was served by a large and dispersed support population in its surrounding hinterlands living in an estimated 1,500 smaller settlements spread throughout the Indus Valley (Kenoyer 2005:27). Most of these were small agricultural villages with areas of between 1 and 10 hectares (between 2.5 and 25 acres), but there were a few larger villages as well of between 10 and 50 hectares in extent (between 25 and 124 acres).

The degree of planning that went into Indus Valley urban sites is unmatched among the earliest civilizations. Mohenjo-daro, Harappa, and Kalibangan follow virtually identical plans (Figure 11.4). There is, as Jane McIntosh (2002:124) phrases it, an "essential unity" to the organization of life in the Indus civilization. In these three cases, a citadel was built up on a platform of mud-brick on the western margin of the city. The citadel was surrounded by large public buildings, including bathhouses and granaries, and this "upper city" was encompassed by a monumental wall. In each of these three cases, the vast expanse of the city—the residential area where tens of thousands of people lived—was spread out to the east of the citadel. The lower city likewise was surrounded by a great wall. In all three cases, it is clear that the cities did not grow simply by accretion, blocks of residences added haphazardly as they were needed in response to population growth. Instead, these cities reflect a pattern of forethought in their construction, with broad main paved thoroughfares separated by secondary streets, which were, in turn, separated by narrow passageways leading to individual residences. Most of the roads were laid out in an often precise grid of parallel and perpendicular pathways. The alignment of the roads is precisely along the cardinal directions, which likely were determined astronomically (Kenoyer 1998:52). The houses themselves were made of mud-bricks that are so regularly and consistently proportioned (most bricks are made in fixed proportions of 1:2:4), it is clear that brick makers, like their modern counterparts in brickyards, adhered to established size and form standards.

Standardization extended to issues of water and sewage. Archaeological excavation of housing blocks at Mohenjo-daro has shown that each of those blocks, and in some cases, each individual house, possessed its own well. For sanitary disposal, excavations at Harappa show that nearly every house possessed its own latrine. Most of these individual toilets led to a large jar with a hole at the bottom

0   30m

to allow waste to drain into the soil. Some were connected to a brick-lined drain that allowed waste to flow out and away from the house, an early version of a sewer system.

Altogether, the Indus civilizations appear to have been highly centralized and tightly controlled, from the layout of their cities, the shapes of their bricks, and even the organization of their economy, including standardized weights and measures found in excavations at Indus cities. The dwellings in the lower cities of Indus urban centers, however, were not built on a standard plan and, instead, exhibit a wide range in size, from single-room apartments to mansions with dozens of rooms and enclosed courtyards. The size and elaborateness of some residences almost certainly reflect vast differences in the wealth and status of the individuals who lived in them. Certain sections of each of the Indus cities were blocked out for the production of goods by specialist craftspeople. McIntosh (2002) enumerates clusters of specialist workshops throughout Indus cities, including those of potters, flint workers, metal workers, brick makers, shell workers, precious-stone workers, ivory carvers, wood workers, textile makers, and seal makers. Other areas of the cities appear to have been the residences of scribes, priests, administrators, and traders (Allchin and Allchin 1982:185). Add to this workshops in which workers baked bread and others where beads were manufactured and you have a picture of a bustling, busy metropolis.

▲ **Figure 11.4**
This map of Mohenjo-daro exhibits the planned nature of the city with its major avenues, parallel and perpendicular streets, and regularly sized buildings and rooms. (From M. Wheeler, *The Indus Civilization*, Fig. 10. Copyright © 2005 Cambridge University Press. Reprinted with the permission of Cambridge University Press.)

Indus Valley cities were also trading centers into which exotic and undoubtedly expensive raw materials flowed and in which finely finished goods were produced. Raw gold, copper, lead, lapis lazuli, turquoise, alabaster, amethyst, agate, chalcedony, and carnelian were brought into the city, although they often originated at sources many hundreds of kilometers distant (Allchin and Allchin 1982:186). Finely made goods made from these exotic materials by Indus Valley artisans are found throughout central Asia in sites in Iran, Afghanistan, and Iraq (Lawler 2008a).

Trade was carried out between these Indus Valley cities and the city-states of ancient Mesopotamia. Harappan seals have been found in Mesopotamia, and a small number of Mesopotamian **cylinder seals** have been found in Indus Valley sites. The island of Bahrain, located in the Persian Gulf, served as a central point in this intercivilization trade network. In other words, more than 4,000 years ago, Mesopotamia and the Indus Valley were part of an international trading system.

The Indus Script

To date, approximately 4,000 Indus inscriptions have been unearthed. Simple symbols have been found dating to as much as 5,200 years ago, but the script was not in widespread use until 800 years later, about 4,400 years ago. There are between 400 and 450 more or less distinct symbols used in the script, most of them in the form of animal pictographs and abstract geometric patterns (Figure 11.5). Unfortunately, there has been no discovery equivalent to the **Rosetta Stone** (see Chapter 10) in the Indus Valley, and the language remains largely indecipherable.

Most of the inscriptions have been found on small clay tablets; some are etched into pottery vessels, others on copper tablets. Kenoyer (2005:30) suggests that the context of the inscriptions and the co-occurrence of symbols indicate that, like the earliest Mesopotamian cuneiform and the first of the Egyptian glyphic writing, the Indus script served a rather mundane, economic purpose: keeping count of lands, goods, and other materials, essentially the record keeping of accountants. Kenoyer (2005:28) calls the Indus script "economic documentation" through a shared set of symbols.

"A Peaceful Realm"

The title of archaeologist Jane McIntosh's (2002) wonderful book on the Indus civilization makes an important point about its development as a complex society: *A Peaceful Realm.* There simply is no evidence that organized warfare or armies or the fear of attack played any role in

▼ **Figure 11.5**
These inscribed ceramic tiles were found in excavations at the Indus Valley city of Mohenjodaro and appear to reflect an early, locally developed form of writing. Though not yet deciphered, the writing appears to represent an accounting of lands, goods, and other materials. (Charles and Josette Lenars/Corbis)

the development of civilization in the Indus Valley. Archaeologists have not found evidence of major military defensive works around Indus cities or villages, no weaponry in the artifact assemblage, no cemeteries filled with skeletons exhibiting mortal wounds that would have resulted from military battles. Though, as we will see in "Issues and Debates" in this chapter, some researchers believe that organized conflict, invasion, and subjugation of a defeated population are key elements in the development of a powerful state society, the Indus Valley civilization provides no evidence to support this scenario. The Indus Valley, indeed, appears to have been a "peaceful realm," showing us that the development of a civilization need not involve the uniquely human invention, war.

The Civilization of Ancient China

It's important to remember that, though I may organize my discussion of the earliest civilizations according to the borders of modern nation-states, I am doing so only as a result of geographic expedience. For example, though I am now going to talk about ancient Chinese civilization, the modern borders of China encompass a vast and diverse landscape through which multiple channels of cultural evolution flowed. Not one, but many of these channels contributed directly to the flowering of East Asian civilization as represented in the first dynastic period called the Shang. As archaeologist Jiang Weidong states it, Chinese civilization cannot be traced to one site, one culture, one river valley, or even one region but, instead, "the origin of Chinese civilization is scattered all over the country" (as cited in Lawler 2009a:935) (Figure 11.6).

One of these early channels is located along the Tiaoxi River, near Liangzhu, in eastern China, about 200 km (125 mi) southwest of the modern city of

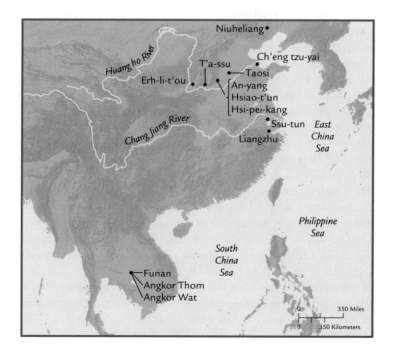

◄ **Figure 11.6**
Archaeological sites in China where evidence of chiefdoms and early state-level societies has been found.

▲ **Figure 11.7**
This beautiful bracelet was carved from a single piece of stone as much as 5,000 years ago. The face is that of a dragon. (Asian Art and Archaeology Inc./Corbis)

Shanghai. Dating to between 5,500 and 4,250 years ago, the principal Liangzhu site is characterized by a monumental defensive wall encircling the village. The wall is about 7 km (almost 23,000 ft) in circumference, enclosing an area of about 3.9 km^2 (1.5 mi^2 or nearly 1,000 acres). Archaeologist Liu Bin estimates that the earthworks would have taken 10,000 workers about 2 years to have constructed them (as cited in Lawler 2009a:930).

Within the encircling wall, archaeologists have identified large earth platforms, some housing the tombs of a rising elite class. The members of this elite were buried with finely made objects (Figure 11.7), including works in jade. This is important at such an early period. It appears that the development of an elite class in early Chinese civilizations is closely associated with the production of beautiful jade objects in several regions. Archaeologist Elizabeth Childs-Johnson (cited in Lawler 2009a) points out that jade is, essentially, the gold of ancient China. It was rare, precious, and highly valued. In quarrying the stone and in having spectacular works of art sculpted from it, the Chinese elite classes were flexing their economic muscles and establishing their position at the apex of the social pyramid.

Far to the north, near the modern city of Liaoning, another channel of increasing complexity is seen at sites in the Hogshan culture. There, even earlier than at Liangzhu, burials of an emerging elite class have been identified dating to as much as 6,500 years ago. Again, archaeologists recognize this from the inclusion of beautiful jade carvings, including those of dragons and Phoenixes in those burials. At one of the Hogshan sites, Niuheliang, in the Liao River Valley, researchers have found the burials of 18 high-status individuals dating to 5,000 years ago. The most elaborate of those burials contained 20 items of carved jade including discs, beads, bracelets, hair tubes, and a fanged plaque (Lawler 2009a).

The Lung-shan Culture

Other examples of emerging complexity and evidence of the development of an economically advantaged elite group of rulers are found throughout China. The best-known example is called the **Lung-shan** culture, located in the Huang ho or Yellow River Valley (Wangping 2005). Its progenitor was the older Yang-shao discussed in Chapter 8. Beginning about 5,000 years ago, a number of new features distinguish Lung-shan sites from earlier Yang-shao sites and presage the development of early Chinese complex civilizations. Rice became the dominant cultigen, and sites are larger and more permanent. For example, at the Lung-shan site of Ch'eng tzu-yai, the village was enclosed by a monumental wall of stamped earth whose size is an indication of the villagers' capacity for communal labor. The Chinese term for the stamped or pounded earth technique used in construction is **hang-t'u.** The hang-t'u technique was used frequently in later periods of Chinese history in making house walls as well as in defensive structures.

The wall at Ch'eng tzu-yai is enormous and far beyond the abilities—and needs—of earlier people to muster the labor of a large population. The wall is measured at 390 m (nearly 1,300 ft) by 450 m (nearly 1,500 ft), is 9 m (29 ft) wide at the top, and is 6 m (more than 19 ft) high (Chang 1986:248). The cemetery at the site reflects another significant element of civilization: status differentiation as reflected in highly differentiated burials. Archaeologist Kwang-chih Chang (1986) notes the existence of a multitiered burial hierarchy. There are large elaborate graves at the site—high-status tombs where the deceased was interred in a wooden casket and accompanied by fine ceramics. In the same cemetery, there are narrow burial pits barely large enough to hold a human body, with no casket or grave goods. In the typical pattern of a stratified society, there were far fewer members of the elite than of the peasant classes, again as reflected in the burial statistics. From most to least elaborate interments, at Ch'eng tzu-yai there were 5 upper-class, 11 second-class, 17 third-class, and 54 fourth-class, or low-class, burials (Chang 1986:249).

Take a look at Table 11.1, compiled by data presented by Shao Wangping (2005), for the giant Lung-shan cemetery at Taosi. The 700 burials excavated at the cemetery (of an estimated 10,000) can be broken down into three, general, socioeconomic status levels: high, medium, and low.

The numbers in Table 11.1 clearly support Wangping's contention that the Lung-shan is characterized by growing differences in economic wealth and social status. The percentages of high-, medium-, and low-status graves are a material reflection of the socioeonomic pyramid that typifies complex societies as depicted in Figure 10.4 with few at the top, more in the middle, and the great majority of the population representing the base.

Along with monumental village walls, which later became a common feature of Chinese civilization, and status-differentiated burials, the period from 5,000 to 4,000 years ago in China is marked by the appearance of a number of other features that represent key elements in the earliest Chinese civilization. The increasing use of metal, especially copper, and the earliest use of bronze is evidenced during this time.

A number of other identifiable hallmarks of later Chinese civilization appear at this time, between 5,000 and 4,000 years ago. The jade *ts'ung* tubes and the practice of **scapulimancy**—divining by interpreting the patterns produced by heating animal shoulder blades in a fire—become geographically widespread, indicating a spatially broad sphere of interaction and the initial unification of people into first a religiously defined and ultimately a politically drawn entity. This pattern is highly reminiscent of the development of a common, unifying iconography in Mesoamerica (Olmec) and western South America (Chavin) discussed in Chapter 9 and also reminiscent of the phenomenon of "cultural convergence" seen in the Indus Valley (discussed earlier in this chapter) immediately prior to the development of civilization there.

In this period we can also perceive evidence of violence on a scale not previously seen in Chinese prehistory. Monumental village walls with ramparts, as well

TABLE 11.1 Breakdown of Lung-shan Burials by Status Level at Taosi

	Wooden Coffin	Number of Grave Goods	% of Graves
High	yes	100–200	1%
Medium	yes	10–20	12%
Low	no	0–2	87%

as the skeletal evidence of trauma, imply that institutional violence with armies clashing had already established itself during Lung-shan times.

Acceleration Toward Civilization

The culmination of these early developments can be seen at the site of Erh-li-t'ou, dated to about 3800 B.P. The site itself is an order of magnitude bigger than anything seen previously, covering an area of 2.5 km (1.6 mi) by 1.5 km (a little less than 1 mi). At its peak, based on the size of the site and the density of its habitation structures, Erh-li-t'ou's population may have been as high as 20,000 (Lawler 2009b).

In both size and configuration, the site is urban in character with what appears to be a well-planned network of streets surrounding a central, walled compound. Two structures far larger than any of the other residences located at the site were found within the compound and appear to be palaces of an elite group. One palace was about 100 m (328 ft) on a side; the second was somewhat smaller. The walls of both palaces consisted of thick berms of stamped earth. Members of the elite class were buried in large, impressive tombs, their bodies placed in wooden, lacquered coffins. Bronze artifacts are common at the site, as are jade *ts'ung* tubes. Some of the bronzes were utilitarian tools, including knives, chisels, axes, adzes, and arrowheads and other weapons. Many of the bronze artifacts at the site, including disks, fancy drinking vessels, and musical instruments, were ceremonial or ornamental. One of the more spectacular artifacts at the site was made of polished jade tiles in the shape of a dragon.

The Shang Civilization

The site of Erh-li-t'ou was a precursor to the early florescence of Chinese civilization as represented by the **Shang Dynasty**. The Shang was China's first true urban civilization. For example, the modern city of An-yang is the site of the ancient city of Yin, a Shang capital city ruled by a succession of 12 kings beginning about 2,400 years ago. Great tombs of the rulers residing at Yin have been found at the sites of Hsiao-t'un and Hsi-pei-kang. These royal interments are enormous and would have required the labor of thousands of peasants. The royal graves are cruciform—in the shape of a giant cross. The king or emperor was buried in the center of the cross, with long, broad access ramps leading to the burial itself. The deceased noble was placed in an elaborate wooden coffin, surrounded by the symbols of rank and wealth that differentiated him or her from the rest of society: jade, bronze (Figure 11.8), and ceramic artifacts and even chariots and sacrificed horses. Along the access ramps to the royal gravesite were found the remains of dozens of humans sacrificed to accompany their leader into the afterlife, decapitated and laid out neatly in rows along the rampways (Figure 11.9).

It is with the Shang that we enter into the historical period of China's past. A written language containing more than 5,000 characters, only a fraction of which have been translated, has been found at Shang sites. Shang set the stage for all subsequent Chinese civilization (see the "Case Study Close-up" of this chapter for one of the most extraordinary manifestations of ancient Chinese civilization). In at least a symbolic sense, the Chinese emperors who ruled well into the twentieth century were the inheritors of a culture that can be traced back to the time of the first dynasty of the Shang civilization.

◀ **Figure 11.8**
Bronze metallurgy played a significant role in the development of ancient Chinese civilization. This is a charming casting of a baby elephant, and notice the little tiger perched on its trunk. This bronze work of art dates to more than 3,100 years ago. (© Asian Art & Archaeology, Inc./Corbis)

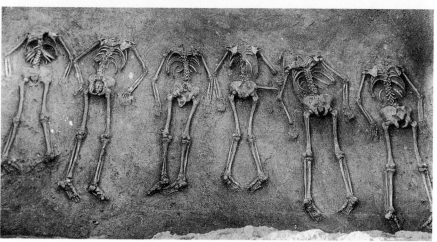

◀ **Figure 11.9**
The burials of beheaded people, sacrificed in ceremonies surrounding the death of a member of the royal class of the Shang civilization in China. (Courtesy of the Institute of History and Philology, Academy Sinica, Taiwan)

Why Were the Elites of State Societies So Conspicuous in Their Consumption?

Monuments like Khufu's Great Pyramid, as well as the pyramids of his son and grandson, the ziggurat at Ur, the temple/palace at Knossos, and the other examples discussed in this book, are enormous and awe-inspiring, to the point of extreme and excess. It would seem, from a modern, economically rationalist perspective, that not just an abundance but an overabundance of the material wealth of ancient states was expended to produce impressive, but otherwise seemingly pointless monuments. It

ISSUES AND DEBATES

would similarly seem that these same societies simply wasted an enormous portion of their precious treasure by burying hoards of gold and silver, precious and semiprecious stones, ivory, alabaster, ceramics, weavings, finely carved wood, and all the rest of the stuff that was deposited in the tombs of the elite classes. What was the point after all? Does it make any sense for these ancient state societies to have expended what clearly appears to be an excess of their time, energy, and wealth in the apparently wasteful practices of piling up prodigious quantities of stone and essentially throwing wealth away by burying it in the ground? Sure, these days that level of over-the-top spending can get you a reality show on cable, but what was the point in antiquity? Wouldn't that wealth have been better expended in other ways: on constructing canals, cleaning the streets, arming the military, or feeding the poor?

It may make perfect sense, however, when one considers the following. The elites of state societies are all about excess; in fact, they rely on it literally from birth to death: excess in the size and richness of their domiciles, excess in the number and value of their possessions, excess even in the concentration of wealth accompanying their mortal remains in their tombs. The elites—in antiquity as well as in the modern world—seem to live by the old adage: "If you've got it, flaunt it."

You've probably heard the term "conspicuous consumption," usually referring to people in modern American society who seem compelled to spend money—on houses bigger than they could possibly need or afford and often on more than one of them, on luxurious and overpriced automobiles, yachts, expensive technology, and on and on—if only, perhaps through profligate spending, to show their "superiority" to the 99% that makes up the rest of us. At least a part of the economic turmoil currently roiling the American economy may be traced to the kind of greed required to support the habit of conspicuous consumption.

The elites of ancient societies appear to have been no different. They too were conspicuous consumers and, in a sense, conspicuous material show-offs, boldly, brazenly, and proudly broadcasting their wealth and position through material consumption, by the use of expensive, exotic raw materials, through their possession of finely crafted goods, and by their sponsorship of the construction of enormous monuments. These monuments and possessions reflect something more than simply elites living large because they can. Conspicuous consumption represents not just one of the side benefits of being in an elite class; it appears to be a requirement, even a responsibility. Large homes, luxurious possessions, and grand monuments are symbols necessary to convey a message of superiority to everyone else in the society. Monuments and possessions are, in a sense, badges of office, symbols that not only reflect but also serve to justify and reify the social inequality on which state societies are based. The masses might not recognize your superiority—and, most dangerously, might not accept it—unless they see it manifested. Conspicuous consumption, in this view, serves as that manifestation, a constant material reminder and reinforcement of that inequality.

The Terra-Cotta Army of the First Emperor of the Qin Dynasty

CASE STUDY CLOSE-UP

Like Twentieth-Dynasty Egyptian pharaoh Tutankhamun, Ying Zheng ascended to the throne when he was just a child, only 13 when he became emperor of the Chinese state of Qin in 246 B.C. Like another Egyptian pharaoh, Narmer of the First Dynasty, Ying Zheng is credited with having unified an array of fractured city-states—Qin was just one of seven such states in China in the third century B.C.—into a single, hugely powerful kingdom in 221 B.C. Ying Zheng, now titled Qin Shihuang, the First Emperor of the Qin Dynasty, was the first ruler of a united China. Upon his death in 207 B.C., Qin Shihuang was placed in a tomb 38 years in the making, the extent and grandeur of which arguably is the most fantastic, the most spectacular, and—following our discussion of the conspicuous consumption that characterizes the elites of ancient as well as modern states—the most excessive investment of time, labor, and treasure for an individual person ever seen before or since.

Located near the Chinese city of Xi'an, Ying Zheng's mausoleum was looted in 206 B.C. and his tomb was pillaged. Fortunately, another part of his mortuary complex remained virtually untouched and was accidentally discovered by workers only in 1974. There, Ying Zheng's subjects had amassed an astonishing simulated army, a brigade of more than 6,000 slightly greater than life-sized warriors and horses, all made from the reddish-brown, firebaked ceramic called terra-cotta (Wu 1986). The men, their horses, and even bronze chariots are arrayed in lengthy columns, an eerily real-looking military formation representing a massive, ceramic army protecting the tomb of the emperor (Figure 11.10).

No standardized molds were used, and each of the clay soldiers excavated and examined to date is unique, each in its own pose. Clay archers kneel in the front of one of the formations, each holding an exquisitely simulated crossbow, while those in the back stand with their weapons, ready to shoot above the heads of their kneeling compatriots in the front. Some of the warriors are depicted wearing armor, others are in clay tunics, and all appear in uniforms that signify their different ranks in the army of the emperor. Perhaps most remarkable of all, just like real people, each terra-cotta warrior has a unique face, each with its own expression (Figure 11.11). It is as if each terra-cotta warrior was not simply an anonymous, imaginary soldier, but the representation of a real living soldier in the emperor's army in the third century B.C. Most of the warrior's hands were shaped to carry weapons, and the terra-cotta army clearly was equipped for war. Thousands of weapons have been found with the soldiers including crossbows, longbows, spears, swords, scimitars, battle axes, daggers, and halberds. The realism of the terra-cotta army was heightened by the ancient artists by their painting the individual soldiers. Their uniforms, their weapons, and even their skin was painted to accurately depict the soldiers as real, individual people (Larmer 2012).

The terra-cotta army represents a massive, almost incomprehensible investment of time, labor, and treasure, all for nothing more than the burial of a dead king. To be sure, it is a spectacular reflection of the

▼ **Figure 11.10**
A small phalanx of soldiers in the greater-than-life-size, 6,000+-man terra-cotta army created for the burial monument of Ying Zheng, the first emperor of the Qin Dynasty in Xi'an, China, who died in 207 B.C. (Bettmann/Corbis)

▲ **Figure 11.11**
Look carefully at the faces of the soldiers in emperor Ying Zheng's terra-cotta army. Each is unique and distinct, as are the thousands created for the emperor's tomb. The labor expended in the creation of the terra-cotta army is a staggering reflection of even ancient state societies to harness the wealth and labor of their citizens. (© Alfred Ko)

power and, it must be admitted, the artistry, of what a state society can create through its ability to harness, coordinate, control, and even monopolize the talents and time of a huge force of laborers and artisans. At the same time, consider the fact that the unimaginable work involved in producing the thousands of soldiers, horses, and chariots did not help feed the hungry in the emperor's kingdom; it did not result in improved systems of roads for transportation or commerce; it did not make the cities of the empire safer or the lives of its citizens more secure or productive. Clay soldiers, no matter how many or how impressive, could never really protect the kingdom from the depredations of nasty neighbors; they couldn't even protect the emperor's mausoleum, looted barely a year after he was buried. But in the desire and ability reflected in the emperor's decision to build this great tomb for his remains, we see reflected a common pattern exhibited by state societies. We may marvel at the beauty of their works, and we may stand in awe of their accomplishments. At the same time, we can recognize that these ancient states survived because their citizens accepted the inequality on which their societies were based and that they did so, at least in part, in their own awe at what the emperor or the pharaoh or the king could command and accomplish.

Summary

The Neolithic set the stage for the development of sedentary farming villages in various places in the Old World. In a select few regions, an acceleration of cultural complexity led to the development of a stratified social system that controlled the excess wealth made possible through the ability to produce an agricultural food surplus. Social elites developed as part of a reorganization of society that allowed for orderly and systematic trade, the construction of irrigation canals to increase the food base, and the construction of monumental defensive fortifications. In these same regions, the new way of organizing and controlling human labor was utilized by the developing elite to construct less practical monumental works—temples, palaces, and mortuary features such as pyramids. This kind of monumental construction, today diagnostic of ancient civilizations, was both cause and effect of the new social dynamic of the world's first civilizations. Large, impressive monuments served as dramatic evidence of the power of the elite and symbolized and reified this power at the same time that it magnified it. In the Old World, the processes that led to the kinds of societies we are calling civilization occurred in Mesopotamia in the Middle East, in the Nile Valley of Egypt, in Sudan, and in the island of Crete in the Mediterranean, discussed in Chapter 10, and in the Indus Valley in Pakistan and in China as discussed here.

Jonnathan Kenoyer's *Ancient Cities of the Indus Valley Civilization* (1998) provides one of the most thorough discussions available on the archaeology of this early state society. Jane R. McIntosh's (2002) *A Peaceful Realm: The Rise and Fall of the Indus Civilization* is another terrific source. K. C. Chang's synthesis work, *The Archaeology of China* (4th ed., 1986), is more than 20 years old but is still a valuable summary of Chinese prehistory and early history and a good source for information about the Shang Dynasty.

For a compendium of more recent articles, see the volume *The Formation of Chinese Civilization: An Archaeological Perspective*, edited by Sarah Allan (2005). For a synthesis of recent discoveries and new interpretations of Chinese antiquity, see the series of articles by science writer Andrew Lawler in the August 21, 2009, issue of *Science*. To see a remarkable artistic recreation of the terracotta army, in full color, check out the June 2012 issue of *National Geographic* (Larmer 2012). It is absolutely astonishing.

TO LEARN MORE

Web links for this chapter can be found at www.oup.com/us/feder

KEY TERMS

cylinder seal, 392	Lung-shan, 394	scapulimancy, 394
hang-t'u, 394	Rosetta Stone, 392	Shang Dynasty, 396

12

An Explosion of Complexity

Mesoamerica

CHAPTER OVERVIEW

Just as seen in the Old World civilizations discussed in Chapters 10 and 11, complex societies exhibiting the construction of monumental edifices, elaborate burials, large armies, full-time artisans, and so on developed in some parts of the New World as fewer people were needed in the subsistence quest and as rulers attempted to legitimize and reinforce their positions of power and wealth. Highland and Lowland Mesoamerica saw the development of the earliest civilizations in the New World including Teotihuacán, the Maya, and Aztecs of Mesoamerica.

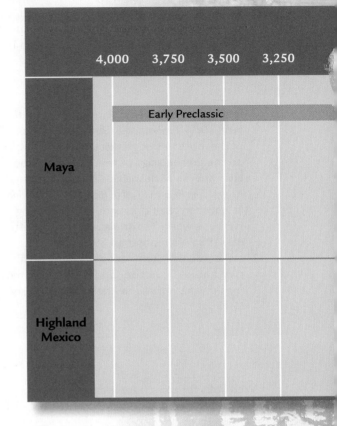

	4,000	3,750	3,500	3,250
Maya	Early Preclassic			
Highland Mexico				

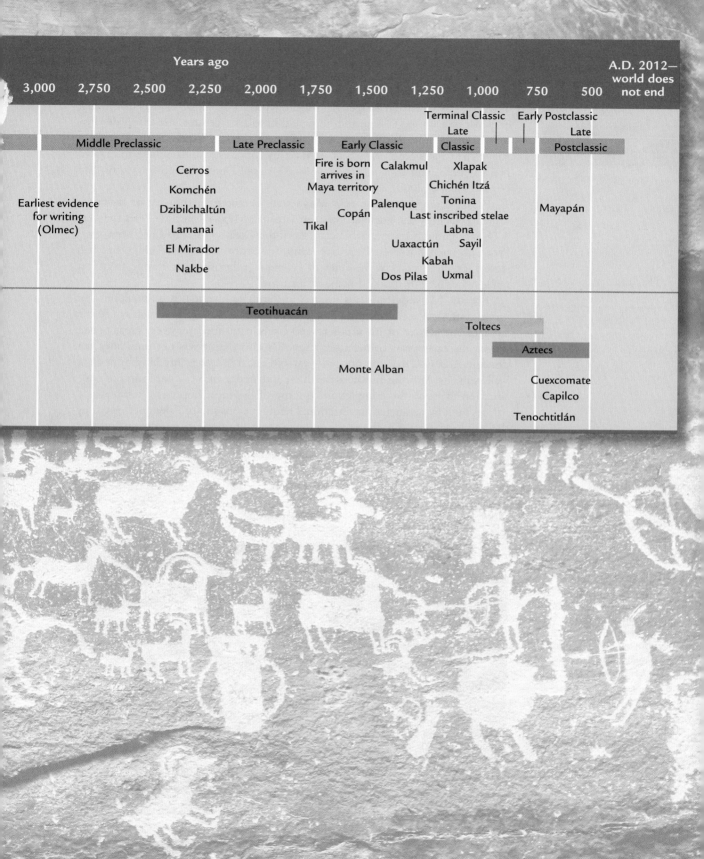

Years ago												A.D. 2012— world does not end
3,000	2,750	2,500	2,250	2,000	1,750	1,500	1,250	1,000	750	500		

Terminal Classic

Late

Early Postclassic

Late

Middle Preclassic   Late Preclassic   Early Classic   Classic   Postclassic

Cerros

Komchén

Dzibilchaltún

Lamanai

El Mirador

Nakbe

Earliest evidence
for writing
(Olmec)

Fire is born
arrives in
Maya territory

Calakmul

Xlapak

Chichén Itzá

Tonina

Palenque

Copán   Last inscribed stelae

Tikal   Labna

Uaxactún   Sayil

Kabah

Dos Pilas   Uxmal

Mayapán

Teotihuacán

Toltecs

Aztecs

Monte Alban

Cuexcomate

Capilco

Tenochtitlán

K'INICH JANAAB PACAL, COMMONLY CALLED PACAL the Great, was 12, just 3 years older than Tutankhamun (Chapter 10) and 1 year younger than Ying Zheng (Chapter 11), when he too ascended to the throne of a great nation. His reign, however, was to last far longer than the Egyptian boy-king's or that of the first emperor of a united China, and he would have a far greater impact on the history of his people. Pacal's story as related here is taken largely from *A Forest of Kings: The Untold Story of the Ancient Maya*, by Mayanists Linda Schele and David Freidel (1990) and *Chronicle of the Maya Kings and Queens* by Simon Martin and Nikolai Grube (2008).

Pacal became the ruler of a **Maya** state centered in the city of Palenque (called Baakal by the ancient Maya) in Chiapas, Mexico, on July 29 in the year A.D. 615. Though from a noble clan, Pacal the Great's father had not been king. Pacal's mother, however, Lady Sak K'uk, was from a family of kings and had served for three years as the ruler of Palenque, inheriting the throne from her uncle, who likely had no offspring of his own.

Because Maya descent was figured in the male line, it was unusual, but not unheard of, for Pacal to become king. That he did so is largely a testament to the strength and power of his mother, who likely continued to wield great power during the early years of her son's reign. It seems that it was not until after her death in A.D. 640 that the now 37-year-old Pacal fully became king in deed as well as in law. After his mother's death, he initiated a vigorous campaign of construction that saw the completion of some of the most impressive temples and palaces built by an ancient civilization. The marvelous site of Palenque, visited by thousands of tourists each year, is largely the result of Pacal's leadership and that of his two sons (Figure 12.1).

▶ **Figure 12.1**
Pacal the Great ruled over the Maya city of Palenque between A.D. 615 and A.D. 683. He oversaw the construction of many of the splendid temples that define this center of Maya civilization. His burial pyramid can be seen in the rear/left of this photograph. (© Fridmar Damm/Corbis)

Perhaps the greatest architectural achievement of Pacal's reign was the temple that would serve as his burial place (Figure 12.2). Not just a tomb, the Temple of the Inscriptions was intended to legitimize Pacal's kingship, to make up for the fact that his father had not been king, and to sanctify and confirm the legitimacy of the ascendance of his son, Kan-Xul II, to the kingship after Pacal's death. In an attempt to solidify his claim to the throne, as well as that of his son and his grandsons and great-grandsons yet to be, Pacal had a detailed king list inscribed in the halls of the temple located atop his imposing burial pyramid. This king list elevated Pacal's mother to the status of a virtual goddess, comparable to the mother of the gods in Maya mythology. Just as the three central gods of Maya religion legitimately ascended to their "godship" through the divinity of their heavenly mother, the Temple of the Inscriptions seems to be asserting that so too had Pacal legitimately ascended to his kingship through his earthly mother.

Pacal died on August 31, A.D. 683, at the age of 80, following a 67-year reign. In the ceremonies that marked the king's journey from this life into the next, his body was first brought up the steeply inclined stairway of the pyramid and then into the temple at its apex. Next, the body of the king was carried down into the pyramid itself; the pyramid had actually been constructed around and over Pacal's

◀ **Figure 12.2**
The Temple of the Inscriptions at the Maya site of Palenque. Pacal the Great, the ruler of Palenque from A.D. 615 to 683, was buried in a limestone sarcophagus at the base of the pyramid. The temple on top houses a detailed king list, validating Pacal's and his sons' descent from the previous kings of Palenque. (© Free Agents Limited/Corbis)

burial chamber, located down a vaulted, internal stairway leading to a chamber excavated by the Maya beneath the pyramid.

At last, the lord and king of Palenque, Pacal the Great, was laid to rest in a sarcophagus carved out of a solid block of limestone. Around the sides of the coffin sculptors carved ten human figures, each depicted as part tree, growing up from out of the ground. These human-trees have been identified as Pacal's mother (Lady Sak K'uk), the first queen of Palenque (Lady Yohl Ik'nal), and a number of previous rulers of the city. On Pacal's face was placed a mask made of obsidian, shell, and jade, bearing a mosaic of Pacal himself. Pieces of jade, a precious stone of enormous significance to the Maya, were placed around the body. The coffin lid is itself an exquisite work of art, perhaps one of the most famous works of Maya fine art, depicting Pacal in his journey from life to death.

There Pacal rested until 1952, when his burial was discovered and the coffin lid raised. That we can tell his story today, more than 1,300 years after Pacal last looked out upon his city in the jungle, is a testament to the ancient Maya. Though perhaps not in the way they intended, in building the Temple of the Inscriptions to house their king for eternity, in placing the king list inscriptions on the temple walls, and in sealing him in his limestone coffin, they assured Pacal a measure of immortality.

As was the case for Tutankhamun, with the burial pyramid of Pacal we are faced with the enormous material and social consequences of the evolution of state societies. The description of Pacal's tomb shows quite clearly that complex, stratified societies such as those discussed in Chapters 10 and 11 evolved in the New World as well as the Old. This chapter focuses on the ancient civilizations of Mesoamerica, and Chapter 13 focuses on South America.

The Maya

CHRONICLE

The Maya was the best-known aboriginal civilization in the New World. Their remarkable culture is the focus of numerous popular books and magazine articles—it is almost impossible to pick up an issue of *National Geographic* and not find an article on the Maya (see, especially, Guy Gugliotta's article in the August 2007 issue)—and the Maya have become a frequent focus of science and history documentaries, especially on cable TV. The movie *2012* has generated even more media buzz about the Maya, and too many people became convinced that the Maya predicted that the world would end on December 21, 2012 (the Maya made no such prediction and the fact that you are alive and reading this is a pretty good indication that the world is still here: Feder 2009).

Evidence of Maya civilization has been found across a huge swath of Mesoamerica, including the eastern Mexican state of Chiapas, the entirety of the Yucatán Peninsula, and the tropical and subtropical lowlands of the modern nations of Guatemala (especially the area known as the Petén), Honduras, Belize, and El Salvador (Figure 12.3). Within what was to become, at the peak of the Maya, a territory of about 324,000 km² (125,000 mi² or a little larger than the state of New Mexico), archaeologists have traced the earliest signs of social and political complexity, reflected by their emerging ability to produce monumental buildings, to more than 2,650 years ago in the tropical lowlands adjacent to those where the Olmec originated (Chapter 9; Coe 1993).

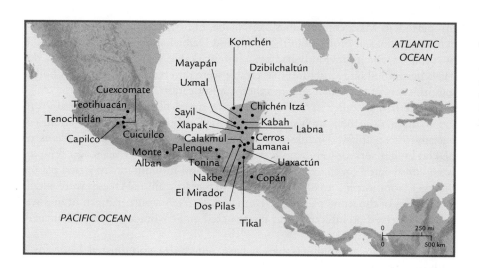

◀ **Figure 12.3**
Archaeological sites in Mesoamerica where evidence of the evolution of chiefdom and early state-level societies has been found.

Though the popular image of the Maya is that of a dead or extinct culture, it is estimated that today more than 5,000,000 people can rightfully claim to be Maya, speakers of the same language and descendants of those who lived in the splendid cities, built the impressive pyramids, and developed a precise astronomically based calendar—and whose culture dominated the Yucatán and tropical lowlands of Mesoamerica for close to 1,500 years (Webster 2002:39).

The earliest glimmerings of a social and political trajectory that would culminate in the flowering of Maya civilization can be seen in the archaeological record beginning about 2,650 years ago in what is called the Middle Preclassic time period (see Table 12.1; Demarest 2007; Sabloff 1994; Webster 2002). During

TABLE 12.1 **Maya Culture Chronology**

Paleoindian	Before 9,000 years ago
Archaic	9,000 to 4,500 years ago
Early Preclassic	4,500 to 3,000 years ago
Middle Preclassic	3,000 to 2,400 years ago
Late Preclassic	2,400 years ago to A.D. 250
Early Classic	A.D. 250 to A.D. 600
Late Classic	A.D. 600 to A.D. 800
Terminal Classic	A.D. 800 to A.D. 1000
Early Postclassic	A.D. 1000 to A.D. 1250
Late Postclassic	A.D. 1250 to A.D. 1519 (arrival of Spanish)
Modern	A.D. 1519 to present

this period, in Maya communities like Nakbe, El Mirador, Lamanai, Cerros, Calakmul, Cuello, and Nohmul in the south and Dzibichaltún and Komchén in the north, all of which previously had been unremarkable, small farming hamlets, the Maya began building structures that clearly were differentiated from other buildings in terms of both their size and their sophistication.

These first so-called civic structures are stepped platforms as much as 20 m (66 ft) high, and their surfaces are sometimes elaborated with decoration, especially stucco (plaster) masks. For example, 2,600 years ago, the residents of Nakbe built a series of enormous stone platforms. By 2,400 years ago, temples were constructed on the top of the platforms and monumentally scaled plaster masks—"zoomorphs," masks in the shape of fantastic animal faces—were added to the sides of the stone platforms (Demarest 2007). A similar pattern of massive, ritually directed architecture was constructed at El Mirador, Cerros, Lamanai, and elsewhere.

Clearly, these monuments would have required a coordinated labor force with sufficient surplus time to build them and a desire to produce structures approaching monumental proportions (Figure 12.4). These structures likely were related to Maya religion, and these villages, like the ceremonial centers of the Olmec, probably housed members of a nascent religious elite and their attendants. Some geographically advantaged settlements such as Cerros—located on a bay by the mouth of a river—became trading centers where raw obsidian and jade, finely crafted goods from these raw materials, agricultural products like cotton and cacao, and perhaps fine ceramics were distributed, adding to the power of the developing religious elite (Sabloff 1994:115).

A highly productive agricultural system focusing on maize and beans provided food for a growing population. Village population grew, and new villages were established during the period from 2600 to 2300 B.P. As a result of this

▶ **Figure 12.4**
Dzibichaltún, located in the north Yucatán, is an early example of a complex Maya settlement and ceremonial center. The platform structure likely was used for ceremonial or religious purposes. (K. L. Feder)

growth as well as an apparent movement of people from the countryside to the population centers, at this time some of the Maya villages evolved into true urban settlements with large, dense populations.

As population grows, the amount of surplus that can be produced and concentrated in the hands of the elite also grows, as does their ability to solidify, sanctify, and symbolize that power. Monumental, communal construction projects among the Maya, as in other early states, were both a cause and an effect of this process. In the Middle and Late Preclassic the elites had the emerging power to command the construction of monuments; and the construction of monuments, in turn, served to further integrate people into the political entity of the emerging state by engaging them in public projects that reflected the socially and politically stratified structure of Maya society. Communal projects, in other words, were microcosms of life among the Maya. At the same time, monuments provided tangible evidence of the power of the elite, further legitimizing their position of power and enabling them to command the construction of ever more impressive pyramids and temples.

These patterns of the concentration of population in a number of centers along with the concentration of economic resources, social status, and political power in the hands of an elite appear to have accelerated in the period following 2,400 years ago in the Late Preclassic period of Maya history. Monumental construction projects dramatically increased in scope. Trade brought in exotic raw materials, which were crafted into finely finished works that ended up being concentrated in the graves of a small segment of each town's population, the increasingly wealthy and powerful elites. Communities began competing with one another—perhaps for land, raw materials, and even the allegiance of the people themselves—and there is evidence, in the form of defensive embankments surrounding Maya communities and in Maya art with depictions of individuals wielding weapons against enemies, for warfare, which would eventually become endemic to Maya society.

Agriculture probably intensified at this time. Of necessity, the Maya employed a number of methods, both extensive and intensive, to feed the large and dense populations in their growing urban settlements. In some regions, the Maya practiced slash-and-burn agriculture, where forest land is cut and burned to produce fields that are abandoned after only a short period of use and allowed to grow over, to be used again after a period of agricultural dormancy. In some regions, however, a more energy-intensive agriculture was practiced with the construction of extensive ridged fields. Here, ridges of land were built up in the rich and fertile floodplains of rivers. The artificial high ground remained dry even when the river flooded. Some Maya sites dating to this period show evidence of canals and even swamp-reclamation projects. The Maya also employed a number of other intensive agricultural techniques, including terracing of hill slopes, planting kitchen gardens, and tree-cropping—the specialized use of tree crops in rain forests and within settlements (McKillop 1994).

Maya Writing

The need for ever-increasing control of information in an increasingly complex cultural system may explain the development of a sophisticated system of writing and mathematics that the Maya derived from the Olmec (Chapter 9; Coe

1992; Harris and Stearns 1997). The oldest evidence in Mesoamerica for the use of symbols among the Olmec dates to about 2,900 years ago in the form of an inscribed stone block found at the Cascajal site in Veracruz (Rodriguez-Martinez et al. 2006). This writing is not yet translatable.

Among the Maya, the information deemed worthy of recording, as determined by the elite who controlled the writing system, related not to accounting or economics, as was the case, for example, in Mesopotamia. Maya writing focused on their history, often emphasizing kingly succession. The desirability of keeping accurate records of time and the Maya ability to do so led to their development of a highly accurate calendar that was based on sophisticated astronomical observations, particularly of the movements of other planets visible in the night sky (Aveni 1977).

Translating the Maya written language has been an extraordinarily difficult undertaking. Even more unfortunately, the vast majority of the Maya screenfold books, works called **codices**, that we know existed in the sixteenth century were destroyed in about 1562, burned upon the order of the sixteenth-century Spanish priest who, 10 years later, would become installed as the Bishop of the Yucatán, Fray Diego de Landa. Only four Maya books have survived into the present, and these all appear to have been produced just before or, in the case of one of the books, immediately after the arrival of the Spanish (Webster 2002:113). The existing codices reflect bits of Maya history but focus primarily on arcane matters of creation and worship.

Though most of the books are gone, there are an estimated 15,000 surviving hieroglyphic inscriptions on buildings, monuments, and stelae (Figure 12.5), and these are under the intense scrutiny of archaeologists and epigraphers (Webster 2002:115). The vast majority of the stelae whose inscriptions can be translated tell stories of warfare and ritual; announce marriages, births, and deaths; tell of the founding of great cities and dynasties; and proclaim the military victories of great leaders and the capture of enemies. It's not a perfect situation, to be sure. Imagine an extraterrestrial archaeologist in the distant future, visiting Earth and attempting to figure out American life if all of our books had been destroyed and the only writing left were the carved inscriptions on presidential memorials in Washington, D.C., and historical monuments in our cities. Certainly, the picture would be incomplete and those extraterrestrials, like modern Mayanists, would need to rely on archaeology to fill in the blanks.

Peak of the Maya

Based on extensive archaeological investigation of their cities and through diligent examination of inscriptions, Mayanists have been able to piece together a detailed accounting of Maya history (Martin and Grube 2008).

▼ **Figure 12.5**
With the destruction by the Spanish of so much of what the Maya wrote about themselves in their hieroglyphic language, archaeologists and historians must rely on the inscriptions written on buildings, monuments, and stelae, like this one, overlooking Copan Valley. (© Macduff Everton/Corbis)

By the end of the Late Preclassic, about 1,900 years ago, the basic elements of Maya civilization were in place, including a socially stratified society with an elite social class headed by a powerful royal family that had, at its apex, a great king or "holy lord"; monumental temples and palaces; use of the corbelled arch; stone altars; an art style and iconography that included depictions of death, human sacrifice, and mutilation; a hieroglyphic written language; a base twenty number system; screenfold, bark paper books bearing lengthy narratives in that written language; stelae—upright stone slabs—also bearing messages in that written language; a written number system; a dual calendar of 365 and 260 days, respectively, that marked time from the beginning of the universe to the end of time or, at least, the end of the current cycle of time as the Maya perceived it; a ritual ballgame; a reverence for jade and related green and blue-green semiprecious stones; and the use of chocolate in preparing a ceremonial beverage imbibed by members of the elite class (Demarest 2007).

With these basic elements in place, the Maya entered into what modern scholars perceive to be the pinnacle of Maya civilization beginning about 1,750 years ago, or A.D. 250 by the reckoning of our modern calendar. This begins the Classic period of Maya history, divided into an Early and Late Classic period (see Table 12.1). For more than 500 years, the Maya civilization dominated the "Peten," the 34,000 km² (13,000 mi²) of northern Guatemala and the surrounding lowlands of Belize, Chiapas, and Tobasco.

Unlike ancient Egypt, in which large population centers up and down the Nile coalesced into a single, geographically dispersed political entity, a nation led by a single, all-powerful leader, the pharaoh, the Maya followed a cultural pathway more similar to that taken in ancient Mesopotamia. Like the Mesopotamians, the Maya developed a series of independent, sovereign, often competing (for land, resources, and people), powerful city-states. Archaeologist David Webster (2002:151) calls them "regal–ritual cities," and at their peak, there were as many as 50 of them. Each was ruled by its own royal dynasties, who lived within the boundaries of the regal–ritual capital of their own states, where they commanded the construction of the impressive pyramids and temples that today so fascinate archaeologists and tourists alike.

Maya city-states were characterized by, essentially, three settlement tiers (Demarest 2007). In the epicenter of each city were the pyramids and palaces, the residences of the highest and offices of the Maya rulers, the tombs of previous rulers, and the centers of political and ritual activities, including the location of the ritual Maya ballgame. Around each city's "central business district" were the neighborhoods of Maya nobility and the craft specialists whose work adorned the temples, burials, and homes of the elites; and spreading farther into the hinterlands were the household compounds of the farmers whose ability to produce a food surplus kept the entire operation in business.

These Maya cities were not the most highly populated among the ancient urban centers discussed in Chapters 10 and 11 or in this chapter. The most extreme estimates for even the most architecturally impressive of the Maya cities do not exceed several tens of thousands. The population of the urban center of Tikal, for example, located in Guatemala, was likely no more than 60,000 and may have been less than half that size (Figure 12.6). The population in the city was organized into a series of neighborhoods where participants in various crafts

▲ Figure 12.6
The impressive Temple I (Temple of the Giant Jaguar) at the Maya site of Tikal in Guatemala. Built around A.D. 700, it towers 45 m (145 ft) above the great plaza in this pre-Columbian city of 60,000. (Cris Wibby)

lived and produced their goods: stone tools, ceramics, and wooden implements. Copán, another major Maya city-state, may have possessed at its peak an urban population of about 20,000 (Fash 2001). Though not enormous by the standards of other ancient civilizations, the cities of the Maya, nevertheless, relied on the contributions of the substantial human populations in the hinterlands. The residents of these hinterlands included primarily farmers, whose surplus provided the economic basis for the existence of the elites, the construction of their monuments, and trade for their exotic raw materials. Remember our previous estimate that, in order to produce a sufficient food surplus to support the apparatus of the ancient Egyptian state, including pyramids, elite burials, temples, palaces, trade for exotics, the army, and so on, likely up to 75% of the population of ancient Egypt had to be farmers? David Webster (2002:140) estimates that, considering the lower agricultural productivity of the tropical and subtropical lowlands in which the Maya developed, up to 90% of the population had to be food producers to support the elements of state societies listed previously and shared by ancient Egyptians and Maya alike.

In their own words, as written down on stelae and other monuments, the Maya believed that their greatest period of growth and expansion was inspired by a military expedition from the great city of Teotihuacán in central Mexico (see the discussion of this vast city later in this chapter), led by a general whose name in English was Fire Is Born (Gugliotta 2007). Apparently, Fire Is Born arrived in the Maya city of Waka in Guatemala on January 8, 378. Either by force or by persuasion, Fire Is Born negotiated an alliance between Teotihuacán and Waka. But that alliance was clearly just a preliminary measure because Fire Is Born next immediately launched an army toward Tikal, just 80 kilometers (50 miles) to the east.

Again, by the Maya's own account, Fire Is Born's forces defeated Tikal's army and subdued the great city within a week of the onset of the battle. Tikal's ruler was executed, many of the city's most important monuments were toppled, and, in a year's time, a new leader was installed to rule over Tikal. His name was Spearthrower Owl and he was not a local. In fact, he was from Teotihuacán, an indication that the great central Mexican city was intent on expanding its power and influence far to the east. Once Spear-thrower Owl was seated as the ruler of Tikal, that city began a series of military excursions against other Maya cities and, as Teotihuacán's representative, began installing their own rulers in Maya cities like Copán. It was a brilliant strategy by Teotihuacán to dominate its universe, and it succeeded, at least for a time.

But Tikal's role as Teotihuacán's power-hub in the Yucatan did not last. An inscription found at the site of Dos Pilas tells the story of a prolonged and bloody war between the enemy cities of Tikal and Calakmul in the seventh century A.D. (Figure 12.7; A. R. Williams 2002).

Dos Pilas is located about 113 km (70 mi) southwest of Tikal and was, at least initially, an outpost of that city, established in the hinterlands of the territory it controlled. When the ruler of Tikal founded Dos Pilas, he installed his own 4-year-old brother, Balaj Chan K'awiil, as its leader, keeping power in the family and ensuring, at least in theory, the allegiance of Dos Pilas to Tikal and maintaining its usefulness as a buffer between Tikal and its powerful enemy, Calakmul. According to the inscription on the steps, this arrangement worked as it was intended for about 20 years, after which Calakmul's invading army attacked Dos Pilas and quickly overran its military defenders. Balaj Chan K'awiil was allowed to live but forced to shift his allegiance, to become now a mortal enemy of his own brother and the city he ruled. Dos Pilas, now as a client state of Calakmul, and at its behest, initiated the protracted, bloody, decade-long war against Tikal that is memorialized in the stairway inscription.

With the backing of its powerful ally, Dos Pilas ultimately defeated the army of Tikal, sacked the city, and took as hostages the rulers of Tikal. The inscription records Balaj Chan K'awiil's dance of victory and the slaughter of Tikal's nobility, including his own brother. As the old saying goes, blood may be thicker than water, but for a chance at life and power, Balaj Chan K'awiil made sure it was his brother's blood that flowed, not his own.

The relationships among the Maya city-states appear always to have been in a state of flux, with fleeting allegiances morphing into states of animosity and then back again to alliance depending on the particular set of circumstances at any given time. Despite the existence of coalitions and partnerships, the Maya city-states appear ultimately, however, always to have been fragmented, always in some state of enmity, friendship, or somewhere in between; warily allied, in the middle of hostilities, or on the way toward one of those extremes. The city-states remained politically autonomous and separate, never coalescing into a powerful, politically unified nation.

The Maya pattern of competing royal dynasties, each ensconced in its own city-state and overseeing the construction of great temples, pyramids, and palaces;

◀ **Figure 12.7**
The detailed and extensive hieroglyphic text carved onto the stairway of the Maya site of Dos Pilas tells the story of a bloody and protracted war between the enemy cites of Tikal and Calakmul in the seventh century A.D. (© Kenneth Garrett/ National Geographic Society Image Collection)

erecting stelae festooned with hieroglyphic messages that advertised its achievements in warfare; controlling widespread trading networks; and presiding over a large and urban population—all of this declined dramatically and rather abruptly after A.D. 800. The last inscribed stelae at Tikal bears a date of A.D. 869, and the final known inscribed monument erected by the Maya dates to A.D. 909 at the site of Tonina. Apparently, there were no more great victories to announce, no important births or deaths of royalty deemed worthy of recording for posterity. Soon thereafter, royal dynasties at least in the southern part of the Maya realm appear largely to have disappeared from the Maya social and political landscape. The last ruler of Copán died in A.D. 820 and was not replaced (see "Issues and Debates," this chapter). During the course of just a few decades following A.D. 800, the majority of the large urban settlements over which those dynasties presided were, again for the most part, abandoned.

Though the Maya world was radically reconfigured at the end of the Classic period, the Maya certainly didn't disappear. In part, their geographic focus shifted to the north where the great Postclassic period centers of Chichén Itzá and Uxmal developed, thrived, engaged in struggles for dominance, and also ultimately collapsed (Figures 12.8 and 12.9). Between A.D. 1250 and 1450, the Maya city of Mayapán was the dominant political entity in the Yucatán, and a number of Maya states continued to thrive outside of Mayapán's reach. Warfare and politics led to the decline of Mayapán, and no single polity rose to take its place in the Yucatán. When the Spanish invaded in the sixteenth century A.D., the much-changed Maya society was largely decentralized and its population was scattered. A few large and impressive sites, for example, Lamanai in Guatemala, continued to be occupied, but the construction of great monuments had ceased entirely. There is, of course, no way of knowing what might have developed in the cycle of Maya history had the Spanish not invaded and imposed their will on the native people.

▶ **Figure 12.8**
The pyramid, known as El Castillo or the Temple of the Feathered Serpent, is located at the site of Chichén Itzá in the northern Yucatán. (K. L. Feder)

The 30-meter (100-foot)-high Temple of the Magician at the Maya site of Uxmal. Typical of Mesoamerican pyramids, the Temple of the Magician consists of superimposed stages and has a stairway (actually two, in the case of this monument) leading to a temple at its apex. Uxmal is located in modern Mexico, in the Yucatan Peninsula. With its pyramids, ballcourt, temples, and palaces, Uxmal is one of several Maya sites open to tourists. Photographs in no way do justice to the splendid architecture and artwork of the ancient Maya; only a visit can convey the beauty of these sites. (K. L. Feder)

The great "mystery of the Maya," among both archaeologists and a public fascinated by this ancient society, has always concerned this apparently abrupt collapse. Why did what appears to have been a thriving civilization close out its time on history's stage? What caused the Maya to abandon their cities, why did the elites fall from positions of power and disappear, and why did it happen apparently so abruptly? Was it invasion, a drought, an epidemic, a catastrophic earthquake, a revolution—or was the Maya collapse rooted in the ecology of slash-and-burn agriculture in a tropical rain forest? These explanations for the fall of the Maya continue to be debated by researchers in the field. The collapse of the Maya is the focus of this chapter's "Issues and Debates."

Teotihuacán

Teotihuacán is so fascinating, at least in part, because it seems so different from other early New World state societies. The city itself stands in marked contrast to the pattern of the Maya with their series of discrete, individual city-states, each one, as art historian Esther Pasztory (1997:7) characterizes them, "small and charming," their structures elaborately decorated, and their scale impressive but quite human. Everything about Teotihuacán, in contrast, is gigantic and singular; its scale is truly monumental, even overwhelming (Headrick 2007). Again in contrast to the Maya's ritual-regal cities, which were characterized by small urban cores, each surrounded by a vast hinterland of rural farmers, Teotihuacán is all city, all urban core, and no hinterland. The densely packed homes of the city's residents spread out across an expanse of more than 23 km^2 (9 mi^2, or 5,760 acres). At its peak, the population of Teotihuacán was vastly larger—by a factor of two, three, or even four—than what has been suggested for even the largest Maya cities, with estimates reaching as high as 200,000.

Teotihuacán's name and, in fact, the names now applied to most of its monuments, are derived from the **Aztecs**, described later in this chapter. The Aztecs frequently visited Teotihuacán even though it was in ruins for more than 700 years when they became the dominant political force in the Valley of Mexico. To the Aztecs, the ancient city was so enormous, so impressive, so awe-inspiring, they called it in their language "Teotihuacán," translated as "The Place of the Gods" or, perhaps more accurately, "Where the Gods Are Made" (Pasztory 1997).

Archaeologist Annabeth Headrick (2007) describes the underpinnings of Teotihuacán as a "trinity," a three-pronged base consisting of a great ruler or king (who, unlike the Maya kings and queens, are anonymous because they did little to advertise their presence, power, and achievements); lineages whose family structure provided the social underpinnings of Teotihuacán life; and the military, whose significance, prestige, and power is ubiquitously depicted in Teotihuacán artwork. With these three elements intertwined, Teotihuacán evolved into one of the most powerful political, economic, and social entities in the ancient world. That focus on the military and militarism is what enabled Teotihuacán's invasion and subjugation of Maya territory as described earlier.

Teotihuacán appears to have been a pilgrimage city, a tradition that was practiced both at its peak and even centuries after its abandonment. Archaeological evidence in the form of Aztec sculptures found in proximity to Teotihuacán's most important monuments supports the notion that the Aztecs visited the ruins and viewed it as a sacred place. Some historical records even indicate that Motecuhzoma (Montezuma), the final Aztec ruler, visited the ruins of Teotihuacán every 20 days to perform various rituals to the gods who he likely believed had built the great monuments located there.

The valley in which the city was located is a part of the Basin of Mexico. Though the area presented its inhabitants with rich agricultural soil, timber, obsidian, and other valuable lithic resources, rainfall is unpredictable, and its high elevation (over 2,200 m, or 7,000 ft) produces a short growing season for agricultural plants.

Teotihuacán History

Teotihuacán began its history as a small farming village, part of the developing settlement system of the Basin of Mexico. Its location afforded its inhabitants decided advantages over their neighbors. The village was located adjacent to a significant source of obsidian, and the site straddles a major trade route to the south and east. The site is also well suited to irrigation-aided agriculture, and so it was well positioned when overall population growth in the Basin of Mexico strained the ability of simple agriculture to feed the increasing number of people living there.

By 2100 B.P. there were a number of growing population centers, but these were all secondary to one of them, Cuicuilco, until a series of devastating volcanic eruptions effectively destroyed that site. In the ensuing struggle for dominance in the basin, Teotihuacán was victorious. The key to its success may have been a combination of its location, its resources, the great potential of irrigation, and the evolution of an elite able to take advantage of this constellation of factors.

As Lamberg-Karlovsky and Sabloff (1995) suggest, the growth of Teotihuacán may have been the result of all of these factors, with each enhancing the other. To take advantage of its obsidian resource, miners of the stone, makers of tools, and full-time traders were needed. A greater emphasis on irrigation developed to produce more food, which in turn allowed a greater proportion of the population to engage in specialties related to the obsidian trade. Enormous responsibility and attendant power and wealth rested in the hands of the elite who controlled both trade and irrigation.

A Monumental City

The monuments of Teotihuacán and their positioning clearly were intended to impress both residents and visitors alike. As archaeologist Annabeth Headrick (2007) describes it, everything about the city, its massive architecture, its location with mountains looming in the background, the configuration of the road by which visitors entered the city, draws you into its heart.

A broad, straight, central avenue, once nearly 5 km (about 3 mi) in length and in places 50 m (164 ft) in width, bisects the city (Figure 12.10). Called the Avenue of the Dead by the Aztecs, the roadbed passes through the center of the city, rising to a summit on top of which, beginning in about A.D. 200, the residents of Teotihuacán built an enormous pyramid. Today it is called the Pyramid of the Moon, again based on its Aztec designation. Its positioning at a naturally high point renders the top of this pyramid a powerful symbol visible from everywhere within the city (Figure 12.11). Off to the side of the Avenue of the Dead is a monument built at about the same time that dwarfs even the Pyramid of the

▼ **Figure 12.10**
Site map of the ancient Mexican city of Teotihuacán. Compare this map with that of the Indus Valley city of Mohenjo-daro in Pakistan (Figure 11.4). One in the Old World, one in the New, both were planned-out settlements, the capitals of vast ancient states. (Reproduced from *Past Worlds: The Times Atlas of Archaeology* by kind permission of Times Books, Ltd., London)

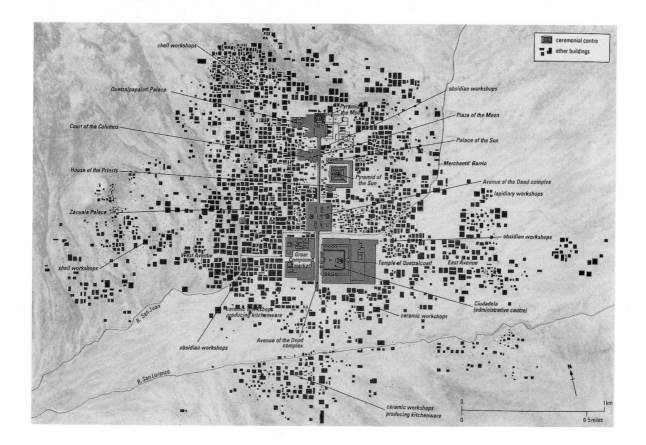

Moon Called the Pyramid of the Sun, it measures 250 m (738 ft) on each side and rises to a height of about 70 m (230 ft). The Pyramid of the Sun has about the same-sized footprint as the Great Pyramid in Egypt (see Chapter 10), but is only about half as tall. Nevertheless, it contains an enormous volume of more than 1 million m^3 (1.5 million yd^3) of material, making it, by most reckonings, the third most massive pyramid in the world (Figure 12.12).

▶ **Figure 12.11**
The Pyramid of the Moon is dramatically positioned at a high point in the natural topography of Teotihuacán and at the terminus of the so-called Avenue of the Dead, a broad roadway that bisects the great city. (Alex Auclair)

▶ **Figure 12.12**
The Pyramid of the Sun is truly monumental, the third most massive pyramid produced by any ancient civilization. It is located alongside the Avenue of the Dead at Teotihuacán. (Alex Auclair)

Many of the 600 or so platform monuments and small pyramids built at Teotihuacán were constructed in a characteristic form of alternating steps together called *talud/tablero*. Built as a series of superimposed blocks of diminishing size as one approaches the monument's apex, the levels alternate between a true block shape (these are the *tablero*) with vertical faces (with recessed panels) and horizontal steps, and blocks whose faces are dramatically sloped inward from bottom to top (these are the *talud*), giving them a triangular shape in cross-section. The *talud/ tablero* form was used repeatedly in Teotihuacán architecture, rendering the resulting monuments both impressive and visually distinctive (Figure 12.13).

Residences of Teotihuacán's Citizens

Archaeological survey work initiated by René Millon (1967, 1981) in the 1960s revealed Teotihuacán's truly urban character. The work exposed the presence of something on the order of 2,000 substantially scaled, multifamily apartment-house compounds, each representing the homes of between 60 and 100 people. These compounds appear to have been built on a consistent and fixed city grid, leaving the clear impression, similar to what is seen in the ancient Indus Valley urban centers (see Figure 11.4), of careful planning and control of housing development on the part of a ruling authority (see Figure 12.10). The compounds likely were the residences of families (Headrick 2007); there is even some skeletal evidence that supports a degree of similarity among the skeletons found within residential compounds (especially among the males) that suggests they were related (Spence 1974).

It is interesting to point out that until the residential compounds were excavated and carefully investigated, many researchers thought they represented the remains of palaces inhabited only by the high elites of Teotihuacán, because they appeared to be that finely made and appointed. Archaeological evidence, however, shows that the compounds were not palaces but the residences of regular Teotihuacános of most every social rank. That's curious. Consider how very unlikely it would be for a future archaeologist to conclude, on examining the residential buildings in one of our modern cities, including the homes of the poorest citizens, that they were all palaces. This is a reflection of what appears to have been a relatively high standard of living, even among the poor of Teotihuacán.

Of course, economic inequality is reflected in the residential compounds. Many of the rooms in individual family units are large, and some apartments open up onto interior patios. These likely were the domiciles of wealthy, socially and politically important families, perhaps administrators, soldiers of high military rank, and priests (Pasztory 1997). Many, perhaps two-thirds of the residential compounds, were lived in by the less-well-off (Millon 1992); likely they were farmers or craft workers. Their apartments were much smaller, crowded, and not as well made and lack interior patios. But even the smallest, most crowded compounds do not evince abject poverty. Large or small, patios or not, many compounds

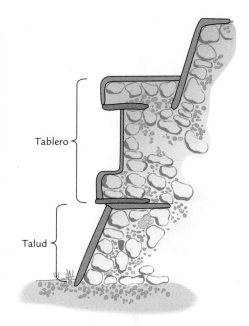

▲ **Figure 12.13**
A schematic representation of talud/ tablero architecture. Characterizing many of the structures at Teotihuacán, the form alternates blocks with vertical faces (the tablero) with blocks whose faces are sloped dramatically inward.

▲ Figure 12.14
Detailed and colorful wall
art decorated the homes
of the Teotihuacán elite.
(Alex Auclair)

were beautifully decorated with remarkable, very artfully rendered and colorful wall paintings (Figure 12.14). There are images of jaguars, birds, plumed serpents, lush plant life, and an abundance of images of water, both as flowing streams and as showers of water droplets flowing from the fingers of what is presumed to be a deity.

Though most of Teotihuacán's inhabitants lived in the sprawl of residential compounds, the highest elites had their own, separate and distinct living quarters in a grand palace built on either side of the Temple of the Feathered Serpent. Their homes are positioned within the monumentally scaled Ciudadela compound, a walled fortress or city within the city located off of the Avenue of the Dead, south of the Pyramid of the Sun.

The Reach of Teotihuacán

The social, economic, political, and, perhaps military reach of Teotihuacán was geographically vast. There is archaeological evidence of Teotihuacán-style objects in the burials of powerful Maya rulers whose cities were located hundreds of kilometers from Teotihuacán. We've already seen how an expeditionary force sent by Teotihuacán and led by Fire Is Born subdued the largest of the Maya city-states, Tikal, and from there dominated the Maya territory for several hundred years.

Also, people throughout Mesoamerica came to Teotihuacán to live and conduct business. A cluster of tombs in the city reflects the cultural practices of people from the ancient city of Monte Albán, located in the Mexican state of Oaxaca. A neighborhood of houses looking markedly different from the standard apartments of most Teotihuacános has been excavated in the eastern part of the city. These houses resemble those found in the Mexican state of Veracruz, located on the Gulf of Mexico; perhaps the people living in these houses were foreign merchants whose business dealings made it sensible for them to live in the big city.

Teotihuacán clearly was a dominant force in ancient Mesoamerica for several hundred years. Its power and impact seem to have diminished after about A.D. 600, and its collapse began to accelerate after A.D. 700, but it is as yet not clear why. There is no indication of a military invasion or a great conflict, but there is some evidence of violence in the form of substantial burning, not in the residential compounds as might be expected in the case of an invader bent on destroying the city, but in ceremonial areas and, especially, in the Ciudadela, the location of what is interpreted to have been the residence of the high elite of the city. Could the end of Teotihuacán have been precipitated by internal social upheaval or even a revolution? Perhaps. After the destruction of the Ciudadela it appears that people simply abandoned the city, occasionally taking the time to burn ceremonial areas, effectively ending Teotihuacán's tenure as Mesoamerica's great urban center.

Monte Albán

Teotihuacán was enormous, both in size and in significance, but it was not the only city-state to develop in Mexico during its tenure. To the south, in the valley of Oaxaca, a people called the **Zapotecs** built a smaller city, Monte Albán. This city, founded in about 500 B.C., became the dominant social and political force in southern Mexico.

Monte Albán's setting is both impressive and reflective of the power of its society. The main part of the settlement was positioned on the top of an artificially flattened hilltop that looms 400 m (1,300 ft) above the surrounding valley floor. It must have taken an enormous body of well-organized laborers just to produce the level surface upon which Monte Albán's many temples, residences, raised platforms, and primary pyramid were built (Figure 12.15). It has been estimated that at its peak, sometime between A.D. 450 and 700, though much smaller than Teotihuacán, the resident population was still large, nearly 25,000 (Sabloff 1989:56). Of course, as a city-state, it is likely that tens of thousands more in the surrounding hinterlands can be considered members of the Monte Albán polity (Marcus and Flannery 1996).

With a natural, easy, and efficient route of communication, trade, and transportation—the Nile—ancient Egypt could develop and maintain a high level of national cohesion across a lengthy geographic distance. Without this kind of natural channel joining distant regions together, the city-states of Mesoamerica remained largely separate political and economic entities. The rulers

▼ Figure 12.15
At its height before A.D. 700, Monte Albán had a resident population as high as 25,000 and was powerful enough to present some competition for its much larger neighbor to the north, Teotihuacán. Luckily, Monte Albán's location was far away from Teotihuacán and distance provided a buffer, allowing it to develop its own identity and wield its own power. (Patrick Escudero/ Hemis/Corbis)

of Teotihuacán could not readily swallow up Monte Albán. Monte Albán may have been too powerful militarily and even had they attempted it, it would have been a great challenge to Teotihuacán simply as a result of the distances involved. Nevertheless, these two powerful city-states were in contact with one another. In fact, a neighborhood at Teotihuacán exhibits an architectural style in its residences and an artistic style in the objects found in those homes that leads researchers to conclude that the people who lived there were not Teotihuacános but were from Monte Albán, perhaps merchants, traders, or even ambassadors to the more powerful entity to the north (Sabloff 1989).

Monte Albán thrived during the middle of the first millennium A.D., becoming militarily powerful, taking control of a large territory, and sitting atop and controlling a multitiered geopolitical system characterized by a hierarchy of smaller ceremonial/population centers. Like Teotihuacán, there were tensions inherent in that system, and as smaller cities previously held under Monte Albán's sway became larger, more powerful, and more demanding of autonomy, Monte Albán lost control and was largely abandoned sometime before A.D. 1000.

The Aztecs

The Aztecs were the reigning civilization encountered by the Spanish conquistadors when they entered the Valley of Mexico in 1519. These Spanish invaders wrote detailed historical accounts of sixteenth-century Aztec culture (Soustelle 1964) that have given us the name of the supreme ruler of the Aztec polity: Motecuhzoma (or Montezuma). We also know that he sat atop a multitiered sociopolitical system that included the rulers of city-states that had been incorporated into the Aztec realm; in turn, these leaders ruled over local nobles. As always, at the base of the social, political, and economic pyramid in complex state societies was the vast majority of the population, made up of the commoners whose labor provided the resources that supported the entire system.

Ordinarily, when we think of an empire, we conjure up in our minds an image of a dominant political force, one with a huge geographic range over which it imposes its will. In a sense, the Aztecs belie that stereotype. Though the geographic reach of the Aztecs was vast, they cared very little about imposing their will over other, smaller states, at least when it came to matters other than economics. In other words, the Aztecs made no effort to convert those under their sway to the Aztec religion. They didn't usurp local political leaders; they didn't attempt to proselytize Aztec cultural practices or change local architectural styles, clothing, or language. The Aztecs, simply, didn't care about making other people into Aztecs. They wanted one thing and one thing alone: wealth. A local group under Aztec rule was basically left on its own as long as the people provided tribute in the form of gold, jade, fine feathers, cloth, and jewels to their Aztec overlords. In a sense, the Aztecs were more like an organized crime syndicate assessing local merchants for "protection" money. If they refused or held back, the Aztec military was called in to slaughter whoever stood in their way.

Aztec merchants played an important role in funneling wealth into the coffers of the empire. Aztec merchants were not just buyers and sellers of goods; they were, effectively, an advance column of unarmed soldiers whose job it was to make sure local people were paying what the Aztec overlords deemed due. Local folks recognized the role played by Aztec merchants and, in some cases, attempted to circumvent the empire by eliminating the merchants. In one instance, several were killed and the feared Aztec ruler Ahuitzotl commanded his army in A.D. 1497 to seek revenge; 2,000 local villagers were rounded up and executed for each merchant that had been assassinated (Draper 2010:134). Apparently, this was a highly effective way of dampening down local resistance to Aztec control.

Motecuhzoma's domain was vast; the Valley of Mexico over which he ruled directly had a population of close to 1 million in the period A.D. 1350–1519. The population of the surrounding territories that can still be considered part of his empire numbered in the millions (M. E. Smith 1997:78). This large population was made possible by an intensive and sophisticated agricultural technology that included substantial irrigation works such as dams and canals. The Aztecs also built walls on hillsides and flattened out slopes naturally too steep for agriculture to produce cultivable terraces. Swamps were drained and artificially raised, and fertilized fields called **chinampas** were produced, resulting in one of the most productive farming patterns seen anywhere before the development of modern agricultural techniques.

The ample historical documentation of the Aztec civilization focuses on the final chapter of that culture. Archaeology has given us an appreciation for how Aztec society evolved. Archaeologist Michael Smith (1997) points out that much of the archaeology conducted in the Aztec realm has focused on the remains discovered at the Aztec capital, Tenochtitlán. The capital of the modern nation of Mexico, Mexico City, was built over the remains of the Aztec capital; and, indeed, it seems that in every construction project in the modern nation's city, ancient remains from the previous inhabitants are brought to light.

Archaeologists, naturally enough, are drawn to these spectacular artifacts, palaces, and pyramids that reflect the great architectural and artistic achievements of the Aztecs. For example, a spectacular array of ceremonial objects was unearthed beginning in 2008 by workers in the middle of a construction project. The centerpiece of the discovery was a 12-ton monolith with a bas-relief of the Aztec earth goddess Tlaltechutli (yes, there are a lot of t's and l's in the Aztec language). She is depicted as being in the process of giving birth and, simultaneously, drinking her own blood (Figure 12.16; Draper 2010). The Tlaltechutli monolith is the third found in the same general area including a 24-ton stone depicting the sun and a smaller, 8-ton bas-relief showing Coyolxauhqui, the Moon Goddess.

Thousands of other objects were found in three distinct layers of offerings beneath the Tlaltechutli monolith by archaeologists called in to excavate the site. In the top layer, researchers found the skeletons of two golden eagles (the Aztec symbol of the sun) surrounded by gold and jade objects and the pelt of a spider monkey. Layer two contained dozens of marine shells and coral. Finally, in layer three the excavators discovered a dog burial, its skeleton showing that in life it had been bejeweled with jade and turquoise. In Aztec tradition, a dog guides the soul of the recently deceased to the underworld. The three layers appear to symbolize the journey of the soul of a deceased king to the Aztec underworld.

▶ **Figure 12.16**
The Tlaltechutli monolith depicts the Aztec Moon Goddess Coyolxauhqui. The stone weighs approximately 24 tons and was discovered in the heart of Mexico City—which was the heart of the Aztec capital, Tenochtitlán—during a construction project. The monolith was one of three that have been found in the area, all part of what appears to have been a funerary complex for an Aztec ruler whose grave has not yet been found. (Kenneth Garrett/ National Geographic Society/Corbis)

Michael Smith (1997) has excavated at two rural villages: Capilco, with a population of about 135, and Cuexcomate, with about 800 people. Agriculture was intense at both villages; terraced slopes allowed for the increased production of corn, beans, and cotton. This agricultural intensity provided the food surplus that passed into the hands of local nobles and from there to the kings of local city-states and ultimately up the line to support the rulers at Tenochtitlán.

The commoners lived in small houses (only about 15 m², about 160 ft², or a room a little more than 12.5 ft on a side). The inhabitants of these houses were, however, part of a complex and interconnected economic system. They produced goods for sale or trade and obtained desired material in exchange. For example, each household grew cotton, and Smith found artifacts used in cotton production (spindle whorls and small bowls used in spinning the cotton) in every excavated house. Cotton textiles were a major product of Aztec peasants and served, for peasants anyway, as the coin of the realm.

Most of the pottery found at Capilco and Cuexcomate had been produced locally, but even the poorest of peasants possessed imported ceramics. Residents also used thousands of obsidian blades, but there is no local source for volcanic glass. It is available 100 km (62 mi) away. Also, though there is no evidence for metallurgy at either site, residents were able to obtain bronze sewing needles, most likely manufactured in western Mexico.

As Smith points out, at least in the outlying sites he excavated, there does not appear to be the kind of grinding poverty that characterizes our modern state societies. In fact, the archaeological record indicates that Aztec commoners did fairly well for themselves. We know from historical records that the Aztecs did not rule with an iron fist; their rule was mostly indirect. As long as each successive rung up the sociopolitical hierarchy received its portion of tribute from those below, people were left alone. In return, they were protected from external threats posed by competitor states, and the goods that people wanted and needed were supplied to the markets.

Why Did the Maya Collapse?

Sometime between the eighth and ninth centuries A.D., the Classic Maya civilization experienced a series of significant changes and dislocations. At least in the Maya heartland in the western Peten (in the central Yucatan), major cities appear to have been abandoned or at least saw their populations decreased dramatically, and monumental construction was severely cut back or stopped altogether (Demarest 2007). Some label this major alteration of Maya society a "**collapse**."

ISSUES AND DEBATES

It is often difficult to tease out of archaeological data the causes and effects of a dramatic change in a culture's trajectory. For example, merely because an environmental change preceded or was contemporaneous with a cultural dislocation does not constitute definitive proof that the former caused the latter. Nevertheless, it can be suggestive and many researchers believe that the fall of the Maya at the end of the ninth century A.D. was caused by a long-term drought that began in A.D. 800 and continued until A.D. 1000.

There is clear paleoenvironmental evidence of such a drought in the Maya homeland at about the time the Maya civilization experienced a dramatic contraction. Recent climate modeling, based on the analysis of lake deposits and stalagmite growth, indicates a 40% reduction in annual rainfall in the ninth and tenth centuries A.D. when compared to earlier precipitation patterns (Medina-Elizalde and Rohling 2012). This certainly would have posed a daunting challenge to the agriculturally based Maya who, of course, relied on rainfall for maintaining levels of crop production sufficient to feed the large populations of their city-states.

The drought hypothesis, however, isn't a slam-dunk in explaining what happened to the Maya in the ninth century. Some Maya city-states in Guatemala had been abandoned before the drought became serious and some, especially those in the northern Yucatan, thrived through the ninth century despite the drop in precipitation (Aimers 2011). Chichén Itzá, for example, was at its peak during the drought and wasn't abandoned until about A.D. 1050. Some smaller, but still substantial, city-states (Tipu, Lamanai, and Tayasal) were occupied into the sixteenth century when the Spanish arrived. Mayanist Elizabeth Graham sees no evidence of collapse along the coast; there's no great population decline, health and nutrition as evidenced in Maya skeletons seems stable, and the people continued to maintain local infrastructure like dams and agricultural terraces (as cited in Lawler 2010). Finally, as archaeologist James Aimers (2011) points out, the archaeological record clearly shows a complex pattern of growth, contraction, and regrowth for many of the Maya city-states regardless of changes in rainfall levels, making it extremely difficult to conclude that such a change was the prime mover in the trajectory of Maya civilization.

David Webster (2002) ascribes the collapse of the Maya to what might seem like a rather mundane and not terribly dramatic cause: He calls it "an ecological trap of their own making" (p. 255). Some habitats lend themselves to the production of the surplus food needed to support monumental architecture, a merchant class, full-time craft specialists, and so on. For example, in the valleys of major rivers outside of the tropics, soil is replenished by the deposition of al luvium during the yearly flood. In other words, at least to a point and for a time, the nutrients removed by producing food at an ever-escalating rate are restored by a natural process, flooding, that in economic terms doesn't cost anything. The Maya civilization, however, developed in a region that is dominated by a tropical and subtropical forest. Soils in the tropics are relatively nutrient-depleted. Instead of nutrients being stored in the soil and replenished by flooding, nutrients in the tropics are stored in the trees themselves; it is estimated that something like 75% of the nutrients in a tropical forest are stored in the vegetation.

Farmers in the tropics all over the world figured this out and realized that the best way to release the nutrients stored in that vegetation back into the soil where it could be used to sustain agricultural plants was to cut the trees down and burn them. That's why this strategy is given the name "slash-and-burn" agriculture. The problem, however, is that once the nutrients are released into the soil by burning, and once those nutrients are taken up by the crops grown, harvested, and then removed, the soil has become depleted and requires an often lengthy rest-ing or fallow period. During this time the soil nutrients are slowly replenished, vegetation becomes reestablished, nutrients become concentrated in the biomass, and eventually the process can be repeated and another burn can take place and another crop can be planted.

Evidence from the bottom of Lake Salpetén in Guatemala shows that almost as soon as the Maya began practicing slash-and-burn, soil erosion was a problem. Researchers have found a thick layer of clay at the bottom of the lake, the result of increased soil erosion, which, in turn, was caused by forest clearing for agriculture (S. Williams 2007). Though most of the clay layer dates to before the collapse of the Maya, researchers suggest that the cumulative effect of erosion over a couple of millennia may have rendered agriculture problematic, especially in the face of a growing population (S. Williams 2007:262).

Webster suggests that while the Maya were able to maintain their complex societies based on a system of intensive agriculture for a time, ultimately it was impossible to sustain that system. As noted by Gugliotta (2007:104), today, the Peten agriculturally supports a population of less than 400,000 people; at their peak, the population of the Maya in that same region may have been as much as 10 million. Perhaps Maya farmland simply could not sustain that population size and their subsistence system collapsed.

Perhaps the Maya were a victim of their own success. The rapacious demands of the elites to sustain their position of power and wealth led to overproduction on thin, depleted soils that were not given sufficient fallow time during which they could replenish their nutrients. This, in turn, led to ever-bloodier conflicts between city-states competing for agricultural lands on which farmers could produce the needed food surplus. Peasant farmers who previously accepted the authority of the elite class and who believed that peace and stability were the result of the sacred legitimacy of the king began to question that legitimacy when crops failed and wars became interminable. Webster (2002:345) goes so far as to suggest that the kings were viewed as being personally responsible when the system failed to provide peace, stability, and food. Without the acquiescence of the peasant farmers, there could be no Maya states; and they may have, in Webster's words, simply voted by their feet and moved beyond the control of the elites living in the regal-ritual centers. The fall of the Maya may have been the result not of a dramatic catastrophe but of a simple but equally devastating problem: "Too many farmers grew too many crops on too much of the landscape" (Webster 2002:347).

What Does "Collapse" Even Mean?

Mesoamericanist Arthur Demarest (2007) questions the validity or, at least, the sufficiency of purely ecological (for instance, a drought) or economic explanations for the Maya collapse/reorganization. As he points out, complex societies regularly face significant challenges—ecological, political, economic, social—and commonly respond in ways that allow them to survive by adapting to new circumstances. The question, as Demarest maintains, is not which ecological challenge caused the collapse of the Maya but, instead, why didn't or couldn't the Maya respond to whatever challenges they were faced with?

Demarest maintains that Maya rule was based on ritual and ideology far more than economics. When faced with a challenge, their rulers—their K'uhul Ajaw—responded in a way that made sense to them and that fell within their purview. Maya rulers were not involved in trade or economics; they did not run their city-state's agricultural system, irrigation networks, or trading policies. As ritual rulers, when faced with an environmental disaster or economic challenge, their response was to intensify ritual behavior, to build more temples, to put more of their state's energy and wealth into a symbolic reaction to the challenge, hoping to placate and pacify the gods or spirits who were causing the problem the Maya were facing. As Demarest (2007:244–245) concludes, "While these activities produced the beautiful corpus of Classic Maya art and ruins admired today, they had a high energetic cost for the supporting populations of the Classic period." In other words, the ritualistic rather than rational or utilitarian reaction to environmental or ecological problems faced by the Maya ironically produced the most spectacular of their monuments, but it was worse than useless, actually diverting energy away from any potentially helpful response. There's the irony; perhaps the coolest elements of Maya archaeology resulted from a misguided ritual approach to a very real, objective problem.

Demarest brings up another, very insightful point. The Maya didn't disappear into the tropical rainforest after their abandonment of the major cities of the Classic period. In fact, not all cities were abandoned. Some, in the north, like Chichén Itzá (see Figure 12.8) and Uxmal (see Figure 12.9), actually saw their populations soar as they became politically and economically dominant. As Demarest (2007:242) points out, millions of Maya continue to live and thrive in their homeland and, just as "the fragmentation of the Western Roman Empire after the fourth century A.D. was not an end of Western Civilization," the fall of the Classic Maya city-states did not mark the collapse of Maya culture.

The Ultimate Sacrifice: Why?

Like ancient civilizations in the Old World, human sacrifice was an important part of religious practice in the New. As in the Old World, some of those sacrificed were war captives; in a recent analysis at a pre-Inca, Wari Empire site in Peru (see Chapter 13), 29 out of 31 of those found ritually buried showed a strontium isotope signature (see Chapter 2) indicating that they were local people. That same form of analysis showed that 14 of the 18 people whose heads ended up as trophies were foreigners and, therefore, likely war captives (Tung and Knudson 2011). In both the Old and New Worlds, some people were sacrificed to accompany the dead ruler to the afterworld (see Chapters 10, 11, and 14). Some cultures in the New World practiced human sacrifice as part of the ceremonial dedication of a sacred building (we cut ribbons, they cut off heads). Additionally, some ancient cultures performed sacrifices on those deemed the most precious and treasured: their own children (here and Chapter 13).

Child sacrifice sounds grotesque to us, of course, but it makes a kind of gruesome sense. Killing an animal or an enemy usually involves very little emotional investment. Those doing the sacrificing aren't really sacrificing all that much by killing animals or people they're not all that fond of in the first place. But a child? That is, truly, the ultimate form of sacrifice and shows one's complete commitment to a god. In the Old Testament of the Bible, God tests Abraham's devotion to him by ordering him to sacrifice his son Isaac. God relents at the last moment, but in nearly killing Isaac on God's command, Abraham exhibits his complete obedience and trust.

There is clear evidence on Crete (Chapter 10) that, when faced with a natural catastrophe (the volcanic eruption of Thera on nearby Santorini Island more than 3,400 years ago), and in an apparent attempt to placate the gods of geology, the Minoans ritually killed children (Warren 1984). The butchered remains of two kids, ages 8 and 11, were found at the Temple of Knossos. There was no evidence of illness or accidental trauma. There was evidence, however, that the children's flesh had been meticulously scraped off their small bones in a manner identical to how the Minoans were known to sacrifice animals. The sacrifice didn't work; Thera blew its top anyway and had a great impact on Minoan civilization.

The ancient Maya practiced child sacrifice as well. Mayanist Stephen Houston reports the 2010 discovery of the sacrificed remains of six small children found in a king's burial at the El Diablo site in Guatemala. The smallest of the children had been killed and their bodies placed whole in individual ceramic jars. The older and larger children (5-year-olds) had been cut up, apparently in order for each to fit into his or her own vessel (as cited in Gibbons 2012c).

When it comes to human sacrifice, the Aztecs appear to have been as committed as anyone to its regular practice. The standard tale told by the Spanish is that the Aztecs slaughtered 80,000 war captives when they consecrated the Great Pyramid at their capital city of Tenochtitlán. While it is almost certainly a gross exaggeration, clear archaeological evidence of human sacrifice has been found at Tenochtitlán. In fact, as a general rule, Aztec warfare was not about getting control of land or real estate. Instead, Aztec wars had two functions: to make sure local people under their sway continued to pay tribute to their Aztec overlords and to capture people for human sacrifice. If you've seen the movie *Apocalypto*, though it is supposed to be about the Maya, (spoiler alert) the human sacrifice scene appears to be based on ethnographic accounts of exactly this kind of real practice by the Aztec in the sacrifice of war captives. Though the great Aztec ruler Ahuitzotl's tomb has yet to be found, historical records related to his death in A.D. 1502 number the slaves sacrificed to follow him to the afterlife at over

200 (Draper 2010). An actual example of this kind of human sacrifice was reflected in one particularly gruesome discovery. Archaeologists at Tenochtitlán excavated the decapitated remains of 47 sacrifice victims, 45 of whom were children (Gibbons 2012c).

Did the Maya Predict That the World Would End on December 21, 2012?

Actually, the Maya did no such thing. Like ours, the Maya calendars (they had several related ways of keeping track of time) express the passage of time as a series of cycles. We have a cycle of weeks (seven days that continuously repeat during the course of a year) and a cycle of months (twelve sets of 28, 30, or 31 days) that repeat each year. Nobody worries when Sunday rolls around that the end of time is upon us. We all know that, after Sunday, it becomes Monday again and another week begins (people may be depressed that they have to go back to work or school, but nobody seriously worries that the universe is going to close down). Similarly, nobody worries when December 31 looms on the calendar that all is lost because that's the *final* day. In an ever-repeating cycle, January 1 has always followed December 31 and always will.

The Maya had the equivalent of months (each one being twenty days in length) and years (made up of 18 of their 20-day months and an additional 5-day period at the end to add up to 365 days). They had longer cycles as well—the equivalent of our decades, centuries, and millennia, only instead of basing these cycles on multiples of ten, the Maya based their longer cycles on multiples of twenty.

One of their longer cycles, indeed, ends on the day that translates in our calendar to December 21, 2012. So what? The Maya did not, in any inscription found anywhere in their realm, maintain that anything particularly momentous would occur then, least of all the end of time. In fact, in Pacal's burial monument mentioned at the beginning of this chapter, the Maya scheduled a big celebration of Pacal's ascension to the throne long after his death. When were the Maya planning this celebration? On our calendar it works out long after 2012; in fact (and mark it on your planners), Pacal's celebration is scheduled for October 15, 4772 (Schele and Freidel 1990:82). You might reasonably accuse the Maya of being a bit obsessive in their planning ahead, but you can't accuse them of being doomsayers. Finally, the fact that you are reading this book after December 21, 2012, is pretty strong proof that whatever the Maya predicted or didn't predict, the world didn't end, and that's that.

THE GREAT KING NAMED YAX PAHSAJ CHAN YOPAT ascended to the throne of the Maya city-state of Copán 1,242 years ago, more precisely on the 2nd of July in the year A.D. 763 (Fash 2001). He was the 16th and final king in Copán's ruling dynasty established by K'inch Yax K'uk Mo' in A.D. 435.

Like his predecessors, Yax Pahsaj recognized the great importance of establishing his legitimacy as ruler of Copán by constructing monumental buildings and erecting stelae verifying, one could even say advertising, in image and word his relationship to the 15 kings who preceded him and, especially, in emphasizing his direct lineal connection to K'inch Yax K'uk Mo', the first in Copán's kingly line. There is no better example of this than Altar Q, a spectacularly carved, four-sided

CASE STUDY CLOSE-UP

monument depicting in bas-relief Yax Pahsaj along with the 15 previous rulers of Copán, positioned in chronological sequence around the entire perimeter of the altar (Figure 12.17). In a sense, Yax Pahsaj is located at the end of the succession of rulers but also physically and symbolically at a point back at the beginning, positioned adjacent to both the previous, 15th ruler of Copán on his left, and to the first, K'inch Yax K'uk Mo', on his right. To make the symbolism even more abundantly clear to the citizens of Copán as well as to modern Mayanists, K'inch Yax K'uk Mo' is shown, precisely as in the words of the old cliché, passing the torch to Yax Pahsaj. It is the equivalent of a monument depicting the inauguration of the U.S. president, with the oath of office being administered by George Washington. To make Yax Pahsaj's legitimacy as the rightful heir to the throne of Copán even clearer and to symbolically show his rightful place in the cycle of powerful kings, a crypt was constructed just east of Altar Q in which the skulls of exactly 15 jaguars were entombed, each representing a ruler in the line of succession leading up to Yax Pahsaj. Jaguars were viewed by the Maya as protectors of their royal houses.

The spectacular Maya city-state of Copán is located within the borders of the modern nation of Honduras, in an agriculturally extremely rich "pocket" of land carved out by the Copán River (Fash 2001). Along with rich soil, Copán is located close to a significant source of volcanic glass, excellent for making sharp-edged stone tools, and near the largest source of jade in Mesoamerica. Granite used for making grinding stones for milling corn, kaolin for making pottery, and volcanic tuff suitable for sculpting were all abundant in the area around Copán.

At its peak of power and size in the late eighth century A.D., Copán had a population estimated at about 20,000, including a dense urban core. That core is characterized by the presence of pyramids, altars, stelae, the large homes of the elites, and a ballcourt where the Maya played a ceremonial game. (The losing side

▶ **Figure 12.17**
One of the four sides of Altar Q at Copán. The altar depicts each of Copán's sixteen historical kings. The builder of this monument, Yax Pahsaj Chan Yopat (the sixteenth in Copán's kingly succession), is shown here, second from the right, being handed the staff of kingship by a figure representing the first king of Copán.
(© Richard A. Cooke/ Corbis)

was sacrificed; according to Mayanist Bill Fash, a lot of the games ended in a tie, which, if you were on one of the teams, you might have found comforting.) This so-called Principal Group of Copán's monumental structures in the urban core covers an area of 12 hectares (about 30 acres; Figure 12.18).

Certainly one of the most spectacular of Copán's monuments in the Principal Group is a pyramid, the top of which can be reached by ascending an intensively carved Hieroglyphic Stairway. The hieroglyphs located on the risers of the stairs (the vertical components of the steps) represent the longest continuous written inscription in the New World (Fash 2001:139a).

The pyramid was constructed by the 13th ruler of Copán over the tomb of the 12th ruler. The detailed message conveyed in the hieroglyphs concerns, as so much of Maya writing seems to, the legitimacy and life histories of the city's rulers, including their births, details of their lineages, their succession to the throne, their important achievements in construction and in war, and then their deaths.

Around the Principal Group archaeologists have found the primary residential wards of Copán where most of the city's population lived. Looking nothing like the regularly laid out neighborhoods of Harappa or Mohenjo-daro of the Indus Valley (Chapter 11) or those of highland Mexico, Teotihuacán (this chapter), Copán's neighborhoods appear to have developed in an informal, ad hoc fashion, growing organically rather than according to some master urban plan. Finally, surrounding Copán's religious, political, and urban residential core there is a broad periphery where the more dispersed settlements of farmers who surely viewed Copán as their capital city were located.

During Copán's tenure as a Classic Maya city, there appear to have been at least four distinct social classes, reflected in the sizes of their residences, the proximity of their residences to the Principal Group, and the elaborateness of their

◀ **Figure 12.18**
Detail of the principal ground of monuments at the Maya site of Copán. The Principal Group covers an area of about 12 hectares (30 acres) and is surrounded by the primary residential wards of the city. (© Craig Lovell/Corbis)

burials. From most powerful to least there were (1) the king and his immediate family, (2) a political elite, (3) landed elites, and (4) commoners. Yax Pahsaj Chan Yopat was the final great ruler of Copán, although at least one additional leader appears to have attempted to succeed him. Bill Fash (2001:178) sees this 17th ruler—if we can really count him on the list—as a rather "tragic figure," an individual who tried to hold Copán together as a great and powerful city-state, but who, in the midst of what appears to be a systemic collapse throughout the Maya world, ultimately failed. Like many of the Maya cities at the end of the ninth and beginning of the tenth century, Copán wasn't destroyed but underwent a dramatic and relatively rapid change, with a large segment of the population moving away from the urban core and even out of the Copán pocket entirely. No more monuments were built, no more stelae were erected, and the royal lineage ended.

Summary

In the New World, just as in the Old, some farming societies eventually developed the ability to produce a food surplus. This surplus enabled the development of social complexity and inequality. Eventually, some of these complex societies developed into true states with a formal government and true power invested in an elite class. The Maya and the complex pre-Aztec cultures of central Mexico developed independently of Old World civilizations. Through their concentration of wealth and power and as members of an elite social class in a stratified society, rulers were able to organize the labor of the many to produce the spectacular monuments—the pyramids and temples—that dominate the ancient landscapes of Teotihuacán and the territory of the Maya. Like the civilizations of the Old World, the complex societies of the New eventually collapsed. Though many suggestions have been proposed to explain the process underlying the fall of ancient civilizations, including resource depletion, environmental catastrophes, invasion, and insurrection, no one of these explanations alone is sufficient. In each case of societal collapse, it is the inability of the society at a particular point in its evolution to respond adequately to a challenge, whatever that challenge may be, that leads to its disintegration.

TO LEARN MORE

Ancient Civilizations: The Near East and Meso-america, by C. C. Lamberg-Karlovsky and Jeremy Sabloff (1995), presents an extremely thorough investigation of the origins of civilization in Mesoamerica (and the Middle East and Indus Valley as well).

There is a wealth of good material aimed at a general readership on the Maya of Mesoamerica—in particular, the wonderfully written *A Forest of Kings,* by Linda Schele and David Freidel (1990). For a virtual encyclopedia of the Maya rulers, take a

look at *Chronicle of Maya Kings and Queens* by Simon Martin and Nikolai Grube (2008). Also, check out Arthur Demarest's (2007) *Ancient Maya: The Rise and Fall of a Rainforest Civilization.*

Don't let the title fool you; David Webster's (2002) wonderful book, *The Fall of the Ancient Maya: Solving the Mystery of the Maya Collapse,* is about so much more than just the collapse of the Classic Maya civilization after A.D. 800. His is a very well-written and inclusive discussion of Maya history from its most ancient origins through its florescence and then on to its collapse, reorganization, and contact with the Spanish invaders. As is often the case, *National Geographic* has published a lavishly illustrated, well-written, and thoughtful summary about the origins and fall of the Maya (by Guy Gugliotta in their August 2007 edition). For Teotihuacán, see Anabeth Headrick's *The Teotihuacán Trinity: The Sociopolitical Structure of an Ancient Mesoamerican City*. A terrific synthesis of Mesoamerican archaeology and culture history is provided by Susan Toby Evans in her book, *Ancient Mexico and Central America* (2008). For about the most beautiful and lavishly illustrated book I have seen in a long time on any topic, see *The Aztec Empire*, (Solis 2004) the published volume that accompanied the Guggenheim Museum's spectacular 2004 exhibit of Aztec and other Mesoamerican art. The book is brimming with incredible photographs of Aztec stonework, metallurgy, and weavings accompanied by short pieces written by experts in Mesoamerican art, history, and archaeology.

Web links for this chapter can be found at www.oup.com/us/feder

KEY TERMS

Aztec, 414	codices, 410	Maya, 404
chinampas, 423	collapse, 425	Teotihuacán, 415

13

An Explosion of Complexity

South America

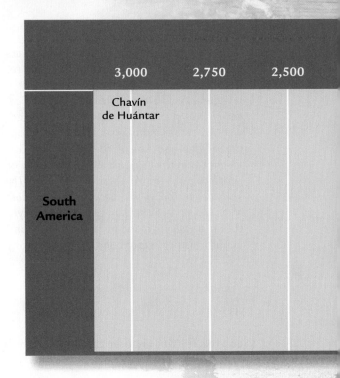

	3,000	2,750	2,500
South America	Chavín de Huántar		

CHAPTER OVERVIEW

Just as seen in the Old World civilizations discussed in Chapters 10 and 11, complex societies exhibiting the construction of monumental edifices, elaborate burials, large armies, full-time artisans, and so on developed in some parts of the New World as fewer people were needed in the subsistence quest and as rulers attempted to legitimize and reinforce their position of power and wealth. South America saw the development of the earliest civilizations in the New World including the Moche, Tiwanaku, Wari, Sicán, Chimu, and Inca.

Years ago

2,250   2,000   1,750   1,500   1,250   1,000   750   500

Moche
Sípan

Tiwanaku
Pampa Koani

Wari
Azángaro

Sicán
Batán Grande

Chimu
Chan Chan

Inca
Cuzco

PRELUDE

READING THE ACCOUNT OF HIS PERUVIAN expedition, one can clearly sense the excitement of Yale University professor Hiram Bingham when the team he was leading entered into a high-altitude saddle in the "cloud forest" in the mountains of Peru, about 97 km (60 mi) from the ancient Incan capital city of Cuzco (Bingham 1913). It was there, on July 24, 1911, that Bingham led a team of archaeologists, historians, and naturalists into an incredible, hidden archaeological world never before seen by outsiders, a world presenting to its visitors what arguably is the most breathtakingly beautiful setting for any archaeological site anywhere on earth (Figure 13.1).

At an elevation of about 2,400 meters (7,900 feet), enfolded by the nearly vertical, ancient granite peaks of mountains sacred to the **Inca**, it is no wonder that Bingham surmised, however incorrectly, that the site he had discovered might be a legendary hidden city. When one considers the setting and surroundings of what local people called Machu Picchu, it is understandable that Bingham speculated that it might have been the final redoubt of a clan of royal Inca, a stronghold into which they made their final desperate retreat from the Spanish conquistadors before they vanished into the haze of history. But Machu Picchu does not represent some romantically doomed last stand of the powerful Incan empire. In fact, it was something far more mundane, though, to be sure, no less fascinating. Machu Picchu simply was a grand royal estate, actually one of many at the disposal of the Inca elite, a "weekend getaway" from the pressures and stresses of running an enormous empire. As archaeologist Lucy Salazar (2004:27) points out, while modern American presidents have their Camp David retreat, the ancient Inca rulers had Machu Picchu, a place where they could relax and entertain guests, among whom might be political allies and even the rulers of other great nations. Machu Picchu was a place where the Inca emperor and his guests—an Incan version of the one-percenters—could, essentially, kick back, do a little hunting and fishing, and simply enjoy the stupendous views.

Likely built by the ninth Inca ruler Pachacuti Inca Yupanqui sometime between A.D. 1450 and 1470, Machu Picchu was a resort consisting of a series of mostly residential compounds whose walls were constructed with precisely shaped granite bricks. Even when the Inca, his family, his entourage, and his guests were in residence, Machu Picchu is unlikely to have housed much more than about 500 people, and certainly not more than 750, of whom only about one-quarter were members of the nobility (Salazar 2004:30).

There are only about 150 individual residences at the site, most with small and not particularly sumptuous living quarters. These likely were lived in year-round, primarily by support staff, individuals whose

▼ **Figure 13.1**
The awesome setting of the Inca settlement of Machu Picchu high in the Andes in Peru. The Inca were a true empire with an enormous geographic reach encompassing close to 1 million km² (380,000 mi²) and extending across 4,000 km (2,500 mi) of western South America. (P. Nute)

job it was to keep the place in shape for its occasional use by the political and economic elites. Some of the ordinary houses were located away from the main part of the site, near the neatly terraced agricultural fields. These likely were lived in by farmers whose produce ended up on the tables of the elite visitors to the estate.

At least three house clusters or compounds look quite different, consisting of larger, more finely made homes, physically isolated from the clusters of the standard structures, providing their residents better views, direct access to flowing water in beautifully made fountains, and considerably more privacy. One of the elite compounds, in particular, stands out, also possessing a private bath and even a private garden; pollen analysis indicates that the residents of this compound, called the King's Group, grew food, including beans, corn, and potatoes, as well as a wide array of flowers, in particular, beautiful and colorful orchids.

Along with the houses of royalty and their support staff, there are also a series of 30 shrines and temples at the site, most of which seem to be aligned to the rising of the sun on the summer solstice, the morning on which the sun rises at its northernmost point on the horizon (Figure 13.2). After that day, June 21 or 22, the sun appears to rise successively farther to the south along the horizon. Along with the shrines and temples, there are 16 fountains at Machu Picchu whose waters are supplied by natural springs at the site, channeled through a stone-lined canal nearly 750 m (2,456 ft) in length. Machu Picchu is an amazing place, one that has reached iconic status as a "must-see" tourist destination; a quick glance at Figure 13.1 is all you need to see why. More than 550 years after Machu Picchu was built, it remains, as archaeologist Lucy Salazar (2004:27) phrases it, "a formal architectural symbol of the power of the ruler and his elite." The ability of the elite classes, the royal rulers of an ancient state society, to have constructed their own haven in the sky is just one more material manifestation of the power concentrated in their hands. This chapter focuses on those material manifestations of ancient state societies in South America.

◄ **Figure 13.2**
Its walls aligned with the rising of the sun on the summer solstice, this Machu Picchu structure is, in fact, called the Temple of the Sun. This photograph shows the beauty and precision of the stonework as well as the dramatic setting of this royal Inca estate.
(© Wolfgang Kaehler/Corbis)

Moche

If asked to enumerate the ancient civilizations of pre-Hispanic South America, most of us would be at a loss after we named the builders of Machu Picchu, the Inca. But this largest and best-known South American state society, first encountered by the Spanish in 1532, was only one in a long sequence of impressively powerful civilizations that characterize the history of western South America (Figure 13.3).

For example, about 1,700 years ago, on Peru's northern coast, a culture called **Moche** developed, with stepped pyramids, hilltop forts, unique pottery styles, and fabulous burials. There are continuities in iconography between Chavín de Huántar (Chapter 9) and Moche, as there are, in fact, between South America's earliest, unifying religious art style and all of the later state societies to be discussed in this chapter.

Beginning construction at their capital in about A.D. 100 and reaching their zenith at about A.D. 400, the Moche produced one of the earliest kingdoms in South America. With a degree of control across an extent of nearly 600 km (370 mi) of coastline, the Moche state constructed enormous monumental works at its primary city, oversaw an extensive trading network that brought in

▶ **Figure 13.3**
Archaeological sites in western South America where evidence of the evolution of chiefdom and early state-level societies has been found.

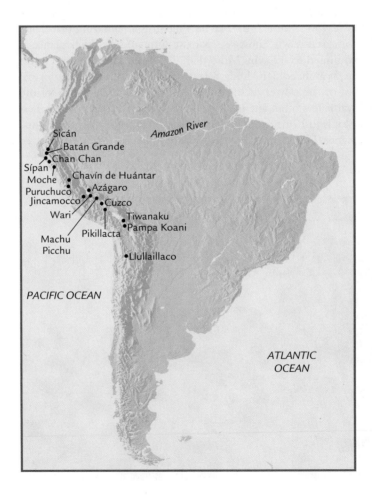

precious raw materials from all over western South America, and ran a large-scale irrigation system of canals and aqueducts.

Following a pattern in South American complex societies established at Caral more than 2,800 years before (see Chapter 9), the Moche built the so-called Pyramid of the Sun (Huaca del Sol) at the heart of its urban center. Construction commenced on this monumental project at about A.D. 100; the pyramid was built in eight distinct phases and ultimately was more than 40 m (130 ft) high. The Moche Pyramid of the Sun covers a vast area; along its longer axis it is 342 m (1,122 ft) in length and nearly 160 m (520 ft) wide. In other words, this one monument covers an area of more than 54,000 m^2 (13.5 acres, or the area covered by more than 12 American football fields). Its enormous volume contains 143,000,000 mold-made, sun-dried adobe bricks (Figure 13.4). Its accompanying, smaller Pyramid of the Moon (Huaca de la Luna) is made of 50,000,000 adobe bricks and rises to a height of 20 m (66 ft).

In the interior of the Egyptian pharaoh Khufu's pyramid, work gangs left graffiti, often referring proudly to their role in building the great burial monument to the absolute leader of their society (see Chapter 10). Archaeologists Charles Hastings and Michael Mosely have examined the construction of the Moche pyramids and have found a similar phenomenon. Though none of the pre-Columbian civilizations in South America, including the Moche, possessed a written language, Hastings and Mosely (1975) found more than 100 different kinds of markings on the adobe bricks in the Pyramid of the Sun. They suggest that such markings may have served to record the material contributions of local groups of people to Moche's great leaders for construction of the pyramid. This record keeping, as Hastings and Mosely suggest, implies a complex, hierarchical political organization in which local people were expected to contribute to the needs of the elite—including the monumental construction projects they ordered.

◀ **Figure 13.4**
The Moche culture Pyramid of the Sun stood over 40 meters in height. Begun in about A.D. 100, it consists of more than 143 million adobe bricks. (© Nathan Benn/Corbis)

▲ **Figure 13.5**
View of one of the spectacular burials of a Moche warrior-priest, filled with artifacts of gold and jade. (© Kevin Shafer/Corbis)

We have already encountered, especially in Chapters 10 through 12, lots of examples of archaeological manifestations of social, political, and economic inequality. The archaeological record of early civilizations is filled with examples of the homes, palaces, and tombs of the original "one-percenters," the folks who controlled those societies and monopolized the wealth. South America's indigenous civilizations were no different. Just such evidence was found in the village of Sípan, located about 150 km (95 mi) north of the Pyramid of the Sun. There, archaeologists Walter Alva and Christopher Donnan (1993, 1994) excavated a royal cemetery of the Moche elite (Figure 13.5).

The first excavated tomb, dating to about 1,660 years ago, was of a man in his late 30s or early 40s. In death he wore an elaborate feathered headdress, nose ornaments, and beaded pectoral ornaments (a chest covering). The tomb was filled with turquoise, copper, silver, and gold jewelry. At his right side lay a gold and silver scepter, and on his left was another scepter of cast silver. Also accompanying this lord of the Moche were hundreds of pottery vessels, some quite elaborate and displaying human shapes; a number were in the form of warriors vanquishing their enemies. As we might expect (see the discussion of sacrifice in "Issues and Debates" in Chapter 12), the chief resident of the grave did not make his voyage to the Moche version of heaven alone; he was buried with llamas, a dog, two men, three women, and a child. The additional males appear to have been sacrificed as part of the burial ceremony. Another royal was found in a plank coffin wearing a headdress of gilded copper. The headdress was in the shape of an owl, with long hanging bands representing the bird's feathered wings. A final burial was also richly appointed with marvelous gold, silver, and turquoise artifacts.

The clothing, ornamentation, and headdresses found in these three burials match quite closely artistic depictions of great warriors from other Moche sites. In those depictions, vanquishing warriors are presented with the hands and feet of their enemies as trophies. Alva and Donnan discovered the remains of additional human hands and feet associated with the major burials at Sípan. As a result, they concluded that the men buried at Sípan represent a class of warrior-priests.

These royal Moche burials are emblematic of civilization. The ability to unify a large population, to control its behavior, and to exploit its labor and monopolize its wealth were the factors that made possible such sumptuous splendor in death for the Moche lords.

To the south of the Moche heartland, another complex culture, the Nazca, developed after about A.D. 400. Along with the construction of large-scale ceremonial centers, the Nazca are today known for their astonishing **geoglyphs**, an elaborate series of amazingly straight, broad lines, extending for miles, etched

◀ **Figure 13.6**
The Naza geoglyphs are among the most notable—and notorious—pieces of ancient, monumentally scaled artworks. Rendered on a giant scale in the Peruvian desert, the ancient Nazcans produced enormous birds, fish, whales, a monkey, and the 150-foot-long spider shown here. The creatures were rendered by sweeping darker rocks away from the lighter underlying surface. The work certainly took great ingenuity and skill but did not, as some very silly authors have suggested, require the assistance of extraterrestrial visitors (whose time would have been better spent fixing their warp drives or flux capacitors rather than directing the production of artwork depicting giant spiders or monkeys). (Yann Arthus-Bertrand/Corbis)

into the desert along with effigies of monumentally scaled animals (the monkey is the best known), birds, fish, and even a spider (Figure 13.6). I don't want to disappoint you, but popular claims that the Nazca lines were airfields employed by extraterrestrial visitors to earth in antiquity are simply ludicrous. Archaeological and ethnohistorical evidence shows that the so-called lines were ceremonial pathways (Bruhns 1994) and the effigies represent gods and spirits.

Empires: Tiwanaku

At an elevation of 3,870 m (12,690 ft), the capital of the **Tiwanaku** civilization, located in Bolivia, just southeast of the enormous and economically productive Lake Titicaca, was one of the highest cities of the ancient world. Beginning in about A.D. 200 and reaching a zenith by about A.D. 400, the builders and sculptors of Tiwanaku constructed a remarkable city encompassing an area of some 4.5 km^2 (1.74 mi^2), filled with a series of palaces, temples, platforms, and massive monoliths, enormous works crafted from single pieces of stone (Figure 13.7).

The stone used by the builders of Tiwanaku included the hard and dense volcanic rock andesite and the softer sandstone; both were abundant in the Tiwanaku region. Quarrying and transporting this stone, often in enormous blocks—one sandstone monolith moved to the capital weighed 118,000 kg (130 tons)—was a truly monumental undertaking. Andesite was quarried at a site located across the lake from Tiwanaku; it was, in all likelihood, floated over to the city on reed boats. Some of the large sandstone blocks were transported 10 km (6 mi) over land.

The intricately carved Gateway of the Sun—the Ponce Monolith—of an enormous Tiwanaku deity, and the Bennett Monolith, a huge sandstone depiction of a Tiwanaku god, are but a small part of the legacy of this civilization (Morris and von Hagen 1993). The amount of labor and the degree of specialization needed to produce these monuments, as well as the impressive architecture of the city of

▲ **Figure 13.7**
The Gateway of the
Sun at Tiwanaku is an
enormous monolith. It
was formed by expert
carvers from a single slab
of extremely hard and
dense volcanic rock.
(© Nathan Benn/Corbis)

Tiwanaku itself, show just how powerful ancient civilizations can become.

Like all complex state societies, Tiwanaku thrived as the result of a highly productive agricultural system. Though the surrounding territory today seems barren, the farmers of Tiwanaku developed an efficient pattern of raised fields. Through communal labor, they constructed huge platforms of rich soil surrounded by lower swales. The largest of the platforms were 200 m (about 650 ft) long and 15 m (50 ft) wide (Morris and von Hagen 1993:105). Excavation of these platforms indicates that they were not simply mounds of earth but carefully engineered agricultural facilities.

At one site, Pampa Koani, the platforms were shown to have been built in stages (Kolata 1986). First, a layer of stone cobbles was laid down as a base. The cobbles were covered with a layer of clay, which was in turn covered with three separate sheets of gravel. The productive topsoil was placed on top. The low-lying areas between the raised fields allowed the waters of Lake Titicaca to flow between the plantings. The complex design of these engineered fields ensured that brackish lake water would not percolate up through the mound to damage plants and that the entire facility would be well drained. As with raised fields elsewhere in the New World, the standing water between the platforms produced a rich organic soup that would then be scooped up and laid over the fields to fertilize the soil. This highly productive agricultural system was at the core of Tiwanaku wealth and power.

As we have seen in all of the civilizations discussed in this book, this wealth and power were invested in an elite class who lived in the palaces of Tiwanaku and who ruled over a vast area of hamlets populated by the commoners of Tiwanaku society—the people whose labor made it all possible. And as in all ancient—and modern—civilizations, there had to be a way to legitimize the rule, wealth, power, and comfort of the few over the many. As archaeologist Craig Morris and journalist Adriana von Hagen (1993) point out, legitimization at Tiwanaku was accomplished through religion. The position of the elite class was seen as part of the natural order of things. A complex social and political order was necessary to produce, maintain, and expand the culture's highly engineered agricultural system. That social and political order was reinforced by religious symbolism and monumental construction of palaces, temples, and monoliths. The influence of Tiwanaku extended across an enormous expanse of South America. Up to 1 million people living in what is now Peru, Bolivia, Ecuador, and Chile were followers of the Tiwanaku state religion.

Empires: Wari

Other civilizations also evolved in highland South America. For example, the **Wari** developed near the modern Peruvian city of Ayacucho. The Wari partly overlapped with Tiwanaku but peaked later, after A.D. 600. The capital of Wari was an enormous enclosure whose walled neighborhoods covered about 2 km^2 (about three-quarters of a square mile, or nearly 500 acres). The construction is truly monumental; some of the walls are 12 m (40 ft) high and several meters thick and extend for hundreds of meters. Much of the city seems to have been multistoried (Figure 13.8; Morris and von Hagen 1993).

Unlike Tiwanaku or the Aztecs, the Wari were not located on the shores of a lake and did not practice raised-field agriculture. They nevertheless practiced a labor-intensive and highly productive, engineered agricultural system that involved the construction of terraced fields, similar to those seen in Mexico at Teotihuacán. Agriculture also depended on an extensive system of irrigation works, including long canals that brought water from the uplands and distributed it across a complex network of branching secondary canals that led to the terraced fields.

Religious iconography centered at Wari is found represented in textiles and pottery across a broad swath of western South America (Figure 13.9). That the Wari gods appear to have been worshipped in a broad area is an indication of the power and influence of the Wari elite who were identified with those gods. As Morris and von Hagen (1993) point out, one of the most fascinating aspects of Wari is the way in which the leaders maintained their far-flung, religion-based empire. In a pattern that was to be followed again by the Inca, the Wari elite controlled outlying regions, funneling surplus labor and wealth to their capital, by the construction of regional administrative centers across Wari territory. For example, Azángaro, located 15 km northwest of Wari itself, was a walled enclosure built as a smaller version of Wari. Wari pottery is found at Azángaro, and the religious iconography is typically Wari. Other large regional centers scattered throughout Wari territory include Pikilacta and Jincamocco. These regional centers likely served

◀ **Figure 13.8**
Located on the southern periphery of Wari territory, the community of Pikilacta was part of the Wari polity and consists of a large number of walled compounds. (Neg. #334818. Courtesy of Department of Library Services, American Museum of Natural History)

as local offices of the elite, perhaps staffed by
Wari nobility, making sure that local populations were participating fully in the Wari state
by sending their surplus food to the capital and
providing labor for the monumental works required by the elite.

Empires: Chimu

The empire of Chimor, or the **Chimu**, extended across more than 1,300 km (800 mi)
of the western coast of South America, essentially the entire northern coast of Peru. Built
beginning sometime before A.D. 900 and expanding at around 1200, the Chimu capital at
Chan Chan was one of the most impressive urban centers constructed in the
ancient world. From the air it is absolutely remarkable (Figure 13.10). Where
Tiwanaku covers an area of 4.5 km^2, Chan Chan's remnants reflect a city some
20 km^2 (almost 8 mi^2) in extent. It is a true city, with neighborhoods divided, in
part, according to which crafts were produced by the inhabitants (Topic 1990).

Irrigation was crucial in the development of the Chimu state and was, perhaps, along with the desire of the elite to incorporate surrounding territories
into its polity, the reason for its expansion across a huge territory. A sophisticated and monumental complex of irrigation canals produced a rich harvest for

the inhabitants of Chan Chan. However, local irrigation in the Moche valley may not have been enough to satisfy the growing population. In addition, as archaeologist Michael Mosely (cited in Morris and von Hagen 1993) points out, irrigated lands build up a concentration of salt, which diminishes harvests and necessitates the incorporation of additional, new lands into the system. Also, as Mosely suggests, the western coast of South America is geologically active. Earthquakes were more than merely a frightening nuisance to the ancient inhabitants of South America, seriously damaging and even destroying irrigation works. Mosely suggests that the Chimu elite found it easier and likely more productive to abandon fields fed by canals if they were destroyed by earthquakes and to annex new territories into their state. This approach would have served the dual purpose of providing more farmland and also new workers—the inhabitants of the annexed territories—for the state.

Empires: The Inca

As seen in this chapter, the Inca civilization that most people have at least heard of did not arise without antecedents in South America. In fact, the Inca were merely the latest in a series of empires that had achieved prominence and hegemony over the Andean region of South America when the Spanish conquistadors, led by Francisco Pizarro, entered their territory in A.D. 1532. In fact, much of what we know about Incan history and culture we know from the records of the Spanish soldiers, missionaries, and colonists who invaded their territory in the sixteenth and seventeenth centuries (for example, the Jesuit missionary Bernabé Cobo: 1979, 1990).

Research led by archaeologist Brian Bauer is beginning to reveal the roots of Inca history (Pringle 2011b). While other, pre-Inca states, like the Wari, were suffering as the result of a sustained drought in the thirteenth century A.D., the Inca people were somewhat insulated from this dry period as a result of their location in a wet, high-altitude river valley near the modern city of Cuzco. While other societies were fragmenting as a result of the drought, the Inca thrived, expanding their agricultural land by terracing higher and wetter slopes. In essence, the drought appears to have created a power vacuum in the Andean highlands of Peru. The Inca took advantage of that and expanded to fill that vacuum, becoming the dominant economic and political force there in the fourteenth century. By the early fifteenth century, Pachacutec, a charismatic leader and brilliant military tactician, arose among the Inca. Under his rule, the Inca achieved a level of economic and political power unseen previously in South America. By A.D. 1500, the Inca, who called their nation Tawantinsuyu (The Four Parts Together"), controlled a broad empire of close to 1 million km^2 (380,000 mi^2; about the size of the modern nation of Egypt), extending across 4,000 km (2,500 mi) of South America's Pacific coast (Figure 13.11). By way of comparison, the length of the eastern coast of the United States, from northernmost Maine to the southern tip of Florida, is only about 3,200 km (2,000 mi) long. It is estimated that as many as 10 million people were citizens of the Inca empire at its peak (D'Altroy 2003:1). That's about the modern population size of Portugal or Bolivia.

The capital at Cuzco was similar to the capitals of older Andean states, only bigger. It was filled with palaces, temples, and plazas. The impressive masonry seen

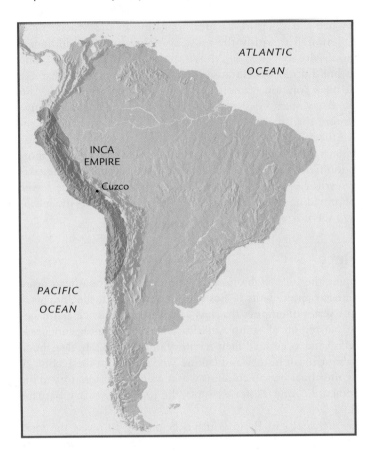

at older sites was raised to a level of perfection at Cuzco, home to the elite of Inca society (Figure 13.12); these are the same folks who, during their downtime, might head off to Machu Picchu for some R & R.

Inca Royalty

The Inca developed a highly regimented and rigid political hierarchy. Their socioeconomic pyramid (see Figure 10.4) was tall, narrow, and steep. At its apex was the king, the supreme ruler, in fact, called "the Inca." Directly under him were his children, especially his sons, along with his grandsons and great-grandsons. Just beneath the immediate family of the Inca king were other people of royal blood, other members of his family.

The next level in this hierarchy consisted of two distinct groups. The first were ethnically Inca aristocrats, bearers of the same culture and representatives of the same ethnicity as the king, but not in his direct family line. People in the second group were called "Incas by Privilege." These were, essentially, "honorary Inca," local people who, though not ethnically Inca, were considered loyal subjects whose ancestors could be traced back in the region of the Inca capital (D'Altroy 2003).

Death, alone, did not remove Inca kings from this political hierarchy. In fact, upon death and after an elaborate funeral, the king's body was mummified and

◄ **Figure 13.12**
The puzzle-piece walls of Sacsayhuman are emblematic of the great skill developed by ancient Inca masons. Enormous stone blocks were individually carved to fit precisely against several neighbors. Take a look at the photograph; you'll see a few simple, four-sided rectangles, but lots of stones with as many as six or seven sides, each butting up against a neighboring stone. It must have taken a tremendous amount of time to make the fit so precise, but as a result of this precision, many of the Inca walls have survived centuries of substantial and frequent earthquake activity, while later walls built by the Spanish have tumbled down.
(Michael Hanson/National Geographic Society/Corbis)

installed in a palace built for his afterlife. Though dead, he was attended to, consulted, and included in royal conversations. The deceased Inca king was feted, given food and drink, and, in fact, treated as if he were still alive and engaged in the important conversations of the Inca state (Pizarro 1986). It would be almost like President Obama making regular visits to Disney's Hall of Presidents to schmooze with the animatronic versions of Washington and Lincoln. All right, not exactly, but you get the point.

The "rich and famous" lifestyle of the deceased king was financially supported through the practice of **split inheritance**. Kingship was passed from father to son. Upon the king's death, the son deemed most able to rule inherited the crown and control of the Inca state, but the personal wealth of the dead king, essentially, stayed with him. The Inca believed, apparently, that you can take it with you when you go. Obviously, the deceased king was in no position to write checks or pay his bills, so those tasks fell to his other relatives. In other words, the king's wealth did not go to his son, but to his other relatives who, in a sense, had power of attorney over his fortune so they could keep him, in death, in the lifestyle to which he had become accustomed in life.

Inca Agricultural Infrastructure

It is easy to become distracted by the incredibly impressive achievements of Inca architects, but the more mundane engineering accomplishments of the Inca deserve our attention as well. For example, the Inca were an agricultural people living in a largely mountainous region where the low-lying, level fields preferred by farmers in antiquity as well as in the modern world were limited. Needless to say, agriculture is challenging in regions characterized by the steeply sloping surfaces that dominate many of the areas where the Inca lived. They responded to this challenge by resculpting the land to better suit their needs. In what must have represented a tremendous investment of time and labor, the Inca converted steep slopes unsuitable for agriculture into a series of enormously productive flat and fertile steps, or terraces.

An examination of the terraces around Machu Picchu (see the "Prelude" for this chapter) provides a detailed picture of how such fields were engineered (Burger 2004). To produce each individual step in a series of such steps, the Inca began by hauling in and laying down a flat layer of stones to build up and level a sloped surface and to aid in drainage. On top of the stones, they deposited another layer, this time of medium-sized gravel, again to aid in drainage. Above this, they placed a layer of fine sand mixed with gravel for drainage and stability. Finally, as the top layer, the Inca deposited a substantial layer of rich and fertile topsoil extracted from the valley below the slope. Each step in the terrace was held in place by constructing a stone-block retaining wall in the front, giving the entire set-up the appearance of a series of stair steps (Figure 13.13). For increased stability, each retaining wall was built so as to lean into the hill at an angle of about 5 degrees. This intense labor converted acres of unusable, steeply sloping hill and mountainsides into valuable, productive farmland. At Machu Picchu, for example, by constructing six sets of terraces, the Inca land engineers created, from unusable land, more than 15,000 m^2 (165,320 ft^2, or nearly 3.8 acres) of arable farmland (Zegarra 2004:79). Archaeologist Alfredo Zegarra (2004:79) estimates that this reclaimed land alone would have produced an annual yield of nearly 2,400 kg (5,280 lb) of maize (off the cob), along with small amounts of other agricultural produce. The productive potential of all of the terraces produced by the Inca is enormous.

How Did the Inca Support Their Economic System?

All complex societies rely on what amounts to skimming a certain percentage of privately held wealth to pay for public projects related to infrastructure, for the military, government services, individual benefits, and so forth. In our own, twenty-first-century complex society, we are in the throes of a series of philosophical debates concerning the appropriate number, kind, extent, and cost of projects run by the government, benefits supplied, and entitlements distributed. Inextricably linked to this discussion is the fundamental challenge posed by the following questions: What is a reasonable and equitable level at which our citizens

▲ **Figure 13.13**
Through careful, time-consuming, and brilliant engineering the Inca transformed steeply sloped land into highly productive agricultural fields. This example from Machu Picchu shows the pattern of wall construction that allowed for the production of flat, agriculturally viable terraces. (© Dave G. Houser/Corbis)

should be taxed to pay for these things? Should everyone contribute, even the poor? Should the rich pay a higher percentage of their incomes in taxes? How much more? And how do we define "rich," anyway?

Regardless of the outcome of this seemingly intractable debate, all citizens of all complex societies expect stuff from their governments: good roads, safe bridges, secure borders, law and order, an economic safety net for those who have fallen on hard times. And there's no such thing as a "free lunch." The various benefits that accrue to the citizens of a complex society must be paid for, and the people—that means you and I—are always left with the check. This fact was no different for the Inca. Part of their solution, as described by the Spanish invaders of their territory, was a system call *mit'a* or *mita*.

You will sometimes hear people today speak in a joking, yet disparaging way about how grateful they are that the government generously "allows" them to keep a small part of their paycheck. This was no joke in the Inca economic system; this perspective was actually enforced as a rule of law. The Inca government legally claimed ownership of *everything* and "generously" allowed those under its sway to use stuff, especially land, only in exchange for labor for the state (D'Altroy 2003). Look around your house; think about that house, your car, your computer. Imagine if the fundamental economic philosophy underpinning our country was the belief that all that stuff you think you own actually belongs to the government and you only get to use it in return for national service for a few months each year—as a soldier, ditch-digger, or construction worker. The *mit'a* was the name given by the Inca to this required labor service (*mit'a* means "turn," as in, "it's your turn to work for the state").

The Inca built roads, bridges, and palaces for their rulers and ran a far-flung empire with a vast and powerful military machine. The government needed workers and soldiers to accomplish these things, who, in turn, needed support services, especially food. All that work was facilitated through the *mit'a*.

In a turn that really is sort of brilliant, the *mit'a* was not a fixed labor contribution required from each head of household. In other words, the *mit'a* contribution was not the equivalent of a fixed tax everyone has to pay each year. According to seventeenth-century Spanish Jesuit missionary Bernabé Cobo, the *mit'a* was calculated on what amounts to a sliding scale proportional to the jobs the government decided needed doing in a given year (Cobo 1979). Imagine if the U.S. government, instead of setting a fixed tax rate of 20% or 35% or 40% of income each year, decided that with ongoing wars, companies requiring bailouts, and the number of unemployed needing benefits just to survive, this year the tax rate will be more like 90%. Maybe it will be lower next year. Sure. You have to admit; that's pretty smart. The *mit'a* applied to household heads between the ages of 25 and 50. That added up to a national labor pool of about 2 million workers (D'Altroy 2003:266). It's no wonder the Inca maintained a vast empire.

The Inca Military Empire

Many early state societies fought wars of plunder, attacking their neighbors, appropriating the wealth of the vanquished, and then absconding with their treasure. The Inca employed this practice early in their history, but their empire then evolved a different strategy. As they reached their ascendancy, the Inca became expansionist, and their goal was not just accumulating the spoils of war but also achieving hegemony over their entire region, incorporating the defeated into their empire. In other words, the Inca fought their wars to actually expand their state geographically. Largely through military conquest enabled by an enormous army estimated to have included as many as 80,000 soldiers (D'Altroy 2003:1), the Inca brought together under their rule an enormous and diverse series of cultures and ethnic groups across a broad swath of western South America. Even just the threat of military action on the part of the Inca sometimes was enough to convince a local non-Incan state to acquiesce and join the empire.

As an expansionist empire that appended the vanquished into their polity, the vast majority of people who were citizens of the Inca state were not culturally or ethnically "Inca." In fact, it is estimated that, at the peak of the empire, those who could claim to be ethnic Incas represented only about 1% of the population (D'Altroy 2003: 231). In other words, while they ruled over a vast empire, the Inca themselves were outnumbered in that empire by a ratio of about 100:1. Ultimately, this may have led to their undoing when the Spanish arrived in 1532 and most citizens of Tawantinsuyu were happy to have an invader dismember the empire that had subjugated them.

Certainly, there was a degree of tension between the Inca and the non-Inca people over whom they ruled. Recognizing this tension, the Inca organized their empire into 80 distinct provinces and built administrative centers in the capitals of the states they subdued. In these centers, the Inca appointed one of their own, an ethnic Inca, to the position of provincial governor. In another clever political strategy, representatives of groups subdued in battle were forced to move to and live in Cuzco, the capital of the Inca empire. Many of those removed from their home territories were members of the local political elite. These political leaders likely played a role in administering their home territories for the Inca. In return, they got to continue to breathe and, in all likelihood, lived under conditions far superior to the situation of the folks back home. In other words, as Morris and von Hagen (1993) maintain, these "guests" of the Inca effectively served as hostages, ensuring the obedience of their homelands to Inca rule.

The Inca elites in Cuzco were able to control their vast empire by constructing an incredible system of roads linking the various provinces. Estimates suggest that, altogether, the Inca road system stretched for more than 48,000 km (30,000 mi), connecting even the most distant communities in the Inca empire, passing through deep jungles, over towering peaks, and across rope bridges spanning vast mountain chasms. Though the Inca possessed no special technology for moving along these roads—no llama-drawn wheeled vehicles, for example—the roads ensured that they could move relatively quickly in response to any real threat or rumor of rebellion that faced their empire.

The governor's job included making certain that the empire's subjects continued to farm and to provide a portion of their produce to the Inca elite, allowing them to live in splendor in places like the royal estate of Machu Picchu discussed in the "Prelude" of this chapter. The governor also administered the system by which local people incorporated into the empire contributed their labor and, at times, even their lives to work and fight for the state. Roads, temples, palaces, and royal estates needed to be built and maintained, and wars needed to be fought to continue to grow the empire. The provincial governor made sure that the people over whom he ruled provided the resources that allowed the empire both to thrive and to expand.

The Inca were more than smart enough to realize that a conquered people will rarely fully accept their subjugation and will subvert that subjugation in whatever ways they can. Recognizing this, the Inca practiced a policy in which they broke up large population units of people over whom they had been militarily victorious and then dispersed those populations through relocation. It is estimated that the Inca commonly removed between one-quarter and one-third of a resident population, often resettling them hundreds or even thousands of kilometers away (D'Altroy 2003). These resettled people were called *mitmaqkuna*.

The cliché is right; there's strength in numbers. By breaking up large groups of "former" enemies into smaller ones and by moving them separately all across the Inca empire, the Inca diminished the possibility that such people could successfully organize an insurrection against the Inca state.

Reading about this policy of relocation, it occurred to me that, while this may have worked initially, different ethnic or cultural groups thrust together by this Inca policy might be drawn to work in tandem to undermine Inca hegemony. Well, the Inca had that figured out as well. When a new group of *mitmaqkuna* were brought into a territory, the Inca gave them lots of perks. The government supported them and confiscated the best farmland from local people and gave it to the new residents. This acted, or course, to generate tremendous resentment against the newcomers among the people already living in the area. The Inca attempted to further isolate the resettled group from others in a region by requiring each to speak only its own language and to continue wearing its own variety of clothing, and by formally restricting their interaction. It didn't always work and it didn't always last, but it was a clever way of putting up roadblocks to organized resistance to the Inca state. Referencing another cliché, the Inca added an additional level to the adage, "divide and conquer." For the Inca it was "conquer, divide those conquered, and in so doing, keep control."

It is remarkable to think how much modern technology has changed this equation. Between texting, tweeting, websites, and YouTube, even people geographically removed from one another can, nevertheless, communicate, organize, rebel, and revolt. The Inca, obviously, didn't have to deal with that and, so, their relocation policy was largely successful in dampening the ability of ethnic and cultural groups who they had defeated militarily to organize, undermine, and regain their sovereignty.

All conquered lands became the property of the Inca state. The previous owners became tenants who were allowed to continue to use those lands only at the discretion of the governor and, ultimately, the emperor himself. The "privilege" of being allowed to work the land that had previously belonged to the groups the Inca had subdued was granted only through payment of a tax—not in cash, but in the bushels of maize, potatoes, manioc, quinoa, jícama, cotton, and so forth needed to supply the enormous needs of the Inca state apparatus.

Certainly, Inca wars and the strategy of annexing defeated territories and their people, at least in part, had the practical aim of supplying the state with ever-increasing, secure, consistent, and reliable sources of food, wealth, labor, and soldiers. Territories were selected for invasion and annexation with the goal of supplying the needs of the elites for rare and exotic raw materials, including gold and the brilliantly colored feathers of tropical birds found in the jungles of South America, spondylus shells available along the coast, and various minerals offered by the territories to the south of Cuzco.

Inca wars had another, less material rationale. One way in which individuals could improve their status and position in Inca society was through service in combat. In a sense, in this regard, the Inca weren't that different from us in the modern world. Certainly, it is no coincidence that of the 44 U.S. presidents who have served as this is being written, 30 (68%) served in the military in some capacity and many were veterans of war—their ability to lead, some have argued, forged in the crucible of combat. It is clearly the case among the Inca that military service, particularly during times of war, provides an opportunity for individuals to display personal characteristics that may allow them to gain the respect of their fellow citizens and later to rise to power in their society. In fact, among the Inca, war may have become a necessary vehicle to provide opportunities for men to exhibit the courage, heroism, patriotism, and dedication to the state required to attain a high level of status and power.

A State Without Writing?

So far in this book we have talked a bit about the world's most ancient writing systems, specifically the cuneiform of Mesopotamia, the hieroglyphics of ancient Egypt, the script of the Indus Valley civilization, the bone writing of the Chinese Shang, and the hieroglyphics of the Maya. In some cases, these early systems of record keeping focused on practical economic issues (especially the earliest writing in Mesopotamia and Egypt) amounting to, essentially and rather unromantically, the archives of accountants keeping track of goods, services, and taxes. Other early writing systems, notably that of the Maya, seem far more focused on genealogy and history, validating in a permanent form the elevated position of the leaders of the Maya city-states. Whatever the particular focus of the specific ancient writing system discussed, they all share the fact that they served the purposes of the state societies in which they were used. Each of the writing systems just mentioned had its own unique way of using conventionalized symbols to keep unambiguous records of things deemed necessary for running the state, intelligible to anyone who knew the code.

Is it possible to have a complex state society in which there was no system of record keeping, no way of keeping track in an unambiguous way, of the production of crops, the manufacture of goods, the payment of taxes, or the lineage and accomplishments of the king? Could the government, bureaucracy, and economy of the United States operate without a writing system; could we function if taxes, laws, business, and banking were all based on the honor system? If the old expression, "knowledge is power," is correct, how can any state society truly possess and wield power if it doesn't have the ability to control the underlying knowledge by codifying it in a clear and concrete way through permanent record keeping?

This question has long vexed those who study the Inca. Clearly the Inca possessed a powerful state society, but there does not appear to have been an Incan writing system. This assertion, however, may reflect our own limited view of what a writing system actually needs to be.

All of the early record-keeping systems discussed so far in this book shared several characteristics in common, including one that may seem so obvious to us it barely warrants mentioning: They were all two-dimensional systems. Records were kept by impressing conventionalized shapes onto soft clay tablets, by applying ink to papyrus or paint to bark, or by carving hieroglyphs onto flat stone surfaces. Though it might seem self-evident that writing is, by definition, a two-dimensional system of record keeping—this certainly is the case with our own system of writing—it appears that the Inca used not a two-dimensional system but a three-dimensional system of record keeping.

The Inca did not ink symbols onto paper or papyrus, they did not press standardized marks onto clay, and they did not carve hieroglyphs onto stelae. Instead, the Inca produced what appear to have been conventionalized, rule-bound symbolic records in the form of knotted strings called **khipu**, and these records could be read by those who understood the underlying code (Figure 13.14). Though it might seem alien to us, that makes the khipu a writing system (Ascher and Ascher 1997; Urton 2003).

The khipu share an unfortunate history with Maya writing; the Spanish missionaries thought they represented idol worship and were banned. Many khipu were destroyed. Nevertheless, today there are about 600 existing khipu in museums and private collections. Some were found individually, but some were found in groups; for example, 21 khipu were discovered under the floor of a single house at the site called Puruchuco and likely were the records of what amounts to an individual Inca accountant (Urton and Brezine 2005).

▶ **Figure 13.14**
The Inca had no system of writing, but they did have khipu; a system of knotted strings by which they kept the records of their empire. (© Peabody Museum, Harvard University, Photo #N21754)

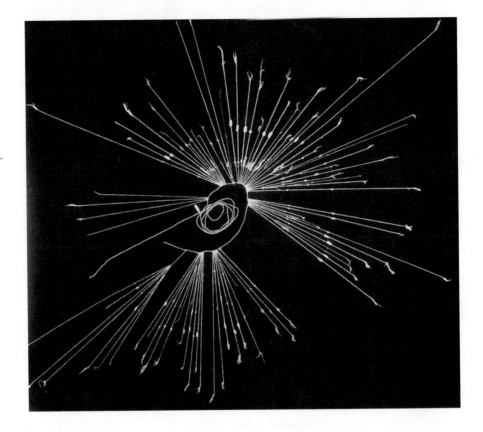

Before they decided they represented the devil's work, the Spanish invaders wrote about the khipu and the way they were read by the record keepers, men called *khipukamayuq*. The Spanish saw the *khipukamayuq* in action, using the khipu, and described the information they clearly seemed to be reading from them: primarily census data, information about quantities of goods in storehouses, amounts of taxes and tribute, calendrical information, and genealogies (Urton 2003:3).

Inca specialist Gary Urton (2003:55) has examined about 450 of the extant khipu and concluded that about two-thirds contain this kind of accounting information. Numbers were coded through the placement of the khipu knots on so-called pendant strings, representing increasing powers of ten as you approach the main string from which the pendant strings are suspended. Urton believes that the other one-third of the khipu he examined may represent actual narratives readable by the *khipukamayuq* in much the same way that an ancient Egyptian or Maya scribe could have read the messages conveyed in their hieroglyphic writing systems.

Though there is, as yet, no equivalent to the Rosetta Stone, no Spanish translation that can be associated with a specific khipu, progress is being made at least in the attempt to figure out the code underlying the khipu system. In a fascinating approach, Urton suggests that the khipu were written in what amounts to a binary code. In his view, the production and placement of each knot on a khipu involved seven discrete steps—six of these steps involve distinct decisions regarding knot production, each with two possible outcomes (raw material: cotton or wool; yarn or string spinning direction: clockwise or counterclockwise; etc.). Combining these binary steps with a seventh step in the selection of one of the 24 string colors used by the Inca, you come up with more than 1,500 ways to produce and place each knot ($2^6 \times 24 = 1,536$), producing a vocabulary at least equal to that of the 1,000 to 1,500 separate cuneiform signs (Mann 2003).

Urton and Brezine (2005:1067) found a consistent feature in the khipu recovered in the excavation of Puruchuco, a series of three figure-eight knots at the beginning of each record. They read this particular series of three knots as the name of the place that the data recorded on the knotted string refer to, in this case Puruchuco. Certainly, a state-required accounting record that enumerates goods or taxes needs to be associated with a particular place and people. Urton and Brezine may have figured out how the khipu accomplished this and, in so doing, they may have translated what amounts to a word written in the khipu's knots: Puruchuco. Though the translation of khipu is only in its infancy, it is hoped that with additional study, the recovery of more of them, and, ultimately, the discovery of an actual khipu alongside a Spanish translation, the Inca may someday be able to speak to us in a manner similar to the scribes of the other early civilizations.

The End of the Inca State

In a sense, the rigidly hierarchical political and social system that had been the source of Inca success was turned against them by the Spanish conquistadors when they invaded Inca territory in 1532. Though armed with guns and having the advantage of being on horseback, the Spanish arrived in small numbers—there were only about 180 of them—and could easily have been defeated by the powerful and enormous Inca army of 80,000, an army that had played a major role in constructing the largest empire seen in the New World. In August 1533, when Pizarro captured the Inca ruler Atawallpa, who, in Inca political culture, was the source of all decisions, the Inca were paralyzed. Though nearly 4,000 Inca soldiers were present when Atawallpa was taken, they were unable to attack the much smaller Spanish force because that would have risked the life of their ruler.

Though the Inca paid a ransom estimated in modern currency to have been the equivalent of 50 million dollars to effect Atawallpa's release (D'Altroy 2003:1), Pizarro realized that in freeing the Inca ruler, he likely would be sealing his own doom. After accepting the ransom, Pizarro killed Atawallpa anyway, throwing the Inca political system into disarray. The empire fell apart as its component parts, always resentful of Inca control, broke away, ending the reign of the most powerful indigenous civilization in the New World.

THE WORLD'S FIRST CIVILIZATIONS HAD MANY features in common. They all were remarkable cultures, spectacularly successful and complex adaptations to their environments. Yet, as successful as they were, all of these early civilizations shared another element that may reflect a fundamental instability in their adaptation. All of these civilizations collapsed.

ISSUES AND DEBATES

Why Do Civilizations Collapse?

The heading used for this section is really shorthand for, "why do civilizations collapse, is collapse inevitable, and what is collapse anyway?" Clearly, state societies run into trouble, are faced with challenges, and devise ways of dealing with those challenges. We saw that in the last chapter when we talked about the so-called collapse of the Maya. As archaeologist Joseph Tainter (1988:37) phrases it: "complex societies are problem-solving organizations." What happens when complex societies can't or simply refuse to come up with solutions to internal or external challenges? And, perhaps even more fundamentally, what if what we interpret as collapse from our examination of the archaeological record—for example, an abandonment of urban centers, a cessation or severe scaling back of monumental construction projects, and a cutback in the wealth placed into the tombs of rulers—doesn't reflect a catastrophic, uncontrolled dissolution of a society, but is the result, instead, of a conscious reorganization, a scaling back of conspicuous consumption, a rational, reasonable, and intentional response by a people facing serious problems in their economic, political, or social systems? But all that verbiage doesn't make for an easy-to-understand sound bite or attention-grabbing heading in a newspaper or, for that matter, in a textbook.

Whether we call it collapse or something else, as archaeologist George Cowgill (1988) points out, state societies historically run into trouble for a number of internal, economic reasons. Expensive bureaucracies proliferate, marked by "increasing corruption, rigidity, incompetence, extravagance, and (perhaps) inefficiency" (Cowgill 1988:263). At the same time, citizens of complex state societies have increasing expectations of services the state should be providing them. All of this sounds disturbingly familiar. Think of our current economic woes. Entitlements make up more than 65% of the U.S. federal budget.

Tainter (1988:89–90) has summarized the causes proposed for the collapse of civilizations in this way:

1. *Resource depletion*—The large, dense populations associated with civilizations and their intensive exploitation of the environment lead to the depletion of key resources and the ultimate collapse of the society.

2. *New resources*—The discovery of new resources eliminates the need for the more complex and stratified social hierarchy of civilizations, and this decentralization leads to the dissolution of the society.

3. *Catastrophes*—Natural catastrophes such as hurricanes, earthquakes, and volcanic eruptions are the root cause of the collapse of civilizations. A book published in 2008 describes historical instances in which major earthquakes destroyed entire cities and changed the course of history (Nur and Burgess 2008). Could not such a catastrophe destroy an ancient civilization?

4. *Insufficient response to circumstances*—As a result of their inherent complexity, civilizations become rigid in their adaptation, and their own inertia makes it difficult, if not impossible, for them to change quickly enough to respond to changes in external or internal conditions.

5. *Other complex societies*—Competition or conflict with other civilizations can lead to the collapse of a civilized society.

6. *Intruders*—Attacks by a more mobile, more aggressive group of intruders can lead to collapse.

7. *Mismanagement*—The elite in a civilization may so abuse their power and direct so much of the surplus wealth and labor of their society to their own benefit that not enough is left for the maintenance of the economic and political system, leading to collapse.

8. *Economic explanations*—Civilizations are expensive to keep going and require increasing amounts of labor and wealth to maintain themselves. As civilizations grow, the upper classes grow—and so does their need for surplus wealth. The overall costs of supporting the system with specialists, servants, slaves, soldiers, police, and so on grow at an increasing rate. Eventually, civilizations simply become top-heavy and economically nonviable. The increasing effort to maintain them produces diminishing returns and leads to their collapse.

As Tainter indicates, most of the enumerated explanations for why civilizations ultimately collapse beg the question. Explanations of environmental catastrophe, the presence of intruders, competition with other civilizations, or resource depletion still leave open the fundamental question: Why can't civilization adequately deal with or respond to such challenges?

The Role of Environment in Collapse

Consider the following question: What would happen, even to our own, technologically very sophisticated society, if the agricultural basis of our subsistence were to be severely disrupted? In thinking about this possibility, researchers have encountered a number of remarkably timed co-occurrences of environmental downturns and the collapse of ancient civilizations. For example, in Chapter 10 we talked about the rise of urban civilization in Mesopotamia and noted that what appears to be the world's first city, Uruk, developed about 5,500 years ago. At that time, Uruk was a city of at least 10,000 people, thriving as the capital of a vast and powerful city-state whose dominance was made possible by a complex and efficient, irrigation-based, agricultural subsistence system. Yet, at the peak of its development, over the relatively short period of the two centuries between 5,200 and 5,000 years ago, Uruk collapsed into chaos. We may know the reason. Analysis of deep-sea cores in the Gulf of Oman shows a sharp increase in dust blowing off of the land and onto the sea at this time. This has led paleoclimatologists to suggest that a relentless drought afflicted Mesopotamia during this period, one that would have severely impaired any agriculturally based economic system (Weiss and Bradley 2001). Another drought, this one dated to about 3,900 years ago, may have had a serious impact on the Indus Valley civilization (Lawler 2007, 2008b). Soon after 3900 B.P., Mohenjo-daro was abandoned, and more than 90% of its surrounding communities disappeared. The city never recovered.

We talked about the possible effect of a two-centuries-long drought on the Maya in Chapter 12. We saw that the drought had an impact, but the Maya response was more complicated than simply falling apart. Similarly, the Moche, discussed earlier in this chapter, didn't just call it quits when faced with a severe environmental challenge. The main Moche site where the inhabitants built the

Huaca del Sol was abandoned by about A.D. 600. This abandonment can be shown to correlate with the drying up of their primary irrigation channels, which provided water to the expansive agricultural fields that allowed a large, dense, urban population to exist in this region (deMenocal 2001). Archaeological evidence at Moche shows that the irrigation channels dried up around A.D. 600 and then were covered by shifting sand dunes, signifying their complete abandonment. Interestingly, however, the Moche did not collapse upon the onset of this dry period; instead, they moved. In apparent response to the onset of aridity, the Moche rapidly shifted to sites farther inland and adjacent to rivers whose waters were a more dependable source than rainfall for irrigation.

Collapse as a Sensible Response

How about our own, modern civilization? How will we respond to a major environmental challenge? Consider the long-term impacts of climate change. How will our modern civilization respond when coastal cities are threatened by sea-level rise? What will happen as currently productive agricultural lands become less productive while the world heats up and precipitation patterns shift? What happens when the "nuclear" club expands yet again, more countries produce stockpiles of nuclear weapons, and the world becomes a substantially more dangerous place? What will be the result as economic power shifts and poor nations become wealthy, and wealthy nations become poor? I guess we'll see.

The point here is pretty simple: All societies, ancient and modern, respond to the various challenges they face. The big questions are as follows: (1) How do they respond and (2) in their response, are they able to continue in a recognizable form? We may call it "collapse" when the new way of life, the new strategy for survival, is so altered, so shifted, so reconfigured that we hardly even recognize the culture anymore. But we need to understand that, short of a response (or lack of response) to an existential threat that results in the actual extinction of a society's people, those social, economic, and political reconfigurations sometimes labeled "collapse" are often sensible, rational, prudent, and viable.

CASE STUDY CLOSE-UP

SHE WAS JUST 15 YEARS OLD when she died, but her life had changed dramatically about a year before her death some 500 years ago. Her body was positioned on the top of a 6,739-m (22,000-ft)-tall mountain in what is today Argentina. Called the Llullaillaco Maiden, she was not alone in her mountaintop shrine. Nearby were the bodies of a 7-year-old boy and a 6-year-old girl. All three were finely clothed and interred with precious treasure: beautiful ceramics, gold bracelets, feathered headdresses, and gold and silver figurines. The Maiden, her legs crossed in a seated position, looks like she's asleep (Figure 13.15). She was placed in her shrine along with a beautiful gold statuette of a woman, which is, itself, wrapped in fine cloth. The boy, seated with his head resting on his knees, was accompanied by an exquisite statuette of a llama, all in gold. He looks, in fact, just like a little boy who has recently fallen asleep. The 6-year-old girl is seated and a gruesome sight: Sometime after her sacrifice it appears that she was struck by lightning; ground strikes of lightning during storms are not uncommon in the high elevations of the Andes. Otherwise, the cold, dry air of this Andean mountaintop has preserved their bodies

◄ **Figure 13.15**
The so-called Llullaillco Maiden was just fifteen years old when she died, the oldest of three children sacrificed by the Inca in a mountain shrine. The Inca viewed mountain peaks like Llullaillco as places imbued with great spiritual power. To placate that power, apparently, the Inca sacrificed individuals from the youngest and most innocent of their population. (ASSOCIATED PRESS/ Natacha Pisarenko)

to a remarkable degree, naturally mummifying them. It is clear from their examination that these children had been ritually sacrificed.

An analysis of their well-preserved hair has enabled researchers to reconstruct their genetic profiles and dietary histories. A DNA analysis shows that none of the three children were closely related; the three do not represent a family (Wilson et al. 2007). As discussed in Chapter 2, the carbon isotope proportions in the body of an animal or human being reflect aspects of their diet. While the carbon isotope proportions in a bone reflect a lifelong dietary pattern, hair preserves a series of snapshots of a diet on a much more precise time frame. Hair grows, on average, about 1 cm a month and, once grown out, doesn't change in its carbon isotope composition. So, by sampling at different points along a strand of hair, the diet during that period of hair growth can be determined and month-by-month dietary changes recognized.

Based on an analysis of their hair (Wilson et al. 2007), researchers determined that all three children had spent most of their short lives eating the diet of Inca commoners. In all likelihood, potatoes made up a significant portion of their diets. However, in the months preceding their deaths, their diets changed dramatically. During their final year, the sacrificed children had eaten well, feasting on meat and maize. Finally, although it is unclear how the children were killed (in other examples of Inca child sacrifice, death came by a blow to the head), at least it is known that all three had been medicated with coca (a common Inca practice intended to mitigate the effects of altitude sickness).

As writer Ann Gibbons (2012c) points out, it seems unlikely that the children were war captives or slaves; the quality and value of their grave goods suggest otherwise. Killed they may have been, but their bodies were treated with enormous respect, reverence, even love. It seems far more likely that these children had been selected from the commoner class to serve an important religious purpose as the sacrificial offerings in an Inca ritual called *capacocha*, the details of which were recorded by the Spanish in the sixteenth century. According to these descriptions, children were selected a year in advance, removed from their families, and then surrounded with comfort and riches. Then, at the appointed time, they began a long trek up into the mountains with their handlers where they were placed in shrines. In some cases they were killed; in some they were left alive to slowly die as a result of the elevation, the cold, and starvation. It sounds like murder to us, but to the Inca, these children were blessed, becoming one with the mountains, closer to their gods, and, in a way, immortalized.

The Inca viewed the mountains as a source of great power and spirit and felt that they needed to be propitiated. To these mountain powers or gods, they sacrificed the most precious, pure, innocent, and beautiful among them: their children. Well, at least the children of poor people.

Summary

In the New World, just as in the Old, some farming societies eventually developed the ability to produce a food surplus. This surplus enabled the development of social complexity and inequality. Eventually, some of these complex societies developed into true states with a formal government and true power invested in an elite class. The Inca and their predecessors in western South America developed independently of Old World civilizations. Through their concentration of wealth and power and as members of an elite social class in a stratified society, rulers were able to organize the labor of the many to produce the spectacular monuments—the pyramids and temples—that dominate the ancient landscapes of the Moche, Tiwanaku, Wari, Chimu, and the Inca.

Like the civilizations of the Old World, the complex societies of the New World eventually collapsed. Though many suggestions have been proposed to explain the process underlying the fall of ancient civilizations, including resource depletion, environmental catastrophes, invasion, and insurrection, no one of these explanations alone is sufficient. In each case of societal collapse, it is the inability of the society at a particular point in its evolution to respond adequately to a challenge, whatever that challenge may be, that leads to its disintegration.

For an excellent treatment of the development of the Inca, check out Terrence N. D'Altroy's (2003) monograph, *The Incas*. For the most recent discussion of khipu, take a look at *Signs of the Inka Khipu*, by Gary Urton (2003). Thomas C. Patterson's *Archaeology: The Historical Development of Civilizations* (1993) is as valuable for its discussion of New World civilization as it is for the Old World. Joseph Tainter's *The Collapse of Complex Societies* (1988) contains a very detailed presentation on the collapse of such societies.

Though its spectacular photographs might give you the impression that it's a coffee-table book, Craig Morris and Adriana von Hagen's *The Inka Empire and Its Andean Origins* (1993) offers detailed information about the evolution of civilization in South America presented in a nontechnical manner. James B. Richardson's *People of the Andes* (1994) provides a useful summary of the evolution and flowering of state societies in western South America. The book *Machu Picchu: Unveiling the Mysteries of the Incas* (2004), edited by Richard L. Burger and Lucy C. Salazar, that accompanied a museum exhibit at Yale University provides a series of wonderfully informative articles that both describe Machu Picchu in detail and place this incredible site in the firm context of Inca history and civilization. For a brief but beautifully illustrated recent article about the Inca and their history, take a look at the April 2011 issue of *National Geographic* (Pringle 2011b). University of California geography professor Jared Diamond is a scientist, well respected in his own academic field, and one of the best syntheses of a broad array of scientific data from a host of specialties. His popular book *Collapse: How Societies Choose to Fail or Succeed* (2005) is a thoughtful and insightful discussion of the collapse of civilizations, both ancient and modern.

TO LEARN MORE

Web links for this chapter can be found at www.oup.com/us/feder

KEY TERMS

Chimu, 444	*mit'a/mita*, 449	Tiwanaku, 441
geoglyphs, 441	*mitmaqkuna*, 451	Wari, 442
Inca, 436	Moche, 428	
khipu, 453	split inheritance, 447	

14

An Explosion of Complexity

North America

CHAPTER OVERVIEW

Beginning more than 5,000 years ago, the ancient inhabitants of the North American Midwest and Southeast began organizing large labor forces to produce enormous and impressive monuments of earth. The Native Americans who built the mounds were part of a socially, politically, and economically complex society whose great rulers could command the labor of thousands and were, in turn, buried in splendor. In the American Southwest, an entirely different pathway led also to complexity, with clear archaeological evidence for the coordination of large groups of people to construct great edifices of adobe brick, clay, and stone. The Mogollon, Hohokam, and Ancestral Puebloan (Anasazi) cultures have left us an archaeological legacy of great irrigation networks, hundreds of miles of ceremonial roadways, Great Houses, and remarkable cliff dwellings.

The "affluent foragers" of the northwest coast of North America provide yet another pathway that led to social and political complexity, producing a society ruled by powerful chiefs who could organize the labor of an extensive population.

The mound-building societies of the American Midwest and Southeast, the pueblo-dwelling people of the American Southwest, and the people of the northwest coast of North America are examples of ancient, complex, non-state societies.

	5,500	3,250	3,000
Mound Builders of American Midwest and Southeast	Watson Brake	Poverty Point	
American Southwest			
Northwest Coast of North America			

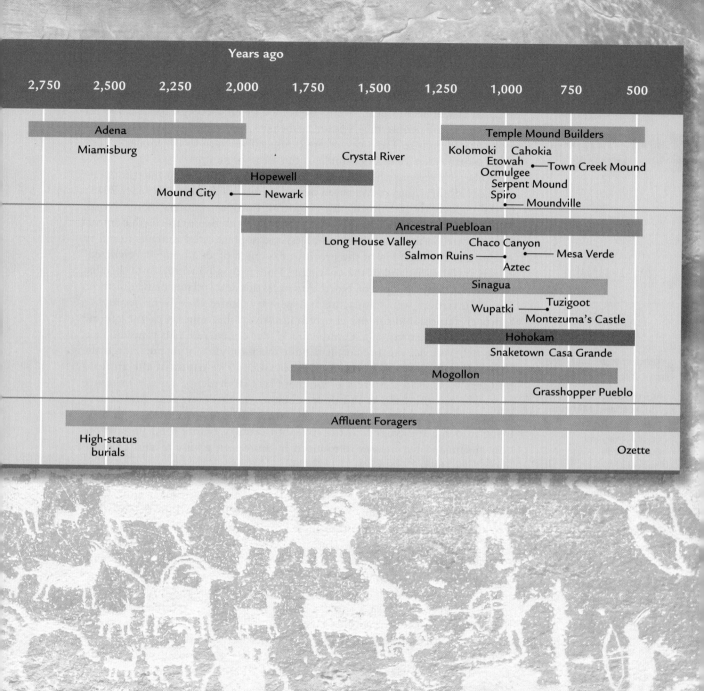

Years ago

| 2,750 | 2,500 | 2,250 | 2,000 | 1,750 | 1,500 | 1,250 | 1,000 | 750 | 500 |

Adena

Miamisburg

Crystal River

Temple Mound Builders

Kolomoki   Cahokia
Etowah
Ocmulgee ●——Town Creek Mound
Serpent Mound
Spiro
●——Moundville

Hopewell

Mound City ●——Newark

Ancestral Puebloan

Long House Valley   Chaco Canyon
Salmon Ruins ——————● ●——Mesa Verde
                    Aztec

Sinagua

Wupatki ●——Tuzigoot
        Montezuma's Castle

Hohokam

Snaketown Casa Grande

Mogollon

Grasshopper Pueblo

Affluent Foragers

High-status
burials

Ozette

PRELUDE

THE FIRST EUROPEANS TO ENCOUNTER THE impressive ruins at Great Zimbabwe presumed that indigenous Africans were not capable of producing such sophisticated and complex architecture. Zimbabwe certainly was not the only instance in which Europeans were confronted by archaeological evidence that the ancestors of people they wished to believe were inferior had produced a sophisticated culture. The story of the European reaction to the mound builders of North America is an example of this form of racism.

Robert Silverberg's book *The Mound Builders* (1989) is a wonderful treatment of this sorry saga in American history (also the Chapter 7 in Feder 2013). In the eighteenth and nineteenth centuries, European settlers of the North American continent were confronted with clear evidence, in the form of monumental works (the mounds themselves) and sophisticated artifacts found in and around the mounds, of the previous existence of an advanced, "civilized" culture in the heartland of the continent. Rather than conclude from this that the ancient native people of North America, the descendants of whom those European settlers were displacing and whose cultures they were destroying, had been responsible for the clearly impressive achievements of the mound builders, instead a myth of a "vanished race" was concocted. This vanished race, many believed, *not* the Indians, had built the mounds and manufactured the beautiful artifacts found in association with them. The **myth of the mound builders** took hold, despite the complete lack of evidence for the existence of anyone but the Indians and their ancestors on this continent. And it took hold even though historical records clearly described mound-building Indians living in dense settlements in the sixteenth century, before their populations were decimated by diseases introduced by European explorers and colonists (de la Vega 1605/1988; Elvas 1611/1966).

The controversy concerning the source of mound-builder culture was a vigorous one until relatively recently. It was an issue of great concern to the Smithsonian Institution, which funded a number of major investigations into the mound-builder question in the nineteenth century. More than 100 years ago a federal agency, the Bureau of American Ethnology, published researcher Cyrus Thomas's (1894/1985) voluminous work on the topic. During the course of his study, Thomas and his assistants examined 2,000 mound sites, collected over 40,000 artifacts, and examined countless historical documents and accounts. Not a shred of the evidence they examined supported the hypothesis of some vanished race of mound builders. Everything showed conclusively that the people who had built the mounds, the people who had produced the sophisticated material culture, the people who had developed the complex society that left these things behind had been none other than the American Indian. Stereotypes of primitive, nomadic tribes of Native Americans were hard to break, but break them Cyrus Thomas did. It is remarkable to think that this issue was resolved only 120 years ago. Today, Cahokia is included on the World Heritage Site list, an honor roll kept by the United Nations of significant archaeological sites worldwide. Its inclusion on this list memorializes the marvelous cultural achievements of the Native Americans who built it.

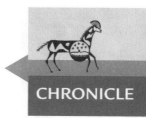

Complexity in Prehistoric America North of Mexico

The Development of Complexity

We saw in Chapter 9 that the Archaic period in the American Southeast is marked by the inception of large-scale communal construction projects involving the movement of copious quantities of earth into ridges and mounds. The specific sites mentioned in Chapter 9, including Watson Brake (dating to 5500 B.P.) and Poverty Point (dating to 3600 B.P.), though impressive in their own right and reflecting the ability of their builders to organize the labor of a substantial population, present only a faint hint of the mound-building abilities of the native peoples in the American Southeast and Midwest in the centuries that followed.

Beginning about 2,800 years ago and centered in the Ohio River valley, people bearing a culture today called **Adena** began constructing conical mounds of earth in which a religious and perhaps economic and social elite were buried (Figure 14.1). Lepper (2005:106) characterizes the period beginning 2,800 years ago as a time of "dramatic, if not revolutionary, cultural transformation." These transformations are, indeed, dramatic; one needs only to examine the remarkable art (Figure 14.2) and impressive earthworks of the Adena that far surpass the art and monuments that preceded them. At the same time, the accomplishments are not really revolutionary but evolutionary. The Adena in the **Early Woodland** period primarily expanded upon and elaborated practices that had their origins in the preceding Archaic; they became more sedentary and built larger and more elaborate earthworks, they increasingly relied on domesticated plants for their subsistence, and they buried their elite dead in increasing splendor (Lepper 2005).

Somewhat later, at about 2200 B.P., in what is called the **Middle Woodland** period, a different burial-mound-building group, the **Hopewell**, appeared with its own unique set of artifacts (Lepper 1995a). Adena and Hopewell traditions overlapped for about 200 years and are differentiated on the basis of certain artifact types. Over that 200-year period of overlap, the Hopewell pattern gradually

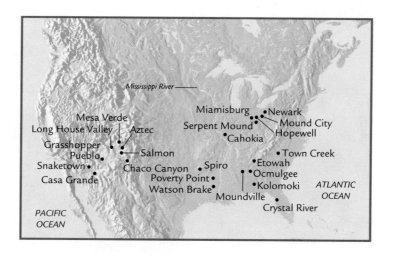

◀ **Figure 14.1**
Archaeological sites in North America where evidence of chiefdom-level societies has been found.

replaced Adena in the Ohio Valley and then spread far more widely throughout the American Midwest.

Again, the changes seen between the Early and Middle Woodland periods in the American Midwest were evolutionary, not revolutionary: Earthworks became larger, the burials of people who appear to have been part of a growing elite class became increasingly elaborate, and nonlocal raw materials from which their grave goods were manufactured were brought in from increasing distances.

The residential settlements of both the Adena and Hopewell people generally were small, consisting of tiny hamlets located across much of southern and central Ohio and surrounding states to the south and west. There were no great urban centers in Adena or Hopewell society. The major river valleys in which the Hopewell lived are enormously rich habitats, and the Hopewell were expert at exploiting the wild foods of their region. Much of the Hopewell diet, in fact, relied on these wild foods; they hunted, fished, and collected nuts, roots, and seeds at a level of intensity that allowed for a large population capable of producing the elaborate earthworks that characterize their society.

The Hopewell produced as well as gathered food by planting many of the crops independently domesticated by Indians north of Mexico, including sunflower, squash, maygrass, knotweed, and goosefoot (Lepper 1995a; see Chapter 8). The major crop that characterized later Indian agricultural societies was not an important component of Hopewell subsistence; evidence for maize agriculture is scanty.

Some of the burial mounds are quite impressive, covering as much as 8,300 m² (2 acres) and stretching up to heights of 21 m (68 ft; Figure 14.3). The volume of earth moved and piled to produce such a monument is enormous and again reflects one of the defining elements of a complex society: its ability to mobilize a large labor force to produce a monumental structure.

▲ **Figure 14.2**
This marvelous Adena sculpture of a person, replete with headdress, ear spools (large, dangling ear jewelry), and loincloth, is actually a pipe. The bowl is between the man's feet and the smoker would place his or her lips on the headdress where the draw hole can be seen. (Dave Barker, Ohio Historical Society)

▶ **Figure 14.3**
The enormous burial mound in Miamisburg, Ohio. This Adena culture mound is the largest in Ohio, standing approximately 21 m (68 ft) high. (K. L. Feder)

The conical mounds were constructed over the remains of either individuals or groups of people. Finely crafted goods, including many made from exotic raw materials not native to the core of the Hopewell region, are found in the mound burials. A widespread trade network brought these natural resources to the Hopewell from all over the United States. Copper and silver were brought in from the Great Lakes region. Turtle shells, pearls, fossil shark teeth, alligator teeth, and conch shells from the Gulf of Mexico traveled up the major river systems of eastern North America also to be included in the burials of the Adena and Hopewell. Obsidian from the Rocky Mountains and quartz crystals and mica from the Appalachian Mountains also made long journeys into the hands of the elite of Hopewell society, often being placed in their tombs (Figure 14.4). Objects made from local materials were also found in these burials, and they are often finely made. For example, beautifully made ceramics, intricately flaked lithics far too delicate to have been used as tools, and whimsically carved stone pipes in the form of animals or even people were also included in the burials. In the enormity of the work necessary to build the actual mounds and in the effort expended to obtain raw materials from distant sources, as well as in the care taken in the manufacture of grave goods, Adena and, especially, Hopewell mound interments represent clear archaeological evidence for the existence of an elite or chieftain class of people in burial-mound society.

Some Hopewell earthworks are not mounds but earth-wall-enclosed spaces of unknown purpose. For example, in Newark, Ohio, a series of long, narrow, earthen walls about 1.5 m (5 ft) high enclose an octagonal plot of more than 200,000 m² (50 acres), which is in turn connected by two parallel earthen walls to an enormous circular area of more than 80,000 m² (20 acres), also enclosed with an earth wall more than a meter in height (Lepper 2002; Figure 14.5). This large earthwork is located at the end point of what appears to have been a ceremonial road, 90 km (60 mi) long, demarcated again by two earth walls approximately 60 m (200 ft) apart and several feet—perhaps as much as 2.5 to 3 m (8–10 ft)—in height (Lepper 1995b). The "Great Hopewell Road" is absolutely straight and seems—geographically and, perhaps, ritually—to connect the earthworks at Newark with a Hopewell necropolis, or "city of the dead," today part of the Hopewell Culture National Historical Park, located in Chillicothe, Ohio (Lepper 1998). The necropolis is an area of about 120,000 m² (30 acres) enclosed by an earth wall, containing 23 burial mounds (Figure 14.6). Connecting these sacred or ceremonial mound sites and enclosures, the Great Hopewell Road may have been used by pilgrims visiting these sites for religious observances—perhaps burial ceremonies or worship services. They are yet another example of the ability of the Hopewell to organize a large labor force and produce works of monumental proportions.

▼ **Figure 14.4**
These carved stone and cut copper (bottom) artifacts reflect the great artistic skill of the ancient Hopewell people. The ability of the makers of objects like these to devote the time necessary to perfect their craft is a hallmark of complex societies. (Tom House/ © Ohio Historical Society)

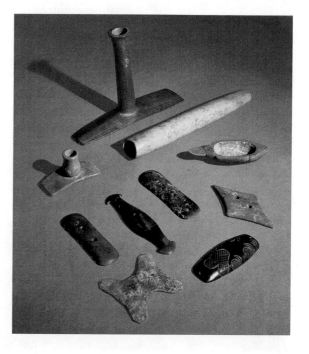

▶ **Figure 14.5**
Nineteenth-century
map of the extensive
prehistoric earthworks
seen in Licking County,
Ohio, in the vicinity of
Newark. The largest of
the areas enclosed by
the mounded earth in
this map is fifty acres,
an enormous expanse
surrounded by a vaguely
square configuration
of linear mounds in the
upper left of the map.
(From *Ancient Monuments
of the Mississippi Valley*,
AMS Press and Peabody
Museum of Archaeology
and Ethnology, Harvard
University)

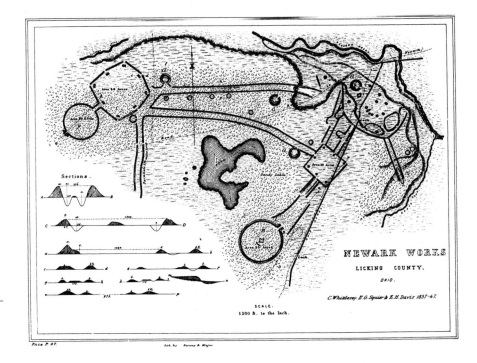

▼ **Figure 14.6**
Mound City in
Chillicothe, Ohio, is a
virtual necropolis or city
of the dead. The site
consists of twenty-three
burial mounds, a few of
which can be seen here,
within a thirteen-acre
area enclosed by an earth
embankment. (K. L. Feder)

As archaeologist Brad Lepper (1996) suggests, the Great Hopewell Road may have served to formalize connections between groups living along it and practicing what we today identify as Hopewell. Hopewell people lacked the formal government or military apparatus of a true state society (see Chapters 10–13), so symbolic activities like building the road and using it for pilgrimages may have served to make connections between people living at great distances more concrete.

Some of the Hopewell earthworks appear to have been intentionally aligned toward particular spots on the horizon. Much as Stonehenge (Chapter 9) was built in such a way as to point to the rising of the sun on the summer solstice (June 21, the longest day of the year and the northernmost location of sunrise), elements of the Newark Earthworks point to the location of the northernmost position of the rising of the moon (Figure 14.7; Lepper 1998, 2002, 2005). As archaeologist Brad Lepper points out, the swing of moonrise from its northernmost location on the horizon, to its southernmost, and then back to the north, is a complicated pattern that takes place over the course of 18.6 years. The Hopewell recognition of that cycle and their memorializing it in the form of

monumentally scaled earthworks was
possible only through long-term, cross-
generational observation possible only
within the context of a complex culture.

Hopewell culture and its construction
of enclosures and burial mounds ceased
by about 1,500 years ago. Among the numerous possible reasons for Hopewell's
decline (Lepper 1995a) are population
growth and warfare: Perhaps the largely informal organization of Hopewell society
was not up to the task of coordinating the activities of an expanding population,
or growing competition among various groups for good farmland may have led
to warfare and the subsequent concentration of the previously dispersed Hopewell
farmers in dense settlements for protection.

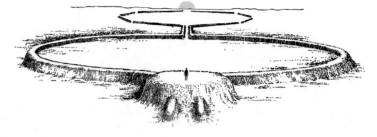

▲ Figure 14.7
Moonrise alignment
of the Great Octagon
earthworks in Newark,
Ohio. (Courtesy, Brad
Lepper and *Timeline*, a
publication of the Ohio
Historical Society)

The Mississippian Civilization

While Hopewell was in apparent decline, the Mississippi River Valley and the
American Southeast saw the rise of another series of complex cultures who produced even larger earthen monuments. These were the Mississippians. Along with
large conical mounds, the Mississippians constructed enormous "truncated" pyramids. These mounds were rectangular at their bases, rising to flat tops on which
archaeological evidence indicates the people constructed elaborate, wooden temples. Cahokia, located in Collinsville, Illinois, was the largest and most impressive
of these **Mississippian culture** sites—and the only one with a resident population of a size and density that approaches an urban character (see Figure 14.10).
But many others, including Town Creek Mounds in North Carolina; Etowah, Ocmulgee, and Kolomoki in Georgia; Crystal River Mounds in Florida; and Moundville in Alabama, although smaller in size and complexity, with fewer and smaller
monumental earthworks, nevertheless present a fascinating picture of developing
complexity and emerging civilization in the period after A.D. 1000 (Figure 14.8).

These **temple mound builders** were able to maintain their society with a
subsistence base primarily of maize and squash agriculture; the use of domesticated beans began relatively later, at about A.D. 1200. Rivers provided fish, and
the forests surrounding their habitations provided wild game as well as wild plant
foods such as acorn and hickory. Many of the larger, impressive sites—Cahokia
in particular—were located on the richest farmland. The enormous food surplus
made possible by the agricultural use of these naturally rich "bottom lands" enabled the evolution of a class of priests and an attendant nobility and artisans. As
we have seen again and again (in Chapters 10–13, and now here), the ability to
produce a food surplus surely was at the heart of the development of stratified,
complex societies. The ability of a chief or king to control that surplus is the
enabling factor in that leader's amassing of the wealth and power that allow or
demand the other characteristics of complex societies.

Cahokia

If you stand at the apex of Monks Mound, thousands of acres of floodplain lie
at your feet. The soil is rich and dark, the surrounding foliage thick and lush.
Construction of this enormous monument in the settlement called Cahokia was

▲ **Figure 14.8**
An assortment of
monumental temple
mound earthworks:
(clockwise from the
upper left) Town Creek
Mound (North Carolina,
with a reconstructed
temple at its summit),
Etowah (Georgia),
Kolomoki Mounds
(Alabama), Moundville
(Alabama). (K. L. Feder)

begun more than 1,000 years ago by the native inhabitants of what is today Collinsville, Illinois (Iseminger 2010).

Monks Mound is impressive, representing a substantial investment of time and energy on the part of the settlement's inhabitants (Figure 14.9). The pyramidal mound of earth covers more than 65,000 m², or some 16 acres. Its volume of earth totals 623,000 m³ (22 million ft³)—moved basketful by basketful by a people who had no animal power or mechanical contrivances. At its summit, the mound stands more than 30 m (100 ft) above the floodplain (all figures for Monks Mound are taken from M. Fowler 1989 and Silverberg 1989). The huge pile of earth served as the platform for a temple that symbolized the power of the political entity that was Cahokia.

From the summit, you can try to look past the paved roads, highways, and commercial structures and imagine what the ancient town of Cahokia with Monks Mound as its focal point must have looked like at its peak more than 800 years ago (Figure 14.10). In the year A.D. 1150, from your vantage point atop the great pyramid, you would have gazed down upon a dense settlement of 5,000 and perhaps as many as 10,000 people, buzzing with activity. In front of the great pyramid were smaller but only slightly less impressive earthworks, delineating an expansive rectangular plaza teeming with people. Scattered across the settlement were dozens of other pyramidal and conical mounds of earth, probably more than 120 in total. To the west was an enormous circle of towering logs, the largest located in the precise center of the monument. To the south was the burial of an important ruler, perhaps a great king of Cahokia (see the "Case Study Close-up" at the end of this chapter).

Surrounding the main part of the settlement was a log fence or palisade with bastions and watchtowers. The wall of logs enclosed an area of more than 800,000 m² (almost 200 acres), and within it were 18 separate earthen mounds, including Monks Mound. Consisting of an estimated 20,000 logs (and it was rebuilt three times), the huge stockade fence was as monumental a feat as Monks Mound itself, enclosing the central part of the settlement, protecting the homes of Cahokia's elite.

Occupation debris from the sprawl of Cahokia's neighborhoods, suburbs, and satellite communities has been found by archaeologists across an area of about 14 km² (5.4 mi²). As archaeologist Melvin Fowler (1989:207) points out, "Cahokia is unique. There is nothing else like it, either in size or complexity, representing Native American achievements within the boundaries of the United States."

Archaeologist Timothy Pauketat's (1994) detailed analysis shows that Cahokia was a central place in a three-tiered hierarchy of communities. Cahokia was at the apex of the sociopolitical pyramid, "a paramount center, a qualitatively different place" (Pauketat 1994:73). Beneath Cahokia was a second level of communities with a few small mounds, perhaps the villages of secondary chiefs. The bottom

▲ **Figure 14.9**
Monks Mound at Cahokia in Collinsville, Illinois. Initial construction began circa A.D. 900; it was continually refined until about A.D. 1300. This complex, four-tiered, truncated pyramid served as the platform on which a chief's house or temple was built. (K. L. Feder)

◀ **Figure 14.10**
Artist's conception of Cahokia at its peak around A.D. 1100. The dense, near-urban character of the settlement is clearly evident in this painting. Cahokia was the political center of an expansive prehistoric chiefdom that flourished more than 800 years ago. (Courtesy of Cahokia Mounds State Historic Site. William R. Iseminger, artist. Reproduced with permission)

tier of sites includes numerous farmsteads in the surrounding hinterlands, inhabited by communities of people who likely supplied most of the food and labor needed to keep the chiefdom running.

Cahokia's geographic spread was enormous. A few miles away, still in Illinois, in what is today East St. Louis, a substantial outlying community—a suburb of ancient Cahokia—had a cluster of 45 mounds and, farther west, in what now is downtown St. Louis in Missouri, was an additional grouping of 26 more mounds (Iseminger 2010). If mound-builder society can be said to have had a capital, the area in and around St. Louis, on both sides of the Mississippi River, can be said to have been that capital. In other words, Cahokia was the equivalent of a city-state, similar in context to those of Mesopotamia or the Maya. It certainly was a major focus of population, monument building, agriculture, manufacturing, trade, and ritual 1,000 years ago.

Thousands more across the American Midwest were within Cahokia's sphere of influence. Communities in some way connected to Cahokia were located as far away as Wisconsin, such as Aztalan, with its small-scale version of Monks Mound. Aztalan may have been built by a breakaway group from Cahokia; it may even have been a colony established there in an effort to control valuable local resources (Birmingham and Goldstein 2005; Figure 14.11).

Clearly, Cahokia was a center of social and political power. The archaeological record at Cahokia shows that craft production was centralized at the site; specialist artisans filled the demands of a powerful elite class for shell and bead pendant necklaces, copper ornaments, fired clay figurines, fine ceramics and lithics, and other items made from exotic raw materials (Pauketat 1994:106; Figure 14.12). The exotic materials from distant sources that made their way into the hands of Cahokia's artisans included copper from Illinois or possibly from as far away as Michigan, shell from the Gulf Coast, and galena (a lead mineral) from the eastern Ozarks (Pauketat 1994). The works of craft and art were produced for the

▶ **Figure 14.11**
Aztalan in Wisconsin looks like a small-scale version of Cahokia replete with its mini-version of a tiered Monks Mound and a log palisade that encompasses the central part of the site. It is uncertain whether Aztalan represents the community of a breakaway group from Cahokia or a colonial outpost to control access to raw material resources. Whichever, it clearly was inspired by what was happening hundreds of miles to the south. (K. L. Feder)

elite class of Cahokians who lived safely within the walls of the palisade and who were buried in the elaborate interments found at the site.

When the Spanish explorer Hernando de Soto and his contingent of more than 600 men traversed much of the American Southeast in the years 1539–1543, they encountered the direct descendants of the builders of the prehistoric temple-mound ceremonial centers (de la Vega 1605/1988; Elvas 1611/1966). They may actually have visited the site of Etowah during a late stage of its occupation (see Figure 14.8). De Soto's chroniclers described a number of large settlements they visited as having populations numbered in the thousands. They also described agricultural fields stretching for miles. They even described the native practice of constructing earthen mounds, upon which the chief's house sat. Ironically, de Soto may have brought more than curiosity and greed with him on his trip. It has been suggested that he and his men unintentionally brought with them infectious diseases (perhaps including smallpox) that the natives had not previously encountered and, as a result, for which they possessed no immunity (Brain 1982; Dobyns 1983; Ramenofsky 1987). Though some of the ceremonial centers had already been abandoned—Cahokia among them—as a result of internal collapse, it is not certain that mound-builder

▲ **Figure 14.12**
This figurine found at Cahokia depicts a tranquil domestic scene: a woman seated on the ground, nursing a baby. A number of similarly styled figurines have been found across the American Southeast, many of which likely were made by Cahokia's artisans (Emerson et al. 2003). (K. L. Feder)

society was destined for disintegration. It may have continued to develop, becoming increasingly complex and more recognizably a civilization.

Later, when the French explorer Le Page du Pratz traveled down the Mississippi River in the mid-eighteenth century, he encountered members of the Natchez tribe living in what is today the state of Mississippi. He saw and wrote about their principal village, today called the Grand Village of the Natchez, describing the presence of large earthen pyramids on which the natives placed the houses of their rulers.

As Timothy Pauketat (1994:6) puts it when assessing the significance of the kind of social stratification and political power evidenced in the archaeological record at Cahokia: "In other regions around the world similar conditions may have been necessary precursors to the rise of early states." But the accidental spread of lethal microbes may have diverted the trajectory of mound-builder culture, and we will never know what might have been.

The American Southwest

As mentioned in Chapter 8, the Mesoamerican domesticates maize and squash appear in the archaeological record of the American Southwest beginning about 3,200 years ago, and beans show up a bit later (Wills 1988). These domesticates initially served to complement and supplement a highly productive indigenous foraging economy based on local wild crops.

Not until over a thousand years later, at approximately 2000 B.P., did maize-based agriculture replace the traditional foraging subsistence system. A number of different cultural traditions based on agriculture then evolved in the prehistoric Southwest with the development of a new variety of maize, Maize de Ocho, that was better suited to the dry conditions and short growing season of this region. The best known of these cultures were the **Ancestral Puebloan**, or **Anasazi**, in the Four Corners region (the broad area around the intersection of Arizona, New Mexico, Utah, and Colorado), the **Mogollon** in the uplands of New Mexico and northeastern Mexico, the **Hohokam** in southern Arizona, and the **Sinagua** in central Arizona (Cordell 1984; Willey 1966). These cultures vary in pottery styles, geography, and settlement patterns, but all relied to varying degrees on a subsistence base of maize, beans, and squash, and all eventually lived a sedentary lifeway before the coming of the Spanish. One more pattern shared by these cultures is social and political complexity, manifested in the archaeological record by the construction of monumental buildings.

Hohokam

The Sonoran Desert is one rather extreme example of the environmental diversity reflected in the myriad settings of the world's ancient complex societies. From A.D. 700 to close to A.D. 1000, the dry Sonoran Desert of southern Arizona served as a backdrop for the flowering of a complex society capable of building huge structures and a complex system of irrigation (Reid and Whittlesey 1997).

The settlement pattern of the Hohokam (literally, "those who have gone" in the Pima Indian language) focused on the major river systems of southern Arizona: the Gila, the Salt, and the Santa Cruz. The reason is obvious. The territory of the Hohokam averages less than 30 cm (12 in) of rain each year. Though the Hohokam included game (deer, bighorn sheep, antelope, and cottontail and jackrabbits) and wild plant foods (mesquite beans and cactus) in their diet, growing corn, beans, and squash was of primary importance and was made possible in this dry environment only by the construction of extensive irrigation networks. The Hohokam irrigated thousands of acres of otherwise dry land through a hierarchical series of canals whose combined length is measured in many kilometers. For example, the Hohokam irrigation network north of the Salt River near modern Phoenix consists of 50 large, primary artificial water channels, hundreds of secondary arteries, and an even greater number of smaller irrigation ditches feeding individual fields (Reid and Whittlesey 1997:76). The labor needed to construct this one irrigation network—and then to maintain it, keeping it clear of clogging silt—must have been enormous and is clear evidence of the Hohokam ability to conscript and organize a substantial workforce far beyond the level of an individual household or family. This, in turn, is a hallmark of social and political complexity.

Hohokam material culture provides additional evidence of the complexity that bloomed in the desert. The Hohokam maintained a trading system that brought in exotic raw materials such as marine shell from the Gulf of California. Hohokam craftspeople produced beautiful and intricate works in carved stone. They also fashioned shell-bead necklaces, shell bracelets, and shell pendants carved into the shapes of animals. They also worked in turquoise and produced an array of finely made ceramics, including red-on-buff painted household wares—a style of pottery that is a defining attribute of Hohokam culture—and whimsical pots in human-like shapes (Figure 14.13). Most individual Hohokam villages consisted of multiple sets of separate residential structure clusters called **courtyard groups**. Each courtyard group consisted of from 2 to 10 family residences surrounding a common area or courtyard.

▲ **Figure 14.13**
Ceramics produced by the Hohokam of the ancient American Southwest were both beautiful and whimsical. (© Richard A. Cooke/Corbis)

The Hohokam also constructed residential compounds called "Great Houses," large apartment buildings that housed most residents of a village. The best example of a Hohokam Great House can be found at the Casa Grande site, located midway between Tucson and Phoenix. Built around A.D. 1350, the main structure at the site is a multistoried, 60-room building surrounded by several smaller adobe structures (Figure 14.14). Casa Grande was built of bricks made of caliche, a desert soil that becomes extremely hard when it dries out. For added strength and stability, the walls of the Great House were massive, 1.2 m (about 4 ft) thick at their base, and set into deep trenches dug into the desert soil. Approximately 600 logs were used in its construction, serving as roof beams and ceilings. An adobe wall more than 2 m (6½ ft) high surrounded the entire complex, enclosing a space of more than 8,000 m² (2 acres). Obviously, a large, well-organized labor force was necessary to construct and maintain Casa Grande; it is likely that a few hundred people lived there.

The largest discovered Hohokam village is Snaketown, located on the Gila River; it was the focus of intensive archaeological excavation in the 1930s and then again in the 1960s (Figure 14.15). The ruins at Snaketown cover more than 2.5 km² (1 mi²), and more than 200 family residences have been excavated in this elaborate town. There is a significant irrigation network at the site. Snaketown has also produced evidence of a ceremonial ballgame that also was played by the native people of Mesoamerica (Figure 14.16; and see Chapter 12). Hohokam ball courts like the one at Snaketown may have been places where disputes between families or villages were worked out on a ritually sanctified stage.

▶ **Figure 14.14**
Casa Grande, a large Hohokam community in southern Arizona. The Great House, shown here, is partially protected from the elements by a large metal superstructure built in the 1930s. (K. L. Feder)

▲ **Figure 14.15**
Aerial photograph of the partially excavated ruins of Snaketown; approximately 60 individual house floors can be seen. (© Arizona State Museum, University of Arizona; photo by Helga Teiwes)

◀ **Figure 14.16**
The reconstructed ball court located at the Wupatki site in Arizona. The trade of turquoise from the American Southwest to the south (see Chapter 2), the presence of architectural features like the ball courts, and agricultural practices and even the use of chocolate are evidence of contact between the native people of what today are the states of Arizona and New Mexico and cultures to the south in the heartland of Mesoamerica. (K. L. Feder)

Clearly, irrigation initially allowed for the development of the agriculture-based Hohokam society in the Sonoran Desert. Intensification of this irrigation technology—building longer and deeper canals that extended the range of arable land ever greater distances from the permanent water-courses—allowed for population growth and the production of a larger food surplus. Elaboration of Hohokam material culture coincided with a probable attendant increase in social and political differentiation among different classes of people as excess wealth became concentrated in the hands of those who controlled, at least to a degree, the irrigation system.

Mogollon

Where the Hohokam were dwellers of the desert, the Mogollon were mountain people, living in the highlands of eastern Arizona and New Mexico—and south into Mexico. Long dependent on hunting and gathering and well adapted to life in the mountains, their shift to agriculture, a sedentary lifestyle, and some degree of social and political complexity occurred rather late in prehistory.

Traced by the diagnostic styles of their artifacts, the Mogollon appear in the archaeological record by about A.D. 200. At this time, they lived in small nomadic groups, hunted deer and turkey, gathered the wild plants that grew abundantly in the mountains, and lived in impermanent villages characterized by small **pit-houses**—semisubterranean structures covered with a thatched roof. Sometime after A.D. 650, the Mogollon began to supplement their diet by farming small garden plots, raising corn, beans, and squash. Not until after A.D. 1150, however, did the Mogollon, probably in contact with the more complex Ancestral Puebloan culture to the north (discussed later in this chapter) and as the result of a significant drought in about A.D. 1300, give up their nomadic, foraging existence, settle down into permanent habitations, and adopt an agricultural mode of subsistence.

The need to increase the agricultural portion of their diet also caused a shift in settlement patterns among the Mogollon. Although before the drought it had made sense for the Mogollon to spread themselves out across the mountains, after A.D. 1300 it made more sense to settle in at those places that offered good agricultural land. These areas experienced a population explosion or, more precisely, an implosion, as the Mogollon began to concentrate their settlements on arable land.

Grasshopper Pueblo, for example, is a large Mogollon settlement dating to this period, located on the best and most extensive agricultural lands in Mogollon territory (Figure 14.17; Reid 1989). Archaeology around the region of Grasshopper shows that before A.D. 1300 there were a total of only about 200 Mogollon dwellings, located in a series of scattered, impermanent communities. After A.D. 1300 in the same region there were 10 times that number, as the scattered Mogollon began concentrating their population on good farmland (Reid and Whittlesey 1997:156). Grasshopper itself consists of 500 rooms arranged in three distinct clusters. Each block possessed its own common area, or plaza.

Great care was taken by the residents of Grasshopper Pueblo in the construction of buildings intended for ceremony and ritual. One of the large plazas at Grasshopper was roofed over at about A.D. 1330, producing an enclosed ritual space called a **kiva** by the historical and modern Hopi. Kivas were places where the community met to engage in and observe important rituals; they were, essentially, churches. The "Great Kiva" at Grasshopper is, as its name implies, an enormous

▶ **Figure 14.17**
Map of room distribution at Grasshopper Pueblo, a Mogollon culture site in Arizona.

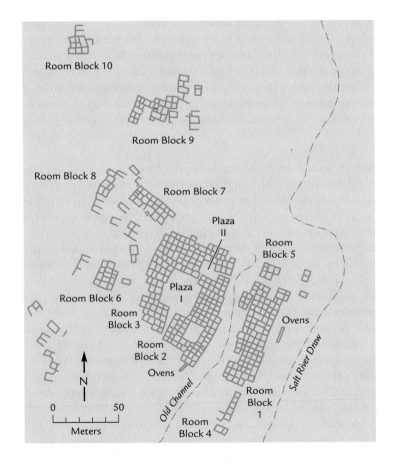

gathering place some 25 m (82 ft) across, with its roof supported by nine huge juniper posts. As archaeologists Jefferson Reid and Stephanie Whittlesey (1997) suggest, the Great Kiva at Grasshopper played an integrative role in Mogollon society. Because large Mogollon communities such as Grasshopper represent the aggregation of previously separate, smaller communities, it is likely that a shared ritual space and communal ceremonies served to bring people together into a more integrated and complex social and political system. A decrease in rainfall after A.D. 1335 made untenable the agricultural way of life to which the Mogollon had become committed. By A.D. 1400, they had left their mountain homeland, lost their separate identity, and merged with other farmers in the Southwest.

Ancestral Puebloan

The Ancestral Puebloans of the Four Corners region, where the modern states of Arizona, New Mexico, Utah, and Colorado meet at right angles, produced the most spectacular masonry architecture in indigenous North America. The largest prehistoric **pueblos** and incredible settings characterize the Ancestral Puebloans. (You will find these people most commonly referred to as the Anasazi. This term means, literally, "ancient enemies" in the language of another group of Native Americans living in the Southwest, the Navajo, many of whom call themselves the Dineh. Many descendants of the people who built the pueblos object to having their ancestors named by another group, especially a group that they have historically been at odds with. It is with that in mind that we will call their predecessors the Ancestral Puebloans.)

Very early in their sequence, beginning about 2,000 years ago, the Ancestral Puebloans developed a subsistence system that, while including a broad array of wild plants and animals, depended quite heavily on maize agriculture. The most diagnostic elements of their culture at this point were baskets, textiles, and nets used in hunting. In fact, the early years of Ancestral Puebloan development are divided into periods called Basketmaker I and II (500 B.C. to A.D. 600) and III (A.D. 600–800).

The florescence of Ancestral Puebloan culture occurred after A.D. 1000. A burst of social and political complexity is demonstrated by the construction of monumental residential structures, including Great Houses exponentially larger than the Great Houses of the Hohokam, remarkable and beautiful cliff dwellings, and enormous ceremonial buildings in the form of Great Kivas. Chaco Canyon is the most obvious manifestation of such complexity; about a dozen Great Houses were built at the base and top of the cliffs demarcating the margins of the arable land along the Chaco River (Figure 14.18). The largest of these, Pueblo Bonito, was a single immense structure made from millions of quarried sandstone blocks (Figure 14.19). Altogether, Pueblo Bonito consisted of about 800 rooms in its five stories. Roofs and ceilings were constructed from thousands of trees cut down and transported from forested areas as much as 80 km (50 mi) distant. The Great Houses at Chaco are monumental structures but likely were not the residences of huge numbers of people. Rather, the Great Houses may have been a kind of public architecture intended by the Ancestral Puebloans, on the practical side, for storage and also, in a metaphorical sense, as symbols of the power of their societies.

In all, about 75 substantial settlements and more than 300 smaller communities have been found that were part of the Chaco Ancestral Puebloan culture,

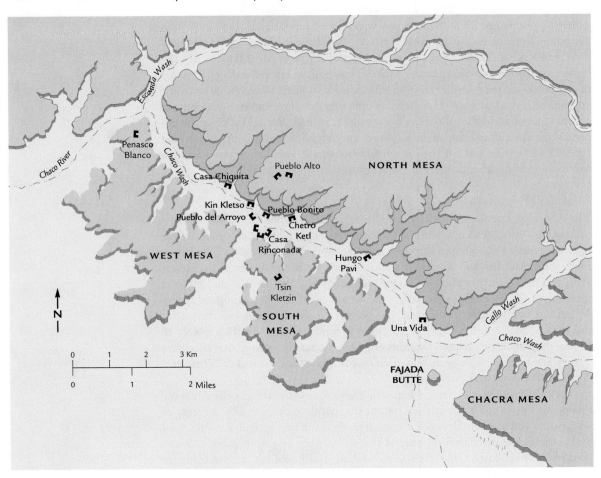

▲ **Figure 14.18**
Locations of most of the
Great Houses of Chaco
Canyon, in New Mexico.
(After the Chaco Canyon
map produced by the
National Park Service)

most of them outside of the canyon itself. The major towns were connected to
Chaco by a series of roads 9 m (30 ft) wide that together measured more than
650 km (about 400 mi) in length. The longest single Chaco road traversed approximately 68 km (42 mi), linking Chaco Canyon with the Great Houses to
the north at the Salmon and Aztec Ruins. These roads were not simply time-
worn trails; they were carefully engineered and constructed and traveled in quite
straight lines. Chaco roads never avoided steep slopes but simply climbed them.
Where the roads traveled over bare rock, walls were built to demarcate them.

The Chaco road system may have served an economic purpose, allowing for
the transportation of precious raw materials and finely made art objects within
the Chaco sphere; but as archaeologist John Kantner (1997) points out, a detailed
analysis of the paths taken by the roads shows that most were not even close to
providing the most efficient or fastest travel between Chaco villages. He feels that
the roads played a far more important role in ritually and symbolically uniting
the far-flung communities in the Chaco universe. Whatever the case, there is little
doubt that economically, politically, and ritually, as more than one writer has put
it, "all roads led to Chaco."

Chaco Great Houses and Great Kivas are enormously impressive, the product
of a large, coordinated labor force. If cultural complexity can be assumed to be

◀ **Figure 14.19**
An aerial view of Pueblo
Bonito, the greatest of the
Great Houses of Chaco
Canyon in New Mexico.
Pueblo Bonito was an
enormous, five-story
structure of more than
800 rooms. (K. L. Feder)

directly proportional to the massiveness of construction projects as manifested in the archaeological record, then the inhabitants of Chaco represent the most complex of the indigenous people of the American Southwest. Though smaller than Chaco's Great Houses, the cliff dwellings of Mesa Verde in southwestern Colorado, built during a 100-year period beginning at the tail end of the twelfth century A.D., are even more striking. These houses look like fairy castles, set into natural depressions in the cliffs that characterize the region (Figure 14.20). There are more than 600 such cliff dwellings at Mesa Verde. Most are quite small, but some consist of a series of residences and storage rooms constructed with stone blocks and stretching across cliff faces more than 100 m (330 ft) in length, with delicate four-story square bastions and graceful round towers (Figure 14.21). It is not clear why the residents of Mesa Verde built their homes in such difficult, inaccessible, though visually striking locations. Perhaps defense from marauding outsiders explains their location, or perhaps it was protection from the elements or ease of access to fresh water seeping through the cliff face. Whatever the case, it is clear that their construction required careful planning and the communal effort of a large force of people.

Though there is little evidence at Mesa Verde for the presence of an elite class, certainly the size of their dwellings and the difficulty posed by their construction are material evidence of the complexity of their society.

A combination of factors may have precipitated abandonment of the majestic cliff homes by the later thirteenth century, soon after Mesa Verde's population peaked. The population of Mesa Verde may have outstripped the environment's ability to support it, especially during the great drought that afflicted the area in the last quarter of the thirteenth century. Shortages of wood for fuel and construction may have played a role. It is also possible that a new religion may have attracted the Mesa Verdeans to the south. The inhabitants of Mesa Verde did not become extinct. They merely moved and today live in modern Hopi villages in New Mexico (see "Issues and Debates" in this chapter).

▶ **Figure 14.20**
Mesa Verde contains some of the most spectacular and monumental of the cliff dwellings. Pictured here is Cliff Palace, a remarkable village built into the side of a mountain. (K. L. Feder)

▶ **Figure 14.21**
The Square Tower House ruin, nestled in a niche at the base of a cliff in Mesa Verde in Colorado. With names like "Cliff Palace," "Balcony House," and "Square Tower House," the cliff dwellings of Mesa Verde were the product of a sophisticated chiefdom society that flourished more than 500 years ago in the American Southwest. (K. L. Feder)

Northwest Coast of North America

In their wide-ranging book, anthropologists Kenneth Ames and Herbert Maschner (1999:13) summarize succinctly European fascination with the native cultures of the northwest coast of North America: These native people simply "contradicted many of the basic assumptions that Europeans held about human societies, particularly the ones that linked cultural complexity with agriculture."

It was apparent from the very earliest contact between Europeans and the native peoples who lived along the coasts of Oregon, Washington, Vancouver

Island, and British Columbia in the late 1700s that the aboriginal inhabitants had long lived in large, sedentary villages with populations as high as 2,000 people, where specialists produced splendid works of art, especially carved and painted objects of wood, including **totem poles** (Figure 14.22). It was also clear to early European observers that the inhabitants of the northwest coast, including people who called themselves the Haida and the Kwakwaka'wakw (Kwakiutl), developed a complex political system headed by powerful, hereditary chiefs and that they lived in a stratified society consisting of two classes: free people and slaves. Free people were further divided into three ranks including an upper rank of noblemen and women, a middle rank of people with some prestige and official titles, and a third rank of common people.

Slaves, often captives from wars fought with neighboring groups, represented the bottom of the social hierarchy. These social categories were largely hereditary; if you were born a slave, your descendants would be slaves, and if you were born to nobility, your descendants would be of noble standing. No one got blindingly wealthy in native Northwest Coast societies. In fact, increased prestige and status was achieved by redistributing excess wealth and not by hoarding it, by, essentially, giving it away in enormous celebrations called **potlatches**. Though historical eyewitnesses to the character of native Northwest Coast societies described no absolute rulers, no one with the all-encompassing power of a King Tut (Chapter 10) or of a Pacal (Chapter 12), clearly Northwest Coast natives had produced a complex society in which authority, privilege, and, to a certain extent, wealth were invested in the hands of a noble class headed by a chief.

Remember in Chapter 9 the discussion about Göbekli Tepe in Turkey and Watson Brake in Louisiana. In both instances we saw evidence for communal labor recruited from a pool far beyond the limits of the immediate family, organized to produce monumental structures (the enormous stone features at Göbekli Tepe and the mounds at Watson Brake). We interpreted those monuments as manifestations of social and political complexity, a complexity that allowed for the organization of a large force. In both cases, subsistence evidence indicated that the people who produced the monuments and exhibited that complexity were foragers and not farmers. Nevertheless, clearly they were not living hand-to-mouth existences and they were not spending all of their time in subsistence pursuits. They were able to produce enough food from wild sources to support the construction of their respective monuments.

Similarly, the indigenous complex societies that developed along the northwestern coast of North America were not agricultural, but relied exclusively on wild foods for their subsistence. What made it possible for large, dense, sedentary populations to develop along the northwest coast of North America was

▼ **Figure 14.22**
Totem poles are emblematic of the native cultures of the American northwest coast.
(© Norbert Wu/Science Faction/Corbis)

the fact that the natural environment of the coast was so fabulously productive, it enabled the kind of food surplus that elsewhere was possible only by artificially raising food productivity through the practice of agriculture. In the terminology of anthropology, the native peoples of the northwest coast of North America were "**affluent foragers**," living in an environment so rich as to allow large, dense, sedentary human populations to thrive there and to develop complex patterns of the production and distribution of wealth and the organization of labor and authority. The forests of the Northwest provided a wide variety of foods including roots, bulbs, berries, acorns, and hazelnuts. Elk, two species of deer, and numerous smaller mammals were hunted, and their meat provided a significant source of protein. Intertidal flats, estuaries, marshes, rocky shores, and extensive shallows attracted a diverse array of birds, fish, and land and sea mammals that were exploited by people living along the coast (Ames and Maschner 1999:47). Fish, especially salmon and marine mammals, including harbor seals, sea lions, porpoises, and gray whales, were hunted as well. Ames and Maschner (1999) suggest that it was the diversity of productive food sources that provided the capacity for the production of a rich food surplus—the equivalent of what can be produced by agriculture—that led to the richness and complexity of Northwest Coast culture.

The origins of social ranking in the southern segment of the northwest coast can be traced in the archaeological record to at least 2,650 years ago. Beginning at this time, about 15% of the human interments that have been excavated archaeologically show evidence of differential wealth and deduced higher status. These high-status burials contain grave goods including things like beads, sometimes in the thousands, made from dentalium shells (a white mollusk); copper artifacts; pendants; rattles; and large stone spearpoints (Ames and Maschner 1999:187). The amount of labor that went into these finely crafted goods signifies their value and reflects the status of the individuals in whose burials such goods were concentrated. It is also important to point out that there were no age restrictions in terms of high-status burials, suggesting that status was inherited, not achieved. Children received high-status interments, almost certainly not because they attained high status through their accomplishments in life but simply because their parents were high-status individuals and this high status was passed down to their offspring.

Ethnographically, much of the architecture and finely and artistically produced work of the Northwest Coast people was made of wood, which preserved very poorly in their wet environment. In one instance, fortunately, this was not the case. Located on the Olympic Peninsula in Washington State, the Ozette site was a village where five houses were destroyed virtually in an instant by a mudslide dated to about A.D. 1491 (Pascua 1991). Ozette was a large and complex village, stretching nearly a mile against the coast (Figure 14.23). The encasing wet slurry of mud prevented aerobic bacteria from eating the organic objects produced by the village's inhabitants. Archaeologists recovered more than 50,000 artifacts in their excavation of the site, including finely made baskets, mats, wooden bowls, and an astonishing block of red cedar, carved into the shape of a whale's dorsal fin, inlaid with more than 700 otter teeth.

An important lesson can be gleaned from the complex societies that developed along the northwest coast of North America. It is something we have seen previously, at the early mound-builder site at Watson Brake (Chapter 8) and at many of the Adena sites discussed in this chapter. A prerequisite in the development of social, economic, and political complexity is the ability to produce a food surplus, but that surplus is not inevitably the result of an agricultural economy. Some world areas, like the northwest coast of North America (coastal Japan is another example), are so naturally productive that social stratification, wealth differentiation, and political inequality can develop. The fascinating cultures of the northwest coast attest to this alternative pathway to complexity.

What Happened to the Ancestral Puebloans?

We saw that Mesa Verde was abandoned in the beginning of the fourteenth century. The reason for this abandonment remains a mystery. In a fascinating bit of analysis on population size, movement, and settlement abandonment by another group of Ancestral Puebloans, researchers produced a computer simulation of population fluctuations in Long House Valley located in northeastern Arizona that is relevant to this question (Axtell et al. 2002; and see Diamond 2002 for a summary).

The simulation began with a small virtual human population of households in A.D. 800 that was programmed to grow or decline at a rate commensurate with fluctuating food availability. As discussed in this chapter, Ancestral Puebloans were agriculturalists and their primary food, both historically and in the simulation, was maize. Yearly variations in probable maize yields were determined for the valley and input into the simulation on the basis of actual, historically determined, yearly rainfall fluctuations. Yearly amounts between A.D. 800 and 1300 could be measured relatively precisely on the basis of tree-ring widths dendrochronologists have determined for the area. So based on the amount of rain falling in a given year, determined by how thick the tree rings in Long House Valley were for that year, the number of bushels of maize that could have been produced by the valley residents was estimated. Thicker rings meant more rain, which in turn meant higher maize yields. Based on ethnographic data, the researchers assigned an average amount of maize needed to sustain an individual during the course of a year. With this in mind, researchers could estimate the total human population in the valley for a given year by dividing the total maize output by the number of bushels needed to sustain an individual for a year.

The next step involved actually running the simulation and determining the fluctuating size of the human population dependent on maize, sustainable each year in the valley. In the mathematical model used in the simulation, the initial,

▲ **Figure 14.23**
This artist's conception of the 500-year-old Ozette village is based on the archaeological and ethnographic records. Ozette was destroyed in a mudslide, which, ironically, contributed to the remarkable preservation of the material culture of the inhabitants. (© Richard Schlecht/ National Geographic Society Image Collection)

small population could grow, as long as the people could produce sufficient food to feed the increasing population based on potential yields that were determined by the amount of rainfall for each given year. The population in the simulation would fall when the potential maize yield fell below that which would have been required to sustain the level the population had grown to.

The final step in the analysis lay in comparing the simulation's predicted human population curve between A.D. 800 and 1300 and the population curve determined archaeologically by counting the number of residences in the valley. The resulting comparison is breathtaking. The two curves—one representing the best estimate determined by archaeological research and the other based on the output of the simulation—are almost identical. In other words, the simulation predicts nearly perfectly the population curve deduced from the archaeological record (Figure 14.24).

Interestingly, the two curves diverge significantly only toward the end of the 1200s, at about the time the Ancestral Puebloans abandoned Long House Valley. Herein lies an interesting lesson. Although, on the basis of the archaeological record, the actual population in the valley declines to effectively zero, the simulation indicates that after A.D. 1270, a reduced but still sizable human population could have survived there. In other words, as the researchers conclude, though rainfall patterns certainly affected crop yield, which then affected human population size, something other than reduced crop yield factored into the abandonment of the valley. The researchers suggest that the final abandonment was a conscious choice on the part of residents, based not on purely economic considerations— they wouldn't have starved but could have survived with a reduced level of population. Sociocultural issues must have affected the choice to abandon Long House Valley, and this must be considered in the case of Mesa Verde as well. Modeling those factors—religious issues or social alliances—however, will be far more difficult to simulate than economic factors like crop yields.

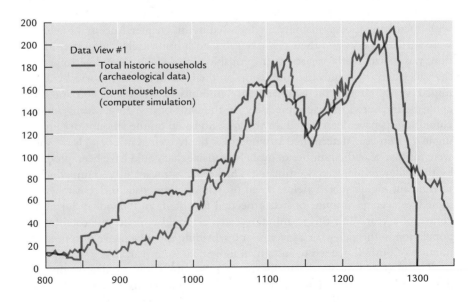

▶ **Figure 14.24**
Graph showing the results of a simulation of population growth and contraction among the Anasazi of Long House Valley. By experimenting with the variables in the simulation, the authors of the study were able to produce a population graph that closely resembles the actual population curve derived from the archaeological analysis of the valley. (From Axtell et al. 2002)

The Death of a King

Almost certainly, when you hear or read about the burial of an ancient ruler, his tomb filled with rare, precious, and finely made goods along with the bodies of dozens of human sacrifices—soldiers, retainers, consorts, and servants—you likely picture ancient Egypt, Mesopotamia, or China. In fact, I've presented examples of exactly this kind of elite burial in those places earlier in the book (Chapters 10 and 11). I discussed these as instances where economic, political, and social inequality in the ancient world had reached such an extreme level that the elite not only controlled the property, surplus wealth, and labor of the great mass of people but also owned their lives.

When you hear or read about such a burial and such an extreme level of the concentration of power, I doubt that an ancient culture that comes to mind is located on the floodplain of the Mississippi River in Collinsville, Illinois. Yet, it should. Cahokia, featured earlier in this chapter, is full of surprises for many people: its monumental mounds, fine works of art, widespread trading networks, and enormous geopolitical reach across much of the midlands of North America 1,000 years ago. Add elite burials to that list, especially and in particular Mound 72, which contained the remains of one of Cahokia's great leaders (Iseminger 2010).

When archaeologists excavated the mound, in sight of Monks Mound, they found the primary burial of a man who had died in his mid-40s. His body had been reverentially placed on a platform consisting of a staggering profusion of 20,000 drilled, conch-shell beads arrayed in the shape of a giant bird, likely a falcon (Iseminger 2010). The source of the shell was more than 1,200 km (750 mi) away, in the Gulf of Mexico. Along with the shell platform, the man was surrounded by more than 700 finely made arrow points, most of which were made from exotic lithic materials available from across the American Midwest and from as far away as Wisconsin (Figure 14.25). Perhaps the Cahokian outpost of Aztalan (discussed earlier) was a source for the Wisconsin stone. Also buried with the man were large sheets of copper whose source was Michigan as well as two large piles of the translucent mineral mica. There is no mica source anywhere near Cahokia and the material in the burial likely originated in North Carolina. In other words, for this one man, raw materials were gathered for his burial from a vast territory around Cahokia. He must have been a very important person to merit all of these precious materials that were so difficult and costly to obtain.

Though his is the most impressive of the Mound 72 internments, there were a lot of other people also buried in the mound (Figure 14.26). In such an elaborate burial feature, we should be surprised if he had not been sent off to the afterlife with human sacrifices. And, indeed, he was. Around the primary grave, archaeologists found six more people, likely the result of human sacrifice.

Altogether, the burials of 272 people have been excavated at Mound 72, and there likely are a few more outside of the mound proper; William Iseminger (2010:80), the director of the Cahokia site, puts the likely total at about 300. Some of the other burials were also of important people, folks who appear to have been among Cahokia's elite, and they too were buried with finely made objects produced from exotic raw materials.

▶ **Figure 14.25**
A sample of the more than 1,000 finely made stone projectile points recovered in the primary burial in Mound 72 at Cahokia. The amount of labor invested in this enormous assemblage of stone points is an indication of the importance of the man with whom they were buried. (Courtesy Cahokia Mounds State Historic Site)

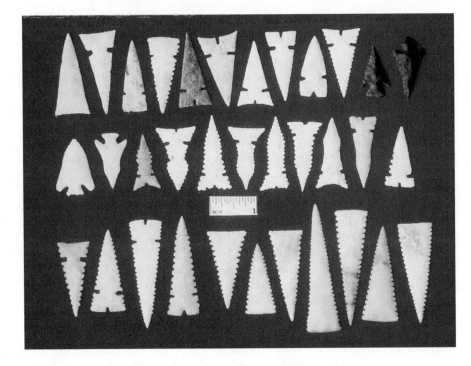

Many interred in Mound 72, however, got there not because of their high status, but as human sacrifices. In one large pit, archaeologists found the remains of 53 women, all between the ages of 15 and 25. Buried simultaneously, it is unlikely in the extreme that these women died natural deaths—what epidemic would selectively wipe out only young women? Almost certainly, these women "earned" their place in Mound 72 as sacrifices intended to serve their masters even in death.

The burials of Mound 72 clearly show the presence of an economic, social, and political elite at Cahokia and are a reflection of their great power, over both wealth and even life itself, at least the lives of commoners. As such, and perhaps ironically, the concentration of wealth in the hands of an elite combined with the practice of human sacrifice at Mound 72 is a clear indication of the presence of a "civilization" in ancient North America.

Summary

Complex societies developed in places where a food surplus could be produced, allowing for the development of wealth that could then be concentrated in the hands of an elite rank or class. In most cases, the ability to produce a food surplus was made possible by the adoption of an agricultural economy where the few could feed the many. However, in some areas the natural food base was so rich, a large, dense, sedentary population developed with attendant cultural complexity without the benefit of agriculture. In some world areas, the development of social complexity, political inequality, and the concentration of wealth culminated in

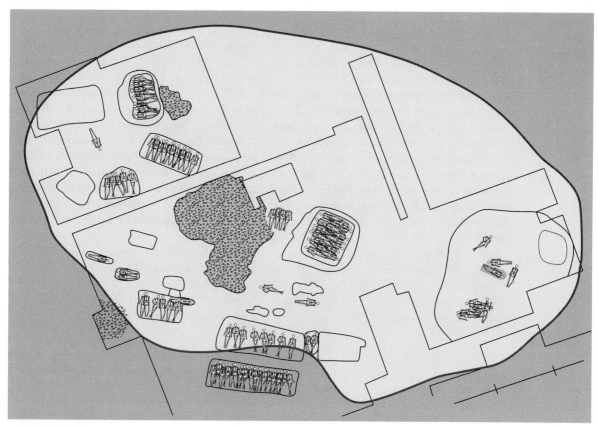

▲ **Figure 14.26**
Layout of burials in Mound 72, Cahokia. The primary burial in Mound 72 is that of a
young man, laid out on a bed of more than 20,000 mother-of-pearl shell beads. In a
practice reminiscent of ancient Egypt (Chapter 10), Mesopotamia (Chapter 10), the
Shang (Chapter 11), and the Moche (Chapter 13), the other interments in Mound 72
are the burials of more than 50 other people, mostly young women, who had been
killed, apparently to accompany the primary individual to his afterlife. (Courtesy of
William Fowler)

the evolution of state societies as described in Chapters 10 through 13. In some
cases, though, society became divided into classes and further subdivided into
various levels of noble and common ranks, and the power to completely control
the lives of the commoners didn't develop. Leaders in such societies maintained a
level of power, not so much by concentrating wealth but by serving as channels
for redistribution of that wealth within their societies. We give these societies a
separate designation—chiefdoms—but there certainly is a continuum from chiefdoms to state societies.

The burial and temple mound builders of the Midwest and Southeast, the
Ancestral Puebloans of the American Southwest, and the native people of the
northwest coast of North America are examples of the various expressions of
cultural complexity that developed in ancient North America.

TO LEARN MORE

Jefferson Reid and Stephanie Whittlesey have written a broad overview of the American Southwest titled *The Archaeology of Ancient Arizona* (1997). Lynne Sebastian's highly readable, theoretical look at the origins and evolution of Ancestral Puebloan society at Chaco Canyon is titled *The Chaco Anasazi: Sociopolitical Evolution in the Prehistoric Southwest* (1992).

For the mound builders and the history of their acceptance as an indigenous American civilization, see Robert Silverberg's wonderful historical summary, *The Mound Builders* (1989). Focusing on the archaeology of Ohio, Brad Lepper's (2005) splendidly illustrated book *Ohio Archaeology: An Illustrated Chronicle of Ohio's Ancient American Indian Cultures* is both beautiful and enormously informative with lots of material about the Adena and Hopewell mound builders. There now are two wonderful books about Cahokia aimed at a popular audience: Timothy Pauketat's *Cahokia: Ancient America's Great City on the Mississippi* (2009), and William Iseminger's *Cahokia Mounds: America's First City* (2010). Read them both! David Roberts's book *In Search of the Old Ones: Exploring the Anasazi World of the Southwest* (1997) provides a detailed look at this region. In the Smithsonian Institution's series, Exploring the Ancient World, Linda S. Cordell's *Ancient Pueblo Peoples* (1994) is an overview of prehistory in the Southwest. For the peoples of the northwest coast, Kenneth Ames and Herbert Maschner's wonderful book titled *Peoples of the Northwest Coast: Their Archaeology and Prehistory* (1999) is a great source of information and a great read.

Web links for this chapter can be found at www.oup.com/us/feder

KEY TERMS

Adena, 465
affluent forager, 484
Anasazi, 474
Ancestral Puebloan, 474
courtyard group, 475
Early Woodland, 465
Hohokam, 474

Hopewell, 465
kiva, 478
Middle Woodland, 465
Mississippian culture, 469
Mogollon, 474
myth of the mound
    builders, 464

pit-house, 477
potlatch, 483
pueblo, 479
Sinagua, 474
temple mound builders, 469
totem pole, 483

Evolutionary Epilogue

CHAPTER OVERVIEW

Our story began with the birth of the universe, the origin of life, the evolution of the primates, and the florescence of the apes. We saw one ape species pushed out onto the savanna at the end of the Miocene that was able to survive as a result of its unique ability to walk on two legs. We witnessed the enormous success of their descendants as their brains expanded and as they relied increasingly on the intellectual power of those big brains to invent tools, tame fire, domesticate plants and animals, and develop complex societies.

We have reached a milepost in our investigation of the human past where we literally have caught up with ourselves on the human evolutionary pathway. We can gaze back, as we have in this book, along its winding and serendipitous route and in the distance we can see, if only dimly, our ancient evolutionary ancestors. Ahead, we can imagine our species racing forward to some unknown and unfathomable point on the horizon of our own future.

Past Perspectives, Future Directions

This book has chronicled our species' long and exciting journey as revealed through the scientific investigation of the period of time literally before history. Together we have traveled a pathway paved with the material remains of those who have passed here before us. Littering the trail have been their bones and their trash, their tools and their monuments. These are the things that have informed us of their story. And *their* story has been *our* story, the physical and cultural evolutionary history of all humankind. It is a tale yet unfolding and of which all living things on earth are a part (Figure E-1).

The Human Adaptation

As we have seen, 2.5 million years ago our human ancestors crossed an intellectual threshold that would forever determine the focus of the human adaptation. In our species' African nursery was born our unique reliance on *culture*— our ability to conceive strategies for survival intellectually, to implement those plans, and to teach our children, who in turn teach theirs. Using the intellectual potential conferred on us by our expanding brains, our *Homo habilis* ancestors initiated a pattern that has continued to define the hominid line. Though nature has not endowed us with great strength or speed, though we lack wings to fly and powerful jaws to bite, though our senses are muted in comparison with those of other animals, we nevertheless have become a hugely successful species. What makes us unique and constitutes the foundation of our success is our intellectual capacity and the manifold cultural adaptations we have invented out of our creative imaginations. Our intelligence enables us to define our evolutionary destinies. We needn't wait for natural selection to slowly shift our adaptations to match our environments. We change ourselves and simultaneously construct our environments, all in the time it takes to formulate a thought or to express an idea.

This process began when *Homo habilis* first visualized a sharp, durable edge within a dull, round rock. A few carefully placed, sharp blows with another stone, and the visualized edge became an actual one, capable of cutting, slicing, or chopping more effectively than any of the bodily "tools" nature had given us. In that instant our ancestors had evolved the equivalent of more powerful, piercing canine teeth, razor-sharp slicing claws, and rock-solid fists. It took no genetic mutation; it merely required the unique genius of our evolutionary family line.

In a sense, all human history is based on the Oldowan stone-tool industry, and all human achievement has been but a series of variations on the theme established 2.5 million years ago on the African savanna. The Acheulean handaxe of *Homo erectus*; the Levallois and Mousterian industries associated with anatomically archaic varieties of our own species, *Homo sapiens*; and even cave paintings and barbed harpoons, domesticated plants and animals, socially stratified societies and walled cities—in fact, civilization itself—all of these things are mere variations on the theme established in the Oldowan tools of the Lower Paleolithic. Throughout our stay on earth, human beings have perceived the need and possessed the intellectual capacity to develop new ways of gathering resources, manipulating the environment, recording and transmitting information, organizing

▲ **Figure E-1**
Space exploration, one of the truly monumental undertakings of our twentieth-century civilization, has provided a unique perspective for all of the inhabitants of earth. We can view the earth from the perspective of another world and truly perceive, for the first time in the history of our species, the fragility and the unity of our home. (Courtesy NASA)

labor—in essence, of living our lives. And cultural adaptation continues today to distinguish us from all other life on the planet.

Many Pathways

Many of us in the West view history as an endless upward spiral of material progress, an inevitable pathway of "improvement" of the human condition leading necessarily to us, to Western civilization. We also often view history as teaching moral lessons—history as a tale of good guys versus bad guys, with the good guys (that would be us) always coming out on top and their destiny being realized.

The belief that all of human prehistory and history followed a single, inevitable pathway—the perspective of **orthogenesis**—provides the philosophical underpinning for a hypothesis of **unilineal evolution** (see the discussion of cultural evolutionist Lewis Henry Morgan in Chapter 1). The view of the universality of cultural evolutionary sequences may be a popular one, but it is not the only view. The ancient Egyptians discussed in Chapter 10, for example, perceived history quite differently. As Egyptologist Barry Kemp (1991) points out, the Egyptians saw history not as a trajectory leading somewhere but as a constant, ordered, linear series of transitions from pharaoh to pharaoh. History, for the ancient Egyptians, leads nowhere in particular but proceeds along a constant line of kingship. When Egyptians wrote their own history, there was no search for meaning or pattern, no saga of a destiny fulfilled. For them, history simply was a list of kings, a succession of rulers. Anthropologists view history differently. History for us is played out on an evolutionary stage where there is no necessary direction, only a common, underlying theme of change and adaptation. We view the ancient past neither as a continual parade of divine and semidivine leaders nor as a parable of the inevitability of material progress. We see a unique series of winding cultural pathways reflecting the myriad ways by which people adapted to their environment and constructed a way of life.

If a pattern leading to increasing technological complexity has been one of the cultural evolutionary pathways followed by our species and navigated in this book, it must be remembered that this has been neither the only nor the inevitable avenue traced by human beings. The trajectories seen in this book exhibit tremendous cultural diversity. Such diversity in the evolutionary pathways followed by human beings may be a key to our species' survival.

"Diversity" has become an American buzzword nowadays in an ongoing argument about what our nation has become and what it should be. Often it refers to so-called racial diversity in neighborhoods, schools, and businesses. But I mean the term to signify variation on a broader geographic and temporal scale, a worldwide and "timewide" diversity of human cultural adaptation, from Arctic hunters to tropical rainforest horticulturists, from desert wanderers to seafaring islanders, from megalith-building farmers to grassland hunters, from urban nation-states to tribal societies. It may take the collective wisdom of the cultures of all these people to ensure the survival of the species, ironically at the very time when cultural homogenization—the Westernization of the world—seems to be overtaking us.

I began this epilogue by likening the human story to a lengthy journey. Now, at last, in this book we have reached a milepost in our investigation. We have literally caught up with ourselves on the human evolutionary pathway; we have reached our present location on the trail. We can gaze back, as we have in this book, along the tortuous, serendipitous route and in the distance see, if only dimly, our ancient evolutionary ancestors. Ahead, we can imagine our species racing forward to some unknown, unfathomable point on the horizon of our future. Though the twists and turns will almost certainly bring us to a point that anthropologists have never even considered, we can all be certain of one thing: The journey will take us where no one has gone before.

KEY TERMS

orthogenesis, 494   unilineal evolution, 494

Hominid Species Glossary

Hominid Species	Location	Timeframe	Evidence of Bipedality	Adult Cranial Capacity	Evidence of Stone Tools	Evidence for Use of Fire
Ardipithecus ramidus	Africa: Ethiopia	4.4 million years ago	pelvis and foramen magnum	300–350 cc	no	no
Australopithecus afarensis	Africa: Ethiopia	4 million–3 million years ago	pelvis, leg and foot bones, footprints	380–430 cc	Indirect, inconclusive evidence; no tools but possible cut marks on animal bones	no
Australopithecus africanus	Africa: South Africa	3 million–2.2 million years ago	foramen magnum, pelvis	400–500 cc	no	no
Australopithecus anamensis	Africa: Kenya and Ethiopia	4.2 million–3.9 million years ago	tibia	?	no	no
Australopithecus sediba	Africa: South Africa	2 million years ago	pelvis	420 cc	no	no
Homo antecessor	Europe: Spain	1.2 million–.8 million years ago	foramen magnum, pelvis, leg bones	1,000 cc	Acheulean handaxes	
Homo erectus	Africa, southwest Asia/Europe, east Asia including China and Java	1.8 million–500,000 years ago	foramen magnum, pelvis, leg bones	800–1,200 cc	symmetrical, Acheulean handaxes, chopping tools, flake tools	yes
Homo ergaster	Africa: Tanzania, Kenya, Ethiopia, and South Africa	1.8 million–1.3 million years ago	foramen magnum, pelvis, leg bones	700–1,100 cc	symmetrical, Acheulean handaxes, chopping tools, flake tools	yes
Homo floresiensis	Island of Flores, western Pacific	35,000–14,000 years ago	foramen magnum, pelvis, leg bones	420 cc	flake tools	?

Hominid Species	Location	Timeframe	Evidence of Bipedality	Adult Cranial Capacity	Evidence of Stone Tools	Evidence for Use of Fire
Homo habilis	Africa: Kenya and Tanzania	2.4 million– 1.4 million years ago	pelvis, foramen magnum	500–800 cc	Oldowan technology; chopping tools and flake tools	no
Homo heidelbergensis	Europe	600,000–400,000 years ago	entire skeletons	1,100–1,400 cc	Acheulean handaxes and chopping tools	yes
Homo neanderthalensis	Europe (France, Spain, Belgium, etc.) and southwest Asia (Israel, Iraq, Iran)	120,000–30,000 years ago	entire skeletons	1,250–1,740 cc	Mousterian, Levallois, Chatleperronian	yes
Homo sapiens (archaic; premodern)	Africa, Europe, Asia	500,000-200,000	entire skeletons	1,100–1,400 cc	Mousterian, Levallois	yes
Homo sapiens neanderthalensis	Europe (France, Spain, Belgium, etc.) and southwest Asia (Israel, Iraq, Iran)	120,000-30,000 years ago	entire skeletons	1,250–1,740 cc	Mousterian, Levallois, Chatleperronian	yes
Homo sapiens sapiens (anatomically modern)	Everywhere	195,000 years ago to the present	entire skeleton	1,200–2,200 cc	numerous technologies dating from as much as 80,000 years ago	yes
Orrorin tugenensis	Africa: Kenya	6.1 million– 5.7 million years ago	femurs	?	no	no
Paranthropus boisei	Africa: Tanzania	2.3 million to 1.2 million years ago	foramen magnum	530 cc	no	no
Paranthropus robustus	Africa: South Africa	2.0 million to 1.2 million years ago	foramen magnum	530 cc	no	no
Sahelanthropus tchadensis	Africa: Chad	7 million–6 million years ago	foramen magnum	350 cc	no	no

497

Glossary

absolute date: Any date where a year or range of years can be applied to a site or artifact. As opposed to a relative date where only a chronological order can be established.

accelerator mass spectrometry (AMS) dating: A variety of radiocarbon dating. In conventional radiocarbon dating, the amount of carbon-14 left in a sample is measured indirectly by the amount of radioactivity the sample gives off. In AMS dating, the amount of carbon-14 left in a sample is measured directly by an actual count of atoms.

Acheulean handaxe: Symmetrical stone tool of the later Early Paleolithic. The bifacially flaked, teardrop-shaped all-purpose handaxe dates to as much as 1.76 million years ago in Africa. There and after about 1.0 million years ago in Europe, the handaxe was manufactured by members of the species *Homo erectus*.

Acheulean tradition: The stone-tool tradition associated with *Homo erectus*. The best-known Acheulean tool type is the symmetrical handaxe, now dating back to 1.76 million years ago at the Kokiselei site in Kenya. Handaxes were multipurpose tools—the Swiss Army rocks of the Paleolithic. The Acheulean tradition also includes flakes—sharp-edged tools produced during production of the handaxes. In their symmetry and, from a twenty-first-century perspective, their beauty, the tools reflect both the technological and the intellectual development of our hominid ancestors.

activity area: A place where an activity or group of activities were carried out in the past. The activity area is transformed into an archaeological feature by the loss or discard of material items used in the activity—stone toolmaking, cooking, butchering, burial—that was carried out there.

adaptation: Mode or strategy for survival. An adaptation can be a physical characteristic; the thick fur of a polar bear is a physical adaptation for life in the Arctic. An adaptation can also be a cultural behavior; the material culture of the Inuit people (Eskimos) including harpoons, igloos, parkas, and dog sleds are their invented, cultural adaptations to life under the same environmental conditions.

adapted: The state of being biologically capable or culturally prepared to survive in a given environment.

Adena: Burial mound-building culture centered in the Ohio River valley. Beginning about 3,000 years ago, this culture developed at the chiefdom level of sociopolitical integration, building sometimes quite impressive tombs for their chiefs.

affluent foragers: Though social, political, and economic complexity is commonly fueled by an agricultural subsistence system, the wild food resource base in some areas is so rich and abundant, complexity may develop without the development of food production. People who live in these resource-privileged regions are called affluent foragers. The Jomon of Japan and the native people of the northwest coast of North America are examples of affluent foragers.

age-mortality profile: Term from the science of demography. A graph showing the number or percentage of animals that reached each age category in a population. In a faunal sample, the age-mortality profile shows the percentage of animals that died or were killed in each age category.

Agricultural Revolution: Period of fundamental change in human economy marked by a shift from foraging wild foods to the production of domesticated plants and animals. This revolution in subsistence occurred in multiple world areas beginning after about 12,000 years ago. This term is synonymous with Neolithic and Food Producing Revolution.

altricial: The condition of being born at an immature stage of development. The term originated in ornithology to describe bird species where hatchlings are entirely dependent upon one or both parents for all of their needs for an extended period. The term is used here to describe a similar circumstance in hominid species both ancient and modern.

Amratian/Nagada: Time period in predynastic Egypt. The Amratian/Nagada I represents the time period between 5,750 and 5,650 years ago in Upper Egypt (the southern part of the Egyptian realm).

Anasazi: Name given by the Navajo to the people who built the ancient cliff dwellings and freestanding pueblos found in the American Four Corners region (where the states of Arizona, New Mexico, Utah, and Colorado come together at right angles). The builders were not Navajo, and the term means "ancient enemies" in the Navajo language. The builders were the ancestors of the modern Hopi, some of whom, not surprisingly, prefer the term Ancestral Puebloan.

anatomically modern *Homo sapiens*: Human beings anatomically indistinguishable from those living today. Anatomically modern *Homo sapiens* are found in the paleoanthropological record dating to more than 190,000 years ago.

Ancestral Puebloan: A prehistoric culture centered in the Four Corners region of the American Southwest. The Ancestral Puebloans constructed large and impressive structures that housed the population of the village. Also called Anasazi.

anthropological linguistics: Subfield of anthropology that focuses on language.

anthropology: The study of humanity. A broad social science with varied foci on human biological and cultural adaptations, human origins, and biological and cultural evolution as well as modern cultures.

arboreal: Life in the trees. Primates, for the most part (our species is a notable exception) possess an arboreal adaptation.

archaeological site: A site is a place where people lived and/or worked and where the material objects that they made, used, lost, or discarded can yet be recovered and analyzed.

archaeologist: A scientist who studies human beings through the analysis of the material remains of behavior: the things that people made and used and that have fortuitously preserved. Archaeologists often focus on human cultural evolution.

archaeology: The study of humanity through the analysis of the material remains of human behavior: the study of the things that people made and used in the past and that have fortuitously preserved. Archaeologists often focus on human cultural evolution.

archaeomagnetism: Orientation of the earth's magnetic field can become fixed in relatively recent cultural deposits like the sediments in a canal or the clay in bricks lining a kiln. The date of a site can be determined where that orientation points to a location of magnetic north already fixed in space and time along a master curve.

Archaic: Chronological period in the New World that follows the Paleoindian period. The Archaic begins at the end of the Pleistocene and represents a period of cultural adaptation to the new, postglacial environment by Native Americans.

archaic *Homo sapiens*: Extinct sub-species of humanity that share much in common with modern or anatomically modern *Homo sapiens*, but who commonly retain primitive skeletal features and possess a somewhat smaller mean cranial capacity than modern people. The Neandertals are the best known archaic variety or subspecies of the human race. Also called premodern *Homo sapiens*.

argon/argon dating: Absolute dating method based on the decay of radioactive potassium to stable argon gas. Argon-argon dating is an updated and more accurate version of potassium-argon dating. Potassium is abundant in rock and is usually applied in the dating of rock strata. Because of the long half-life of radioactive potassium, there is no upper chronological limit to the application of the technique.

articular surfaces: The surfaces of two adjacent bones marking the point at which they attach or "articulate." By examining the articular surfaces of a bone, scientists can determine the mechanics of joint movement.

artifact: Any object manufactured by a human being or human ancestor. Usually defined further as a portable object like a stone spearpoint or clay pot to distinguish it from larger more complex archaeological features.

artificial selection: The process used in the domestication and refinement of plants and animals whereby human beings select which members of a species will live and produce offspring. Humans make such decisions on the basis of their needs or desires concerning the form or behavior of the species: plants that produce larger seeds; animals that produce woollier coats; animals that produce more milk.

association: Term relating to the spatial relationships among archaeological artifacts, ecofacts, and features. Objects found in proximity to each other are said to be in association.

attritional profile: An age-mortality profile in which most deaths in the sample occur in the very young and very old age categories. Proportionally fewer deaths occur in the prime of life. Such a profile results when deaths are due to routine causes like disease and predation. Compare to catastrophic profile.

Aurignacian: Lithic tool technology associated with anatomically modern human beings in Europe about 40,000 years ago. Includes long, narrow blade tools.

Aurignacian blade: A blade tool produced in the Aurignacian technology dating between 40,000 and 27,000 years ago.

Australian Small Tool Phase: Cultural phase beginning in Australia around 6,000 years ago and became widespread within about a thousand years. The phase is marked by the production of blade tools, reflecting a more efficient use of stone than in earlier technologies.

australopithecine: Any members of the genus *Australopithecus*, including several species: *ramidus, afarensis, africanus,* and *sediba*. Oldest members of the genus date back to at least 4.4 million years ago. The genus is extinct by 1 million years ago. Characterized by an ape-sized brain but with the modern human behavioral trait of bipedal locomotion.

Aztec: Calling themselves the Mexica, the Aztecs were the historical civilization encountered by the Spanish invaders of Mexico in the sixteenth century. When the Spanish arrived, the Aztecs were the dominant political and military force in Mesoamerica. The Aztec capital of Tenochtitlán was located on an island in Lake Texcoco; Spanish accounts remark on the majesty of the city's architecture. Aztec wealth was dependent on the tribute demanded of those under its military sway, but they never fully integrated surrounding groups into their empire.

backed blade: Stone blade tool in which one edge has been dulled or "backed" so it can be more readily held in the hand while being used.

Badarian Time: Period in predynastic Egypt. The Badarian represents the time period between 6,400 and 5,750 years ago in Upper Egypt (the southern part of the Egyptian realm).

basicranium: The base of the cranium. Since the soft parts of hominid anatomy involved in the production of sound do not preserve but are connected to the base of the skull, the basicranium is a crucial part of the anatomy when assessing the ability of human ancestors to produce human speech.

Bering Land Bridge: A broad connection of land more than 1,500 kilometers (1,000 miles) across connecting northeast Asia with northwest North America during periods of sea level depression in the Pleistocene. People living in Asia walked east across the land bridge into the lands of the Western Hemisphere at least 15,000 years ago and possibly more.

blades: Long thin stone flakes, commonly twice as long as they are wide. Blades represent an efficient use of stone, producing a high proportion of edge for the amount (weight) of stone used.

brachiation: The ability to swing, arm over arm, through the trees. Many primates are expert brachiators.

burin: Sharp and durable stone tool used in engraving. Burins were used in etching out thin slivers of antler or bone which then were modified further to make awls and needles.

C3 pathway: The photosynthetic process employed by most trees. In the C3 pathway, a radioactive isotope of carbon, ^{13}C, is differentially filtered out.

C4 pathway: The photosynthetic process employed by most grasses and sedges. In the C4 pathway, a radioactive isotope of carbon, ^{13}C, is more readily used than in plants that follow the C3 pathway.

cache: A stash of stuff placed away for safe keeping by ancient people. When the archaeologist is lucky, a cache was not returned to in the past and whatever was stored therein was not retrieved. A cache becomes the equivalent of an unintentional time capsule, providing a cluster of artifacts representing a single time period.

calibration curve: Curve resulting from the graphing of dendrochronologically derived dates for an extensive series of tree rings and the carbon dates determined for each of those same rings.

calvarium: The top part of a skull, lacking the lower jaw (mandible) and facial bones.

camelid: Large ruminant animal including bachtrian and dromedary camels in the Old World and llamas, alpacas, guanacos, and vicuñas in the New World.

Capsian: Northwest African culture dating to after 10,000 years ago. Characterized by hunting of wild sheep, collection of shellfish and snails, and the harvesting of wild grains.

carbon dating: Radiometric dating technique based on the decay of a radioactive isotope of carbon: ^{14}C or radiocarbon. Carbon dating can be applied to virtually anything that was once part of a living organism within a range from about 50,000 to 500 years ago. Also called radiocarbon dating.

carbon isotope analysis: Analysis of the proportion of ^{12}C and ^{13}C in a bone or soil sample. Useful in dietary and environmental reconstruction because different groupings of plants use carbon compounds containing ^{12}C and ^{13}C differentially.

carrying capacity: The number of organisms a given region or habitat can support without degrading the environment.

catastrophist: An adherent to the perspective that the current appearance of the earth can be best explained as having resulted from a series of natural catastrophes—for example, floods and volcanoes. Catastrophism was quite popular prior to the nineteenth century and lent support to the claim of a recent age for the earth.

central place: Concept from the field of cultural geography. Central places are the geographic focal points of a political entity. A large city or ceremonial center with religious structures often is a central place for a state or chiefdom.

cereal: Plants, especially grasses, that produce starchy grains. Cereal plants were among the first domesticated foods produced during the Neolithic.

Châtelperronian: Lithic technology including the use of blades that appears to be intermediate in form and time between Mousterian and Aurignacian. Associated with some late populations of Neandertals.

Chavin: A distinctive art style that developed in western South America beginning about 3,000 years ago. The religious iconography of Chavin seems to have served as a unifying influence, setting the stage for the later development of geographically broad empires.

chiefdom: A level of socio-political integration more complex than the tribe but less so than the state. The social system is ranked, not egalitarian. Individuals are placed in a hierarchy of power and prestige. Chiefdoms are less rigidly structured than state societies and a chief's power is less than that of a king or pharaoh.

Chimu: One of the pre-Inca complex societies that developed in South America. The Chimu produced a true empire that spread across more than 1,300 km (800 mi) of the coast of South America, including the entire northern coast of Peru. Its capital, Chan Chan, was truly urban in character; its many neighborhoods and compounds covered an expanse of 20 km² (8 mi²).

chinampas: Artificial islands in lakes and swamps produced by the Aztecs of central Mexico. These artificial islands were intensively farmed.

Chindadn: A teardrop-shaped spearpoint found in the Nenana Complex in Alaska. Chindadn points are similar to a form found in the Ushki sites located on the Kamchatka Peninsula of eastern Siberia.

city-state: Political entity characteristic of some early civilizations, especially in Mesopotamia. A central population center dominates the surrounding hinterlands. The wealth of the countryside flows into the city where it is concentrated in the hands of the elite classes.

civilization: As used here, cultures exhibiting social stratification, labor and craft specialization, a food surplus used to support a political and/or religious elite, monumental construction, and a system of record keeping.

clay tokens: Small geometric shapes of clay, some bearing impressed symbols, dating back to as much as 10,000 years ago in the Middle East that appear to represent an early system of record keeping that led ultimately to a system of writing.

Clovis: Fluted point type of the Paleoindians. Large, laurel-leaf-shaped stone blades exhibiting a channel or "flute" (as in a fluted column) on both faces to aid in hafting the stone point onto a wooden shaft. The channel begins at the base and generally extends from one-third to no more than one-half the length of the point. Clovis points date from about 13,200 to 11,900 years ago (compare to Folsom).

codices (sing., codex): The screenfold books of the Maya. Written in their hieroglyphic language, the vast majority of the codices were collected and destroyed by the Spanish in A.D. 1562. Only four codices survived this tragic period of book burning.

collapse: All civilizations experience "collapse." Collapse may involve the complete dissolution of a social/economic/political entity as the result of revolution, military defeat, a descent into anarchy, and social chaos. What we sometimes perceive as "collapse" in the archaeological record may also reflect, instead, the reconfiguring of a social/economic/political system involving a general strategy of "downsizing": population decline, a decrease in the scope and number of monumental construction projects, and a decline in the level of economic inequality.

complex foraging: A system of hunting animals and gathering wild plants in which subsistence is focused on a few, highly productive resources. These foods are collected and stored, allowing for a more sedentary settlement system. Compare to simple foraging.

conflict models: Models of the development of complex societies that maintain that complexity evolved as a way to reduce, control, and mediate conflict among people living in a society. In other words, in conflict models, social rules developed to dampen resentment among people concerning the development of economic inequality and, in essence, to normalize that inequality.

coprolite: Fossilized feces, useful in the reconstruction of an ancient animal's diet.

Cordilleran: The Pleistocene mountain ice mass in North America centered in the Rocky Mountains.

cortex: The exterior surface or rind of a core, usually removed in the process of stone-tool manufacturing.

courtyard groups: Clusters of separate residential structures in Hohokam villages surrounding a common area or courtyard. Most individual villages consisted of multiple courtyard groups. Each courtyard group consisted of from two to ten family residences.

cranial suture: Lines of connection between cranial bones. Sutures appear as squiggly lines on both the interior and exterior surfaces of the skull. Sutures progressively disappear with age and can be used to provide a general estimate for age at death.

craniometrics: Measurement of the shape of the cranium.

cranium: The bones of the head and face (excluding the lower jaw).

creation story: Legend, myth, or folk tale intending to explain the origin of the universe, the earth, life, and humanity. Not intended as a scientific hypothesis, but, instead, an internally consistent, satisfying explanation for why we are here.

creationist: One who believes that the universe, the earth, life, and humanity are the product of the creation of an all-powerful god.

cultural evolution: Just as biological evolution posits ordered change through time among biological organisms, cultural evolution posits ordered change through time among cultures. Cultures change in response to changes in their physical environments (for example, changes in climate) and cultural environments (contact with other human groups), as well as through the development of new technologies.

culture: The invented, taught, and learned patterns of behavior of human groups. The extrasomatic (beyond the body or beyond the biological) means of adaptation of a human group.

cuneiform: Early form of written records in Mesopotamia, involving the impression of standardized symbols on wet clay. Dating to close to 6,000 years ago, cuneiform is the earliest writing in the world.

cylinder seal: Mesopotamian system of impressing symbolic notation onto wet clay by using a marked cylinder.

dagga: A high-quality, clay-based building material used in southern Africa. Dagga construction is commonly found in the homes of the people of Great Zimbabwe.

debitage: Waste flakes produced during the process of making stone tools. Usually small, unusable bits of stone.

deciduous dentition: Baby teeth. The teeth that are shed like the leaves of deciduous trees.

deffufa: Monumental mud-brick towers built by the inhabitants of the ancient Nubian civilization of Kerma located south of the third cataract of the Nile in modern Sudan. Kerma dates to more than 3,500 years ago.

Denali Complex: A lithic technology seen in the Arctic consisting of wedge-shaped cores, microblades, bifacial knives, and burins. Dating to about 10,000 years ago, several features of the Denali Complex are reminiscent of elements of older complexes in northeast Asia, particularly that of Dyuktai Cave.

dendrochronology: Tree-ring dating. By placing a tree section found at an archaeological site within a master sequence of tree-ring widths through time, the age of the tree (when it died or was cut down) can be determined and associated with the site at which it was found.

diaphysis: The shaft of a long bone. On either end of the diaphysis there is an epiphysis.

diastema: Gap in the teeth of both the mandible (lower jaw) and maxilla (upper jaw). The large canine teeth fit into the diastemas of their opposing jaws when those jaws are closed.

DNA: Shorthand for deoxyribonucleic acid. The genetic code; the genetic instructions for each life form on the planet.

dolmen: Standing stones found throughout western Europe, erected by the same Megalithic culture that produced Stonehenge. Though they range widely in size, dolmen can be quite tall and heavy stones that must have taken an enormous effort to move into place and then to erect.

domesticated: A plant or animal that has been altered by human beings through selective breeding. Some plants and animals have been so altered in this way, they can no longer survive without human intervention.

domestication: Through artificial selection, the production of new species of plants and animals that owe their existence to human intervention. Some domesticated species become so highly specialized to the demands of human beings, they can no longer survive and propagate without human assistance.

Early Woodland: Time period in ancient eastern North America, usually dated between 3,000 and 2,200 years ago.

ecofact: Element found in archaeological contexts that exhibit human activity, but were not made by people and so are not, strictly speaking, artifacts. Burned wood in a fireplace, butchered animal bone in a trash pit, and charred seeds or nuts in a midden are all ecofacts.

egalitarian: Social systems in which all members of the same age/sex category are equal in the sense that they all possess the same amount of wealth, social standing, and political influence.

einkorn: Variety of wheat; *Tripsicum monococcum*. Einkorn possesses hulled grains and was an important domesticate in the Neolithic. Today it is not a significant agricultural crop (compare to emmer).

ejecta: All the material thrown out of a volcano during an eruption.

electron spin resonance dating: Radiation damage dating technique based on measurement of build-up of electrons in crystalline materials. Can be applied to sites more than a few thousand years old. The upper limit of the technique is estimated to be more than 10 million years.

emmer: A variety of wheat: *Tripsicum turgidum*. Emmer wheat was soon established as the primary stock of early agricultural wheat. It is the source of cultivated wheat in the modern world (compare to einkorn).

enamel hypoplasia: Medical condition affecting the outside layers of teeth. Horizontal cracks develop on the enamel in individuals who experience bouts of malnutrition during their early years.

endocast: Mold of the brain produced naturally by sediment entering the skull and then mineralizing. Also produced artificially by coating the inside of the skull with a latex-based material. Endocasts can exhibit features of the exterior surface of the brain.

envelope: Name given to clay containers used to store clay tokens in the Middle East beginning 5,500 years ago. The clay tokens were of various shapes and used as an information storage system, the different shapes representing different categories of goods—jars of oil, sheep, cattle, etc. Markings were made on the clay envelope to indicate the kind and number of tokens they contained. Ultimately, the tokens were eliminated and these markings developed into the world's first writing system.

epiphyseal fusion: The epiphyses of each long bone join to the diaphyses during the process of physical maturation. The age of death of a juvenile individual can be assessed by reference to the degree of epiphyseal fusion exhibited.

epiphysis (pl.—epiphyses): The endcaps of the long bones. The epiphyses join at the ends of the diaphysis of each long bone.

erosion: The disintegration and transportation of geological material by wind, water, or ice.

ethnoarchaeology: The archaeological study of a living group of people. Often focuses on the processes by which human behavior becomes translated into the archaeological record.

ethnographer: Cultural anthropologist who lives among a group of people or a cultural group. Interacts with them on a daily basis, often for an extended period of time, observing their behavior.

ethnology: The comparative study of culture. Ethnologists study human behavior cross-culturally, looking for similarities and differences in how people behave: how they raise their children, how they treat elders, how they organize their labor, etc.

evolution: Systematic change through time of biological organisms or human cultural systems.

experimental replication: The reproduction, under laboratory conditions, of facsimiles of archaeological artifacts. Process employed to analyze ancient technology.

faunal assemblage: The animal bones found at a site and the species represented by those bones.

Fayum/Merimden: Time period in predynastic Egypt. The Fayum/Merimden represents the time period between 7,200 and 6,400 years ago in Lower Egypt (the northern part of the Egyptian realm).

feature: Combination of artifacts and/or ecofacts at a site, reflecting a location where some human activity took place. Features include fireplaces, middens, burials, cooking hearths, activity areas, and buildings. Features are also defined as nonportable, complex artifacts.

femur: The upper leg bone.

Fertile Crescent: A crescent-shaped region extending from the eastern Mediterranean coast of modern Israel, Lebanon, and Syria, north into the Zagros Mountains, and then south toward the Persian Gulf (see Figure 8.15). An area marked by an abundance of wild cereal grain at the beginning of the Holocene. Not coincidentally the region where some of the world's first domestication of plants took place.

fission track dating: Radiation damage dating technique that measures the age of an artifact as a function of the amount of physical damage in the form of damage tracks left in a material by radioactive decay.

flake: Stone fragment removed from a core with the blow of a hammerstone, antler baton, or pressure flaker. The flake can be either discarded or it can be used as is or further modified for use as a specific tool.

fluted point: Projectile points made by Paleoindians in the New World between about 13,200 and 10,000 B.P. The points exhibit a distinctive channel or "flute" (as in the flutes in a fluted column) on both faces. These channels aided in hafting the spearpoint onto its wooden shaft. The two major forms of fluted point are Clovis and Folsom.

Folsom: Fluted point type of the Paleoindians. Generally smaller than Clovis points, Folsom points are later in time than Clovis, dating to after 11,000 B.P. Where Clovis points have been found in association with the bones of extinct elephants, Folsom points have been found in association with the bones of bison. Folsom points are fluted, with the channels commonly extending nearly the entire length of the point (compare to Clovis).

Food Producing Revolution: Period of fundamental change in human economy marked by a shift from foraging wild foods to the production of domesticated plants and animals. This revolution in subsistence occurred in multiple world areas beginning after about 12,000 years ago. This term is synonymous with Neolithic and Agricultural Revolution.

food surplus: That food that can be produced beyond the needs of the producer and his or her family. A food surplus is a necessary concomitant of civilization, freeing entire classes of people from the subsistence quest, and allowing for the existence of full-time rulers, soldiers, merchants, and priests.

foraging: A subsistence system based on the collection of wild foods. May include any combination of hunting wild game, gathering wild plants, fishing, and shellfish collecting.

foramen magnum: Large hole at the base or back of the skull through which veins, arteries, and nerves pass. The location of the foramen magnum in a fossil skull is an indicator of how the skull was attached to the vertebral column and, by inference, the form of locomotion employed by the creature.

foraminifera: Microorganisms used in the study of ancient environments. By measuring the ratio of $^{16}O:^{18}O$ in foraminifera fossils, the amount of the earth's surface covered in ice at any given point of time can be indirectly determined.

forensic anthropologist: A biological anthropologist who specializes in the identification of the human skeleton, often in the investigation of a crime. Forensic anthropologists are often employed by police agencies to assist in the identification of human remains.

gene flow: The movement and exchange of genetic material among populations of a species through interbreeding.

gene pool: All of the genetic variants in a population.

genera (sing. genus): The level in biological taxonomy between family and species. For example, chimpanzees are classified as *Pan troglodytes* while their cousins, the bonobos, are classified as *Pan paniscus*; they are members of the same taxonomic family, the *Pongidae*, and the same genus, *Pan*, but different species, *troglodytes* and *paniscus*.

geoglyphs: Large-scaled artwork, usually produced by piling up stones or sweeping them away from the surface. The Nazca lines and depictions of fish, animals, birds, and spiders are among the most famous. Geoglyphs are often of such a large scale that they can only be fully appreciated from nearby mountain peaks.

Geometric Kebaran: Pre-Neolithic culture in the Middle East, dating to the period 14,500 to 12,500 B.P. Located in the moist Mediterranean woodlands of the central Levant and extending into the margins of the Negev and Sinai Deserts, and across southern Jordan. Subsistence was based on foraging.

glacial: Period of ice advance during the Pleistocene. Glacials are generally long-lived, their tenure measured in the many thousands of years. Cold glacials were interrupted by equally long, warmer periods called interglacials.

glacier: A massive body of ice that, through a number of processes, can expand and actually move.

glume: Case in which individual cereal grain is enclosed.

glyph: A carved figure or symbol in a written language.

gracile: Lightly constructed, referring to the overall appearance of a hominid skeleton. Modern humans are gracile and when the term is applied to the fossils of extinct hominids, it is in reference to their appearance relative to anatomically modern human beings. Bones that are more massive than those of modern humans are said to be robust.

grave goods: Cultural materials placed into a grave, sometimes in a conscious attempt to provide the deceased with items it is believed are needed in the afterlife.

Gravettian: Toolmaking tradition of the Upper Paleolithic, characterized by the production of small blades and denticulate knives. Dated from 27,000 to 21,000 B.P.

ground-penetrating radar (GPR): A noninvasive technique to investigate the subsurface. An electromagnetic pulse is passed through the soil. The pulse encounters objects or differently compacted soil layers and bounces a signal back to a receiver. The signal can be interpreted and imaged, revealing buried walls, earthworks, or other cultural features.

Halafian: Culture in Mesopotamia dating from 7,500 to 6,700 B.P. Halafian sites generally are small farming villages.

half-life: Measurement of the amount of time it takes for half of the radioactive isotope in a given sample to decay into a stable form. The half-life of radiocarbon, for example, is 5,730 years while that of radioactive potassium is 1.3 billion years.

Hamburgian: Culture of the northern European Upper Paleolithic.

hammerstone: In stone toolmaking, the hammerstone is the lithic tool used in percussion flaking to remove flakes or blades from a core, or to detach additional flakes from flakes or blades.

handaxe: Bifacially chipped, symmetrical stone tool associated with *Homo erectus* populations in Africa and Europe. The sequence of steps needed to produce a handaxe is longer and more complex than those necessary to produce the older Oldowan choppers. The oldest handaxes have been found in Africa and date to 1.76 million years ago in Kenya.

hang-t'u: Chinese term for stamped or pounded and compacted earth used to make structures.

haplogroup: A cluster of DNA variants that are found together in individual members of a population. Five major mitochondrial haplogroups have been identified among Native Americans; all five are also found in central and eastern Asian populations.

Harris lines: Longitudinal cracks located at the ends of long bones; indicative of dietary stress during physical development.

Hassunan: Culture in Mesopotamia dating from 8,000 to 7,200 B.P. Characterized by small farming villages where subsistence was based on the growing of wheat, barley, peas, and lentils. Hunting supplemented the diet.

hieroglyphic: A writing system in which pictorial symbols are used to convey a particular sound, object, or idea—or some combination of these three things.

Hoabinhian: Southeast Asian Mesolithic stone-tool tradition based on the manufacture of tools from chipped pebbles.

Hohokam: Culture in the American Southwest, centered in southern Arizona. The Hohokam people constructed irrigation canals to water the fields in which they grew maize, beans, and squash.

Holocene epoch: The recent and current geological epoch. The Holocene followed the Pleistocene and may represent a break with that glacial epoch. On the other hand, the Holocene may, in actuality, merely represent a short-lived respite in glaciation, an interglacial rather than a new and different epoch.

Holocene Warm Maximum: Period when worldwide temperatures rose beginning about 8,700 years ago. Depending on your location temperatures were between 0.5°C (0.9°F) and 3°C (5.4°F) higher than they are currently.

hominid: Any creature believed to be in the direct human line. Bipedal locomotion is the single most salient characteristic of the hominids.

Hopewell: Burial mound building culture centered in the Ohio River valley. Beginning about 2,400 years ago, this culture developed at the chiefdom level of sociopolitical integration, building sometimes quite impressive tombs for their chiefs. Hopewell is generally later than Adena.

humerus: The upper arm bone.

hypothesis: A proposed explanation for some phenomenon. A hypothesis may be derived initially from empirical observation of the phenomenon; the process called induction. Hypotheses must be tested; predictions are deduced of what new data must be found if the hypothesis is to be supported. When data are found that contradict these predictions, the hypothesis is rejected or modified.

Iberomaurusians: Northwest African culture dating to after 16,000 B.P. Iberomaurusians inhabited the coastal plain and interior of modern Tunisia and Morocco. Subsistence was based on hunting wild cattle, gazelle, Hartebeest, and Barbary sheep and the collection of marine mollusks.

ice-free corridor: A proposed route of safe passage in North America between the farthest west extent of the Laurentide ice field and the farthest east extent of the Cordilleran glacier. Paleoindians may have traveled down this corridor from the western Arctic into the heartland of America. Also called the McKenzie Corridor.

ilium: The upper blade of the pelvis.

impact wear: Distinctive damage scars on stone tools that can be experimentally shown to have resulted from the tool being used as a projectile.

Inca: Calling themselves *Tawantinsuyu*, the Inca were the dominant social, economic, and political force in South America when the Spanish invaded in the late fifteenth century. The Inca possessed a huge empire that they controlled with their military might. The Inca strategy for control included installing their own people into leadership roles in the territories they incorporated into their empire and the movement of local residents out of their homelands in an attempt to marginalize their ability to resist Inca hegemony.

innominate: The left or right side of the pelvis. The innominate consists of the ilium, the ischium, and the pubis.

integration model: Models of the development of complex societies that maintain that complexity evolved as a way to respond to significant challenges faced by a society, including the need to construct large-scale irrigation works or defensive walls. In this view, social and political inequality are the tools by which the power of the few to organize and oversee the work of the many is rationalized and justified.

interglacial: Period during the Pleistocene when temperature ameliorated. Interglacials lasted for thousands of years, and were preceded and followed by glacials.

interstadial: Short periods during glacials when temperature increased and glaciers receded.

Iron Age: The final of the three periods in the National Museum of Denmark's C. J. Thomsen's three-age system. Period of time in human history when the iron metallurgy became the dominant technology for producing metal tools.

ischium: The bottom rear portion of the innominate bone of the pelvis.

isotope: Variety of an element's atomic form. Isotopes are distinguished by the number of neutrons in their atomic nuclei. Some isotopes are unstable and decay into other forms. These are said to be radioactive. Some radioactive isotopes can be used in dating paleontological or archaeological material.

Jomon: Ancient Japanese culture dating from 13,000 years ago. The Jomon people were foragers, relying on hunting wild animals, gathering wild plants, and, especially, collecting food from the sea. The rich resource base exploited by the Jomon allowed for dense population and complex social patterns before their adoption of agriculture.

K/Ar dating: Potassium/argon dating. The half-life of radioactive potassium has been measured to be 1.3 billion years. Since potassium is an abundant element in the earth's crust and since argon collects in rock at a fixed rate as a result of the decay of radioactive potassium, this technique is widely applicable.

Karim Shahirian: Pre-Neolithic culture located in the foothills of the Zagros Mountains in modern Turkey.

khipu: Record-keeping system of the Inca in which a series of knotted strings were used as mnemonic devices to help record keepers remember information (also quipu).

Kibish formation: Ancient stratum in Ethiopia in which the Omo I and Omo II crania were found. The specific part of the stratum (Member I) in which the crania were recovered has now been dated to 195,000 years ago, making Omo I the oldest anatomically modern human cranium yet found and dated.

kiva: A round structure used in religious ceremonies by Native American societies in the Southwest. Most kivas were relatively small, but so-called great kivas were enormous. Casa Rinconada in Chaco Canyon, for example, was nearly 20 m (63.5 ft) across.

knapper: One who makes stone tools. To knapp is to make stone tools through the application of percussion and pressure.

Knossos: Enormous and impressive site representing the culmination of Minoan civilization. The temple at Knossos was built beginning in 3,880 B.P. and at its height it covered an area to about 20,000 square meters with 1,000 rooms built up to three and, in sections, four stories.

Kush: The Egyptian name for the land south of their territory. Kush began at the first cataract of the Nile in southern Egypt and extended to the sixth cataract near the modern Sudanese city of Khartoum.

lacustrine: Having to do with lakes.

Lake Forest Archaic: Archaic culture of eastern North America, centered in, though not restricted to, the region of the Great Lakes. Lake Forest people exploited the food resources of the large lakes of eastern North America.

Lapita: Pottery style known from the inhabited Pacific Islands. The movement of people from the western to eastern Pacific can be traced by the presence and spread of Lapita pottery.

Late Gerzean: Time period in predynastic Egypt. The Late Gerzean (Nagada II) represents the time period between 5,400 and 5,300 years ago in Upper Egypt (the southern part of the Egyptian realm). The Late Gerzean (Maadian) represents the time period between 5,400 and 5,300 years ago in Lower Egypt (the northern part of the Egyptian realm).

Laurentide: The massive continental ice sheet of Pleistocene North America, centered in central northeastern Canada.

legume: Legumes comprise a large family of flowering plants. All legumes produce fruits which grow in the form of a pod that splits along its seams when mature and opens to reveal the seeds. Garden peas, snap beans, lima beans, lentils, and chick peas are all legumes domesticated during the Neolithic.

Levallois: Stone-tool technology involving the production of consistently shaped flakes from carefully prepared cores. Levallois technology is associated with archaic forms of *Homo sapiens*.

Levant: Name applied to the areas along the eastern shore of the Mediterranean, including present-day Greece, Turkey, Syria, Lebanon, Israel, and Egypt.

Levantine Corridor: A natural geographic passageway of low-lying land hugging the eastern margin of the Mediterranean, linking Africa, Asia, and Eurasia.

Linearbandkeramik: Early Neolithic culture of central Europe. Dating to about 6,500 B.P., the subsistence base was domesticated emmer wheat, barley, and pulses.

lintels: Horizontal cross-members of the Stonehenge monument. The thirty lintels at Stonehenge rest on top of and connect the thirty upright sarsens.

littoral: Related to the sea shore.

logistical collecting: A settlement-subsistence strategy that involves the movement of a group in a fixed seasonal round. The food collectors know when resources are available and where during the course of a year. They plan the movements of their settlements to coincide with the availability of food resources in their territory.

Lower Paleolithic: Period from 2.5 million to 250,000 years ago. Encompasses the stone-tool industries of *Homo habilis* and *Homo erectus*.

luminescence dating: Determining the age of an object by releasing as light the energy it has accumulated during its existence. The amount of light it emits in this process is directly proportional to its age. Light (optically stimulated luminescence) or heat (thermoluminescence) can be used to release this energy.

Lung-shan: Chinese culture that followed the Neolithic Yang-shao. Dated to 5,000 B.P., Lung-shan sites are larger with evidence of substantial hang-t'u construction. Lung-shan cemeteries have produced clear evidence of a socioeconomically stratified society. Lung-shan laid the foundation for China's first complex state, the Shang.

Maadian: Time period in predynastic Egypt. The Late Gerzean (Maadian) represents the time period between 5,400 and 5,300 years ago in Lower Egypt (the northern part of the Egyptian realm).

macroband: Hunter-gatherers often arrange themselves into communities or "bands" of 25 to 75 people. A group of bands of people who interact on a regular basis—they may intermarry, conduct group hunts, share resources—is called a macroband.

Magdelanian: Late Paleolithic culture in Europe dating from 16,000 to 11,000 B.P. Known from sites primarily in France and Spain, the Magdelanian material culture included finely made barbed harpoons, carved decorative objects, and cave paintings.

Maglemosian: Early Mesolithic culture of Europe. Adapted to a forest and lakeside environment. The famous site of Star Carr is a Maglemosian site.

mandible: The lower jaw (compare to maxilla).

Maritime Archaic: Archaic period culture of northeast North America. Centered along the coast of northern New England and the Canadian Maritime provinces, the Maritime Archaic people's subsistence focus was on the sea where they fished and hunted sea mammals. Burials with rather elaborate grave goods mark the Maritime Archaic.

mastaba: Mud-brick structures built over the tombs of a developing elite in Egypt before the pharaohs. Mastabas became larger through time, were stacked on top of each other, and ultimately evolved into the pyramid tomb emblematic of ancient Egyptian civilization.

master sequence: The regional pattern of tree-ring width yearly variations. The master sequence for the American West extends back some 9,000 years. When an archaeological tree-ring section can be placed within the master sequence, it can be dated directly and this date can be associated with the archaeological site at which it was found.

Mast Forest Archaic: Archaic period culture of northeastern North America. Centered in central New England, Mast Forest sites reflect a subsistence focus on the interior forest of New England, especially on the resources of the mast forest: nut foods like acorn, hickory, chestnut, and walnut and animals, especially deer.

mattock: A digging tool with a working blade set at right angles to the handle. Antler mattocks have been found in European Mesolithic sites like Star Carr.

maxilla: The upper jaw (compare to mandible).

Maya civilization: centered in Guatemala, Belize, Honduras, and eastern Mexico, especially the Yucatán Peninsula, the Maya was one of the most spectacular ancient civilizations in the world. The Maya built cities with spectacular pyramids, temples, astronomical observatories, and ball courts. They used a hieroglyphic writing system, developed a complex mathematical system (that included the concept of "zero"), and developed a series of very accurate calendars. They did not predict the world would end on December 21, 2012.

McKenzie corridor: A proposed route of safe passage between the farthest west extent of the Laurentide ice field and the farthest east extent of the Cordilleran glacier. Paleoindians may have traveled down this corridor from the western Arctic into the heartland of America. Also called the Ice-free corridor.

megafauna: Very large animals; commonly used to describe the large, now extinct herbivores of the Pleistocene world.

megalithic: Related to the construction of large stone monuments. The Megalithic culture erected thousands of these monuments beginning more than 5,000 years ago. Stonehenge is the most famous of the Megalithic monuments.

Melanesia: Islands located north of New Guinea in the western Pacific.

Mesolithic: Culture period after the Paleolithic and before the Neolithic. A period of the proliferation of many regional adaptations and an explosion of local cultural diversity.

Mesopotamia: The land between the Tigris and Euphrates Rivers in modern Iraq. The world's first cities and complex civilization developed in Mesopotamia.

metatarsal: Any of the long bones of the feet, located between the bones of the ankles and the toes.

microbands: Small co-habiting groups of people. Microbands commonly consist of ten or fifteen people who move together in a pattern of seasonally nomadic movement.

microblade: Very small stone blade, often with a very sharp cutting edge. Microblades often were set in groups into wooden, bone, or antler handles.

microcephaly: A congenital condition characterized by a very small head and incomplete development of the brain. Some suggested, at least initially, that the cranium found on the island of Flores and called the Hobbit was not an ancestral form of hominid but a pathological individual, a victim of microcephaly.

microlith: Very small stone tool.

Micronesia: Small islands in the western Pacific, east of New Guinea.

midden: An archaeological feature that consists of a refuse heap. A preserved pile of trash, often food remains.

Middle Paleolithic: The Middle Stone Age. Period after the Lower Paleolithic and before the Upper Paleolithic. Covers the span of about 250,000 to 40,000 years ago and includes the cultures of archaic varieties of human beings.

Middle Woodland: Time period in ancient eastern North America, usually dated between 2,200 and 1,600 years ago.

Minoan: Name given by Sir Arthur Evans to the early European civilization that evolved on the island of Crete. The temple at Knossos is the best-known manifestation of this culture.

Miocene: Period of time from 25 to 5 million years ago. Forests were more extensive during the Miocene than they are today. A broad array of arboreally adapted ape species thrived during this epic; most became extinct at the end of the Miocene when the forests diminished in their geographical extent.

Mississippian: Peaking at about A.D. 1000, the Mississippian culture developed in the American Midsouth and Southeast and is characterized by the construction of sometimes monumentally scaled temple mounds—truncated pyramids of earth up to 100 feet in height with a footprint covering several acres—in large ceremonial centers, a few of which, especially Cahokia, also had a substantial resident population. The Mississippian were an indigenous North American complex culture that, at its peak, and centered at Cahokia, was an indigenous North American civilization.

Mississippian culture: The people responsible for the construction of the Temple Mounds. The Mississippian culture flourished between approximately 1,500 and 500 years ago.

mit'a/mita: The Inca term for the labor required of its citizens devoted to state projects. The amount of work demanded by the state was determined on the basis of the amount of work needed in any given year: to construct buildings, build and maintain roads, prepare agricultural fields, and so on.

mitmaqkuna: The Inca term for the people of conquered lands who the Inca then separated and disbursed by resettling them, all in an effort to prevent their rebelling against the Inca state.

mobiliary art: Art that is portable. Mobiliary art made during the Upper Paleolithic includes Venus figurines, animal carvings, and geometrically incised bone and antler.

Moche: One of the pre-Inca complex societies that developed in western South America. Located on the northern Peruvian coast, the Moche were at their peak at about A.D. 400. Located in the heart of the Moche population center, the Pyramid of the Sun was constructed of more than 143 million adobe bricks and, at its peak, stood more than 40 m (131 ft) in height.

Mogollon: Prehistoric culture located in the American Southwest. Centered in the uplands of New Mexico and northeastern Mexico. The Mogollon people grew maize, beans, and squash, relying for the most part on rainfall agriculture.

monumental works: Large-scale, communal construction projects characteristic of civilizations.

morphology: Literally, the study of form. An analysis of the shape and form of skeletons or artifacts.

mosaic: Environments characterized by patches of different habitats rather then a single, homogeneous habitat. It is believed that the first hominids lived in a mosaic environment characterized by a mixture of woodlands and savannas.

mound builder: The people of the American Midwest and Midsouth who constructed earthworks or mounds, including conical burial mounds, truncated pyramid platform mounds, enclosure mounds, and effigy mounds. Though the precise origin and identity of the mound builders was a point of controversy in the eighteenth and nineteenth centuries, we now know that Native Americans were responsible for their construction, beginning more than 5,000 years ago and continuing into the period of earliest European exploration of North America.

Mousterian: The stone-tool tradition of the Neandertals and early anatomically modern human beings. A core and flake technology in which a series of different, standardized tool types were produced from stone flakes struck from cores.

multilinear cultural evolution: The view that there are many pathways of change a culture may take over the time span of its existence. Multilineal evolutionary schemes recognize that cultures experience ordered change, but that there is no single pathway that all cultures take.

multiregional model: The view that anatomically modern *Homo sapiens* evolved from premodern humans in several regions simultaneously.

musculoskeletal hypertrophy: Great size and associated strength in the muscles and bones of a species or individual. Among recent human ancestors, the Neandertals exhibit an extreme level of musculoskeletal hypertrophy.

Mushabian: Pre-Neolithic culture located in the steppe and arid zones of the Negev and Sinai Deserts in modern Israel and Egypt. Contemporary with the Geometric Kebaran, dating from 14,500 to 12,500 B.P.

Mycenaeans: Southern European civilization that followed the Minoans and preceded the Greeks.

myth of the mound builders: When Europeans first entered into the American Midwest, they were confronted by ancient monuments and artifacts that belied the stereotype many of them harbored concerning the intelligence and sophistication of the native people of North America. Rather than reassess, reevaluate, and abandon those stereotypes, many Europeans instead concocted a just-so story that ascribed the earthworks and finely made artifacts to a missing and mysterious "race" of mound builders, separate and distinct from American Indians. Thus was born the myth of a mound-builder race.

Nagada II: Time period in predynastic Egypt. The Early Gerzean/Nagada II represents the time period between 5,650 and 5,300 years ago in Upper Egypt (the southern part of the Egyptian realm).

Nagada III: Time period in predynastic Egypt. The Nagada III represents the time period between 5,300 and 5,100 years ago in both Upper (southern) and Lower (northern) Egypt.

Natufian: Middle Eastern culture dated from 13,000 to 9,000 B.P. Located in the Mediterranean woodland zone, the Natufian reliance on wild wheat and barley set the stage for the Neolithic.

natural selection: The process proposed by Charles Darwin for how species evolve. Those individuals in a species that possess advantageous characteristics are more likely to survive and pass down those characteristics than are individuals that do not possess those advantages.

Nenana Complex: Perhaps the oldest stone-tool complex identified in Alaska dating from 11,800 to 11,000 B.P. Predating the Denali Complex, Nenana includes bifacially flaked, un-fluted spear points. Nenana bifaces are similar and perhaps related to tools made in eastern Russia about 14,000 years ago.

Neolithic: The "New Stone Age." In the past Neolithic was defined on the basis of the appearance of ground stone as opposed to chipped stone tools. Today, Neolithic refers to the period after 12,000 years ago when food producing through the domestication of plants and animals replaced foraging as the dominant mode of subsistence.

Neolithic Revolution: Period of fundamental change in human economy marked by a shift from foraging wild foods to the production of domesticated plants and animals. This revolution in subsistence occurred in multiple world areas beginning after about 12,000 years ago. This term is synonymous with Agricultural and Food Producing Revolution.

neotony: Literally means "holding on to youth." Neotony is usually used to describe a feature of modern human beings. The cranial morphology of modern adult human beings is more similar to that of subadult chimpanzees than it is to adults of that ape species. Compared to chimps, therefore, we exhibit neotony.

neutron activation analysis: Form of trace element analysis. The precise and unique chemical makeup of numerous raw material sources have been determined through neutron activation analysis. Archaeological artifacts can be analyzed for their chemical makeup as well. When the artifact's chemistry matches that of a source area, it is concluded that the ancient people obtained the material from the chemically matching source.

New Temple Period: Culture period defined for Minoan Crete dating from 3,650 to 3,420 B.P. The New Temple Period followed a catastrophic earthquake that badly damaged the temple at Knossos, but marks a florescence of Minoan culture.

niche: The actual physical space occupied by an organism as well as its functional role in a community of organisms. Sometimes refered to as an organism's ecological address.

Nubia: The territory south of the ancient Egyptian nation; primarily between the first and sixth cataract of the Nile, from southern Egypt to Sudan. The ancient Egyptians called this area Kush.

nuclear DNA: The genetic instructions contained in the nucleus of the cell. These instructions determine the biological make-up of the organism.

object piece: In the manufacturing of stone tools, the object piece is the stone that is being worked through the application of either percussion or pressure.

obsidian hydration: Dating method based on the rate that a freshly exposed surface of obsidian begins to physically alter by chemically combining with water in the air or soil. The thickness of the hydration layer that develops in a given environment is a factor of time.

occipital: Area to the rear of the skull. In ancient hominids, the occipital area tends to be massive and robust. In anatomically modern human beings, the occipital tends to be smooth and gracile.

Oldowan: The earliest stone tools. Simple chopping tools and sharp flakes, Oldowan tools date to about 2.4 million years ago. These tools were probably made by *Homo habilis*. Some evidence suggests they may also have been produced by *Paranthropus robustus*.

Olmec: Ancient culture of lowland Mesoamerica. Dating to 3,200 years ago, the Olmec produced a number of large ceremonial centers where they produced great earthworks, finely carved jade sculptures, and massive basalt carvings of human heads. The religious iconography of Olmec art seems to have served as a unifying element in ancient Mesoamerica.

Omari A: Time period in predynastic Egypt. The Omari A represents the time period between 5,750 and 5,650 years ago in Lower Egypt (the northern part of the Egyptian realm).

opportunistic foragers: Groups that follow a subsistence pattern in which they take advantage of whatever resources become available without much patterning or planning in advance.

optically stimulated luminescence: Method of luminescence dating in which the time-dependent energy stored in an archaeological specimen is released by the application of laser light.

orthogenesis: The invalid notion of a predestined and progressive pattern of evolutionary change.

osteological comparative collection: A bone library. A collection of bones used as models to aid in identifying the bones (species, sex, anatomical part) recovered in a paleontological or archaeological excavation.

osteological: Related to bones.

Paleo-Arctic tradition: Stone-tool tradition in the Arctic, dating to the period before 10,000 years ago. The technology involved the production of microblades detached from wedge-shaped cores.

paleoanthropology: Anthropological study of the evolution of our species. Paleoanthropologists study the skeletal remains and cultures of ancient hominids.

paleoecological: Reference to the relationship between an ancient organism and its environment by reference to that physical evidence that has preserved.

Paleoindian: Period and culture in the New World dating from about 13,200 to about 10,000 B.P. Fluted points are the most distinctive element in the Paleoindian stone-tool kit. Paleoindians hunted the late Pleistocene megafauna of the New World. Many archaeologists believe that the Paleoindians were the first human settlers of the New World.

paleomagnetic dating: Dating method based on the movement of the earth's magnetic poles.

paleopathology: The study of ancient disease, trauma, or dietary deficiency. Hominid skeletons often bear evidence of these.

palynology: The identification of plants through the remains of their pollen grains. Pollen is morphologically species specific; the pollen grains of each species are recognizably different from the pollen of all other plant species. Recovery at an archaeological site of the preserved pollen of particular species allows for the reconstruction of the plant community present when the site was occupied which can, in turn, inform us of the climate at the time.

paradigm: An overarching perspective, a broad view that underlies a scientific discipline.

parietal art: Art on the walls of a cave like the cave paintings of the Upper Paleolithic.

pastoralists: People who raise and tend livestock like sheep or cattle as the focus of their subsistence.

patrilocality: A postmarital residence pattern in which the married couple lives with the family of the husband, as compared to matrilocality, where the couple lives with the wife's family.

pedestrian survey: A systematic walkover of an area in the search for archaeological remains. A pedestrian survey is a useful tool in the search for sites especially where ancient people built structures with durable materials, where natural processes did not cover up materials on the ground, or where natural or cultural processes have exposed buried layers on the surface.

Peiligang: Earliest Neolithic culture in north China with well-established farming villages dating to 8,500 to 7,000 years ago.

pelagic: Anything related to or that lives in the open sea, far from shore.

petroglyph: Designs etched into rock faces. Darker, weathered rock surface is removed, creating a design or pattern by exposing lighter-colored rock beneath.

photosynthesis pathways: Different specific modes of photosynthesis various plant groups employ in the production of energy from sunlight. Most trees employ one such photosynthesis pathway (called C3); most grasses another (called C4).

phylogeny: The evolutionary histories of different kinds of organisms and their relationships to each other. A phylogeny can be a chart showing the evolutionary connections among organisms as well as the timing of those connections.

phytoliths: Microscopic, inorganic particles produced by plants. Phytoliths are extremely durable and their morphology is species specific. Enormous databases have been compiled that allow the researcher to examine individual phytoliths recovered in the soils or adhering to artifacts recovered at archaeological sites and to identify the species from which the phytoliths originated.

pit-houses: Semisubterranean houses constructed by the ancient inhabitants of the American Southwest. Pit-houses commonly were circular pole-and-mud-covered residences.

Pleistocene epoch: Geological epoch beginning about 2.6 million years ago and, perhaps, ending about 10,000 years ago. Marked by a succession of colder periods (glacials) interrupted by warmer periods (interglacials). During glacials, large portions of the earth were covered by ice and sea level was depressed.

Pliocene: Geological epoch of the Tertiary Period, following the Miocene Epoch and preceding the Pleistocene Epoch of the Quaternary Period. The Pliocene is defined as beginning about 5 million years ago and lasting until about 2.6 million years ago.

pluvial: Period of increased rainfall in areas far south of large glacial masses during the Pleistocene.

pollen: Pollen grains are the male gametes in plant sexual reproduction. Pollen grains are durable and morphologically species specific. When preserved at or near an archaeological site and recovered from the same stratigraphic level as a site, a general picture of the local plant community present when the location was occupied can be reconstructed.

pollen rain: The overall count or percentage of pollens of different plant species falling at a particular place and time.

Polynesia: Islands of the central and eastern Pacific. Polynesian islands are volcanic in origin.

pongid: A member of the taxonomic family Pongidae. An ape.

postcranial: All of the bones below the cranium.

potlatch: Celebrations held by chiefs among the native peoples of the northwest coast of North America in which much of their wealth—in the form of food, animal skins and furs, etc.—is distributed to members of the group. Potlatches allowed for the redistribution of wealth, conferred increased status on chiefs, and, at the same time, prevented individual chiefs from accumulating a permanent reservoir of wealth.

Poverty Point culture: Marked by extensive earthworks, the Poverty Point site located in Louisiana and dating to 3,600 years ago appears to have been a ceremonial center for a geographically widespread culture located across the American South. Sharing a common hunting-and-gathering subsistence focus, pottery styles, and religious iconography, these people are referred to as the Poverty Point culture.

pre-Clovis: It was a long-held archaeological consensus that Clovis spearpoints exhibiting their channeled or "fluted" faces were the earliest stone tools found in the New World and, by implication, their makers the first human settlers here some 13,000 years ago. However, archaeologists have now found reliably dated sites older than this in the New World, including the Debra L. Friedkin site in Texas, Meadowcroft Rockshelter in Pennsylvania, Monte Verde in Chile, and Manis in Washington State. These sites and a host of others are labeled "pre-Clovis."

preform: Partially worked core, flake, or blade. In a preform, the first general steps have been made in producing a tool. When a finished tool is needed, final finishing can be efficiently accomplished.

premodern *Homo sapiens*: Extinct sub-species of humanity that share much in common with modern or anatomically modern *Homo sapiens*, but who commonly retain primitive skeletal features and possess a somewhat smaller mean cranial capacity than modern people. The Neandertals are the best-known archaic variety or sub-species of the human race. Also called archaic *Homo sapiens*.

pressure flaking: Flaking and shaping a stone tool by the application of precisely focused pressure, often with the pointed tip of an antler.

primary refuse: Archaeological artifacts and ecofacts left at the place they were used or produced.

primate: Members of the taxonomic order Primates. Animals possessed of grasping hands and feet, stereoscopic vision, and relatively large brains (in proportion to body size). Most, but not all primates have nails instead of claws, tails, and an arboreal adaptation.

primatologist: A person who studies primates: prosimians, monkeys, or apes.

prognathous: The quality of having a forward-thrusting lower face. Apes are prognathous as are extinct hominids. Anatomically modern human beings tend to have flat, nonprognathous faces.

proton magnetometer: A noninvasive technique to investigate the subsurface. The magnetometer measures the strength of the earth's magnetic field from the surface and detects anomalies or small variations that may result from the presence of buried walls or soil disturbances from, for example, a filled canal or an earthwork.

pubic symphysis: Point of articulation between the two pubic bones of the pelvis. Changes in the appearance of the pubic symphysis occur fairly regularly during an individual's life and so can be used to determine the age of death.

pueblo: Apartment house-type structures of the ancient and some modern inhabitants of the American Southwest. Constructed of adobe brick, rubble, and shaped stone.

pumice: A light and porous volcanic rock. Pumice forms when a glassy molten froth cools and solidifies quickly.

punctuated equilibrium: Mode of evolution in which long periods of stasis or "equilibrium" in a species are interrupted by short, relatively rapid bursts ("punctuations") of great change producing a new species. Initially proposed by Niles Eldridge and Stephen Jay Gould, punctuated equilibrium is now widely accepted as the primary pattern of evolutionary change.

pyroclastic: A swiftly flowing mass of ash, molten rock, and gas spewing from an erupting volcano. Essentially a burning avalanche, the pyroclastic flow that overwhelmed the Roman cities of Pompeii and Herculaneum traveled at speeds of up to 200 kmh (almost 125 mph).

Qadan: Sites along the Nile in Egypt dating to the period 15,000 to 11,000 years ago. Evidence at Qadan sites shows a reliance on fishing, hunting, and the collection of wild grains. Microblades found at Qadan sites exhibit polish that may indicate their use in the harvesting of wild cereal crops.

quadruped: Any animal that habitually walks on four feet. Most animals, including most primates, are quadrupeds.

quipu: Record-keeping system of the Inca in which a series of knotted strings were used as mnemonic devices to help record keepers remember information (also khipu).

rachis: Area of attachment between seeds and other seeds or between seeds and other parts of the plant. A brittle rachis is an adaptive feature under natural conditions but, since it makes harvesting more difficult, is selected against by humans through artificial selection.

radiocarbon dating: Radiometric dating technique based on the decay of a radioactive isotope of carbon: ^{14}C or radiocarbon. Carbon dating can be applied to virtually anything that was once part of a living organism within a range from about 50,000 to 500 years ago. Also called carbon dating.

radiometric: Any dating technique based on the measurement of radioactive decay.

rank societies: Societies in which there are a few sociopolitical levels filled by a relatively small number of people.

Regal–ritual cities: Term used by archaeologist David Webster (2002) to describe Maya population centers. These centers were the home of Maya nobility and served also as the central location for Maya religion and ritual.

relative date: A date that places fossil or archaeological site or artifact in a sequence with other specimens, but does not allow for the assignment of an age in terms of years or even a range of years (compare to absolute date).

remote sensing: Procedure that allows for the discovery of archaeological sites or artifacts without digging. Remote sensing may include aerial photography and a number of technologies that allow for scanning below ground without disturbing the soil (proton magnetometry, electrical resistivity survey).

replacement model: The view that anatomically modern *Homo sapiens* evolved from premodern humans in one place at one time (usually Africa between 100,000 and 200,000 years ago) and spread out from that point of origin, replacing premodern human beings as they encountered them especially in Asia and Europe.

robust: Term applied to skeletal features that are heavily built.

Rosetta Stone: Discovered in 1799, the Rosetta Stone bore the same message in three scripts: Greek and two versions of the written language of ancient Egypt, demotic and hieroglyphic. The Greek on the stone was known when the stone was discovered, and provided, therefore, a key to deciphering the Egyptian written language.

sagittal crest: A ridge of bone that runs along the top of the skull from front to back. The sagittal crest provides added surface area for the attachment of powerful temporalis muscles that attach to the jaws. Male gorillas and some ancient hominid fossils possess a sagittal crest.

Sahul: The land mass of "Greater Australia" including Australia proper, New Guinea, and Tasmania. During periods of glacial maxima in the Pleistocene these three islands were combined in the single land mass of Sahul.

Samarran: Neolithic culture of southern Mesopotamia. Dating to after 7,500 years ago, Samarran sites are located on the floodplain of the Tigris and Euphrates Rivers. There is evidence of communal works including the construction of irrigation canals, fortification walls, and communal grain storage structures.

sarsen: The thirty upright stones at Stonehenge are called the sarsens. Each sarsen is over 3 m (10 ft) tall and weighs 25,000 kg (55,000 lb).

savanna: Grasslands. The replacement of the Miocene forests of Africa with savannas set the stage for the evolution of an upright primate adapted for life under conditions of flat, open expanses and few trees.

scapulimancy: A process of divining the future in which the scapulae (shoulder blades) of animals are burned and the pattern of burning and breakage is "read" by a diviner. Scapulimancy was popular in ancient China.

seal: Carved or molded symbol (on a ring, stamp, or cylinder) that was impressed into soft clay to leave one's official mark. Used in early Mesopotamia as a system of record keeping (also see cylinder seal).

secondarily altricial: Human infants are born at an advanced—precocial—state in terms of sensory and brain development, but at an immature and dependent—altricial—state physically. This combined condition is labeled secondarily altricial.

secondary refuse: Archaeological artifacts and ecofacts that were removed by the people who made, used, or produced them from the place where they were made, used, or produced, to a designated refuse area or areas: for example, a trash pile or pit.

sedentism: A pattern of settlement in which a community of people tends to remain in one place over the course of a year or years. A sedentary settlement pattern differs from nomadism in which a community may move seasonally, following the availability of resources.

seedbed selection: Process wherein the seeds of wild plants are tended in planted seedbeds. As later-germinating and slower-growing plants are weeded out of the seedbed, plants that sprout and grow quickly because they have larger seeds and thinner seed coats are selected for unintentionally. This can be a first step in the domestication of plants.

settlement pattern: The location, size, function, and seasonality of the various communities or activity areas within a given cultural system. The pattern of land use.

sexual dimorphism: Differences in the form and size of the two sexes. Among most primates, males tend to be larger and physically more powerful than females.

Shang dynasty: The first Chinese urban civilization. The ancient city of Yin was the capital of the Shang polity. Beginning in 2,400 B.P., a series of 12 kings or emperors ruled the Shang.

Shell Mound Archaic: Reflecting a worldwide pattern, after the end of the Pleistocene epoch, cultural diversity appears to have increased dramatically as people became adapted to the modern environments established after deglaciation and the accompanying sea-level rise. Various **Mesolithic** cultures in the Old World and **Archaic** cultures in the New World are now recognized by archaeologists. The Shell Mound Archaic in the American Midsouth is one of these post-Pleistocene Archaic cultures. Shell Mound Archaic sites reflect a subsistence focus on freshwater shellfish and exhibit some level of social and economic differentiation in their burials.

simple foragers: Hunters and gatherers with no particular focus on or commitment to any one food source.

Sinagua: In Spanish, *Sinagua* literally means "without water." It refers to one of the prehistoric cultures of the American Southwest, which also include the **Hohokam**, **Mogollon**, and Anasazi or **Ancestral Puebloan**. Located in central Arizona, Montezuma's Castle (Figure 1.3, left) and Wupatki (Figure 14.16) are Sinagua sites characterized by impressive, multistory pueblos.

site: A place where people lived and/or worked and where the physical evidence of their existence in the form of artifacts, ecofacts, and features can be or have been recovered.

social stratification: Pattern of social integration in which individuals are placed into a hierarchy of social levels. The presence of a hierarchy of differences in status and wealth in a society.

Solutrean: Stone-toolmaking tradition of the European Upper Paleolithic. Dating from 21,000 to 16,000 B.P., Solutrean bifaces are often exquisitely made, symmetrical, leaf-shaped projectile points.

spear-thrower: A tool used to increase the range and accuracy of the hand-thrown spear. The spear-thrower is a straight rod or board with a hook at one end. The hook articulates with the end of the spear. The spear-thrower effectively increases the length of the arm of the individual throwing the spear. Called an "atlatl" by the Aztecs who perfected the weapon in the New World.

specialization of labor: Cultural pattern in which some individuals can focus all or most of their labors on some specialty: metal working, pottery manufacturing, stone working, weaving, architectural design, etc. By specializing, these individuals can become quite proficient at their craft, art, or science. The specialization of labor is characteristic of complex civilizations.

split inheritance: Practiced by the Inca, a son of the king inherited the Inca throne, but the dead king's wealth passed to other relatives who were then required to use it to support his memorial. In other words, the Inca king contradicted the old saying "You can't take it with you."

stadial: Short period of increased glaciation. Stadials can occur during either glacials or interglacials and are separated by interstadials.

starch grains: Small fragments of starch produced by plants. Starch grain shapes are unique to individual plant species. As a result, when starch grains preserve on tools used to process plants, they can be recovered and the plant species identified.

state: Class societies, often rigidly stratified into social levels. The ruling class controls the populace not by consensus but by coercion and force. The rulers in a state society have the power to levy and collect taxes, to establish and enforce laws, and to conscript people to do the work of the state.

stela (pl.—stelae): Columns on which images or written messages have been inscribed. The Maya of Mesoamerica left a large number of stelae.

stratigraphic (stratigraphy): Related to the geological or cultural layer in which something has been found. Stratigraphic layering represents a relative sequence of geological time and/or cultural chronology.

striking platform: Part of a stone core or worked flake that presents an area where the desired flake can be removed when struck with a hammerstone or antler hammer.

subsistence: The material necessary to sustain life: water, food, clothing, and shelter. Here used usually in reference to the food quest.

Sunda (Sundaland): The combined land mass of the modern islands of Java, Sumatra, Bali, and Borneo. These islands became a single, continuous land mass during periods of glaciation and attendant lowered sea level during the Pleistocene.

supraorbital torus: A continuous ridge of bone above and across the eye orbits. A projecting, bony ridge commonly seen in apes as well as in ancient hominids. A supraorbital torus is lacking in anatomically modern human beings, though less conspicuous brow ridges are present in some individuals, especially John Travolta.

system of record keeping: Any symbolic system, usually but not always involving some form of writing, for keeping track of economic transactions, historical events, religious rules, etc. A system of record keeping is a fundamental tool needed to keep complex civilizations running.

talus: Material that accumulates at the base of a cliff. As rock erodes off the cliff face, gravity accumulates the eroded rock at the base of the slope; this is talus. Talus also refers to a large bone in the ankle that articulates the tibia with the bones of the foot.

taphonomy: How materials become part of the paleontological or archaeological record.

taro: A tropical plant with edible roots and leaves.

taxonomy: A systematic classification based on similarities and differences among the things being classified. Organisms, artifacts, or even whole cultures can be classified in this way.

Tehuacán: A valley in central, highland Mexico. The Tehuacán Valley was the focus of a multidisciplinary research project that produced important archaeological data concerning the domestication of plants in the New World, particularly the domestication of maize and squash.

temple mound builders: People of the American Midwest and Midsouth who constructed large platform mounds in the shape of truncated pyramids. Based on archaeological and ethnohistorical data, these mounds served as platforms on top of which were built the palaces of chiefs as well as temples for worship. Cahokia was the largest of these sites and is home to Monk's Mound, the largest of the temple mounds.

teosinte: The wild ancestor of domesticated maize. Teosinte grew and grows wild throughout the American tropics. The mutation of a very few teosinte genes change the spikey stem with its small, encased seeds, into a cob with a larger number of bigger, naked kernels.

Teotihuacán city-state: Teotihuacán was the Rome of Mesoamerica. The largest city built in the ancient New World, its population likely approached 200,000. We do not know what its inhabitants called the city; "Teotihuacán" is the name given the place by the later Aztecs. In their language, it means "The Place of the Gods." Reaching its zenith between A.D. 200 and 500, Teotihuacán was the dominant political and military force in central Mexico. The tentacles of its military reached as far as Maya territory to the west where they installed some of their own people as rulers after military victories.

test pit: A hole or boring into soil in the search for archaeological evidence. In some parts of the world, a pattern of test pits spread out across an area is a primary method by which archaeological sites are searched for and by which the spatial distribution of buried materials at a site is first identified.

thermoluminescence: A "trapped charge," radiation damage technique for dating archaeological objects. Energy produced by natural radiation in soil becomes stored in nearby objects. The amount of energy stored is a function of the level of the background radiation (this can be measured) and time. Once you know the level of background radiation at a particular place, you can measure how much has accumulated in an archaeological object, and from that determine how old the object is (how long it has been accumulating the energy).

tholoi: A new architectural form seen at Halafian sites in Mesopotamia, dating to after 7,500 years ago. Tholoi appear to have been communal storage facilities for these Neolithic people. Tholoi may also have served as burial chambers for a growing class of socioeconomically important individuals.

three-age system: Chronological breakdown of the history of human culture into a stone, bronze, and iron age. Developed in 1836 by J. C. Thomsen as part of a guidebook for the archaeological collections at the Danish National Museum, this evolutionary system achieved great popularity.

three-dimensional computed tomography: Technique for producing a three-dimensional virtual image. This technique has been used to produce a virtual image of the interior of hominid crania and, in this way, a three-dimensional image of the exterior surface of hominid brains which can then be compared to the brain of modern *Homo sapiens*.

tibia: The larger of the two long bones making up the lower leg. The shin bone.

Tiwanaku: One of the pre-Inca complex societies that developed in western South America. Located in Bolivia and at its peak at around A.D. 400, Tiwanaku is a vast, highland ceremonial complex characterized by the impressive and monumental stonework including the iconic Gateway of the Sun (Figure 13.7).

token: Small pieces of shaped clay (southwest Asia) or inscribed tags of bone or ivory (Egypt) that represent early steps in the development of a written language. The clay tokens of southwest Asia date to 9,000 years ago and appear to have been used to tabulate amounts of goods.

tool kit: A set of tools used together in performing a single task (e.g., a butchering tool kit including all of the tools used in the dismemberment of an animal carcass). A tool kit can also refer to the entire range of tools used at a particular site or during a given time period, or produced by a particular group of hominids.

totem pole: A wooden pole, along which have been carved and painted the images of animals or mythical beasts who are a family or clan's symbol or "totem." Totem poles are emblematic of the native peoples of the Northwest Coast of North America.

trace element analysis: Determining the geographic source of the materials used by an ancient people through the analysis of small or "trace" concentrations of elements or chemicals in those raw materials. The levels measured in archaeological artifacts are compared to the levels present in various possible sources. Where the concentrations in an artifact and a source closely match, it is suggested that the prehistoric people obtained the raw material from that source.

trilithon: Set of three stones, two uprights and one lintel, at Stonehenge. There are five trilithons at Stonehenge. The largest of the trilithon uprights stands about 8 m (24 ft) above the surface, with an additional 2 m (6 ft) of stone nestled in the ground. The largest of the trilithon uprights weighs 45,000 kg (50 tons) and the associated lintel weighs 9,000 kg (10 tons).

tuber: A relatively short, fleshy, usually underground stem of a plant. Tubers are often rich in starch and carbohydrates and have long contributed to the human food quest.

tumuli (sing., tumulus): An artificial pile of earth, often placed over an individual's grave.

Ubaid: Name given to the culture of southern Mesopotamia at 6,300 B.P. Irrigation canals constructed by the Ubaidic people made agriculture possible and larger settlements grew up in the Mesopotamian flood plain at this time. Evidence of the growing power of the religious elite is seen at Ubaidic sites with wealth becoming concentrated in the temples.

ulna: One of the bones of the forearm. The ulna is the more interior bone, closer to the body, while the radius is more exterior (on the thumb side of the arm).

Umm Dabaghiyah: Neolithic culture in northern Mesopotamia dating to more than 8,000 years ago characterized by a subsistence base of wheat, barley, sheep, and goats. Hunting was still important and their settlements were small.

uniformitarianism: The belief that the appearance of the earth could best be understood as resulting from the slow action of known processes over a very long period of time. Uniformitarianism, first championed in the late eighteenth and early nineteenth centuries, allowed for a great age of the earth.

unilineal evolution: The no longer accepted view that all cultures change or evolve along the same pathway, usually one of increasing complexity. In some unilineal evolutionary views, cultures can become "stuck" at a particular evolutionary step when some particular, necessary technological development is lacking. Nineteenth-century scholar Lewis Henry Morgan's sequence of savagery, barbarism, and civilization is an example.

Upper Paleolithic: Final phase of the Paleolithic, dating to after 40,000 years ago. The Upper Paleolithic is associated with the first appearance of anatomically modern humans in Europe.

Uruk Period: Period of time dating between 5500 and 5200 B.P. when the Mesopotamian city-state of Uruk became a sizable population center. By processes of internal growth as well as centrifugal forces drawing people from the hinterlands into the city, Uruk grew to a population estimated to have been over 10,000 during the Uruk Period.

varve: Layers of sediment laid down annually in a body of water, usually a lake. Varves may preserve evidence of yearly fluctuations in the environmental conditions in and around the body of water in which they were deposited.

Venus figurines: Upper Paleolithic sculptures of females, often, but not always, with exaggerated secondary sexual characteristics. Venus figurines have been found in geographic clusters in western, central, and eastern Europe. Most date to a rather narrow time span of between 27,000 and 20,000 years ago.

Wallacea: Name given to the sea over the Wallace Trench.

Wallace Trench: An undersea chasm located between New Guinea/Australia and Java/Borneo. Nearly 7,500 m deep (almost 25,000 ft), the Wallace Trench was not breached during periods of lowered Pleistocene sea levels so population movement from southeast Asia and Sahul were accomplished, of necessity, by a water route.

Wari: One of the pre-Inca complex societies that developed in South America. Located in the Peruvian highlands near the modern city of Ayacucho, the Wari peaked at about A.D. 600. Their capital consisted of a large, multistoried compound that spread out over an area of nearly 500 acres.

wear patterns: Characteristic and diagnostic traces of damage or polish left on stone tools as a result of their use. Analysis of wear patterns can often tell the researcher how the tool was used and on what material it was used.

weathering: The decomposition and disintegration of rock, usually at or near the earth's surface.

wedge-shaped cores: Cores shaped like wedges from which blades were struck; found as part of the Paleo-Arctic tradition in northeastern Asia and also found as part of the Denali Complex in the American Arctic.

X-ray fluorescence: A technique for identifying the chemical makeup of a raw material. Each chemical element in the raw material of an artifact—for example, a flint spearpoint—gives off a unique set of energies when bombarded with X-rays. The energies released can be read and then used to determine the precise elemental composition of the raw material. The geographic source of the raw material can be determined when its composition as determined by X-ray fluorescence is similar to the composition of a possible source determined in the same way.

Yang-shao: Early Neolithic culture of China. Dating to about 7,000 B.P., Yang-shao settlements appear to have been planned out. Subsistence was based on the cultivation of foxtail millet. Domesticated rice, though a minor component in the diet, appears at Yang-shao sites.

Younger Dryas: Name given in Europe to a stadial that lasted between 12,900 to 11,600 years ago. Though a relatively short interlude of renewed glacial expansion during a general warming trend at the end of the Pleistocene, the Younger Dryas may have been severe enough to have caused the temporary abandonment by humans of much of northwest Europe.

Zapotecs: The Mesoamerican group responsible for the ancient city of Monte Albán in Oaxaca, Mexico. The Zapotecs founded Monte Albán in 500 B.C.

Zarzian: Pre-Neolithic culture identified in the foothills of the Zagros Mountains in Turkey.

ziggurat: A large, pyramidlike platform made primarily of mud-brick in Mesopotamia. Constructed more than 4,000 years ago, the Great Ziggurat of Ur (Figure 10.8) is an early example of the ability of ancient complex societies to organize a large labor force capable of building monumental structures for the state.

References

Abi-Rached, L., et al. 2011. The shaping of modern human immune systems by multiregional admixture with archaic humans. *Science* 334:89–92.

Adams, R. M., and H. J. Nissen. 1972. *The Uruk Countryside: The Natural Setting of Urban Societies.* Chicago: University of Chicago Press.

Adovasio, J., O. Soffer, and B. Kilma 1996. Upper Paleolithic fibre technology: Interlaced woven finds from Pavlov I, Czech republic, c. 26,000 years ago. *Antiquity* 70:269.

Adovasio, J. M., J. Donahue, and R. Stuckenrath 1990. The Meadowcroft rockshelter radiocarbon chronology—1975–1990. *American Antiquity* 55:348–353.

Adovasio, J. M., J. D. Gunn, J. Donahue, R. Stuckenrath, J. Guilday, and K. Lord. 1979–80a. Meadowcroft Rockshelter—Retrospect 1977: Part 1. *North American Archaeologist* 1(1):3–44.

Adovasio, J. M., J. D. Gunn, J. Donahue, R. Stuckenrath, J. Guilday, K. Lord, and K. Volman. 1979–80b. Meadowcroft Rockshelter—Retrospect 1977: Part 2. *North American Archaeologist* 1(2):99–138.

Agenbroad, L. D. 1988. Clovis people: The human factor in the Pleistocene megafauna extinction question. In *Americans Before Columbus: Ice-Age Origins,* ed. R. C. Carlisle, 63–74. Ethnology Monographs, vol. 12. Pittsburgh, PA: University of Pittsburgh.

Ahler, S. R. 1993. Stratigraphy and radiocarbon chronology of Modoc Rockshelter, Illinois. *American Antiquity* 58:462–489.

Aiello, L. C. 1994. Variable but singular. *Nature* 368:399–400.

Aiello, L. C., and M. Collard. 2001. Our newest oldest ancestor? *Nature* 410:526–527.

Aimers, J. 2011. Drought and the Maya: The story of the artefacts. *Nature* 479:44.

Alemseged, Z., F. Spoor, W. H. Kimbel, R. Bobe, D. Geraads, D. Reed, and J. G. Wynn. 2006. A juvenile early hominin skeleton from Dikika, Ethiopia. *Nature* 443:296–301.

Alexander, C. 2008. If the stones could speak: Searching for the meaning of Stonehenge. *National Geographic* 213 (6):34–59.

Allan, S. (ed.). 2005. *The Formation of Chinese Civilization: An Archaeological Perspective.* New Haven: Yale University Press.

Allchin, B., and R. Allchin. 1982. *The Rise of Civilization in India and Pakistan.* Cambridge, England: Cambridge University Press.

Allison, M. J. 1984. Paleopathology in Peruvian and Chilean populations. In *Paleopathology at the Origins of Agriculture,* ed. M. N. Cohen and G. J. Armelagos, 515–529. New York: Academic Press.

Allsworth-Jones, P. 1990. The Szeletian and the stratigraphic succession in central Euorpe and adjacent areas: Main trends, recent results and problems for resolution. In *The Emergence of Modern Humans: An Archaeological Perspective,* ed. P. Mellars, 160–242. Ithaca: Cornell University Press.

Alva, W., and C. B. Donnan. 1993. *Royal Tombs of Sípan.* Los Angeles: Fowler Museum of Culture History.

———. 1994. Tales from a Peruvian crypt. *Natural History* 103:26–34.

Ames, K. M., and H. D. G. Maschner. 1999. *Peoples of the Northwest Coast: Their Archaeology and Prehistory.* London: Thames and Hudson.

Anderson, D. 1990. The Paleoindian colonization of eastern North America. *Research in Economic Anthroplogy* Suppl. no. 5:163–216.

Anderson, D. D. 1968. A stone age campsite at the gateway to America. *Scientific American* 218(6):24–33.

———. 1970. Microblade traditions in northwestern Alaska. *Arctic Anthropology* 7(2):2–16.

Appenzeller, T. 2012. Eastern odyssey. *Nature* 485:24–26.

Armitage, S. J., S. A. Jasim, A. E. Marks, A. G. Parker, V. I. Usik, and H.-P. Uepermann. 2011. The southern route "Out of Africa": Evidence for an early expansion of modern humans into Arabia. *Science* 331:453–456.

Arnheim, R. 1956. *Art and Visual Perception: A Psychology of the Creative Eye.* London: Faber and Faber.

Arnold, D. 1991. *Building in Egypt: Pharaonic Stone Masonry.* Oxford, England: Oxford University Press.

Arsuaga, J.-L., I. Martinez, A. Garcia, J.-M. Carretero, and E. Carbonell. 1993. Three new human skulls from the Sima de los Huesos Middle Pleistocene site in Sierra de Atapuerca, Spain. *Nature* 362:534–537.

Arsuaga, J. L. 2002. *The Neanderthal's Necklace: In Search of the Fast Thinkers.* New York: Four Walls Eight Windows Press.

Ascher, M., and R. Ascher. 1997. *Mathematics of the Incas: Code of the Quipu.* Mineola, NY: Dover.

Asfaw, B., et al. 2002. "Remains of *Homo erectus* from Bouri, Middle Awash, Ethiopia." *Nature* 416: 317–319.

Ashmore, W., and R. J. Sharer. 2009. *Discovering Our Past: A Brief Introduction to Archaeology.* Mountain View, CA: Mayfield Publishing.

Atkinson, T., and M. Leeder. 2008. Canyon cutting on a grand time scale. *Science* 319:1343–1344.

Aveni, A., ed. 1977. *Native American Astronomy.* Austin: University of Texas Press.

Axtell, R. L., J. M. Epstein, J. S. Dean, G. J. Gumerman, A. C. Swedlund, J. Harburger, S. Chakravarty, R. Hammond, J. Parker, and M. Parker 2002. Population growth and collapse in a multiagent model of Kayenta Anasazi in Long House. *Proceedings of the National Academy of Sciences* 99:7275–7279.

Baadsgaard, A., J. Monge, S. Cox, and R. L. Zettler. 2011. Human sacrifice and intentional corpse preservation in the Royal Cemetery of Ur. *Antiquity* 85:27–42.

Bahn, P. G. 1998. Neanderthals emancipated. *Nature* 394:719–721.

Bahn, P. G., and J. Vertut. 1997. *Journey Through the Ice Age.* Berkeley: University of California Press.

Bailey, G. N. 1978. Shell middens as indicators of postglacial economies: a territorial perspective. In *The Early Postglacial Settlement of Northern Europe: An Ecological Perspective,* ed. P. Mellars, 37–63. Pittsburgh, PA: University of Pittsburgh Press.

Balter, M. 1998. Why settle down? The mystery of communities. *Science* 282:1442–1445.

———. 2001. Stone age artists—or art lovers—unmasked. *Science* 294:31.

———. 2004a. Dressed for success: Neandertal culture wins respect. *Science* 306:40–41.

———. 2004b. Earliest signs of human-controlled fire uncovered in Israel. *Science* 304:663–665.

———. 2005. *The Goddess and the Bull: Çatalhoyuk: An Archaeological Journey to the Dawn of Civilization.* New York: The Free Press.

———. 2007a. An Incan feast before death. http://news.sciencemag.org/sciencenow/2007/10/02–01.html

———. 2007b. In search of the world's most ancient mariners. *Science* 218:388–389.

———. 2008a. Early Stonehenge pilgrims came from afar, with cattle in tow. *Science* 320:1704–1705.

———. 2008b. Going deeper into the Grotte Chauvet. *Science* 321:904–905.

———. 2009a. Early start for human art? Ochre may revise timeline. *Science* 323:569.

———. 2009b. New work may complicate history of Neandertals and H. Sapiens. *Science* 326:224–225.

———. 2009c. On the origin of art and symbolism. *Science* 323:709–711.

———. 2010. Neandertal jewelry shows their symbolic smarts. *Science* 327:255–256.

———. 2010b. The tangled roots of agriculture. *Science* 327:404–406.

———. 2012. "Early dates for artistic Europeans." *Science* 336:1086–1087.

Bard, K. A. 2000. The emergence of the Egyptian state (c.3200–2686 BC). In *The Oxford History of Ancient Egypt,* ed. I. Shaw, 61–88. Oxford, England: Oxford University Press.

Barker, G. 1978. Economic models for the Manekweni Zimbabwe, Mozambique. *Azania* 13:71–100.

Barclay, E. 2008. Oldest skeleton in Americas found in underwater cave? *National Geographic News.* http://news.nationalgeographic.com/news/2008/09/080903-oldest-skeletons.html.

Barnosky, A. D., P. L. Koch, R. S. Feranec, S. L. Wing, and A. B. Shabel. 2004. Assessing the causes of Late Pleistocene extinctions on the continents. *Science* 306:70–75.

Barry, C. 2007. Rolling back the years: Radiocarbon dating gets a remake. *Science News* 172:344–345.

Bar-Yosef, O. 1980. Prehistory of the Levant. *Annual reviews of Anthropology* 9:101–133.

———. 1998. The Natufian culture of the Levant, threshold to the origins of agriculture. *Evolutionary Anthropology*: 159–177.

Bar-Yosef, O., B. Vandermeersch, B. Arensburg, A. Belfer-Cohen, P. Goldberg, H. Laville, L. Meignen, et al. 1992. The excavations in Kebara Cave, Mt. Carmel. *Current Anthropology* 33:497–534.

Beadle, G. 1977. The origin of *Zea mays.* In *The Origins of Agriculture,* ed. C. A. Reed, 615–635. The Hague: Mouton.

Bednarik, R. G. 1993. Oldest dated rock art in the world. *International Newsletter on Rock Art* 4:5–6.

Begun, D., and A. Walker. 1993. The endocast. In *The Nariokotome Homo erectus Skeleton,* ed. A. Walker and R. Leakey, 326–358. Cambridge, MA: Harvard University Press.

Beja-Pereira, A., P. R. England, N. Ferrand, S. Jordan, A. O. Bakhiet, M. A. Abdalla, M. Mashkour, J. Jordana, P. Taberlet, and G. Luikart 2004. African origins of the domestic donkey. *Science* 304:1781.

Belfer-Cohen, A., and N. Goren-Inbar. 1994. Cognition and communication in the Levantine Lower Paleolithic. *World Archaeology* 26(2):144–157.

Belfer-Cohen, A., and E. Hovers. 1992. In the eye of the beholder: Mousterian and Natufian burials in the Levant. *Current Anthropology* 33:463–471.

Ben-Itzhak, S., P. Smith, and R. A. Bloom. 1988. Radiographic study of the humerus in Neandertals and *Homo sapiens sapiens. American Journal of Physical Anthropology* 77:231–242.

Bennett, M. R., J. W. K. Harris, B. G. Richmond, D. R. Braun, E. Mbua, P. Kiura, D. Olago, et al. 2009. Early hominin foot morphology based on 1.5-million-year-old footprints from Ileret, Kenya. *Science* 323:1197–1201.

Berger, L. R., D. J. d. Ruiter, S. E. Churchill, P. Schmid, K. J. Carlson, P. H. G. M. Dirks, and J. M. Kibii. 2010. *Australopithecus sediba:* A new species of *Homo*-like australopith from South Africa. *Science* 328:195–204.

Bermúdez de Castro, J. M., J. L. Arsuaga, E. Carboneli, A. Rosas, I. Matinez, and M. Mosquera. 1997. A hominid from the Lower Pleistocene of Atapuerca, Spain: Possible ancestor to Neandertals and modern humans. *Science* 276:1392–1395.

Berna, F., P. Goldberg, L. K. Horwitz, J. Brink, S. Holt, M. Bamford, and M. Chazen. 2012. Microstratigraphic evidence of in situ fire in the Acheulean strata of Wonderwerk Cave, Northern Cape Province, South Africa. *Proceedings of the National Academy of Sciences* 109:E1215–E1220.

Binford, L. 1984. *Faunal Remains from Klasies River Mouth.* Orlando, FL: Academic Press.

Bingham, H. 1913. The discovery of Machu Picchu. In *Harper's Monthly* 127:709–719.

Birdsell, J. H. 1977. The recalibration of a paradigm for the first peopling of Greater Australia. In *Sunda and Sahul: Prehistoric Studies in Southeast Asia, Melanesia, and Australia,* ed. J. Allen, J. Golson, and R. Jones, 113–167. New York: Academic Press.

Birmingham, R. A., and L. G. Goldstein. 2005. *Aztalan: Mysteries of an Ancient Indian Town.* Madison, WI: Wisconsin Historical Society Press.

Bischoff, J. L., N. Soler, J. Maroto, and R. Julià. 1989. Abrupt Mousterian/Aurignacian boundary at c. 40 ka bp: Accelerator 14C dates from l'Arbreda Cave (Catalunya, Spain). *Journal of Archaeological Science* 16:563–576.

Blomster, J. P., H. Neff, and M. D. Glascock. 2005. Olmec pottery production and export in ancient Mexico determined through elemental analysis. *Science* 307:1068–1072.

Bocquet-Appel, J. P. 2011. When the world's population took off: The springboard of the Neolithic demographic transition. *Science* 333:560–561.

Boëda, E., J. M. Geneste, C. Griggo, N. Mercier, S. Muhesen, J. L. Reyss, A. Taha, and H. Valladas. 1999. A Levallois point embedded in the vertebra of a wild ass (*Equus africanus*): hafting projectiles and Mousterian hunting weapons. *Antiquity* 73:394–402.

Bolnick, D. A., K. L. Feder, B. T. Lepper, and T. A. Barnhart. 2012. Civilizations lost and found: Fabricating history. Part Three: Real messages in DNA. *Skeptical Inquirer* 36(1):48–51.

Bolnick, D. A., and D. G. Smith. 2007. Migration and social structure among the Hopewell: Evidence from ancient DNA. *American Antiquity* 72:627–644.

Bonnichsen, R., and A. L. Schneider. 2001–02. The case for a pre-Clovis people. *American Archaeology* 5(4):35–39.

Bonnichsen, R., and K. L. Turnmire, eds. 1991. *Clovis: Origins and Adaptations.* Cornvallis, OR: Center for the Study of the First Americans.

Bordaz, J. 1970. *Tools of the Old and New Stone Age.* Newton Abbot, England: David and Charles Publishing.

Bordes, F. 1972. *A Tale of Two Caves.* New York: Harper and Row.

Bordes, F., and J. Labrot. 1967. "La stratigraphie du gisement de Roc de Combe et ses implications." *Bulletin de la Société Préhistorique Française* 64: 15–28.

Bortolini, M.-C., F. M. Salzano, M. G. Thomas, S. Stuart, S. P. K. Nasanen, C. H. D. Bau, M. H. Hutz, et al. 2003. Y-chromosome evidence for differing ancient demographic histories in the Americas. *American Journal of Human Genetics* 73:524–539.

Borziyak, I. A. 1993. Subsistence practices of Late Paleolithic groups along the Dnestr River and its tributaries. In *From Kostenki to Clovis: Upper Paleolithic-Paleoindian Adaptations,* ed. O. Soffer and N. Preslov, 67–84. New York: Plenum.

Boucher de Perthes, J. 1864. *Antiquités Celtiques et Antédiliviennes.* Paris.

Boule, M., and H. V. Vallois. 1923. *Fossil Men.* New York: Dryden Press.

Bowdler, S. 1974. Pleistocene date for man in Tasmania. *Nature* 252:697–698.

———. 1977. The coastal colonisation of Australia. In *Sunda and Sahul: Prehistoric Studies in Southeast Asia, Melanesia, and Australia,* ed. J. Allen, J. Golson, and R. Jones, 205–246. New York: Academic Press.

———. 1990. Peopling Australasia: The "Coastal Colonization" hypothesis re-examined. In *The Emergence of Modern Humans: An Archaeological Perspective,* ed. P. Mellars, 327–343. Ithaca, NY: Cornell University Press.

Bower, B. 1993a. Fossil jaw offers clue to human ancestry. *Science News* 144:277.

———. 1993b. Fossil may extend antiquity of human line. *Science News* 141:134.

———. 1993c. Lucy's new kin take a powerful stand. *Science News* 144:324.

———. 1996. Visions on the rocks. *Science News* 150:216–217.

———. 1997. Early humans make their marks as hunters. *Science News* 151:222.

———. 2000. Early New World settlers rise in the east. *Science News* 157:244.

———. 2003. *Erectus* ahoy: Prehistoric seafaring floats into view. *Science News* 164:248–250.

———. 2007. Ancient beads found in northern Africa. *Science News* 171:397.

———. 2009a. Apes get sweets, tookits in hand. *Science News* 175:9.

———. 2009b. Hunter-gatherers stored wild crops. *Science News* 176(2):13.

———. 2010. Groovy eggshell designs. *Science News* 177:10.

Bower, B. 2012. "Stone age art gets animated." *Science News* 181(13): 12.

Bowlby, J. 1990. *Charles Darwin: A New Life.* New York: W. W. Norton & Company.

Bowler, J. M., H. Johnston, J. M. Olley, J. R. Prescott, R. G. Roberts, W. Shawcross, and N. A. Spooner. 2003. New ages for human occupation and climatic change at Lake Mungo, Australia. *Nature* 421:837–840.

Bowler, J. M., R. Jones, H. Allen, and A. G. Thorne. 1970. Pleistocene human remains from Australia: A living site and human cremation from Lake Mungo, western New South Wales. *World Archaeology* 2:39–60.

Bowler, J. M., A. G. Thorne, and H. A. Polach. 1972. Pleistocene man in Australia: Age and significance of the Lake Mungo skeleton. *Nature* 240:48–50.

Bradbury, R. 2006. *The Martian Chronicles.* New York: William Morrow.

Bradley, D. G., et al. 1998. "Genetics and domestic cattle origins." *Evolutionary Anthropology* 6(3):79–86.

Brain, J. P. 1982. *Tunica Treasure.* Peabody Museum of Archaeology and Ethnology Papers 71. Cambridge, MA: Harvard University Press.

Bramble, D. M., and D. E. Lieberman. 2004. Endurance running and the evolution of *Homo. Nature* 432: 345–352.

Bräuer, G., H. J. Deacon, and F. Zipfel. 1992. Comments on the new maxillary finds from Klasies River Mouth, South Africa. *Journal of Human Evolution* 23: 419–422.

Brennan, M. U. 1991. Health and Disease in the Middle and Upper Paleolithic of Southwestern France: A Bioarchaeological Study. PhD diss., New York University.

Brewer, D. J., and E. Teeter 1999. *Egypt and the Egyptians.* Cambridge, England: Cambridge University Press.

Brice, W. R. 1982. Bishop Ussher, John Lightfoot, and the age of creation. *Journal of Geological Education* 30:18–24.

Brier, B., and J.-P. Houdin. 2008. *The Secret of the Great Pyramid.* New York: Harper.

Brooks, A. S. 2010. What does it mean to be human? A behavioral perspective. *AnthroNotes* 31(1):1–10.

Brown, F., J. Harris, R. Leakey, and A. Walker. 1985. Early *Homo erectus* skeleton from west Lake Turkana, Kenya. *Nature* 316:788–792.

Brown, K. 2001. New trips through the back alleys of agriculture. *Science* 292:631–633.

Brown, P., T. Sutikna, M. J. Morwood, R. P. Soejono, Jatmiko, E. W. Saptomo, and R. A. Due. 2004. A new small-bodied hominin from the Late Pleistocene of Flores, Indonesia. *Nature* 431:1055–1061.

Bruhns, K. O. 1994. *Ancient South America.* Cambridge World Archaeology. Cambridge, England: Cambridge University Press.

Brumm, A., G. M. Jensen, G. D. v. d. Bergh, M. J. Morwood, I. Kurniawan, F. Aziz, and M. Storey. 2010. Hominins on Flores, Indonesia, by one million years ago. *Nature* 464:748–752.

Brunet, M., F. Guy, D. Pilbeam, D. E. Lieberman, A. Likius, H. T. Machaye, M. S. P. d. Leon, et al. 2005. New material of the earliest hominid from the Upper Miocene of Chad. *Nature* 434:752–755.

Buckley, T. 1976. The discovery of Tutankhamun's tomb. In *The Treasures of Tutankhamun*, ed. K. S. Gilbert, J. K. Holt, and S. Hudson, 9–18. New York: The Metropolitan Museum of Art.

Buikstra, J. E. 1984. The lower Illinois River region: A prehistoric context for the study of ancient diet and health. In *Paleopathology at the Origins of Agriculture*, ed. M. N. Cohen and G. J. Armelagos, 215–234. New York: Academic Press.

Burger, R. L. 1988. Unity and heterogeneity within the Chavin Horizon. In *Peruvian Prehistory*, ed. R. W. Keatinge, 99–144. Cambridge, England: Cambridge University Press.

———. 1995. *Chavin and the Origins of Andean Civilization.* London: Thames and Hudson.

———. 2004. Scientific insights into daily life at Machu Picchu. In *Machu Picchu: Unveiling the Mystery of the Incas*, ed. R. L. Burger and L. C. Salazar, 85–106. New Haven, CT: Yale University Press.

Burger, R. L., and R. B. Gordon. 1998. Early central Andean metalworking from Mina Perdida, Peru. *Science* 282:1108–111.

Burger, R. L., and L. C. Salazar, eds. 2004. *Machu-Picchu: Unveiling the Mystery of the Incas.* New Haven, CT: Yale University Press.

Burks, J. 2010. Rediscovering prehistoric earthworks in Ohio, USA: It all starts in the archives. In *Landscapes Through the Lens: Aerial Photographs and Historic Environment*, ed. D. C. Cowley, R. A. Standing, and M. J. Abicht. Oxford, England: Oxbow Books.

Burks, J., and R. A. Cook. 2011. Beyond Squier and Davis: Rediscovering Ohio's earthworks using geophysical remote sensing. *American Antiquity* 76:667–689.

Burl, A. 1995. *A Guide to the Stone Circles of Britain, Ireland, and Brittany.* New Haven, CT: Yale University Press.

Burl, A. 2005. *A Guide to the Stone Circles of Britain, Ireland, and Brittany*. New Haven: Yale University Press.

Burley, D.V., and W. R. Dickinson. 2001. Origin and significance of a founding settlement in Polynesia. *Proceedings of the National Academy of Sciences* 98:11829–11831.

Byers, D., ed. 1967. *Prehistory of the Tehuacan Valley*. Austin: University of Texas Press.

Carbonell, E., J. M. Bermúdez de Castro, J. L. Arsuaga, J. C. Diez, A. Rosas, G. Cuenca-Bescos, R. Sala, et al. 1995. Lower Pleistocene hominids and artifacts from Atapuerca-TD6 (Spain). *Science* 269:826–830.

Carbonell, E., J. M. Bermúdez de Castro, J. M. Parés, A. Pérez-Gonzalez, et al. 2008. The first hominin of Europe. *Nature* 452:465–469.

Carlisle, R. C., and J. M. Adovasio, eds. 1982. *Meadowcroft: Collected Papers on the Archaeology of Meadowcroft Rockshelter and the Cross Creek Drainage*. Minneapolis, MN: Society of American Archaeologists.

Carmody, R. N., G. S. Weintraub, and R. W. Wrangham. 2011. Energetic consequences of thermal and nonthermal food processing. *Proceedings of the National Academy of Sciences* 108:19199–19203.

Carniero, R. 1970. A theory of the origin of the state. *Scientific American* 265:104–110.

Carrier, D. R. 1984. The energetic paradox of human running and hominid evolution. *Current Anthropology* 25:483–495.

Caspari, R., and S.-H. Lee. 2004. Older age becomes common late in human evolution. *Proceedings of the National Academy of Science* 101(30):10895–10900.

Castleden, R. 1990a. *The Knossos Labyrinth*. London: Routledge.

———. 1990b. *Minoans: Life in Bronze Age Crete*. London: Routledge.

Catto, N., and C. Mandryk. 1990. Geology of the postulated ice-free corridor. In *Megafauna and Man: Discovery of America's Heartland*, ed. L. D. Agenbroad, J. I. Mead, and L. W. Nelson, 80–85. Hot Springs, SD: The Mammoth Site of Hot Springs and Northern Arizona University.

Cerling, T., Y. Wang, and J. Quade. 1993. Expansion of C4 ecosystems as an indicator of global ecological change in the late Miocene. *Nature* 361:344–345.

Cerling, T. E., J. G. Wynn, S. A. Andanje, M. I. Bird, D. K. Korir, N. E. Levin, W. Mace, et al. 2011. Woody cover and hominin environments in the past 6 million years. *Nature* 476:51–55.

Chang, K.-C. 1986. *The Archaeology of Ancient China*, 4th ed. New Haven, CT: Yale University Press.

Chapman, J., and G. D. Crites. 1987. Evidence for early maize (*Zea mays*) from Icehouse Bottom Site, Tennessee. *American Antiquity* 52:318–329.

Chard, C. 1974. *Northeast Asia in Prehistory*. Madison: University of Wisconsin Press.

Charteris, J., J. C. Wall, and J. W. Nottrodt. 1981. Functional reconstruction of gait from the Pliocene hominid footprints at Laetoli, northern Tanzania. *Nature* 290:496–498.

Chase, P. G., and H. L. Dibble. 1987. Middle Paleolithic symbolism: A review of current evidence and interpretations. *Journal of Anthropological Archaeology* 6:263–296.

Chauvet, J.-M., É. Deschamps, and C. Hillaire. 1996. *Dawn of Art: The Chauvet Cave*. New York: Harry N. Abrams.

Chippendale, C. 2004. *Stonehenge Complete*. London: Thames and Hudson.

Churchill, S. E., and E. Trinkaus. 1990. Neandertal scapular glenoid morphology. *American Journal of Physical Anthropology* 83:147–160.

Cinque-Mars, J. 1978. Bluefish Cave I: A Late Pleistocene eastern Beringian cave deposit in the northern Yukon. *Canadian Journal of Anthropology* 3:1–32.

Ciochon, R. L., and E. A. Bettis III. 2009. Paleoanthropology: Asian *Homo erectus* converges in time. *Nature* 458:153–154.

Clayton, P. A. 1994. *Chronicle of the Pharaohs: The Reign-by-Reign Record of the Rulers and Dynasties of Ancient Egypt*. London: Thames and Hudson.

Clement, C. R., M. d. Cristo-Araújo, G. C. d'Eeckenbrugge, A. A. A. Pereria, and D. Picanço-Rodrigues. 2010. Origin and domestication of native Amazonian crops. *Diversity* 2:71–106.

Clottes, J., and J. Courtin. 1996. *The Cave Beneath the Sea: Paleolithic Images at Cosquer*. New York: Harry N. Abrams, Inc.

Clottes, J., and D. Lewis-Williams. 1998. *The Shamans of Prehistory: Trance and Magic in the Painted Caves*. New York: Harry N. Abrams, Inc.

Cobo, B. 1979. *History of the Inca Empire: An Account of the Indians' Customs and Their Origin Together with a Treatise on Inca Legends, History, and Social Institutions*. Austin: University of Texas Press.

———. 1990. *Inca Religion and Customs*. Austin: University of Texas Press.

Coe, M. 1968. *America's First Civilization*. New York: Van Nostrand.

Coe, M. D. 1992. *Breaking the Maya Code*. New York: Thames and Hudson.

———. 1993. *The Maya*. New York: Thames and Hudson.

———. 1996. *The Olmec World: Ritual and Rulership*. Princeton, NJ: Art Museum at Princeton University.

Cohen, M. N., and G. J. Armelagos. 1984. Paleopathology at the origins of agriculture: Editors' summation. In *Paleopathology at the Origins of Agriculture*, ed. M. N. Cohen and G. J. Armelagos, 585–601. New York: Academic Press.

Conkey, M. W. 1980. The identification of prehistoric hunter-gatherer aggregation sites: The case of Altamira. *Current Anthropology* 21:609–630.

———. 1981. A century of Paleolithic cave art. *Archaeology* 34(4):20–28.

Connah, G. 1987. *African Civilization: Precolonial Cities and States in Tropical Africa; An Archaeological Perspective.* Cambridge, England: Cambridge University Press.

Conrad, N. J. 2003. Palaeolithic ivory sculptures from southwestern Germany and the origins of figurative art. *Nature* 426:830–832.

———. 2009. A female figurine from the Basal Aurignacian of Hohle Fels Cave in southwestern Germany. *Nature* 459:248–252.

Conrad, N. J., M. Malina, and S. C. Münzel. 2009. New flutes document the earliest musical tradition in southwestern Germany. *Nature* 460:737–740.

Constable, G., and the editors of Time-Life Books. 1973. *The Neanderthals.* New York: Time-Life Books.

Conyers, L. B. 2004. *Ground Penetrating Radar for Archaeology.* Walnut Creek, CA: AltaMira Press.

Cooley, A. E. 2003. *Pompeii.* London: Duckworth.

Cope, J. 1998. *The Modern Antiquarian.* London: Thorsons.

Copeland, S. R., M. Sponheimer, D. J. de Ruiter, J. A. Lee-Thorp, D. Condron, P. J. le Roux, W. Grimes, and M. P. Richards. 2011. Strontium isotope evidence for landscape use by early hominins. *Nature* 474:76–78.

Cordell, L. 1984. *The Archaeology of the Southwest.* New York: Academic Press.

———. 1994. *Ancient Pueblo Peoples.* Exploring the Ancient World. Washington, DC: Smithsonian Books.

Cosgrove, R., J. Allen, and B. Marshall. 1990. Palaeo-ecology and Pleistocene human occupation in south central Tasmania. *Antiquity* 64:59–78.

Cowgill, G. L. 1988. Onward and upward with collapse. In *The Collapse of Ancient States and Civilizations*, ed. N. Yoffe and G. L. Cowgill, 244–276. Tuscon: University of Arizona Press.

Crawford, G. W. 1992. Prehistoric plant domestication in East Asia. In *The Origins of Agriculture: An International Perspective*, ed. C. W. Cowan and P. J. Watson, 7–38. Washington, DC: Smithsonian Institution Press.

Crawford, H. 1991. *Sumer and the Sumerians.* New York: Cambridge University Press.

Crown, P. L., and W. J. Hurst. 2009. Evidence of Cacao Use in the Prehispanic American Southwest. *Proceedings of the National Academy of Sciences* 106:2110–2113.

Culotta, E. 2008. When Hobbits (slowly) walked the earth. *Science* 320:433–435.

Cummins, J., ed. 1992. *The Voyage of Christopher Columbus: Columbus' Own Journal of Discovery.* New York: St. Martin's Press.

Curry, A. 2008a. Gobekli Tepe: The World's First Temple. *Smithsonian,* January 18, 2008. http://www.smithsonianmag.com/history-archaeology/30706129.html.

———. 2008b. Seeking the roots of ritual. *Science* 319:278–280.

———. 2012. Coming to America. *Nature* 485:30–32.

Dalrymple, G. B., and M. A. Lanphere. 1969. *Potassium-Argon Dating: Principles, Techniques, and Applications to Geochronology.* San Francisco: W. H. Freeman.

D'Altroy, T. N. 2003. *The Incas.* Oxford, England: Blackwell.

Daniel, G., and C. Renfrew. 1988. *The Idea of Prehistory.* Edinburgh, Scotland: Edinburgh University Press.

Darwin, C. 1859. *The Origin of Species by Means of Natural Selection.* Great Books of the Western World 49. Chicago, IL: Encyclopaedia Britanica, 1952.

Darwin, F., ed. 1961. *Charles Darwin's Autobiography.* New York: Collier Books.

David, B., R. Roberts, C. Tuniz, R. Jones, and J. Head. 1997. New optical and radiocarbon dated from Ngarrabullgan Cave, a Pleistocene archaeological site in Australia: Implications for the comparability of time clocks and for the human colonization of Australia. *Antiquity* 71:183–188.

Davis, M. B. 1969. Climatic changes in southern Connecticut recorded by pollen deposition at Rogers Lake. *Ecology* 50:409–422.

Day, M., and E. H. Wickens. 1980. Laetoli Pliocene hominid footprints and bipedalism. *Nature* 286:385–387.

Day, M. H. 1969. Omo human skeletal remains. *Nature* 222:1135–1138.

———. 1986. *Guide to Fossil Man.* Chicago, IL: University of Chicago Press.

Deacon, H. J., and R. Shuurman. 1992. The origins of modern people: The evidence from Klasies River. In *Continuity or Replacement: Controversies in* Homo sapiens *Evolution*, ed. G. Bräuer and F. Smith, 121–130. Rotterdam, The Netherlands: Balkema.

Dean, M. C., C. B. Stringer, and T. G. Bromage. 1986. Age at death of the Neandertal child from Devil's Tower, Gibraltar and the implications for students of general growth and development in Neandertals. *American Journal of Physical Anthropology* 70:301–301.

Deino, A., P. R. Renne, and C. C. Swisher III. 1998. 40Ar/39Ar dating in paleoanthropology and archaeology. *Evolutionary Anthropology* 6(2):63–75.

de la Vega, G. 1988. *The Florida of the Inca.* 1605 ed. Trans. J. Varner and J. Varner. Austin: University of Texas Press.

Demarest, A. 2007. *Ancient Maya: The Rise and Fall of a Rainforest Civilization.* Cambridge, England: Cambridge University Press.

deMenocal, P. 2001. Cultural responses to climate change during the Holocene. *Science* 292:667–672.

Denham, T. P., S. G. Haberle, C. Lentfer, R. Fullagar, J. Field, M. Therin, N. Porch, and B. Winsborough. 2003. Origins of agriculture at Kuk Swamp in the highlands of New Guinea. *Science* 301:189–193.

Denison, S. 1995. Mesolithic food industry on Colonsay. *British Archaeology* 5. http://www.britarch.ac.uk/ba/ba5/BA5NEWS.HTML.

Dennell, R. 1986. Needles and spear-throwers. *Natural History* 95:70–78.

Dennell, R. W. 1992. The origins of crop agriculture in Europe. In *The Origins of Agriculture: An International Perspective*, ed. C. W. Cowan and P. J. Watson, 71–100. Washington, DC: Smithsonian Institution Press.

Derenko, M.V., T. Grzybowski, B. A. Malyarchuk, J. Czarny, D. Miscicka-Sliwka, and I. A. Zakharov. 2001. The presence of mitochondiral haplogroup X in Altaians from south Siberia. *American Journal of Human Genetics* 69:237–241.

De Tapia, E. M. 1992. The origins of agriculture in Mesoamerica and South America. In *The Origins of Agriculture: An International Perspective*, ed. C. W. Cowan and P. J. Watson, 143–171. Washington, DC: Smithsonian Institution Press.

Diamond, J. 1987. The worst mistake in the history of the human race. *Discover* 8:50–60.

———. 1994. How to tame a wild plant. *Discover* 15:100–106.

———. 2002. Life with the artificial Anasazi. *Nature* 419:567–569.

———. 2004. The astonishing micropygmies. *Science* 306:2047–2048.

———. 2005. *Collapse: How Societies Choose to Fail or Succeed*. New York: Penguin.

Dibble, H. 1987. The interpretation of Middle Paleolithic scraper morphology. *American Antiquity* 52:108–118.

Diehl, R. A. 1989. Olmec archaeology: What we know and what we wish we knew. In *Regional Perspectives on the Olmec*, ed. R. J. Sharer and D. C. Grove, 17–32. New York: Cambridge University Press.

———. 2004. *The Olmecs: America's First Civilization*. London: Thames and Hudson.

Dikov, N. N. 1978. Ancestors of Paleoindians and proto-Eskimo-Aleuts in the Paleolithic of Kamchatka. In *Early Man in America From a Circum-Pacific Perspective*, ed. A. L. Bryan, 68–69. Edmonton, Canada: Archaeological Researches International.

DiLeo, J. H. 1970. *Young Children and Their Drawings*. New York: Brunner/Mazel.

Dillehay, T. D. 1987. By the banks of the Chinchihuapi. In *Natural History* 96(8):9–12.

———. 1989. *Monte Verde: A Late Pleistocene Settlement in Chile, Vol. 1: Paleoenvironment and Site Context*. Washington, DC: Smithsonian Institution Press.

———. 1996. *Monte Verde—A Late Pleistocene Settlement in Chile, Vol. 2: The Archaeological Context and Interpretation*. Washington, DC: Smithsonian Institution Press.

———. 1997. The battle of Monte Verde. *The Sciences* January/February:28–33.

Dillehay, T. D., and M. B. Collins. 1988. Early cultural evidence from Monte Verde in Chile. *Nature* 332:150–152.

Dillehay, T. D., C. Ramirez, M. Pino, M. B. Collins, J. Rossen, and J. D. Pino-Navarro. 2008. Monte Verde: Seaweed, food, medicine, and the peopling of South America. *Science* 320:784–786.

Dincauze, D. 1993. Fluted points in the eastern forests. In *From Kostenki to Clovis: Upper Paleolithic-Paleoindian Adaptations*, ed. O. Soffer and N. Preslov, 279–292. New York: Plenum.

Dixon, E. J. 1999. *Bones, Boats, and Bison: Archaeology and the First Colonization of Western North America*. Albuquerque: University of New Mexico Press.

Dobyns, H. 1983. *Their Numbers Became Thinned*. Knoxville: The University of Tennessee Press.

Doebley, J., A. Stec, and L. Hubbard. 1997. The evolution of apical dominance in maize. *Nature* 386:485–488.

Draper, R. 2010. Unburying the Aztec. *National Geographic* 218(5):110–135.

Duarte, C., J. Maurîcio, P. B. Pettitt, P. Souto, E. Trinkaus, H. v. d. Plicht, and J. Zilhao. 1999. The early Upper Paleolithic human skeleton from the Abrigo do Lagar Velho, Portugal and modern emergence in Iberia. *Proceedings of the National Academy of Sciences* 96:7604–7609.

Dubois, E. 1894. *Pithecanthropus erectus. Eine Menschenähnliche Übergangsform Aus Java* [*Pithecanthropus erectus:* A manlike transition form from Java]. Batavia: Landersdruckerei.

Dunne, J., R. E. Evershed, M. Salque, L. Cramp, S. Bruni, K. Ryan, S. Biagetti, and S. d. Lernia. 2012. First dairying in green Saharan Africa in the fifth millennium BC. *Nature* 486:390–394.

Dwyer, E. 2010. *Pompeii's Living Statues*. Ann Arbor: University of Michigan Press.

Edwards, E., et al. 2010. The origins of C4 grasslands: Integrating evolutionary and ecosystem science. *Science* 328:587–591.

Eighmy, J. L., and J. B. Howard. 1991. Direct dating of prehistoric canal sediments using archaeomagnetism. *American Antiquity* 56:88–102.

Eighmy, J. L., and R. S. Sternberg, eds. 1990. *Archaeomagnetic Dating*. Tuscon: University of Arizona Press.

Elias, S. A., S. K. Short, C. H. Nelson, and H. H. Birks. 1996. Life and times of the Bering land bridge. *Nature* 382:60–63.

Elvas, a Gentleman of. 1611. *The Discovery and Conquest of Tierra Florida by Don Ferdinando de Soto and Six Hundred Spaniards, His Followers*. Reprinted in 1966. New York: Burt Franklin.

Emerson, T. E., R. E. Hughes, H. R. Hynes, and S. U. Wisseman. 2003. The sourcing and interpretation of Cahokia-style figurines in the trans-Mississippi south and southeast. *American Antiquity* 68:287–313.

Erlandson, J. M., T. C. Rick, T. J. Braje, M. Casperson, B. Culleton, B. Fulfrost, T. Garcia, et al. 2011. Paleoindian seafaring, maritime technologies, and coastal foraging on California's Channel Islands. *Science* 331:1181–1184.

Evans, J. D. 1968. Neolithic Knossos: The growth of a settlement. *Proceedings of the Prehistoric Society* 37(2):95–117.

Evans, S. A. 1921–1936. *Palace of Minos*. 4 vols. Oxford, England: Oxford University Press.

Evans, S. T. 2008. *Ancient Mexico and Central America*. New York: Thames and Hudson.

Evershed, R. P., S. Payne, A. G. Sherratt, M. S. Copley, J. Coolidge, D. Urem-Kotsu, K. Kotsakis, et al. 2008. Earliest date for milk use in the Near East and south-eastern Europe linked to cattle herding. *Nature* 455:528–531.

Fagan, B. M. 1994. *Quest for the Past: Great Discoveries in Archaeology*. Prospect Heights, IL: Waveland Press.

———. 2005. *Ancient North America: The Archaeology of a Continent*. London: Thames and Hudson.

———. 2008. *In The Beginning: An Introduction to Archaeology*, 7th ed. New York: Prentice Hall.

———. 2011. *Archaeology: A Brief Introduction*, 4th ed. New York: Prentice Hall.

Falk, D. 2012. *The Fossil Chronicles: How Two Controversial Discoveries Changed Our View of Human Evolution*. Berkeley: University of California Press.

Falk, D., C. Hildebolt, K. Smith, M. J. Morwood, T. Sutikna, P. Brown, Jatmiko, et al. 2005. The brain of LB1, *Homo floresiensis*. *Science* 308:242–245.

Farnsworth, P., J. E. Brady, M. J. DeNiro, and R. S. MacNeish. 1985. A re-evaluation of the isotopic and archaeological reconstruction of diet in the Tehuacán Valley. *American Antiquity* 50:102–116.

Fash, W. L. 2001. *Scribes, Warriors and Kings: The City of Copan and the Ancient Maya*. New York: Thames and Hudson.

Feder, K. L. 2008. *Linking to the Past: A Brief Introduction to Archaeology*. New York: Oxford University Press.

———. 2009. "2012": Maya calendar misconception results in only a Hollywood ending. *Chicago Tribune*.

———. 2013. *Frauds, Myths, and Mysteries: Science and Pseudoscience in Archaeology*. New York: McGraw-Hill.

Feder, K. L., and M. A. Park. 2007. *Human Antiquity: An Introduction to Physical Anthropology and Archaeology*. New York: McGraw-Hill.

Fedoroff, N. V. 2003. Prehistoric GM corn. *Science* 302: 1158–1159.

Feibel, C. S., F. H. Brown, and I. McDougal. 1989. Stratigraphic context of fossil hominids from the Omo Group deposits: Northern Turkana Basin, Kenya and Ethiopea. *American Journal of Physical Anthropology* 78:595–622.

Firestone, R. B., et al. 2007. Evidence for an extraterrestrial impact 12,900 years ago that contributed to the megafaunal extinction and the Younger Dryas cooling. *Proceedings of the National Academy of Sciences* 104(41):16016–16021.

Fladmark, K. 1986. Getting one's Berings. In *Natural History* 95:8–10, 14, 16–19.

Flannery, K., ed. 1986. *Guilá Naquitz: Archaic Foraging and Early Agriculture in Oaxaca, Mexico*. New York: Academic Press.

Flannery, K. V. 1968. Archaeological systems theory and early Mesoamerica. In *Anthropological Archaeology in the Americas*, ed. B. Meggars, 67–87. Washington, DC: Anthropological Society of Washington.

Flint, R. F. 1971. *Glacial and Quarternary Geology*. New York: Wiley.

Ford, R. 1985. Patterns of prehistoric food production in North America. In *Prehistoric Food Production in North America*, ed. R. Ford, 341–364. Anthropological Papers, Vol. 75. Ann Arbor: University of Michigan, Museum of Anthropology.

Fowler, B. 2007. Written in bone. *Archaeology*. http://www.archaeology.org/0705/abstracts/isotopes.html.

Fowler, M. 1989. *The Cahokia Atlas: A Historical Atlas of Cahokia Archaeology*. Studies in Illinois Archaeology 6. Springfield: Illinois Historic Preservation Agency.

Fowler, M. L. 1959. *Summary Report of Modoc Rockshelter: 1952, 1953, 1955, 1956*. Report of Investigations 8. Springfield: Illinois State Museum.

Frayer, D. W., M. H. Wolpoff, A. G. Thorne, F. H. Smith, and G. G. Pope. 1993. Theories of modern human origins: The paleontological test. *American Anthropologist* 95:14–50.

Frere, J. 1800. Account of flint weapons discovered in Hoxne in Suffolk. *Archaeologia* 13:204–205.

Frink, D. S. 1997. OCR Carbon dating of the Watson Brake mound complex. Paper presented at the 53rd annual meeting of the Southeastern Archaeological Conference, Birmingham, AL.

Gabunia, L., A. Vekua, D. Lordkipanidze, C. C. S. III, R. Ferring, A. Justus, M. Nioradze, M. Tvalchrelidze, et al. 2000. Earliest Pleistocene cranial remains from Dmanisi, Republic of Georgia: Taxonomy, geological setting, and age. *Science* 288:1019–1025.

Galinat, W. C. 1992. Maize: Gift from America's first people. In *Chilies to Chocolate: Food the Americas Gave the World*, ed. N. Foster and L. S. Cordell, 47–60. Tuscon: University of Arizona Press.

Gamble, C. 1982. Interaction and alliance in Paleolithic society. *Man* 17:92–107.

———. 1986. *The Paleolithic settlement of Europe*. Cambridge, England: Cambridge University Press.

Gardner, H. 1980. *Artful Scribbles: The Significance of Children's Drawings*. New York: Basic Books.

Garlake, P. S. 1973. *Great Zimbabwe*. London: Thames and Hudson.

Gibbons, A. 1996. Did Neandertals lose an evolutionary "arms" race? *Science* 272:1586–1587.

———. 2001. The riddle of coexistence. *Science* 291: 1725–1729.

———. 2002. In search of the first hominids. *Science* 295: 1214–1219.

———. 2007a. Coastal artifacts suggest early beginnings for modern behavior. *Science* 318:377.

———. 2007b. Food for thought. *Science* 316:1558–1560.

———. 2007c. Hobbit's status as a new species gets a hand up. *Science* 316:34.

———. 2008a. The birth of childhood. *Science* 322:1040–1043.

———. 2008b. Brainy babies and risky birth for Neandertals. *Science* 312:1429.

———. 2009a. Civilization's cost: The decline and fall of human health. *Science* 324:588.

———. 2009b. First globetrotters had primitive tool kits. *Science* 323:999.

———. 2009c. Of tools and tubers. *Science* 324:588–589.

———. 2009d. Oldest stone blades uncovered. *ScienceNOW*. April 2, 2009. http://sciencenow.sciencemag.org/cgi/content/full/2009/402/2.

———. 2010. Lucy's 'big brother' reveals new facets of her species. *Science* 328:1619.

———. 2011a. A battle over bones. *Science* 336:654.

———. 2011b. A new view of the birth of *Homo sapiens*. *Science* 331:392–394.

———. 2011c. Who were the Denisovans. *Science* 333: 1084–1087.

———. 2012a. A new face reveals multiple lineages alive at the dawn of our genus *Homo*. *Science* 337:635.

———. 2012b. An evolutionary theory of dentistry. *Science* 336:973–975.

———. 2012c. The ultimate sacrifice. *Science* 336:834–837.

Gibson, J. L. 2001. *The Ancient Mounds of Poverty Point: Place of Rings*. Gainesville: University of Florida Press.

Gilbert, M. T. P., D. L. Jenkins, A. Götherstrom, N. Naveran, J. J. Sanchez, M. Hofreiter, P. F. Thomsen, et al. 2008. DNA from pre-clovis human coprolites in Oregon, North America. *Science* 320:786–789.

Gill, J. L., J. W. Williams, S. T. Jackson, K. B. Lininger, and G. S. Robinson. 2009. Pleistocene megafaunal collapse, novel plant communities, and enhanced fire regimes in North America. *Science* 326:1100–1103.

Glover, I. C. 1993. Tools and cultures in Late Paleolithic southeast Asia. In *The First Humans: Human Origins and History to 10,000 B.C.*, ed. G. Burenhult, 128–130. San Francisco: HarperSanFrancisco.

Goebel, T., R. Powers, and N. Bigelow. 1991. The Nenana Complex of Alaska and Clovis origins. In *Clovis: Origins and Adaptations*, ed. R. Bonnichsen and K. L. Turnmire, 49–79. Corvallis, OR: Center for the Study of the First Americans.

Goebel, T., M. R. Waters, and M. Dikova. 2003. The archaeology of Ushki Lake, Kamchatka, and the Pleistocene peopling of America. *Science* 301:501–506.

Goebel, T., M. R. Waters, and D. H. O'Rourke. 2008. The late Pleistocene dispersal of modern humans in the Americas. *Science* 319:1497–1502.

Goodall, J. 1986. *The Chimpanzees of Gombe: Patterns of Behavior*. Cambridge, MA: Belknap Press.

Goren-Inbar, N., G. Sharon, Y. Melamed, and M. Kislev 2002. Nuts, nut cracking, and pitted stones at Gesher Benot Ya'aqov, Israel. *Proceedings of the National Academy of Sciences* 99:2455–2460.

Gorman, C. 1972. Excavations at Spirit Cave, North Thailand: Some interim impressions. *Asian Perpsectives* 13:79–107.

Gould, S. J. 1977. *Ever Since Darwin*, 70–75. New York: Norton.

———. 1984. Human equality is a contingent fact of history. In *Natural History* 93:26–33.

———. 1988. A novel notion of Neanderthal. In *Natural History* 97:16–21.

———. 1991. Fall in the house of Ussher. In *Natural History* 100:12,14–16,18–21.

———. 1994. Lucy on the earth in stasis. In *Natural History* 103:12,14,16,18–20.

Gowlett, J. 1984. Mental abilities of early man. In *Hominid Evolution and Community Ecology*, ed. G. N. Bailey and P. Callow, 169–192. London: Academic Press.

Gowlett, J. A. J. 1986. Culture and conceptualisation: The Oldowan-Acheulian gradient. In *Stone Age Prehistory: Studies in Memory of Charles McBurney*, ed. G. N. Bailey and P. Callow, 243–260. Cambridge, England: Cambridge University Press.

Gramly, R. M. 1982. *The Vail Site: A Palaeo-Indian Encampment in Maine*. Bulletin of the Buffalo Society of Natural Sciences 30. Buffalo, NY: Buffalo Society of Natural Sciences.

———. 1993. *The Richey Clovis Cache*. Buffalo, NY: Persimmon Press.

Gray, D. 1996. Champion of Aboriginal Art. *Archaeology* 46(4):44–47.

Grayson, D. K. 1983. *The Establishment of Human Antiquity*. New York: Academic Press.

———. 1987. Death by natural causes. In *Natural History* 96:8, 10, 12–13.

Green, R. E., et al. 2010. A draft sequence of the Neanderthal genome. *Science* 328:710–722.

Groube, L., J. Chappell, J. Muke, and D. Price. 1986. A 40,000 year-old human occupation site at Huon Peninsula, Papua New Guinea. *Nature* 324:453–455.

Grove, D. 1996. The Olmec. *Arqueologia Mexicana* 12:26–33.

Grün, R., P. B. Beaumont, and C. B. Stringer. 1990. ESR dating evidence for early modern humans at Border Cave in South Africa. *Nature* 344:537–539.

Grün, R., N. J. Shackleton, and H. J. Deacon. 1990. Electron-spin-resonance dating of tooth enamel from Klasies River Mouth cave. *Current Anthropology* 31(4):427–432.

Guanjun, S., G. Xing, G. Bin, and D. E. Granger. 2009. Age of Zhoukoudian *Homo erectus* determined with ^{26}Al/^{10}Be burial dating. *Nature* 458:198–200.

Gugliotta, G. 2007. The Maya glory and ruin. *National Geographic* 212(2):68–109.

Gutin, J. 1995. Archaeology: Do Kenya tools root birth of modern thought in Africa? *Science* 270:1118–1119.

Gunz, P., S. Neubauer, B. Maureille, and J.-J. Hublin. 2010. Brain development after birth differs between Neanderthals and modern humans. *Current Biology* 20(21): pR921–pR922.

Haak, W., et al. 2010. Ancient DNA from European early Neolithic farmers reveals their Near Eastern affinities. http://www.plosbiology.org/article/info%3Adoi%2F10 .1371%2Fjournal.pbi0.1000536

Haas, J. 1982. *The Evolution of the Prehistoric State*. New York: Columbia University Press.

Haas, J., W. Creamer, and A. Ruiz. 2004. Dating the Late Archaic occupation of the Norte Chico region of Peru. *Nature* 432:1020–1024.

Hager, L. D. 1994. Fashioning the primitive: 100 years of looking at Neandertals, looking at us. Paper presented at the annual meeting of the Society for American Archaeology, Anaheim, CA.

Halvorson, J. 1987. Art for art's sake in the Paleolithic. *Current Anthropology* 28:63–71.

Hammer, M. F., A. E. Woerner, P. L. Menendez, J. C. Watkins, and J. D. Wall. 2011. Genetic evidence for archaic admixture in Africa. *Proceedings of the National Academy of Sciences* 108(37):15123–15128.

Hanotte, O., D. G. Bradley, J. W. Ochieng, Y. Verjee, E. W. Hill, and J. E. O. Rege. 2002. African pastoralism: Genetic imprints of origins and migrations. *Science* 296: 336–339.

Hard, R. J., and J. R. Roney. 1998. A massive terraced village complex in Chihuahua, Mexico: 3000 years before present. *Science* 279:1661–1664.

Harlan, J. 1992. Indigenous African agriculture. In *The Origins of Agriculture: An International Perspective*, ed. C. W. Cowan and P. J. Watson, 59–70. Washington, DC: Smithsonian Institution Press.

Harper, A. 1999. Forensic archaeology and the woodchipper murder. In *Lessons From the Past: An Introductory Reader in Archaeology*, ed. K. L. Feder, 189–193. Mountain View, CA: Mayfield.

Harris, J. F., and S. K. Stearns. 1997. *Understanding Maya Inscriptions*. Philadelphia, PA: The University Museum, University of Pennsylvania.

Harrison, T. 2010. Apes among the tangled branches of human origins. *Science* 327:532–533.

Harrold, F. B. 1980. A comparative analysis of Eurasian Palaeolithic burials. *World Archaeology* 12:195–211.

Hastings, M. C., and M. Mosely. 1975. The adobes of Huaca del Sol and Huaca de la Luna. *American Antiquity* 40:196–203.

Hay, R. L., and M. Leakey. 1982. The fossil footprints of Laetoli. *Scientific American* 246:50–57.

Haynes, C. V. 1982. Were Clovis progenitors in Beringia? In *Paleoecology of Beringia*, ed. D. M. Hopkins, J. V. M. Jr., C. E. Schweger, and S. B. Young, 383–398. New York: Academic Press.

———. 1987. Clovis origins update. *The Kiva* 52(2):83–93.

———. 1992. Contributions of radiocarbon dating to the geochronology of the peopling of the New World. In *Radiocarbon Dating After Four Decades: An Interdisciplinary Perspective*, ed. R. R. Taylor, A. Long, and R. S. Kra, 355–374. New York: Springer-Verlag.

Headrick, A. 2007. *The Teotihuacan Trinity: The Sociopolitical Structure of an Ancient Mesoamerican City*. Austin: University of Texas Press.

Heizer, R. F., and L. K. Napton. 1970. Archaeology as seen from Lovelock Cave, Nevada. *Univerisity of California Research Facility Contributions* 10(1).

Helbaek, H. 1965. Early Hassunan vegetable food at Tell es-Sawwan near Samarra. *Sumer* 20:45–48.

Henderson, J. S., R. A. Joyce, G. R. Hall, W. J. Hurst, and P. E. McGovern. 2007. Chemical and archaeological evidence for earliest cacao beverages. *Proceedings of the National Academy of Sciences* 107:18937–18940.

Henry, A. G., P. S. Ungar, B. H. Passey, M. Sponheimer, L. Rossouw, M. Bamford, P. Sandberg, et al. 2012. The diet of *Australopithecus sediba*. *Nature* 487:90–93.

Henry, D. O. 1989. *From Foraging to Agriculture: The Levant at the End of the Ice Age*. Philadelphia: University of Pennsylvania Press.

Henshilwood, C. S., F. d'Errico, K. L. van Niekerk, Y. Coquinot, Z. Jacobs, S.-E. Lauritzen, M. Menu, and R. García-Moreno. 2011. A 100,000-year-old ochre-processing workshop at Blombos Cave, South Africa. *Science* 334:219–222.

Henshilwood, C., F. d'Errico, M. Vanhaeren, K. van Niekerk, and Z. Jacobs. 2004. Middle Stone Age shell beads from South Africa. *Science* 304:404.

Henshilwood, C. S., F. d'Errico, C. W. Marean, R. G. Milo, and R. Yates. 2001. An early bone tool industry from the Middle Stone Age at Blombos Cave, South Africa: Implications for the origins of modern human behaviour, symbolism, and language. *Journal of Human Evolution* 41:631–678.

Henshilwood, C. S., F. d'Errico, R. Yates, Z. Jacobs, C. Tribolo, G. A. T. Duller, N. Mercier, et al. 2002. Emergence of modern human behavior: Middle Stone Age engravings from South Africa. *Science* 295:1278–1280.

Heun, M., R. Schäfer-Pregl, D. Klawan, R. Castagna, M. Accerbi, B. Borghi, and F. Salamini. 1997. Site of einkorn wheat domestication identified by genetic fingerprinting. *Science* 278:1312–1313.

Higham, C. 1989. *The Archaeology of Mainland Southeast Asia.* Cambridge, England: Cambridge University Press.

Higham, T., L. Basell, R. Jacobi, W. Wood, C. B. Ramsay, and N. J. Conrad. 2012. Testing models for the beginnings of the Aurignacian and the advent of figurative art and music: The radiocarbon chronology of Beibenklösterle. *Journal of Human Evolution* 62:664–676.

Higham, T., T. Compton, C. Stringer, R. Jacobi, B. Shapiro, E. Trinkaus, B. Chandler, et al. 2011. The earliest evidence for anatomically modern humans in northwestern Europe. *Nature* 479:521–524.

Hill, A., S. Ward, and B. Brown. 1992. Anatomy and age of the Lothagam mandible. *Journal of Human Evolution* 22:439–451.

Hodder, I. 2005. Women and men at Çatalhöyük. *Scientific American: Special Edition* 15(1):35–41.

Hodder, I., and C. Cessford. 2004. Daily practice and social memory at Çatalhöyük. *American Antiquity* 69:17–40.

Hoffman, M. A. 1979. *Egypt Before the Pharaohs: The Prehistoric Foundations of Egyptian Civilization.* New York: Alfred A. Knopf.

———. 1983. Where nations began. In *Science '83* 4:42–51.

Holden, C. 2001. Ancient stepping-stones to Australia. *Science* 292:47.

———. 2002. Very old tools. *Science* 295:795.

———. 2003a. Dmanisi hominds get legs. *Science* 301:1469.

———. 2003b. Leftovers spur edible debate. *Science News* 300:1653.

———. 2007. Modern humans in Borneo. *Science* 315:1773.

———. 2008. Natufian toolbox. *Science* 319:15.

———. 2009. Ancient granaries. *Science* 325:15.

———. 2010. Tangled turkey tale. *Science* 327:765.

Holloway, R. 1980. Indonesian "Solo" (Ngandong) endocranial reconstructions: Preliminary observations and comparisons with Neandertal and *Homo erectus* groups. *American Journal of Physical Anthropology* 53:285–295.

Holloway, R. L. 1981. The Indonesian *Homo erectus* brain endocasts revisited. *American Journal of Physical Anthropology* 55:503–521.

Hoppe, K. 1992. Antiquity of oldest American confirmed. *Science News* 142:334.

Hublin, J.-J., F. Spoor, M. Braun, F. Zonneveld, and S. Condemi. 1996. A late Neanderthal associated with Upper Paleolithic artefacts. *Nature* 381:224–226.

Hughes, R. 1995. Behold the Stone Age. *Time* 145:52–57, 60, 62.

Hurst, W. J., S. M. Tarka Jr., T. G. Powis, F. Valdez Jr., and T. R. Hester. 2002. Cacao usage by the earliest Maya civilization. *Nature* 418:289–290.

Hutton, J. 1795. *Theory of the Earth: With Proofs and Illustrations* (2 vols.). Weinheim, Germany: H. R. Engelmann (J. Cramer) and Wheldon & Wesley, 1959.

Iriarte, J., I. Holst, O. Marozzi, C. Listopad, E. Alonso, A. Rinderknecht, and J. Montana. 2004. Evidence for cultivar adoption and emerging complexity during the mid-Holocene in the La Plata basin. *Nature* 432:614–617.

Irwin, G. 1993. *The Prehistoric Exploration and Colonisation of the Pacific.* Cambridge, England: Cambridge University Press.

Irwin, G., S. H. Bickler, and P. Quirke. 1990. Voyaging by canoe and computer experiments in the settlement of the Pacific. *Antiquity* 64:34–50.

Iseminger, W. 2010. *Cahokia Mounds: America's First City.* Charleston, SC: The History Press.

Jackson, K., and J. Stamp. 2003. *Building the Great Pyramid.* Buffalo, NY: Firefly Books.

Jaenicke-Després, V., E. S. Buckler, B. D. Smith, M. Gilkbert, A. Cooper, J. Doebley, and S. Paabo. 2003. Early allelic selection in maize as revealed by ancient DNA. *Science* 302:1206–1208.

Jelinek, A. J. 1994. Hominids, energy, environment, and behavior in the Late Pleistocene. In *Origins of Anatomically Modern Humans*, ed. M. Nitecki and D. Nitecki, 67–92. New York: Plenum.

Jenkins, D. L., et al. 2012. Clovis age western stemmed projectile points and human coprolites at the Paisley Caves. *Science* 337:223–228.

Jia, L., and H. Weiwen. 1990. *The Story of Peking Man.* New York: Oxford University Press.

Jian, G., and J. A. Rice. 1990. The dragon bones of Tongxin. *Natural History* 99(9):60–67.

Jochim, M. 1983. Paleolithic cave art in ecological perspective. In *Hunter-Gatherer Economy in Prehistory: A European Perspective*, ed. G. Bailey, 212–219. Cambridge, England: Cambridge University Press.

Jochim, M. A. 1998. *A Hunter-Gatherer Landscape: Southwest Germany in the Late Paleolithic and Mesolithic.* New York: Plenum.

Johanson, D. 1993. A skull to chew on. In *Natural History* 102(5):52–53.

Johanson, D., and M. Edey. 1981. *Lucy: The Beginnings of Humankind.* New York: Warner Books.

Johanson, D., and B. Edgar. 1996. *From Lucy to Language.* New York: Simon and Schuster.

Johanson, D., L. Johanson, and B. Edgar. 1994. *Ancestors: In Search of Human Origins.* New York: Villard.

Johanson, D., and J. Shreeve. 1989. *Lucy's Child: The Discovery of a Human Ancestor.* New York: William Morrow and Company.

Johanson, D. C., and K. Wong. 2009. *Lucy's Legacy: The Quest for Human Origins.* New York: Harmony Books.

Johnson, E. 1991. Late Pleistocene cultural occupation on the southern Plains. In *Clovis: Origins and Adaptations*, ed. R. Bonnichsen and K. L. Turnmire, 215–236. Corvallis, OR: Center for the Study of the First Americans.

Johnson, T. 2008. *Solving Stonehenge: The New Key to an Ancient Enigma*. London: Thames and Hudson.

Jones, R. 1987. Pleistocene life in the dead heart of Australia. *Nature* 328:666.

———. 1989. East of Wallace's Line: Issues and problems in the colonisation of the Australian continent. In *The Human Revolution: Behavioural and Biological Perspectives in the Origins of Modern Humans*, ed. P. Mellars and C. Stringer, 741–782. Princeton, NJ: Princeton University Press.

———. 1992. The human colonisation of the Australian continent. In *Continuity or Replacement: Controversies in* Homo sapiens *Evolution*, ed. G. Bräuer and F. Smith, 289–301. Rotterdam, The Netherlands: Balkema.

Jones, M. K., and Xinyi Liu. 2009. Origins of agriculture in East Asia. *Science* 324:730–731.

Jordaan, H. V. F. 1976. Newborn:adult brain ratios in hominid evolution. *American Journal of Physical Anthropology* 44:271–278.

Jordan, P. 2001a. *The Atlantis Syndrome*. Phoenix Mill, England: Sutton Publishing.

———. 2001b. *Neanderthal*. London: Sutton.

Joyce, D. J. 2006. Chronology and new research on the Schaefer mammoth (?*Mammuthus primigenius*) site, Kenosha County, Wisconsin. *Quaternary Journal* 142–143:44–57.

Jungers, W. L., W. E. H. Harcourt-Smith, R. E. Wunderlich, W. W. Tocheri, S. G. Larson, T. Sutikna, R. A. Due, and M. J. Morwood. 2009. The foot of *Homo floresiensis*. *Nature* 459:81–84.

Kantker, J. 1997. Ancient Roads, modern mapping: Evaluating Chaco Anasazi roadways using GIS technology. *Expedition* 39(3):49–60.

Kaplan, L. 1981. What is the origin of the common bean? *Economic Botany* 35:241–254.

Kaplan, L., and L. N. Kaplan. 1992. Beans of the Americas. In *Chilies to Chocolate: Food the Americas Gave the World*, ed. N. Foster and L. S. Cordell, 61–79. Tuscon: University of Arizona Press.

Kaplan, L., T. F. Lynch, and C. E. Smith Jr. 1973. Early cultivated beans (*Phaseolus vulgaris*) from an intermontaine Peruvian valley. *Science* 179:76–77.

Karl, W., and L. Bruchert. 1997. Spearthrower performance: Ethnographic and experimental research. *Antiquity* 71:890–897.

Keeley, L. 1980. *Experimental Determination of Stone Tool Use: A Microwear Analysis*. Chicago, IL: University of Chicago Press.

Keeley, L. 1997. *War Before Civilization: The Myth of the Peaceful Savage*. New York: Oxford University Press.

Keeley, L., and N. Toth. 1981. Microwear polishes on early stone tools from Koobi Fora, Kenya. *Nature* 293:464–465.

Kelly, R. L., and D. H. Thomas. 2010. *Archaeology: Down to Earth*. New York: Wadsworth Publishing.

Kelly, R. L., and D. H. Thomas. 2012. *Archaeology*. New York: Wadsworth Publishing.

Kemp, B. 1977. The early development of towns in Egypt. *Antiquity* 51:185–199.

Kemp, B. J. 1991. *Ancient Egypt*. New York: Routledge.

Kenoyer, J. M. 1998. *Ancient Cities of the Indus Valley Civilization*. Oxford, England: Oxford University Press.

———. 2005. Uncovering the keys to the lost Indus cities. *Scientific American: Special Edition* 15(1):24–33.

Kent, J. 1987. The most ancient south: A review of the domestication of the South American camelids. In *Studies in the Neolithic and Urban Revolutions*, ed. L. Manzanilla, 169–184. BAR International Series, Vol. 349. Oxford, England: British Archaeological Review.

Kenyon, K. 1954. Ancient Jericho. *Scientific American* 190:76–82.

Kerr, R. A. 2009. The Quaternary Period wins out in the end. *Science* 324:1249.

Kerr, R. A. 2010. Mammoth-killer impact flunks out. *Science* 329:1140–1141.

Kidder, T. R. 2010. Hunter-gatherer ritual and complexity: New Evidence from Poverty Point, Louisiana. In *Ancient Complexities: New Perspectives in Pre-Columbian North America*, ed. S. Alt, 32–51. Salt Lake City: University of Utah Press.

Kiernan, K., R. Jones, and D. Ranson. 1983. New evidence from Fraser Cave for glacial age man in south-west Tasmania. *Nature* 301:28–32.

Kimbel, W. H., D. C. Johanson, and Y. Rak. 1994. The first skull and other new discoveries of *Australopithecus afarensis* at Hadar, Ethiopia. *Nature* 368:449–451.

Kirch, P. V. 1984. *The Evolution of Polynesian Chiefdoms*. Cambridge, England: Cambridge University Press.

Kislev, M. E., and N. D. Carmi. 1992. Epi-Paleolithic (19,000 BP) cereal and fruit diet at Ohalo II, Sea of Galilee, Israel. *Review of Paleoethnobotany Palyonolgy* 71:161–166.

Kitagawa, H., and J. van der Plicht. 1998. Atmospheric radiocarbon calibration to 45,000 BP: Late Glacial fluctuations and cosmogenic istope production. *Science* 279:1187–1190.

Kitchen, A., M. M. Miyamoto, and C. J. Mulligan. 2008. A three-stage colonization model for the peopling of the Americas. *PLoS One* 3(2), January 16, 2008. http://www.plosone.org/article/info%3Adoi%2F10.1371%2Fjournal.pone.0001596.

Klein, R. 1983. The stone age prehistory of southern Africa. *Annual Review of Anthropology* 12:25–48.

Klein, R. G. 1969. *Man and Culture in the Late Pleistocene: A Case Study*. San Francisco, CA: Chandler Publishing.

———. 1977. The ecology of early man in Southern Africa. *Science* 197:115–126.

———. 1989. *The Human Career: Human Biological and Cultural Origins*. Chicago, IL: University of Chicago Press.

————. 1993. Hunter-gatherers and farmers in Africa: The transformation of a continent. In *People of the Stone Age: Hunter-gatherers and Early Farmers*, ed. G. Burenhult, 39–47, 50–55. San Francisco, CA: HarperSanFrancisco.

Knapp, S. 2008. Celebrating spuds. *Science* 321:206–207.

Knudson, K. J., T. D. Price, J. E. Buikstra, and D. E. Blom. 2004. The use of strontium isotope analysis to investigate Tiwanaku Migration and Mortuary Ritual in Bolivia and Peru. *Archaeometry* 46:5–18.

Knudson, K. J., T. A. Tung, K. C. Nystrom, T. D. Price, and P. D. Fullagar. 2005. The origin of the Juch'uypampa Cave mummies: Strontium analysis of archaeological remains from Bolivia. *Journal of Archaeological Science* 32:903–913.

Kolata, A. 1986. The agricultural foundations of the Tiwanaku state: A view from the heartland. *American Antiquity* 51:748–762.

Kopper, P. 1986. *The Smithsonian Book of North American Indians Before the Coming of the Europeans*. Washington, DC: Smithsonian Books.

Krogman, W. M. 1973. *The Human Skeleton in Forensic Medicine*. Springfield, IL: Charles C. Thomas.

Kuiper, K. F., A. Deino, F. J. Hilgen, W. Krijgsman, P. R. Renne, and J. R. Wijbrans. 2008. Synchronizing rock clocks of earth history. *Science* 320:500–504.

Kurtén, B. 1976. *The Cave Bear Story: Life and Death of a Vanished Animal*. New York: Columbia University Press.

Lahdenpera, M., V. Lummaa, S. Helle, M. Tremblay, and A. F. Russel. 2004. Fitness benefits of prolonged post-reproductive lifespan in women. *Nature* 428:178–181.

Lalueza-Fox, C., et al. 2010. Genetic evidence for patrilocal mating behavior among Neandertal groups. *Proceedings of the National Academy of Sciences* 108(1):250–253.

Lamberg-Karlovsky, C. C., and J. A. Sabloff. 1995. *Ancient Civilizations: The Near East and Mesoamerica*. Prospect Heights, IL: Waveland Press.

Larick, R., R. L. Ciochon, Y. Zaim, Sudijono, Suminto, Y. Rizal, F. Azizi, et al. 2001. Early Pleistocene 40Ar/39Ar ages for Bapang Formation hominins, Central Java, indonesia. *Proceedings of the National Academy of Sciences* 98:4866–4871.

Larmer, B. 2012. Terra-cotta warriors in color. *National Geographic* 221(6):74–87.

Lawler, A. 2001. Writing gets a rewrite. *Science* 292:2418–2420.

————. 2007. Climate spurred later Indus decline. *Science* 316:978–979.

————. 2008a. Boring no more, a trade-savvy Indus emerges. *Science* 320:1276–1281.

————. 2008b. Indus collapse: The end of the beginning of an Asian culture. *Science* 320:1281–1283.

————. 2009a. Beyond the Yellow River: How China became China. *Science* 325:930–935.

————. 2009b. Founding dynasty or myth? *Science* 325:934.

————. 2009c. Millet on the move. *Science* 325:942–943.

————. 2010. Collapse? What collapse? Societal change revisited. *Science* 330:907–909.

————. 2012a. The battle over violence. *Science* 336:829–830.

————. 2012b. Civilization's double-edged sword. *Science* 336:832–833.

————. 2012c. Near Eastern archaeology works to dig out of a crisis. *Science* 336:796–797.

Leakey, M. 1971. *Olduvai Gorge* 3. Cambridge, England: Cambridge University Press.

Leakey, M. D., and R. L. Hay. 1979. Pliocene footprints in the Laetolil Beds at Laetoli, northern Tanzania. *Nature* 278:317–323.

Leakey, M. G., C. S. Feibel, I. McDougal, C. Ward, and A. Walker. 1998. New specimens and confirmation of an early age for *Australopithecus anamensis*. *Nature* 393:62–65.

Leakey, M. G., F. Spoor, F. H. Brown, P. N. Gathogo, C. Klarie, L. N. Leakey, and I. McDougall. 2001. New hominin genus from eastern African shows diverse middle Pliocene lineages. *Nature* 410:433–440.

Leakey, M. G., F. Spoor, M. C. Dean, C. S. Feibel, S. C. Antón, C. Kiarie, and L. N. Leakey. 2012. New fossils from Koobi Fora in northern Kenya confirm taxonomic diversity in early *Homo*. *Nature* 488:201–204.

Leakey, R., and R. Lewin 1992. *Origins Reconsidered: In Search of What Makes Us Human*. New York: Doubleday.

Leakey, R., and A. Walker. 1985. Further hominids from the Plio-Pleistocene of Koobi Fora, Kenya. *American Journal of Physical Anthropology* 64:135–163.

Lebel, S., E. Trinkaus, M. Faure, P. Fernandez, C. Guérin, D. Richter, N. Mercier, et al. 2000. Comparative morphology and paleobiology of Middle Pleistocene human remains from the Bau de l'Aubesier, Vaucluse, France. *Proceedings of the National Academy of Sciences* 98:11097–11102.

Lehner, M. 1997. *The Complete Pyramids*. New York: Thames and Hudson.

Lepper, B. T. 1995a. *People of the Mounds: Ohio's Hopewell Culture*. Hopewell, OH: Hopewell Culture National Historical Park.

————. 1995b. Tracking Ohio's Great Hopewell Road. *Archaeology* 48(6):52–56.

————. 1996. The Newark Earthworks and the geometric enclosures of the Scioto Valley: Connections and conjectures. In *A View From the Core: A Synthesis of Ohio Hopewell Archaeology*, ed. P. Pacheco, 226–241. Columbus: The Ohio Archaeological Council.

————. 1998. The archaeology of the Newark Earthworks. In *Ancient Earthen Enclosures of the Eastern Woodlands*, ed. R. C. Mainfort Jr. and L. P. Sullivan, 114–134. Gainesville: University Press of Florida.

———. 2002. *The Newark Earthworks*. Columbus: Ohio Historical Society.

———. 2005. *Ohio Archaeology: An Illustrated Chronicle of Ohio's Ancient American Indian*. Wilmington, OH: Orange Frazer Press.

Lepre, C. J., H. Roche, D.V. Kent, S. Harmand, R. L. Quinn, J.-P. Brugal, P.-J. Texier, et al. 2011. An earlier origin for Acheulian. *Nature* 477:82–85.

Leroi-Gourhan, A. 1982. *The Dawn of European Art: An Introduction to Paleolithic Cave Painting*. Cambridge, England: Cambridge University Press.

Lewis-Williams, J. D., and T. A. Dowson. 1988. The signs of all times. *Current Anthropology* 29(2): 201–217.

Lieberman, P., E. Crelin, and D. H. Klatt. 1972. Phonetic ability and related anatomy of the newborn and adult human, Neanderthal Man, and the chimpanzee. *American Anthropologist* 74:287–307.

Lieberman, P., J. T. Laitman, J. S. Reidenberg, and P. J. Gannon. 1992. The anatomy, physiology, acoustics, and perception of speech: Essential elements in analysis of the evolution of human speech. *Journal of Human Evolution* 23:447–467.

Lombard, M., and I. Phillipson. 2010. Indications of bow and stone-tipped arrow use 64,000 years ago in Kwa-Zulu-Natal, South Africa. *Antiquity* 84:635–648.

Lordkipanidze, D., T. Jashashvili, A. Vekua, M. S. Ponce de Leon, C. P. E. Zollikofer, P. Rightmire, H. Pontzer, et al. 2007. Postcranial evidence from early *Homo* from Dmanisi, Georgia. *Nature* 449:305–310.

Lourandos, H. 1997. *Continent of Hunter-Gatherers*. Cambridge, England: Cambridge University Press.

Lovejoy, C. O. 1981. The origin of man. *Science* 211:341–350.

———. 1984. The natural detective. *Natural History* 93:24–28.

———. 1988. Evolution of human walking. *Scientific American* 259(5):118–125.

———. 2009. Reexamining human origins in light of *Ardipithecus ramidus*. *Science* 326:74, 74e1–74e8.

Lovejoy, C. O., K. G. Heiple, and A. Burnstein. 1973. The gait of *Australopithecus*. *American Journal of Physical Anthropology* 38:757–780.

Lowe, G.W. 1989. The heartland Olmec: Evolution of material culture. In *Regional Perspectives on the Olmec*, ed. R. J. Sharer and D. C. Grove, 33–67. Cambridge, England: Cambridge University Press.

Lowell, T. V., and M. A. Kelly 2008. Was the Younger Dryas global? *Science* 321:348–349.

Lowenthal, D. 1988. *The Past Is a Foreign Country*. Cambridge, England: Cambridge University Press.

Luikart, G., L. Gielly, L. Excoffier, J.-D.Vigne, J. Bouvet, and P. Taberlet. 2001. Multiple maternal origins and weak phylogeographic structure in domestic goats. *Proceedings of the National Academy of Sciences* 98:5927–5932.

Lyell, C. 1863. *The Geological Evidences of the Antiquity of Man*. London: Murray.

———. 1990. *Principles of Geology; Being an Attempt to Explain the Former Changes of the Earth's Surface, By Reference to Causes Now in Operation*, 1830 ed. (2 vols.). Chicago, IL: University of Chicago Press.

Lynch, T. F., R. Gillespie, J. A. J. Gowlett, and R. E. M. Hedges. 1985. Chronology of Guitarrero Cave, Peru. *Science* 229: 864–867.

MacDonald, G. F. 1985. *Debert: A Paleo-Indian Site in Central Nova Scotia*. Buffalo, NY: Persimmon Press.

MacNeish, R. S. 1964. Ancient Mesoamerican civilization. *Science* 143:531–537.

———. 1967. An interdiscipinary approach to an archaeological problem. In *Prehistory of the Tehuacan Valley, Volume One: Environment and Subsistence*, ed. D. Beyers, 14–23. Austin: University of Texas Press.

Magnusson, M., and H. Paulsson. 1965. *The Vinland Sagas*. New York: Penguin.

Maisels, C. K. 1990. *The Emergence of Civilization: From Hunting and Gathering to Agriculture, Cities, and the State in the Near East*. New York: Routledge.

Manley, B., ed. 2003. *The Seventy Great Mysteries of Ancient Egypt*. London: Thames and Hudson.

Mann, C. C. 2003. Cracking the khipu code. *Science* 300: 1650–1651.

———. 2005. Oldest civilization in the Americas revealed. *Science* 307:34–35.

———. 2011. The birth of religion. *National Geographic* 219(6):34–59.

Mannikka, E. 1996. *Angkor Wat: Time, Space, and Kingship*. Honolulu: University of Hawai'i Press.

Marchant, J. 2011. Spring comes to ancient Egypt. *Nature* 479:464–467.

Marcus, J., and K. Flannery. 1996. *Zapotec Civilization: How Urban Society Evolved in Mexico's Oaxaca Valley*. London: Thames and Hudson.

Marinatos, S. 1972. Thera: Key to the riddle of Minos. In *National Geographic*, 141:702–726.

Marks, A. E. 1990. The Middle and Upper Paleolithic of the Near East and the Nile Valley: The problem of cultural transformations. In *The Emergence of Modern Humans: An Archaeological Perspective*, ed. P. Mellars, 56–80. Ithaca, NY: Cornell University Press.

———. 1993. The early Upper Paleolithic: The view from the Levant. In *Before Lascaux: The Complex Record of the Early Upper Paleolithic*, ed. H. Knecht, A. Pike-Tay, and R. White, 5–21. Boca Raton, FL: CRC Press.

Martin, P. S. 1967. Prehistoric overkill. In *Pleistocene Extinctions: The Search for a Cause*, ed. P. S. Martin and H. E. Wright, 75–120. New Haven, CT: Yale University Press.

Martin, P. S., and H. E. Wright, eds. 1967. *Pleistocene Extinctions: The Search for a Cause.* New Haven, CT: Yale University Press.

Martin, R. D. 1989. Evolution of the brain in early hominids. *Ossa* 14:49–62.

Martin, S., and N. Grube. 2008. *Chronicle of the Maya Kings and Queens.* London: Thames and Hudson.

Mascarelli, A. L. 2009. Quaternary geologists win timescale vote. *Nature* 459:624.

Matsuoka, Y., Y. Vigouroux, M. Goodman, J. Sanchez G., E. Buckler, and J. Doebley. 2002. A single domestication for maize shown by multilocus microsatellite genotyping. *Proceedings of the National Academy of Science* 99:6080–6084.

Maureille, B. 2002. A lost Neanderthal neonate found. *Nature* 419:33.

McCamant, J. F. 1992. Quinoa's roundabout journey to world use. In *Chilies to Chocolate: Food the Americas Gave the World,* ed. N. Foster and L. S. Cordell, 123–141. Tuscon: University of Arizona Press.

McDermott, F., R. Grün, C. B. Stringer, and C. J. Hawkesworth. 1993. Mass-spectrometric U-series dates for Israeli Neanderthal/early modern hominid sites. *Nature* 363:252–255.

McDougall, I., F. H. Brown, and J. G. Fleagle. 2005. Stratigraphic placement and age of modern humans from Kibish, Ethiopia. *Nature* 433:733–736.

McGrew, W. C. 2010. Chimpanzee technology. *Science* 328:579–580.

McHenry, H. M. 1991. Sexual dimorphism in *Australopithecus afarensis. Journal of Human Evolution* 20:21–32.

McIntosh, J. R. 2002. *A Peaceful Realm: The Rise and Fall of the Indus Civilization.* Boulder, CO: Westview Press.

McKillop, H. 1994. Ancient Maya tree-cropping. *Ancient Mesoamerica* 5:129–140.

McMahon, A., A. Soltysiak, and J. Weber. 2011. Late Chalcolithic mass graves at Tell Brak, Syria, and violent conflict during the growth of early city-states. *Journal of Field Archaeology* 36:201–220.

McPherron, S. P., Z. Alemseged, C. W. Marean, J. G. Wynn, D. Reed, D. Geraads, R. Bobe, and H. A. Béarat. 2010. Evidence for stone-tool-assisted consumption of animal tissues before 3.39 million years ago at Dikika, Ethiopia. *Nature* 466:857–860.

Medina-Elizalde, M., and E. J. Rohling. 2012. Collapse of Classic Maya civilization related to modest reduction in precipitation. *Science* 335:956–959.

Megaw, J. V. S., and D. D. A. Simpson, eds. 1979. *Introduction to British Prehistory.* Leicester, England: Leicester University Press.

Mehringer, P. J., and F. F. Foit Jr. 1990. Volcanic ash dating of the Clovis cache at East Wenatchee, Washington. *National Geographic Research* 6(4):495–503.

Meikeljohn, C. 1978. Ecological aspects of population size and growth in late-glacial and early postglacial northwestern Europe. In *The Early Postglacial Settlement of Northern Europe: An Ecological Perspective,* ed. P. Mellars, 65–79. Pittsburgh, PA: University of Pittsburgh Press.

Mellaart, J. 1965. *Earliest Civilizations of the Near East.* London: Thames and Hudson.

Mellars, P. 1978. Excavation and economic analysis of Mesolithic shell middens on the Island of Oronsay (Inner Hebrides). In *The Early Postglacial Settlement of Northern Europe: An Ecological Perspective,* ed. P. Mellars, 371–396. Pittsburgh, PA: University of Pittsburgh Press.

———, ed. 1990. *The Emergence of Modern Humans: An Archaeological Perspective.* Ithaca, NY: Cornell University Press.

———. 2004. Neanderthals and the modern human colonization of Europe. *Nature* 432:461–465.

Mellars, P., and P. Dark. 1998. *Star Carr in Context.* Cambridge, England: McDonald Institute for Archaeological Research.

Mellars, P., and J. C. French. 2011. Tenfold population increase in Western Europe at the Neandertal-to-modern transition. *Science* 333:623–627.

Meltzer, D. 1989. Why don't we know when the first people came to North America? *American Antiquity* 54:471–490.

———. 1993a. Is there a Clovis adaptation? In *From Kostenki to Clovis: Upper Paleolithic-Paleoindian Adaptations,* ed. O. Soffer and N. Preslov, 293–310. New York: Plenum.

Meltzer, D. J. 1993b. Pleistocene peopling of the Americas. *Evolutionary Anthropology* 1(5):157–169.

———. 1997. Monte Verde and the Plesitocene peopling of America. *Science* 276:754–755.

———. 2009. *First Peoples in a New World: Colonizing Ice Age America.* Berkeley: University of California Press.

Mercader, J., M. Panger, and C. Boesch. 2002. Excavation of a chimpanzee stone tool site in the African rainforest. *Science* 296:1452–1455.

Mercier, N., H. Valladas, J.-L. Joron, J.-L. Reyss, F. Léveque, and B. Vandermeersch. 1991. Thermoluminescence dating of the late Neanderthal remains from Saint-Césaire. *Nature* 351:737–739.

Merpert, N. Y., and R. M. Munchaev. 1987. The earliest levels at Yarim Tepe I and Yarim Tepe II in northern Iraq. *Iraq* 49:1–36.

Miller, N. 1992. The origins of plant cultivation in the Near East. In *The Origins of Agriculture: An International Perspective,* ed. C. W. Cowan and P. J. Watson, 39–58. Washington, DC: Smithsonian Institution Press.

Millon, R. 1967. Teotihuacán. *Scientific American* 216:38–49.

———. 1981. Teotihucán: City, state, and civilization. In *Supplement to the Handbook of Middle American Indians,* Vol. 1, ed. J. Sabloff, 198–243. Austin: University of Texas Press.

———. 1992. Teotihuacan residential architecture. Paper presented at the 57th annual meeting of the Society for American Archaeology, Pittsburgh.

Minnis, P. E. 1992. Earliest plant cultivation in the desert borderlands of North America. In *The Origins of Agriculture: An International Perspective*, ed. C. W. Cowan and P. J. Watson, 121–141. Washington, DC: Smithsonian Institution Press.

Mitchell, L. 1999. Earliest Egyptian glyphs. *Archaeology* 52 (2):28–29.

Moeller, R. 1980. *6LF21: A Paleo-Indian Site in Western Connecticut*. Washington, CT: American Indian Archaeological Institute.

Molnar, S., and I. M. Molnar. 1985. The incidence of enamel hypoplasia among the Krapina Neandertals. *American Anthropologist* 87:536–549.

Morgan, J. 2008. Dig pinpoints Stonehenge Origins. September 21, 2008. http://ncws.bbc.co.uk/2/hi/science/nature/7625145.stm.

Morgan, L. H. 1877. *Ancient Society*. Cambridge, MA: Belknap Press.

Morgan, M., J. Kingston, and B. Marino. 1994. Carbon isotope evidence for the emergence of C4 plants in the Neogene from Pakistan and Kenya. *Nature* 367: 162–165.

Morlan, R. E. 1970. Wedge-shaped core technology in northern North America. *Arctic Anthropology* 7(2):17–37.

Morris, C., and A. von Hagen 1993. *The Inka Empire and Its Andean Origins*. New York: American Museum of Natural History.

Morwood, M. J., P. B. O'Sullivan, F. Aziz, and A. Raza. 1998. Fission-track ages of stone tools and fossils on the east Indonesian island of Flores. *Nature* 392:173–176.

Morwood, M. J., R. P. Soejono, R. G. Roberts, T. Sutikna, C. S. M. Turney, K. E. Westaway, W. J. Rink, et al. 2004. Archaeology and age of a new hominin from Flores in eastern Indonesia. *Nature* 431:1087–1091.

Morwood, M. J., and P. v. Oosterzee. 2006. *Discovery of the Hobbit: The Scientific Breakthrough that Changed the Face of Human History*. New York: Random House.

Mourre, V., P. Villa, and C. S. Henshilwood. 2010. Early use of pressure flaking on lithic artifacts at Blombos Cave, South Africa. *Science* 330:659–662.

Mowat, F. 1987. *Woman in the Mists*. New York: Warner Books.

Mulvaney, J., and J. Kamminga. 1999. *Prehistory of Australia*. Washington, DC: Smithsonian Institution Press.

Napier, J. 1967. The antiquity of human wallking. *Scientific American* 216(4):56–66.

Ndoro, W. 1997. Great Zimbabwe. *Scientific American* 277(5): 62–67.

Nelson, S. M. 1993. *The Archaeology of Korea*. Cambridge, England: Cambridge University Press.

Newcomer, M. 1971. Some quantitative experiments in handaxe manufacture. *World Archaeology* 3:85–94.

Niewoehner, W. A. 2001. Behavioral inferences from the Skhul/Qafzeh early modern human hand remains. *Proceedings of the National Academy of Sciences* 98:2979–2984.

Normille, D. 1997. Yangtze seen as earliest rice site. *Science* 275:309.

———. 2012. Experiments probe language's origins and development. *Science* 336:408–411.

Nur, A., and D. Burgess. 2008. *Apocalypse: Earthquakes, Archaeology, and the Wrath of God*. Princeton, NJ: Princeton University Press.

Oates, J. 1973. The background and development of early farming communities in Mesopotamia and the Zagros. *Proceedings of the Prehistoric Society (London)* 39:147–181.

O'Connell, J. F., and J. Allen. 1998. When did humans first arrive in Greater Australia and why is it important to know? *Evolutionary Anthropology* 6(4):132–146.

O'Connor, D. 1993. *Ancient Nubia: Egypt's Rival in Africa*. Philadelphia, PA: University of Pennsylvania, University Museum.

Oglivie, M. D., B. K. Curran, and E. Trinkaus. 1989. Incidence and patterning of dental enamel hypoplasia among the Neandertals. *American Journal of Physical Anthropology* 79:25–41.

Ohnuma, K., and C. A. Bergman. 1990. A technological analysis of the Upper Paleolithic levels (XXV–VI) of Ksar Akil. In *The Emergence of Modern Humans: An Archaeological Perspective*, ed. P. Mellars, 91–138. Ithaca, NY: Cornell University Press.

Olding-Smee, L. 2007. Dig links Stonehenge to circle of life. *Nature* 445:574.

Oliva, M. 1993. The Aurignacian in Moravia. In *Before Lascaux: The Complex Record of the Early Upper Paleolithic*, ed. H. Knecht, A. Pike-Tay, and R. White, 37–55. Boca Raton, FL: CRC Press.

Outram, A. K., N. A. Stear, R. Bendrey, S. Olsen, A. Kasparov, V. Zaibert, N. Thorpe, and R. P. Evershed. 2009. The earliest horse harnessing and milking. *Science* 323: 1332–1335.

Owen, R. C. 1984. The Americas: The case against an Ice-Age human population. In *The Origins of Modern Humans: A World Survey of the Fossil Evidence*, ed. F. H. Smith and F. Spencer, 517–564. New York: Liss.

Pääbo, S. 1989. Ancient DNA: extraction, characterization, molecular cloning, and enzymatic amplification. *Proceedings of the National Academy of Sciences* 86:1939–1943.

Page, C., and J. Cort. 1997. *Secrets of Lost Empires: Stonehenge*. Boston: WGBH.

Pappu, S., Y. Gunnell, K. Akhilesh, R. Braucher, M. Taieb, F. Demory, and N. Thouveny. 2011. Early Pleistocene presence of Acheulian hominins in South India. *Science* 331:1596–1598.

Parés, J. M., and A. Pérez-González. 1995. Paleomagnetic age for hominid fossils at Atapuerca archaeological site, Spain. *Science* 269:830–832.

Parfit, M. 2000. The hunt for the first Americans. *National Geographic* 198(6):35–39.

Parfitt, S. A., N. M. Ashton, S. G. Lewis, R. L. Able, G. R. Coope, M. H. Field, R. Gale, et al. 2010. Early Pleistocene human occupation at the edge of the boreal zone in northwest Europe. *Nature* 466:229–233.

Park, M. P. 2012. *Exploring Evolution*. London: Vivays.

Pascua, M. P. 1991. A Makah village in 1491: Ozette. *National Geographic* 180(4):38–53.

Pasztory, E. 1997. *Teotihuacan: An Experiment in Living*. Norman: University of Oklahoma Press.

Patterson, T. C. 1993. *Archaeology: The Historical Development of Civilizations*. Englewood Cliffs, NJ: Prentice Hall.

Pauketat, T. R. 1994. *The Ascent of Chiefs: Cahokia and Mississippian Politics in Native America*. Tuscaloosa: University of Alabama Press.

Pauketat, T. R. 2009. *Cahokia: Ancient America's Great City on the Mississippi*. New York: Viking.

Pavlov, P., J. I. Svendsen, and S. Indrelid. 2001. Human presence in the European Arctic nearly 40,000 years ago. *Nature* 413:64–68.

Pearsall, D. 1992. The origins of plant cultivation in South America. In *The Origins of Agriculture: An International Perspective*, ed. C. W. Cowan and P. J. Watson, 173–205. Washington, DC: Smithsonian Institution Press.

Peck, A., and C. Andrade-Watkins. 1980. *Other People's Garbage*. DVD. Watertown, MA: Documentary Educational Resources.

Perkins, S. 2007. North by northwest: The planet's wandering magnetic poles help reveal history of Earth and humans. *Science News* 172:392–394.

Phelan, A. H. 1988. *Gorillas in the Mist: The Story of Dian Fossey*. Film. Directed by Michael Apted. Universal City, CA: Universal Studios.

Phillipson, D. W. 1993. *African Archaeology*, 2nd ed. Cambridge, England: Cambridge University Press.

Piaget, J., and B. Inhelder. 1969. *The Psychology of the Child*. London: Routledge and Kegan Paul.

Pickering, R., P. H. G. M. Dirks, Z. Jinnah, D. J. d. Ruiter, S. E. Churchill, A. I. R. Herries, J. D. Woodhead, et al. 2011. *Australopithecus sediba* at 1.977 ma and implications for the origins of the genus *Homo*. *Science* 333:1421–1422.

Pike, A. W. G., D. L. Hoffman, M. García-Diez, P. B. Pettitt, J. Alcolea, R. D. Balbín, C. González-Sainz, et al. 2012. U-series dating of Paleolithic art in 11 caves in Spain. *Science* 336:1409–1413.

Pineda, R. F. 1988. The late Preceramic and Initial Period. In *Peruvian Prehistory*, ed. R. W. Keatinge, 67–96. Cambridge, England: Cambridge University Press.

Piperno, D., and K. A. Stothert. 2003. Phytolith evidence for early Holocene *Cucurbita* domestication in southwest Ecuador. *Science* 299:1054–1057.

Piperno, D. R., and D. M. Pearsall. 1998. *The Origins of Agriculture in the Lowland Neotropics*. Orlando, FL: Academic Press.

Piperno, D. R., A. J. Ranere, I. Holst, and P. Hansell. 2000. Starch grains reveal early root crop horticulture in the Panamanian tropical forest. *Nature* 407:894–897.

Piperno, D. R., E. Weiss, I. Holst, and D. Nadel. 2004. Processing of wild cereal grains in the Upper Paleolithic revealed by starch grain analysis. *Nature* 430:670–673.

Pitts, M., and M. Roberts. 2000. *Fairweather Eden: Life Half a Million Years Ago as Revealed by the Excavations at Boxgrove*. New York: Fromm International.

Pitulko, V. V., P. A. Nikolsky, E. Y. Girya, A. E. Basilyan, V. E. Tumskoy, S. A. Koulakov, S. N. Astakhov, et al. 2004. The Yana RHS site: Humans in the Arctic before the last glacial maximum. *Science* 303: 52–56.

Pizarro, P. 1986. *Relación del descubrimiento y conquista de los reinos del Perú*. Lima: Pontificia Universidad Católica del Perú.

Polyak, V., C. Hill, and Y. Asmerom. 2008. Age and evolution of the Grand Canyon revealed by U-Pb dating of water table-type speleothems. *Science* 319:1377–1380.

Ponce de Léon, M., and C. Zollikofer. 2001. Neanderthal cranial ontogeny and its implications for late hominid diversity. *Nature* 412:534–538.

Pool, C. 2007. *Olmec Archaeology and Early Mesoamerica*. Cambridge, England: Cambridge University Press.

Pope, G. G. 1992. Craniofacial evidence for the origin of modern humans in China. *Yearbook of Physical Anthropology* 35:243–298.

Pope, K. O., M. E. D. Pohl, J. G. Jones, D. L. Lentz, V. von Nagy, F. J. Vega, and I. R. Quitmyer. 2001. Origin and environmental setting of ancient agriculture in the lowlands of Mesoamerica. *Science* 292:1370–1373.

Possehl, G. L. 1980. *Indus Civilization in Saurashtra*. Delhi, India: B. R. Publishing.

Potter, B. A., J. D. Irish, J. D. Reuther, C. Gelvin-Reymiller, and V. T. Holliday. 2011. A terminal Pleistocene child cremation and residential structure from eastern Beringia. *Science* 331:1058–1061.

Potts, R., A. K. Behrensmeyer, A. Deino, P. Ditchfield, and J. Clark. 2004. Small mid-Pleistocene hominin associated with East African Acheulean technology. *Science* 305:75–77.

Powell, E. 2005. The turquoise trail. *Archaeology* 58(1): 24–29.

Powers, W. R., and T. D. Hamilton. 1978. Dry Creek: A Late Pleistocene human occupation in central Alaska. In *Early Man in America From a Circum-Pacific Perspective*, ed. A. L. Bryan, 72–77. Edmonton, Canada: Archaeological Researches International.

Powers, W. R., and J. F. Hoffecker. 1989. Late Pleistocene settlement in the Nenana Valley, central Alaska. *American Antiquity* 54:263–287.

Price, A. G., ed. 1971. *The Explorations of Captain James Cook in the Pacific: As Told by Selections of His Own Journals 1768–1779.* New York: Dover Publications.

Price, T. D. 1987. The Mesolithic of western Europe. *Journal of World Prehistory* 1:225–305.

———. 1991. The view from Europe: Concepts and questions about terminal Pleistocene societies. In *The First Americans: Search and Research*, ed. T. D. Dillehay and D. J. Meltzer, 185–208. Boca Raton, FL: CRC Press.

———. 2000. *Europe's First Farmers.* Cambridge, England: Cambridge University Press.

Pringle, H. 1997. Ice Age communities may be earliest known net hunters. *Science* 277:1203–1204.

———. 1998. New women of the Ice Age. *Discover* April: 62–69.

———. 2001. The first urban center in the Americas. *Science* 292:621–622.

Pringle, H. 2011a. The curse of the mummy's arteries. *Science* 332:157.

———. 2011b. Lofty ambitions of the Inca. *National Geographic* 219(4):34–61.

Purugganan, M. D., and D. Q. Fuller. 2009. The nature of selection during plant domestication. *Nature* 457:843–848.

Quade, J., N. Levin, S. Semaw, S. Sileshi, R. Dietrich, P. Renne, M. Rogers, and S. Simpson. 2004. Paleoenvironments of the earliest stone tool makers, Gona, Ethiopia. *Geological Society of America Bulletin* 116:1529–1544.

Quilter, J., B. Ojeda E., D. M. Pearsall, D. H. Sandweiss, J. G. Jones, and E. S. Wing. 1991. Subsistence economy of El Paraíso, an early Peruvian site. *Science* 251:277–283.

Raloff, J. 1993. Corn's slow path to stardom. *Science News* 143:248–250.

Ramenofsky, A. F. 1987. *Vectors of Death.* Albuquerque: University of New Mexico Press.

Ramsey, C. B., M. W. Dee, J. M. R. F. G. Higham, S. A. Harris, F. Brock, A. Quiles, E. M. Wild, et al. 2010. Radiocarbon-based chronology for dynastic Egypt. *Science* 328:1554–1557.

Rasmussen, M., et al. 2011. An Aboriginal Australian genome reveals separate human dispersals into Asia. *Science* 334:94–98.

Raven, C. E. 1950. *John Ray, Naturalist: His Life and Works.* Cambridge, England: Cambridge University Press.

Ray, J. 1691. *The Wisdom of God Manifested in the Works of the Creation.* New York: Georg Olms Verlag, 1974.

Reich, D., et al. 2010. Genetic history of an archaic hominin group from Denisova Cave in Siberia. *Nature* 468:1053–1060.

Reich, D., et al. 2012. Reconstructing Native American population history. *Nature* 488:370–374.

Reid, J. 1989. A Grasshopper perspective on the Mogollon of the Arizona mountains. In *Dynamics of Southwest Prehistory*, ed. L. S. Cordell and G. J. Gummerman, 65–97. Washington, DC: Smithsonian Institution Press.

Reid, J., and S. Whittlesey. 1997. *The Archaeology of Ancient Arizona.* Tuscon: University of Arizona Press.

Reimer, P. J., et al. 2004. Radiocarbon calibration from 0–26 cal kyr BP. *Radiocarbon* 46:1029–1058.

Renfrew, C. 1972. *The Emergence of Civilization.* London: Methuen.

———. 1979. *Before Civilization: The Radiocarbon Revolution and Prehistoric Europe.* Cambridge, England: Cambridge University Press.

Rice, P. 1981. Prehistoric Venuses: Symbols of motherhood or womanhood. *Journal of Anthropological Research* 37:402–414.

Rice, P., and A. Paterson. 1985. Cave art and bones: Exploring the interrelationships. *American Anthropologist* 87: 94–100.

———. 1986. Validating the cave art-archaeofaunal relationship in Cantabrian Spain. *American Anthropologist* 88:658–667.

———. 1988. Anthropomorphs in cave art: An empirical assessment. *American Anthropologist* 90:664–774.

Richards, M. P., P. P. Pettitt, E. Trinkaus, F. H. Smith, M., Paunovi, and I. Karavani. 2000. Neanderthal diet at Vindija and Neanderthal predation: The evidence from stable isotopes. *Proceedings of the National Academy of Sciences* 97:7663–7666.

Richards, M. P., R. J. Schulting, and R. E. M. Hedges. 2003. Sharp shift in diet at onset of Neolithic. *Nature* 425:366.

Richardson, J. B. III. 1994. *People of the Andes.* Exploring the Ancient World. Washington, DC: Smithsonian Books.

Richmond, B. G., and W. L. Jungers. 2008. *Orrorin tugenensis* femoral morphology and the evolution of Hominin bipedalism. *Science* 319:1662–1665.

Rightmire, G. P. 1979. Implications of Border Cave skeletal remains for later Pleistocene evolution. *Current Anthropology* 20:23–35.

———. 1984. *Homo sapiens* in sub-Saharan Africa. In *The Origins of Modern Humans: A World Survey of the Fossil Evidence*, ed. F. H. Smith and F. Spencer, 295–326. New York: Liss.

———. 1990. *The Evolution of Homo Erectus: Comparative Anatomical Studies of an Extinct Human Species.* New York: Cambridge University Press.

———. 1991. Comparative studies of late Pleistocene human remains from Klasies River Mouth, South Africa. *Journal of Human Evolution* 20:131–156.

Rindos, D. 1984. *The Origins of Agriculture: An Evolutionary Perseptive.* New York: Academic Press.

Ritchie, W. A. 1971. *A Typology and Nomenclature for New York State Projectile Points*. Albany: New York State Museum.

Roberts, D. 1997. *In Search of the Old Ones: Exploring the Anasazi World of the Southwest*. New York: Simon & Schuster.

Roberts, R. G., and B. W. Brook. 2010. And then there were none? *Science* 327:420–422.

Roberts, R., T. F. Flannery, L. K. Ayliffe, H. Yoshida, J. M. Olley, G. J. Prideaux, G. M. Laslett, et al. 2001. New ages for the last Australian megafauna: Continent-wide extinction about 46,000 years ago. *Science* 292:1888–1892.

Rodriguez-Martinez, M. d. C., P. O. Ceballos, M. D. Coe, R. A. Diehl, S. D. Houston, K. A. Taube, and A. D. Calderon. 2006. Oldest writing in the New World. *Science* 313:1610–1614.

Rose, M. 1993. Early skull found in Java. *Archaeology* 46 (5):18.

———. 1995. The last Neandertals. *Archaeology* 48:12–13.

Rose, M. D. 1983. Miocene hominoid postcranial morphology: Monkey-like, ape-like, neither, or both? In *New Interpretations of Ape and Human Ancestry*, ed. R. L. Ciochon and R. S. Corruccini, 405–420. New York: Plenum.

Rosenberg, K. R. 1992. The evolution of modern human childbirth. *Yearbook of Physical Anthropology* 35:89–124.

Ross, P. E. 1991. Mutt and Jeff: Did Cro-Magnons and Neanderthals co-exist? *Scientific American* September:40–48.

Ruff, C. B. 1993. Climatic adaptation and hominid evolution: The thermoregulatory imperative. *Evolutionary Anthropology* 2(2):53–60.

Ruff, C. B., E. Trinkaus, A. Walker, and C. S. Larsen. 1993. Postcranial robusticity in *Homo*. I: Temporal trends and mechanical interpretation. *American Journal of Physical Anthropology* 91:21–53.

Ruggles, C. 1996. Stonehenge for the 1990s. *Nature* 381: 278–279.

Rule, S., B. W. Brook, S. G. Harberle, C. S. M. Turney, A. P. Kershaw, and C. N. Johnson. 2012. The aftermath of megafaunal extinction: Ecosystem transformation in Pleistocene Australia. *Science* 335:1483–1486.

Ruspoli, M. 1986. *The Cave of Lascaux: The Final Photographs*. New York: Henry N. Abrams.

Russo, M. 1996. Southeastern Archaic mounds. In *Archaeology of the Mid-Holocene Southeast*, ed. K. E. Sassaman and D. G. Anderson, 259–287. Gainesville: University Press of Florida.

Sabloff, J. 1994. *The New Archaeology and the Ancient Maya*. New York: Scientific American Library.

Sabloff, J. A. 1989. *The Cities of Ancient Mexico: Reconstructing a Lost World*. London: Thames and Hudson.

Salazar, L. C. 2004. Machu Picchu: Mysterious royal estate in the cloud forest. In *Machu Picchu: Unveiling the Mystery of the Incas*, ed. R. L. Burger and L. C. Salazar, 21–47. New Haven, CT: Yale University Press.

Saunders, J. W., R. D. Mandel, R. T. Saucier, E. T. Allen, C. T. Hallmark, J. K. Johnson, E. H. Jackson, et al. 1997. A mound complex in Louisiana at 5400–5000 years before the present. *Science* 277:1796–1799.

Saura Ramos, P. A. 1998. *The Cave of Altamira*. New York: Harry N. Abrams.

Schele, L., and D. Freidel. 1990. *A Forest of Kings: The Untold Story of the Ancient Maya*. New York: Quill William.

Schiffer, M. B. 1976. *Behavioral Archaeology*. New York: Academic Press.

Schmandt-Besserat, D. 1992. *Before Writing: From Counting to Cuneiform* (2 vols.). Austin: University of Texas Press.

———. 1996. *How Writing Came About*. Austin: University of Texas Press.

———. 2002. Signs of life. *Odyssey* January/February:6–7, 63.

Schmid, R. E. 2008. Study: Stonehenge was a burial site for centuries. May 29, 2008. http://esciencenews.com/sources/newsvine/2008/05/29/study.stonehenge.was.a.burial.site.centuries

Scholz, M., L. Bachmann, G. J. Nicholson, J. Bachmann, I. Giddings, B. Rüschoff-Thale, A. Czarnetzki, and C. M. Pusch. 2000. Genomic differentiation of Neanderthals and anatomically modern man allows a fossil-DNA-based classification of morphologically indistinguishable hominid bones. *American Journal of Human Genetics* 66:1927–1932.

Schrenk, F., T. Bromage, C. Betzler, U. Ring, and Y. Juwayayi. 1993. Oldest *Homo* and Pliocene biogeography of the Malawi Rift. *Nature* 365:833–836.

Schwartz, J. H. 2004. Getting to know *Homo erectus*. *Science* 305:53–54.

Scott, G. R., and L. Gibert. 2009. The oldest hand-axes in Europe. *Nature* 461:82–85.

Sebastian, L. 1992. *The Chaco Anasazi: Sociopolitical Evolution in the Prehistoric Southwest*. Cambridge, England: Cambridge University Press.

Semaw, S., P. Renne, J. W. K. Harris, C. S. Feibel, R. L. Bernor, N. Fesseha, and K. Mowbray. 1997. 2.5-million-year-old stone tools from Gona, Ethiopia. *Nature* 385:333–336.

Service, E. 1975. *The Origins of the State and Civilization: The Process of Cultural Evolution*. New York: W. W. Norton & Company.

Severinghaus, J. P., T. Sowers, E. J. Brook, R. B. Alley, and M. L. Bender. 1998. Timing of the abrupt climate change at the end of the Younger Dryas interval from thermally fractionated gases in polar ice. *Nature* 391:141–146.

Shackleton, N., and N. Opdyke. 1973. Oxygen isotope and paleomagnetic stratigraphy of equatorial Pacific core V28–238: Oxygen isotope temperatures and ice volumes on a 10^5 and 10^6 year scale. *Quaternary Research* 3:39–55.

———. 1976. Oxygen-isotope and paleomagnetic stratigraphy of Pacific core V28–239 Late Pliocene and latest Pleistocene. In *Investigation of Late Quaternary Paleoceanography and Paleoclimatology,* Vol. 145, ed. R. M. Cline and J. Hays, 449–464. Boulder, CO: Geological Society of America.

Shapiro, H. L. 1974. *Peking Man.* New York: Simon & Schuster.

Sharer, R. J., and W. Ashmore. 1993. *Archaeology: Discovering Our Past.* Mountain View, CA: Mayfield Publishing.

Sharer, R., and D. Grove. 1989. *Regional Perspectives on the Olmec.* New York: Cambridge University Press.

Shaw, I., ed. 2000. *The Oxford History of Ancient Egypt.* Oxford, England: Oxford University Press.

Shaw, J. 2003. Who built the pyramids? *Harvard Magazine* July/August:43–49, 99.

Shea, J. J. 1990. A further note on Mousterian spear points. *Journal of Field Archaeology* 17:111–114.

———. 1992. Lithic microwear analysis in archaeology. *Evolutionary Anthropology* 1(4):143–150.

Shea, J. 2007. Behavioral differences between Middle and Upper Paleolithic *Homo sapiens* in the East Mediterranen Levant. *Journal of Anthropological Research* 63:449–488.

Shermer, M., and A. Grobman. 2000. *Denying History: Who Says the Holocaust Never Happened and Why Do They Say It?* Berkeley: University of California Press.

Shipman, P. 1984. Scavenger hunt. *Natural History* 93:20–27.

———. 1986. Scavenging or hunting in early hominids: Theoretical framework and tests. *American Anthropologist* 88:27–43.

———. 1990. Old masters. *Discover* 11:60–65.

———. 2000. Doubting Dmanisi. *American Scientist* 88(6):491.

———. 2011. *The Animal Connection: A New Perspective on What Makes Us Human.* New York: W. W. Norton.

Shipman, P., and J. Rose. 1983. Evidence of butchery and hominid activities at Torralba and Ambrona: An evaluation using microscopic techniques. *Journal of Archaeological Science* 10:465–474.

Shreeve, J. 1996. New skeleton gives path from trees to ground an odd turn. *Science* 272:654.

Shreeve, J. 2010. The evolutionary road. *National Geographic* 218:34–67.

Silverberg, R. 1989. *The Mound Builders.* Athens: Ohio University Press.

Simek, J. F. 1992. Neanderthal cognition and the Middle to Upper Paleolithic transition. In *Continuity or Replacement: Controversies in* Homo sapiens *Evolution,* ed. G. Bräuer and F. Smith, 231–246. Rotterdam, The Netherlands: Balkema.

Simmons, A. H. 1986. New evidence for the early use of cultigens in the American Southwest. *American Antiquity* 51:73–89.

Simpson, S. W., J. Quade, N. E. Levin, R. Butler, G. Dupont-Nivet, M. Everett, and S. Semaw. 2008. A female *Homo erectus* pelvis from Gona, Ethiopia. *Science* 322:1089–1091.

Sinclair, A. 2003. Art of the ancients. *Nature* 426:774–775.

Singer, R., and J. Wymer. 1982. *The Middle Stone Age at Klasies River Mouth in South Africa.* Chicago, IL: University of Chicago Press.

Skoglund, P., H. Malmström, M. Raghavan, J. Storå, P. Hall, E. Willerslev, M. T. P. Gilbert, et al. 2012. Origins and genetic legacy of Neolithic farmers and hunter-gatherers in Europe. *Science* 336:466–469.

Slimak, L., J. I. Svendsen, J. Mangerud, H. Plisson, H. P. Heggen, A. Brugère, and P. Y. Pavlov. 2011. Late Mousterian persistence near the Arctic Circle. *Science* 332: 841–844.

Smith, B. 1989. Origins of agriculture in eastern North America. *Science* 246:1566–1570.

———. 1997. The initial domestication of *Cucurbita pepo* in the Americas 10,000 years ago. *Science* 276:932–934.

Smith, B. D. 1992. Prehistoric plant husbandry in eastern North America. In *The Origins of Agriculture: An International Perspective,* ed. C. W. Cowan and P. J. Watson, 101–119. Washington, DC: Smithsonian Institution Press.

———. 1995. *The Emergence of Agriculture.* New York: Scientific American Library.

———. 2007. The ultimate ecosystem engineers. *Science* 315:1797–1798.

Smith, B. H. 1993. The physiological age of KNM-WT 15000. In *The Nariokotome* Homo erectus *Skeleton,* ed. A. Walker and R. Leakey, 195–220. Cambridge, MA: Harvard University Press.

Smith, C. 1992. *Late Stone Age Hunters of the British Isles.* London: Routledge.

Smith, F. H. 1991. The Neandertals: Evolutionary dead ends or ancestors of modern people? *Journal of Anthropological Research* 47(2):219–238.

Smith, F. H., E. Trinkaus, P. B. Pettitt, I. Karavani, and M. Paunovic. 1999. Direct radiocarbon dates for Vindija G1 and Velika Peina Late Pleistocene hominid remains. *Proceedings of the National Academy of Sciences* 96:12281–12286.

Smith, M. A. 1987. Pleistocene occupation in arid Central Australia. *Nature* 328:710–711.

Smith, M. E. 1997. Life in the provinces of the Aztec Empire. *Scientific American* 277(3):76–83.

Smith, P., O. Bar-Yosef, and A. Sillen. 1985. Archaeological and skeletal evidence for dietary change during the Late Pleistocene/Early Holocene in the Levant. In *Paleopathology at the Origin of Agriculture,* ed. M. N. Cohen and G. J. Armelagos, 101–130. New York: Academic Press.

Snow, D. 1980. *The Archaeology of New England.* New York: Academic Press.

Sockol, M. D., D. A. Raichlen, and H. Pontzer. 2007. Chimpanzee locomotor energetics and the origin of human bipedalism. *Proceedings of the National Academy of Sciences* 104:12265–12269.

———. 1993. Upper-Paleolithic adaptations in central and eastern Europe and man-mammoth interactions. In *From Kostenki to Clovis: Upper Paleolithic-Paleoindian Adaptations*, ed. O. Soffer and N. Preslov, 31–50. New York: Plenum.

———. 1994. Ancestral lifeways in Eurasia: The Middle and Upper Paleolithic record. In *Origins of Anatomically Modern Humans*, ed. M. Nitecki and D. Nitecki, 101–119. New York: Plenum.

Solecki, R. 1971. *Shanidar: The First Flower People*. New York: Knopf.

Solis, F. 2004. *The Aztec Empire*. New York: Solomon G. Guggenheim Foundation.

Solis, R. S., J. Haas, and W. Creamer. 2001. Dating Caral, a preceramic site in the Supe Valley on the central coast of Peru. *Science* 292:723–726.

Soustelle, J. 1964. *Daily Life of the Aztecs*. London, Pelican.

Spence, M. W. 1974. Residential practices and the distribution of skeletal traits in Teotihuacan, Mexico. *Man* 9:262–273.

Spencer, H. 1967. *The Evolution of Society (selections from Principles of Sociology: vol. 1, 1876; vol. 2, 1882; vol. 3, 1896)*. Chicago, IL: University of Chicago Press.

Spinney, L. 2008. The lost world. *Nature* 454:151–153.

Sponheimer, M., B. H. Passey, D. J. de Ruiter, D. Guatelli-Steinberg, T. E. Cerling, and J. A. Lee-Thorp. 2006. Isotopic evidence for dietary variability in the early Hominin *Paranthropus robustus*. *Science* 314:980–981.

Spoor, F., M. G. Leakey, P. N. Gathogo, F. H. Brown, S. C. Antón, I. McDougall, C. Kiarie, and F. K. Manthi 2007. Implications of new early *Homo* fossils from Ileret, East of Lake Turkana, Kenya. *Nature* 448:688–691.

Squier, E. G., and E. H. Davis. 1848. *Ancient Monuments of the Mississippi Valley: Comprising the Results of Extensive Original Surveys and Excavations*. Smithsonian Contributions to Knowledge, Vol 1. 1973 reprint. New York: AMS Press.

Stanford, D., and B. Bradley. 2000. The Solutrean solution: Did some ancient Americans come from Europe? *Discovering Archaeology* 2(1):54–55.

Stanford, D. J., and B. Bradley. 2012. *Across the Atlantic Ice: The Origin of America's Clovis Culture*. Berkeley: University of California Press.

Stiebing W. H. Jr. 1993. *Uncovering the Past: A History of Archaeology*. New York: Oxford University Press.

Stiles, D. 1991. Early hominid behaviour and culture tradition: Raw material studies in Bed II, Olduvai Gorge. *The African Archaeological Review* 9:1–19.

Stiner, M. 1994. *Honor Among Thieves: A Zooarchaeological Study of Neandertal Ecology*. Princeton, NJ: Princeton University Press.

Stone, R. 2009. Signs of early *Homo sapiens* in China? *Science* 326:655.

Straus, L. G. 1989. Age of the modern Europeans. *Nature* 342:476–477.

———. 2000. Solutrean settlement of North America? A review of reality. *American Antiquity* 65:219–226.

Stringer, C. 2012a. *Lone Survivors: How We Came to Be the Only Humans on Earth*. New York: Times Books.

———. 2012b. *The Origin of Our Species*. London: Penguin Books.

Stringer, C., and P. Andrews. 2012. *The Complete World of Human Evolution*. London: Thames and Hudson.

Stringer, C., and C. Gamble. 1993. *In Search of the Neanderthals*. New York: Thames and Hudson.

Stringer, C. B. 1990. The emergence of modern humans. *Scientific American* 263:1263–1268.

———. 1992a. Reconstructing recent human evolution. *Philosophical Transactions of the Royal Society of London (B)* 337:217–224.

———. 1992b. Replacement, continuity, and the origin of *Homo sapiens*. In *Continuity or Replacement: Controversies in* Homo sapiens *Evolution*, ed. G. Bräuer and F. Smith, 9–24. Rotterdam, The Netherlands: Balkema.

———. 1994. Out of Africa: A personal history. In *Origins of Anatomically Modern Humans*, ed. M. Nitecki and D. Nitecki, 149–174. New York: Plenum.

Stringer, C. B., and P. Andrews. 1988. Genetic and fossil evidence for the origin of modern humans. *Science* 239:1263–1268.

Stringer, C. B., and R. Grün. 1991. Time for the last Neandertals. *Nature* 351:701–702.

Struever, S., and F. A. Holton. 1979. *Koster: Americans in Search of Their Prehistoric Past*, ed. Garden City, NY: Anchor Press/Doubleday.

———. 2000. *Koster: Americans in Search of Their Prehistoric Past*, 2nd ed. Prospect Heights, IL: Waveland Press.

Summerhayes, G. R., M. Leavesley, A. Fairbairn, H. Mandui, J. Field, A. Ford, and R. Fullagar. 2010. Human adaptation and plant use in Highland New Guinea 49,000 to 44,000 years ago. *Science* 330:78–82.

Suwa, G., B. Asfaw, Y. Beyene, T. D. White, S. Katoh, S. Nagaoka, H. Nakaya, et al. 1997. The first skull of *Australopithecus boisei*. *Nature* 389:489–492.

Svoboda, J. 1993. The complex origin of the Upper Paleolithic in the Czech and Slovak Republics. In *Before Lascaux: The Complex Record of the Early Upper Paleolithic*, ed. H. Knecht, A. Pike-Tay, and R. White, 23–36. Boca Raton, FL: CRC Press.

Swisher, C. C., G. H. Curtis, T. Jacob, A. G. Getty, A. Suprijo, and Widiasmoro. 1994. Age of the earliest known hominids in Java, Indonesia. *Science* 263:1118–1121.

Swisher C. C. III, W. J. Rink, S. C. Antón, H. P. Schwarcz, G. H. Curtis, A. Suprijo, and Widiasmoro. 1996. Latest *Homo erectus* of Java: Potential contemporaneity with *Homo sapiens* in Southeast Asia. *Science* 274:1870–1874.

Tague, R. G., and C. O. Lovejoy. 1986. The obstetric pelvis of A.L. 288–1 (Lucy). *Journal of Human Evolution* 15:237–255.

Tainter, J. 1988. *The Collapse of Complex Societies.* New York: Cambridge University Press.

Tanner, N. 1981. *On Becoming Human.* Cambridge, England: Cambridge University Press.

Tattersall, I. 2012. *Masters of the Planet: The Search for Human Origins.* New York: Palgrave Macmillan.

Terrell, J. 1986. *Prehistory in the Pacific Islands.* Cambridge, England: Cambridge University Press.

Thieme, H. 1997. Lower Paleolithic hunting spears from Germany. *Nature* 385:807–810.

Thomas, C. 1894. *Report on the Mound Explorations of the Bureau of American Ethnology,* 1985 ed. Washington DC: BAE (reprinted by the Smithsonian Institution).

Thomas, D. H. 2000. *Skull Wars: Kennewick Man, Archaeology, and the Battle for Native American Identity.* New York: Basic Books.

Thomas, G.V., and A. M. J. Silk. 1990. *An Introduction to the Psychology of Children's Drawings.* New York: New York University Press.

Thorne, A. G., and M. H. Wolpoff. 1992. The multiregional evolution of humans. *Scientific American* April:76–83.

Tocheri, M. W., C. M. Orr, S. G. Larson, T. Sutikna, Jatmiko, E. W. Saptomo, R. A. Due, et al. 2007. The primitive wrist of *Homo floresiensis* and its implications for hominin evolution. *Science* 317:1743–1745.

Topic, J. 1990. Craft production in the kingdom of Chimor. In *The Northern Dynasties: Kingship and Statecraft in Chimor,* ed. M. Moseley and A. Cordy-Collins. 145–176. Washington, DC: Dumbarton Oaks.

Toth, N. 1985. The Oldowan reassessed: A close look at early stone artifacts. *Journal of Archaeological Science* 2:101–120.

Travis, J. 2010. Grave disputes. *Science* 330:166–173.

Trinkaus, E. 1983a. Neandertal postcrania and the adaptive shift to modern humans. In *The Mousterian Legacy,* Vol. 164, 165–200. Oxford, England: British Archaeological Reports, International Series.

———. 1983b. *The Shanidar Neandertals.* New York: Academic Press.

———. 1986. The Neandertals and modern human origins. *Annual Review of Anthropology* 15:193–218.

———. 1989. The Upper Pleistocene transition. In *The Emergence of Modern Humans: Biocultural Adaptations in the Later Pleistocene,* ed. E. Trinkaus, 42–46. Cambridge, MA: Cambridge University Press.

Trinkaus, E., and P. Shipman. 1993. *The Neandertals: Changing Images of Mankind.* New York: Knopf.

Troy, C. C., D. E. MacHugh, J. F. Bailey, D. A. Magee, R. T. Loftus, P. Cunningham, A. T. Chamberlain, et al. 2001. Genetic evidence for Near-Eastern origins of European cattle. *Nature* 410:1088–1091.

Tung, T. A., and K. J. Knudson. 2011. Identifying locals, migrants, and captives in the Wari heartland: A bioarchaeological and biogeochemical study of human remains from Conchopata, Peru. *Journal of Anthropological Archaeology* 30(3):247–261.

Turney, C. S. M., T. F. Flannery, R. G. Roberts, C. Reid, L. K. Fifield, T. F. G. Higham, Z. Jacobs, et al. 2008. Late-surviving megafauna in Tasmania, Australia, implicate human involvement in their extinction. *Proceedings of the National Academy of Sciences* 105:12150–12153.

Two-Bears, D. R. 2006. Navajo archaeologist is not an oxymoron: A tribal archaeologist's experience. *American Indian Quarterly* 30(3&4):381–387.

Tyldesley, J. 2012. *Tutankhamen: The Search for an Egyptian King.* New York: Basic Books.

Ungar, P. S., and M. Sponheimer. 2011. The diets of early hominins. *Science* 334:190–193.

Unger-Hamilton, R. 1989. The epi-Paleolithic southern Levant and the origins of cultivation. *Current Anthropology* 30:88–103.

Urton, G. 2003 *Signs of the Inka Khipu.* Austin: University of Texas Press.

Urton, G., and C. J. Brezine. 2005. Khipu accounting in ancient Peru. *Science* 309:1065–1067.

Valdes, V. C., and J. L. Bischoff. 1989. Accelerator ^{14}C dates for Early Upper Paleolithic (Basal Aurignacian) at El Castillo Cave (Spain). *Journal of Archaeoogical Science* 16:577–584.

Van Der Veen, M., ed. 1999. *The Exploitation of Plant Resources in Ancient Africa.* New York: Kluwer Academic Publishers.

Van Peer, P., and P. M. Vermeersch. 1990. Middle to Upper Paleolithic transition: The evidence for the Nile Valley. In *The Emergence of Modern Humans: An Archaeological Perspective,* ed. P. Mellars, 139–159. Ithaca, NY: Cornell University Press.

Van Riper, A. B. 1993. *Men Among the Mammoths: Victorian Science and the Discovery of Human Prehistory.* Chicago, IL: University of Chicago Press.

Vekua, A., D. Lordkipanidze, G. P. Rightmire, J. Agusti, R. Ferring, G. Maisuradze, A. Mouskhelishvili, et al. 2002. A new skull of early *Homo* from Dmanisi, Georgia. *Science* 297:85–89.

Vercors. 1953. *You Shall Know Them,* trans. R. Barisse. Boston: Little, Brown and Company.

Vietmeyer, N. 1992. Forgotten roots of the Incas. In *Chilies to Chocolate: Food the Americas Gave the World,* ed. N. Foster and L. S. Cordell, 95–104. Tuscon: University of Arizona Press.

Villa, P. 1990. Torralba and Aridos: Elephant exploitation in Middle Pleistocene Spain. *Journal of Human Evolution* 19:299–309.

vonHoldt, B. M., J. P. Pollinger, K. E. Lohmueller, et al. 2010. Genome-wide SNP and haplotype analyses reveal a rich history underlying dog domestication. *Nature* 464:898–902.

Wadley, L. 2010. Were snares and traps used in the Middle Stone Age and does it matter? A review and a case study from Sidubu, South Africa. *Journal of Human Evolution* 58(2):179–192.

Wadley, L., T. Hodgskiss, and M. Grant. 2009. Implications for complex cognition from the hafting of tools with compound adhesives in the Middle Stone Age, South Africa. *Proceedings of the National Academy of Sciences* 106(24):9590–9594.

Wadley, L., C. Sievers, M. Bamford, P. Goldberg, F. Berna, and C. Miller. 2011. Middle Stone Age bedding construction and settlement patterns at Sibudu, South Africa. *Science* 334:1388–1391.

Walker, A., R. E. Leakey, J. M. Harris, and F. H. Brown. 1986. 2.5 Myr *Australopithecus boisei* from west of Lake Turkana, Kenya. *Nature* 322:517–522.

Walker, A., and P. Shipman. 1996. *The Wisdom of the Bones.* New York: Vintage Books.

Wang, H., T. Nussbaum-Wagler, B. Li, Q. Zhao, Y. Vigouroux, M. Faller, K. Bomblies, et al. 2005. The origin of the naked grains of maize. *Nature* 436:714–719.

Wangping, S. 2005. The formation of civilization: The interaction sphere of the Longshan period. In *The Formation of Chinese Civilization: An Archaeological Perspective*, ed. S. Allan, 85–123. New Haven, CT: Yale University Press.

Ward, C. V., W. H. Kimbel, and D. C. Johanson. 2011. Complete fourth metatarsal and arches in the foot of *Australopithecus afarensis. Science* 331:750–752.

Warren, P. 1984. Knossos: New excavations and discoveries. *Archaeology* 37:48–55.

———. 1987. Crete: The Minoans and their gods. In *Origins: The Roots of European Civilisation*, ed. B. Cunliffe, 30–41. Chicago: Dorsey Press.

Waters, M., S. L. Forman, and J. M. Pierson. 1997. Diring Yuriakh A Lower Paleolithic site in central Siberia. *Science* 275:1281–1283.

Waters, M. R., S. L. Forman, T. A. Jennings, L. C. Nordt, S. G. Driese, J. M. Feinberg, J. L. Keene, et al. 2011. The Buttermilk Creek Complex and the Origins of Clovis at the Debra L. Friedkin Site, Texas. *Science* 331:1599–1603.

Waters, M. R., C. D. Pevny, and D. L. Carlson. 2011. *Clovis Lithic Technology: Investigation of a Stratified Workshop at the Gault Site, Texas.* College Station: Texas A&M University Press.

Waters, M. R., T. W. Stafford Jr., H. G. McDonald, C. Gustafson, M. Rasmussen, E. Cappellini, J. V. Olsen, et al. 2011. Pre-Clovis mastodon hunting 13,800 years ago at the Manis Site, Washington. *Science* 334:351–353.

Webster, D. 2002. *The Fall of the Ancient Maya: Solving the Mystery of the Maya Collapse.* London: Thames and Hudson.

Weiss, H., and R. S. Bradley. 2001. What drives societal collapse? *Science* 291:609–610.

Wendorf, F., A. E. Close, R. Schild, K. Wasylikowa, R. A. Housley, J. R. Harlan, and H. Królik. 1992. Saharan exploitation of plants 8,000 years B.P. *Nature* 359: 721–724.

Wendorf, F., R. Schild, and A.E. Close. eds. 1989. *The Prehistory of Waddi Kubbaniya.* Dallas: Southern Methodist University Press.

Wendorf, F., R. Schild, N. E. Hadidi, A. Close, M. Kobusiewicz, H. Wieckowska, B. Issawa, and H. Hass. 1979. Use of barley in the Egyptian Late Paleolithic. *Science* 205:1341–1347.

Wenming, Y. 2005. The beginning of farming. In *The Formation of Chinese Civilization: An Archaeological Perspective*, ed. S. Allan, 27–41. New Haven, CT: Yale University Press.

Wenming, Y., and W. Youping 2005. Early humans in China. In *The Formation of Chinese Civilization: An Archaeological Perspective*, ed. S. Allan, 10–23. New Haven, CT: Yale University Press.

West, F. H. 1967. The Donnelly Ridge site and the definition of an early core and blade complex in central Alaska. *American Antiquity* 32:360–382.

———. 1975. Dating the Denali Complex. *Arctic Anthropology* 11(1):76–81.

———. 1981. *The Archaeology of Beringia.* New York: Columbia University Press.

———. 1996. *American Beginnings: The Prehistory and Paleoecology of Beringia.* Chicago: University of Chicago Press.

Wheeler, M. 1968. *The Indus Civilization.* Cambridge, England: Cambridge University Press.

White, J. P. 1993. The settlement of ancient Australia. In *The First Humans: Human Origins and History to 10,000 B.C.*, ed. G. Burenhult, 147–151,153–157, 160–165. New York: Harper Collins.

White, J. P., and J. F. O'Connell. 1982. *A Prehistory of Australia, New Guinea, and Sahul.* New York: Academic Press.

White, R. 1982. Rethinking the Middle/Upper Paleolithic transition. *Current Anthropology* 23:169–192.

———. 1993. Technological and social dimensions of "Aurignacian-age" body ornaments across Europe. In *Before Lascaux: The Complex Record of the Early Upper Paleolithic*, ed. H. Knecht, A. Pike-Tay, and R. White, 277–299. Boca Raton, FL: CRC Press.

White, T. 1980. Evolutionary implications of Pliocene hominid footprints. *Science* 208:175–176.

White, T., and P. A. Folkens. 1991. *Human Osteology.* San Diego, CA: Academic Press.

White, T. D. 2003. Early hominids—Diversity or distortion? *Science* 299:1994–1997.

White, T. D., B. Asfaw, Y. Beyene, Y. Haile-Selassie, O. C. Lovejoy, G. Suwa, and G. WoldeGabriel. 2009. *Ardipithecus ramidus* and the paleobiology of early hominids. *Science* 326:64–86.

White, T. D., and G. Suwa. 1987. Hominid footprints at Laetoli: Facts and interpretations. *American Journal of Physical Anthropology* 72:485–514.

Whittle, A. 1985. *Neolithic Europe: A Survey*. New York: Cambridge University Press.

Wildman, D. E., L. I. Grossman, and M. Goodman. 2001. Human and chimp functional DNA shows they are more similar to each other than either is to other apes. Paper presented at the Development of the Human Species and Its Adaptation to the Environment, Cambridge, MA.

Wilkinson, T. 2003a. Did the Egyptians invent writing? In *The Seventy Great Mysteries of Ancient Egypt*, ed. B. Manley, 24–27. London: Thames and Hudson.

———. 2003b. Who were the first kings of Egypt? In *The Seventy Great Mysteries of Ancient Egypt*, ed. B. Manley, 28–32. London: Thames and Hudson.

Willey, G. R. 1966. *An Introduction to American Archaeology Vol. 1: North and Middle America*. Englewood Cliffs, NJ: Prentice Hall.

Williams, A. R. 2002. A new chapter in Maya history: All-out war, shifting alliances, bloody sacrifice. *National Geographic* 202(4). Geographica section.

Williams, S. 2007. Not so clear-cut. *Science News* 172:262.

Willoughby, C. C. 1935. *Antiquities of the New England Indians*. Cambridge, MA: Peabody Museum of American Archaeology and Ethnology..

Wills, W. H. 1988. *Early Prehistoric Agriculture in the American Southwest*. Santa Fe, NM: School of American Research.

Wilmshurst, J. M., A. J. Anderson, T. F. G. Higham, and T. H. Worthy. 2010. Dating the late prehistoric dispersal of Polynesians to New Zealand using the commensal Pacific rat. *Proceedings of the National Academy of Sciences* 105:7676–7680.

Wilmshurst, J. M., T. L. Hunt, C. P. Lipo, and A. J. Anderson. 2008. High-precision radiocarbon dating shows recent and rapid initial human colonization of East Polynesia. *Proceedings of the National Academy of Sciences* 108:1815–1820.

Wilson, A. S., T. Taylor, M. C. Certuti, J. A. Chavez, J. Reinhard, V. Grimes, W. Meier-Augenstein, et al. 2007. Stable isotope and DNA evidence for ritual sequences in Inca child sacrifice. *Proceedings of the National Academy of Sciences* 104:16456–16461.

Wing, E. 1977. Animal domestication in the Andes. In *Origins of Agriculture*, ed. C. A. Reed, 837–860. The Hague: Mouton.

Wittfogel, K. 1957. *Oriental Despotism: A Comparative Study of Total Power*. New Haven, CT: Yale University Press.

Wolpoff, M. H. 1989a. Multiregional evolution: The fossil alternative to Eden. In *The Human Revolution: Behavioral and Biological Perspectives in the Origins of Modern Humans*, ed. P. Mellars and C. Stringer, 62–108. Princeton, NJ: Princeton University Press.

———. 1989b. The place of the Neandertals in human evolution. In *The Emergence of Modern Humans: Biocultural Adaptations in the Later Pleistocene*, ed. E. Trinkaus, 97–141. Cambridge, England: Cambridge University Press.

———. 1992. Theories of modern human origins. In *Continuity or Replacement: Controversies in* Homo sapiens *Evolution*, ed. G. Bräuer and F. Smith, 25–64. Rotterdam, The Netherlands: Balkema.

Wolpoff, M. H., and R. Caspari. 1990. Metric analysis of the skeletal material from Klasies River mouth, Republic of South Africa. *American Journal of Physical Anthropology* 81:319.

———. 1997. *Race and Human Evolution*. New York: Simon & Schuster.

Wolpoff, M. H., A. G. Thorne, F. H. Smith, D. W. Frayer, and G. G. Pope. 1994. Multiregional evolution: A worldwide source for modern human populations. In *Origins of Anatomically Modern Humans*, ed. M. Nitecki and D. Nitecki, 175–199. New York: Plenum.

Wolpoff, M. H., X. Z. Wu, and A. G. Thorne. 1984. Modern *Homo sapiens* origins: A general theory of hominid evolution involving the fossil evidence from East Asia. In *The Origins of Modern Human: A World Survey of the Fossil Evidence*, ed. F. H. Smith and F. Spencer, 411–484. New York: Liss.

Wood, B. 1992a. Early hominid species and speciation. *Journal of Human Evolution* 22:351–365.

———. 1992b. Origin and evolution of the genus *Homo*. *Nature* 355:783–790.

Wrangham, R. 2009. *Catching Fire: How Cooking Made Us Human*. New York: Basic Books.

Wright, G. 1971. Origins of food production in southwestern Asia: A survey of current ideas. *Current Anthropology* 12:447–477.

Wu, X., C. Zhang, P. Goldberg, D. Cohen, Y. Pan, T. Arpin, and O. Ben-Yosef. 2012. Early pottery at 20,000 years ago in Xianrendong Cave, China. *Science* 336:1696–1700.

Wu, Z. 1986. *Terra-cotta Figures and Bronze Chariots and Horses at Qin Mausoleum*. Xian, China: Museum of the Emperor.

Yamei, H., R. Potts, Y. Baoyin, G. Zhengtang, A. Deino, W. Wei, J. Clark, et al. 2000. Mid-Pleistocene Acheulean-like stone technology of the Bose Basin, South China. *Science* 287:1622–1626.

Yi, S., and G. Clark. 1985. The "Dyuktai Culture" and New World origins. *Current Anthropology* 26:1–13.

Yokoyama, Y., K. Lambeck, P. D. Deckker, P. Johnsston, and L. K. Fifield. 2000. Timing of the Last Glacial Maximum from observed sea-level minima. *Nature* 406:713–716.

Zeder, M., and B. Hesse. 2000. The initial domestication of goats (*Capra hircus*) in the Zagros Mountains 10,000 years ago. *Science* 287:2254–2257.

Zeder, M. A. 1994a. After the revolution: Post-Neolithic subsistence in northern Mesopotamia. *American Anthropologist* 96:97–126.

———. 1994b. New perspectives on agricultural origins in the ancient Near East. *AnthroNotes* 16(2):1–7.

Zegarra, A. V. 2004. Recent archaeological investigations at Machu Picchu. In *Machu Picchu: Unveiling the Mystery of the Incas*, ed. R. L. Burger and L. C. Salazar, 71–82. New Haven, CT: Yale University Press.

Zhu, R. X., K. A. Hoffman, R. Potts, C. L. Deng, Y. X. Pan, B. Guo, C. D. Shi, et al. 2001. Earliest presence of humans in northeast Asia. *Nature* 413:413–417.

Zhu, R. X., R. Potts, F. Xie, K. A. Hoffman, C. L. Deng, C. D. Shi, Y. X. Pan, et al. 2004. New evidence on the earliest human presence at high northern latitudes in northeast Asia. *Nature* 431:559–562.

Zihlman, A., and N. Tanner. 1978. Gathering and the hominid adaptation. In *Female Hierarchies*, ed. L. Tiger and H. M. Fowler, 163–194. Chicago: Beresford Book Service.

Zilhão, J., and E. Trinkaus, eds. 2003. *Portrait of the Artist as a Child: The Gravettian Human Skeleton from the Abrigo do Lagar Velho and Its Archaeoloigcal Context*. Lisbon, Portugal: Instituto Portugues de Arqueologia.

Zimmer, C. 2004. Faster than a hyena? Running may make humans special. *Nature* 306:1283.

Zohary, D., and M. Hopf. 2001. *Domestication of Plants in the Old World: The Origin and Spread of Cultivated Plants in West Asia, Europe, and the Nile Valley*. Oxford, England: Oxford University Press.

Index

Page numbers in bold indicate figures or tables.